Kevin Roy

THE IVP NEW TESTAMENT COMMENTARY SERIES

Matthew

Craig S. Keener

Grant R. Osborne
series editor

D. Stuart Briscoe
Haddon Robinson
consulting editors

INTERVARSITY PRESS
DOWNERS GROVE, ILLINOIS, USA
LEICESTER, ENGLAND

InterVarsity Press, USA
P.O. Box 1400, Downers Grove, IL 60515, USA
World Wide Web: www.ivpress.com
E-mail: mail@ivpress.com

Inter-Varsity Press, England
38 De Montfort Street, Leicester LE1 7GP, England

InterVarsity Press®, USA., is the book-publishing division of InterVarsity Christian Fellowship®, a student movement active on campus at hundreds of universities, colleges and schools of nursing in the United States of America, and a member movement of the International Fellowship of Evangelical Students. For information about local and regional activities, write Public Relations Dept., InterVarsity Christian Fellowship, 6400 Schroeder Rd., P.O. Box 7895, Madison, WI 53707-7895.

Inter-Varsity Press, England, is the book-publishing division of the Universities and Colleges Christian Fellowship (formerly the Inter-Varsity Fellowship), a student movement linking Christian Unions in universities and colleges throughout the United Kingdom and the Republic of Ireland, and a member movement of the International Fellowship of Evangelical Students. For information about local and national activities write to UCCF, 38 De Montfort Street, Leicester LE1 7GP.

USA ISBN 0-8308-1801-4
UK ISBN 0-85111-682-5

Printed in the United States of America

Library of Congress Cataloging-in-Publication Data

Keener, Craig S., 1960-
    Matthew / Craig S. Keener.
        p.   cm. —(IVP New Testament commentary series; 1)
    Includes bibliographical references.
    ISBN 0-8308-1801-4 (alk. paper)
        1. Bible.   N.T.   Matthew—Commentaries.   I. Title.   II. Series.
    BS2575.3.K44   1997
    226.2'07—dc21   *96-36847*
                                                                                                            CIP

British Library Cataloguing in Publication Data

A catalogue record for this book is available from the British Library.

20	21	19	18	17	16	15	14	13	12	11	10	9	8	7	6
16	15	14	13	12	11	10	09	08	07	06					

*To my dear brothers and sisters in Christ
at Orange Grove Missionary Baptist Church and
Mount Zion Missionary Baptist Church, in North Carolina,
and the intensely devoted students
of New Generation Campus Ministries' and Youth United's
Leadership Training School*

General Preface

In an age of proliferating commentary series, one might easily ask why add yet another to the seeming glut. The simplest answer is that no other series has yet achieved what we had in mind—a series to and from the church, that seeks to move from the text to its contemporary relevance and application.

No other series offers the unique combination of solid, biblical exposition and helpful explanatory notes in the same user-friendly format. No other series has tapped the unique blend of scholars and pastors who share both a passion for faithful exegesis and a deep concern for the church. Based on the New International Version of the Bible, one of the most widely used modern translations, the IVP New Testament Commentary Series builds on the NIV's reputation for clarity and accuracy. Individual commentators indicate clearly whenever they depart from the standard translation as required by their understanding of the original Greek text.

The series contributors represent a wide range of theological traditions, united by a common commitment to the authority of Scripture for Christian faith and practice. Their efforts here are directed toward applying the unchanging message of the New Testament to the ever-changing world in which we live.

Readers will find in each volume not only traditional discussions of authorship and backgrounds, but useful summaries of principal themes and approaches to contemporary application. To bridge the gap between commentaries that stress the flow of an author's argument but skip over exegetical nettles and those that simply jump from one difficulty to another, we have developed our unique format that expounds the text in uninterrupted form on the upper portion of each page while dealing with other issues underneath in verse-keyed notes. To avoid clutter we have also adopted a social studies note system that keys references to the bibliography.

We offer the series in hope that pastors, students, Bible teachers and small group leaders of all sorts will find it a valuable aid—one that stretches the mind and moves the heart to ever-growing faithfulness and obedience to our Lord Jesus Christ.

Acknowledgments

I am especially grateful to my Matthew seminars at Hood Theological Seminary in Salisbury, North Carolina, and Eastern Baptist Theological Seminary in Philadelphia for the opportunity to practice the academic side of this commentary on them; and to Mount Zion Missionary Baptist Church in Salisbury, North Carolina, for the opportunity to practice the application side of this commentary on them. I am also grateful to my series editors for welcoming this contribution and to Ruth Goring for her usual fine work in copyediting it.

Abbreviations

1QH	*Hôdāyôt* or *Thanksgiving Hymns* from Qumran Cave 1
1QM	*Milḥāmāh* or *War Scroll* from Qumran Cave 1
1QpHab	*Pesher on Habakkuk* from Qumran Cave 1
1QS	*Serek hayyaḥad* or *Manual of Discipline* from Qumran Cave 1
2 Baruch	*2 Apocalpyse of Baruch*
4QFlor	*Florilegium* or *Eschatological Midrashim* from Qumran Cave 4
4QPs 37	Commentary on Ps 37 from Qumran Cave 4
11QTemple	*Temple Scroll* from Qumran Cave 11
Ach. Tat.	Achilles Tatius *Clitophon and Leucippe*
Apol.	*Apology*
Apul. *Metam.*	Apuleius *Metamorphosis* (=*The Golden Ass*)
Arist. *E.E.*	Aristotle *Ethica Eudemia*
Arist. *Rhet.*	Aristotle *Rhetoric*
Arist. *V.V.*	Aristotle *On Virtues and Vices*
ARN	*'Abot de Rabbi Nathan*
Artem.	Artemidorus *Oneirocriticon*
b.	Babylonian (Talmud)
bar.	baraita
CD	Cairo *Damascus Document* from Qumran
Char. *Chaer.*	Chariton *Chaereas and Callirhoe*
CIJ	*Corpus Inscriptionum Iudaicarum*
CPJ	*Corpus Papyrorum Iudaicarum*
Did.	*Didache*

Diog. Laert.	Diogenes Laertius *Lives of Eminent Philosophers*
Epict. *Disc.*	Epictetus *Discourses*
Ep.	*Epistle*
Ep. Arist.	*Epistle of Aristeas*
Euseb. *H.E.*	Eusebius *Ecclesiastical History*
Euseb. *P.E.*	Eusebius *Preparation for the Gospel*
Gaius *Inst.*	Gaius *Institutes*
Herod. *Hist.*	Herodotus *History*
Incant. text	Aramaic incantation text
Isoc. *Demon.*	Isocrates *Demonicus*
Isoc. *Nic.*	Isocrates *Nicocles*
Isoc. *Or.*	Isocrates *Orations*
Jos. *Ant.*	Josephus *Antiquities of the Jews*
Jos. *Apion*	Josephus *Against Apion*
Jos. *War*	Josephus *The Jewish War*
Jub.	*Jubilees*
Justin *1 Apol.*	Justin Martyr *1 Apology*
Justin *Dial.*	Justin Martyr *Dialogue with Trypho*
Juv. *Sat.*	Juvenal *Satires*
Lucr. *Nat.*	Lucretius *De Rerum Natura*
m.	Mishnah
Macc	Maccabees
Marc. Aur.	Marcus Aurelius *Meditations*
Mart. *Epig.*	Martial *Epigrams*
Mek.	*Mekilta*
Ode Sol.	*Odes of Solomon*
p.	Palestinian (Talmud)
P. Oxy.	*Papyrus Oxyrhynchus*
par.	parallel to
PDM	*Papyri Demoticae Magicae*
Pes. Rab.	*Pesiqta Rabbati*
Pes. Rab Kah.	*Pesiqta de Rab Kahana*
Petr. *Sat.*	Petronius *Satyricon*
PGM	*Papyri Graecae Magicae*
Philo *Decal.*	Philo *De Decalogo*

Phil *Leg. Gai.*	Philo *Legatio ad Gaium*
Phil *Mut.*	Philo *De Mutatione Nominum*
Phil *Migr. Abr.*	Philo *De Migratione Abrahami*
Philo *Spec. Leg.*	Philo *De Specialibus Legibus*
Philostr. *V.A.*	Philostratus *Vita Apollonii*
Pliny *N.H.*	Pliny *Natural History*
Plut. *Mor.*	Plutarch *Moralia*
pq.	pereq
Ps-Philo	Pseudo-Philo *Biblical Antiquities*
Ps-Phocyl.	Pseudo-Phocylides
Ps. Sol.	*Psalms of Solomon*
Quint.	Quintilian *Institutes of Oratory*
Rab.	*Rabbah* (Rabbinic commentaries preceded by abbreviation for name of biblical book; thus, *Gen. Rab.=Genesis Rabbah*)
Rhet. ad Herenn.	*Rhetorica ad Herennium*
Sen. *Dial.*	Seneca *Dialogues*
Sen. *Ep.*	Seneca *Epistles to Lucilius*
Sib. Or.	*Sibylline Oracles*
Sipra Behuq.	*Sipra Behuqotai*
Sipra Qid.	*Sipra Qiddušin*
Sipra Sav Mek. deMiluim	*Sipra Sav Mekilta deMiluim*
Sipra Shem. Mek. deMil.	*Sipra Shemini Mekilta deMiluim*
Sipra VDDeho.	Sipra Vayyiqra Dibura Dehobah
Sipre Deut.	*Sipre Deuteronomy*
Sipre Num.	*Sipre Numbers*
Strabo	Strabo *Geography*
Suet.	Suetonius
Syr. Men. Sent.	Sentences of the Syriac Menander
t.	Tosefta
Tac.	Tacitus
Tert. *Spect.*	Tertullian *De Spectaculis*
Test.	*Testament*
Test. Ab.	*Testament of Abraham*
Test. Asher	*Testament of Asher*
Test. Benj.	*Testament of Benjamin*

Test. Dan	*Testament of Dan*
Test. Gad	*Testament of Gad*
Test. Iss.	*Testament of Issachar*
Test. Jos.	*Testament of Joseph*
Test. Judah	*Testament of Judah*
Test. Levi	*Testament of Levi*
Test. Naph.	*Testament of Naphtali*
Test. Reub.	*Testament of Reuben*
Test. Sim.	*Testament of Simeon*
Test. Zeb.	*Testament of Zebulon*
Theon *Progymn.*	Theon *Progymnasmata*

Introduction

This commentary focuses on the lessons Matthew may have drawn from his narratives—lessons we may find helpful when preaching, teaching and living this Gospel today. Although I include some documentation here, those who need further documentation or background which the scope and character of this volume prohibits will find it in my forthcoming larger academic commentary on Matthew with Eerdmans.

This commentary also focuses on sample applications, with the necessary emphasis on *sample*. Because Scripture is rich enough to speak to Christians throughout the world from different backgrounds, all modern illustrations are at most samples of how we can grapple with Matthew's message in our own lives. Applications can never be more than such examples; the principles in the text may be transcultural, but most of the particular situations we address in preaching and teaching Scripture are limited to our own cultures or settings.

My applications and illustrations rise especially from my own preaching context, but I hope they can stimulate readers to consider practical applications for their own situations. (Much of my own ministry is in the African-American church in North America, where issues and illustrations differ radically not only from situations on other continents but even from most white North American constituencies.) I readily acknowledge that despite my attempts to communicate Matthew's graphic images, Matthew portrays his point with far greater narrative artistry than my illustrations could hope to do!

In seeking to echo and apply Matthew's own message, I have endeavored as much as possible to let the radical force of that message come home with stark principles or modern illustrations. In some passages that force may sound harsh. Yet in the context of the whole Gospel of Matthew the demands of the kingdom are seasoned with the grace of the God of the cross. Matthew expected his audience to read his Gospel as a whole and in the context of the Christian message they had already embraced, not to take it piecemeal (the way we often must do for sermons and Bible studies). Matthew's narratives also further qualify the force of Jesus' sayings in Matthew (see, for example, comment on 12:3-8), but I have tried to bring out the rhetorical force of each passage by itself rather than risking toning down Jesus' exhortations (against which 5:19 warns).

Jesus ate with sinners as he won them to God's kingdom, and reserved his fiercest denunciations for those who claimed to be doing God's will but were not doing so. I fear that much of Western Christendom has become so familiar with the Gospels that we fail to hear the "shock effect" of Jesus' sayings in their original context (such as his warning that those who value material possessions more than God's will are lost). I therefore have tried to gear my illustrations to replicating that shock value, which I believe should also be replicated in preaching and teaching, provided it remains in the context of grace. The church tradition in which my own preaching has developed often preaches "hard," but we also try to show unconditional affirmation and concern for people's needs, and most of our listeners prefer to hear the message "straight" rather than watered down. I pray that this commentary will be one tool helping us to better submit our lives to the yoke of the kingdom of heaven and its meek and lowly-hearted King.

□ Approaches to the Gospels

Because Matthew is the first of the four Gospels in our canon, it is appropriate that the commentary on Matthew in a series introduce some basic issues historians ask when they study the Gospels. Scholars over the past century have developed various methods of approaching the Gospels. Some of these methods help our case for the historical accuracy of the Gospels; others help us better understand the Gospels.

The historical questions are important for apologetics, for defending the faith in a society that doubts Jesus' claims; the literary questions are important for preaching, because we want to communicate the same inspired message we find in the biblical text. Both kinds of questions have been addressed by scholars from across the theological spectrum, both those who are more conservative (such as Robert Gundry, I. Howard Marshall, Ralph Martin) and those who are more liberal (such as Rudolf Bultmann, Hans Conzelmann, Willi Marxsen). When more conservative scholars ask historical questions, they emphasize that even when we use methods developed by skeptics, enough of the Gospel tradition is *demonstrably* true that those prejudiced against the Christian faith should consider its claims.

Source Criticism

Nineteenth- and early twentieth-century scholars asking how historically reliable the Gospels are first turned to *source criticism* (for more detailed discussion see Carson, Moo and Morris 1992:26-38; France 1985:34-38). Source criticism asks the question: What written sources might the author of a Gospel have used? Although various source theories have come and gone, most scholars today agree (though a significant and capable minority demur) that Matthew used Mark, Q (that is, another source shared by both Matthew and Luke) and some other material not employed by Mark or Luke. Scholars commonly call this view the "Two-Source Hypothesis."

Where we can check his work, Matthew follows Mark and Q closely (by ancient literary standards). Thus it is logical to assume that Matthew is no less reliable where we cannot check him. His basically conservative editing at most points will impress those who begin with neither a thoroughgoing skepticism nor a naive literalism, but with the standards of ancient texts in general.

At any rate, Matthew's audience certainly had other Palestinian traditions beside Mark and Q, and these traditions had undoubtedly been interacting with Mark and Q long before Matthew wrote his Gospel (Meier in Brown and Meier 1983:55). Matthew sometimes removes ambiguities in Mark (for example, Mt 12:3-4 par. Mk 2:25-26; Mt 3:3 par. Mk 1:2-3; Mt 14:1 par. Mk 6:14) and sometimes makes his language more like the Palestinian Jewish way Jesus may have spoken ("kingdom of heaven/God": Mt 19:3, 9 par. Mk 10:2, 11-12). At least on some occasions Matthew makes his changes because of traditions older than Mark (Mt 12:28 par. Lk 11:20, missing in Mk 3:23-29).

Form Criticism

Because early Christians told the stories about Jesus orally before writing Gospels, scholars began to ask about the way early Christians transmitted them. Thus they developed *form criticism* (see Carson, Moo and Morris 1992:21-25). Many form critics noted that Jesus used teaching forms popular among his contemporaries (such as parables and witty sayings) and that early Christians transmitted Jesus' sayings and deeds in forms used by other biographers and storytellers of their day.

Some criteria for authenticity the form critics developed were reasonable (if one's purpose is to convince skeptics about the Gospels with purely historical evidence): for instance, a saying of Jesus attested in a variety of independent sources or which would not have been made up by the later church was probably authentic. Some form critics, however, started with skeptical presuppositions and consequently produced predictably skeptical conclusions (for example, Bultmann 1968); others started with less skeptical premises and produced more positive conclusions (for example, Dibelius 1971; Jeremias 1971; Taylor 1935). The conclusions varied in part because of the premises with which scholars started and in part because flaws existed in the methodology (see E. Sanders 1969). The best criteria of form criticism work much better when used to argue for the reliability of the Gospels than to argue the reverse (see France 1976).

Redaction Criticism

While source and form criticism were sometimes helpful for understanding the nature of Jesus' teachings and the way the Gospels are written, scholars asked these questions mainly to determine how historically reliable the Gospel stories were, not to understand the Gospels' message. Inevitably scholars began to ask, "Given that Matthew used Mark and Q, *why* does Matthew edit Mark and Q the way he does? What is Matthew's *point?*" This question became the focus of the editorial critics, called *redaction critics* (see Carson, Moo and Morris 1992:38-45; Blomberg 1987:35-43).

Some writers have used redaction criticism in a negative way. Some redaction critics assumed that any material Matthew or Luke added to their main sources was not historical; their view stemmed not from redaction criticism per se, however, but from unlikely presuppositions. They wrongly wrote as if Matthew and Luke had no other information except in Mark and Q, and as if editing a source for literary style or theological emphasis renders one's information unhistorical. Many scholars today question those presuppositions.

By contrast, other scholars used redaction criticism to determine more accurately the distinctive emphases of each Gospel, so we could preach texts from each Gospel with greater faithfulness to that Gospel writer's emphasis. By focusing on how Matthew consistently edits his sources, we can observe some of his emphases, which in turn helps us interpret more obscure passages in light of his whole Gospel (see, for example, Gundry 1982:624-25). Conservative redaction critics could argue that God inspired four accounts of the Gospels so Christians would understand these events "from numerous perspectives" (Blomberg 1992:11-12).

Although this commentary's focus and length do not allow me to indulge in many redaction-critical observations, one important social-historical pattern warrants mention. Where possible, Matthew has made Mark's Jesus "more Jewish." That is, where Mark was preaching Jesus in a relevant way to a broader (more "universal") Greco-Roman audience, Matthew has consistently re-Judaized Jesus for his Jewish audience. (As early as Papias, the early church also recognized Matthew's Jewishness.) In some detail, Matthew may have been following rhetorical practices of his day, such as speech-in-character and historical verisimilitude, making Jesus fit what was known about him in general (for example, as a Jewish teacher he should have introduced parables with the sorts of formulas used by Jewish teachers; he may have used "kingdom of heaven"). Yet even in these cases, a purely historical approach would suggest that given Matthew's proximity to Jesus' situation, his conclusions are more apt to be correct than those of modern scholars. In other cases, however, I am reasonably sure that Matthew has re-Judaized Jesus based on solid traditions available to him (just as he removes some ambiguities from Mark, as noted above).

Contemporary Literary Criticism

Because redaction critics focused on locating the Gospel writers' emphasis, redaction critical questions naturally led to a new set of questions that were more concerned with the point of the Gospel writers than with their accuracy. Scholarship in the 1970s began to expose more of the weaknesses of traditional redactional assumptions (such as that all changes were theologically motivated and that what writers change is more significant than what they retain), paving the way for a more holistic interpretation of each Gospel (see Spencer 1993:385-86).

Literary critics began examining themes that ran through a particular Gospel and asking, "What does this Gospel mean as a whole?" But though literary questions are essential, not all literary approaches will be equally helpful for the purposes of this commentary. Because readers of this commentary are less interested in all possible ways to read a text than in the points the authors were inspired to communicate to their readers, we want to reconstruct as well as possible what Matthew sought to communicate to his readers in the historical and social context he shared with them. How Matthew's original message then translates into various situations today (that is, how we apply it) will vary depending on the situations we must address, but this commentary will give examples of some applications hopefully relevant to contemporary readers.

The insights of narrative critics are very important. Giving attention to the completed Gospels and not just to the traditions behind them is crucial if we want to understand and apply them today. Rather than reading a story about Jesus here and there, skipping from one Gospel to another, Christians should read the Gospels the way God chose to give them to us, one Gospel at a time. Further, we should read the Gospels as narratives, as stories (in this case *true* stories). Like the first

Christian readers, we must ask, "What is the moral or point of this story?" This was the way early Christians learned from their Bibles (1 Cor 10:11); they understood that Scripture's stories, like other parts of Scripture, taught God's truth (2 Tim 3:16). The Gospel writers wanted the first readers to apply Jesus' life and teaching to their own situation, and we understand the Gospels best when we see how the Gospel writers were "preaching" Jesus to their original readers. (Knowing the social and historical background of what was going on among those readers helps us understand what the writer was emphasizing to them.)

Christian Interpretation

But the final step in interpretation goes beyond traditional scholarly options. Some contemporary interpreters speak of "communities of interpretation"; in their language we recognize the church as a distinct community of interpretation. The secular academy can ask questions about history, about literary structure, about themes in a given book or even about how people in given religious traditions interpret a book, but as Christians we also read each book of the Bible as a message from God. We ask a final question: "Given what God inspired the author to say to the book's first audience, how does this message address God's people and our society today?"

When pastors and missionaries read the problems Paul faced as a pastor and a missionary, we can identify with his struggles. When Christians in poor countries or in the inner city read how the early Christians faced poverty and violence, they can resonate with the needs and faith of those early Christians. When a loved one is dying, we can identify with those people who flocked to Jesus, desperately seeking healing. (Indeed, those of us who have experienced or witnessed Jesus' continuing power are as skeptical of the Enlightenment prejudice against miracles as many secular intellectuals are of miracles.) Again and again the inspired authors confront us in situations where we need to hear from God, and in these common human situations they deliver to us a message from God.

Most of all, the biblical texts reveal to us Jesus' character and so unveil to us the heart of God. When we receive a communication from someone we know well, we read that communication in the context of what we know about that person and our relationship with him or her. The Bible always expands our knowledge of God by showing us how he relates to different people in various situations, but we also read it in a special way because we are coming to know the Bible's main character better and better as we follow him in our struggles, joys, prayers and witness. For us the Bible is both history and literature, but it is far more: it is a message from God that we live by. "Let anyone with ears listen!" (Mt 13:9 NRSV).

□ Matthew as Biography

A reader who expected an exciting novel would be disappointed by most commentaries; a reader who approached a Frank Peretti novel expecting a dry theological treatise on spiritual warfare would likewise be caught off guard. How would ancient readers have approached Matthew?

Through most of history, readers understood the Gospels as biographies (Stanton 1989:15-17), but after 1915 scholars tried to find some other classification for them, mainly because these scholars confused ancient and modern biography and noticed that the Gospels differed from the latter (Talbert 1977:2-3). The current trend, however, is again to recognize the Gospels as ancient biographies (as in Aune 1987:46-76; Stanton 1974:117-36; Stanton 1992; Burridge 1992; Robbins 1992:2-3).

The Nature of Biographies

Ancient biographers did not write the way modern biographers do. For instance, they could start in the subject's adulthood (so Mark or *Life of Aesop*); they also had the freedom to arrange their material topically rather than in chronological sequence (4 Macc 12:7; Aune 1987:31-32; Stanton 1974:119-21). We should not be surprised, then, when many sayings occur in a different location in Matthew from where they fall in Luke or Mark. Further, ancient writers could expand or shorten accounts freely (2 Macc 2:24-25; Theon *Progymn.* 3.224-40; 4.37-42, 80-82; E. Sanders 1969:19, 46-189, 272). We should thus not be surprised when Matthew condenses accounts in Mark. (Greco-Roman readers may have also appreciated conciseness—Theon *Progymn.* 5.39-43, 52-53.)

Although the historical accuracy of biographers varied from one biographer to another, biographies were always *primarily* historical works (see Aune 1988:125). Historians wanted to make their accounts interesting (2 Macc 2:24-25; Aune 1987:80, 95) and had specific emphases in writing (Momigliano 1977:71-73; Mason 1992:60-71, 77-81), but such practices do not keep one from writing good history (Vermes 1984:19-20; Lyons 1985:66).

To what extent writers' historical interest determined historical accuracy varies from one to the next, depending on how they used their sources. Biographers like Plutarch and Livy spice up their accounts and often depend on centuries-old legends; but Plutarch and Livy often wrote about people who had lived centuries before their own time. By contrast, biographers like Tacitus and Suetonius, who wrote about events closer to their own time, are much more accurate. Despite Josephus's self-serving agendas, he gets various details correct—including the color of paint on Herod's bedroom wall! However creative they may have been with many details, even Plutarch and Livy apparently did not create for their accounts entire *events* where events did not appear in their sources.

Some scholars suggest that Matthew interprets Jesus in light of the Old Testament and that he therefore does not stick very close to the history of Jesus. But while it is true that Matthew interprets Jesus in light of the Old Testament, he also interprets the Old Testament record in light of Jesus. If Matthew simply invented stories about Jesus' infancy to fit Old Testament messianic texts, he should have chosen more obvious texts to start with and created stories that matched them better (compare Soares Prabhu 1976:159-60). Like *most* Greek-speaking Jewish biographers, Matthew is more interested in interpreting tradition than in creating it.

Implications for Matthew's Accuracy

Whether we read Greek-speaking Jewish historical writers or Roman historians, we must compare the sources to evaluate the degree to which each writer was faithful to his sources. When we check the Gospel writers, we can be encouraged by how they used the sources that we can evaluate. A Gospel writer like Luke was among the most accurate of ancient historians, if we may judge by his use of Mark (see Marshall

1978) and his historiography in Acts (see, for example, Sherwin-White 1978). Luke had both written (Lk 1:1) and oral (1:2) sources available, and his literary patron Theophilus already knew much of this Christian tradition (1:4). Luke undoubtedly researched this material (1:3) during his sojourn with Paul in Palestine (Acts 21:17; 27:1; on the "we narratives"—which I, against many scholars, accept as an accurate reflection that the author traveled with Paul—compare, for example, Maddox 1982:7). Although Luke writes more in the tradition of Greco-Roman historians than Matthew does, Matthew's normally rather conservative use of Mark likewise suggests that we may trust the history behind his accounts.

But Matthew's genre also gives us a clue to the hard work he put into his Gospel. Matthew did not write his Gospel off the top of his head; he was a historian-biographer and interpreter, not just a storyteller. Just as speechwriters carefully premeditated their works (Quint. 10.6.1-2), writers of narratives began with a rough draft, then revised and polished it (Aune 1987:82, 128; compare Hata 1975). Like other writers, Matthew would follow one main source (in this case Mark) and weave his other sources around it (Aune 1987:65, 139; see also Downing 1988). Matthew also had to plan the length of his Gospel; the Gospels conform to the standardized lengths of the scrolls on which they are written. (Thus Luke, Acts and Matthew are about the same length; John falls within 1 percent of three-quarters of this length, and Mark is about half this length [Metzger 1968:5-6; see also F. Bruce 1963:12; Palmer 1993:5].)

If Matthew's basic genre suggests historical *intention,* his relatively conservative use of sources (where we can check him, especially Mark) indicates that his other purposes did not obscure this historical intention. The following survey of data will suggest that the sources on which Matthew depends also preserved a substantially reliable picture of Jesus, the tradition being "carefully transmitted and relatively stable" as well as quite close in time to the events described (Hagner 1993:xliii).

□ The Reliability of Jesus' Teachings in Matthew

Scholars who start with the working assumption that material is probably inaccurate until proven otherwise are likely to arrive at conclusions quite different from those who start with the opposite assumption. If Matthew was ancient biography, we should start with the assumption of basic accuracy and leave the burden of proof in specific cases with those who argue against historicity.

With his five major blocks of Jesus' sayings (Mt 5—7; 10; 13; 18; 23—25), Matthew clearly wants to emphasize Jesus' teachings (28:19-20). Many scholars even suggest that Matthew intends Christian scribes to use the collections of Jesus' teachings in his Gospel as a teaching manual (28:19-20; see F. Bruce 1972a:62-63). Matthew's emphasis on Jesus' teaching highlights one of Jesus' historical activities. Whatever Jesus' other roles, he was undoubtedly a sage. Matthew deepens this emphasis, however, so that the wording of Jesus' teachings in his Gospel often comes closer to Jewish rabbis' formulations than those in Mark and Luke, whose audiences included more Gentiles.

Accurate Memory in Matthew's Day

But assuming that Matthew wants to convey Jesus' teachings, a historian will want to know how accurately Matthew could have known Jesus' teachings. Would Jesus' followers still have remembered his teachings? Scholars who deny essentially reliable transmission must suppose that disciples who considered Jesus Lord were far more careless with his words in the earliest generations of Christianity than first- and second-generation students of other ancient teachers were (see W. Davies 1966a:115-16; Benoit 1973-1974:1:33). Especially given how much of Jesus' teaching was disseminated in public during his lifetime, the sort of "radical amnesia" this skepticism requires of Jesus' first followers (Witherington 1990:14) would certainly not have been typical of schools of other early sages.

The disciples may have had more than their memories available. Disciples of Greek teachers normally took notes on what their teachers said (Stowers 1988:74; Gempf 1993:299) and sometimes published them afterward (Kennedy 1980:19). Such notes often reflected the teacher's own style (Epict. *Disc.* 1 preface), and the teachers themselves might later attest the accuracy of the notes (Quint. 1 preface 7-8). Jewish students emphasized oral transmission far more than Greek students did, but they could also take some notes to help prod them in memorizing larger bodies of oral tradition (Gerhardsson 1961:160-62;

see also Safrai 1974-1976a:966). Eventually many sayings were gathered into collections (like Proverbs and *'Abot;* see also Diog. Laert. 2.18-47; Plut. *Sayings of Kings, Mor.* 172B-194E).

Even without notes, however, disciples' memories in the first generation should have preserved Jesus' teachings quite accurately, because the larger ancient Mediterranean society also emphasized memory. Thus, for example, Roman orators regularly memorized their speeches even when these were several hours long (Quint. 11.2.1-51); *memoria,* "learning the speech by heart in preparation for delivery," was one of the orator's five primary tasks (Satterthwaite 1993:344). Members of Greek schools passed on sayings of founders from one generation to the next (Culpepper 1975:193; compare Diog. Laert. 10.1.12).

Greco-Roman education as a whole emphasized memorization (as in Quint. 1.3.1; 2.4.15; Isoc. *Demonicus* 18, Or. 1), and Jewish education, as part of that larger world, was no exception (see Jos. *Life* 8; *m. 'Abot* 6:6). At least by the second century and probably earlier, rabbis expected their disciples to memorize their teachings through repeated practice (as in *Sipre Deut.* 48.1.1-4; Goodman 1983:79). Although disciples undoubtedly confused some sayings as generations passed, this would happen less often in the first generation or two; concrete evidence suggests that Jewish teachers highly valued careful transmission of teachings (*t. Yebamot* 3:1; *Mek. Pisḥa* 1.135-36; *ARN* 24 A).

Of course this does not mean that sayings were always passed on verbatim. The wording of some of Jesus' sayings in Matthew differs, for instance, from that of some of his sayings in Luke, and this difference is to be expected. Just as students memorized, they also regularly paraphrased sayings of teachers; paraphrase was a standard school exercise even in Greco-Roman education (Theon *Progymn.* 1.93-171). Liberal and conservative scholars alike thus agree that Jewish and Christian sources preserved but also adapted earlier tradition (W. Davies 1967:156; Draper 1984; Bock 1995).

Such changes of wording, however, are relatively minor given the way ancient history was written. Early Christians resisted the temptation to read major theological issues of their own day into Gospel materials (Stein 1980:225-28). Although Paul was writing about very different issues, some of his letters show that years before our Gospels were written down he knew some of the same sayings of Jesus (1 Cor 7:10-12; 11:23; 15:3; 1 Thess 4:15). Likewise, many sayings in the Gospels imply a setting relevant only to Palestine and/or the specific time of Jesus (see Theissen 1991:25-59).

Other Incentives for Accuracy

More to the point, written Gospels were appearing within three decades of Jesus' ministry, while eyewitnesses maintained positions of prominence in the church (Davids 1980:89-90; France 1986:100-101; compare also Blomberg 1995:22; pace Koester 1990; 1994). Luke thus attests his reader's awareness of many existing written sources (Lk 1:1-4). Had early Christian storytellers and writers in various geographical regions freely invented different stories about Jesus, we could have expected Gospels much more diverse than our Synoptics are (Gundry 1975:191)—more like the later Gnostic materials formed under exactly such conditions (as discussed in Hill 1979:163, 172; compare *P. Oxy.* 1).

Matthew's method may be, if anything, more conservative than that of many of his predecessors in preserving what he believes to be the substance of Jesus' teaching, although he freely rearranges and develops his material. As E. P. Sanders observes (1993:193), "The gospel writers did not wildly invent material. They developed it, shaped it and directed it in the ways they wished. But even Matthew did not create a sizeable body of material in favour of the Gentile mission, though he seems to have enhanced what he had."

We need only read afresh Jesus' sayings in many of Matthew's discourses to see that they represent collections of isolated sayings or groups of sayings that Matthew has arranged as topically as possible, often even without very helpful explanatory transitions. Had Matthew wanted to *create* teaching material for Jesus (apart from minor transitions), literary unity provided him plenty of incentive to do so. But the evidence of Matthew's text suggests that he exercised both freedom to rearrange sayings and conservatism in reporting rather than inventing them.

☐ Structure, Authorship, Provenance and Date

While we can make a strong case that Matthew is historically reliable, many other introductory questions are more difficult.

Structure

As noted above, many biographers arranged their material topically. Matthew arranges not only the structure of his Gospel but even many sayings thematically (see Davies and Allison 1988:87-88). This Gospel divides chronologically into three sections (Kingsbury 1975:7-25); its teaching material divides topically into five. Some scholars think that "from that time on Jesus began" provides a chronological marker (Mt 4:17; 16:21). Most scholars identify the five discourses by the closing formula "when he had finished . . ." in 7:28; 11:1; 13:53; 19:1; 26:1 (for example, Aune 1987:19, 49; Kee 1980:141; Beare 1981:200). The threefold chronological narrative structure and the fivefold discourse structure are not incompatible (Senior 1983:26-27; Blomberg 1992:24-25). (From Papias in the second century to B. W. Bacon in the twentieth, some scholars have compared Matthew's five discourse sections to the five books of the Pentateuch. Some other Jewish works also exist in five divisions, such as Psalms, *1 Enoch* and *Pirqe 'Abot,* but even if the number of sections recalls the Pentateuch, one cannot draw specific parallels with books of the Pentateuch.) For a full survey of views concerning Matthew's structure, see Bauer 1988:21-55.

One can divide the Gospel in various ways. Matthew arranged his material more topically than some other Gospel writers, but still did not have our modern system of outlining in mind. Thus, for example, 6:1-18 is a tightly knit literary structure, a virtual three-point sermon. Verse 1 provides the thesis statement, followed by three partly balanced sections (6:2-4; 6:5-15; 6:16-18). The middle section, however, contains so much additional material on prayer (6:7-13) that it breaks the symmetry; a modern preacher might not have time to fully expound the Lord's Prayer (6:9-13) *and* the entire rest of Matthew's structure. Yet on the level of this outline, verse 1 is a larger heading than 6:9-13. Matthew probably expected congregations to read his Gospel as a whole unit publicly, or at least to treat it in larger segments than we do today. Limited by the time available, preachers are often forced to approach the text a paragraph at a time. In personal study, however, we are wise to read the Gospel in larger sections.

Authorship

The minority of scholars who believe Matthew wrote this Gospel (such as Gundry 1982:609-22) have marshaled important arguments and provided answers to those more skeptical that Matthew was the author. Clearly Matthew is the best *named* candidate offered; but the lack of evidence for any other author does not necessarily make the limited evidence for Matthew's authorship compelling.

Arguments for Matthew as Author. The titles of the Gospels were unanimously accepted over a large geographical region in the second century (see Hengel 1985:81-82), a point that may favor Matthew as the author. External evidence (church tradition) stemming from Papias in the early second century (in Euseb. *H.E.* 3.39) and confirmed by the unanimous title (added after early Christians identified the extant Gospels as one genre, though possibly before they were collected) supports Matthew as the author. Because travelers networked early Christian assemblies throughout the Roman Empire and word traveled quickly among them, early traditions concerning the authors of popular Christian works are probably generally correct.

Arguments Against Matthew as Author. But these arguments depend on church tradition, not on the text of the Gospel itself; and in this instance, scholars have reason to suspect the tradition because of an apparent mistake Papias made. Even if Matthew wrote an earlier stage of the tradition (say, Q), we have no guarantee that the finished product is largely from Matthew's hand. Matthew's use of Mark also may speak against the author's having been a firsthand witness of the events he describes, as much as the church would have liked him to have been. This point may make Matthew's claim for authorship the weakest among the four Gospels, a claim that I at one time therefore dismissed without further consideration.

Tentative Conclusions Regarding Authorship. Still, Papias's tradition probably dates to within half a century of Matthew's publication, and no one in the years surrounding Papias challenged Matthew's authorship; nor, if one had to guess at an author, was Matthew the most obvious name to attach to the Gospel (apostles like Peter, Andrew and perhaps even Thomas might commend themselves with greater authority; see Carson 1984:17-19; Blomberg 1992:44; Hagner 1993:lxxvi). Many thus accept a Matthew tradition edited among a community of Matthew's disciples or by one of his disciples (for example, Hagner 1993:lxxvii; compare Hill 1972:55).

In contrast to my earlier opinion (Keener 1993:43), rereading the earliest patristic materials that depend most heavily on apostolic Christianity has currently inclined me to give more weight to the voice of early Christian tradition than I did previously. Authorship would be the *last* point forgotten. That this Gospel originally circulated without oral reports of its authorship is unlikely; as an anonymous work it would not have quickly commanded the wide acceptance it received, and authors of biographies of this length normally were named (though persecution could have demanded a special case of anonymity here). At the moment I therefore accept the probability that Matthew was at least associated with some stage of the production of this Gospel or the tradition on which it depends; scholars who argue for Matthew's authorship should be given a fairer hearing than they often receive.

In any case, neither the authority nor accuracy of the Gospel of Matthew is at stake; it does not name its author (the titles were added to all four Gospels later). The evidence warrants the caution of some recent evangelical commentators like R. T. France, who, though he remains open to the possibility of Matthew's influence in the Gospel, admits that we cannot be sure to what extent Matthew contributed (1985:34). Likewise D. A. Carson, who ultimately considers Matthew's authorship "the most defensible" single position, nevertheless concurs that "none of the arguments for Matthew's authorship is conclusive" and "we cannot be entirely certain who the author of the first Gospel is" (1984:19). Craig Blomberg, finding the arguments of both sides too easy to refute, accepts Matthew as the author only "tentatively" (1992:43-44).

In the same way, some who reject Matthew as the author are troubled by the antiquity of the Gospel titles and the tradition of authorship; Ulrich Luz complains that too many scholars simply ignore these difficulties (1989:94-95). What does affect our reading of the Gospel is what we can say for sure: Matthew is Jewish, in dialogue with contemporary Jewish thought and skilled in traditional Jewish interpretation of the Old Testament.

Provenance and Date

When we turn to provenance and date, however, we return to shaky ground. The best (though far from certain) and most common case for provenance fits some urban center in Syro-Palestine (often thought to be Antioch) where Greek was spoken, which included a sizable Jewish community residentially segregated from Gentiles—Jews who perhaps remained bitter about the recent massacres of 66-70 and remained in contact with theological issues in Judea.

Although some scholars have made a good case that Matthew could precede A.D. 70 (for example, Gundry 1982:599-608; Robinson 1977:76-78), many suggest a date after 70, perhaps as late as the mid- to late 80s (for example, P. Ellis 1974:5; F. Bruce 1980:40; Senior 1983:13-14; Davies and Allison 1988:127-38). A later date need not imply that Matthew is inaccurate; as noted above, he depends on earlier sources. But like preachers today, Matthew emphasized those features of his tradition that best addressed the pastoral situation of his readers. In my opinion the following evidence seems to favor a date after A.D. 70:

1. More so than Mark or Luke (but less than John, who writes in the 90s), Matthew particularly engages Pharisaism, which became early Syro-Palestinian Christians' primary opposition only after 70.

2. Matthew reflects a Jewish worldview closer to that of the rabbis than probably any other writer in the New Testament (although many other parts of the New Testament are equally Jewish). But the rabbinic movement began achieving prominence only after 70 (and even then not everyone paid attention to it).

3. Matthew and Luke both probably depend on Mark, which probably (though not certainly) derives from the mid-60s and may have addressed the church in Rome. The early church was well networked, so Mark may have circulated quickly; nevertheless, Matthew must have read and assimilated Mark, then invested a great deal of time arranging, drafting and polishing his own Gospel. Matthew uses Mark as a backbone for his Gospel, not merely one source among many, which may indicate that Mark had become established as a standard. All this suggests a date some time after 70. (This argument of course falters if, with a substantial minority of conservative scholars, we date Mark before the 60s; contrary to accepted scholarly tradition, we cannot date it with certainty to the 60s or early 70s.)

4. Matthew more clearly separates the disciples' questions about the temple's destruction and the world's end for his readers than Mark does (Mt 24:3 par. Mk 13:2-4), even though Matthew's Jewish readers would have been more familiar with the traditional prophetic perspective that arranged events according to their kind rather than their timing.

Those who argue for an earlier date dispute each of the above points and provide counterarguments; I could also cite more arguments for a later date. Suffice it to note here that at present I tentatively favor a date in the late 70s, which is somewhat earlier than I previously would have dated this Gospel. I originally believed that the situation the Gospel addresses could suggest a date in the mid-80s, making it (in my opinion) later than both Mark and Luke. Yet some clues suggest to me that the hostilities of the Judean-Roman war (A.D. 66-70) remain fresh: I suspect that Matthew's audience retains some bitterness toward Gentiles (hence the need for stressing the Gentile mission, even if Matthew wrote near Antioch, a home of that mission); other recollections of Jerusalem's destruction also appear to remain relevant to Matthew's audience (see comment on 24:1-3). Such memories probably remained fresh for a long time, but because they appear an unresolved issue I am guessing that no more than a decade has passed. But as France, a scholar who tentatively advances a pre-70 date, rightly warns all scholars, "any 'publication date' can be advanced only very tentatively" (1985:30), whether that date is "early" or "late."

□ The Situation Matthew Addresses

Although Matthew's dependence on earlier tradition prevents him from adapting everything in his Gospel to his readers' situation, he does have particular emphases, and these fit what we know of the issues of his day. Matthew is engaged in polemic against Jewish authorities (see Van Tilborg 1972; Senior 1983:6-10). As noted above, Matthew's special target appears to be the successors of Pharisaism, probably the founders of what became the rabbinic movement at Jamnia and those Jewish leaders throughout Syro-Palestine who may have been aligned with them. (He has far less concern with the Sadducees, a group that had ceased to provide much of a threat after A.D. 70.) Like his teacher Jesus, Matthew agrees with some of the Pharisees' teaching (23:2-3), but he resents their behavior and opposition to the truth of Jesus and his followers (23:29-37).

Some read the First Gospel as if Matthew's audience has decisively broken with Judaism; on my reading of this Gospel, though, that suggestion could be true only in a highly qualified sense. Although a severe conflict may have forced much of Matthew's audience out of their synagogues, it is very unlikely that they view themselves as cut off from their biblical or cultural heritage (see most fully Saldarini 1994). Why would they reject their own heritage in Israel's history simply because they were debating with others who claimed that heritage for themselves? Such a reconstruction would make sense only to later Gentile Christians who assumed that all mature Christians would want to be Gentiles—a strange idea that probably would not have even occurred to Matthew.

Instead Matthew remains committed to his Jewish heritage while struggling with those he believes to be its illegitimate spokespersons. Of all four Gospels, Matthew's language and method most closely resemble those of the part of Pharisaism growing into the emerging rabbinic movement (perhaps his circle of congregations even includes Christian scribes, as some have suggested; Mt 13:52). Probably Matthew responds to non-Christian Jewish charges that Christians oppose the law, a charge his Gospel therefore emphatically denies (5:17-20). Thus as early as the sixteenth century Sebastian Münster called Matthew a "new Torah" (Lapide 1984:55).

Of course Matthew's readers are not so fortunate as to be facing only one problem. We may note that condemnations of scribes and Pharisees (3:7-10; 12:24, 33-34) blend together with warnings regarding false prophets (7:15-23; 24:24). Likewise, judgments against the false religious leaders of Jesus' day (23:13-29) serve as a warning to religious leaders of the end-time generation (24:45-51), which Matthew undoubtedly understood as potentially relevant to Christian teachers in his own generation. But most of all, Matthew probably functions as a discipling manual, a "handbook" of Jesus' basic life and teaching, relevant to a Jewish Christian community engaged in the Gentile mission and deadlocked in scriptural polemic with their local synagogue communities.

□ Matthew and the Jesus of History

History has passed a negative verdict on most of the past two centuries of "historical Jesus" research. (For summaries of the first quest, see Schweitzer 1968; for the current quest, see especially Boyd 1995; Witherington 1995.) If quests for the historical Jesus have started with the reasonable assumption that later orthodox Christology should not be automatically read into our earliest accounts of Jesus, they have almost invariably read Jesus in light of too narrow a background (a revolutionary, a teacher, a prophet or otherwise, but rarely more than one at a time) or as a reflection of their own values. Although scholars after Schweitzer temporarily gave up the comfortable picture of Jesus as merely a noneschatological sage, some have today returned to this position, prompting one critic to remark, "There is something disturbingly familiar about a mildly reforming, sagacious teacher, who . . . does not use language and imagery that promises the reversal of the rulers of the world" (Overman 1990:195). As John P. Meier complains (1991:177), a Jesus

> who spent his time spinning out parables and Japanese koans, a literary aesthete who toyed with 1st-century deconstructionism, or a bland Jesus who simply told people to look at the lilies of the field—such a Jesus would threaten no one, just as the university professors who create him threaten no one.

It is hard to explain how the harmless, noneschatological sage of the Jesus Seminar, Crossan, Mack and others, like that of the nineteenth-century lives of Jesus, would get himself crucified (compare Meier 1991:177). Admittedly the historical method can give us only a partial picture of the Jesus who lived in history (Meier 1991:21-31), but the broader the base of evidence, the fuller the picture we can likely construct.

Because the commentary proper cannot provide full background for recurrent themes every time they occur, I provide a brief treatment of some of Matthew's primary christological motifs here.

Jesus as Teacher and Prophet

Matthew portrays Jesus in a variety of ways. First, he presents Jesus as a teacher, such as in the Sermon on the Mount. Our available evidence clearly indicates that Matthew is historically correct: Jesus was a teacher. Jewish teachers ranged from traditional sages like Joshua ben Sira (in the book called Sirach or Ecclesiasticus) to local legal experts and children's Bible teachers. Many teachers apparently performed both wisdom and legal functions (for example, *m. 'Abot* 1—3; see Keener 1991a:23, 145-46). Jesus often employed the rhetorical techniques of his contemporaries, such as hyperbole and rhetorical overstatement (similar to *m. 'Abot* 2:8; *ARN* 36A) or parables (see comments on chap. 13).

Second, and closely connected with Jesus' teaching role, Jesus is a prophet like Jeremiah (Mt 16:14; 21:12; 23:29-32) and especially a prophet-healer like Elijah and Elisha (as in the healings of Mt 8—9). Those who insist that because Jesus was a sage he was not a prophet (for example, Mack 1988:57, 87 n. 7) are manipulating forced-choice logic; in Jesus' day most popular figures fit several roles (see, for example, Keener 1995; Witherington 1990:180).

All strata of Gospel tradition (such as Mark, Q, John and Matthew's special material) confirm that Jesus performed miracles like those of Elijah and Elisha (see Meier 1994:1044-45). That an associate of John should have been considered a prophet is hardly surprising. Because various categories of charismatic leaders overlapped in ancient sources, and because the Gospels portray Jesus as legal teacher, healer and prophet, a forced choice among these options would do injustice to some of our evidence. Observers probably approached Jesus in terms of whichever role they needed him to fill, although this probably meant in practice that most people approached him as a charismatic signs-prophet (as in Mt 4:24-25).

Third, some such signs-prophets also became messianic (hence in some sense end-time) figures as well. First-century Jewish Palestine's most popular figures were probably prophets of deliverance, leading messianic movements and modeling their ministries after those of Moses and Joshua. These were signs-prophets like Theudas, who tried to part the Jordan, and the Egyptian false prophet who expected Jerusalem's walls to collapse before him, both seeking to anticipate eschatological deliverance by working Moses- or Joshua-like miracles (see E. Sanders 1985:138, 171; Meeks 1967:163-64; Horsley 1985). Some of these figures undoubtedly saw their task as messianic (Freyne 1988:194-95; Witherington 1990:83). Jesus' popularity as a prophet thus leads us to inquire whether many people would have also speculated about his being a messiah.

Jesus as Messiah/King

More important than his portrayals of Jesus as teacher and prophet, Matthew hails Jesus as the true King of Israel (21:5-9; 27:29), that is, the Messiah (Christ; 16:16-20). Jesus' teachings have such authority precisely because he is God's appointed King. Israel's prophets had promised a final king or dynasty descended from David (as in Is 9:7; Jer 23:5), a theme that continued in early Judaism (for example, *Ps. Sol.* 17.21; Fitzmyer 1974:113-26).

Because the king was the "anointed one," Jewish people often labeled this ultimate king "the anointed one" or "the Messiah," which the Greek translation of the Hebrew Bible regularly renders "the Christ." Later Christians and Jews outside Palestine were far less interested in a "Messiah" than the Gospels were, which indicates how unlikely it would have been for the Gospel writers to have simply invented the tradition of Jesus' messiahship (pace Mack 1993:4-5).

Even the earliest strands of Gospel tradition indicate that Jesus taught that his disciples would have a role in the messianic kingdom, which would naturally imply that he attributed to himself the role of Israel's king (E. Sanders 1985:234). Despite the subsequent course of events (not conforming to any contemporary pattern for the Messiah's career), his disciples claimed him to be Messiah, and his execution as king indicates that others believed that he considered himself King, even though he was reticent to employ the title "Messiah" publicly (E. Sanders 1985:307). One might add to this case other factors such as the Palestinian features of the triumphal entry narrative (including the Hallel) that suggest the authenticity of the entry, when Jesus approached Jerusalem as a king. Although E. P. Sanders distinguishes "king" from "messiah," he thus thinks that many scholars have been too cautious about assuming that Jesus believed he was a king (1985:307; see also R. Brown 1994:480). At the same time Jesus limited public testimony to his messiahship, probably because his mission redefined the meaning of the term (see Marshall 1990:89-90).

Matthew also frequently uses the expression "Son of God," which he regards as virtually interchangeable with "Christ" (compare 16:16 with Mk 8:29). Jack Dean Kingsbury may well be correct that this represents Matthew's primary christological title (1975:40-83), although other scholars have challenged this contention (Hill 1980; Meier 1979:218-19); at any rate, it represents an important title expressing Jesus' authority under the Father. The Aramaic expression in Mark 14:36 indicates that Jesus historically did call God his Father; Jesus undoubtedly saw himself as the special Son of God, the Davidic King (2 Sam 7:14; Ps 2:7; 4QFlor 1.10-11).

Other Facets of Jesus' Identity in Matthew

"Son of Man" represents another important christological term for Matthew. He borrows it from sources like Mark, who develops an eschatological Christology related to the Son of Man in Daniel 7:13-14 (a possible source of Jesus' "kingdom" emphasis as well). Jesus' allusion to Daniel 7:13-14 becomes most explicit in Matthew 24:30 par. Mark 13:26 (to Jesus' disciples) and in Matthew 26:64 par. Mark 14:62 (to Jesus' opponents, ending Mark's "messianic secret").

Although some more skeptical scholars have argued that the later church made up many or all of Jesus' "Son of Man" sayings, "Son of Man" in early Christian texts appears almost exclusively on Jesus' lips. Thus if *any* title of Jesus is authentic, this one surely is (even by older, radical form critics' most negative use of the "criterion of dissimilarity"). If the title is authentic and barely used by anyone except Jesus, and if Jesus proclaimed a kingdom and implied his messiahship, future-oriented Son of Man sayings are likely authentic.

From our perspective of hindsight, the most significant christological emphases in Matthew and his sources may cluster more around images than titles. In the Q traditions Jesus portrays himself not as a mere human teacher but as judge in the day of judgment who will be addressed as "Lord, Lord" (Mt 7:21 par. Lk 13:25; Mt 7:24-27 par. Lk 6:46-49).

Also in early Q tradition, even John the Baptist recognizes that the Coming One is greater than a merely human, natural messiah or teacher. He presents him as one whose sandals he was unworthy to unloose or carry (Mt 3:11; Lk 3:16), that is, as one whose servant he is unworthy to be (see comment on Mt 3:11)—though biblical prophets had readily owned the honorary title "servants of God." This supernatural figure would baptize not in mere water but in the Spirit of God and (for the wicked) fire—a purely divine role in the Old Testament (who but God can pour out God's Spirit? Is 44:3; Ezek 39:29; Joel 2:28; perhaps Zech 12:10).

In the same passage the Coming One would likewise perform the divine role of judge, separating the righteous for eternal life and the wicked for damnation (Mt 3:11-12; Lk 3:16-17). A skeptic may dispute the extant witness of Q and other early evidence for a "high" Christology, but we should be clear about what the skeptic is doing: dismissing the earliest evidence wherever it does not fit traditional critical theories so he or she can build a picture on the basis of what coheres with a prior theory—and doing so without explicit concrete evidence requiring this dismissal.

Early Christian writers preferred to make their case through a variety of images rather than to focus on answering a small number of precise christological questions no one was yet asking; but their images of Jesus from the start include a suprahuman role subordinate to the authority of the Father (in material particular to Matthew, for example, Mt 25:31-34). Matthew, like John, represents a strain of Jewish Christianity less Hellenized than Mark's or Luke's; and like John, Matthew emphasizes Jesus' divine authority to monotheistic readers. Whereas John uses especially the image of Wisdom to develop his Christology, however, Matthew may also use the image of the Shekinah, the divine presence. Jesus is not only God present with his people (1:23), after his exaltation as Son of Man (28:18) equal to the Father and divine Spirit (28:19) and virtually omnipresent (28:20); Jesus is God's presence among his people (18:20), fulfilling a function Jewish teachers ascribed to the Shekinah, God's presence.

Yet for all his teaching indicating Jesus as divine, this is hardly Matthew's most frequent emphasis; Matthew devotes far more space to Jesus as authoritative teacher, Messiah (rightful King of Israel), the fulfillment of ancient Israel's history and prophecies, and so forth (on Matthew's Christology see especially Kingsbury 1975). One of the most prominent characteristics of Matthew's Jesus is how he fulfills Scripture, sometimes literally and sometimes as the embodiment of Israel's history. Matthew is clear that Jesus is the goal of the Law and Prophets; hence anyone faithful to the heritage and the Bible of Israel must recognize and follow him.

☐ The Kingdom of Heaven

Some earlier traditional dispensationalists contrasted the kingdom of heaven and the kingdom of God, but few hold this view today, and it is no longer a necessary part of modern dispensationalism (Saucy 1993:19; also see Carson 1984:100-101). Indeed, a simple comparison of parallel passages in Matthew and Mark would demonstrate that whereas Mark (like Luke) always employs "kingdom of God," Matthew employs "kingdom of heaven" consistently with but four exceptions. Some other Jewish texts use "kingdom of heaven" as a periphrasis for "kingdom of God" (for example, *Sipra Qid*. pq. 9.207.2.13; *p. Qiddušin* 1:2, §24), as many scholars note (for example, Bonsirven 1964:7; Marmorstein 1968:93; Moore 1971:1:119).

Although the English word *kingdom* may connote to us a place or a people, most scholars agree that the Hebrew, Aramaic and Greek terms especially communicate the concept of reign, authority or rule (Dodd 1961:34; Perrin 1963:24; Betz 1968:33). Like the Old Testament (for example, Is 6:5), Jewish teachers could speak of God's present rule (especially among the people who obeyed his law; for example, *m. Berakot* 2:2). But Jewish people also looked for the kingdom as God's future rule, when he would reign unchallenged (Is 24:23; *Jub*. 1:28; *Mek. Shirata* 10.42-45), as attested in regular Jewish prayers (see, for example, Oesterley 1925:65, 70). Jesus' picture of the kingdom, as well as of the Son of Man, may derive especially from Daniel 7, a passage less frequently mined by Jesus' followers (Witherington 1990:242); he may also allude to Daniel 2:30, 44.

Clear evidence indicates that Jesus announced a future (impending) kingdom (E. Sanders 1985:151-54, 231-32; compare Burkitt 1910:69; Schweitzer 1968:223-397). Yet many have also noted an emphasis on the presence of the kingdom in the Gospels, especially in the kingdom parables and sayings like the one about entering the kingdom as a child (for example, Dodd 1961; Vermes 1993:147-49). If one examines the whole picture of the Gospels, the kingdom is both present and future (see Stein 1978:60-79; Ladd 1974b:70-80; Witherington 1992:51-74; Meier 1994:10, 289-506). It was only natural for Jesus and his first followers, once they recognized that Jesus would come again to establish his kingdom fully, to recognize that the future kingdom would come in two stages corresponding to Jesus' first and second comings.

As Jesus' resurrection is the first installment on the future resurrection of the righteous, guaranteeing that it will occur (1 Cor 15:20), so Jesus' demonstrations of God's rule at his first coming foreshadow the completed revelation of his rule when he returns. In the interim believers enjoy the Spirit as the "down payment" of their future hope (Rom 8:23; 2 Cor 1:22; 5:5; Eph 1:13-14; Heb 6:4-5). The present significance of the future kingdom is thus that God's people in the present age are citizens of the coming age; their identity is determined by what Jesus has done and what they will be, not by what they were or by their status in this world.

Too many Christians do not understand that God's kingdom became present in Jesus and that where the King is, his kingdom or reign is established among his followers. When Christians dare to believe that they are citizens of a future age, empowered by the Spirit who rules among them, they will begin to live like people of the future age instead of letting the world define their identity and establish their values. Through the Spirit, Christians can live out the reality that Jesus is King of the deepest values and sentiments of their hearts (Gal 5:16).

□ Concluding Summary

Matthew recognizes Jesus as the supreme teacher (Mt 23:8-10) and indicates that Jesus' disciples must make more disciples for his teachings (28:19). But Jesus' teaching is supremely authoritative precisely because he is the rightful ruler of Israel, God's Son, the Messiah (16:16-17) who will return to judge the world (3:12; 25:31-32). Matthew derives each aspect of his portrait of Jesus from accurate historical traditions but emphasizes these particular aspects to encourage his audience in their difficult situation.

After A.D. 70, one relatively small group of Pharisees became a dominant influence in Syro-Palestinian Judaism. This group of Pharisees and many synagogue leaders allied with their agendas set out to define Judaism according to their traditions, bringing them into direct conflict with the mission of the more numerous but less socially powerful Jewish Christians. Matthew writes to equip his audience in their responses to the Jewish legal scholars who challenged them, and also to call them to look beyond the horizons of Israel to another mission that had to be completed before Israel as a whole would come to repentance: the mission to the Gentiles (24:14; 28:19). The Christians faced persecution (10:17; 24:9), counterfeit prophets (7:22; 24:11, 24), apostasy (13:21-22; 24:10, 12) and a continuing need for more laborers with Jesus' heart (9:37)—in short, the hostility of their society and the apparent inadequacy of their church to transform the situation for good.

Matthew counters the despair of the situation with Jesus' call to radical discipleship (8:20-22; 16:24-27; 24:13), Jesus' demand for obedient and holy living (chaps. 5—7) and Jesus' promise of ultimate success in the believers' mission (24:14; 28:19-20), albeit probably at the cost of most of their lives (10:17-39). But above all this teaching towers the figure of our Lord Jesus himself: King Messiah, Son of Man, the rightful Lord of Israel whom their people would one day acknowledge (1:21; 23:39). The final judge, the true revelation of the Father (11:27), was the meek and lowly One who had walked among the first disciples and died for his people (11:29; 20:28; 21:5), the One who would also empower Matthew's readers to fulfill the task he had given them (10:19-20; 11:28-30). That is the same Jesus we must follow today.

Outline of Matthew

19:1—22:46 ___ THE FINAL JOURNEY
19:1—20:16 ___ Inverting the World's Values
    19:1-12 _____ Grounds for Divorce in God's Law
    19:13-15 _____ The Kingdom Belongs to Children
    19:16-22 _____ The Cost of Discipleship
    19:23-30 _____ Sacrifice and Reward
    19:30—20:16 _ Reversal of Fortunes

20:17—21:16 __ The Price of Jesus' Mission
    20:17-19 _____ Suffering for the Kingdom
    20:20-28 _____ The Reign of a Suffering Servant
    20:29-34 _____ Persistent Prayer
    21:1-11 _____ Jerusalem's King Enters Its Gates
    21:12-16 _____ Judgment on the Temple Establishment

21:17—22:46 __ Jesus Debates Jerusalem's Leaders
    21:17-22 _____ Faith to Accomplish the Impossible
    21:23-27 _____ The Source of Jesus' Authority
    21:28-32 _____ Pretend Obedience Versus Delayed Obedience
    21:33-44 _____ The Murderous Tenants
    21:45-46 _____ The Cowardly Politicians
    22:1-14 _____ Scorning the King's Son
    22:15-22 _____ Caesar or God
    22:23-33 _____ Proving the Resurrection
    22:34-40 _____ Love God and Neighbor
    22:41-46 _____ David's Son, David's Lord

23:1—25:46 ___ THE FUTURE AND THE KINGDOM
23:1-39 _____ Judgment on the Religious Elite
    23:1-12 _____ Religion for Show
    23:13-32 _____ Woes Against Human Religion
    23:33-39 _____ Impending Judgment on the Establishment

24:1-31 _____ Judgment on the Temple and the World
    24:1-3 _____ The Temple's Destruction
    24:4-14 _____ Not Yet the End
    24:15-28 _____ The Tribulation in History
    24:29-31 _____ Jesus' Return

24:32—25:46 __ Parables of the Future Kingdom
    24:32-44 _____ Neither the Day Nor the Hour

COMMENTARY

INTRODUCTION TO THE KINGDOM (1:1—4:23)

Ancient biographies could open with the subject's public vocation, as in Mark, but often began by rehearsing the background of the central character. Such background might include a noble or prominent ancestry (Mt 1:1-17), virtuous parents (1:18-25), childhood background that introduced themes relevant to the subject's later public activity (2:1-23), the attestation of others to the person's character (3:1-17), including that of the person's adherents (4:18-25), and qualifying tests through which the person's character was proved (4:1-11). Such introductory comments set the tone for the whole of the work that would follow.

□ History and the Mixed-Race Messiah (1:1-17)

Matthew opens his Gospel by showing that Jesus is part of Israel's history—as well as part of God's plan for the mission to the Gentiles, a plan already implied in that history. To make this point Matthew lists Jesus' ancestors who evoke Israel's rich Old Testament heritage, notably including four Gentile women who came to participate in that heritage. The opening verse of the Gospel introduces two ancestors who become pivotal characters in the genealogy: Jesus is son of Abraham (thus the ideal Israelite) and son of David (thus the Messiah).

Matthew does have to omit some unhelpful generations and otherwise adjust the genealogy to fit his scheme; but skipping some generations was common enough in ancient genealogies. A more relevant question might be: Could Matthew have really had a list of Jesus' ancestors? That he does not simply fabricate a fourteenth generation to add to his thirteen generations in the final segment of his genealogy may suggest that he is genuinely bound to some prior source (Davies and Allison 1988:186). The temple records preserved priestly genealogies, and families interested in their lineage (such as those descended from David might be) may have preserved records of their own ancestry. Taxation status at times required peoples elsewhere in the Empire to be able to trace their lineage back as many as seven generations (see N. Lewis 1983:41-42).

Jesus Is Son of David and Son of Abraham (1:1) First Matthew calls Jesus *son of David,* a title of the rightful heir to Israel's throne (as in Jer 23:5; 33:15; *Ps. Sol.* 17:21-23; 4QFlor). Other lines of evidence support the claim that Jesus' family stemmed from this royal lineage (for example, Rom 1:3; *b. Sanhedrin* 43a bar.; Euseb. *H.E.* 3.20; see also Meier 1991:216-19), and ancient Jewish polemicists never bothered to try to refute it. Thus Matthew opens and closes the genealogy with a title for Jesus that is significant but rare in his Gospel: *Jesus Christ,* that is, the messianic king (1:1, 18).

Next Matthew calls Jesus *son of Abraham.* This is especially significant because subsequent chapters further portray Jesus as Israel's representative, the epitome of its history (for example, 2:15; 4:2; see Kingsbury 1975:12; Longenecker 1975:141-43). As the heir of Abraham par excellence, Jesus can communicate Abraham's promised blessings to his

---

1:1 Some have also seen an allusion to David in the number of generations Matthew enumerates in three sets of names: *fourteen* is the total numerical value of the three letters of David's name in Hebrew. But this allusion would have been hardly obvious to Greek readers and seems questionable; perhaps fourteen was simply Matthew's rough estimate of the generations from one period in Israel's history to the next, showing that Israel was due for its Messiah when Jesus came (compare *2 Baruch* 53—74). Matthew may have also preferred a round number for each set of generations, perhaps for ease of memorization (compare 2 Macc 2:25).

1:2-17 Many commentators note the striking differences between the genealogies in Matthew and Luke. The best alternative to harmonizing the lists in these ways is to suggest

people. (Some teachers regarded Abraham as the first Gentile convert to Judaism, which may also fit Matthew's theme.)

Jesus Is the Goal and Climax of Israel's History. (1:2-17) As important as Jesus' familial background may have been, that was not quite what a reader who read the genealogy would emphasize (see 1:18-25). In this section Matthew is most interested in Jesus' spiritual ancestry in Israel's history (Johnson 1988:209-10). The names in Matthew's genealogy—like Judah, Ruth, David, Uzziah, Hezekiah, Josiah—would immediately evoke for Matthew's audience a whole range of stories they had learned about their heritage from the time of their childhood. By evoking great heroes of the past like David and Josiah, Matthew reminds his audience of the ultimate hero of Israel's history to whom all those stories pointed.

Matthew makes this point clear in the opening words of his genealogy: a record of the genealogy of Jesus Christ, literally, the "book of the genesis of Jesus Christ" (1:1). Matthew gets this phrase from passages in Genesis ("the book of the generations of" in Gen 2:4; 5:1; 10:1, translated "account of" in the NIV), but his use of the phrase contrasts starkly with the use in Genesis. Genealogies like those in Genesis typically list a person's descendants after this phrase, rather than his ancestors. Matthew's point here is profound: so much is Jesus the focal point of history that his ancestors depend on him for their meaning. In other words, God sovereignly directed the history of Israel and preserved David's line because of his plan to send Jesus (Gundry 1982:10, 13; Patte 1987:18).

As the genealogies of Genesis 5 and 11 unify history between major figures (Adam, Noah and Abraham; see Johnson 1988:78), Matthew's genealogy unifies the defining periods of Israel's history and points them

---

that Matthew emphasizes the nature of Jesus' lineage as royalty rather than trying to formulate a biologically precise list (contrast possibly Luke) to which he did not have access. The following are among proposals that seek to harmonize the lists.

Luther suggested that Matthew offers Joseph's ancestry, whereas Luke provides Mary's; but his grammatical evidence for the position is not compelling (M. Johnson 1988:143-44). Utilizing levirate marriages, Africanus harmonized Matthew's genealogy (Joseph's biological ancestry) with Luke's (Joseph's legal ancestry by inheritance; Euseb. *H.E.* 1.7; M. Johnson 1988:141). Modern scholars more frequently argue that Matthew provides the legal line of royal inheritance (Hagner 1993:8); some connect this lineage with Luke's physical line by means of two adoptions (see M. Johnson 1988:142).

to Jesus. Jewish people also viewed genealogies as a testimony of God's providence in their ancestry. Many people regarded ancestry and the joining of couples as a sign of divine rule (for example, Epict. *Disc.* 1.12.28-29). Jewish people in particular believed that husbands and wives came together by an act of divine providence; some later rabbis even called it a miracle as great as the parting of the Red Sea (*b. Sanhedrin* 22a). History is important: it defines our identity and shapes our preparation for the future; and because we are God's people, Israel's history in the Bible has more to say to us about our eternal identity than does the heritage of any other culture we may claim as our own.

The Gentile mission. Through four interracial marriages Matthew teaches us about missions and racial reconciliation (1:3, 5-6). While Matthew's most obvious point is the connection of Jesus with Israel's history, another point would also strike his biblically sensitive readers forcefully. Genealogies need include only men (those in 1 Chron exemplify this pattern), so the unexpected appearance of four women draws attention to them. Had Matthew merely meant to evoke the history of Israel in a general way, one would have expected him to have named the matriarchs of Israel: Sarah, Rebekah, Leah and Rachel. Or to evoke supernatural births as a prelude to Mary's, he could cite Sarah, Rebekah and Rachel, whose wombs God opened. Instead he names four women whose primary common link is their apparent Gentile ancestry: Tamar of Canaan, Rahab of Jericho, Ruth the Moabite and the ex-wife of Uriah the Hittite.

In a world divided by races and cultures, an interracial marriage can appear scandalous, an act of treachery. The traditional white prejudice in some parts of the United States against black-white intermarriage is rooted in the history of slavery and racism (see Bennett 1966:242-73). Yet a genuinely divinely ordained interracial marriage can testify that Christ is a bond that runs deeper than race. One Tamil-Sinhalese couple in racially torn Sri Lanka declared, "Our marriage crosses the ethnic lines that divide our nation" (Williams 1992:10). By contrast, many North American Christians fail to actively pursue even interracial *friendships*.

Jewish people regarded genealogies as important to establish the purity of their lineage (as in 1 Esdras 5:39-40), yet it is the mixed nature of Jesus' lineage that Matthew purposely highlights. When Matthew cites these four women, he is reminding his readers that three ancestors of King David and the mother of King Solomon were Gentiles. Matthew thus declares that the Gentiles were never an afterthought in God's plan but had been part of his work in history from the beginning. This point fits an emphasis that runs throughout Matthew's Gospel (for example, 2:1; 3:9; 4:15; 8:11; 28:19), that God is not only for people of our own race or culture; we must cross racial and cultural boundaries to evangelize the whole world, humbly learn from other cultures, and serve with our brothers and sisters there.

☐ Accounts of Jesus' Childhood (1:18—2:23)

Matthew's accounts of Jesus' childhood set the stage for Jesus' ministry depicted in the rest of the Gospel, "defining his origin and goal" (Meier 1980:1-2). Matthew builds almost every paragraph following the genealogy and preceding the Sermon on the Mount around at least one text of Scripture. He thus invites us to read Jesus in light of Scripture and Scripture in light of Jesus—to recognize that the person and work of Jesus are central to Scripture's character. Some have suggested that Matthew made up the infancy stories to fit Scripture texts about Jesus, but the evidence suggests that he instead chose the Scripture texts to fit the stories. Matthew hardly cites the most obvious messianic texts here (see Soares Prabhu 1976); he probably depends on earlier tradition for the stories (Davies and Allison 1988:190-95; see more fully France 1981).

Because skeptical scholars often challenge the historical accuracy of these stories, we pause to consider some responses here. First, because Matthew builds each paragraph around Scripture, it should not surprise us that the passages contain midrashic (Jewish interpretive) elements, but we should not a priori assume that these passages are therefore necessarily unhistorical (see Hagner 1993:lviii; against Bourke 1960; Beare 1981:82). While midrashic interpretation can lead to fanciful elaborations of biblical accounts, it need not do so; at its core midrash simply requires reflection on Scripture. It is thus too simplistic to simply define Matthew's narratives as midrash and to define midrash as historically inaccurate embellishment (see P. Payne 1983; Cunningham and Bock 1987).

Second, were Matthew embroidering the stories of Jesus' birth, one might expect him to do so far more thoroughly, as various Jewish accounts embroidered biblical births (such as *1 Enoch* 106:2-3) or later apocryphal infancy Gospels embroidered Jesus' childhood.

Third, many texts Matthew cites are hardly obvious ones if he started with texts and then created stories around them (the stories do not fit the texts as well as one would expect if he had started with the texts first). While ignoring obvious messianic texts like Isaiah 9:6, Matthew selects texts that his contemporaries did not regard as messianic (Gundry 1975:194, despite his later view). This suggests that Matthew started with the infancy traditions and found biblical texts that fit (albeit adjusting the telling of both in the process). As R. T. France observes, "The only conceivable reason for introducing these texts is that it was already known that Jesus went to Egypt, that there was a slaughter of children, and that Jesus' home was in Nazareth, and that scriptural justification was desired for these elements in his background" (France 1985:71).

Fourth, scholars concerned to trace each detail of their narrative to extant sources can easily abuse midrash. Whereas some Matthew scholars suggest that some of Matthew's infancy material is midrash on traditions later incorporated into Luke (for example, Gundry 1982:20), some scholars who specialize in Luke suggest that Luke has midrashically interpreted Matthew (Drury 1976:123-25).

Fifth, the infancy narratives' vocabulary is not much more characteristic of Matthew than the rest of the Gospel is (Soares Prabhu 1976:167-70). Indeed, substantial evidence supports the possibility that earlier narratives stand behind Matthew's infancy stories (Davies and Allison 1988:190-95).

Finally, midrashic elements do not make these accounts strictly midrash in themselves (see Wright 1966:454-56). Given the literary unity and Luke's occasional confirmation of Matthew's birth narratives apart from the Old Testament citations, Matthew probably added the quotations to the narratives rather than simply the reverse (Down 1978; also see Soares Prabhu 1976:159-60, 165).

Had Luke reported the same undoubtedly pre-Matthew traditions, many scholars would be inclined to accept their historical core on the basis of multiple attestation or at least a pre-Synoptic tradition. Yet Luke's and Matthew's divergences do help us historically in one way: because these infancy narratives are independent (so also, for example, Hagner 1993:14-15), the points where they do overlap provide independent attestation for pre-Synoptic tradition—such as the virgin birth.

When a Virgin Gave Birth (1:18-25) If the genealogy indicates that Joseph descended from King David, this narrative explains in what sense this son of David (1:20) became Jesus' legal father by adoption. In this brief narrative Matthew provides not only an account of the virgin birth but reinforcement of the Christian view of Scripture and of Christ along with various principles of Christian ethics. Because this is Matthew's opening narrative, I treat it in rather extensive detail as a sample of the kinds of applications we can draw from Matthew's accounts. I must first, however, respond briefly to the skepticism with which some have challenged this account.

Arguments raised by more skeptical scholars against the virgin birth account are open to challenge. Whether this account makes historical sense rests largely on one's presuppositions. Would anyone whose logic was not shaped by Enlightenment thought doubt that of all the miraculous births of history, the Messiah's should be the most miraculous? One cannot deny testimony for a miracle by dismissing it on the grounds that miracles cannot happen; that is circular reasoning (see Craig 1986; compare Borg 1987:33-34; Meier 1994:11, 519-21; R. Brown 1994:143-44; on the historical context of modern skepticism, see Kee 1983:3-16; Bockmuehl 1988). Further, the proposed parallels to the virgin birth are inadequate (see Davies and Allison 1988:214-15).

We must evaluate the function and reliability of the virgin birth story by tools more reliable than philosophical presuppositions. On the one hand, ancient writers did like to recount miraculous births when possible. Greco-Roman biographies, or "lives," frequently included birth narratives (Aune 1987:65), including miraculous signs such as dreams when appropriate (Schuler 1982:94). Thus it is not surprising that Matthew would focus on such events, although his birth narratives do not perfectly fit this genre, since they lack the typical structure of miracle stories (see Theissen 1991:123).

Yet on the other hand an inclination to report a kind of event does not render evidence for that event unhistorical. The basic account of the virgin birth is earlier than either of the Gospels that describe Jesus' infancy; neither Gospel is clearly dependent on the other (see R. Brown 1977:162; pace Drury 1976:123-25). Reliable sources also stand behind the account; Jesus' birth is likely one of the stories whose reliability Luke investigated (Lk 1:3), since he had direct access to a younger son of Mary (Acts 21:18; see introduction). Members of Jesus' family remained in positions of prominence in early Christianity (1 Cor 15:7; Gal 1:19; 2:9), when this pre-Matthew tradition (shared with Luke) was circulating.

But Matthew is less concerned to prove the virgin birth to his audience, which both accepted Jesus as Messiah and acknowledged the miraculous. Matthew is more interested in teaching, and an important lesson his narrative teaches is that Jesus' birth fulfills Scripture (1:22-23).

Matthew affirms the inviolability of God's plan promised in Scripture. Theologians debate why Jesus had to be born from a virgin, sometimes suggesting, for instance, that God sent Jesus through a virgin so he could escape the sin nature. Yet for whatever other reasons God incarnated Jesus through a virgin, the only reason Matthew states is that Scripture might be fulfilled (1:22). Thus Matthew trusts the authority of Scripture.

This basic point is clearer than the actual nature of Matthew's argument from Isaiah, however. Because the Hebrew term *'almâh* in Isaiah 7:14 need not always mean virgin, most Jewish interpreters reject the messianic interpretation of this text (Berger and Wyschogrod 1978:41). Yet Matthew knows the context. In context, the child of Isaiah 7:14 was an urgent sign to Ahaz and would still be young when the kings oppressing Ahaz were carried into captivity (Is 7:7-25); Isaiah probably thus referred to his own son "Quick to the plunder, swift to the spoil" (Is 8:1, 3 mg), who would perform exactly the same function as Immanuel (8:1-4). But because Isaiah's children were for "signs" (8:18), Matthew was right to recognize in Immanuel (compare Is 8:8) a

---

1:20 That Joseph obeyed a revelation through a *dream* would not surprise ancient readers; most ancient Mediterranean sources regarded dreams as potentially revelatory. Of all New Testament writers, Matthew especially stresses revelation through dreams (2:12, 13, 19, 22; 27:19), though others recognize that God can speak (and sometimes today continues to

sign pointing to the ultimate presence of God and triumph for Judah in the Davidic Messiah who would be born to Israel (Is 9:1-7; Blomberg 1992:60; Keener 1993:48). Matthew recognizes that Scripture reveals the divine plan, and those who trust its authority need doubt no miracle it promises.

At much greater length, Matthew provides us various lessons from a righteous man's obedience. Matthew emphasizes Jesus' purity by recounting the obedience of the family who raised him, and in the process teaches us much about how we should live (Mt 1:19, 24-25). One of Matthew's purposes in his Gospel is to transmit Jesus' ethics (28:19); here he portrays a righteous young man and woman as models for Christian living. Luke focuses on God's revelation to Mary; Matthew focuses on the revelation to Joseph.

In this passage Matthew may work from an assumption that some people, both in his day and in ours, would challenge: the ability to obey God does not depend on age. Many modern cultures could learn from the valuable emphasis in Matthew's culture on respect for the aged; yet Matthew's culture, and sometimes our own, made seniority too great a criterion for such respect. (In the whole of Matthew's Gospel he praises not only young adults the age of Mary and Joseph but also children—18:2-6; 19:14; 21:16). Jewish men in Joseph's day generally married around the age of eighteen or twenty, after working to save some money (see, for example, *m. 'Abot* 5:21; N. Lewis 1983:55). Jewish women could marry as young as twelve or fourteen, upon reaching puberty (Jeremias 1969:365), though, like Greek and Roman women, they could be married much older.

Yet aside from his background assumptions, Matthew also provides clearer lessons in this narrative. First, he affirms, against any possible misinterpretations of the virgin birth, that Joseph controlled himself, practicing sexual restraint. By calling Joseph *righteous* (1:19) Matthew invites us to learn from Joseph's character about fidelity, discipline and preferring God's honor above our own. This paragraph assumes the

---

speak) in this manner (Acts 2:17). The character of the dream is noteworthy. Pagan (e.g., Apul. *Metam.* 8.8; 9.31; Plut. *Bravery of Women, Mor.* 252F) and sometimes Jewish (*ARN* 40A; *Pes. Rab Kab.* 11:23) dreams often included apparitions of deceased persons; like earlier biblical tradition, however, Matthew limits apparitions to angels.

principles of sexual fidelity and discipline that both Jesus and his Jewish contemporaries demanded (see 5:27-30).

Like most first-century Jewish people, Joseph was faithful to his future spouse in advance, awaiting marriage, and he expected the same in return. So clearly does Matthew want his audience to understand that this was part of Joseph's character that he points out that even once he and Mary were married, they refrained from marital relations until Jesus' birth (1:25). This would have taken considerable self-control; in many Middle Eastern societies observers simply assume that "if a man and woman are alone together for more than twenty minutes they have had intercourse" (Delaney 1987:41). The self-control of this young couple challenges those today who doubt their ability to control their passions.

Second, Matthew implicitly teaches about the nature of commitment in marriage: infidelity is always unjust, whereas divorce is just under some circumstances. Because Matthew wrote his Gospel as a whole, his narratives often illustrate principles that he teaches more explicitly in other contexts, and this is one such case (see 5:32). Some modern readers of the Gospels have treated divorce as sinful regardless of the reason, including cases of adultery, abandonment or abuse. This text challenges that prejudice, inviting readers of Matthew's divorce teaching in 5:32 and 19:9 to remember Joseph's righteousness and the exception that Matthew's Jewish audience would have understood permitted Joseph divorce and remarriage (see Allison 1993a).

For Joseph to "put Mary away" (1:19, literally) meant for Joseph to *divorce her* (NIV). Ancient Mediterranean fathers generally arranged their daughters' marriages through a custom called betrothal. Betrothal was much more serious than our modern practice of "engagement": it left the survivor of the man's death a widow, and if both partners lived it could be ended only by divorce (for example, *m. Ketubot* 1:2; *Yebamot* 4:10). Yet though Joseph was preparing to divorce Mary, the text calls him righteous.

At the same time we should observe that the circumstances under which Joseph was planning to divorce Mary were hardly light. Unlike today, Joseph had no option of giving Mary a second chance, even if he wanted to. Jewish and Roman law both demanded that a man divorce his wife if she were guilty of adultery (Keener 1991a:31, 156). Roman law actually treated a husband who failed to divorce an unfaithful wife as a panderer exploiting his wife as a prostitute (Gardner 1986:131-32; Richlin 1981:227).

Further, Joseph had another reason to divorce her. Because others would assume that Joseph himself must have gotten her pregnant unless he divorced her, his reputation was at stake for the rest of his life. Joseph probably also did not know Mary as well as we would expect of engaged couples today and had little reason to trust her innocence; if our sources are reliable, Galilean couples apparently enjoyed no privacy together until the wedding (Safrai 1974-1976b:756-57; Finkelstein 1962:1:45; though Matthew, unlike Luke, does not clarify at this point that the family already settled in Galilee). Joseph hence experiences the pain of betrayal, the breach of a contract more binding than a business deal in his culture (unfortunately our culture has less respect for commitment and fidelity). Because a wife's adultery could imply the husband's inadequacy or his family's poor choice of a mate, Mary's apparent unfaithfulness shamed Joseph as well (compare *2 Enoch* 71:6-11).

Under these circumstances, Joseph would be righteous in divorcing Mary; to fail to do so would violate law and custom, would bring enduring reproach on his household and would constitute embracing as wife one who had betrayed him in the worst manner conceivable in his culture. Modern Western society offers little sympathy for Joseph's pain. Our culture encourages marital betrayal that wounds trusting hearts, devastating homes where children should be nurtured in love and crushing whole families with the despair of abandonment. Unfortunately our churches often understand such pain no better than the culture does, counting as "unrighteous" those who legally divorce an unrepentantly unfaithful spouse. Unlike Matthew, we treat all kinds of divorce harshly yet often excuse adultery. Some of the same Christians who clamor for greater punishment for violent crimes or drug dealing counsel betrayed or abused spouses to be perpetually patient as if no consequences were appropriate for the betrayers or abusers.

By calling Joseph *righteous* Matthew challenges both our culture and our church in their lax views of sexual fidelity. The evil of divorce is in the breaking apart of what God has put together, but a person who abandons, betrays or abuses his or her spouse has already done just that. Matthew thus does not permit us to punish the innocent party in a divorce (in cases where one exists) any more than we should punish the innocent party in a rape (Deut 22:25-27) or any other crime. Yet for Joseph and for Matthew the exception remains a last resort, not a rationalization for a dissatisfied spouse to seek greener pastures.

Third, Matthew exhorts us to temper justice with compassion, a central principle in his Gospel (9:13; 12:7). Joseph was righteous not because he was divorcing Mary (although, as noted, this did not make him unrighteous); rather, Joseph was righteous for divorcing Mary *quietly* or privately—that is, for not bringing unnecessary shame on her. He knew suffering already awaited her: her premarital pregnancy had likely already ruined any chance of her ever marrying (see Delaney 1987:42), a horrible fate in an economically and honor-driven male-centered society. (Deut 22:21-24 mandated execution for this offense, but that penalty could rarely be carried out in this period; see, for example, Jos. *War* 2.117; Sherwin-White 1978:32-45.)

Yet Joseph could have profited by divorcing Mary publicly. By taking her to court, Joseph could have impounded her dowry—the total assets she brought into the marriage—and perhaps recouped the bride price if he had paid one at betrothal. By simply providing her a certificate of divorce in front of two or three witnesses, he would forfeit this economic reimbursement—simply to minimize her public dishonor (see *m. Gittin* 2:5; 9:3, 4, 8). Even though Jewish tradition ruled that a wife could lose her dowry for infidelity or for as little as scolding her husband (*m. Ketubot* 7:6), in normal divorces where the wife was not charged she kept her dowry (N. Lewis 1983:56). Joseph would have to enlist the help of a village scribe or elders to get the money, and this would increase Mary's public shame.

I have known of some churches that publicly shamed a young woman who became pregnant, usually leaving the less obvious father of the child concealed from public reproach. Joseph's "justness" or "righteousness" reminds us that justice is not merely a matter of punishment and shame but also a matter of mercy. Joseph was going to divorce Mary, but wounded though he felt, he would do everything in his power to minimize her shame.

Fourth, Joseph values commitment to God above his own honor, another principle Matthew articulates elsewhere (compare 7:21-27; 23:5-11). When God reveals the truth to Joseph, he immediately believes and obeys God's will, unbelievable as the truth would seem without a deep trust in God's power (compare Lk 1:37). (By contrast, many unmarried men today refuse to take responsibility even when they are the father!)

Joseph trusted God enough to obey him. Yet such obedience was costly. Because Joseph married Mary, outsiders would assume that he had gotten Mary pregnant before the wedding. Joseph would remain an object of shame in a society dominated by the value of honor. This was a stressful way to begin a marriage! By waiting to have intercourse (1:25), hence failing to provide the bloody sheet that would prove Mary's virginity on the wedding night (Deut 22:15; *p. Ketubot* 1:1, §§7-8; Eickelman 1989:174), Mary and Joseph also chose to embrace shame to preserve the sanctity of God's call.

Joseph's obedience to God cost him the right to value his own reputation. Many Christians today, probably much older than Joseph and claiming the power of the Holy Spirit in their lives, have yet to learn his lesson.

Matthew also emphasizes that Jesus is the Savior (1:20-21). At times when I have preached principles of sexual fidelity and betrayal from this passage, many hearers have been moved to repentance. At that point I am happy to turn to the other main character in the passage. Not only does Matthew teach us about the authority of Scripture through Isaiah and about fidelity, commitment and obedience through Joseph, he also provides teaching about salvation from sin through Christ. Even while Jesus is in Mary's womb, the angel declares that his name will be Yeshua (here in its Greek form *Iēsous,* translated "Joshua" in the Old Testament and *Jesus* in the New), which means "salvation." Jesus would bear this name because he would save his people from their sins (1:21). Jesus' other acts of "salvation" (8:25; 9:22; 10:22; the Greek term is broad in meaning) point to his ultimate redemption of his people. One who expounds this paragraph in public thus may want to echo Matthew's call to accept Christ's salvation.

But Matthew speaks of more than personal repentance; he evokes the Old Testament hope of the salvation of God's people, including the justice and peace of God's kingdom. For Matthew, and for us, salvation from sin cannot end with a prayer. Matthew promises salvation not only from sin's penalty but also from its power. Christ's followers are not merely heirs of his coming kingdom but servants of the King, committed to exemplifying the values of that future world in the midst of this present evil age.

More than anything, Matthew's narrative of the virgin birth, like every other event in Matthew, explains and exalts the character of his Lord. Many Bible readers today want to hear the Bible made "relevant" and "practical" to issues like those Matthew teaches through the example of Joseph, but nothing Matthew tells us is more practical than the way he reveals the heart and character of our Lord. As we get to know Jesus better through the Scriptures, we get to know Scripture's author and our character becomes more like his (see 2 Cor 3:14-18).

In view of Matthew 18:20 and 28:20, Matthew clearly understands *God with us* in Isaiah 7:14 to mean that Jesus is truly God (Mt 1:23). But as God "*with* us," Jesus is also the fully human one who *save[s] his people* by the cross. Matthew thus invites us to consider and worship the God who accepted the ultimate vulnerability, born as an infant to poor and humiliated parents into a world hostile to his presence. Oppressors must hate such a God, for his abandonment of power for love is contrary to everything they stand for. But the broken and oppressed find in him a Savior they can trust in a world where trust is generally dangerous. Of all the world's faiths, only Christianity announces a God who embraced our pain with us.

The First Star Trek (Matthew 2:1-12) As early as the second century, Bethlehemites believed they could identify the exact cave where, following Luke's account of the manger, Jesus had been born (Stauffer 1960:21; Finegan 1969:20-23; for echoes of Jesus' birth in Bethlehem in early rabbinic disputes, see Herford 1966:253-55).

A microcosm of Matthew's Gospel as a whole, this passage reminds us that we must preach the gospel to all people because we cannot always predict who will hear the message and who will not. Those we least expect to honor Jesus may worship him, and those we least expect to oppose him may seek his death. This passage confronts Matthew's readers with a summons to personal decision by contrasting the main characters (contrasting characters was a standard ancient literary device; see, for example, Schuler 1982:50). The Magi worship Jesus; Herod seeks his death; Jerusalem's religious elite—forerunners of the opponents of Matthew's audience—take Jesus for granted. The reader must identify with the pagan Magi rather than with Herod or Jerusalem's religious elite, and hence are compelled to recognize God's interest in the mission to the Gentiles. The God who sought servants like the Roman centurion (8:5-13) from the pagan west also sought previously pagan servants *from the east* (2:1; compare Is 2:6) like the Magi (see 8:11).

Matthew challenges prejudice against pagans. The first story after Jesus' birth opens with Magi who have traveled a long distance to offer homage to a new king born in Judea. They enter Jerusalem with a large enough caravan to attract the city's attention (2:3); they must have assumed that they would find the newborn king in Herod's palace in Jerusalem.

Magi were astrologers from the royal court of the king of Persia. Part of their job description was to make the king of Persia look good, but here they come to promote another king. Kings would often send congratulations to new rulers in other realms, but the king of Persia called himself "king of kings," that is, the highest of kings (compare, for example, Ezra 7:12; Dan 2:37). We might not expect the Magi to worship Jesus, especially if they found him not in the royal palace but in a cave.

More unexpectedly, these Magi are astrologers, which is why they noticed the star to begin with. Many sources from this period report the skill of Magi in divination, but Matthew's audience would probably recall first the Magi of their Greek translation of the Old Testament: Daniel's enemies, whom Daniel's narratives portray in a negative light as selfish, incompetent and brutal pagans (Dan 2:2, 10). (Their identity is even clearer in some later Greek versions of the Old Testament. In this period the Magi probably would have been Zoroastrian, but Matthew's readers would think more of Daniel's pagan accusers.)

Although the Bible forbade divination (Deut 18:9-13), which includes astrology (Is 47:13; see also Deut 4:19), for one special event in history the God who rules the heavens chose to reveal himself where the pagans were looking (compare Acts 19:12, 15-20). Without condoning astrology, Matthew's narrative challenges our prejudice against outsiders to our faith (see also 8:5-13; 15:21-28): even the most pagan of pagans may respond to Jesus if given the opportunity (compare Jon 1:13-16; 3:6-10). What a resounding call for the church today to pursue a culturally sensitive yet uncompromising commitment to missions!

Yet even supernatural guidance like the star can take the astrologers only so far; for more specific direction they must ask the leaders in Jerusalem where the king is to be born (2:2). That is, their celestial revelation was only partial; they must finally submit to God's revelation in the Scriptures, preserved by the Jewish people (see Meier 1980:11).

Matthew challenges prejudice that favors political power. Another central character in this narrative is Herod (2:3, 7-8). That Herod is dismayed by the Magi's announcement is not surprising (2:3); in this period most Greeks, Romans and even Jews respected astrological predictions. Further, a cosmic signal of another ruler would necessarily indicate the end of the current ruler's reign (as in Suet. *Vespasian* 23; Artem. 2.36). Other rulers also proved paranoid about astrologers (see MacMullen 1966:133; Kee 1980:71), and some had been ready to kill their own descendants to keep the throne (Herod. *Hist.* 1.107-10). But as many incidents during Herod's reign illustrate, he was more paranoid than most other rulers (see comment on 2:16). For Herod, little room existed for two kings in his realm: although he was Idumean by birth (Jos. *War* 1.123, 313; see Deut 17:15), he considered himself *king of the Jews* (compare 2:2). Here the one who reigns as king of God's people acts just like the oppressors of old: in Jewish tradition, both Pharaoh and his people feared when they learned in advance of the coming of Israel's deliverer (Jos. *Ant.* 2.206; Allison 1993b:146).

Herod's brutal power, played out in the following narrative, contrasts starkly with the human defenselessness of the Child and his mother (2:11, 19, 21). Whereas pagan Magi act like God's people (v. 11), the king of God's people acts like a notorious pagan king of old (v. 16; compare Ex 1:16). When we side with the politically powerful to seek human help against common foes, we could actually find ourselves

---

2:9-10 Without a tail extending to earth, a celestial light could have pointed them only in the most general way or by symbolic means toward Judea, and could now "move" before them to Bethlehem only in the sense that stationary objects in the sky appeared to move as travelers did. (Astronomers have proposed a variety of celestial phenomena around the time of Jesus' birth, perhaps 7 B.C., which could be the Magi's "star.") Why then does

fighting God's agendas (compare Is 30:1-5; 31:1-3). Jesus came and served among the weakest, depending solely on God's vindication (Mt 11:29; 12:19-21; 18:3-4; 19:14).

Matthew challenges the prejudice that respects spiritually complacent religion. Not knowing himself where the king would be born, Herod gathers the religious experts, the chief priests and scribes (2:4), most of whom in this period were loyal to his agendas (compare Jos. *Ant.* 15.2, 5). These experts immediately identify the place where the Messiah will be born on the basis of Micah 5:2 (Mt 2:5-6). But while the religious leaders know where the Messiah will be born, they do not join the Magi in their quest. These are the religious leaders, but they fail to act on all their Bible knowledge. Jesus is just a baby, and they take him for granted.

Although these authorities did not desire to kill Jesus as Herod did, their successors a generation later—when Jesus could no longer be taken for granted—did seek his death (26:57, 59). One is tempted to note that the line between taking Jesus for granted and wanting him out of the way may remain very thin today as well. And we must not forget that the sin of taking Jesus for granted is the sin not of pagans who know little about him, but of religious folk and Bible teachers.

Matthew reinforces these points by reminding us that it is the pagans who worshiped Jesus. After the Magi have left Jerusalem, they come and worship Jesus (2:9-11). A road led south to Bethlehem, which was about six miles from Jerusalem, so the rest of the Magi's journey probably did not take very long. That they offer Jesus both homage and standard gifts from the East (2:11) fits Eastern practices; for instance, royal courts there used frankincense and myrrh (though these spices also had many other uses). The Magi's homage to Jesus may reflect biblical language alluding to the pilgrimage and homage of nations in Psalm 72:10 or Isaiah 60:6, or to the queen of Sheba's visit to Solomon (1 Kings 10:1-13), or to all three texts; a late midrash on the queen of Sheba story includes a miraculous star (Bruns 1961). If Matthew has Psalm 72 or 1 Kings 10 in

---

Matthew describe the star's "movement" in these terms? Possibly the moving star in Matthew alludes to the pillar of cloud guiding Israel in the wilderness (Soares Prabhu 1976:280), suggesting that however the astrologers viewed the star, God used it in a manner that recalled Israel's salvation history.

mind, he expects us to recognize Jesus as King Solomon's greatest son (compare Mt 1:6-7; 12:42).

At any rate, the threefold repetition of homage (2:2, 8, 11) reinforces the point of the narrative: if God's people will not honor Jesus, former pagans will (Harrington 1982:17). Throughout this Gospel, homage to Jesus reflects some degree of recognition of his identity (as in 8:2; 9:18; 14:33; 15:25), climaxing in the ultimate homage of 28:9, 17, a context that declares Jesus' royal authority equivalent to the Father's (28:18-20). But such a hint may be present even in this Gospel's first example of homage: Matthew's audience may have expected Persians like the Magi to have intended more than merely human respect when they offered homage (compare Esther 3:2).

That the Magi needed a supernatural revelation to warn them not to return by way of Jerusalem (2:12) suggests their innocent naiveté. Even without Herod's unadmirable character (see comment on 2:16), few kings would be ready to surrender their own rule to a nonrelative some foreigners hailed as king! (For that matter, not only powerful people in society but many others today seem reluctant to acknowledge Jesus' right to direct their lives.) The Magi's innocence compared to Herod's murderous shrewdness again reminds Matthew's readers not to prejudge the appropriate recipients of the gospel (compare 13:3-23). Jesus is for all who will receive him, and God may provide Jesus' servants with allies in unexpected places if we have the wisdom to recognize them.

The Persecuted Child (2:13-18) This passage provides some important lessons for Matthew's first audience and for us today.

God Protects Jesus and His Family (2:13) Matthew here narrates God's protection for Jesus (2:13-15) and Herod's brutal massacre of

---

2:13-16 Skeptics often raise arguments against this account, especially because the other Gospels do not cover this part of Jesus' life. On one hand, to be sure, little historical evidence has survived that directly confirms the account in this paragraph; but on the other hand it is consistent with what we do know historically, and no historical evidence argues against it. In support of this passage, some cite second-century Jewish tradition confirming Jesus' stay in Egypt (which it associates with the sorcery Jewish people believed prevailed there; Dalman 1973:33). This tradition may be based on Christian claims (besides Matthew, compare later "infancy Gospels"). At the same time, the tradition could well stem from the

other children (2:16-18). Although the narrative rings with inspired grief and rage against Herod's act, God does not stop the injustice in this narrative any more than in most of the narratives we hear played on the evening news. Yet this narrative contains a kernel of good news that human reporters often cannot adequately discern until after the fact: the injustice of a world run by rebels against God cannot thwart his ultimate purposes for justice in that world.

Jesus Is a Refugee, a Model for Suffering (2:14) If we read 2:13-14 in the context of Matthew's Gospel, we realize that even in his childhood the Son of Man already lacked a place to lay his head (8:20). Disciples would face the same kind of test (10:23; 24:16).

Jesus' miraculous escape here should not lead us to overlook the nature of his deliverance (compare, for example, 1 Kings 17:2-6). Jesus and his family survived, but they survived as refugees, abandoning any livelihood Joseph may have developed in Bethlehem and undoubtedly traveling lightly. Although travel within Egypt was easy for visitors with means (Casson 1974:257), many Judeans had traditionally regarded refuge in Egypt as a last resort (2 Macc 5:8-9; compare 1 Kings 11:17, 40; Jer 26:21).

Some Christians in the West act as if an easy life were their divine right, as if to imply that suffering Christians elsewhere lack faith or virtue. Yet from its very beginning the story of Jesus challenges such a premise. Of the millions of refugees and other impoverished people throughout the world (for reports, see, for example, B. Thompson 1987), some are our brothers and sisters in Christ; many others have never yet heard how much he loves them. Reports of hundreds of thousands of civilians being tortured or slaughtered each year for political, ethnic or religious reasons can inoculate us against the reality of the human pain involved, but firsthand accounts from some of my closest African friends have brought

---

first century, when Egypt boasted a large Jewish population, perhaps one-third of Alexandria; early in the second century that community was mostly obliterated.
2:13 Extrabiblical Jewish traditions about Moses' birth further illustrate the parallel: a "scribe" notified Pharaoh that Israel's deliverer would be born, and a dream warned Moses' father to protect him (see Jos. *Ant.* 2.205-17, 234-36; Crossan 1986; Soares Prabhu 1976:289-90). In rabbinic tradition astrologers foretell Moses' birth (*b. Sanhedrin* 101a; *Soṭa* 12b), and the *Jerusalem Targum* on Exodus 1:15 calls them "magicians" (Allison 1993b:145).

the tragedy of this plight home to me. Many could resonate with the story of Jesus the refugee who identified with their suffering. Indeed, Western Christians should not be so arrogant as to think that we could never face such affliction ourselves; in due time Christians in all nations will receive their share of hardship (see 24:9).

Like other episodes in Matthew's first narrative section (1:18—4:25), the accounts of Jesus' childhood fulfill Scripture, with at least one explicit quotation per section. But all four stories in chapter 2 also surround place names rooted in Scripture. Jesus is "forced to wander from place to place," King of a world hostile to him (Schweizer 1975:41, 45). The world's treatment of Jesus likewise promises little better for his followers (10:23-25). While Christians are right to work for change within this world, we should not be surprised when we face hostility, false accusations or even death for Jesus' name (10:17-39; 13:21; 16:24-27; 24:9-14; compare 1 Thess 3:3; 1 Pet 4:12-13).

In Jesus the Anticipated Salvation of God's People Has Begun (2:15)

When Matthew quotes Hosea, he knows Hosea's context. The past exodus with which Jesus identified (Hos 11:1) was the historic sign of the covenant anticipating a new exodus (Hos 11:11). By quoting the beginning of the passage, Matthew evokes the passage as a whole and shows how Jesus is the forerunner of the new exodus, the time of ultimate salvation. Matthew uses God's pattern in history to remind us that our call and destiny, not the ridicule of outsiders, must define us. We are the people of the new exodus, the people of God's kingdom.

Matthew declares (2:15) that Jesus' sojourn in Egypt fulfills Hosea's prophecy *Out of Egypt I called my son* (Hos 11:1). But this second line in Hosea's verse directly parallels the first, "When Israel was a child, I loved him." Thus by citing Hosea 11:1 Matthew evokes the new exodus in Jesus, who embodies Israel's purpose and mission (Longenecker 1975:144-45). But by emphasizing that Jesus' return from *Egypt* reveals his sonship, Matthew again emphasizes that Jesus' mission is for all peoples (compare Acts 6:13; 7:33).

2:15 The Scriptures often called Israel God's *son* (e.g., Ex 4:22) or children (e.g., Deut 32:19), and both ancient Jewish sources understood the text as referring to Israel (see Daube 1973:191). Matthew corrects the Greek mistranslation of Hosea 11:1 to fit the Hebrew, so he presumably knew the context as well. Matthew emphasizes Jesus' solidarity

Matthew's quotation from Hosea also reminds us that Jesus identifies with his people's heritage. Jesus appears as the promised one greater than Moses (Deut 18:18; compare Mt 4:2; 17:2) and the heir of God's call to Israel. As God protected Moses when Pharaoh killed the male Israelite children, so God protects Jesus.

Further, Jesus goes to Egypt like Israel under the first Joseph, and like Pharaoh, Herod slays male Israelite children (Ex 1:16-2:5; Ps-Philo 9:1). To persecuted Christians, Herod's Pharaoh-like behavior is significant. Infanticide and more frequently child abandonment constituted typically pagan offenses that the Jewish people despised (for example, Wis 12:5-6; 14:23; Ps-Philo 2:10; 4:16); only such pagan evildoers as Antiochus IV Epiphanes had repeated Pharaoh's murder of Israelite babies (1 Macc 1:60-61; 2 Macc 6:10; 8:4).

Part of the moral of the story is therefore how it reflects on rulers among God's people: if a supposed "king of the Jews" can be a new Pharaoh, one cannot necessarily count on one's own people for allies. Matthew again challenges his readers' prejudice against Gentiles, reminding them of their opposition from fellow Jews. In a world still divided by racial and national ties, Christians from all peoples must remember that no group of people is incapable of producing evil. Herod's behavior may thus summon us to examine the sins of our own people first (compare 7:1-5).

A Ruler's Injustice Is Denounced (2:16-17) We lack concrete historical record for Matthew's next episode (except a garbled account from Macrobius; Ramsay 1898:219), but it certainly fits Herod's character (France 1979; compare Soares Prabhu 1976:227-28; Stauffer 1960:35-41). When Herod's young brother-in-law was becoming too popular, he had a "drowning accident" in what archaeology shows was a rather shallow pool; later, falsely accused officials were cudgeled to death on Herod's order (Jos. *War* 1.550-51). Wrongly suspecting two of his sons of plotting against him, he had them strangled (Jos. *Ant.* 16.394; *War* 1.550-51), and five days before

---

with Israel elsewhere (compare 1:1; 4:2); like the messianic servant (Is 49:5-7; 52:13—53:12) who fulfills the mission Israel had failed (Is 42:18-22), Jesus fulfills Israel's call (compare Is 42:1-4; 43:10; 49:1-3).

his own death the dying Herod had a more treacherous, Absalom-like son executed (*Ant.* 17.187, 191; *War* 1.664-65). Thus many modern writers repeat the probably apocryphal story that Augustus remarked, "Better to be Herod's pig than his son" (Ramsay 1898:219-20).

The murder of the children of Bethlehem thus fits Herod's character; yet it is not surprising that other early writers do not mention this particular atrocity. Herod's reign was an era of many highly placed political murders, and our accounts come from well-to-do reporters focused on the royal house and national events. In such circles the execution of perhaps twenty children in a small town would warrant little attention—except from God (see France 1979:114-19).

Matthew does not simply report this act of injustice dispassionately; he chooses an ancient lament from one of the most sorrowful times of his people's history. Jeremiah 31:15 speaks of Rachel weeping for her children, poetically describing the favored mother of Benjamin (standing for all Judah) mourning because her descendants were led into exile (see Montefiore 1968:2:10-11). Rachel, who wept from her grave in Bethlehem during the captivity, was now weeping at another, nearer crisis significant in salvation history (compare Mt 1:12, 17).

More important, however, the context in Jeremiah 31 also implies future hope. Rachel weeps for her children, but God comforts her, promising the restoration of his people (Jer 31:15-17), because Israel is "my dear son, the child in whom I delight" (Jer 31:20; compare Mt 2:15; 3:17). This time of new salvation will be the time of a new covenant (Jer 31:31-34). The painful events of Jesus' persecuted childhood are the anvil on which God will forge the fulfillment of his promises to his people, just as the cross will usher in the new covenant (Mt 26:28).

This text shows that God called his son Jesus to identify with the suffering and exile of his people (as in 1:12, 17; compare Jer 43:5-7) as he identified with their exodus (Mt 2:15). In his incarnation Jesus identified not only with humanity in an abstract sense but with the history

---

2:18 Rachel had been buried in Bethlehem (Gen 35:19), some six miles south of Jerusalem; Ramah was roughly six miles to the north of Jerusalem, on the road by which the Babylonians would lead the captive Judeans from their land (see Fenton 1977:49). That her cry was *heard in Ramah* indicates the loudness of her wailing in this image. Some later

of a people whose history is also spiritually the history of all believers (because we have been grafted into their history and use their Scriptures).

Yet we may also suspect that this identification speaks of a God who feels our human pain as deeply as we do. While philosophers and theologians must address the problem of evil intellectually, many grieving people inside and outside our churches face it existentially. To broken people wounded by this world's evil, Jesus' sharing our pain offers a consolation deeper than reasoned arguments: God truly understands and cares—and paid an awful price to begin to make things better.

Growing Up in a Small Town (2:19-23) Whereas modern Western readers generally expect a series of neat, concise theological statements, God chose to reveal himself in more concrete historical forms. Matthew does not just provide abstract statements about Jesus; he explains the character of his Lord by the history that was sanctified by his presence.

Jesus Is Granted a Respite from Trouble (2:19-20) Although Jesus would face more persecution in his adult years, Herod's death granted him a time of relative respite until his public ministry. Although Matthew mentions Herod's murder of the children, he notes Herod's own death three times—indicating that God alone holds the ultimate power of life and death (Patte 1987:36). Every unjust empire in history has ultimately fallen, but God's church continues to endure (Rev 18:1-3; 19:1-3). To oppressed Christians, whether persecuted for their faith (Mt 10:22; 1 Pet 4:13-14) or repressed for other unjust reasons (Mt 5:39-41; Jas 5:1-7), this reminder of the oppressors' mortality is a reminder that all trials are temporary and our loving Father remains in control (Mt 10:28-31; see also 1 Pet 5:10).

The angelic orders to return to the land of Israel because those seeking the child's life were dead (2:19-21) explicitly recall Exodus 4:19-20. Jewish readers would have immediately recognized the allusion: like Moses, Jesus had outlived his persecutor and would lead his people to salvation (Mt 1:21; Acts 7:35).

---

rabbis even said Jacob buried Rachel in Bethlehem so she could pray for the exiles when they later passed that way (e.g., *Gen. Rab.* 82:10). Matthew may connect the two passages (Gen 35:19; Jer 31:15) by using Rachel as a common link (Jewish teachers often linked texts on the basis of a common key word).

Wisdom Protects the Family from a Potential Danger (2:21-22)
God again protects his purpose in history from human oppressors.
Joseph was wise to avoid Judea and Archelaus (compare Prov 22:3;
27:12), as a dream confirmed. Archelaus shared all his father's
negative qualities and quickly provoked the opposition of many of
the people (Suet. *Tiberius* 8; Jos. *Ant.* 17.311-17). Although he
maintained his position as ethnarch for some time, the opposition of
A.D. 6 led to his banishment to Vienna in Gaul (Strabo 16.2.46; Jos.
Ant. 17.342-44).

By God's Plan, They Settle in an Obscure Place (2:23) Jewish leaders
who opposed Matthew's community undoubtedly reviled Jesus by won-
dering how a great Messiah could come from politically insignificant
Nazareth (compare Jn 1:46). Nazareth was, like many Galilean towns, "a
tiny agricultural village." Earlier estimates suggested that it contained as
many as sixteen hundred to two thousand inhabitants (Meyers and Strange
1981:27, 56), but more recent estimates have suggested five hundred
(Stanton 1993:112). It was the sort of community where everyone would
know everyone else's business, but it was a religiously orthodox town (see
Meyers and Strange 1981:27; Finegan 1969:29). Though Nazareth existed
in the shadow of the large, Hellenized Jewish city of Sepphoris, Galilean
villages and towns were not very dependent economically on the two
Hellenized cities (Goodman 1983:27, 60).

But while Nazareth was humanly insignificant, Matthew emphasizes
that it was divinely significant. Jewish leaders may have been inclined
to question, "Can any good thing come out of Nazareth?" (Jn 1:46 NASB),
but Matthew turns their objection around by showing divine significance
in the choice of Nazareth as Jesus' hometown. Matthew accomplishes
this exercise by a wordplay, a standard and accepted form of argumen-
tation in both Jewish and Greco-Roman rhetoric (Keener 1992b:54 n.
101). Although we would not use an argument based on wordplay today
(in English wordplays usually constitute bad puns rather than arguments), Matthew's argument demonstrates that we, like Matthew, should
be prepared to answer our culture's objections and questions regarding
our Lord Jesus in culturally relevant ways. His case for Nazareth also

---

2:23 *Nēṣer ("branch") recurs in the Dead Sea Scrolls as a messianic title (1QH 6.15; 7.19;*

reminds us that God often uses the despised things of the world to accomplish his purposes (1 Cor 1:27).

That Matthew is making a play on the name Nazareth is easier to recognize than the specific word with which he is playing, and scholars divide in their opinions here. Two views are most common. Those who believe that Matthew would not use a wordplay that worked only in Hebrew usually hold that Matthew intended "Nazirite" (Patte 1987:39-40; Meier 1980:16). Scholars who argue this position typically assume that Matthew drew a typological application from Samson in Judges 13:5 (part of the former prophets), which he attributed for some reason to the Messiah.

But whereas Matthew's less skillful readers would have to have satisfied themselves that the text was in their Bible somewhere, those skillful enough to recognize that no single text said this would also recognize Matthew's method; many might also know Hebrew. Thus other scholars appeal to the prophets' messianic title "the branch" (Is 4:2; Jer 23:5; 33:15; Zech 3:8; 6:12); Isaiah 11:1 uses the same term, which is more clearly messianic than "Nazirite."

□ Preparation for Public Ministry (3:1—4:25)

Matthew's introduction to Jesus' public ministry does not end with the stories of Jesus' childhood. Ancient biographies could include other introductory qualifications, and Matthew is no exception: he reports the attestation of the prophet John, of the heavenly voice and of Jesus' success in testing (3:1—4:11). Jesus' public ministry begins in 4:17.

Warnings of a Wilderness Prophet (3:1-12) Just as God revealed his purposes in advance to his prophets in ancient Israel (Amos 3:7; compare Is 41:22-29; 42:9; 43:9, 19; 44:7-8, 24-26; 45:21; 46:10; 48:6), God sent John the Baptist to prepare Israel for his climactic revelation in history. John was a wilderness prophet proclaiming impending judgment; for him repentance (Mt 3:2, 6, 8) was the only appropriate response to the coming kingdom (3:2), its fiery judgment (3:7, 10-12) and its final judge, who would prove to be more than a merely political Messiah (3:11-12).

8.6, 8, 10) and may be associated with Jesus in later rabbinic texts (*b. Sanhedrin* 43a, bar.; compare Herford 1966:95-96).

Given the widespread view in early Judaism that prophecy in the formal sense had ceased (Keener 1991b:77-91), John's appearance naturally drew crowds (3:5). (Modern proponents of the view that miraculous gifts have ceased have not been the first people in history surprised when God's sovereign activity challenges their presuppositions; see Judges 6:13; Deere 1993.)

The warnings in this passage serve two functions for Matthew's persecuted readers: judgment against persecutors both vindicates the righteous they oppress and warns the righteous not to become wicked (Ezek 18:21-24). Matthew's tradition probably mentioned the "crowds" in general (compare Lk 3:7), but Matthew focuses in on a specific part of the crowds: *Pharisees and Sadducees* (Mt 3:7). Like a good pastor, Matthew thus applies the text to the needs of his own congregations: their Pharisaic opponents were spiritual Gentiles (3:6, 9). Yet later chapters in this Gospel warn Matthew's audience that they can also become like these Pharisees if they are not careful (24:48-51; compare Amos 5:18-20).

John's Lifestyle Summons Us to Heed God's Call (3:1-4) John's location, garb and diet suggest a radical servant of God whose lifestyle challenges the values of our society even more than it did his own, and may demand the attention of modern Western society even more than his preaching does.

First, John's location suggests that the biblical prophets' promise of a new exodus was about to take place in Jesus. So significant is the wilderness (3:1) to John's mission that all four Gospels justify it from Scripture (3:3; Mk 1:3; Lk 3:4; Jn 1:23; Is 40:3): Israel's prophets had predicted a new exodus in the wilderness (Hos 2:14-15; Is 40:3). Thus Jewish people in John's day acknowledged the wilderness as the appropriate place for prophets and messiahs (Mt 24:26; Acts 21:38; Jos. *Ant.* 20.189; *War* 2.259, 261-62).

Further and no less important to John's mission, the wilderness was

---

3:3 The Qumran community applied the same Isaiah text to their own mission in the wilderness (1QS 8.13-16). If John was aware how others used the text, however, he undoubtedly felt that it applied better to himself; rather than separating himself totally from Israel as the Qumran sectarians did (1QS 8.13-14; 9.19-20; F. Bruce 1956:177), he preached directly to the crowds that came to him there (3:5).

3:4 Honey was the regular Palestinian sweetener (e.g., Ex 3:8; Prov 24:13; *Jub.* 1:7; Sirach 11:3; 24:20) and was available to the poor (e.g., Judg 14:8; 1 Sam 14:25; Is 7:22). Domestic

a natural place for fugitives from a hostile society (as in Heb 11:38; Rev 12:6; *Ps. Sol.* 17:17), including prophets like Elijah (1 Kings 17:2-6; 2 Kings 6:1-2). John could safely draw crowds (Mt 3:5) there as he could nowhere else (compare Jos. *Ant.* 18.118), and it provided him the best accommodations for public baptisms not sanctioned by establishment leaders (see Jos. *Ant.* 18.117). Thus John's location symbolizes both the coming of a new exodus, the final time of salvation, and the price a true prophet of God must be willing to pay for his or her call: exclusion from all that society values—its comforts, status symbols and even basic necessities (compare 1 Kings 13:8-9, 22; 20:37; Is 20:2; Jer 15:15-18; 16:1-9; 1 Cor 4:8-13).

Although true prophets could function within society under godly governments (as in 2 Sam 12:1-25; 24:11-12), in evil times it was mainly corrupt prophets who remained in royal courts (1 Kings 22:6-28; compare Mt 11:8) as God's true messengers were forced into exile (1 Kings 17:3; 18:13). Most Jewish people in the first century practiced their religion seriously; but the religious establishment could not accommodate a prophet like John whose lifestyle dramatically challenged the status quo. A prophet with a message and values like John's might not feel very welcome in many contemporary Western churches either. (Imagine, for example, a prophet overturning our Communion table, demanding how we can claim to partake of Christ's body while attending a racially segregated church or ignoring the needs of the poor. In most churches we would throw him out on his ear.)

John's garment (Mt 3:4) in general resembled the typical garb of the poor, as would befit a wilderness prophet cut off from all society's comforts. But more important, his clothing specifically evokes that of the Israelite prophet Elijah (2 Kings 1:8 LXX). Malachi had promised Elijah's return in the end time (Mal 4:5-6), a promise that subsequent Jewish tradition developed (for example, Sirach 48:10; compare 4 Ezra

---

beekeepers produced honey (*m. Baba Batra* 5:3), but John may have acquired wild honey by smoking bees out and breaking the honeycomb (see *m. 'Uqsin* 3:11). Because the Gospels provide no further explanation, bee honey rather than the less-known vegetable "honey" (Jos. *War* 4.468-69) is probably in view. In the wilderness, both refugees (*Eccl. Rab.* 10:8, §1) and pietists with special kosher requirements (*CD* 12.14; 11QTemple 48.1-5; compare S. Davies 1983) might subsist on locusts.

6:26; *t. 'Eduyyot* 3:4). Although Matthew did not regard John as Elijah literally (17:3; compare Lk 1:17), he believed that John had fulfilled the prophecy of Elijah's mission (Mt 11:14-15; 17:11-13).

John's Elijah-like garb thus tells Matthew's readers two things: first, their Lord arrived exactly on schedule, following the promised end-time prophet; and second, John's harsh mission required him to be a wilderness prophet like Elijah. Following God's call in our lives may demand intense sacrifice.

John's diet also sends a message to complacent Christians. Disgusted though we might be today by a diet of bugs with natural sweetener, some other poor people in antiquity also ate locusts (3:4), and honey was the usual sweetener in the Palestinian diet, regularly available even to the poor. But locusts sweetened with honey constituted John's entire diet. First-century readers would have placed him in the category of a highly committed holy man: the pietists who lived in the wilderness and dressed simply normally ate only the kinds of food that grew by themselves (2 Macc 5:27; Jos. *Life* 11). Matthew is telling us that John lived simply, with only the barest forms of necessary sustenance. Although God calls only some disciples to such a lifestyle (Mt 11:18-19), this lifestyle challenges all of us to adjust our own values. Others' needs must come before our luxuries (Lk 3:11; 12:33; 14:33), and proclaiming the kingdom is worth any cost (Mt 8:20; 10:9-19).

For that matter, John's lifestyle, like that of St. Anthony, St. Francis, John Wesley or Mother Teresa, may challenge affluent Western Christianity even more deeply than John's message does. John's lifestyle declares that he lived fully for the will of God, not valuing possessions, comfort or status. Blinded by our society's values, we too often preach a Christianity that merely "meets our needs" rather than one that calls us to sacrifice our highest desires for the kingdom. Too many Western Christians live a religion that costs nothing, treats the kingdom cheaply and therefore does not demand saving faith. Saving faith includes

---

3:6 Jewish "proselyte baptism" appears in relatively early sources (e.g., *m. Pesaḥim* 8:8; *t. 'Aboda Zara* 3:11; Pusey 1984), was known outside Palestine in the first century (Epict. *Disc.* 2.9.20; perhaps Juv. *Sat.* 14.104; *Sib. Or.* 4.162-65), is demanded by Jewish purification customs in view of the uncleanness of Gentiles, and, most significantly, was surely not borrowed from Christian baptism, with which it is analogous. See further documentation in Keener 1997.

believing God's grace so sincerely that we live as if his message is true and stake our lives on it. May we have the courage to trust God as John did, to stake everything on the kingdom (13:46) and to relinquish our own popularity, when necessary, by summoning others to stake everything on the kingdom as well.

John Has an Uncomfortable Message for Israel (3:5-10) Although most Jewish traditions acknowledged that all people need some repentance (see 1 Kings 8:46; 1 Esdras 4:37-38; Sirach 8:5), John's call to his people (Mt 3:5-6, 8-9) is more radical. John's "repentance" refers not to a regular turning from sin after a specific act but to a once-for-all repentance, the kind of turning from an old way of life to a new that Judaism associated with Gentiles' converting to Judaism. True repentance is costly: the kingdom "demands a response, a radical decision. . . . Nominalism is the curse of modern western Christianity" (Ladd 1978a:100). In various ways John warns his hearers against depending on the special privileges of their heritage.

First, John's baptism confirms that he is calling for a once-for-all turning from the old way of life to the new, as when Gentiles convert to Judaism. Although Judaism practiced various kinds of regular ceremonial washings, only the baptism of Gentiles into Judaism paralleled the kind of radical, once-for-all change John was demanding. In other words, John was treating Jewish people as if they were Gentiles, calling them to turn to God on the same terms they believed God demanded of Gentiles. As F. F. Bruce puts it, "If John's baptism was an extension of proselyte baptism to the chosen people, then his baptism, like his preaching, meant that even the descendants of Abraham must . . . enter . . . by repentance and baptism just as Gentiles had to do" (1978:61).

Second, John's hearers were not all good descendants of their ancestors anyway. "Viper" was certainly an insult, and *brood of vipers* (offspring of vipers) carries the insult further. In the ancient Mediterranean many people thought of vipers as mother killers. In the fifth century

---

3:7 Ancient Mediterranean peoples considered parent murder one of the most hideous crimes conceivable (Plutarch *Romulus* 22.4; Apul. *Metam.* 10.8; 1 Tim 1:9). Most people believed that even children who justly avenged their fathers did evil if they personally carried out vengeance against their mothers, and thus the Furies would torment them (e.g., Euripides *Electra* 1238-91; *Orestes* 531-32, 549-63).

B.C. Herodotus declared that newborn Arabian vipers chewed their way out of their mothers' wombs, killing their mothers in the process. Herodotus believed that they did so to avenge their fathers, who were slain by the mothers during procreation (Herod. *Hist.* 3.109). Later writers applied his words to serpents everywhere (Aelian *On Animals* 1.24; Pliny *N.H.* 10.170; Plut. *Divine Vengeance* 32, *Mor.* 567F). Calling John's hearers vipers would have been an insult, but calling them a *brood of vipers* accused them of killing their own mothers, indicating the utmost moral depravity. That Matthew applies this phrase to religious leaders may be unfortunately significant.

Third, employing the image of a tree's *fruit*, both John and Jesus demand that one's life match one's profession (3:8; 7:16-17; 12:33; 13:22-23; 21:34, 43). In contrast to some forms of modern Christianity, Judaism also insisted that repentance be demonstrated practically (*m. Yoma* 8:8-9; Montefiore 1968:2:15). Thus no one could simply appeal to ethnic character or descent from Abraham (compare Deut 26:5). Biblical tradition had already applied the image of a *tree* being *cut down* (Ezek 31:12-18; Dan 4:23) or burned (Jer 11:16) to the judgment of a nation. Most small trees that could not bear fruit would have been useful, especially for firewood (N. Lewis 1983:139).

Fourth, John's admonition that out of stones God could raise up children for Abraham (compare Gen 1:24; 2:9) warns his hearers not to take their status as God's people for granted. Jewish people had long believed they were chosen in Abraham (Neh 9:7; Mic 7:20; E. Sanders 1977:87-101), but John responds that this ethnic chosenness is insufficient to guarantee salvation unless it is accompanied by righteousness (compare Amos 3:2; 9:7). Prophets were not above using witty wordplay at times (Amos 8:1-2; Mic 1:10-15; Jer 1:11-12), and *children* and *stones* probably represent a wordplay in Aramaic; the two words sound very similar (Manson 1979:40). (At any rate, John's symbolism should not have been obscure: God had previously used stones to symbolize his people in Ex 24:4; 28:9-12; Josh 4:20-21.)

Salvation demands personal commitment, not merely being part of a religious or ethnic group. No one can take one's spiritual status for granted simply because one is Jewish, Catholic, Baptist, evangelical or anything else. As the saying goes, God has no grandchildren; the piety of our upbringing cannot save us if we are not personally committed to Christ. Even depending on our past religious experience is precarious. Whereas historic Calvinism teaches that the elect will persevere to the end and Arminianism allows that apostate converts may be lost, neither supports the now-common view that those who pray the sinner's prayer but return to a life of ignoring God will be saved. Yet at a popular level, vast numbers of people believe they are saved because they once prayed a prayer. If this modern popular misunderstanding of the once-saved-always-saved doctrine is false, it may be responsible for millions of people's assuming they are saved when they are in fact lost. John's message constituted a decisive challenge to false doctrines of his day that cost people their salvation; John's successors in our day must be prepared to issue the same sort of unpopular challenges.

John Proclaims the Coming Judge and Judgment (3:10-12) In Matthew, John is mostly what narrative critics call a "reliable character": we can trust the perspective of most of what he says (11:7-11). The only point at which Matthew needs to qualify John's proclamation is John's inability to distinguish works inaugurated at the first coming of Jesus (such as baptism in the Spirit) from those inaugurated at the second (such as baptism in fire); Jesus addresses this lack of nuance in 11:2-5 (see comment there).

Although Matthew and Luke retain Mark's emphasis on the Spirit (the Spirit-baptizer himself becomes the model of the Spirit-empowered life—Mk 1:8-12; see Keener 1996: 29-30), they report more of John's preaching of imminent judgment than Mark does. Matthew emphasizes the kingdom, the Coming One and the judgment he is bringing (Mt 3:2, 7-12).

First, John emphasizes that the *kingdom* is coming. In Matthew's summary of their preaching, both John and Jesus announce the same message: *Repent, for the kingdom of heaven is near* (3:2; 4:17). Matthew intends us to see John's and Jesus' preaching about the kingdom as models for our preaching as well (10:7); the Lord is not looking the other way in a world of injustice but is coming to set matters straight. Therefore those who believe his warnings had better get their lives in order.

Most Jewish people in Palestine expected a time of impending judgment against the wicked and deliverance for the righteous. But most expected judgment on other peoples and on only the most wicked in

Israel (compare *m. Sanhedrin* 10:1; E. Sanders 1985:96); Jewish people, after all, had certain privileges. Oppressed by surrounding nations, Israel had good reason to long for deliverance, but many people within the nation, including its political leaders, needed to look first to themselves. Amos sounded a clear warning, to his generation, to Jesus' generation and to ours, when we prove more quick to judge others than ourselves: "Woe to you who long for the day of the LORD," for it will be a day of reckoning (Amos 5:18). Sometimes skeptics appeal to evil in the world to deny God's existence; instead they should be applauding his mercy in giving them time to repent, because when God decisively abolishes evil, he will have to abolish them (see 2 Pet 3:3-9).

Second, John warns that the wicked will be burned, just as farmers destroy useless products after the harvest. Harvest and the threshing floor (3:8, 10, 12) were natural images to use in agrarian, rural Palestine. Earlier biblical writers had used these images to symbolize judgment and the end time (as in Ps 1:4; Is 17:13; Hos 13:3; Joel 3:13); Jesus (Mt 9:38; 13:39; 21:34) and his contemporaries (4 Ezra 4:30-32; *Jub.* 36:10) also used the image. (Fire naturally symbolized future judgment, as in Is 66:15-16, 24; *1 Enoch* 103:8.) Villagers carried grain to village threshing floors; large estates worked by tenants would have their own (N. Lewis 1983:123). When threshers tossed grain in the air, the wind separated out the lighter, inedible chaff. The most prominent use of this chaff was for fuel (*CPJ* 1:199). But while chaff burned quickly, John depicts the wicked's fire as *unquenchable.* Many of his contemporaries believed that hell was only temporary (for example, *t. Sanhedrin* 13:3, 4), but John specifically affirmed that it involved eternal torment, drawing on the most horrible image for hell available in his day.

Many of us today are as uncomfortable as John's contemporaries with the doctrine of eternal torment; yet genuinely considering and believing

---

3:11 Some think John's original proclamation addressed only the threshing-floor image of wind blowing *chaff* so it could be separated from the *wheat* and burned. In this case John would have thought not of *the Holy Spirit* but of a "purifying wind," which would be translated much the same way (A. Bruce 1979:84; Flowers 1953). But four reasons militate against taking John's original words as merely "wind and fire": Jewish people usually understood "holy spirit" as a reference to God's Spirit (occasionally to a purified human spirit); wind, like fire, can represent God's purifying Spirit in the Old Testament; many—especially John's contemporaries in the wilderness—associated the Spirit with purification

it would radically affect the way we live. That John directs his harshest preaching toward religious people (Mt 3:7) should also arouse some introspection on our part (see also Blomberg 1992:142-43). Even for the saved, the knowledge that all private thoughts will be brought to light (10:26) should inspire self-discipline when other humans are not watching. Our culture prefers a comfortable message of God's blessing on whatever we choose to do with our lives; God reminds us that his Word and not our culture remains the final arbiter of our destiny.

Finally, John warns of the coming judge, who is incomparably powerful. Judgment is coming, but the coming judge John announces is superhuman in rank (3:11-12). Only God could pour out the gift of the Spirit (Is 44:3; 59:21; Ezek 36:27; 37:14; 39:29; Joel 2:29; Zech 12:10), and no mere mortal would baptize in fire (in the context, this clearly means judge the wicked—3:10, 12).

Further, whereas Israel's prophets had called themselves "servants of God" (as in 2 Kings 9:7, 36; Jer 7:25; Dan 9:6, 10; Amos 3:7), John declares himself unworthy even to be the coming judge's slave! In ancient Mediterranean thought, a household servant's basest tasks involved the master's feet, such as washing his feet, carrying his sandals or unfastening the thongs of his sandals (see, for example, Diog. Laert. 6.2.44; *b. Baba Batra* 53b). Although ancient teachers usually expected disciples to function as servants (as in Diog. Laert. 7.1.12; 7.5.170; *t. Baba Meṣi'a* 2:30), later rabbis made one exception explicit: disciples did not tend to the teacher's sandals (*b. Ketubot* 96a). John thus claims to be unworthy to even be the Coming One's slave. Indeed, the One whose way John prepares is none other than the Lord himself (Is 40:3; Mt 3:3). Matthew's readers would not need to know Hebrew to realize that John was preparing the way for "God with us" (1:23). No wonder John is nervous about baptizing Jesus (3:14)!

(see Keener 1991b:65-69); and all extant traditions apply the saying to God's Spirit (see F. Bruce 1966:50; Aune 1983:132).

3:12 Many of John's contemporaries believed hell was eternal for at least the worst sinners (4 Macc 9:9; 12:12; *t. Sanhedrin* 13:5). In the most common Jewish view, however, most sinners endure hell only temporarily and are then destroyed (compare 1QS 4.13-14; *t. Sanhedrin* 13:3-4) or released (*Num. Rab.* 18:20; other texts are unclear, e.g., Sirach 7:16; *Sipre Num.* 40.1.9). John is not simply accommodating the views of his culture.

God Honors His Humble Son (3:13-17) Given the embarrassment of some early Christian traditions that Jesus accepted baptism from one of lower status than himself, it is now inconceivable that early Christians made up the story of John baptizing Jesus (E. Sanders 1985:11; 1993:94; Meier 1994:100-105; pace Bultmann 1968:251).

Although Jesus alone did not need John's baptism—he was the giver of the true baptism (3:11)—he submitted to it to fulfill God's plan (3:14-15). In a traditional Mediterranean culture where society stressed honor and shame (Malina 1993), Jesus relinquishes his rightful honor to embrace others' shame. After Jesus' public act of humility, God publicly honors Jesus as his own Son (3:16-17; compare 2:15)—that is, as the mightier One whose coming to bestow the Spirit John had prophesied (3:11-12).

John Recognizes Jesus as the Ultimate Baptizer (3:14) Why would the fire-baptizer seek baptism like an ordinary mortal? Whereas John recognizes Jesus' superiority, Jesus humbly identifies himself with John's mission: *It is proper for us to do this to fulfill all righteousness* (Meier 1980:26-27). Although John undoubtedly recognized the Spirit's empowerment in his own ministry (Lk 1:15-17), he recognized that Jesus had come to bestow the Spirit in fuller measure than even he as a prophet had received, and he desired this baptism (Mt 3:11; compare 11:11-13).

Various schools of thought today dispute exactly what the New Testament writers meant by Spirit baptism; some think the term refers to conversion only, and others only to a subsequent experience. It may be that John applied the expression to the entire sphere of the Spirit's work in our lives, including both conversion and subsequent experiences of empowerment (see Keener 1996:17-78), in which case both main schools of thought would be correct. But regardless of our view about the specific meaning of his language, most of us fail to grasp the power God has provided us. If Jesus has bestowed on us even more spiritual power than he bestowed on John and the Old Testament prophets, today's church should be trusting God for a much deeper empowerment in our life and witness than most of us currently experience.

3:14 That John himself would admit Jesus' greater status here is not unreasonable given John's witness to a mightier one (3:11-12), subsequent witness to the Spirit descending on

Jesus "Fulfills All Righteousness" by Identifying with His People (3:15) As noted above, on behalf of others Jesus voluntarily accepted a lower status than he deserved. Since "fulfilling righteousness" elsewhere in Matthew may pertain to obeying the principles of the law (5:17, 20; compare, for example, *Sib. Or.* 3.246), Jesus presumably here expresses his obedience to God's plan revealed in the Scriptures. But Jesus sometimes also fulfilled the prophetic Scriptures by identifying with Israel's history and completing its mission (Mt 2:15, 18). This baptism hence probably represents Jesus' ultimate identification with Israel at the climactic stage in its history: confessing its sins to prepare for the kingdom (3:2, 6).

If this suggestion is correct, then Jesus' baptism, like his impending death (compare Mk 10:38-39 with Mk 14:23-24, 36), is vicarious, embraced on behalf of others with whom the Father has called him to identify (Lampe 1951:39). This text declares the marvelous love of God for an undeserving world—especially for us who by undeserved grace have become his disciples. Jesus' example also calls us to offer ourselves sacrificially for an undeserving world as he offered himself for us. In a world that regards moral boundaries as impractical, where nothing higher than selfish passion guides many lives around us, Jesus reminds us of a higher mission and purpose for our lives. By submitting to baptism by one of lower rank who was nevertheless fulfilling his calling, Jesus also models humility for us.

God Declares His Approval of Jesus (3:16-17) After Jesus submits humbly to others in God's plan, God publicly acknowledges Jesus' own rank. First, *heaven was opened,* reflecting biblical language for God's revelation or future deliverance (Is 64:1 [LXX 63:19]; Ezek 1:1; Kingsbury 1983:64; Schweizer 1970:37; compare *Joseph and Asenath* 14:2/3).

Second, Jesus saw *the Spirit descending like a dove and lighting on him.* The background for this sign of God's approval may require further comment. Scholars have often suspected that the dove has symbolic value and have proposed a variety of possible backgrounds for it. Jewish use of the dove to symbolize God's Spirit (Abrahams 1917:48-49; Barrett

Jesus (3:16-17), and subsequent witness that he had at least initially assumed Jesus was the Christ (11:3; see comment there).

1966:38) is both rare and late, as is the rabbinic comparison of the brooding Spirit in Genesis 1 with a dove (Taylor 1952:160-61). More frequently the dove represents Israel (as in Ps-Philo 39:5; *b. Šabbat* 49a; 130a); but while Jesus identifies with Israel in the context (as in Mt 2:11), this passage portrays the Spirit, not Jesus, as a dove. Genesis 8:8-12 probably provides the most suitable background (see also 4 Baruch 7:8): here the dove appears as the harbinger of the new world after the flood, which other early Christian literature employs as a prototype of the coming age (Mt 24:38; 1 Pet 3:20-21; 2 Pet 3:6-7). Jesus is the inaugurator of the kingdom era that John has been proclaiming.

Third, God shows his approval of Jesus by a *voice from heaven*, a concept with which Matthew's Jewish audience was undoubtedly familiar. Many Jewish teachers considered this *bat qôl* the primary source of revelation apart from Scripture exposition while the Spirit of prophecy was quenched. The Gospels show that three voices—Scripture, a prophetic voice in the wilderness and the heavenly voice—all attest Jesus' identity. The heavenly voice alone would have been inadequate, but here it confirms the witness of Scripture and a prophet. Jesus is not a mere prophet but the subject of other prophets' messages.

The fact of the voice is important, but what the voice says is most important, for this is what officially declares Jesus' identity to Matthew's biblically informed implied audience. The voice rehearses ancient biblical language, probably adapting Psalm 2:7 ("You are my Son") into an announcement to the bystanders *(This is my Son)*. Psalm 2, originally an enthronement psalm, is here used to announce in advance Jesus' messianic enthronement. The second proposed biblical allusion here, Isaiah 42:1, is more controversial, despite its many proponents. But whether or not Mark saw Isaiah's servant as background here, Matthew surely did, for he reads the wording of this voice's recognition oracle

---

3:17 Rabbinic texts frequently mention the *bat qôl*, or "daughter of a voice" (e.g., *b. Baba Batra* 73b; *Makkot* 23b), which also has conceptual parallels outside rabbinic literature (Jos. *Ant.* 13.282-83; Artapanus in Euseb. *P.E.* 9.27.36). That the *voice* supplements John's witness rather than replaces it is important; in Jewish tradition the *bat qôl* testified of others as well (e.g., *Sipre Deut.* 357.10.3), and it remained subordinate to Scripture (*p. Mo'ed Qaṭan* 3:1, §6). Some find in the *voice from heaven* an allusion to the sacrifice of Isaac (Gen 22:11-12; compare *Test. Levi* 18), but given the dove, one might also appeal to a voice in Noah's time (Gen 9:1; *Sib. Or.* 1:127, 267).

into his own translation of Isaiah (Mt 12:18). Jesus' mission includes suffering opposition as well as reigning, and so does the mission of his followers (5:11-12; 10:22; 16:24-27; 19:27-29; 24:9-13).

The Father's acclamation of the Son may suggest various principles to Matthew's readers. First, it reveals how central Jesus is to the Father's heart and plan; no one can reject Jesus and simultaneously please the Father. Jesus is not one prophet among many, but God's ultimate revelation; that he is God's "beloved" Son underlines the magnitude of God's sacrifice (compare Jn 3:16). Though in many contemporary circles worship properly exhorts and encourages the people of God (Col 3:16), we also need the kind of worship that tells Jesus how great he is, praising him for what he has done and for who he is (Ps 150:2).

Second, the Father's acclamation reveals that the meek Jesus is also the ultimate ruler who will usher in justice and peace. The beginning of his story tells his persecuted followers the end of the story in advance, providing us firm hope for the future.

Finally, the voice reveals Jesus as the Son obedient to the point of death, who willingly divests himself of his proper honor by identifying with us in baptism and death. We who often trifle with obedience in the smallest matters—for instance, the discipline of our thoughts or words for God's honor—are shamed by our Lord's obedience. May we worship him so intensely that his desires become our own and we, like our Lord, become obedient servants with whom the Father is *well pleased*.

God's Son Passes the Test (4:1-11) Scholars' interpretations of the temptation narrative broadly fall into three primary categories (Theissen 1991:218-19): (1) Jesus' testing recalls that of Israel in the wilderness; whatever God commanded Israel his child in the wilderness, much more he would require of his Son the Messiah. (2) Jesus provides a model for

---

The word order of Psalm 2:7 LXX differs from Mark's (Cranfield 1955:61), but the voice may place *son* later to keep the added "beloved" with "in whom I am well pleased," and early Christians used Psalm 2 for Jesus regularly (e.g., Acts 13:32-33; Heb 1:5); see Marshall 1969:332-33. More scholars find Isaiah 42 in Mark 1:11 than find Genesis 22:2 there, but in Mark's wording the Genesis allusion is probably paramount (compare Best 1983:81; Stegner 1985; Suder 1982); the Greek version sometimes uses "beloved" to translate *yāḥîd* ("only son"), including in Genesis 22 (Dodd 1961:130 n. 1), increasing the pathos of the sacrifice; compare Mk 14:36; 15:39.

tested believers. (3) The narrative affirms a correct understanding of Jesus' messiahship as against contemporary political or militaristic interpretations. Clues within the narrative (such as 4:2) and the rest of Matthew (such as 6:13; 26:41; 27:42-43) indicate that the narrative functions in all three ways.

Matthew emphasizes that Jesus, unlike Israel, passed his test in the wilderness. Matthew makes this biblical background clear even in simple ways like saying the Spirit *led* Jesus into the wilderness, reflecting a common biblical motif of God guiding his people in the wilderness (as in Ex 13:18, 21; 15:13, 22; Deut 8:2). We should also note that Jesus quotes three texts from Deuteronomy, all of them commandments that Israel failed to obey but that Jesus is determined to obey.

Like John, Jesus had to exit the confines of society for his supernatural encounter (see comment on 3:1-12). The wilderness (translated *desert* in the NIV because few people lived there) was not a pleasant place: some believed the wilderness to be a special haunt of demons (see comment on 12:43; compare *1 Enoch* 10:4; 4 Macc 18:8). Apart from a few rugged people like John who made the "wilderness" between the Jordan Valley and Judean hills their home, it represented a dangerous and inhospitable setting (E. Sanders 1993:113).

But when we think of applying this passage today, we may meditate at greater length on the other two lessons scholars often draw from the narrative: what Jesus' victory models for us as his disciples and what the passage tells us about the true character of Jesus' mission. No less than Matthew's discourse sections (28:19), this narrative provides a model for us. (Jewish teachers instructed by example as well as by word, and

---

4:1 Much of the past cannot be recovered by purely historical methods, and it would naturally be difficult to find historical evidence for this temptation narrative outside the Gospels. Nevertheless, at barest and most skeptical minimum we must acknowledge that Jesus undoubtedly sometimes felt tempted, sometimes sought to get alone to pray, and probably would have fasted before starting his public ministry (E. Sanders 1993:112). Jesus used "twelve" symbolically in calling disciples; it is no less reasonable to surmise that he himself also would use *forty days* to allude to Israel's forty years in the desert (Sanders 1993:112-13). Those of us who know people who undertake forty-day fasts will also find the fast more credible than those who cannot imagine it. Elements of the narrative are consistent with Jesus' known practice (Sanders 1993:117).

In form the narrative is closest to a "controversy dialogue" (Travis 1977:69), or the kind of debate one expects from two experts in the law (e.g., Jeremias 1971:158). The Bible

biographers taught moral lessons through their accounts. So narratives about Jesus teach us no less than his direct commandments do.) For instance, if John had been a model of sacrificial obedience for living in the wilderness and subsisting on locusts, Jesus who *fasts* in the wilderness is even more so.

This narrative underlines the biblical principle that God's calling must be tested. The Spirit, having empowered Jesus for his mission as God's Son (3:16-17), now is the one who leads him into the wilderness where his call must be tested (4:1, 3, 6). Matthew expressly informs us that the purpose of the Spirit's first leading of God's Son was that he might be tested! Like most of his heroic predecessors in biblical history (Abraham, Joseph, Moses, David, Job), Jesus had to pass a period of testing before beginning his public ministry. Some of his predecessors almost snapped under pressure, restrained only by God's favor (for example, 1 Sam 25:13-34; 1 Kings 19:4; Jer 20:7-18), but our Lord Jesus provides the perfect model for triumphing in testing.

If God is calling and empowering you to do something for him (3:16-17), you can expect to be tested (compare comment on 6:13), and you can expect testing commensurate with the seriousness of your call. The devil may not show up in person or test you on the same supernatural level that he tested Jesus, but your hardships may seem unbearable apart from the grace of God. Nevertheless, testing is for our good: when biblical heroes had matured through the time of testing, they knew the depth of God's grace that had sustained them. The truly triumphant boast not in their success in the test but in God's empowerment, without which they could not have over-come. Jesus went into this testing only after the Father had empow-

---

usually makes God the author of "testing" (Gen 22:1; Deut 13:3), as does much later Jewish literature (e.g., *Jub.* 17:17; Sirach 2:1; 36:1; Wisdom 3:5-6), but in the sense that he proves the depth of a person's commitment (translated "trial"), not in the sense of seeking to make a person fall (translated "temptation"; compare Jas 1:13-15; Best 1965:49-50). The latter was the devil's work.

4:2 Jesus' fast especially recalls that of Moses in Exodus 24:18 and 34:28, as does that of Elijah in 1 Kings 19:8. Later Jewish literature had others repeat Moses' forty-day fast (e.g., *Life of Adam and Eve* 6:1; compare *History of Rechabites* 1:1). Yet Jesus is fully human and hungry: contrast Abaris's continual magical fast (Blackburn 1986:191) and Baruch's seven-day fast, which did not make him hungry (*2 Baruch* 21:1). Ancients recognized that forty days without food could precipitate death by starvation (Diog. Laert. 8.1.40).

ered him in the Spirit (3:16).

This narrative presents Jesus as our vicarious advocate, relinquishing his own power for his mission to save us from our sins. In this narrative Matthew presents Jesus as Israel's—and our—champion, the One who succeeded in the wilderness where Israel had failed. (A champion was one who fought another on behalf of and as a representative of his people, the way David fought Goliath.) Christians are destined for testing (6:13; 26:41), but Jesus our forerunner has gone before us and shown us how to overcome.

The devil tempts Jesus to abuse his calling and power for selfish ends. The "christological" interpretation of this passage noted above has much to teach us. In 3:16-17 God identifies Jesus as his Son; now the devil tries to redefine the nature of Jesus' sonship (4:3, 5-6, 8-9). *If you are the Son of God* can also be translated "*Since* you are the Son of God," which may be more likely in this context: the devil invites Jesus not so much to deny his sonship as to act according to various worldly expectations for that role. This narrative warns all of us whom God has called not to let the world define the content of our call. For instance, some pulpit ministers ought to be ministering as public school teachers or social workers in addition to or instead of pulpit ministry, and some in other professions should be training to become expounders of God's Word.

In other words, we must acknowledge God's right not only to determine what to label our calling but also to determine what that label should mean. A call to evangelism may be a call to bring Christ to people on the streets or in hospitals rather than in a traditional pulpit—yet such a ministry may bring more people to Christ than most traditional pulpit ministries can. Disregarding the church hierarchy and the "ministerial ethics" of his day, John Wesley went into other ministers' parishes to reach the people those ministers were not reaching—the poor and alienated. Wesley's call did not fit traditional categories of ministry, but the revival that ensued turned Britain inside out. We, like Jesus, can begin our mission only once we have demonstrated that our commitment is to God who called us and that we will let him rather than human honor define the nature of our call.

Note *how* the devil seeks to redefine Jesus' call: he appeals to various culturally prevalent models of power to suggest how Jesus should use his God-given power. God's empowerment does not guarantee that we are doing his will in all details (compare 1 Cor 13:1-3). One example of exploiting God's power for selfish ends is the minority of clergy and other professional authority figures who abuse their calling for sexual or other advantages. When we confuse others' dependence on our office with dependence on us as persons, we endanger our own relationship with God as his humble servants (Mt 23:5-12; 24:45-51; Prov 16:18; 18:12).

The devil tests Jesus with three roles into which other Palestinian charismatic leaders had fallen—from the crassly demonic sorcerer's role to that of an apparently pious leader. Jesus' refusal in each case allows Matthew to define Jesus' call over against the charges of his opponents (12:24; 26:55; 27:11, 40-43).

First, Jesus was not a magician (4:3). Magicians typically sought to transform one substance into another to demonstrate their power over nature (as in *p. Ḥagiga* 2:2, §5; *Sanhedrin* 6:6, §2). Jesus' opponents could not deny his power but wished to attribute it to Satan, as if he were a magician (Mt 12:24); many Jews associated demons with the worst kind of sorcery (Ps-Philo 34.2-3; *b. Sanhedrin* 67b). Unlike most of Jesus' religious contemporaries, however, the reader knows the true story and just how false the charge of Jesus' association with magic was. Even after a forty-day fast, and though Jesus had power to multiply food for the crowds (Mt 14:13-21; 15:29-38; 16:9-10), he resisted the temptation to turn stones into bread. Where magicians manipulated spiritual power and formulas, Jesus acted from an intimate, obedient personal relationship with his Father (6:7-9). Like a father disciplining his children, God humbled Israel in the wilderness, teaching his people that he would provide their bread while they were unemployed if they would just look to him (Deut 8:1-5). Jesus accepts his Father's call in the wilderness and waits for his Father to act for him (Mt 4:11).

Second (pace Albert Schweitzer), Jesus was not a deluded visionary (4:5-6) like Josephus's "false prophets" who wrongly expected God to back up their miraculous claims (Jos. *Ant.* 20.168; *War* 2.259). By wanting Jesus to jump over an abyss (perhaps on the southeast corner of the temple area overlooking the Kidron Valley) known to invite certain death without God's intervention (see Jos. *Ant.* 15.412), the devil wants Jesus to presume on his relationship with God, to act as if God were there to serve his Son rather than the reverse. Religious teachers later echo Satan's theology: if Jesus is God's Son, let God rescue him from the cross (Mt 27:40-43). When people become so arrogant as to think we have God figured out, we can easily miss God's true purposes and become Satan's mouthpieces.

Among contemporary charismatics (of whom I am one) I observe two prominent models for being "charismatic." One is to "claim" blessings on the basis of spiritual formulas, a method whose success God never guaranteed. Like the first-century false prophets who promised the pious Jerusalemites the deliverance they wanted to hear (as in Jos. *War* 6.285-87), our brothers and sisters who follow this method without the Spirit may encounter some uncomfortable surprises. (Matthew would also have balked at some charismatics' claim to be able to "send" angels—4:6; 26:53.) The other method is to sensitively follow the Spirit's leading to do what God has called us to do. When God has genuinely spoken and his servants act in obedience, he will accomplish his purposes—even if those purposes must lead us through the cross. For "who can speak and have it happen if the Lord has not decreed it?" (Lam 3:37).

Jesus did not get himself into testing presumptuously; like Elijah of old, he did what he did at God's command (1 Kings 18:36). Jesus understood Scripture accurately and alluded not only to the passage he cited but to its context. When he warns against putting *the Lord your God to the test* (Mt 4:7; Deut 6:16), he alludes to Israel's dissatisfaction in the wilderness (as in Ex 17:2-3). Although God graciously supplied their needs, they harshly demanded more, forgetting how much God had delivered them from. We, like Israel, serve a living God and must be prepared to do his will whether or not it is to our immediate liking (Mt 26:42).

Finally, Jesus was not a political revolutionary, contrary to the assumptions and charges of the Jewish aristocracy (26:55, 61; 27:11-12; compare P. Ellis 1974:108). As another Gospel puts it, "My kingdom is not of this world. If it were, my servants would fight to prevent my arrest" (Jn 18:36). Many citizens of the Roman Empire felt that Rome ruled the earth's kingdoms (for example, Rev 17:18; Jos. *War* 2.361; 3.473); to rule the earth would include the subjection of the Roman emperor. If Matthew writes after A.D. 70, his audience knows how Roman forces had slaughtered the Jewish revolutionaries and how resounding defeat had dashed their people's hopes for a worldly kingdom; how would deliverance come?

The devil offered Jesus the kingdom without the cross, a temptation that has never lost its appeal. Corrupted once it achieved political power and popularity, its members' motives no longer purified by persecution, the medieval church too often was marked by corruption and repression that we today repudiate; but we can face the same temptations. Upon facing this temptation, not Jesus' opponents but his own star disciple Peter echoes Satan's theology exactly: the messianic kingdom without the cross (Mt 16:22). Jesus thus pushes away Peter in disgust as he had Satan—even to the point of calling Peter *Satan* (16:23; compare 4:10). Jesus' mission involved the cross (26:54), and whether we like it or not, so does our mission (16:23-26).

Political and social involvement are important; marketing strategies are not necessarily wrong; but when we substitute any other means of transforming society for dependence on God, we undercut the very purpose for our mission. Where the church flirts with political power to enforce public morality, it must become all the more conscious of its own need for spiritual renewal. Atheists and Christians often use the same methods of social change; but if we genuinely embrace a faith worth defending, can we also have the faith to go beyond those methods and depend on *God* to give us revival? The temptation narrative strikes at the heart of human religion and worldly conceptions of power—and reminds us of how close that danger can come to believers.

The narrative also emphasizes that we can use Scripture for righteous or unrighteous causes. Jesus and the devil argue Scripture, and both are adept in it (as some later rabbis expected the devil and some demons were; for example, *b. Sanhedrin* 89b), though the devil quotes Scripture out of context and so values its wording over its meaning (4:6). (Psalm 91:3-10 addresses protection from dangers that approach the righteous, not testing God to see whether he will really do what Scripture promises.) That the devil quotes Scripture out of context should not surprise us, since he does it even today in many pulpits every Sunday morning. (I say this only partly tongue in cheek; religious leaders in Mt 27:40 become mouthpieces for the devil's lie in 4:3, and Jesus' leading disciple in 16:22 echoes 4:8-9. Piety, whether feigned or genuine, does not necessarily preserve us from communicating false ideologies from our culture or spiritual tradition that we have never taken the time to examine from God's revealed Word.) Notice too that whereas Jesus uses Scripture to teach him God's will, the devil presents it merely as promises to be exploited for one's own purposes— as some of the more extreme radio preachers today have put it, "how to get God to work for you."

But the devil's abuse of Scripture should not lead us to neglect Scripture's real power when rightly interpreted and applied. Our Lord himself submitted his life to its claims (compare 3:15) and calls us to do the same (5:17-20). Jesus' three responses in this testing narrative share the phrase *It is written* (NIV) or "It has been written" (4:4, 7, 10). It comes as no surprise that Jesus' first citation declares the primacy of God's words, on which we his people should feed as on necessary food (4:4; compare Jer 15:16). Not worldly categories but God's will revealed in Scripture defined the character of Jesus' call.

Jesus' specific Spirit-led behavior in this model is significant: he already knew God's commands and their context, and for him to know was to obey. He adds no reasoning to God's simple commands. "I have hidden your word in my heart that I might not sin against you" (Ps 119:11). We must learn Scripture well and, empowered by the Spirit, choose to obey it rather than flirting with temptation. We can overcome temptation in any given case; hence no matter how great we feel our temptations are, there is no temptation too great to endure (1 Cor 10:13). As many modern authors emphasize, we need to be honest about temptation and not say, "I can't help it"; if we are tempted, we must be honest and say, "I won't." Jesus' victory for us has taken away our excuse; he has provided us the power to overcome if we dare to believe him.

4:12 That Jesus "withdrew" to Galilee may suggest that he was himself in the wilderness

Finally, God brings triumph to those who remain faithful in testing (4:11). Without Jesus' submitting to the devil (compare Mt 4:6: *his angels . . . will lift you up*), God's agents provide Jesus' needs as soon as he has vanquished his foe. After three high-stake tests the devil leaves, so that Jesus can later say that he is freeing Satan's possessions because he has already bound the strong man (12:29). Jesus is the new Moses who will provide bread for his people (see commentary on 14:13-21; 16:29-38), whom God will deliver by the resurrection and who will eventually rule the nations (Ps 2:7, cited by God in Mt 3:17). According to Jesus' call, all these things belonged to him; but the ends of God's call in the long term do not justify inappropriate means in the short term (such as affirming unjust denominational policies or cheating on seminary exams). Our mission is most of all obedience to our Father's will, both in our destiny and in the details. God's vindication does not always come in this life, but in the end he always delivers his own.

Moving to a Bigger Town (4:12-16) John's imprisonment—which foreshadows Jesus' own suffering—becomes the signal for Jesus to begin public ministry (4:12; compare Jn 3:23-30). The forerunner has completed his mission of preparing the way (3:3).

Matthew may address three issues in Jesus' move to Capernaum. First, the move may indicate a concerted missions strategy. Although Jesus had grown up in a relatively unpretentious town (see commentary on 2:23), the time apparently had come for him to find a more suitable base for his urgent mission—a town with more people, with greater notoriety and from which news would spread quickly around the perimeters of the lake of Galilee and perhaps also via the nearby trade route. (Capernaum probably held at least fifteen hundred people—E. Sanders 1993:103.) Capernaum would also prove more responsive than Nazareth (compare 9:1-2; 11:23; 13:54-57). That Capernaum appears in later rabbinic accounts solely in connection with "schismatics," presumably Jesus' followers (Theissen 1991:50), suggests that Jesus' missionary

of Perea, where John was probably arrested. If Matthew's audience was in Syria (as many scholars hold), they might have supposed this geographical setting.

strategy was ultimately successful.

Although God may intend for many of us to serve in places like Nazareth for years, he is undoubtedly calling many of us to larger challenges at some point in our lives. I say "undoubtedly" because the vast majority of full-time Christian workers serve among peoples where the gospel is widely available, while fewer than thirty thousand serve the half of the world's population that has never received an adequate witness of the gospel. Given both Jesus' mission for us (28:19) and the love we should have for our fellow human beings, should we not be seeking God as to whether he wants us to serve him by staying or going?

But besides Jesus' own mission strategy, Matthew stresses Jesus' Galilean ministry base for two other reasons more directly relevant to his audience. The second issue is that Matthew's opponents undoubtedly criticized the Jesus movement's Galilean origins. The Pharisees and their successors, centered in Judea, retained considerable prejudice against Galilee, which they also used against Jesus' followers. Matthew thus cites Scripture about a messianic role in Galilee to counter regional prejudice against the gospel.

Third, and probably most important, what Isaiah says about Galilee foreshadows the Gentile mission that Matthew keeps urging on his readers (4:14). Jesus again acts in obedience to Scripture (4:14-15), and this passage (Is 9:1-2; compare Lk 1:79)—which in context addresses the work of the Davidic Messiah (Is 9:6-7)—indicates that he will work in *Galilee of the Gentiles*. This is not to say that Jesus directed much of his own ministry to Gentiles; but the text allows Matthew to foreshadow Jesus' command to proclaim the kingdom to the nations (Mt 24:14; 28:19). Capernaum was actually in Naphtali's territory, not directly Zebulon's (Meier 1980:32); yet Zebulon, sometimes associated with the fishing industry (Gen 49:13; *Test. Zeb.* 5:5), was not far away. At any rate, this Isaiah text would refute the claims of scribes who insisted that a Messiah must hail

---

4:17 Jesus' proclamation probably implies that the kingdom "has drawn near" (Kümmel 1957:19-25; Black 1967:208-11; Nineham 1977:69) rather than "has arrived" (Dodd 1961:44; Argyle 1963:42), but in either case the sense of its intrusive imminence compels an immediate response (26:45-46; see France 1985:90). One may compare the demands implied

directly only from Bethlehem (Mt 2:5-6; Jn 7:42).

Abandoning All for the Kingdom (4:17-22) Once God had commissioned Jesus (3:17), the devil had tested him (4:3-11), the forerunner had completed his mission (4:12) and Jesus had settled in Capernaum (4:12-16), he was ready to begin his public ministry (*from that time on*, 4:17). Matthew opens this section with a summary of Jesus' message (v. 17). As this message summarizes Jesus' proclamation of God's authority, so verses 18-22 demonstrate people's proper response to God's rule; verses 23-25 demonstrate God's rule over sickness and demons; and chapters 5—7 flesh out the nature of the ethic of repentance one must live to be prepared in advance for the kingdom.

For Matthew, the message for both Galilean Jews (10:5-7) and eventually Gentiles (28:18-19) is the same as John the Baptist's (3:2) and that of Jesus: Get your lives in order, for God's kingdom is approaching (4:17). Only those who submit to God's reign in advance (as in 4:18-22) will be ready when he comes to rule the whole world. Just as Jesus' message concurred with that of John, so the message of Jesus' followers must accord with that of Jesus. We must proclaim the imminence of the kingdom (10:7; compare 28:18), demonstrate God's rule over sickness and demons (10:8), and pass on our Master's teachings (28:19).

In 4:18-22 the One whom the Father called now calls others who will advance his mission. Jesus' call to leave profession and family was radical, the sort of demand that only the most radical teacher would make. This text provides us several examples of servant-leadership and radical discipleship.

Jesus Calls a Nucleus of Disciples (4:18-19) Early Jewish and Greek tradition normally assumes that disciples are responsible for acquiring their own teachers of the law (*m. 'Abot* 1:6, 16; *ARN* 3, 8A; Socrates *Ep.* 4). The more radical teachers who, like Jesus, sometimes even rejected prospective disciples (see commentary on Mt 19:21-22)

---

by the prophets' "day of the Lord" (Is 13:6, 9; Joel 1:15; 3:14). Although some writers in the past denied it, the Bible is clear that the good news of the kingdom is the good news of grace the church must continue to proclaim (Acts 8:12; 19:8; 20:25; 28:23, 31).

probably considered the disciple's responsibility so weighty that it would be dishonorable for the teacher to seek out the disciple.

Jesus' seeking out disciples himself may thus represent a serious breach of custom (Malina 1981:78; though compare Jer 1:4-10), "coming down to their level" socially. This would be like itinerant preachers going out to the unchurched instead of expecting them to visit our churches and appreciate our well-prepared sermons. Probably Jesus is choosing as his model the prophetic way of choosing one's successor found in 1 Kings 19:19-21 (see also Lk 9:61-62).

Jesus Relates to His Hearers in Terms They Can Understand (4:19) Although most scholars agree that Matthew's community included Christian scribes (Mt 13:52; 23:34), Jesus did not call professionally trained rabbis (who might have had a lot to *unlearn* first) to be his disciples. He called artisans and encouraged them that the skills they already had were serviceable in the kingdom. If God called shepherds like Moses and David to shepherd his people Israel, Jesus could call fishermen to be gatherers of people. Some great men and women of God in the Bible never even became public expositors of Scripture; aside from his prophetic gifts, Joseph's witness involved especially public administration, learned in Potiphar's house and a prison and then applied to all Egypt. Social workers, teachers and many others have skills and backgrounds on which we must draw to be an effective church today. It is to our loss that congregations disregard the insights of the various professions among us.

Jesus' Call Involves Downward Mobility (4:20) Although artisans had far less income than the wealthy (who made up perhaps 1 percent of the ancient population), they were not among the roughly 90 percent of the ancient population we may call peasants either (popular jokes about low-class disciples "mending their nets" aside—the expression

---

4:18-19 The essential material in this section seems to genuinely reflect Jesus tradition (for fuller discussion, see E. Sanders 1993:119; Davies and Allison 1991:393-94; Witherington 1990:129-30; little reflects the Christology or other editorial language of later Christians). Some scholars favor an Old Testament background for *fishers of men* (Hab 1:15; Jer 16:16; Mt 13:47; see also Ezek 47:10; later, *CD* 4.15-17; 1QH 5.7-8; Ps-Philo 3:11); but the Old Testament use is a judgment metaphor, which may make it less relevant here.
4:20-22 Torah teachers did praise those who honored Torah above their families (*ARN* 6A; 13, §30B). Although disciples of rabbis normally remained with their wives during study

can mean *preparing their nets*—v. 21). Family businesses like these were especially profitable. Even if disciples followed Jesus only during certain seasons of the year, they could not easily return to abandoned businesses.

The disciples thus paid a price economically to follow Jesus. Jewish people told stories of pagans' relinquishing their wealth on converting to Judaism (*Sipre Num.* 115.5.7), and Greek philosophers told stories of converts to philosophy who abandoned wealth to become disciples (Diog. Laert. 6.5.87; Diogenes *Ep.* 38). These stories demonstrate not only the relative worthlessness of possessions but also the incomparable value of what the converts gained. The kingdom is like a precious treasure, worth the abandonment of all other treasures (Mt 13:44-46). Many of us today respond defensively, "I would abandon everything if Jesus asked me to, but he has not asked me to." Yet if we value the priorities of the kingdom—people and proclamation more than possessions—I wonder whether Jesus is not speaking to us through the world's need for the gospel and daily bread. Let the one who has ears to hear, hear.

Jesus' Scandalous Call Costs Comfort and Challenges the Priority of Family (4:21-22) James and John abandoned not only the boat—representing their livelihood—but also their father and the family business (4:22). In a society where teachers normally stressed no higher responsibility than honor of parents (Jos. *Apion* 2.206; Keener 1991a:98, 197), including economic responsibility for them, some people would view such behavior as scandalous. Jesus elsewhere affirms the importance of marriage (19:9) and filial (15:4-6) relationships; the kingdom is never an excuse to downplay our crucial responsibilities to our families (see Keener 1991a:98-99, 102). They too warrant our attention and our ministry. At the same time God has called his servants, and that means

---

(see Safrai 1974-1976a:965), the rabbis praised those said to have endured hardship for Torah study (Hillel), including those who stayed away from home for years of Torah study (Sandmel 1978b:246-47; *Gen. Rab.* 95 MSV). The stories are probably fictitious—many Jewish teachers forbade leaving one's wife for more than thirty days to study Torah (Safrai 1974-1976b:763)—but they would not even make sense unless some Jewish men did leave home to study with famous teachers of the law (see *Sipre Deut.* 48.2.4, 6). Jesus' demands were, however, greater than those of most teachers.

we are not our own. Those of us who are single dare not choose marriage partners who cannot bear our calling, and we must recognize the demands of God's kingdom—announcing its good news—more highly than the shame it brings on our families or the way they feel about that shame (10:35-37; compare 1:24).

Jesus Demonstrates God's Reign with Power (4:23-25) No less a historian than E. P. Sanders declares it an "almost indisputable" historical fact that "Jesus was a Galilean who preached and healed" (1985:11) and that "the sheer volume of evidence makes it extremely likely that Jesus actually had a reputation as an exorcist" (1993:149; see also Meier 1994:646-77).

Technically this paragraph in Matthew serves as part of the narrative introduction to the Sermon on the Mount, although it is included in the "introduction" to Jesus' ministry here (1:1—4:23) because of the title I have chosen for the next section. Before each of the first two discourse sections, Matthew includes a summary of Jesus' kingdom works (4:23-25; 9:35). Jesus was *teaching* and *preaching the good news of the kingdom*. Teaching generally involved ethical or apologetic instruction, whereas preaching was proclamation aimed at bringing about conversion (Dodd 1980:7-8; compare Guelich 1982:43). Yet Jesus not only proclaimed and explained the kingdom; he demonstrated God's authority by healing the sick and expelling demons (Ladd 1978a:47). That he healed "all" diseases (4:23; NIV *every disease*) may mean every kind of sickness rather than every sick person, since the *all* of verse 24 is necessarily hyperbole; surely suppliants did not bring *every* sick person in Syria to him (Blomberg 1992:92 n. 5)!

Jesus Begins Where the People Are (4:23) Where possible, Jesus worked through existing institutions. He taught in the synagogues, the educational and community centers of the day.

Jesus Ministers to His Hearers Both Physically and Spiritually (4:23-24) Many conservative Christians rightly stress personal conver-

---

4:24-25 Jesus' popularity with crowds seeking healing is not surprising. Vast numbers of people flocked to healing springs like Hammath Tiberias in Galilee, seeking cures for their ailments. "Signs prophets" who claimed to be able to perform miracles (like making the

sion but wrongly ignore the desperate physical needs around them (both for miracles and for social intervention). Many other churches rightly address societal injustices but neglect spiritual needs and personal human pain. Jesus cared about people in their totality and was concerned for their pressing needs. His example summons us to a more well-rounded ministry that preaches the gospel through evangelism and demonstrates the gospel through ministries of compassion, justice and Spirit-empowered healing (see Sider 1993).

This renewed vision of Jesus' compassion can encourage us in our prayers. When we care for people's brokenness as Jesus does, we can bring their pain to God in prayer with greater confidence. The Jesus who healed people then can heal people today, both emotionally and physically (see Deere 1993). Too many of us offer prayers while secretly doubting that God can hear us. Although God always has the right to do as he wills, we would pray with greater faith if we recognized his compassion.

Word About Jesus Spreads Widely (4:25) Ancient narratives about popular teachers (as opposed to more aristocratic figures who often disdained the masses) praised them by emphasizing their popularity (for example, Philostr. *V.A.* 1.40; Robbins 1992:122 n. 74). Matthew is also interested in the geographical distribution of this popularity. Josephus indicates that many Jews lived in Syria in Jesus' day (Jos. *War* 2.461-68); if Matthew writes to believers in Syria (see Meier 1980:36; see also introduction), he may use the mention of Jewish followers from Syria (Mt 4:24) to encourage his own audience.

In the context of the whole Gospel, however, Jesus' popularity in this passage provides a warning. God's call demands faithfulness with or without popularity. Jesus had awaited God's time for him to minister (4:12); now word about him was spreading quickly. Subsequent narratives in this Gospel, however, warn that momentary popularity is just an opportunity to convey the word to those who really have ears to hear. Popularity does not always translate into deep commitment in the

---

walls of Jerusalem collapse) drew crowds as well, although there is not much evidence that their promises proved successful.

end (27:20). Thus Matthew warns his first audience and us as well not to build our assurance of God's call on others' responses to our message; our knowledge of our God-given mission in life must go unshakably deeper than that (3:16—4:11).

THE ETHICS OF GOD'S KINGDOM (5—7)

Jesus summons those who would be his followers to radical devotion and radical dependence on God. His followers must be meek, must not retaliate, must go beyond the letter's law to its spirit, must do what is right when only God is looking, must depend on God for their needs and pursue his interests rather than their own, and must leave spiritual measurements of others' hearts to God. In short, true people of the kingdom live for God, not for themselves. (My overall approach to the Sermon on the Mount combines some approaches, but still remains one among many. For a more complete summary of various views on this sermon's message, see, for example, Guelich 1982:14-22; Cranford 1992; Allen 1992.)

Readers should contemplate the message of this sermon. Having summarized Jesus' message as repentance in view of the coming kingdom (4:17), Matthew now collects Jesus' teachings that explain how a repentant person ready for God's rule should live. Only those submitted to God's reign now are truly prepared for the time when he will judge the world and reign there unchallenged. This sermon provides examples of the self-sacrificial ethics of the kingdom, which its citizens must learn to exemplify even in the present world before the rest of the world recognizes that kingdom (6:10).

To be faithful to the text, we must let Jesus' radical demands confront us with all the unnerving force with which they would have struck their first hearers. At the same time, the rest of the Gospel narrative, where Jesus does not repudiate disciples who miserably fail yet repent (for example, 26:31-32), does season the text with grace. Most Jewish people understood God's commandments in the context of grace (E. Sanders 1977; though compare also Thielman 1994:48-68); given Jesus' demands for greater grace in practice (9:13; 12:7; 18:21-35), we must remember that Jesus embraces those who humble themselves, acknowledging God's right to rule, even if in practice they are not yet perfect (5:48).

Jesus preached hard to the religiously and socially arrogant, but his words come as comfort to the meek and brokenhearted.

Of course one also needs to read grace in light of the kingdom demands; grace transforms as well as forgives. Jesus is meek and lowly in heart to the broken and heals and restores the needy who seek him; it is the arrogant, the religiously and socially satisfied, against whom Jesus lays the kingdom demands harshly (compare Mt 23).

Although the sermon's structure does not fit some modern outlines, it reflects a consistent pattern. Matthew gathers a variety of Jesus' teachings on related topics that appear in the source he shares with Luke. Ancient writers exercised the freedom to rearrange sayings, often topically; sometimes they also gathered sayings of their teachers into collections. Evidence within the sermon itself suggesting various audiences (5:1; 7:28) may also support the view that the sermon is composite. Scholars debate its precise structure, but 5:17-48, 6:1-18 and 6:19-34 are its largest complete units.

☐ Kingdom Blessings for True Disciples (5:1-16)

The Setting of Jesus' Sermon (5:1-2) Various features of the setting contribute to Matthew's portrait of Jesus.

First, "mountain" settings in Matthew are usually significant (17:1; compare 15:29; 28:16; although Moses is not alluded to in 4:8). Many scholars think that Matthew probably recalls Moses' revelation on Mount Sinai (Ex 19:3) here. If so, Jesus' superior revelation also makes him superior to those who "sit in Moses' seat" (Mt 23:2); the One greater than Moses, first encountered in 2:13-20, has begun his mission.

Second, Matthew's depiction of Jesus' teaching is appropriate. That Jesus sat to teach (5:1; compare 13:1-2; 23:2) fits expected patterns of Jewish instruction (see also Lk 4:20). Thus Jesus takes the role of the scribes, but Matthew also indicates that Jesus is greater than the scribes (Mt 7:29).

Finally, Jesus' audience is also relevant to Matthew's point. Jesus' ethics specifically address disciples, but Jesus also invites those who are not disciples to become disciples and live according to the values of God's kingdom. The crowds following Jesus (4:25—5:1) function as at least potential disciples; disciples in the Gospel provide models for later believers (Guelich 1982:53). Matthew explicitly indicates that Jesus taught his disciples (5:1-2) but also that the crowds were present (5:1; 7:28—8:1), implying that Jesus wanted both to hear, calling both to decision (7:24-27; see Guelich 1982:60).

Kingdom Rewards for the Repentant (5:3-9) If we truly repent in light of the coming kingdom, we will treat our neighbors rightly. No one who has humbled himself or herself before God can act with wanton self-interest in relationships. Those with the faith to await the vindication of the righteous in God's kingdom can afford to be righteous, to relinquish the pursuit of their own rights (5:38-42; compare 1 Cor 9:3-23), because they know the just judge will vindicate them as they seek his ways of justice.

Jesus employs a standard Jewish literary form to express this point, a beatitude, which runs like this: "It will go well with the one who . . . for that one shall receive . . ." ("Fortunate" or "it will be well with" may convey the point better than *blessed* or "happy.") In this context Jesus' beatitudes mean that it will ultimately be well with those who seek first God's kingdom (Mt 6:33).

Because various themes pervade all or many of Matthew's beatitudes here, the principles are summarized by topic rather than by verse in this section of the commentary. Matthew intends his audience to hear all the beatitudes together (his Gospel would have been read in church assemblies), not for them to be taken piecemeal. What themes emerge from these brief pronouncements of blessing?

Jesus lists promises that pertain to the coming kingdom. Theirs is the kingdom of heaven frames most of this section (5:3, 10). All the blessings listed are blessings of the kingdom time. In the time of the kingdom God will "comfort all who mourn in Zion" (Is 61:2); he will satisfy the hunger and thirst of his people (Mt 8:11; 22:2; 26:29; Is 25:6) as in the first exodus (Deut 6:11; 8:17). God's ultimate mercy will be revealed on the day of judgment (*1 Enoch* 5:5; 12:6; 92:4; *Ps. Sol.* 16:15). At that time

---

5:5 When Jewish people thought of the *meek* "inheriting the earth," they went beyond the minimal interpretation of Psalm 37:9, 11, 29 (where those who hope in God alone "will

he will ultimately declare the righteous to be his children (Rev 21:7; *Jub.* 1:24), as he had to a lesser degree at the first exodus (Ex 4:22). God is technically invisible (1QS 11.20; Jos. *Apion* 2.191), but in the future the righteous will fully see God (*1 Enoch* 90:35; *ARN* 1A).

The blessings he promises come only by God's intervention. Because the future kingdom is in some sense present in Jesus, who provides bread (Mt 14:19-20) and comforts the brokenhearted (14:14; compare Lk 4:18), we participate in the spiritual down payment of these blessings in Christ in the present (see Gal 3:14; Eph 1:3). But such blessings come only to the meek—those who wait on God to fight God's battles.

The blessings of the beatitudes are for a people ready for the kingdom's coming. This passage shows what kingdom-ready people should be like; hence it shows us prerequisites for the kingdom as well as kingdom promises.

First, kingdom people do not try to force God's whole will on a world unprepared for it. Many first-century Jews had begun to think that revolutionary violence was the only adequate response to the violence of oppression they experienced. Matthew's first audience no doubt could recall the bankruptcy of this approach, which led to crushing defeat in the war of A.D. 66-73. But Jesus promises the kingdom not to those who try to force God's hand in their time but to those who patiently and humbly wait for it—the meek, the poor in spirit, the merciful, the peacemakers.

Of course Jesus' demand does not merely challenge the bloodshed of revolution. *Peacemakers* means not only living at peace but bringing harmony among others; this role requires us to work for reconciliation with spouses, neighbors and all people—insofar as the matter is up to us (Rom 12:18).

Second, God favors the humble, who trust in him rather than their own strength (5:3-9). For one thing, the humble are not easily provoked to anger. These are *the poor in spirit, . . . the meek,* those who appear in Jewish texts as the lowly and oppressed. Because the oppressed poor become wholly dependent on God (Jas 2:5), some Jewish people used

---

inherit the land"; compare Ps 25:13) and thought of inheriting the entire world (Rom 4:13; 4QPs 37).

"poor [in spirit]" as a positive religious as well as economic designation. Thus it refers not merely to the materially poor and oppressed but to those "who have taken that condition to their very heart, by not allowing themselves to be deceived by the attraction of wealth" (Freyne 1988:72).

Jesus promises the kingdom to the powerless, the oppressed who embrace the poverty of their condition by trusting in God rather than favors from the powerful for their deliverance. The inequities of this world will not forever taunt the justice of God: he will ultimately vindicate the oppressed. This promise provides us both hope to work for justice and grace to endure the hard path of love.

There are, of course, exceptions, but as a rule it is more common for the poor to be "poor in spirit"; Matthew's *poor in spirit* does have something to do with Luke's "poor." Surveys in the United States, for example, show that religious commitment is generally somewhat higher among people with less income (Barna 1991:178-81; Gallup and Jones 1992), and Christians in less affluent countries like Nepal, Guatemala, Kenya or China often are prepared to pay a higher price for their faith than most Western Christians. In Bible studies among students from different kinds of colleges and backgrounds I have found that students from poor homes, struggling to pay their way through college, frequently understand this passage better than those students for whom the road is easier. Feeling impressed by the wealth and status of others, the less privileged students are amazed to learn how special they are to God and embrace this message as good news. Those of us who have attained more income or education would do well to imitate their meekness, lest the self-satisfaction and complacency that often accompany such attainments corrupt our faith in Christ (13:22).

Further, these humble people are also those who yearn for God above all else. Luke emphasizes those who hunger physically (Lk 6:21); Matthew emphasizes yearning for God's righteousness more than for food and drink, perhaps also implying that those who hunger physically are in a better position to begin to value God more than food (Mt 5:6; this may include fasting). In this context hungering for *righteousness*

5:11-12 Literarily these verses seem to be a somewhat different unit, meant to drive home

probably includes yearning for God's justice, for his vindication of the oppressed (see Gundry 1982:70); the context also implies that it includes yearning to do God's will (5:20; 6:33; 21:32; 23:29). This passage reflects biblical images of passion for God, longing for him more than for daily food or drink (Job 23:12; Ps 42:1-2; 63:1, 5; Jer 15:16; compare Mt 4:4). God and his Word should be the ultimate object of our longing (Ps 119:40, 47, 70, 92, 97, 103).

"Mourners" here (5:4) may thus refer especially to the repentant (Joel 1:13; see also Jas 4:9-10; Lev 23:29; 26:41), those who grieve over their people's sin (Tobit 13:14). Given the promise of comfort, however, the term probably also applies more broadly to those who are broken, who suffer or have sustained personal grief and responded humbly (see Fenton 1977:368). God is near the brokenhearted (Ps 51:17) and will comfort those who mourn (Is 61:1-3); the people of the kingdom are the humble, not the arrogant. *The pure in heart* (Mt 5:8) in Psalm 73 refers to those who recognize that God alone is their hope.

Likewise, this lifestyle of meekness Jesus teaches challenges not only Jewish revolutionaries but all Christians in our daily lives. If we are to walk in love toward our enemies (Mt 5:43), how much more should we walk in love toward those closest us (compare 5:46-47; 22:36-40)? I am always awed by the presence of the truly humble—like three of my friends from Ethiopia, one of whom was imprisoned by the old Marxist regime for a year and two of whom led about two thousand fellow Ethiopians to Christ in their refugee camp. Not only did these brothers regularly offer me their most gracious hospitality when I visited them, but every time I came they would insist on my teaching them the Bible—though I am sure that I had far more to learn from them!

Encouragement for Those Persecuted for the Gospel (5:10-12) In his final beatitudes Jesus declares not "Happy are those," but "Happy are *you*." Here Jesus takes his ethic of nonretaliation (5:38-47) to its furthest possible length: not only must we refuse to strike back, but we are to rejoice when persecuted. The persecution itself confirms our trust

---

the impact of what precedes in the light of persecution, including the rejection experienced by Matthew's audience.

in God's promise of reward, because the prophets suffered likewise (13:57; 23:37; 26:68; 2 Chron 36:15-16; Jer 26:11, 23). The prophetic role of a disciple is analogous to (Mt 10:41-42; 23:34) and greater than (11:9, 11; 13:17) that of an Old Testament prophet. When we represent Jesus and his message faithfully and suffer rejection accordingly, we may identify with ancient prophetic leaders like Jeremiah, Isaiah and Ezekiel.

But here Jesus summons us to a greater honor than being prophets; he summons us to bear the name—the honor—of Jesus. The characteristics Jesus lists as belonging to the people of the kingdom are also those Jesus himself exemplifies as the leading servant of the kingdom and Son par excellence of the Father (11:27; 20:28). Jesus is meek and lowly in heart (11:29); he mourns over the unrepentant (11:20-24); he shows mercy (9:13, 27; 12:7; 20:30); he is a peacemaker (5:43-45; 26:52). If he is lowly, how much more must be his disciples, who are to imitate his ways (10:24-25; 23:8-12)—in contrast to worldly paradigms for religious celebrities (23:5-7).

Worthless Disciples (5:13-16) Jesus' audience at least partly includes "disciples" (5:1-2). Having described the appropriate lifestyle of disciples, Jesus now explains that a professed disciple who does not live this lifestyle of the kingdom is worth about as much as tasteless salt or invisible light—nothing.

Until my conversion in 1975 I professed to be an atheist in part because I looked at the roughly 85 percent of my fellow U.S. citizens who claimed to be Christians and could not see that their faith genuinely affected their lives. I reasoned that if even Christians did not believe in Jesus' teachings, why should I? My excuse for unbelief—and the excuse of many other secularists I knew—continued until God's Spirit confronted me with the reality that the truth of Christ does not rise or fall on the claims of his professed followers, but on Jesus himself. The faith of nominal Christians may appeal to non-Christians who can use it to justify their own unbelief, but such "Christians" will have no part in God's kingdom. Instead they will be *thrown out and trampled* (5:13).

5:14 Jewish teachers applied the image of a "light for the world" to especially pious sages (Sirach 50:6-7; *ARN* 25A), as well as to heroes such as Adam (*ARN* 9, §25B), Abraham (*Test. Ab.* 7B; *Gen. Rab.* 2:3), Moses (*Sipre Num.* 93.1.3), the Messiah (*1 Enoch* 48:4; *Pes. Rab*

Jesus refers here to more than good deeds; he refers to a good character (compare 7:17-20; 12:33-37). Such character comes only by embracing God's kingship as a gift (as in 10:40; 18:4, 12-14, 27). The images of salt and light evoke consideration less of what we do than of what we are. If only true disciples count before God (5:13-16) and true discipleship means treating both friends and enemies kindly (5:3-12), the salt-and-light paragraph becomes a resounding warning to heed Jesus' teaching on meekness in the preceding paragraph.

A disciple who rejects the beatitudes' values is like tasteless salt: worthless. Salt had a variety of uses (see Davies and Allison 1988:472-73); probably the most evident use was as a flavoring agent (Plut. *Isis* 5, *Mor.* 352F; *Table-Talk* 4.4.3, *Mor.* 669B). In any case the point is, what is to be done with salt that no longer functions as salt should?

A later Jewish story may illustrate how first-century hearers would have grasped Jesus' point. An inquirer reportedly asked a late first-century rabbi what to salt tasteless salt with; he responded, "The afterbirth of a mule" (*b. Bekarot* 8b). In that society everyone knew that mules are sterile; the point is, "You ask a stupid question, you get a stupid answer. Salt can't stop being salt!" But of course if it were to do so, it would no longer be of any value as salt.

Just as tasteless salt lacks value to the person who uses it, so does a professed disciple without genuine commitment prove valueless for the work of the kingdom.

A disciple whose life reveals none of the Father's works is like invisible light for vision: useless. Jesus reinforces his point with various images. A disciple should be as obvious as a city set on a hill (as most cities were), and a light in a home should be no easier to hide than a torchlit city at night (5:14-15; most homes had only one room). As a popular sage had put it, "What is the value of concealed wisdom, any more than of treasure that is invisible?" (Sirach 41:14).

Jesus depicts his disciples' mission in stark biblical terms for the mission of Israel. God called his people to be lights to the nations (for example, Is 42:6; 49:6—that is, the whole world (compare Mt 18:7).

Kah. Supplement 6:5) and ultimately God himself (1QH 7.24-25; *4 Baruch* 9:3; *Sipre Num.* 41.1.1; see Ps 27:1). But they also applied this image more generally to Israel (Sirach 17:19), Jerusalem (*Pes. Rab Kah.* 21:4) and the temple (*Gen. Rab.* 3:4).

Christians are light because—contrary to some psychoanalytic theories—their destiny (13:43) more than their past must define them.

But Christians cannot be content to remain the world's light in a merely theoretical sense; they must "be what they are," letting their light shine for their Father's honor (5:16). Ministers of the Word must equip all other Christians for their ministry as lights in their various neighborhoods and occupations (Eph 4:11-13; Tit 2:1, 5, 8, 10). While Jesus is opposed to our doing good works publicly for our own honor (6:1, "to be seen" by people), he exhorts us to do those good works publicly for God's honor (5:16; cf. 6:9). This distinction exhorts us to guard the motives of our hearts and consider the effects our public activities and pronouncements have on the spread of the gospel and the honoring of God among all groups of people.

□ Jesus Applies Principles in God's Law (5:17-48)

As if Jesus' words in 5:3-16 were not strong enough, he presents even more stringent demands of the kingdom in these verses. While various groups of Christians today may differ concerning exactly how Jesus intended his disciples to interpret the law, one point is clear: Jesus was not an antinomian. He expected his followers to understand and apply the moral principles already revealed in Scripture.

Christians Must Obey God's Law (5:17-20) Matthew uses Jesus' words in 5:17-20 as a thesis statement for the whole of 5:21-48 which follows. Jesus essentially says, "Look, if you thought the law was tough, wait till you see this. If you really want to be my disciples, give me your hearts without reservation" (see 5:17).

This passage seems to suggest that an uncommitted Christian is not a Christian at all (see 5:20). Like other Jewish teachers, Jesus demanded whole obedience to the Scriptures (5:18-19); unlike most of his contemporaries, however, he was not satisfied with the performance of scribes and Pharisees, observing that this law observance fell short even of the

---

5:18 The story about the *yôd* from Sarai's name appears often in rabbinic texts (e.g., *b. Sanhedrin* 107a-b; *p. Sanhedrin* 2:6, §2; *Gen. Rab.* 47:1; *Lev. Rab.* 19:2). Likewise, sages declared that when Solomon threatened to uproot a *yôd* from the law, God responded that he would uproot a thousand Solomons rather than a word of his law (*p. Sanhedrin* 2:6,

demands of salvation (5:20). After grabbing his hearers' attention with such a statement, Jesus goes on to define God's law not simply in terms of how people behave but in terms of who they really are (5:21-48).

Jesus' High View of Scripture (5:17-18) Jesus' view of Scripture did not simply accommodate his culture, a fact that has implications for the view of Scripture Jesus' followers should hold (J. Wenham 1977:21; D. Wenham 1979). Here Jesus responds to false charges that he and his followers undermine the law. First, when Jesus says that he came not to *abolish the Law or the Prophets* but to *fulfill them,* he uses terms that in his culture would have conveyed his faithfulness to the Scriptures (v. 17).

Second, Jesus illustrates the eternality of God's law with a popular story line from contemporary Jewish teachers (5:18). Jesus' *smallest letter* (NIV), or "jot" (KJV), undoubtedly refers to the Hebrew letter *yôd,* which Jewish teachers said would not pass from the law. They said that when Sarai's name was changed to Sarah, the *yôd* removed from her name cried out from one generation to another, protesting its removal from Scripture, until finally, when Moses changed Oshea's name to Joshua, the *yôd* was returned to Scripture. "So you see," the teachers would say, "not even this smallest letter can pass from the Bible." Jesus makes the same point from this tradition that later rabbis did: even the smallest details of God's law are essential.

We Will Be Judged by Our Response to God's Word (5:19) Jesus here provides a graphic example of the law's authority. Jewish teachers typically depicted various persons as "greatest" before God; the emphasis was not on numerical precision but on praising worthy people (for example, *m. 'Abot* 2:8). When Jesus speaks of *the least of these commandments,* he also reflects Jewish legal language. Jewish teachers regularly distinguished "light" and "heavy" commandments (as in *Sipra VDDebo.* parasha 1.34.1.3; compare Mt 23:23) and in fact determined which commandments were the "least" and "greatest." Noting that both the "greatest" commandment about honoring parents (Ex 20:12; Deut 5:16) and the "least" commandment about the bird's nest (Deut 22:6-7)

---

§2). That nothing will pass away *until everything is accomplished* means until the consummation of the kingdom, when heaven and earth pass away (Mt 24:34-35; compare Jer 31:35-37; Ps-Philo 11:5; *Sib. Or.* 3:570-72).

included the same promise, "Do this and you will live," later rabbis decided that "live" meant "in the world to come" and concluded that God would reward equally for obedience of any commandment. One who kept the law regulating the bird's nest merited eternal life, whereas one who broke it merited damnation (see, for example, Urbach 1979:1:350; Keener 1991a:116). In the same way, those who merely honored the highest standards of their religion would fall short of entering the kingdom at all (Mt 5:20).

Other sages used such language to grab attention and emphasize the importance of the law. But like Jesus, they did not want anyone to miss the point: God has not given us the right to pick and choose among his commandments. As some teachers put it, one should be as "careful with regard to a light commandment as you would be with a heavy one, since you do not know the allotment of the reward" (*m. 'Abot* 2:1). The sages were not suggesting that they never broke commandments (see Moore 1971:1:467-68), but rather believed that one who cast off any commandment or principle of the law was discarding the authority of the law as a whole (*m. Horayot* 1:3; Keener 1991a:115-17).

Jesus concurs: God does not allow us the right to say, "I will obey his teaching about murder but not his teaching about adultery or fornication"; or, "I will obey his teaching about theft but not about divorce." To refuse his right to rule any of our ethics or behavior is to deny his lordship.

In this passage Jesus also warns that teachers who undermine students' faith in any portion of the Bible are in trouble with God. This text addresses not only obedience to the commandments but also how one teaches others (*and teaches others to do the same;* compare Jas 3:1). I have occasionally taught alongside colleagues who actively sought to undermine students' faith in the name of "critical thinking"; sometimes they succeeded. Critical thinking is important, but it functions best with the firm foundation of the fear of God (Prov 1:7).

Bible-Believing People Without Transformed Hearts Are Lost (5:20) Like John the Baptist in 3:7-12, Jesus savages the false security

---

5:21-48 Even skeptics who accept as authentic only what can be definitely argued on purely historical grounds should accept much of the material in this section. Mark, Q and even Paul, for instance, attest to Jesus' teaching about divorce; that the early Christians had to

of the religious establishment. To grasp the full impact in today's language we might compare the scribes with ministers or religious educators and the Pharisees with the most pious, Bible-believing laypeople (although there was some overlap between the two groups). Pharisaic ethics emphasized "inwardness" as much as Jesus did, but Jesus challenges not their traditional ethics but the actual condition of their hearts (Odeberg 1964).

It is possible to agree with everything Jesus taught in this sermon yet fail to live accordingly (23:3). That is why Jesus indicates that the best of human piety is inadequate for salvation—whether it be Pharisaic or Christian. Nothing short of a radical transformation, what other early Christian writers called a new birth (Jn 3:3-6; 1 Pet 1:23), can enable one to live as a disciple (compare Mt 18:3).

Angry Enough to Kill (5:21-26) This paragraph opens the section that runs from verse 21 through verse 48, which requires some introductory comment. Once Jesus has made it clear that he is not opposing the law itself but interpreting it, he shows how the customary practice of the law in his day is inadequate.

In 5:21-48 Jesus explains six legal texts from the Old Testament, interpreting as a good Jewish scholar of his day would (see Flusser 1988:494; Keener 1991a:113-20). Jesus makes the law more stringent in this passage (building a sort of "fence" around the law, which his contemporaries felt was respectful toward the law).

Other Jewish teachers also offered phrases like *You have heard . . . but I tell you* when expounding Scripture. Paul, in fact, uses roughly the same formula when applying one of Jesus' sayings in this context to a new situation (1 Cor 7:10-12). When Jewish teachers offered statements like this, they saw themselves not as contradicting the law but as explaining it, so we might read the passage thus: "You understand the Bible to mean only this, but I offer a fuller interpretation" (see Schechter 1900:427; Daube 1973:55-58). At the same time, Jesus does not speak with merely scribal authority (7:28-29); there is no academic debate or

qualify and explain Jesus' teaching on the subject also suggests that it did not originate with them (E. Sanders 1993:200).

citation of other teachers, but solemn pronouncements. Jesus upholds the law (5:17-19) but is the decisive arbiter of its meaning, not one scholar among many (Daube 1973:58-60). Matthew 5:21-48 provides concrete examples of the "greater righteousness" of verse 20. Jesus addresses not just how we act but who we are.

The heavenly court will judge all offenses of intention. Earthly courts could not usually judge such offenses as displays of anger (for exceptions see 1QS 7.5; Gaius *Inst.* 3.220). But God's heavenly court would judge all such offenses (Mt 5:25-26; see more fully Keener 1991a:14-16). Jesus begins by citing the crime of murder in Exodus 20:13, for which biblical law required a Jewish court to execute the sentence of death (Gen 9:5-6; Deut 21:1-9). But Jesus presses beyond behavior specifically punished by law to the kind of heart that generates such behavior. Anger that would generate murder if unimpeded is the spiritual equivalent of murder (1 Jn 3:15). God has never merely wanted people to obey rules; he wants them to be holy as he is, to value what he values.

Anger, calling someone a fool and calling the person *Raca* (an "emptyhead"; Mt 5:22) are roughly equivalent offenses. Likewise Jesus probably reads the *judgment* of verse 21 as the day of God's judgment, *the Sanhedrin* (v. 22) as God's heavenly court (compare vv. 25-26; also portrayed as the Sanhedrin in Jewish texts—Keener 1987), and both as equivalent to the sentence to be decreed there: damnation to eternal hell. Because every word is uttered before the heavenly court, slander of another merits for the accuser the eternal punishment that would have been due the accused (cf. 12:35-37; Deut 19:16-19; Susanna 62).

Jesus' prohibition of acting in anger is a general principle. As in each of his six examples, Jesus graphically portrays a general principle, although some of these principles (like anger and divorce) must be qualified in specific circumstances. Most people understood that such general principles expressed in proverbs and similar sayings sometimes needed to be qualified in specific situations (see Du Plessis 1967:17; Keener 1991a:22-28); Jesus elsewhere qualifies principles of the law more than most of his contemporaries did (as in Mt 12:3-8).

Although condemning anger and insults, Jesus himself expressed grieved indignation and called people "fools" under appropriate circumstances (23:17; see also 23:13-33). Yet our own indignation is too easily excused as "righteous" (see Jas 1:20), and even just anger must be expressed productively, never in a manner harmful to another person (Eph 4:26, 29-32; Col 3:8). Thus when debating with those like the religious leaders in Jesus' day, we must speak responsibly for their correction and accept the personal consequences. When dealing with those closest to us, such as a spouse, we must humble ourselves and seek the other person's best interests in love (as in, for example, Eph 5:21-25; Keener 1992b:133-83).

Our relationship with God is partly contingent on how we treat others. God will not accept our gift at the altar until we reconcile with our neighbor (see similarly *m. Yoma* 8:9). Again Jesus depicts the situation graphically, since his Galilean hearers might have to travel a considerable distance to leave the Jerusalem temple and then return (vv. 23-24). Jesus' following crisis parable shows how urgent the situation is (vv. 25-26). Imprisonment was generally a temporary holding place until punishment; here, however, a longer penalty is envisaged. *The last penny* (Greek *kodrantēs,* Roman *quadrans*) refers to the second-smallest Roman coin, only a few minutes' wages for even a day laborer.

Through a variety of terrible images, Jesus indicates that when we damage our relationships with others, we damage our relationship with God, leading to eternal punishment (compare 18:21-35). A man who beats his wife, a woman who continually ridicules her husband, and a thousand other concrete examples could illustrate the principle. We must profess our faith with our lives as well as with our lips.

God sees what we are each made of. We judge by what we can see of a person's actions; God evaluates the heart's motivation. Some can act more moral by society's standards because it is to their advantage to do so, but this behavior does not necessarily imply that their hearts are purer than those with less social incentive to behave morally. Although their options differ, most drug dealers operate on the same moral principle as the media networks, the junk food industry or, for that matter, some Christian publishers: "We just give people what they want; it's not our fault if what they want isn't what's good for them." This excuse does not absolve them of guilt, but the person with a straight track through college and into the work force has more incentive to choose a different path. Indeed, the intellectual elite in Western universities laid the groundwork for the sexual promiscuity that has destroyed family structures in many ghettos and made drugs popular. God evaluates us not only by our deeds but also by our character—what we are made of when no one else sees us.

Do Not Covet Others Sexually (5:27-30) Jesus' warning against lust would have challenged some ancient hearers' values. Many men in the ancient Mediterranean thought lust healthy and normal (for example, Ach. Tat. 1.4-6; Apul. *Metam.* 2.8); some magical spells even describe self-stimulation as a way to secure intercourse with the object of one's desire (*PGM* 36.291-94), even if she was married (*PDM* 61.197-216). Jewish writers, however, viewed lust far more harshly (for example, Sirach 9:8; 41:21; 1QS 1.6-7; *CD* 2.16); some, in fact, viewed it as visual fornication or adultery (see Keener 1991a:16-17). Yet Jesus is not challenging his hearers' ethics; the scribes and Pharisees may have agreed with his basic premise, but Jesus challenges their hearts, not just their doctrine. Many Christians today similarly profess to agree with Jesus' doctrine here but do not obey it.

Jesus offers an implicit argument from Scripture, not just a cultural critique. The seventh of the Ten Commandments declares, "You shall not commit adultery" (Ex 20:14), while the tenth commandment declares, "You shall not covet [that is, desire] . . . anything that belongs to your neighbor" (Ex 20:17). In the popular Greek version of Jesus' day the tenth commandment began, "You shall not covet your neighbor's wife," and used the same word for "covet" that Jesus uses here for "lust." In other words, Jesus reads the humanly unenforceable tenth commandment as if it matters as much as the other, more humanly enforceable commandments. If you do not break the letter of the other commandments, but you *want* to do so in your heart, you are guilty. God judges a sinful heart, and hearts that desire what belongs to others are guilty.

Jesus does, however, go beyond his contemporaries' customary views on lust. Jewish men expected married Jewish women to wear head coverings to prevent lust. Jewish writers often warned of women as dangerous because they could invite lust (as in Sirach 25:21; *Ps. Sol.* 16:7-8), but Jesus placed the responsibility for lust on the person doing the lusting (Mt 5:28; Witherington 1984:28). Lust and anger are sins of the heart, and rapists who protest in earthly courts, "She asked for it!"

have no defense before God's court. Jesus says that it is better to suffer corporal punishment in the present—amputating one's lustful eye or other offending appendages—than to spend eternity in hell after the resurrection of the damned (5:29-30; 18:8-9).

Of course gouging out one's eye cannot stop lust; people can lust with their eyes closed. (Thus Tertullian warns that Christians need not blind themselves as Democritus did, but must simply guard their minds; he contends that "the Christian is born masculine for his wife and for no other woman"—*Apol.* 46.11-12.) Jesus is declaring in a graphic manner that by whatever means necessary, one should cast off this sin (compare Col 3:5). One must repent to be ready for the kingdom of heaven (Mt 4:17).

Herod Antipas, driven by lust, ended up murdering a prophet (14:6, 10; compare 5:11-12), illustrating the principle of both this paragraph and the preceding one (5:21-30), as well as the prohibition of oaths (5:33-37; 14:7). Most of us lack Herod's power to indulge our desires, but God knows what our hearts desire, whether we have power to execute that desire or not. How different the model of Joseph and Mary (1:25) and virtuous single persons like John the Baptist and Jesus, who suffered persecution for righteousness!

From this warning we learn the value that God places on marital and premarital fidelity. Even our thoughts should be only for our spouse; our spouse, rather than a given culture's idealization, should redefine our standard of beauty (compare Song 1:15-16). Of course, since the Bible demands faithfulness in advance to our *future* spouse (Deut 22:13-21; see also Mt 1:19), the principle Jesus illustrates with "adultery of the heart" could apply to premarital "fornication of the heart" just as well.

Jesus does not, of course, refer here to passing attraction. The Greek tense probably suggests "the deliberate harboring of desire for an illicit relationship" (France 1985:121). In our culture, where young people generally have to arrange their marriages without their parents' help, we might be in trouble if Jesus meant mere attraction! Jesus refers not to noticing a person's beauty but to imbibing it, meditating on it, seeking to possess it.

Lust is antithetical to true love: it dehumanizes another person into an object of passion, leading us to act as if the other were a visual or emotional prostitute for our use. Fueled by selfish passion, adultery violates the sanctity of another person's being and relationships; love, by contrast, seeks what is best for a person, including strengthening their marriage. Adultery usually involves considerable rationalization, justifying one's behavior as necessary or loving; but lust is the mother of adultery, the demonic force that allows human beings to justify exploiting one another sexually, at the same time betraying the most intimate of commitments where trust ought to abide secure even if it can flourish nowhere else. Lust demands possession; love values, respects and seeks to serve other persons with what is genuinely good for them. Lust is always incompatible with acknowledging God as the supreme desire of our hearts, because it is contrary to his will.

Legalism cannot change the heart and destroy lust or any other sin; only transformation of the heart to view reality in a new way can. Matthew frames Jesus' commandments in this section with that warning (compare 5:20, 48). Whereas lust distorts relationships, proper relationships in Christ's family can meet the need that lust pretends to fill. Paul and his contemporaries prescribed marriage as a helpful solution (1 Cor 7:2, 5, 9; Keener 1991a:72-74, 79-82), but many godly people today do not find marriage partners for years—and not all have the gift to easily embrace that state (Mt 19:11). How can they best guard against lust?

Once we begin to appreciate our brothers and sisters in Christ as members of our spiritual family, we are less apt to dehumanize them as temptations—whether temptations to be avoided or indulged. Our video culture has cheated us by reducing the meaning of gender to sexual gratification, as if we could relate to members of the other gender best as sleeping partners. God ideally gave people families in part so we could learn how to relate to other people in a variety of ways (motherly, fatherly, brotherly, sisterly—1 Tim 5:1-2); our Christian family is no different (1 Tim 5:1-2; see also Mt 12:49; 23:8; 25:40).

5:29-30 The word translated *sin* in the NIV here means "stumble." A bad foot or eye could cause one to stumble literally, but stumbling here (compare 13:41; 16:23; 18:6; 17:27; 18:8, 26:31) is a transparent metaphor for sin or apostasy (Ezek 14:3-7; Sirach 9:5; 25:21; 1QS 2.12; 3.24).

5:32 Rhetorical overstatement and hyperbole were common Jewish teaching techniques (*m.* '*Abot* 2:8) and appear elsewhere in the ancient Mediterranean as well (e.g., Arist. *Rhet.* 3.11.15, 1413a; *Rhet. ad Herenn.* 4.33.44; in Jesus' teaching, see especially Tannehill 1975).

Thus giving and receiving genuine Christian love within the appropriate boundaries—dealing with people as human beings like ourselves rather than objects of our passion (22:39)—is an important defense against lust. Perhaps an even greater defense remains being so wrapped up in Jesus' presence and work that one can wait either for God to send a spouse or for the ultimate unity that transcends the need for marriage altogether (see 22:30). In the meantime, one can pray for God's blessings on and prepare one's own life for the person God may send, or pour one's whole commitment into the work of the kingdom (6:33). I suggest these insights not as a married man paternalistically advising singles, but as one who remains single at the time of writing. The longer we resist a particular temptation, the less power that temptation can exercise in our lives.

Do Not Betray Your Spouse by Divorce (5:31-32) Adultery is unfaithfulness to one's spouse or accommodating another person's unfaithfulness to that person's spouse. Lust is one form of such unfaithfulness; divorce is another. The person who betrays his or her spouse by divorce is no less unfaithful to his or her marriage than the adulterer or lustful person and presumably warrants the same punishment prescribed by the preceding passage—damnation (5:29-30). Although Matthew does qualify the force of the saying, he wants us to hear its demand: marriage is sacred and must not be betrayed.

In principle, remarriage is adulterous because God rejects the validity of divorce. Employing the same teaching technique of rhetorical overstatement that pervades the context (as in 5:18-19, 29-30; 6:3; Stein 1978:8-12, 1979:119 and 1992:198; Keener 1991a:12-25), Jesus declares that God does not accept divorce; hence a divorced woman remains married in God's sight to her first husband, making her remarriage adulterous (5:32). (The image presumably addresses the woman be-

Maxims and proverbs, general statements of principle requiring qualification (compare Prov 18:22 with Mt 11:22; 12:4; 21:9; others in Keener 1993:235), were common throughout the ancient Mediterranean (Isoc. *Demon.* 12, *Or.* 1; Plut. *Poetry* 14, *Mor.* 35E-F) and in other societies (Mbiti 1970:2). Legal principles also had to be qualified (Quint. 7.6.1, 5); even the brief quips concluding many controversy chreiai or accents (as in Matthew 19:9) functioned thus (compare Plut. *Agesilaus* 21.4-5; Diog. Laert. 1.35).

cause the Palestinian Jewish law in Matthew's milieu permitted men to marry more than one wife anyway, whereas the sharing of a woman involved adultery—Keener 1991a:35, 47-48; Easton 1940:82; but compare, somewhat differently, Luck 1987:103-7.) Precisely because the very term for legal "divorce" meant freedom to remarry, everyone understood that a woman without a valid certificate of divorce was not free to remarry (as in *m. Giṭṭin* 2:1); but Jesus declares that if God does not accept the divorce as valid, remarriage is adulterous (19:6, 9; see similarly France 1985:123).

A few churches today take this passage completely literally and demand that remarried partners break up and return to their original spouses. If this passage did not employ rhetorical overstatement, their interpretation would be right; but their interpretation does not square with the rest of the biblical data (such as Jn 4:18, where the woman had five "husbands"). As common as divorce and remarriage were in antiquity (Carcopino 1940:95-100), Paul's letters would surely have reflected it had he been spending time breaking up new converts' second and third marriages. The Roman authorities, already concerned about subversive religious groups disrupting families (Keener 1992b:139-42), would have also noticed and acted swiftly! In practice, the strict position of churches that break up second marriages actually leads to new divorces—a position God surely disapproves of (Mt 5:19). (Supporters of breaking up second marriages sometimes cite 2 Sam 3:13-16, but because David had never actually divorced Michal, Saul's arrangement of Michal's marriage to Paltiel was illegal and adulterous; compare 1 Sam 19:11-17. Had that marriage been legally valid, Israelite law would have prohibited David from taking Michal back; see Deut 24:1-4.)

"Adultery" meant unfaithfulness to one's spouse, and remarriage is adulterous here precisely because in God's sight the original couple remains married. The moral issue of the image, however, is not remarriage but the validity of the divorce; although most people accepted most divorces as valid, everyone recognized that one could not remarry without a valid divorce. Jesus is prohibiting divorce in an incomparably graphic fashion (Keener 1991a:34-40, 43-44; Stein 1979).

In practice, this text demands that we love and serve our spouse. If integrity forbids us to violate vows in general (Mt 5:33-37), this principle applies most plainly to marriage vows (see also Mal 2:14). But most marriage vows promise more than "I won't commit adultery, lust after someone else or divorce you." Most people marry with the explicit or implicit expectation of enduring, mutual love; only in a secure relationship like marriage can people trust enough to intimately expose the depths of their hearts. Yet in all divorces, one or both parties is unfaithful to this implicit promise of marriage.

While Jesus gives divorce as an explicit example of marital infidelity, his principle of challenging all unfaithfulness to one's marriage as adulterous forces his followers to examine their own marriages more clearly. A man may never divorce his wife yet also fail to show her love; a woman may avoid affairs yet despise her husband. These too are acts of unfaithfulness to marriage (though they are not biblical grounds for divorce). If I am to love my neighbor as myself, how much more should I love my wife as my own body, to sacrifice myself for her willingly as Christ offered himself for the church (Eph 5:25)! Provided that my love for my spouse expresses rather than competes with my love for God (Mt 10:37; Lk 14:26; 18:29; Eph 5:1-2, 18-21), any gift of love I offer this daughter of God is too small a gift for the treasure of her sharing her life with me.

In warning against the sin of abandoning one's marriage, Jesus is defending rather than oppressing those divorced against their will. Yet instead of examining our own hearts and marriages as Jesus wills, some Christians today resort to the very kind of Bible interpretation Jesus was opposing. Jesus' words protected married people from the schism of divorce, but we sometimes turn them into a weapon against wounded Christians. Assuming that anger (Mt 5:21-22) and lust (5:27-28) are forgivable offenses because we have committed them, some nevertheless look askance at those who divorced in the past, as if that sin were unforgivable. Not content with that, some condescendingly claim to "forgive" innocent parties in divorces (such as a young mother who is single because she was abandoned by a drug-abusing husband). Perhaps none of us is a perfect spouse, and many of us live in a culture that confuses right and wrong, but the Bible does take sides on some issues. For instance, it plainly assigns guilt to the adulterer without assuming guilt on the part of the adulterer's spouse (Lev 20:10); nor may one automatically assume any more guilt for the abandoned spouse than for a spouse who is not abandoned (see Stephen 1993:14). Punishing one divorced against his or her will to show that we are against divorce makes as much sense as punishing a mugging victim to express our disdain for mugging.

Although many marriages do end by default, I have witnessed countless Christians who fought to preserve their marriages while spouses left them against their will; David Seamands tells me he has seen hundreds of such cases. Some in the church compassionlessly explain devastating illnesses as evidence of lack of faith, perhaps to assure themselves that they could never suffer them (compare Job 6:21; 12:5; Ps 38:11). Many other Christians do the same with divorce.

Matthew specifically states an exception. When Jesus offered a proverb stating a general principle (Mk 10:11; Lk 16:18), ancient hearers understood that such sayings often needed to be qualified for specific situations (Keener 1991a:22-25). Two similar divorce sayings in different contexts actually conflict if pressed literally: Mark 10:9 assumes that divorce should not but can occur, while the Q saying in Matthew 5:32 par. Luke 16:18 assumes that marriage is indissoluble and a genuine divorce cannot occur. But the conflict arises when we ignore Jesus' teaching style (Catchpole 1993:238): such a disharmony simply means that each saying must be read as a demand rather than a law, and the overarching social function of both must be recognized. That function is a call for absolute faithfulness in and to marriage.

To put the matter differently, Jesus' "purpose was not to lay down the law but to reassert an ideal and make divorce a sin, thereby disturbing then current complacency" (Davies and Allison 1988:532; compare Down 1984). In practice, the early Christians immediately began to qualify Jesus' divorce saying; other principles of Jesus, like not condemning the innocent (12:7) and the principle of mercy (23:23), would have forced them to do so in some circumstances.

For instance, when confronted by Christians wanting to divorce unbelieving spouses, Paul used Jesus' saying to forbid such an intention, but noted that if instead the spouse left, the believer was "not bound" (1 Cor 7:15). (Some others also view Paul's exception as implying that Jesus' prohibition is "not comprehensive"; see Blomberg 1992:111-12;

Vermes 1993:34 n. 34.) Paul's words recall the exact language for freedom to remarry in ancient divorce contracts, and his ancient readers, unable to be confused by modern writers' debates on the subject, would surely have understood his words thus (see, for example, *m. Giṭṭin* 9:3; *CPJ* 2:10-12, §144; Carmon 1973:90-91, 200-201, §189; Keener 1991a:61-62). Subsequent history has nevertheless saddled Christians with prejudices; thus, for example, after the NIV rightly notes that one who is married should "not seek a divorce," it translates the same Greek word for divorce as "unmarried" in the next line, where remarriage is permitted (1 Cor 7:27-28). One could presume that both uses of the Greek term "loosed" mean "widowed," of course—provided one consistently translates "seeking to be widowed" in this passage, which rather improbably suggests some lethal activity such as adding arsenic or cyanide to a spouse's tea. But most likely Paul addresses especially divorce and remarriage in this passage.

Paul's and Matthew's exceptions (Mt 5:32; 19:9; 1 Cor 7:15, 27-28) constitute two-thirds of the New Testament references to divorce, and both point to the same kind of exception: the person whose marriage is ended against his or her will. As Craig Blomberg reasons, other exceptions probably exist, but they must be governed by the principles that unite the two biblical exceptions: (1) both infidelity and abandonment destroy one of the basic components of marriage; (2) "both leave one party without any other options if attempts at reconciliation are spurned"; (3) both use divorce "as a last resort." That some will abuse this freedom (as Blomberg also warns) cannot make us insensitive to the innocent party who genuinely needs that freedom (Blomberg 1992:293). In other words, Jesus' exceptions do not constitute an excuse to escape a difficult marriage (compare 1 Cor 7:10-14); they exonerate those who genuinely wished to save their marriage but were unable to do so because their spouse's unrepentant adultery, abandonment or abuse de facto destroyed the marriage bonds.

Admitting the exceptional cases does not excuse us from taking Jesus' actual point seriously. Palestinian Jewish husbands could divorce for virtually any reason (Jos. *Ant.* 4.253), explicitly including their wives' disobedience (*ARN* 1A; Jos. *Life* 426), even burning the toast (*m. Giṭṭin* 9:10; *Sipre Deut.* 269.1.1). In broader Greco-Roman culture (which Paul addresses in 1 Cor 7:10-16) either husband or wife could unilaterally divorce the other spouse without obtaining consent (Cary and Haarhoff 1946:144; O'Rourke 1971:181). By removing the right of divorce, Jesus is protecting a person from being betrayed by her or his spouse and demanding that we respect one another enough to do our own utmost to make our marriage work rather than abandoning the partner with whom we entered into covenant for life.

Although the thrust of this passage is faithfulness to one's marriage, Matthew's exception clause does not allow his readers to apply his rhetorical overstatement legalistically. Indeed, to read the Sermon on the Mount "legalistically as a set of rules is to miss the point; it represents a demand more radical than any legislator could conceive" (France 1985:106), still less enforce. Jesus' real point, which the hyperbolic image is meant to evoke, is the sanctity of marriage (see also 19:4-6; Efird 1985:57-59). Addressing the hardness of legal interpreters' hearts (19:8), Jesus opposed divorce to protect marriage and family, thereby seeking to prevent the betrayal of innocent spouses.

I believe that churches who punish innocent parties in divorces today interpret Jesus legalistically with hearts as hard as those of Jesus' opponents. They understand neither the point of Jesus' teaching nor the heart of God that motivated him (compare 9:11-13; 12:2-14; 23:23-24). But we do the same when we condone inappropriate divorce or the hardness of heart in marriage (19:8) that can lead to divorce or in other ways ruin the intimacy of one flesh that God commanded.

Oaths Are a Poor Substitute for Integrity (5:33-37) When Jesus quotes his Bible as prohibiting false vows and other oaths (Deut 23:23), he probably also has in view the Ten Commandments, as in Matthew 5:21, 27. In this case he alludes to the third commandment: a false oath "misuses" or takes in vain God's name, since oaths by definition called on a deity to witness them (Ex 20:7). Breaking an oath was dangerous, for in all societies oaths contained curses that deities would avenge if the person who swore by them broke the oath. The Bible's point in prohibiting false oaths, however, was that one should tell the truth and keep one's promises. The Hebrew Bible approved of some oaths and vows (as in Num 5:19-22; 6:2), but Jesus again summons us beyond the law's letter to its intention. His own point is not so much that oaths are evil as that the motivation for engaging in them is; one should simply tell the truth (Mt 5:37).

Although Jesus' position on oaths is not wholly unique, it was rare enough to be distinctive. Although some Jewish teachers warned against customary oath-taking, nearly all accepted oath-taking as valid; in daily life, it was surely common in the marketplace. Some groups of Essenes may have avoided oaths altogether (Jos. *War* 2.135), except for their initiatory oath for joining the sect (Jos. *War* 2.139-42; see also 1QS 5.8). Josephus declares that one could trust an Essene's word more than an oath, however (*War* 2.135); Philo indicates that their abstention from oaths declared their commitment to truth (*Every Good Man Free* 84; also Vermes 1993:35). Jesus and the Essenes probably intended the same as Pythagoras: let your word carry such conviction that you need not call deities to witness (Diog. Laert. 8.1.22; compare Philo *Spec. Leg.* 2.2; Isoc. *Nic.* 22, *Or.* 2).

The point of this passage is integrity. Jesus observes that since God witnesses every word we say anyway, we should be able to tell the truth without having to call God to witness by a formal oath. Jesus is addressing a popular abuse of oaths in his day. To protect the sanctity of the divine name against inadvertent oath-breaking, common Jewish practice introduced surrogate objects by which to swear (Vermes 1993:34-35). Some people apparently thought it harmless to deceive if they swore oaths by something like their right hand (*t. Nedarim* 1:1; cf. Jos. *War* 2.451). The further removed the oath was from the actual name of God, the less danger they faced for violating it (Schiffman 1983:137-38; E. Sanders 1990:53-54). Jewish teachers had to arbitrate which oaths were actually binding as allusions to God's name (*m. Šebi'it* 4.13; see also *CD* 15.1-5). Jesus teaches that all oaths invoke God's witness equally. Just as heaven, earth (Is 66:1-2) and Jerusalem (Ps 48:2; Mt 4:5; 27:53) belong to God (Mt 5:34-35), so do the hairs on our heads (5:36); although we can dye our hair, we have no genuine control over its aging (compare 6:27). All oaths implicitly call God to witness, because everything that exists was made by him. For Jesus, no aspect of life except sin is purely secular.

Avoiding oaths is thus inadequate; the issue is telling the truth, because God witnesses every word we speak. Although many passages in the Bible allow some degree of deception to preserve life (Keener 1991a:22), such exceptions are rare in our daily lives. When we lie to cover our own wrong motives from those we think would disdain us, we forget that one day God will expose all the secrets of our hearts anyway (Mt 10:26). When we lightly commit ourselves to meet people at particular times and then unnecessarily delay them (as if their time were a commodity less precious than our own), we treat them unjustly and deceitfully, even if in a relatively minor way. How much more when we make promises in business deals or make still more lasting vows (such as the marriage covenant—5:31-32).

Making vows (promises) to God lightly is a severe offense (compare Acts 5:1-11). Although Jesus' first followers continued to call on God to witness the truth of some of their statements, apparently taking Jesus' words as rhetorical overstatement (examples appear in Rom 1:9; 9:1; Gal 1:20), they seem to have refrained from more overt oaths (2 Cor 1:17; Jas 5:12). Oaths that invite penalties on oneself for violating them ("cross my heart and hope to die") are unnecessary for people of truth.

Avoid Retribution and Resistance (5:38-42) Jesus here warns against legal retribution (vv. 38-39) and goes so far as to undercut legal resistance altogether with a verse that, if followed literally, would leave most Christians stark naked (v. 40). He also advocates not only compliance but actual cooperation with a member of an occupying army who might be keeping you from your livelihood (v. 41), as well as with the beggar or others who seek our help (v. 42). (Taking the last verse literally would also break most of us financially. Consider how many requests for money come in the mail each week!) If Jesus is not genuinely advocating nudity and living on the street—that is, if he is speaking the language of rhetorical overstatement (5:18-19, 29-32; 6:3)—this still does

---

5:38 *Eye for eye, and tooth for tooth* (Ex 21:23-25; Deut 19:21) was standard ancient Near Eastern law, except that legal collections besides the Old Testament often varied the punishments according to one's social class (Hammurabi 196-223). This *eye for eye* form of law, called *lex talionis,* provides the foundation for legal ethics by making punishment commensurate with offense (Jeremias 1963:28; Meier 1979:261; Guelich 1982:224). In the classless Old Testament version these laws made a just point: each person must recognize that another person's life and members are worth no less than one's own. But whereas some Israelite laws could serve as deterrents (Deut 19:20; 21:21) or provide benefit for the

not absolve us from taking his demand seriously. Jesus utilized hyperbole precisely to challenge his hearers, to force us to consider what we value.

Jesus' words strike at the very core of human selfishness, summoning us to value others above ourselves in concrete and consistent ways. Some misread this text as if it says not to oppose injustice; what it really says, however, is that we should be so unselfish and trust God so much that we leave our vindication with him. We have no honor or property worth defending compared with the opportunity to show how much we love God and everyone else. By not retaliating, by not coming down to the oppressors' level, we necessarily will appear unrealistic to the world. Jesus' way scorns the world's honor and appears realistic only to those with the eyes of faith. It is the lifestyle of those who anticipate his coming kingdom (4:17).

Jesus Challenges Our Desire for Personal Vindication (5:38) *Eye for eye* never meant that a person could exact vengeance directly for his or her own eye; it meant that one should take the offender to court, where the sentence could be executed legally. People sometimes cite this example as a case of Jesus' disagreeing with the Old Testament. But a society could recognize the legal justice of *eye for eye* while its sages warned against descending to oppressors' moral level by fighting evil with evil (Akkadian wisdom in Pritchard 1955:426). Jesus is not so much revoking a standard for justice as calling his followers not to make use of it; we qualify justice with mercy because we do not need to avenge our honor. Jesus calls for this humble response of faith in God; God alone is the final arbiter of justice, and we must trust him to fulfill it.

Turning the Other Cheek, Letting God Vindicate Us (5:39) As in much of Jesus' teaching, pressing his illustration the wrong way may obscure his point. In fact, this would read Scripture the very way he was

person injured (Ex 21:19, 26-27), the *lex talionis* regulations simply avenged the person's honor, vindicating the victim by punishing the assailant. Contemporary Jewish law sought to remedy this weakness by providing monetary restitution as an alternative to maiming the offender (Jos. *Ant.* 4.280; see also Cohen 1966:1:18; Belkin 1940:97-103).

5:39 Although it was never the corporate norm (1 Macc 2:67), both ancient Israel (Ex 23:4-5; Lev 19:18; Job 31:29-30; Prov 24:17-18, 29; 25:21-22) and later Judaism (Sirach 28:1-8; 1QS 10.17-19; *CD* 9.3-6; Ps-Phocyl. 77; Ps-Philo 8:10) sometimes advocated nonresistance.

warning against: if someone hits us in the nose, or has already struck us on both cheeks, are we finally free to hit back? Jesus gives us a radical example so we will avoid retaliation, not so we will explore the limits of his example (see Tannehill 1975:73). A backhanded blow to the right cheek did not imply shattered teeth (tooth for tooth was a separate statement); it was an insult, the severest public affront to a person's dignity (Lam 3:30; Jeremias 1963:28 and 1971:239). God's prophets sometimes suffered such ill-treatment (1 Kings 22:24; Is 50:6). Yet though this was more an affront to honor, a challenge, than a physical injury, ancient societies typically provided legal recourse for this offense within the *lex talionis* regulations (Pritchard 1955:163, 175; see also Gaius *Inst.* 3.220).

In the case of an offense to our personal dignity, Jesus not only warns us not to avenge our honor by retaliating but suggests that we indulge the offender further. By freely offering our other cheek, we show that those who are secure in their status before God do not value human honor. Indeed, in some sense we practice resistance by showing our contempt for the value of our insulter's (and perhaps the onlookers') opinions! Because we value God's honor rather than our own (Mt 5:16; 6:1-18), because our very lives become forfeit to us when we begin to follow Jesus Christ (16:24-27), we have no honor of our own to lose. In this way we testify to those who insult us of a higher allegiance of which they should take notice.

Legal Nonresistance (5:40) Rather than trying to get an inner garment back by legal recourse, one should relinquish the outer one too! If taken literally, this practice would quickly lead to nudity (see also Stein 1978:10), an intolerable dishonor in Palestinian Jewish society (for example, *Jub.* 7:8-10, 20; 1QS 7.12). Many peasants (at least in poorer areas like Egypt) had only one outer cloak and pursued whatever legal recourse necessary to get it back if it was seized (*CPJ* 1:239-40, §129.5). Because the outer cloak doubled as a poor man's bedding, biblical law permitted no one to take it, even as a pledge overnight (Ex 22:26-27; Deut 24:12-13). Thus Jesus demands that we surrender the very possession the law explicitly protects from legal seizure (Guelich 1982:222). To force his hearers to think, then, Jesus provides a shockingly graphic, almost humorous illustration of what he means by nonresistance. His hearers value honor and things more than they value the kingdom.

This passage is a graphic image, but if we read it literally, believers should never take anyone to court. How far do we press Jesus' image here, or Paul's in 1 Corinthians 6:1-8?

A driver had slammed into (and demolished) the car of one of my students, a new Christian, and the student feared that reporting him to her insurance company would violate the spirit of this passage. In such cases I suspect that insurance is our society's way of providing for the parties involved with a minimum of pain to both. But our very questions regarding how far to press Jesus' words force us to grapple with his principle here. Nothing a person can take from us matters in the end anyway; we must love our enemies and seek to turn them into friends.

Love Even Your Oppressors (5:41) Here Matthew probably means submission to a Roman soldier's demands. Because tax revenues did not cover all the Roman army's needs, soldiers could requisition what they required (N. Lewis 1983:172-73; Rapske 1994:14). Romans could legally demand local inhabitants to provide forced labor if they wanted (as in Mt 27:32) and were known to abuse this privilege (for example, Apul. *Metam.* 9.39). Yet "going the extra mile" represents not only submitting to unjust demands but actually exceeding them—showing our oppressors that we love them and take no offense, although our associates may wrongly view this love as collaboration with an enemy occupation. The truth of this passage is a life-and-death matter for many believers. Members of both sides in wars have often killed Christians for refusing to take sides; gangs in inner cities can present similar pressures.

Such courageous love is not easy to come by and is easily stifled by patriotism. To take but one example that challenges my own culture, many white U.S. citizens may wish to rethink the patriotic lens through which they view the American colonies' revolt against Britain in the 1770s—did they really have grounds for secession of which Jesus would have approved if they had been his disciples? Past oppression is also easily recalled. British Christians might consider their feelings for Germans; Korean and Chinese Christians, for the Japanese. In some form the principle can apply to most national, racial and cultural groups. While early Christians responded to their persecutors with defiant love (a humility the persecutors often viewed as arrogance), many politically zealous Christians in the United States guard their rights so fiercely that they are easily given to anger (which opponents also view as arrogance).

Jesus and Paul responded firmly to unjust blows in the face (Jn 18:22-23; Acts 23:2-5) and in other circumstances (Jn 8:40-44; Acts 16:37; 22:25; 25:11; 26:25) without retaliating in their own interests. Thus the text need not rule out all forms of resistance (see Clavier 1957; France 1985:126; Vermes 1993:36). But whether persecuted as Christians or for other reasons, we must respond with love and kindness (like the workers at a pregnancy-support clinic who brought food out to abortion-rights picketers). We must resist injustice and refuse to comply with demands that compromise justice; but we must do so in kindness and love, not with violence or retribution.

Jesus' words are designed to shock us into considering our values, but how far do we press Jesus' meaning? Is he calling for personal or societal nonviolence? Within a week after my conversion, my first reading of Matthew 5 led me to abandon my peace-through-strength militarism for a thoroughgoing, martyrdom-anticipating pacifism, at least on the personal level. Yet I have come to wonder whether on a corporate level just military interventions might not sometimes be a lesser evil than tolerating unjust military actions tantamount to genocide (such as those of Hitler). Can meek and weaponless police officers enforce laws designed to restrain drug dealers? Possessions may not matter, but human life clearly does (Mt 6:25).

Still, it is easy for nations to abuse the rhetoric of justice for self-serving violence, and unlike C. S. Lewis and some other Christian thinkers I respect, I continue to struggle with the idea of "loving your enemy" while you are trying to kill him. Dietrich Bonhoeffer, a pacifist Christian who opposed Hitler's regime, ultimately decided to participate in an assassination attempt against Hitler. He preferred to "do evil rather than to be evil," arguing that tolerating such evil as Hitler was tantamount to supporting that evil. The plot failed, and Bonhoeffer was executed with his coconspirators. What would we have done had we been in Bonhoeffer's place? For some of us, at least, this seems to be a hard question demanding charity toward those whose conclusions differ from our own.

At least on a personal level, however, Jesus' point is both uncomfortable and difficult to evade. The life of Martin Luther King Jr. reminds us that the meek rarely advance their cause without paying a high personal price, even martyrdom. Do we have the courage to stand for justice yet do so without this world's weapons of violence and hatred (see Thurman 1981:88)? While Jesus' teaching cannot be conformed to the agendas of those who advocate violent revolution, no matter how just their cause, neither does it mean total passivity in the face of evil. It does not mean that an abused wife must remain in the home in the face of abuse; it does not mean that God expects people being massacred to remain instead of fleeing (compare Mt 2:13-20; 10:23). James, an advocate of peace (Jas 2:11; 3:13-18; 4:1-2), was unrestrained in his denunciation of those who oppressed the poor (Jas 5:1-6; see Keener 1991c).

Rather, Jesus' teaching does mean that we depend on God rather than on human weapons, although God may sovereignly raise up human weapons to fight the oppressors. If we value justice and compassion for persons rather than merely utopian idealism, we must also calculate the human cost of opposing various degrees of injustice. In first-century Palestine, few "safe" vehicles existed for nonviolent social protest against the Romans; Romans viewed most public protest as linked with revolution, and punished it accordingly. In a society like ours where Christian egalitarianism has helped shape conceptions of justice, nonviolent protest stands a much better chance of working. Neither violent revolutionaries (whose cause may be more just than their methods) nor the well-fed who complacently ignore the rest of the world's pain (and whose cause is merely personal advancement) may embrace Jesus without either distorting him or transforming themselves in the process.

Yet Jesus' own life explains the meekness he prescribes. When the time appointed by his Father arrived, Jesus allowed people to crucify him, trusting his Father's coming vindication to raise him from the dead (Mt 17:11; 20:18-19). He was too meek to cry out or bruise a reed until the time would come to bring "justice to victory" (12:19-20). Yet he proclaimed justice (12:18), openly denounced the unjust (23:13-36) and actively, even somewhat "violently," protested unrighteousness although he knew what it would cost him (21:12-13). Jesus was meek (11:29), but he was not a wimp. He called his disciples to be both harmless as doves and wise as serpents (10:16)—in short, to be ruled by the law of love (22:39). Love of neighbor not only does no harm to a neighbor but bids us place ourselves in harm's way to protect our neighbor.

Surrender Your Possessions to Whoever Requests Them (5:42)

Judaism recognized giving to beggars as a moral obligation. Judaism stressed both charity and a high work ethic; most beggars genuinely had no alternative means of income. Unlike some of Jesus' contemporaries (Hengel 1974:20; see also Jeremias 1969:127), he places no cap on giving. While Jesus lived simply, he did have a home (4:13), like most other Galileans (albeit probably a modest one, like most of his townspeople). Yet if Jesus merely counseled "Live simply" without confronting us with concrete, graphic illustrations, many of us would define simplicity in terms of our desires rather than in terms of the world's great needs. Jesus forces us to decide how much we love others—and him.

Again Jesus invites us to grapple with his point, to which he will return with far greater force in 6:19-34. If nonresistance means disdaining our right to personal honor (5:38-39), our most basic possessions (v. 40) and our labor and time (v. 41) when others seek them by force, we must also disdain these things in view of the needs of the poor (v. 42). When the kingdom comes, our deeds rather than our wealth will matter (6:19-21; compare 25:34-46). In the meantime those who disdain everything else for the kingdom (13:44-45) must do with these other possessions what Jesus wills: give them to those who need them more (19:21). Our "vested interests" must be in heaven, not on earth (6:19-21). If we cannot value the kingdom that much, Jesus says, it will not belong to us (19:29-30).

Love Your Enemies (5:43-48) Jesus demands not only that we not resist evil people assaulting our honor or possessions (vv. 38-42) but that we go so far as to actively love our enemies.

Jesus Demands Love Even for Enemies (5:43-44) When Jesus

5:42 In a society dominated by honor and shame, some considered it better to die than to beg (Sirach 40:28-30); few would resort to that lifestyle unnecessarily. Work normally generated more income than begging anyway.

5:43 Both Jewish (Ps-Phocyl. 152; *Test. Benj.* 4:2; Flusser 1988:506; E. Sanders 1992:234-35) and Greek (Diog. Laert. 1.78; 6.1.12; compare Plut. *Profit by Enemies, Mor.* 86B-92F) sages sometimes admonished against hating one's enemies, although the more common sentiment in practice—then as today—was to make sure you did your enemy more harm than he did to you (Isoc. *Demon.* 26, *Or.* 1).

5:44 Some rightly observe that Jesus' warnings against resistance address personal resistance rather than nations at war (Neil 1976:160-62); they do not summon non-Christian

explains his final quotation from the Bible, *Love your neighbor,* he adds to the quote an implication some of his contemporaries found there: *hate your enemy.* He is probably speaking of all kinds of enemies. Personal enemies were common enough in the setting of Galilean villages (Horsley 1986; Freyne 1988:154), but Jesus' contemporaries may have also thought of corporate threats to Israel or the moral fabric of the community (see Borg 1987:139). Whereas the biblical command to love neighbors (Lev 19:18) extends to foreigners in the land (Lev 19:33-34; compare Lk 10:27-37), other texts hold up a passionate devotion to God's cause that bred hatred of those who opposed it (Ps 139:21-22; see also 137:7-9). Popular piety, exemplified in the Qumran community's oath to "hate the children of darkness," may have extended such biblical ideology in Jesus' day (see Sutcliffe 1960). Jesus may well mean both personal and corporate enemies (Moulder 1978).

Jesus builds a fence around the law of love (Mt 22:39), amplifying it to its ultimate conclusion (compare Ex 23:4-5). In so doing, he makes demands more stringent than the law. He also makes a demand that can require more than merely human resources for forgiveness. Corrie ten Boom, who had lost most of her family in a Nazi concentration camp, often lectured on grace. But one day a man who came to shake her hand after such a talk turned out to be a former prison guard. Only by asking God to love through her did she find the grace to take his hand and offer him Christian forgiveness.

Since Jesus does not say exactly what to pray for our persecutors, some of us have been tempted to pray, "God, kill that person!" Needless to say, the context makes clear that Jesus means to pray good things for our enemies. Old Testament prayers for vindication (such as 2 Chron 24:22; Jer 15:15) still have their place (2 Tim 4:14; Rev 6:10), but our

---

national governments or government police forces to Christian self-sacrifice. Yet others make a reasonable case that the prohibition of personal involvement in violence also prohibits Christians' participation as combatants in national wars, "just" or unjust (e.g., Sider 1979). Even just wars such as international police actions invariably kill unwilling participants unjustly; to what extent should Christians participate in such wars, and to what extent is it appropriate to wait for God to raise up others, like the Babylonians or Assyrians of old, to do the job? God's kingdom is no longer tied with the nation-state as in the Old Testament (Craigie 1978:102, 110-11), and Christians going to war for one country or tribe now may kill Christians warring for another country or tribe.

attitude toward individuals who hurt us personally or corporately must be love (Lk 23:34; Acts 7:60). Again, Jesus' words are graphic pictures that force us to probe our hearts; they do not cancel the Old Testament belief in divine vindication (Mt 23:33, 38; Rev 6:10-11), but summon us to leave our vindication with God and seek others' best interests in love.

Jesus Appeals to a Positive and Negative Example (5:45-47) First he provides the ultimate moral example: God (vv. 45, 48). Jewish teachers generally recognized, as Jesus did, that God was gracious to all humanity, including the morally undeserving (for example, *Sipre Deut.* 43.3.6); they also saw rain as one of God's universal signs of beneficence. But after adducing the ultimate moral example, Jesus adduces an example from the opposite end of his hearers' moral spectrum (vv. 46-47): he provokes his hearers to shame by comparing their ability to obey the love commandment with that of tax-gatherers and Gentile idolaters, the epitome of moral reprobates (Mt 6:7; 20:25; 18:17; compare, for example, *Sipre Deut.* 43.16.1). One whose righteousness would surpass that of scribes and Pharisees (5:20) must exemplify a higher standard of righteousness than loving those friendly to their interests.

Jesus Demands That We Be Perfect like God (5:48) What Jesus illustrated with graphic, concrete examples earlier in the sermon (vv. 21-47) he now epitomizes in a summary statement that forces us to go beyond mere examples. We can appeal to no law to tell us that we are righteous enough—that would be legalism. Instead, we must desire God's will so much that we seek to please him in every area of our lives—that is holiness. Jesus says that God's law was never about mere rules; instead, God desires a complete righteousness of the heart, a total devotion to God's purposes in this world.

That God becomes the standard of comparison suggests that Jesus' instruction here is exhortation, setting a goal, not assuming a state to which the hearers have already come. (The issue of whether any Christian *is* perfect is irrelevant here. All of us can learn to better reflect God's character; at the same time, God promises us power to overcome any given temptation; and if we can overcome *any* temptation, we should choose to say no to *every* temptation.) And as long as God represents the moral standard, none of us has room to boast; all of us must unite as brothers and sisters in need and seek God's kingdom and righteousness with all our hearts.

□ Showing Righteousness to God Alone (6:1-18)

Jesus begins this section of his teaching with a thesis statement summarizing his point: Do your righteousness for God to see you, not others (6:1). Jesus then illustrates his point with the examples of secret charity (vv. 2-4), prayer (vv. 5-15) and fasting (vv. 16-18). The middle section on prayer is the longest (following accepted practices of arrangement in his day, Matthew may have inserted the Lord's Prayer from a different context; compare Lk 11:1-4).

Righteousness When Only God Sees (6:1) Several observations concerning 6:1, the thesis statement for this section, are appropriate before we approach the following paragraphs of the passage in more detail.

First, we must impress God alone. In all three examples Jesus warns his followers not to be like the *hypocrites* (6:2, 5, 16; also 15:7; 22:18; 23:13-29; 24:51). This term originally designated actors in the theater, though both Greek and Jewish texts had long before come to apply it figuratively.

One of human religion's greatest temptations is to act piously to elicit the praise of others. A secret atheist could practice religion in that form without the slightest element of faith (compare 23:5). Such temptations were part and parcel of ancient religion; for instance, when some first-century Jewish leaders called a fast for unrighteous reasons, others feared not to observe it, lest anyone question their piety (Jos. *Life* 290-91). Yet the same temptation is no less real today. Jesus reminds us that true piety means impressing God alone—living our lives in the recognition that God knows every thought and deed, and it is his approval alone that matters. Matthew again praises the meek, whose only hope is in God, not in others' opinions of them. Those of us who are "religious professionals," making our living from public ministry, should take special heed: if we value the approval or pay of our congregations more than what God has called us to do, we will have no reward left when we stand before him.

Second, Jesus' warning does not preclude public acts of righteousness.

Public righteousness, even when carried out in the knowledge that such acts will draw attention, is not wrong so long as we seek to be seen for God's glory rather than our own (5:16). This text warns us, however, how easy it is to justify our own desire to impress others as "being a light." We should do everything for God (Rom 14:6-8; 1 Cor 10:31; Col 3:17); the repentant person who lives in view of the coming kingdom (4:17) is concerned more with God's evaluation than with that of others. Many people practice religion without paying attention to God, and this warns us to search our motives.

Third, Jesus demands practice, not just theory. Jesus' Jewish contemporaries agreed with most of what he was teaching here (*ARN* 28A; 40A; 46, §129B). Thus Jesus is not satisfied that we claim to agree with his ethics; he wants us to live accordingly.

Fourth, Jesus' three examples are random, so secrecy must apply to all acts of righteousness. Judaism often listed righteous works, sometimes in sets of threes (Jesus' list here resembles Tobit 12:8), but such lists were never more than random examples. We must thus apply Jesus' principle to all our acts of righteousness.

Fifth, Jesus promises eternal reward for those who seek to please God rather than mortals. Jesus concludes his warnings with another graphic image: businessmen regularly wrote the phrase *received their reward in full* (see 6:2, 5, 16) on receipts to indicate that no further payment was required (Deissmann 1978:110). Jesus is saying that those who give charity to be admired by others, or pray and fast to people rather than to God, already have what they wanted: others' approval. They will not be rewarded again for their deeds on the day of judgment.

Finally, Jesus defines true religion differently from the way many Christians do. If it is possible to pray, fast and give alms extensively and yet do it from wrong motives, we must reevaluate our religious values. Most people I know who pray four hours a day have a very close walk with God. But I know others whose calling may allow them only an hour a day of concerted prayer, yet their walk is probably just as close to God, since they are living according to his will. We should pray, fast and serve the needy because we love God—not in order to convince anyone, including ourselves, that we do.

Doing Charity Secretly (6:2-4) This paragraph assumes that disciples give to the poor (compare 6:19-24 at greater length); what it evaluates is *how* we give to the poor.

Jesus again employs hyperbole in his descriptions (as in 5:19, 29-30), thereby adding graphic force to his warnings. Although some scholars have argued that people actually blew trumpets during giving in the synagogues, Jesus probably simply uses rhetorical exaggeration to reinforce his point, as when picturing the Pharisees who swallow a camel whole but strain out a mere gnat (23:24). Jesus adds to this stark image still another: we should be so secretive in giving that we should not let our left hand know what our right hand is doing (6:3; 1 Cor 4:3-5). He challenges us about the danger of public piety with such forceful language precisely "because our assurance that such hypocrisy is no great problem with us is a major part of the problem" (Tannehill 1975:85).

Jesus emphasizes future reward for those who forgo present honor. He promises something better than a charitable deduction on one's income tax, nice as that may be (vv. 1, 2, 4). Many of his contemporaries believed that charity delivers the giver from death and stores up treasure in heaven (Tobit 4:10; 12:8; 14:10; *t. Pe'a* 4:21; *Pes. Rab.* 25:2); Jesus likewise emphasizes heavenly reward for serving those truly in need (6:19-21). In contrast to nineteenth-century evangelicalism, much of today's church is divided between those who emphasize personal intimacy with God in prayer and those who emphasize justice for the true poor (see Sider 1993). Like the prophets of old, however, Jesus demanded both (6:2-13; Mk 12:40); he also recognized that without keeping God himself in view, we can pervert either form of piety.

We should care for the poor. The phrase *when you give to the needy* implies the expectation, standard in Judaism, that one would care for the needs of the poor (Tobit 4:7), just as the phrase *when you pray* (6:5) takes for granted that the hearer will pray (*m. 'Abot* 2:10). Jesus' Jewish contemporaries emphasized that one must give charity from the right kind of heart (*m. 'Abot* 5:13) and sometimes objected to ostentation in charity (*Test. Job* 9:7-8; *m. Šeqalim* 5:6).

If more of us Christians feared God, this realization would scare some sense into us. We like to think that Jesus was condemning the "legalistic" religion of Judaism, but we are wrong. Jesus was not condemning an officially legalistic religion, but the ostentatious practice of those whose religion taught purity of heart. In other words, on many points the Pharisees believed the same things we do, the same things Jesus was teaching. When we parade up to the altar to give our money (in some churches) or make sure the ushers see us contribute a significant offering when they pass the plate (in other churches), our hearts stand condemned regardless of our doctrine. True religion demands sufficient faith to settle for God's approval, to do what pleases him no matter what others may think.

The Right Way to Pray (6:5-15) This section parallels the sections on giving charity (vv. 2-4) and fasting (vv. 16-18) secretly, but adds to its material on praying secretly (vv. 5-6) much other material on prayer, including the Lord's Prayer (vv. 9-13). Because of the abundance of material here, someone preaching or teaching on verses 1-18 who is limited by time constraints might wish to treat verses 7-13 in a separate sermon or teaching block.

Jesus emphasizes that we should not pray *like the hypocrites,* to be seen by others (v.5); instead we should pray privately (v. 6). He also emphasizes that we should not pray *like pagans,* that is, Gentiles, expecting to manipulate an answer from their deities (v. 7); instead we should offer a simple prayer to our Father (vv. 8-13).

Pray in Secret (6:5-6) Jesus seizes our attention here with forceful language, warning against seeking to pray in the synagogues (where prayers were customarily offered) and in the most visible location, the streets (Tannehill 1975:82; compare 12:19). We should thus enter into a private room, but this is not *your room* (NIV), for the only room in the average Palestinian home that had its own door would be the much smaller "closet" (KJV) or "storeroom" (Schweizer 1975:145). Jewish people did not normally pray in the street, but Jesus again graphically reduces the questionable behavior to the absurd: one who craves notice so much that he arranges to find himself in the street during the regular daily prayer times. This illustration, like Jesus' preceding one (vv. 2-3), is rhetorical overstatement: none of Jesus' own reported private prayers were prayed in a storeroom. This text precludes not public prayer (18:19-20; 1 Tim 2:8) but prayer to be seen and glorified by others. At the same time, Jesus' point is quite literal. When Jesus prayed privately, he normally sought a place more secluded than a storeroom, going into the Galilean hills (Mt 14:23).

Being religious or faithful to church traditions is thus inadequate. Contemporary Judaism emphasized regular and efficacious prayer far more than most modern Western Christians do (though less than, say, most Korean Christians do). Because prayer promises the hearing of an Advocate more powerful than any other, it goes without saying that those who spend little time in prayer do not in practice believe much in a God who answers prayer; but Jesus goes one step beyond this charge. Those who spend much time in prayer so they may impress others with their piety likewise lack faith in a God who rewards us by answering prayer or at the coming of his kingdom. Slicing through the veneer of human religion, Jesus exposes the functional atheism of our hearts.

Jesus' point of contention with his Jewish contemporaries was not the form of their prayers (which his own prayer in 6:9-13 closely matches) but their motivation. Again his words strike not at a practice foreign to Christians today, but at the very heart of our outward piety. God demands that we genuinely pray to *him*.

Do Not Pray like the Pagans (6:7-8) But Jesus not only warns against the "hypocrites' " prayers that invite human rather than divine attention; he criticizes pagan prayers designed to manipulate the deities. Pagans piled up as many names of the deity they were entreating as possible, hoping at least one would be effective. Pagans also reminded a deity of favors owed, seeking an answer on contractual grounds (Burkert 1985:74-75). One may note that whereas ancient Israel shared with its neighbors thank offerings, atonement offerings and so forth, Israel had no sacrifices to secure rain or any favors from God; God gave these blessings only in response to Israel's obedience to his covenant (Deut 27—28).

To compare Jewish hearers' behavior with that of pagans would have shamed them deeply (Mt 6:7; pace Meier 1980:59). Both Matthew (5:47; 18:17; 20:25) and his Bible (Lev 18:3; Deut 18:9; Jer 10:2) contain warnings not to be like the pagans. This contrast has some implications for Christians today. First, we should understand the Lord's Prayer (6:9-13) rather than simply repeat it by rote in our churches (compare

Did. 8: do not pray like the hypocrites, rather pray the Lord's Prayer three times a day). Second, whatever one's views on school prayer, the "Lord's Prayer" is not a prayer for pagans, but only for those who may rightly call God *Father* (v. 9). Only *hypocrites* (v. 5) can pray it yet remain unconcerned for God's honor in the world (vv. 9-10). Finally, Christians who seek answers to prayer on "contractual" grounds—with formulas rather than out of an intimate and mature trust in God our Father—pray like pagans.

Genuine faith grows out of a relationship with God and cannot be simulated by formulas, no matter how invested our culture becomes in instant products, academic cramming and slothful shortcuts to prosperity. We pray not because we think our prayers earn God's favor, but as an expression of our trust in a Father who already knows our need and merely waits for us to express our dependence on him (v. 8). Many Jewish writers of Jesus' day stressed that prayer involves a heartfelt relationship with God and not just petition (Abelson 1969:325). Is it possible that Jesus' contemporaries understood prayer better without the empowerment of the Spirit than many of us do with this empowerment? It need not only be pagans who shame us.

Jesus Teaches His Disciples the Kingdom Prayer (6:9-13)
Versions of this prayer appear in both Matthew (6:9-13) and Luke (11:2-4); most scholars accept the original form of the prayer that stands behind these Gospels as authentic (Witherington 1990:204). Jesus here probably adapts an early form of what became a basic synagogue prayer, the Kaddish (Vermes 1984:43; Davies and Allison 1988:595), which began something like this (Jeremias 1964:98):

Exalted and hallowed be his great name

in the world which he created according to his will.

May he let his kingdom rule . . .

Although Jesus' ministry sets the elements of the prayer in a new context—the future kingdom is present in a hidden way in the future

---

6:9 The parallel between the *Kaddish* and the first stanza of Jesus' model prayer was so obvious that an eighth-century translation of the Lord's Prayer from Latin into Hebrew borrows some of its wording directly from the *Kaddish* (Lapide 1984:8). A benediction in one standard Jewish prayer acknowledged the holiness of God's name in the present (the *Amida*—m. *Roš Haššana* 4:5; *Sipra Emor* par. 11.234.2.3), but Jesus' prayer, like the *Kaddish* (cited above), yearns for the future day when God's name alone would be hallowed—that

King, Jesus of Nazareth (Mt 8:29; 13:31-33)—the first disciples must have heard in Jesus' words an exhortation to seek God's coming kingdom (4:17; 6:33) by praying for it to come. Neither the Kaddish nor Jesus' sample prayer is a prayer for the complacent person satisfied with the treasures of this age. This is a prayer for the desperate, who recognize that this world is not as it should be and that only God can set things straight—for the broken to whom Jesus promises the blessings of the kingdom (5:3-12).

Various features of this prayer are significant. First, Jesus predicates it on the basis of an intimate relationship with God: *Father* (v. 9). This is a relationship that denotes both respectful dependence and affectionate intimacy. We must understand what God's "fatherhood" would have meant to most of Jesus' hearers. In first-century Jewish Palestine children were powerless social dependents, and fathers were viewed as strong providers and examples on whom their children could depend. Jesus summons us to pray not like the pagans (v. 7), but with a dependence on God as our Father (vv. 8-9) who watches over us (Deut 8:3-5 in Mt 4:4).

Yet just as many middle-class suburbanites cannot resonate with the Gospel portrait of Jesus as the object of unjust oppression, many inner-city children cannot resonate with the image of God as "Father" (see Malina 1993:96). For many children today, fathers have abandoned them, are powerless to provide for them or have even abused them. Thus it is always important for us to explain how Jesus and his Jewish ancestors and contemporaries meant the title: referring to someone who loves us, someone we can depend on when what we seek from him is truly for our good (see also 7:7-11). Many modern Westerners also have indulgent fathers and see love and discipline as irreconcilable; we need to realize that God, like most ancient fathers, loves us enough to firmly discipline us for our good (Heb 12:5-11). A caring parent will not let us run out in front of cars for fear of limiting our independence; God

---

is, sanctified or shown holy, special above every other name.

If "Abba" (Mk 14:36) stands behind "Father," as many scholars think (and Jesus surely taught his disciples that title at some point—Rom 8:15; Gal 4:6), Jesus uses for God a term so intimate that few of his contemporaries ever used it to address God (the suggested exception is a comparison, not a prayer).

disciplines us in love, but he remains intimate and loving toward us.

Perhaps more significantly, the context (Mt 6:7-8) indicates that *our Father* implies intimate communion. Effective prayer is not a complex ritual but a simple cry of faith predicated on an assured relationship (again, 7:7-11). The earnest brevity and simplicity of this prayer fits not the cry of the complacent and the self-satisfied, but that of the humble, the lowly, the broken, the desperate. This is the prayer of those who have nowhere to turn but to God—the "meek" who "will inherit the earth" (5:5).

When Jewish people called God by the Old Testament title "Father," the title connoted intimacy as well as respect and dependence. Jesus summons his disciples to appropriate this intimacy still more deeply (see also Mk 14:36; Rom 8:15; Gal 4:6).

Second, the prayer seeks first God's glory, not our own. The "you-petitions," for God's kingdom and glory, precede the "we-petitions" for our own needs, and *your* is repeatedly in an emphatic final position in the Greek. When we worship God, both praising him directly and seeking his glory in the world, other competing claims to our attention fade before the majesty of our King's glory.

The first petition is for God's *name* to be *hallowed* in the future. Although many profane God's name—his honor—in this age (acting as if it were unholy), God will see to it that his name will be hallowed in the coming time of the kingdom (Is 5:16; 29:23; Ezek 39:7, 27). But as nineteenth-century evangelist Charles Finney emphasized, people who seek the day when God's name is hallowed throughout the earth must not only pray for his name to be hallowed; they must live as if they value the honor of his name right now (Finney 1965:8).

Jesus' Jewish hearers would have understood this message implicit in the lines of the prayer itself. Hallowing God's name *(qiddûš ha-šēm)* was "the most characteristic feature of Jewish ethics" (Moore 1971:2:101). Later rabbis said, for instance, that a Bible teacher who does not pay his bills on time profanes God's name (Montefiore and Loewe 1974:397). Some went so far as to say that if a Jew must sin, he ought to go somewhere where no one knows him and pretend to be a Gentile. Of course secret sin does not ultimately hallow God's name, since he will reveal the thoughts of all hearts when his kingdom comes. Nevertheless, these Jewish teachers longed for the honor of God's name more seriously than the vast majority of Christians do today. As an example, many of us were embarrassed by the practices of some televangelists before public scandals broke, but it took the secular media to address openly what we should have already addressed in Christian love (see Rom 2:24).

Third, believers long for the coming of God's *kingdom* and the doing of his *will* (Mt 6:9-10). The hallowing of God's name, the consummation of his reign and the doing of his will are all versions of the same end-time promise: everything will be set right someday. No more crime, no more discrimination and hatred, no more sickness or grief. Of course that day will bring an end to those not doing God's will, so his mercy has delayed it for their sake (2 Pet 3:9, 15). But we who long for God's will *on earth* in the future ought to live consistently with our longing in the present, working for God's righteousness and seeking his will here (Mt 26:39; see Grenz 1992). We who believe that God's kingdom has invaded history in the person of Jesus of Nazareth (Mt 13:31-33) must exemplify his reign in our own lives in the present. The world around should be able to look at how God's people treat one another and see what heaven is like, so much so that they want to have a share in that future kingdom we live out among them in this age.

The Lord's Prayer concludes with the "we-petitions." Many think that these petitions also address the end time; I and many others think that they primarily address the present, as such petitions normally did in other Jewish prayers. The fourth petition expresses dependence on God for daily sustenance (6:11). While in this context the text clearly indicates trust in God for sustenance (see 6:25-34), scholars still debate some points, particularly the meaning of the phrase *daily bread*. Frequently proposed meanings are "daily rations," "essential for survival" and (most commonly) "bread for tomorrow."

Whether we ask for "today's" bread or "tomorrow's," the prayer stresses that the requester needs it *today* (in Greek "today" appears in an emphatic position), and all ancient Mediterranean peoples acknowledged their need for daily bread (Yamauchi 1966:148-53). While seeking the future kingdom, Jesus' followers also needed bread in the present (6:31-33; 7:9; 15:32). In virtually every class or Bible study group when I ask, "Where in the Old Testament did God provide daily bread?" students recall what would have been even more obvious to Jesus' hearers: manna (see, for example, Grelot 1979). If God provided for a whole people through forty years of landless wandering and unemployment, how much more should we trust him for our basic needs!

This prayer fits the audience of the rest of the sermon. A prayer expressing dependence on God for daily bread and asking only for bread was the prayer of a person willing to live simply, satisfied with the basics (Prov 30:8-9; compare 1 Tim 6:8). Jesus too showed that he depended on his Father, the God of the exodus, to supply his bread (Mt 4:3-4, 11).

The fifth petition entreats God to *forgive us our debts* (6:12). This line of Jesus' prayer, too, would remind his hearers of a standard Jewish prayer: the sixth of the Eighteen Benedictions entreated God's forgiveness. Yet if we have truly embraced the principle of grace in God's forgiveness, we must also extend it to our fellow servants who are of equal worth in his sight (18:35; compare Sirach 28:1-8).

Literally Jesus invites us to ask God to release the debts that we owe against his account book. The image of debts was a graphic one to most of Jesus' contemporaries. While debts include money, most of Jesus' hearers would have been borrowers rather than lenders, so Jesus probably includes more than merely economic debts. It is clear that *debts* before God represent "sins," as they normally did both in Jewish teaching and in the Aramaic term used for both concepts (*boba;* Black 1967:140; Lk 11:4). This text helps us forgive by reminding us of the magnitude of God's forgiveness.

The final petitions plead for God's protection in testing (Mt 6:13). *Temptation* here means "testing," as in trials of suffering; the English word *temptation,* which includes the connotation that the tester seeks the person's fall through the trials, is too narrow unless the context warrants it (as in Jas 1:13-18; Sirach 2:1-6). In this context the person is praying precisely that the testing will not lead to falling: testing with a view to bringing people to succumb was the business of *the evil one* (Mt 6:13). The primary test early Christians would face, and which Jewish heroes of old had faced, was persecution, the temptation to apostasy (compare 1 Pet 5:8-9).

6:13 The familiar doxology closing the modern version of the Lord's Prayer appears in a textual note in the NIV because the earliest manuscripts of the New Testament do not include it (Bandstra 1981:18-25). But just as Jewish worshipers often closed regular prayers with spontaneous doxologies (Jeremias 1964:106), some very much like this one (compare

Those inclined to see all these petitions as addressing the end time usually see the *temptation* or "test" as the final period of testing that Jewish people anticipated before the kingdom. But for suffering believers who recognize that Jesus can return soon, the present may fulfill the expected time of tribulation. Most other Jewish prayers requesting protection from temptation spoke of testing in the present time (Montefiore 1968:2:103). In the whole context of Matthew, "testing" here probably includes the final tribulation but is not limited to it. If a specific allusion is intended in this context, it may be to the time of the exodus. God released his people from slavery and fed them with manna (Mt 6:11), and they, like Jesus, were tested in the wilderness (v. 13; also see 4:1-2).

Jesus is calling disciples to pray for deliverance from and protection in testing, not proposing that disciples can avoid tests of their faith. A prayer suggesting that we could avoid tests of faith would contradict God's dealings with his people in ancient Israel (Gen 22:1; Deut 13:3; 1 Cor 10:13) and the model of Jesus (Mt 4:1). The Aramaic construction Jesus may have originally used can mean "Do not let me succumb to the test" or "fall prey to the test." Indeed, Jesus' prayer resembles the kind of prayer Jewish people later began to offer daily, which sought not to avoid testing but to stand firm when tested (Jeremias 1971:202). Whereas God's purpose in testing is to confirm our faith, the evil one's purpose in testing is to weaken it. We should seek to minimize rather than increase our testing. But when it comes, only God's strength can see us through.

But if Matthew's first readers wondered at all whether *lead us not into temptation* meant "let us not succumb to testing," Matthew 26:41 should have settled the matter. There Jesus warns the disciples to watch and pray lest they "fall [literally, enter] into temptation," but in the context testing is already inevitably on the way (26:45). The issue is not whether some testing will come, but whether it will find the disciples unprepared (it did). Thus this is a prayer that God bring us safely through testing (compare, for example, Ps 141:3-4; Is 63:17; 64:7 NRSV; Rev 3:10; *Jub.* 11:17; 21:22; 22:23), rather than deliver us from experiencing it.

1QM 18.13), earliest Christians probably added a doxology like this one when praying the Lord's Prayer in public (*Did.* 8, 10) and naturally later added this liturgical feature (perhaps from the *Did.*) to the text of Matthew. Although its substance is biblical and thus appropriate to pray, there is little chance that it was part of the original text of the Bible.

Finally, we may note that the kingdom prayer is a communal or corporate prayer. The plural pronouns (*our Father . . . give us,* and the like) remind us that just as we approach God as our Father, we must remember God's other children as our brothers and sisters. I must seek not only my own daily bread but also the needs of my brothers and sisters in Christ. No matter how individualistic our culture, our own intimacy with God must lead to prayer for and active commitment to the needs of all his people.

Those Who Do Not Forgive Will Not Be Forgiven (6:14-15) Jesus concludes his words on prayer by returning to the warning implicit in verse 12 (compare Mk 11:25). The day of judgment belongs to God alone, and when we assume his sole prerogatives we idolatrously impinge on his deity, hence meriting judgment for ourselves (compare Jas 5:9; 2 Pet 3:7, 12).

Fasting Secretly (6:16-18) In this case (as opposed to generally) the *hypocrites* who *disfigure* [literally, ruin!] *their faces* may well evoke the original sense of "hypocrites" as actors in the theater, who typically wore large theatrical masks. Fasting typically accompanied grief, often the sorrow of penitence (Neh 1:4-7; 9:1-2; Zech 7:5; Sirach 31:26; Judith 4:9-13). Yet as Joel put it, the true penitent must rend his or her heart and not merely garments (2:13); Isaiah declared that the true fast was to act for justice (Is 58:6-10). Fasting is a time of drawing close to God by demonstrating our commitment to him. Normally coupled with prayer in the New Testament (Acts 9:9; 13:2-3; 14:23; compare Ezra 8:23; Neh 1:4), biblical fasting is not asceticism for asceticism's sake (Col 2:18-23). Many Pharisees may have fasted twice a week as a mark of piety (Lk 18:12; *b. Ta'anit* 12a); but I fear that some early Christians missed the point of this passage when they insisted that believers should not fast on Mondays and Thursdays like the "hypocrites," but rather on Wednesdays and Fridays (*Did.* 8:1).

Under normal circumstances people trimmed beards or changed clothes before appearing in public, as well as anointing themselves. (Palestinian Jews used oil to clean and anoint their skin, especially on their heads; *t. Šebi'it* 6:9; *ARN* 3A, probably to lubricate dry scalps.) Because penitent fasting included afflicting oneself (Lev 23:32), for most

Jewish people the most extreme fasts meant not only abstaining from food but also practicing other forms of self-abasement like not shaving, washing one's clothes, anointing or having intercourse (*m. Ta'anit* 1:6; 4:7; *Yoma* 8:1). Jesus is so concerned with keeping one's righteousness private that he prohibits customary features of what his contemporaries considered a strict fast.

It may be difficult for a member of a family to get around explaining why he or she is not sharing a meal, but in normal circumstances we may wish to observe Jesus' warning as literally as possible to guard our own motives before God. If we want our credit with God, we need to be satisfied that he alone knows, for we can trust that his reward will be more than adequate.

☐ Do Not Value Possessions (6:19-34)

Jesus exhorts us not to value possessions enough to seek them (6:19-24), quite in contrast to today's prosperity preachers and most of Western society. Yet he also exhorts us not to value possessions enough to worry about them (vv. 25-34), a fault shared by most believers who rightly reject the prosperity teaching. Jesus' words strike at the core of human selfishness, challenging both the well-to-do who have possessions to guard and the poor who wish they could acquire them. His words are so uncomfortable that even those of us who say we love him and fight to defend Scripture's authority find ourselves looking for ways around what he says.

Do Not Value Possessions Enough to Seek Them (6:19-24) So prominent in Jesus' parables and wisdom sayings is his emphasis on utter faith in God and relinquishment of possessions that Geza Vermes (1993:148) considers this a central element in Jesus' teaching. Paul S. Minear declared that it was no wonder those with vested interests hated Jesus: "So insidious was [his] attack upon earthly treasures that he became, according to Kierkegaard, a 'far more terrible robber' than those who assault travelers along a highway. Jesus assaulted the whole human race at the point where that race is most sensitive: its desire for security and superiority" (Minear 1954:133).

We like to point out Jesus' rhetorical overstatement in this passage while ignoring why he used it to secure our attention. Most Christians disagree with what the prosperity preachers say over the radio and television, but the main difference between us and them in practice is often that they provide a theological justification for their materialism, where we do not.

Seek Treasure in Heaven (6:19-21) Jesus teaches that if we really trust God, we will act as if treasure in heaven is what matters (compare 1 Tim 6:8-10). Although Jesus illustrates his point here with images about treasure in heaven shared by many of his contemporaries (such as Sirach 29:10-11; 4 Ezra 7:77; *2 Baruch* 14:12), only the most radical sages of antiquity shared Jesus' view that earthly possessions were essentially worthless. Yet for Jesus the treasure is not merely in heaven (Mt 19:21); it represents the kingdom of heaven (13:44). Idolaters who value Mammon too highly to abandon it for what Jesus values will have no place in his kingdom (19:21-30; compare Lk 14:33).

Some other countercultural sages in antiquity also advocated lack of attachment to material possessions (Epict. *Disc.* 1.18.15-16). Unlike some philosophers, however, Jesus is not against possessions because he supposes them to be evil (compare Lucr. *Nat.* 5.1105-42; Sen. *Dial.* 5.33.1); the issue is not that possessions themselves are bad but that a higher priority demands our resources. If we value what our Lord values rather than what our society values, he demands that we meet the basic needs of people lacking adequate resources before we seek to accumulate possessions beyond our basic needs (19:21; compare Lk 3:11; 12:33-34).

Someone will object that we have to stop sacrificing at some point because we will never finish meeting all this world's needs (Mt 26:11). But could not the abundance of this world's needs represent a call to keep sacrificing? Do we use the behavior of many of our fellow Christians to justify reinterpreting Jesus' explicit call to value what he cares about more highly than possessions? Many professing Christians before Luther were wrong about justification by faith; is it possible that most Western Christians today wrongly miss Jesus' explicit teaching about sacrifice?

One researcher suggests that professed followers of Christ take in 68 percent of the world's income, yet only 3 percent of that goes to the church and a tiny percentage to world missions. Perhaps if more Westerners lived even briefly among the desperately hungry or developed friendships with people from lands where laborers for the gospel are few, our priorities would change. Meanwhile Jesus, who already sees the needs of all people, summons us to value what matters to him—if not yet out of love for them, then out of love for our Lord who loves them.

Can we claim not to love wealth more than our brothers and sisters in Christ when we see them hurting and do not sacrifice what should matter to us less than their need? While many of us pursue status symbols that television suggests are "necessities," evangelical ministries to the poor claim that forty thousand people die of starvation and malnutrition daily. That means roughly twenty-seven a minute, twenty of whom are children under five years old. (This represents a loss of life roughly equivalent to the first atom bomb being dropped again—every three days.) Wherever possible, people should earn their own wages and not become dependent on charity. But children under five cannot "pull themselves up by their bootstraps," nor can our brothers and sisters in drought- and famine-stricken areas. Those who say, "For the sake of everyone it is better to let the weak die off," are social Darwinists, not Christians; Christians are called to serve the weak.

The world's need is overwhelming, but if as individuals we calculate what resources we do not need and contribute them to ministries like World Vision and Food for the Hungry, we can at least do our part to make a difference in the world, trusting that God will raise up others to join us. One wonders, too, what a witness it would be among the world's poor who are not Christians if they saw that wealthier Christians cared more about the poor than about their own affluence.

Materialism Blinds People to God's Truth (6:22-23) If we justify valuing material possessions because "everyone does it" or "other people do it more," our self-justification will blind us to the truth of our disobedience and affect our whole relationship with God. Jesus' illustration about the "single" (NIV *good*) eye and the evil eye would immediately make sense to his hearers: a "good" eye was literally a healthy eye, but figuratively also an eye that looked on others generously (Sirach 32:8). In the Greek text of the Gospels, Jesus literally calls the eye a "single" eye, which is a wordplay: the Greek version of the Hebrew Bible also uses this word for "single" to translate the Hebrew term for "perfect"—thus "single-minded" devotion to God, with one's heart set on God alone. An "evil eye," conversely, was a stingy, jealous or greedy eye; yet it also signifies here a *bad* eye (Mt 6:23), one that cannot see properly. Jesus uses the "single" eye as a transition to his next point, for the "single" eye is literally undivided, having the whole picture: thus one is not divided between two masters, as the text goes on to explain (v. 24).

Many leaders in past revival movements have warned that Christians ought not to pray for revival if they want to hold on to their money, because we cannot have both. For John Wesley, defying material prosperity was part of holiness, separation to God away from the things the world valued (Jennings 1990:157-79). He warned that riches would increase believers' conformity to the world and attacked those who preached in favor of the accumulation of wealth (Jennings 1990:36, 98-102). He felt that Acts 2 was for today—including the part about sharing possessions (2:44-45; Jennings 1990:111-16). He chose to live as simply as possible so as to give all else to the poor, and called on his followers to do the same (Jennings 1990:119-23; Sider 1990:152). In contrast to most contemporary Western Christians, Wesley felt that "stewardship means giving to the poor. . . . *We give to God not by giving to the church, but by giving to the poor*" (Jennings 1990:105). If one did not give all one could, Wesley taught, one was in disobedience to Jesus' teaching and would end up in hell (Jennings 1990:133).

Noting that the church has adequate funds to evangelize the world if we would choose to do so, nineteenth-century evangelist Charles G. Finney warned that God requires us to surrender to him the *ownership* of everything, so that we never again consider it as our own; we must do with it only what he would do (Finney 1869:353-54). Finney further exhorted that "young converts should be taught that they have renounced the ownership of all their possessions, and of themselves, or if they have not done this they are not Christians" (ibid., p. 127).

Years ago I eagerly read Ron Sider's *Rich Christians in an Age of*

6:23 In Jewish literature, an "evil" eye (NIV *bad*) was a jealous or greedy one (compare

Hunger (rev. 1990) after I heard Gordon Fee state that every American Christian should read it. While I cannot evaluate Sider's macroeconomic proposals (for important proposals in this area see also National Conference of Catholic Bishops 1986), I appreciate his emphasis on the Bible's commitment to serving the poor. Yet some critics wrongly criticized Sider's motives as Marxist (he is not a Marxist). Some consider Wesley and Finney, who preached more strongly than Sider, legalists. When Jesus, John the Baptist or James (Lk 3:10-11; 14:33; Jas 2:14-16) preaches far more strongly than Sider, Wesley or Finney, we call it hyperbole. I fear that many of us hear what we want because we have vested interests to guard—interests many Christians value more than they value the agendas of God's kingdom. Our eyes are not "single."

We Must Love Either God or Money (6:24) One must serve someone, but a person whose service is divided will love one master and hate the other. Masters only rarely owned a slave jointly (for example, *m. 'Eduyyot* 1:13; *Giṭṭin* 4:5), but when they did, the slave naturally preferred one master to the other. Jesus warns us that we must choose: if we work for possessions, we will end up hating God; if we work for God, we will end up hating possessions. (*Hate* may mean by comparison of one's love for something else—10:37 par. Lk 14:26.)

"Mammon," translated *Money* in the NIV, was a common Aramaic term for money or property (Flusser 1988:153), but its contrast with God as an object of service here suggests that it has been deified as well as personified (compare Sirach 34:7). Early Christians extended the principle of not serving two masters to avoiding theaters (where other humans were routinely slaughtered for public entertainment, perhaps akin to some movies today; Tert. *Spect.* 26) and to gaining the world and thereby forfeiting one's soul (*2 Clement* 6). But Jesus here applies the principle to one of the greatest temptations: the idolatry of materialism (compare possibly Col 3:5).

Unfortunately, covetousness (materialism) has achieved nearly cultic status as a traditional American value (with some other Western cultures not far behind), under such euphemisms as "the good life" and "getting ahead." As Craig Blomberg (1992:124) laments, "Many perceptive observers have sensed that the greatest danger to Western Christianity is

---

Deut 15:9; Prov 23:6; 28:22; Sirach 14:8-10; 34:13; Tobit 4:7, 16; *m. 'Abot* 2:9, 11).

not, as is sometimes alleged, prevailing ideologies such as Marxism, Islam, the New Age movement or humanism but rather the all-pervasive materialism of our affluent culture." Reminding us that the New Testament summons churches in one part of the world to look out for the needs of the church elsewhere (2 Cor 8:13-15), Blomberg further reminds us that because "over 50 percent of all believers now live in the Two-Thirds World . . . a huge challenge to First-World Christianity emerges. Without a doubt, most individual and church budgets need drastic realignment" (1992:126-27). Unlike the rich man in Luke 16:19-31, however, few suburban First World Christians could go to hell for allowing a man to starve at our doorstep: those who are starving rarely are able to get near our doorstep.

North American Christians can pour nearly a billion dollars a year into new church construction. Church buildings are helpful tools in our culture, but the Bible does not require them—and the Bible does expressly command serving the poor. How many churches pour equivalent resources into church-sponsored homeless shelters and other means of service (and witness) to the needy of our communities? The streets of our most affluent Western cities host hundreds of thousands of homeless people, many of them children. Many young people sell their bodies on those streets to get a place to sleep at night, and mere sermons against prostitution are not going to do anything about it.

Church buildings are important in our present culture, but the early church did live without them for its first three centuries, and in a time of persecution we would be obliged to do the same. The early church therefore had funds for other purposes: second-century pagans continually noted Christians' charity toward both Christian and non-Christian poor. Church buildings are valuable, but when they take precedence over caring for the poor or evangelism, our priorities appear to focus more on our comfort than on the world's need—as if we desire padded pews more than new brothers and sisters filling the kingdom. Have we altogether forgotten the spiritual passion of the early church and nineteenth-century evangelicalism?

Jesus in this passage uses graphic imagery about idolatry not to force us into legalism but to prevent us from rationalizing away his point. First World Protestants are quick to judge Christians in other parts of the world who venerate their ancestors or worship the saints. When symbols of respect become objects of worship, our concerns are surely justified. But in condemning such practices we may be sporting a "plank" in our own eye (7:3), for those concerned with wealth become as sterile in their Christianity as those who forget their faith or fall away under persecution (13:19-22).

Most of us respond to Jesus' devaluation of possessions in one of two ways: (1) we retort that there is nothing wrong with making money, or (2) we claim we do not love wealth, we just accumulate it. The first response is tangential: the issue is never how much money we make (as long as it is made honestly, the more the better), but what we do with what we make. The second response is simply dishonest, like the man immersed in television six hours every evening who says that it does not really interest or affect him. If we are seeking and accumulating wealth for ourselves, then we do love it.

Do Not Value Possessions Enough to Worry About Them (6:25-34)

Jesus' message here picks up his earlier discussion of secret charity (6:1-4). If many prosperity preachers err in urging Christians to seek material gain (see vv. 19-24), many of us err by doubting God's power to provide. Yet in this passage while Jesus emphasizes God's power, he also stresses that God guarantees only what we need. If God sustains life and protects our bodies, will we complain if he does it differently from the ways our culture values (v. 25)? If he feeds us like the birds (v. 26; compare 1 Kings 17:6) or clothes us like the flowers (v. 28), he will have provided us more than what our culture values, not less (v. 29). Yet if God provides for birds and flowers, he will also provide for us (v. 30).

God promises the basics. This theme is important to the passage (vv. 25-26, 28-30). Jesus twice uses a standard type of Jewish argument traditionally called *qal waḥomer*—"how much more?" (vv. 26, 30). If God cares for birds and for perishable flowers, how much more for his own beloved children (compare vv. 8, 32)!

We generally expect biologists today to examine and classify data without making many ethical or theological pronouncements. But ancient naturalists were sometimes also sages who regarded all God's creation as a legitimate field for inquiry. Wisdom sayings often addressed nature (for example, 1 Kings 4:33; Ahiqar column 6; Sirach 43:33).

Jesus draws a lesson from God's care for birds and flowers (Mt 6:26, 30). Some other Jewish teachers also recognized that God provides for creatures (compare Ps 104:24-27) and that people are worth much more than birds (compare *m. Qiddušin* 4:14). Jesus, who regards God's original creation purpose as still valid (Mt 19:4-6), believes that the God who cares for unemployed animals will care still more for his children, regardless of their economic situation.

People in Jesus' day considered their cloaks essential, and the law in fact took this for granted (Ex 22:26-27; Guelich 1982:339). Paul (less given to hyperbole than his Palestinian Master) declares that Christians need nothing more than food and clothing (1 Tim 6:8). But Jesus declares that God can provide for us adequately even if we lack clothing (Mt 6:25)! He then goes on to assure us that God will supply covering for our bodies, pointing to the splendor of the fields, whose vegetation is nevertheless used as fuel for baking bread. Solomon's splendor had become proverbial (for example, *CIJ* 2:83, §837; *m. Baba Meşi'a* 7:1), but it remained minuscule compared to the splendor of God's creation (compare Ps 8:1-9). In the end, wealth does not matter, but God will supply what we genuinely need.

Jesus again shames his hearers by reminding them that even Gentiles seek material things. Pagans seek (NIV *run after*) their own needs (Mt 6:31-32; compare *Ep. Arist.* 140-41); God's children should seek instead God's agendas, assured that God will also care for them in the process (6:33). Even in Jesus' model prayer, disciples seek God's kingdom first (vv. 9-10). Faith is not an intricate ritual to get what we want for ourselves; faith is obeying God's will with the assurance that he will ultimately fulfill for us what is in our best interests. That kind of faith grows only in the context of an intimate relationship of love between the heavenly Father and his children.

Some people today associate faith with being able to obtain possessions from God, but Jesus did not even associate it with *seeking* basic needs from God. Pagans seek those things, he warned (v. 32; compare 5:47; 6:7); we should seek instead God's kingdom and his righteous will

---

6:34 Some other sages would have agreed with Jesus' teaching in this verse (*b. Sanhedrin*

(6:33). It is when his people care for others in need among them that God supplies the needs of his people as a whole, perhaps because then he can best trust them to use his gifts righteously (Deut 15:1-11; Blomberg 1992:126). In our lifelong plans and each day as we decide what to do with our life and resources, we have fresh opportunities to prove to God our love for him—or our lack of it.

Anxiety does no good. Jesus highlights this theme in Matthew 6:26, 34. Anxiety will not add even the smallest unit of time to one's life. Not only is it true that we cannot extend our life by worrying, but daily experience in our comparatively fast-paced culture confirms the wisdom of an earlier Jewish sage, who observed that worry and a troubled heart actually shorten life (Sirach 30:19-24). If much study is wearying to the flesh (Eccl 12:12—undoubtedly many a scholar's favorite verse), *worry* about wealth also banishes sleep and destroys the flesh (Sirach 34:1).

Unlike some ancient philosophers, Jesus never condemns people for recognizing their basic needs; their Father *knows* they need food and clothing. Yet he calls them to depend on God for their daily sustenance. Those who can trust their heavenly Father to care for them (as most first-century Jewish children could depend on their earthly fathers) need not be anxious concerning clothes or food.

Jesus paints his point in graphic word pictures. Like a typical sage, he finally notes that one has enough to worry about for the day without adding tomorrow's worries (Mt 6:34; compare Prov 27:1). Employing the typical rhetorical technique of personification (Kennedy 1984:60), Jesus further admonishes his hearers to let *tomorrow* worry about itself. Yet when Jesus forbids us to worry about tomorrow, this does not mean that concerns will never press upon us. It means instead that we should express dependence on God in each of these concerns. We should pray for our genuine needs (v. 11), provided we pray for God's kingdom most of all (vv. 9-10; most of Paul's "concerns" fit this category: 2 Cor 11:28; 1 Thess 3:1-5). The part of the future we must concern ourselves with and work toward is what he has revealed to us and called us to do (compare Mt 10:5-25).

100b; *Yebamot* 63b; Epict. *Disc.* 3.24.26).

□ Appropriate Judgment (7:1-27)

The rest of the Sermon on the Mount does not fit into a tightly knit structure beyond the level of the individual paragraphs; some elements (such as 7:6) are actually difficult to fit into their context! This reminds us how important Jesus' teachings are to Matthew. Even though Matthew carefully organizes most of his material, he wants us to know all of Jesus' teachings, even when he cannot fit them into the structure of his argument.

Nevertheless, Matthew continues to arrange Jesus' teaching in a relevant, pastoral way for his readers. Just as outward acts of righteousness can be misleading (6:1-18), we should avoid any external evaluations of individuals (7:1-5) and certainly should not trust all religious claims (7:15-23). Jesus' promise concerning prayer (7:7-11) expands his earlier discussion of private prayer (6:5-15) and seeking the kingdom first (6:32-33). (NIV obscures the flow of thought by translating the first "seek" as *run after;* that Greek term can be stronger, but in this context it contrasts with the closely related term in the next verse.) Jesus' admonition to self-examination (7:1-5), warning that few will enter God's kingdom (vv. 13-14), observation that one's behavior reveals one's character (vv. 15-20) and caution that our lives and not just lips must acknowledge Christ (vv. 21-23) suitably climax in his final warning that only those who obey his teaching will endure the judgment (vv. 24-27).

Do Not Judge Others (7:1-6) Jesus declares that the person judging *will be judged* (v. 1) because judging assumes a divine prerogative; final judgment belongs to God alone, and those who seek to judge others now will answer then for usurping God's position (see also 6:12-15).

God Will Judge Us the Way We Judge Others (7:1-2) By this point in the sermon, no one who has been taking Jesus' words seriously will feel much like judging anyone else anyway. Still, we humans tend to prefer applying ethics to other people rather than ourselves. (For example, husbands tend to prefer quoting Paul's instructions on marriage to their wives rather than his admonitions to them, and vice-versa.

7:2 In the marketplace one would measure out to others appropriate portions of what they were purchasing (*m. Beṣa* 3:8). This image had become a Jewish maxim, however: "By the

Likewise, I have sometimes listened to a sermon thinking, *I wish so-and-so had shown up for church today*.) So just in case we have been too obtuse to grasp that Jesus addresses us rather than others in 5:3—6:34, Jesus renders the point explicit in 7:1-5. We are objects of God's evaluation, and God evaluates most graciously the meek, who recognize God alone as judge.

Even if we knew people's hearts, we could not evaluate degrees of personal guilt as if we understood all the genetic and social influences that combine with personal sinful choices in making some people more vulnerable to particular temptations (such as alcohol or spouse abuse) than others. Most important, Jesus warns us that even if we knew people's hearts, we would be in no position to judge unless we had lived sinless lives, never needing God's forgiveness (vv. 3-5; compare 6:12, 14-15).

Many people have ripped this passage out of context, however. Jesus warns us not to assume God's prerogative to condemn the guilty; he is not warning us not to discern truth from error (see 7:15-23). Further, Jesus does not oppose offering correction, but only offering correction in the wrong spirit (v. 5; compare 18:15-17; Gal 6:1-5).

Having right beliefs about judging is not enough. Although Jesus regards scribal and Pharisaic righteousness as inadequate (Mt 5:20), it is not because scribes and Pharisees professed the wrong doctrine on this issue. Most of the sages would have probably agreed with his basic perspective here (compare, for example, Sirach 28:1-3; *m. 'Abot* 2:5), and even the particular image of measuring back what one measures out (Mt 7:2—as in "what goes around comes around") was proverbial wisdom. Jesus' contemporaries often affirmed his principle and even used the same illustration, but Jesus demands more than agreement from disciples: he demands obedience (vv. 24-27).

We Blind Ourselves When We Rationalize Away Our Guilt (7:3-5) We rationalize away our guilt but not that of others, and our double standard itself renders our own behavior inexcusable (compare 6:22-23; Rom 2:1-3). A splinter or wood chip in a neighbor's eye might

---

measure by which a man metes it is measured to him" (judgment in the present era in *m. Sota* 1:7).

render that person blind, but a plank embedded in one's own eye would certainly render one blind. The image is graphic hyperbole: imagine a zealous Christian walking around with a log protruding from his eye (as if one end of it would even fit!), totally ignorant of his impossibly grotesque state. Just as we would not want a blind guide leading us into a pit (Mt 15:14; 23:16), we would not want a blind surgeon operating on our eyes; only one who sees well is competent to heal others' blindness (compare 9:27-31; 20:29-34).

At a Bible study Joe Bayly once met a former Nazi, a participant in the Holocaust, who complained that had missed a promotion in the army because he objected to social dancing. Bayly remarked tongue in cheek that "Christians were the same everywhere—they weren't afraid to speak out, even against Hitler, when it came to social dancing." Likewise, some conservative Christians who are quick to judge those who do not uphold the Bible's authority have spent little time in personal study of the Bible themselves. If Jesus minced no words with those blinded by religious tradition in his day, we who claim devotion to his cause must beware lest we share more in common with them than with him.

Even When You Are Right, Do Not Impose the Truth on Others (7:6) This saying seems to make little sense in this context; hence varied interpretations of verse 6 abound. Some think that *dogs* here are the Gentiles (15:26) and the *pearls* the gospel of the kingdom (13:45). But Jewish teachers used dogs to represent different things (not just Gentiles) in their parables, and even in 15:26 "dogs" is not wholly negative as it is here (see comment there). Other attempts to narrow the saying's object to prohibiting sinners from the Eucharist (as in *Did.* 9:5) also go beyond the evidence.

In its most general sense 7:6 was probably simply a wisdom saying like Proverbs 23:9: "Do not speak to a fool, for he will scorn the wisdom of your words" (compare also *Syr. Men. Sent.* 328-32). *Dogs* may refer to the wicked or oppressors more generally (compare Ps 22:16, 20; 59:14-15; Prov 26:11). It was also commonly known that stray scavenger dogs—the main

_____

7:3-5 The Talmud complains of those who resent "the mildest criticism. If someone is told, 'Take the chip out of your eye!' he retorts, 'Take the beam out of yours!' (*b. 'Arakin.* 16b; *b. Baba Batra* 15b)" (Vermes 1993:80). If this is not a polemical distortion of Jesus' saying,

kind encountered in the towns of Jewish Palestine—growled at those feeding them as much as at passing strangers (Isoc. *Demon.* 29, *Or.* 1). Clearly these are people who do not value what we have to offer them; swine also proverbially lacked appreciation of value (Prov 11:22).

But why did Matthew include this saying here? Some connect the saying to the preceding context by suggesting that it means it is worthless to try to correct (7:1-5) one unwilling to listen. Others note that while we should not judge, some people should be avoided or we must exercise discernment. Yet taken by themselves, none of these suggestions explain the lack of disjunction in verse 6.

Most likely verse 6 provides a transition between the preceding and following contexts. Correcting those who will not receive correction is futile (vv. 1-5; Prov 9:8; 23:9); we should discerningly continue to offer wisdom (or the gift of the kingdom) only to those willing to receive what we offer, just as God does (Mt 7:7-11). In this case the text sounds a note of reciprocity to be repeated in verse 12 (Keener 1993:64). If verse 6 means something along these lines, it does not allow us to prejudge who may receive our message (13:3-23), but does forbid us to try to force it on those who show no inclination to accept it (10:13-16; compare Carson 1984:185; Blomberg 1992:128-29; Hagner 1993:172).

Good Gifts Guaranteed (7:7-12) Although Matthew has already offered a longer section on prayer (6:5-15), he emphasizes prayer again here. Because in the context the supreme object of "seeking" is the kingdom (6:33) and the door to be opened is the gate of salvation (7:13; contrast Lk 11:5-13), this prayer may especially represent a prayer for God's rule (compare 6:9-10 and the prayer for empowerment by the Spirit in Lk 11:2-13). But in any case, the specific application of the saying depends on its more general principle concerning how God hears prayers of faith (21:21-22; compare 14:28-31).

God Can Supply Anything to the Righteous Who Seek His Purposes (7:7-10) This text indicates some important lessons for us today. First, Jesus promises his disciples extraordinary power from God,

it probably reflects a common figure of speech, in which case Jesus is graphically saying that those who resent our criticism have a point until we get our lives in order.

like that of Elijah of old. In this case the Gospel narratives (such as 14:28-31) and other "charismatic" sayings (such as 21:21-22) demonstrate that Jesus was not speaking figuratively, but training disciples to express bold faith. Early Jewish teaching did celebrate God's kindness in answering prayer (Hagner 1993:174), but rarely promised such universal answers to prayer to all of God's people as the language here suggests; only a small number of sages were considered pious enough to have such power with God. But both the Hebrew Bible (for example, Gen 32:26-30; Ex 33:12—34:9; 1 Kings 18:36-37, 41-46; 2 Kings 2:2, 4, 6, 9; 4:14-28) and the Gospel tradition (Mk 5:27-34; 7:24-30; 10:46-52; Mt 8:7-13; Jn 2:3-5) provide examples of such bold faith. The most crucial model for bold holy persons in Jewish tradition is probably Elijah, who despite his human frailty (1 Kings 19:4) could summon fire from heaven against those potentially threatening his life simply by declaring, "If I am a man of God, may fire come down from heaven" (2 Kings 1:10, 12-15).

James likewise tells us that Elijah was a person of flesh and blood just like us; if we begin to see ourselves as and act as men and women of God, we will have access to the kind of miracles that Elijah had (Jas 5:16-18). Scripture shows us Elijah's frailties as well as his faith. We are likewise men and women of God by God's grace, and as we dare to believe that and to live according to the relationship our Father has given us with himself in Christ, that confidence will transform our prayer lives.

Second, this empowerment presupposes that we are ready to be as committed to God's purposes as Elijah and like-minded servants of God were. Such a call to believing prayer supposes a heart of piety submitted to God's will; it would not apply to a man praying to obtain another man's wife or to a woman praying for a nicer car as a status symbol of conspicuous consumption. Although Jesus states the promise graphically, he implicitly addresses only men and women of God who will seek the things God would have them to seek for the good of his kingdom and their basic needs (Mt 6:11, 19-34). Jesus' promise is for the righteous—people who share kingdom values—asking basic needs and requests concerning the kingdom. Jesus' disciples were to be prophets (5:12) and holy persons, like Elijah, whose requests God would hear.

Third, this passage's context suggests the kinds of prayers such righteous people offer. They seek first in prayer the purposes of God's kingdom (6:9-10, 31-33; compare Ps 9:10; 24:6; 27:4, 8; 34:14; 63:1; 69:6, 32; 70:4; 119:45; 122:6-9; and especially Prov 2:4-5; 8:17; Is 55:6; Jer 29:13), and also request that God meet their own basic needs (Mt 6:11). The specific examples Jesus gives that children would request are basic staples in the Palestinian diet—bread and fish; and Jesus has already promised his hearers the basics (6:25-34). Jesus later provided bread and fish for his followers (14:19-20; 15:36-37), encouraging us that he will also hear our requests for provision today. While such basics do not include mere status symbols or other objects of fleshly appetites, they do include whatever is ultimately for God's kingdom—anything necessary for us to fulfill our life and call.

God's Fatherly Care Is Our Assurance That He Will Answer (7:11) Jesus uses the familiar Jewish method of arguing by a "how much more" analogy. God who gives *good gifts* to children may not give everything every child asks, but he will not withhold his gifts from those who desire and seek what is right (Ps 37:4; 84:11). Our Father will give appropriate consideration to each request his children make, watching out for their true needs (compare Mt 6:8).

Reciprocate Good Deeds in Faith (7:12) If those who condemn others are condemned (7:1-5), God clearly operates on a principle of reciprocity; we must do good to people in advance of their doing good to us, trusting God to reward us later. The principle in this context is that as we give, it will be given to us by God in the day of judgment. If God is the example of giving (vv. 7-11), we should give whatever people need (5:42). How we treat others (7:12) reveals our character (vv. 16-20) and hence reveals our eternal destiny (vv. 13-14, 21-23). At least since a sermon of John Wesley in 1750 this has been called the "Golden Rule" (Guy 1959); over a millennium earlier, a Christian Roman emperor allegedly engraved the saying on his wall in gold (France 1985:145).

This rule was a widespread principle of ancient ethics. The positive form of the rule appears as early as Homer and recurs in Herodotus, Isocrates and Seneca. The negative form ("And what you hate, do not do to anyone") appears in Tobit 4:15, Philo (*Hypothetica* 7.6) and elsewhere; one Jewish work straddles both forms (*Ep. Arist.* 207). Although some commentators have tried to disparage the negative form by contrast with the positive, both forms mean essentially the same thing; both biblical law (Lev 19:18) and Paul (Rom 13:10) define the positive commandment of love by means of negative commandments (E. Sanders 1992:258-59).

The principle appears in cultures totally isolated from the ancient Mediterranean; it appears, for example, in Confucian teaching from sixth-century B.C. China (see Jochim 1986:125). That others would discover this same principle should not surprise us, because one of the most natural foundations for ethics is for a person to extrapolate from one's own worth to that of others, hence to value others as oneself (compare, for example, Sirach 31:15). Thus every person is morally responsible to recognize how one ought to treat every other person. When we treat others (such as waitresses, store clerks or children) the way people of higher status treated people of lower status in Jesus' day, we invite God's judgment against us. No one so insensitive as to demean another human being on account of social station warrants God's mercy (Mt 5:7; 6:14-15; 7:1-5).

One who observes this basic principle will fulfill all the basic principles of the law the way God intended them (compare 5:21-48; 22:37-39). Later Jewish tradition declares that the sage Hillel, who taught before Jesus did, had already seen this rule as a good summary of the law. As the story goes, a Gentile approached both Hillel and his rival sage, promising each that he would convert to Judaism if the sage could teach him the law concisely. Hillel declared, "Whatever you do not want someone to do to you, do not do to your neighbor. This is the whole Law; the rest of it is just explanation" (*b. Šabbat* 31a; compare *ARN* 25, §53B).

This is the law of love, the principle by which Jesus epitomizes the entire humanward aspect of God's law (22:39-40; compare Jn 13:34-35), a principle Jesus' earliest followers never forgot (Rom 13:8-10; Gal 5:14; 6:2; Jas 2:8). What is distinctive about the principle as it appears in Matthew is its relation to the day of judgment (Mt 7:1-2, 13-14).

The Narrow Way (7:13-14) Within this chapter, verses 1-12 fit together somewhat loosely, but the paragraphs in verses 13-27 make more sense together. Most first-century Jewish people believed they were saved by virtue of descent from Abraham (3:9). Yet Jesus regards the assumption of salvation as a deception; most of his contemporaries were unsaved (7:13-14). Those who led them showed by their lives that they were not God's true representatives (vv. 15-20); indeed, many professing servants of Jesus will themselves be banished from God's presence in the judgment (vv. 21-23), for only those who truly obeyed his teaching will stand (vv. 24-27). When one compares the great numbers of people today who cavalierly identify themselves as Christians yet never consider the claims of Christ, one shudders to realize how deadly such deception remains. May we present Christ's radical claims boldly so that more professing Christians may reckon with the reality of his lordship.

Jesus' image of the narrow way should have made sense to his hearers (v. 13). Greek, Roman and Jewish writers often employed the image of the two paths in life (for example, Sen. *Ep.* 8.3; 27.4; Diogenes *Ep.* 30; Deut 30:15; Ps 1:1; *m. 'Abot* 2:9), and those particularly concerned with the future judgment especially employed the image of the two ways, the narrow one leading to life and the broad one to destruction (as in 4 Ezra 7:3-16, 60-61; 8:1-3; *Test. Ab.* 11A; 8B).

Some people's assurance of salvation is a delusion (Mt 7:13-14). To enter the narrow gate of the kingdom we must knock, that is, request that God make us citizens of his kingdom (vv. 7-8). The difficulty of Jesus' way includes embracing by repentance both persecution (5:10-12) and the ethics of the kingdom taught in the Sermon on the Mount.

Most Jewish people in Jesus' day were religious; respecting God and keeping his commandments were an important part of their culture. These would be the *many* people of whom Jesus' hearers would think when they heard him. Yet Jesus, like a few contemporaries who were particularly scrupulous (4 Ezra 7:45-61; 8:1-3), declared that most people were lost. Jesus intends his words to jar us from complacency, to consider the genuineness of our commitment to him.

One wonders how many members in our churches today assume that they are saved when in fact they treat Jesus' teachings lightly—people who give no thought to their temper, their mental chastity, their integrity and so forth during the week (compare 5:21-48), then pretend to be religious or even spiritually gifted in church. Do we have the courage to communicate Jesus' message as clearly as he meant it to be conveyed, to warn ourselves and others that it is possible for people to assume they are saved and yet be damned? Some texts in the Bible provide assurance to suffering Christians that the kingdom is theirs; this text challenges "cultural Christians," those following only Christian tradition rather than Christ himself, to realize that they need conversion.

Discern by Fruits, Not Gifts (7:15-23) True prophets obey Jesus' teachings. Like the false prophets of old (Jer 6:13-14; 8:11; 23:13-17; Ezek 13:1-16; Mic 3:5-8), those Matthew warns against in 7:15 probably proclaim a gospel of false peace, an easy way that neglects God's true demands (vv. 13-14; France 1985:147). Matthew elsewhere warns against false prophets (7:22; 24:5, 24) and apostate Christians and leaders in the church (24:12, 48-51). Jesus elsewhere applies the present denunciations of fruitless trees against the religious leaders of his day (12:33; compare 3:8, 10; 21:19; 23:3), but because his words in this context address prophets (which most Pharisees thought no longer existed in their day), one suspects that Matthew wants Christians of his own generation to take notice.

Jesus' words are not only polemic against enemies of the faith from the outside; they are also warnings to us who claim to be Jesus' followers. We dare not restrict the title "hypocrites" to Jesus' religious contemporaries (6:2, 5, 16; pace *Did.* 8:1-2); God's subsequent servants may share the same fate (24:51). This passage presents us with several lessons.

False Prophets and Their Teaching Pose a Real Danger to Believers (7:15) They are like hungry wolves who disguise themselves as sheep. People in Jesus' day could disguise themselves in sheepskins in the hope of being taken for stray dogs or other animals (Jos. *War* 3.192). Jesus' image is, however, more graphic than that, employing hyperbole: wolves do not wear clothes, and changing one's hide was a metaphor for the impossible (Jer 13:23; *Jub.* 37:20). By coming in sheep's clothing, the false prophets pretend to be sheep (Acts 20:29-30) though they are in fact hungry wolves who have come to prey on sheep (compare Mt 10:16).

Some denominations that once evangelized peoples and held orthodox teachings now encompass a much wider range of moral and spiritual teaching, and many movements that remain orthodox in general nevertheless remain susceptible to dangerous winds of doctrine. We who should be challenging unjust reasoning in the world instead often find ourselves fighting a defensive battle within our own ranks. For the sake

_____
7:15 The enmity of lambs and wolves was by now proverbial (*1 Enoch* 89:15; *Jub.* 37:21;

of the flock, we must exercise discernment, especially within the church.

Evaluate Prophets by Their Fruits (7:16-20) These false prophets (v. 15) claim to have prophesied, exorcised and effected miracles by Jesus' name (v. 22). Although Matthew is surely charismatic in a positive way (compare, for example, 5:12; 10:8, 40-42; 23:34), here he challenges false Christian charismatics whose disobedience Christ will finally reveal (10:26). Although some could prophesy and work signs by demonic power (for example, 2 Thess 2:9; Rev 13:13-16; compare Jer 2:8; 23:13), one could also manifest genuine gifts of God's Spirit yet be lost (1 Sam 19:24).

Once we acknowledge that God can inspire people to speak his message (and this would apply to gifts like teaching as well as prophecy), how do we discern his genuine representatives? Like his follower Paul, Jesus subordinates the gifts of the Spirit to the fruit of the Spirit (compare 1 Cor 13) and submission to Jesus' lordship (1 Cor 12:1-3). Jesus' words about fruit thus refer to repentant works (Mt 7:21; 3:8, 10), recalling Jesus' ethical teachings in 5:21—7:12.

Much of today's church may miss out on prophecy altogether, which is not a healthy situation (1 Thess 5:20). Prophecy remains a valid gift until Jesus' return (1 Cor 13:9-12), and we should seek it for our churches (1 Cor 14:1, 39; Grudem 1982; Keener 1996:79-130). But wherever the real is practiced, the counterfeit will also appear (a phenomenon I as a charismatic have witnessed frequently; compare 1 Cor 14:29; 1 Thess 5:21).

An adulterous minister may exhibit many divinely bestowed gifts— sometimes because God is answering the prayers of people in the congregation—but such ministers are unworthy of our trust as God's spokespersons as long as they continue in sin. Yet Jesus wants us to look even closer to home. Do we become so occupied with "the Lord's work" that we lose sight of the precious people God has called us to serve? Do we become so preoccupied with our mission and our gifts that we neglect a charitable attitude toward our families and other people around us?

Yet the image of the tree and the fruit also reminds us that behavior flows from character, and in Christian teaching character comes through

Horace *Epode* 4.1-2). Aesop's fable of the wolf in sheep's clothing may have been influential (see Davies and Allison 1988:704).

being born again rather than merely through self-discipline (see Ode-berg 1964:72). Our own best efforts at restructuring unregenerate human nature are doomed to failure (Gal 5:19-21). By contrast, a person transformed by and consistently dependent on the power of God's Spirit will live according to the traits of God's character because of God's empowerment, just as trees bear fruit according to their own kind (Gal 5:18, 22-23).

God Will Expose Our Hearts on the Day of Judgment (7:21-23) Some people claim to accept Jesus as a great teacher, but no more than a teacher. Yet a central component of Jesus' teaching is the revelation of his identity, and in this passage as in Matthew 25:31-46, Jesus claims the role of final judge.

Churchgoers today are no more automatically saved than those who ate with Jesus in the past (as is often noted, attending a church no more makes one a Christian than entering a garage makes one a car). Not those who claim to "know" Jesus but only those who do the Father's will have any claim on Jesus (12:50). Jesus thus borrows biblical language for righteous enmity toward the wicked (Ps 6:8; 119:115) to banish them from his presence (Mt 7:23; compare 7:19). *I never knew you* is a formal repudiation of the person (25:12; compare 26:70, 72, 74; France 1985:149).

Obeying Jesus' Words (7:24-27) Another early Jewish teacher, while illustrating this point with many examples, went so far as to say that one who studies Torah and has good works "may be likened to" one who lays a foundation of stones and then of bricks, so that rising water or rain cannot overturn it. But one who studies Torah and has no good works is like one who builds with bricks on the bottom, so that even a small amount of water overturns it (*ARN* 24A).

7:22 Matthew is not "anticharismatic"—that he must warn his community against the wrong kind of prophets, yet fails to attack prophecy in general, strongly suggests that he and his community both accept some prophets as genuine (5:12; 10:8, 40-42; 23:34; see Michaels 1976; Hill 1979:156; Aune 1983:215). The *Didache* similarly provides moral tests for prophets precisely because its audience accepts the validity of prophets (*Did.* 11.3-12).

7:28 Each of Jesus' five major discourses in Matthew concludes with the formula "And when Jesus had finished speaking these words" (or, in 13:53, "these parables"), which was

But Jesus here refers to his own words the way other Jewish teachers referred to God's law (Jeremias 1972:194). The language at least implies that Jesus is God's prophetic spokesperson (Ezek 33:32-33) but is more authoritative than is typical even for prophets; in this context (Mt 7:21-23; see also 18:20), the claim is far more radical. One cannot be content with calling Jesus a great teacher, for he taught that he was more than a mere teacher; one must either accept all his teachings, including those that demand we submit to his lordship, or reject him altogether. Jesus is not one way among many; he is the standard of judgment.

The Hebrew Bible often employed the rock image for the security Israel had in God if they obeyed him (for example, Deut 32:4, 18, 31; Ps 18:2, 31, 46; 19:14), including in a time of flood and disaster (Is 28:14-19). The storm could represent any test, but surely represents especially the final test, the day of judgment (for example, Jeremias 1963:8-9; compare Mt 24:37-39). Jesus' clear assurance of deliverance in the final test contrasts with the fears of some of his contemporaries; many people had little certainty of the afterlife (see, for example, Plato *Apol.* 29AB, *Phaedo* 64A; Bonsirven 1964:167-68). Jesus spoke with unparalleled authority (Mt 7:28-29).

□ Epilogue: Jesus' Hearers Recognize His Authority (7:28-29)

The crowds respond to Jesus' teaching as disciples and crowds often responded to his other acts: with awe (8:27; 9:8; 12:23; 22:33; compare Jn 7:46). What astonished them so much about Jesus' teaching was not his use of proverbs, parables, hyperboles or other standard pedagogic devices of his day; what astonished them was his claim to authority, a theme that climaxes in Matthew 28:18. Other Jewish teachers regularly cited earlier sages' opinions, and though later teachers sometimes came

---

a relatively natural way to conclude a section (*Jub.* 32:20; 50:13).
7:29 From at least the early second century on, some rabbis identified earlier traditions with the law itself as a sort of "oral law" (*Sipre Deut.* 306.25.1; 351.1.2, 3) and eventually viewed oral tradition as greater than written Torah (*p. 'Aboda Zara* 2:7, §3) because oral law encompassed and explained written law (*Sipre Deut.* 313.2.4). The words of the scribes were nearly always on a lower level than the words of Torah in the earliest rabbinic sources, however (E. Sanders 1990:115-25), and the identification of the two may not have been widespread in the early period (Sanders 1990:97-130).

to regard their tradition as tantamount to God's Word, Jesus' contemporaries never would have claimed, like Jesus, that people would be judged according to how they treated their words.

With greater authority than the scribes who expound the law, greater authority than Moses who gave it (5:1), the authority indeed of the One who will judge humanity on the final day (7:21-23), Jesus declares God's word, and the people recognize that he speaks with authority unlike their other teachers.

JESUS RULES NATURE—AND DISCIPLES (8:1—9:38)

After completing Jesus' sermon, Matthew begins recounting signs reported in Mark and some other source(s) Matthew shares with Luke. Matthew arranges these accounts about Jesus' authority in a special way. Many scholars count ten specific miracles in this section, some emphasizing the view that this points to the ten signs of a new Moses (Teeple 1957:82). Others emphasize the whole narrative's structure: because two of the miracles appear in one miracle story, Matthew narrates a total of nine miracle stories, which break into sets of three, separated by blocks of Jesus' teaching (Meier 1979:67 and 1980:80). Matthew 8:1-17 shows Jesus' authority over sickness; 8:23-28 shows his authority over nature, demons and paralysis; and 9:18-34 demonstrates his authority over disabilities and death.

Whereas these narratives demonstrate how much authority Jesus has in creation, the intervening paragraphs teach that we humans should also acknowledge Jesus' rightful authority over us (8:18-22; 9:9-17). The concluding summary of miracles (9:35) also contains another declaration of Christ's authority: we must ask the Lord to send out workers to demonstrate Jesus' authority over these needs (9:36-37). That final summary section (9:35-38), like the one preceding the Sermon on the Mount (4:23-25), could also be classified (with 10:1-5) as the narrative introduction for the discourse that follows in chapter 10.

□ Jesus' Authority over Sickness (8:1-22)

Even the best of ancient historians were interested in the meaning of history, its moral, as well as its information; most biographers especially explored their characters as positive or negative examples. (Many ancient writers, unlike many modern ones, had a sense of responsibility to their society!) The Gospel writers are interested in more than listing all Jesus' deeds (as if that were possible anyway—see Jn 21:25); they select examples from their materials to emphasize relevant points for their own readers (compare Jn 20:30-31). In narrating events like Jesus' healings, Matthew encourages his audience that the Lord to whom they pray for their needs in the present demonstrated his ability to meet those needs during his earthly ministry. While Matthew addresses particularly the need to trust Jesus to heal, the principles can apply to other desperate needs in our lives.

Jesus' Willingness to Heal (8:1-4) One could draw a number of lessons from this narrative. Because this is Matthew's first extended healing miracle, I will treat some elements in greater detail here than in some subsequent narratives.

The Leper Does Not Beseech Cavalierly (8:1-2) This leper was in a desperate and apparently lifelong situation. Biblical leprosy (distinct from modern Hansen's disease) was an assortment of serious skin problems that isolated the leper from the rest of society (Trapnell 1982:459). Sometimes we pray passively, almost unconcerned as to whether God hears a particular prayer or not; the leper did not have this luxury. For another expression of desperate faith, see comment on 9:20-21.

The Leper Approaches Jesus with Humility (8:2) Bowing down before another person was a great act of respect for the other's dignity, especially for a Jewish person (as in *Test. Ab.* 3-4, 9, 16A). The leper not only shows physical signs of respect toward Jesus; he acknowledges that Jesus has the right to decide whether to grant the request. To acknowledge that God has the right to grant or refuse a request is not lack of faith (8:2; compare, for example, Gen 18:27, 30-32; 2 Sam 10:12; Dan 3:18); it is the ultimate act of dependence on God's compassion and takes great trust and commitment for a desperate person.

The Leper Has Perfect Trust in Jesus' Power (8:2) He knows Jesus is able to make him clean if he wants to; he is not using *if you are willing* as a religious way of saying, "I doubt that you can, but I would be happy if you might do something for me anyway." Yet the text demonstrates, as has been already noted, that his trust in Jesus' power is not presumption either.

Jesus Not Only Heals but Touches the Untouchable (8:3) Jewish law forbade touching lepers (Lev 5:3) and quarantined lepers from regular society (Lev 13:45-46); people avoided most contact with them (2 Kings 7:3; Jos. *Ant.* 9.74). Some ruled that the defilement of leprosy was one of the greatest defilements, for a leper could communicate it even by entering a house (*m. Kelim* 1:4). It is thus no small matter for Jesus to compassionately touch the man. Yet by touching Jesus does not actually undermine the law of Moses, but fulfills its purpose by providing cleansing (Mt 5:17-48; compare Lev 13:3, 8, 10, 13, 17).

Some Christians today would fear to touch a Christian brother or sister who, through blood transfusion, past lifestyle or a spouse's infidelity, was HIV-positive, even though HIV is less contagious than many people thought leprosy was. As often happens today, some people in antiquity constructed theological rationalizations for others' misfortune perhaps to escape from the fear that they too were vulnerable; hence some later teachers decided that leprosy was divine punishment (*m. Šeqalim* 5:3; *Lev. Rab.* 17:3).

Jesus Wants to Make the Man Whole (8:3) Verse 3 implies what is elsewhere explicit: Matthew views compassion as a primary motivation in Jesus' acts of healing (9:36). Even if in some cases God has some higher purpose in mind than an immediate answer to our request (as in 26:39, 42), he is never sadistic. Jesus demonstrated his feeling toward our infirmities by bearing them with us and for us (8:17) and by healing all who sought his help (8:16). Matthew hardly expects us to suppose that Jesus has lost any of his power (28:18) or compassion since the resurrection. Unfortunately, many of us Western Christians today feel more at home with the Enlightenment rationalism in which we were trained than we do with the desperate faith of Christians who dare to believe God for miracles. Those in desperate need cannot afford to rationalize away God's power and compassion.

Jesus Does Not Seek Human Honor for Himself (8:4) This healing would be viewed as no small miracle; later Jewish teachers

---

8:4 Scholars offer various reasons for the messianic secret in the Gospels (it is most prominent in Mark); not all are mutually exclusive. Some suggest that Jesus rejects the title initially due to its military connotations (Cullmann 1956b:26); no public acclamation of Jesus' messiahship could be understood accurately until after the crucifixion and resurrection (Mk 15:26; Hurtado 1983:xxiii). Others argue that Jesus was only Messiah-designate

regarded leprosy as akin to death (compare Num 12:12; 2 Kings 5:7) and cleansing a leper as akin to raising the dead (*b. Sanhedrin* 47a). Yet not only does Jesus refuse to take advantage of the opportunity for publicity, he attempts to suppress it. Some other prominent biblical prophets at times worked clandestinely, endeavoring to accomplish their mission without seeking their own honor (for example, 1 Kings 11:29; 13:8-9; 21:18; 2 Kings 9:1-10), partly because they were investing their time especially in a small circle of disciples (1 Sam 19:20; 2 Kings 4:38; 6:1-3; Keener 1993:134). There are also other important reasons for the messianic secret, but whatever the other reasons, Jesus is not interested in getting credit from others for everything he does (compare Mt 6:1-18).

Jesus Honors the Requirements of the Law of Moses (8:4) Jesus upholds the law (Mt 5:17-20): the law commanded lepers who thought they were cleansed to submit to priestly inspection and offer sacrifice (Lev 14:1-9; *CD* 13.6-7; *m. Nega'im*). Jesus may not seek credit for the miracle, but his faithfulness to the law takes precedence over his personal prohibition against announcing the work.

A Roman Exception (8:5-13) The Gentile mission was at most peripheral to Jesus' earthly ministry: he did not actively seek out Gentiles for ministry (Mt 10:5), and both occasions on which he heals Gentiles he does so from a distance (8:13; 15:28). The Gentile mission became central to the early church, however, and early Christians naturally looked to accounts of Jesus' life for examples of ministry to the Gentiles (compare 1:3, 5-6; 2:1-2, 11; 3:9; 4:15). Matthew here draws from Q material (on the Q hypothesis, see the introduction) to emphasize his theme favoring the Gentile mission.

The significance of the passage is clarified by some basic information about Roman centurions and what they represented to Jewish people in the first century. In this period soldiers in the Roman legions served twenty years (Ferguson 1987:39). Unlike aristocrats, who could become

---

till after the resurrection anyway (Longenecker 1981:68-73). Thus messianic acclamations could and did lead the authorities to wrongly classify Jesus as a revolutionary and seek his execution. Undue publicity drew uncontrollable crowds (Mk 1:45; 2:2; 3:9-10, 20); the crowds and the rumors they might spread could have invited further "incriminating charges," which Jesus sought to delay until the appropriate time (see Rhoads and Michie 1982:87).

tribunes or higher officials immediately, most centurions rose to their position from within the ranks and became members of the equestrian (knight) class when they retired (J. Jones 1971:201-3). Roman soldiers participated in pagan religious oaths to the divine emperor (J. Jones 1971:212).

Matthew here demonstrates that a call to missions work demands that disciples first abandon ethnic and cultural prejudice. His Jewish readers would be tempted to hate Romans, especially Roman soldiers, and perhaps their officers even more; this would be especially true after A.D. 70. Jesus' teaching about accommodating a Roman soldier's unjust request (5:41), paying taxes to a pagan state that used the funds in part for armies (22:21) or paying a temple tax that the Romans later confiscated for pagan worship (17:24-27) would seem intolerable to anyone whose allegiance to Christ was not greater than his or her allegiance to family and community. But Jesus is not satisfied by our treating an enemy respectfully; he demands that we actually love that enemy (5:44). No one challenges our prejudices—and sometimes provokes our antagonism—more than a "good" member of a group that has unjustly treated people we love. This narrative challenges prejudice in a number of ways.

The Centurion Humbles Himself on Behalf of a Servant (8:5-6)
This Roman soldier was one that Jewish people would have to count as an exception (compare explicitly in Lk 7:4-5). The slave was probably the centurion's entire "family" (Roman soldiers were not permitted to have legal families during their two decades of military service; A. Jones 1970:155-56). (Matthew's audience may even think of Jewish relatives enslaved by the Romans after Jerusalem's fall in A.D. 70.)

The Centurion Acknowledges His Inferior Status as a Gentile (8:7-8)
Matthew reports such self-humbling on the part of both Gentiles who entreat Jesus for help (here and 15:27). The centurion's initial announcement of the need (8:6) is an oblique form of request; one rarely simply presumed on others' favor (compare Lk 24:28-29; Jn 1:38-39), and one of higher social status rarely would utter a direct request unless

---

8:6 Although many soldiers took unofficial concubines (Fabius Maximus 4 in Plut. *Sayings of Romans, Mor.* 195E-F), centurions were frequently transferred from one legion to another, preventing permanent ties with local women; a code of dignity may have also lessened the likelihood of their liaisons with concubines (Scipio the Elder 2, Plut. *Sayings of Romans,*

desperate (compare Jn 2:3). But Jesus forces the centurion to admit his status as a suppliant.

The emphatic Greek *I* in 8:7 suggests that Jesus' words there are probably better translated as a question: "Shall *I* come and heal him?" (France 1977:257). Most Palestinian Jews, after all, considered entering Gentile homes questionable (compare Acts 10:28; *m. Pesaḥim* 8:8; *Oholot* 18:7). Here Jesus erects a barrier the Gentile must surmount, as in 15:24, 26: an outsider who would entreat his favor must first acknowledge the privilege of Israel, whom other peoples had oppressed or disregarded (compare Jn 4:22). Such initial rejection was a not uncommon ploy for demanding greater commitment (see comment on Mt 19:16-22). Rather than protesting, the centurion acknowledges his questionable merit before Jesus (compare Lk 7:4, 6), adopting the appropriate role of a suppliant totally dependent on a patron's benefaction—a role centurions themselves often filled for local populations (Malina 1981:78; Malina and Rohrbaugh 1992:70).

The Centurion Recognizes Jesus' Unlimited Authority to Heal (8:8-9) The man shows faith not only by acknowledging his own unworthiness but also by recognizing that Jesus' power is so great that this request is small to him. Most of the centurion's contemporaries would have balked at such faith; even Jewish people considered long-distance miracles especially difficult and rare, the domain of only the most powerful holy men like Hanina ben Dosa. The centurion reasons, however, from what he knows: he himself can issue commands and receive obedience because he is *under authority,* that is, backed by the full authority of the Roman Empire, which he represents to his troops. In the same way, the authority of Israel's God backs Jesus, and a mere command from his lips banishes powers in subjection under him, such as sickness.

Do we have such faith to recognize the greatness of God's power? Those who are submitted to Jesus' will may act on it today, recognizing that the authority he provides to carry out his work is his and not our own (10:8, 40).

Mor. 196B). This centurion thus may have had no family except for this servant.
8:9 To say "Go," and others go, and "come," and others come, was a standard summary representation of personal authority (Epict. *Disc.* 1.25.10-11).

Jesus Accepts This Attitude as Faith (8:10) Jesus accepts the centurion's recognition of Jesus' great authority as faith and heals the servant (8:13). But the text also offers a second lesson, a lesson about our prejudices. Jesus "marvels" (NIV *was astonished*) only twice in the Gospel traditions, here at a Gentile's faith (v. 10) and in Mark 6:6 at his hometown's unbelief (France 1977:259). It is often those closest to the truth who most take it for granted and those who have had the least exposure to it who most recognize its power when it confronts them (Mt 2:1-12).

Many church workers focus on getting people saved in churches where new people rarely visit; we may need to focus more on sharing the faith by word and deed in our communities outside church walls, and across cultural barriers as well. As one missionary statesman put it, "I do not see why anyone should hear the gospel twice when so many people have never heard it once." Or as R. T. France muses (1985:157):

The centurion's story has thus highlighted faith as the "one thing needful." It is a practical faith which expects and receives results. Such faith renders tradition and heredity meaningless, and "of such is the kingdom of God." Schweizer draws an appropriately uncomfortable moral: "The warning in this story may be especially urgent in an age when Africans and Asians in the community of Jesus may well be called on to show 'Christian' Europe what Christian life really is."

The Centurion Is a Promise of More Gentiles to Come (8:11-12) Evidence supports this as an authentic saying of Jesus (Semitisms and background in Jeremias 1958:55-62). Matthew may draw Jesus' words here from another context (Lk 13:28-29) to reinforce the point that this story prefigures the Gentile mission, which Jesus endorsed in advance (France 1977:260).

Subjects of the kingdom (literally "sons of the kingdom"; compare Mt 13:38; 23:15) refers to Jewish people—those who expected salvation based on their descent from Abraham (3:9). The damnation of those who thought themselves destined for the kingdom sounded a sober

---

8:12 Outer darkness represents damnation (13:42; 22:13; 25:30; *1 Enoch* 10:4-6; 92:5; 103:8; 108:14) and sometimes is conjoined with burning (1QS 4.12-13; *Sib. Or.* 4.43). *Weeping* indicates mourning over damnation (Judith 16:17; *Test. Judah* 25:5); *gnashing of teeth*

warning to nationalist Jews of Matthew's day; it sounds a similar warning
to complacent Christians today (Goldingay 1977:254; compare 13:38).

Rome was the great power that lay to the west, and Matthew had
earlier illustrated the coming of pagans from the east (2:1). Pagans thus
would recline at table (the standard posture for feasts and banquets) in
the kingdom with the patriarchs—the messianic banquet Israel expected
for itself (5:6; 22:2; Lk 16:23; 4 Macc 13:17; *1 Enoch* 70:4).

"Exceptions" can make a difference. When one white minister living
in the U.S. South was experiencing the deepest trauma of his life, some
African-American Christians took him under their wing and nursed him
back to spiritual and emotional health. The white minister began to
experience the spiritual resources and strength that the black American
church had developed through slavery, segregation and contemporary
urban crises and was eventually ordained in a black Baptist church.
Subsequently he discovered slave narratives and other accounts that
brought him face to face with what people who looked like him had
done to the near ancestors of his closest friends. He became so ashamed
of the color of his skin that he wanted to rip it off. But the love of his
African-American friends and the good news of Christ's love restored
him, and soon he began to feel part of the community that had embraced
him.

He often joined his friends in lamenting the agony of racism and its
effects. But one day after a Sunday-school lesson, a minister friend said
something about white people in general that he suddenly took
personally. "I didn't mean *you*," the black minister explained quickly.
"You're like a brother to me." The black minister made an exception
because he knew the white Christian, but the white Christian wondered
about all the people who didn't know him. He had experienced a taste
of what most of his black friends regularly encountered in predominantly
white circles.

The next week the ministers were studying together the story of the
centurion's servant in Luke, and they noted that the centurion's Jewish
contemporaries viewed him as an exception to the rule that Gentiles

sometimes signifies anger (Ps 112:10; Acts 7:54) but probably signifies anguish here (*Sib. Or.* 2:203, 305; 8.86, 105, 125).

were oppressors. They also noted that the Gospels tell this story because that exception in Jesus' ministry points to a huge number of Gentile converts pouring in at the time when the Gospels were being written.

If even a few people become exceptions and really care enough about their brothers and sisters of other races to listen, these exceptions can show us that the racial and cultural barriers that exist in our societies do not need to continue. If we are willing to pay the price—which will sometimes include hints of rejection from people we have come to love—we can begin to bring down those barriers.

Jesus the Healer (8:14-17) Despite our claim to believe the Bible, we often reject those of its teachings that violate our traditions. Although Matthew employs Jesus' past healings as a proof of Jesus' messianic claim, he spends much of his narrative presenting Jesus as healer also because he expected his audience to experience Jesus as continuing healer, as the One who now holds all authority in heaven and on earth (28:18; see also 9:35-38). Yet just as many Protestants before William Carey doubted that the Great Commission (28:19) was for today, many Christians seem reluctant to embrace Jesus' power to touch physical illness today. Their reluctance is understandable as a reaction against the many excesses of some prominent figures, but it nevertheless betrays an inadequate attention to many biblical texts. Too many of us still read the Gospels as if they were merely history without preaching, instead of hearing God's Spirit preaching through the history.

Jesus and Disciples Should Always Be Ready to Minister (8:14-15) We should be ready to serve others wherever we encounter need, not just when "on duty." Jesus exercised God's power in regular human settings, in this case within the fairly typical living arrangements of a disciple's family.

Donald Hagner (1993:208-9) points out a minor chiastic structure in these verses, in which Jesus first ministers to Peter's wife's mother and she in turn ministers to him. This structure may make emphatic the model for discipleship: after Jesus transforms a person, the person serves him. If so, this is not the only text where Matthew chooses women disciples as a paradigm for discipleship in general (27:55-61; 28:1-10). That Jesus touches her to cure her may also indicate the way he values people over traditions, given some evidence for prejudice against touching people with fevers (Witherington 1984:67); compare 8:3; 9:20, 25.

Word Spreads, and Jesus Heals All Who Come (8:16) Having heard of Jesus' power, those who were diligent enough to come to him at evening undoubtedly had faith, removing the primary obstacle to his healing activity (compare 13:58). As throughout the book of Acts, healing both meets people's needs directly and draws them to the One who can transform their lives. Various examples elsewhere in the Bible demonstrate that God does not always heal instantly (Job 2:7-8; Mt 25:36; Gal 4:13; Phil 2:26-27) and sometimes chooses not to heal physically at all (1 Kings 1:1; 14:14; 2 Kings 13:14, 20-21; 2 Tim 4:20), perhaps because of issues that matter more than physical healing.

Modern medicine, based much more on the empirical character of our bodies that God created than ancient medicine was, can also be a tool in God's hands to bring healing. Nevertheless, modern medicine has its limitations, and this passage demonstrates Jesus' abundant authority and compassion to heal. The passage may suggest to us that Western Christians often unnecessarily forgo healing because our heritage of rationalism has unduly prejudiced us against it.

Jesus' Power: Healing and Expelling Demons with a Mere Word (8:16) Many of Jesus' contemporaries sought to chase away demons by means of incantations, pain compliance techniques like smelly roots, or invocation of higher spirits to get rid of lower ones (as in Tobit 6:7-8, 16-17; 8:2-3; Jos. *Ant.* 8.45-49; *Jub.* 10:10-13). (One thinks of the children's story of the king who hired cats to chase away mice from his palace, then had to hire dogs to drive off the cats, lions to be rid of the dogs, elephants to scare out the lions—and finally mice to chase the elephants from his now ruined palace.) Jesus instead expelled demons simply by his word (Mt 8:16; compare Twelftree 1986:383). Perhaps in view of the predicted nearness of God's kingdom, Satan's kingdom had initiated a counteroffensive raising the visibility of demon possession in this period (Alexander 1980:249).

Healing Is Part of Jesus' Mission (8:17) The context in Isaiah 53 suggests that the suffering servant's death would heal the nation from its sin (Is 53:4-6, 8-9; compare 1 Pet 2:22-25), a figurative expression frequent in the Prophets (Mt 13:15; Is 6:10; 57:18; Jer 3:22; 6:14; 8:11;

14:19; Hos 14:4). But the broader context of Isaiah shows God's promise for his people's complete wellness in the era of the kingdom (Is 29:18; 32:3-4; 35:5-6), suggesting secondary nuances of physical healing in 53:4-5 as well. The servant's suffering would, after all, restore to Israel all the benefits lost through sin (compare Ex 15:26; Deut 27—28). Thus Matthew cites Isaiah 53:4 to demonstrate that Jesus' mission of healing fulfills the character of the mission of the servant, who at the ultimate cost of his own life would reveal God's concern for a broken humanity.

Matthew himself also recognizes that genuine physical healings can illustrate principles of spiritual healing (9:5-7, 12; 13:15). But we should note the correct caution of D. A. Carson (1984:207):

> This text and others clearly teach that there is healing in the Atonement; but similarly there is the promise of a resurrection body in the Atonement, even if believers do not inherit it until the Parousia. From the perspectives of the NT writers, the Cross is the basis for all the benefits that accrue to believers; but this does not mean that all such benefits can be secured at the present time on demand, any more than we have the right and power to demand our resurrection bodies.

Because the kingdom is present as well as future, God often heals in the present, but what he does not choose to heal now he has promised to heal in the end (Blomberg 1992:145). More practically than simply quoting a few verses that address healing, we should meditate on biblical examples of healing and what we can learn thereby about how God feels about human pain. By doing so we can develop deeper intimacy in our relationship with Jesus, trusting his compassion, which is the basis for every kind of healing he graciously performs.

Following Where Jesus Leads (8:18-22) The same Jesus who has authority over nature (Mt 8:23-27), demons (8:28-34) and paralysis (9:2-8) is the One whose authority we should acknowledge over our

---

8:17 Although the miracles of Elijah and Elisha provide the role model for many of Jesus' miracles, the closest (yet not perfect) Old Testament model for someone performing exorcisms would be David in 1 Samuel 16:14-23 (see Betz 1968:66; Barrett 1966:53; Ps-Philo 60).
8:22 A few teachers did insist that they would honor their teachers above their parents (*p.*

own lives. David Bryant tells of a people movement in India in which twenty thousand poor Christians have divested themselves of virtually all their meager resources, mobilized to send forth as many of their number as possible to reach unreached peoples of India with the gospel (Bryant 1984:52). By contrast, it is difficult to engage many Western church members in such small gestures of self-discipline as fasting a meal or giving up an evening of television for door-to-door witnessing. In view of the way Jesus defines what it means to be his follower, one might well wonder how many of these church members are genuinely following the Jesus who speaks to us in the Gospels.

Following Jesus May Cost Us the Most Basic Security (8:18-20) The scribe no doubt supposes that he is paying a high price in volunteering to *follow* Jesus; such a decision will cost popularity in some circles, and going through the process of discipleship after already being a scribe would be a humbling experience (like having to repeat high school after finding out that one's school was unaccredited).

Jesus, however, warns his prospective disciple that even such a sacrifice may be inadequate. Jesus is, after all, *the Son of Man* who must suffer before his exaltation (compare Dan 7:13-22). As the Arab Christian commentator Ibn Sa'id remarked on this passage, the disciple "does not understand that 'follow' means Gethsemane, and Golgotha, and the tomb" (Bailey 1980:24). Although Jesus still had a home base in Capernaum (Mt 4:13), his traveling ministry left him and his disciples at the mercy of others' hospitality. In practice, then, Jesus was essentially homeless. Matthew records Jesus' words not merely as a matter of historical interest but as a call to his own generation, and by implication to ours: are we ready to follow Jesus even at the cost of all securities (10:5-14; compare Heb 11:38)?

Following Jesus Takes Precedence over All Social Obligations (8:21-22) Jesus' priority over social obligations includes even those family obligations one's society and religion declare to be ultimate. *Let*

Ḥagiga 2:1, §10); that one should honor one's teacher as one honors God (*m. 'Abot* 4:12) was a graphic way of increasing the honor due a teacher without diminishing that due God. But in no other case did a teacher demand that a disciple follow him instead of fulfilling the burial obligation.

the dead bury their own dead may refer to the "spiritually dead" (compare Lk 15:24, 32); others suggest, "Let the other physically dead in your father's tomb see to your physically dead father," a manifest impossibility characteristic of Jesus' typically shocking and graphic style (compare McCane 1990:41).

Jesus' demand may prove less harsh in some respects than it sounds to us at first. The *disciple* (by calling him this Matthew makes the narrative explicitly relevant for Christians' commitment) is probably not asking permission to attend his father's funeral later that day; his father likely either was not yet dead or had been buried once already.

When a father died, mourners would gather immediately and a funeral procession would take his body to the tomb (see Mt 27:59-60; Mk 5:35, 38; Lk 7:12), leaving no time for a bereaved son to be talking with rabbis. For a week afterward the family would remain mourning at home and not go out in public (Sirach 22:12; Judith 16:24). But current Semitic idioms show that "I must first bury my father" can function as a request to wait until one's father dies—perhaps for years—so that one may fulfill the ultimate filial obligation before leaving home (Bailey 1980:26).

A custom practiced only in the period immediately surrounding the time of Jesus may illumine this passage more directly, however. In Jesus' day the eldest son would return to the tomb a year after the father's death to "rebury" his father by neatly arranging his now bare bones in a container and sliding it into a slot in the wall. If the father of the man in Matthew's account has died, this young man cannot be referring to his father's initial burial and so must be asking for as much as a year's delay for a secondary burial (see McCane 1990).

At the same time, Jesus' demand also proves harsher than it sounds to us at first. The offense lies not in the immediacy of the demand but in the priority the demand takes over family obligations (Mt 10:21, 35-37). Many Jewish people considered honoring parents the supreme commandment (*Ep. Arist.* 228; Jos. *Apion* 2.206) and burial of one's parents one of the most important implications of that commandment, regardless of the circumstances (Tobit 4:3-4; 6:14; 1 Macc 2:70). In most current interpretations of biblical law, only the honor due to God took precedence over the honor shown to parents (Deut

13:6; 4 Macc 2:10-12; Jos. *Apion* 2.206). Jesus does insist on honoring parents (Mt 15:4-6), yet he demands a greater affection toward himself. Jesus scandalously claims the supreme position of attention in his followers' lives. If we devote ourselves to anyone or anything more than to him, our claim to be his followers becomes hollow, no matter how many "disciples" around us live the same way. And lest we think that Jesus could never demand the immediate abandonment of family obligations we would have otherwise read into the demand, Luke adds a third account that requires just that (Lk 9:61-62; see Keener 1993:215).

Jesus' words in Matthew 8:18-22 were probably intended mainly to weed out would-be disciples who would prove weak in commitment. Jesus wanted people to follow him and welcomed the masses; he did not actually want prospective disciples to abandon him. Mark tells us that Jesus loved a prospective disciple—just before he effectively discouraged the man from following him (Mk 10:21-22). But those who would genuinely be disciples of the King must count the cost before they begin following him (Lk 14:26-35). (Parallels from some other radical ancient teachers demonstrate that commitment rather than harshness was Jesus' intent; see comments on Mt 19:16-22.)

☐ Jesus' Authority over Nature and Disciples (8:23—9:17)

As in the preceding section (8:1-22), here Matthew recounts three signs of Jesus' authority over creation (8:23—9:8), then turns to Jesus' proper authority over humanity and our response to him (9:9-17).

Jesus' Authority over Nature (8:23-27) This passage affirms Jesus' authority over nature (8:26), and if over nature, then over any crisis his followers may face. Many ancient accounts of nature miracles were purely legendary, but these generally surrounded characters of the distant past (compare R. Grant 1986:62) rather than arising when eyewitnesses remained. The tradition behind this particular story is very likely Palestinian, describing in traditional Galilean (contrary to foreign) fashion the Lake of Galilee as a "sea" (v. 24, literally, against the NIV; see Mk 4:39; see Theissen 1991:105-8).

Jesus' Ministry Exhausts Him (8:23-24) Jesus' exhausted slumber in the boat passage incidentally illustrates his statement in verse 20 that the Son of Man has nowhere to lay his head. Perhaps as if to underline the point, Matthew omits Mark's mention of the makeshift cushion (Mk 4:38). Matthew also purposely emphasizes that Jesus' true disciples *followed* him (8:22-23).

Jesus Reproves the Disciples for Their Fear (8:25-26) Jesus' peace (v. 24) contrasts starkly with the disciples' fear (v. 25); they are *of little faith* (v. 26), just like those who are anxious for tomorrow (6:30) or who doubt Jesus' power to work extraordinary miracles (14:31; 16:8; 17:20). Ability to sleep during trouble was often a sign of faith in God (Ps 3:5; 4:8), and the Greeks also praised philosophers who demonstrated consistency with their teaching by maintaining a serene attitude during a storm (Diog. Laert. 1.86; 2.71; 9.11.68). Just as Jesus demands that we express our love for God by trusting him for material provision (Mt 6:25-34), he demands that we trust him for safety. Our heavenly Father may not always protect us from earthly ills, but he will do with our lives what is best for us (10:29-31). By this point in the narrative the disciples appear without excuse for their unbelief, like Israel in the wilderness; "Jesus expects them to have taken charge of the storm themselves" (Rhoads and Michie 1982:90, 93).

Jesus' Power Reveals His Identity (8:27) If the disciples thought the boat might sink with Jesus aboard, it was because they did not understand Jesus' identity. His power over the sea, however, forces them to grapple afresh with that question. Faith in Jesus' authority flows from conviction concerning his true identity (compare 8:8; 9:6).

Stories about nature miracles occasionally circulated in antiquity, usually either stories about deities (R. Grant 1986:62) or legends about heroes of the distant past (as in Diog. Laert. 8.2.59; Blackburn 1986:190; compare *t. Ta'anit* 2:13). Parallels to the Jonah story (Cope 1976:96-98) can link the disciples' amazement at Jesus' stilling of the storm to God's stilling the storm in the Jonah story (Jon 1:15-16); other backgrounds in

---

8:28 Matthew's *Gadarenes* represents a different city from Mark's "Gerasenes" (Mk 5:1). Gerasa was larger and more powerful in Mark's time; hence Mark used the more prominent city to identify the region (see Vander Broek 1983:89-102); Matthew, probably writing to Christians in Syria who knew the region better, names the city nearer the lake (six miles away as opposed to thirty—Anderson 1976:147-48).

the Hebrew Bible also point to Jesus' identity with God (see in Lane 1974:176). In biblical tradition it was God whom the seas obeyed (as in Job 38:8-11; Ps 65:5-8; 89:8-9; France 1985:162). The astonishment of Jesus' disciples is therefore understandable (Mk 4:41; 6:51)! Their cry for Jesus to *save* them reflects one sense of the Greek term *save* ("deliver safely") but probably also alludes on a literary level to Jesus' broader mission (Mt 1:21).

Jesus' Authority over Demons (8:28-34) The setting builds suspense. Gadara and (Mark's) Gerasa were both part of the Decapolis, a primarily Gentile area with a large Jewish population (Jos. *War* 1.155). That tombs were unclean (for example, *m. Nazir* 3:5; 7:3; *t. Baba Batra* 1:10-11) and considered the usual haunts of demons and magic (*PGM* 101.1-3; Nineham 1977:153) increases the audience's suspicion that these demons are inordinately powerful—hence the narrative's opening suspense and christological impact.

Even Demons Know Who Their Lord and Judge Is (8:28-29) The demoniacs ran to Jesus (Mt 8:28), and the demons protested his coming to torture them (compare *Test. Sol.* 5:5). Jesus' presence also reduced them to entreating permission just to enter some pigs (v. 30). Yet in contrast to demons, many people remain unaware of Jesus as Lord and Judge.

The Kingdom Is "Already" As Well As "Not Yet" (8:29) Because the King of the future age arrived in the first century, his kingdom also invaded this world in a way hidden to people but recognized by the evil one and his forces (see also Cullmann 1950:71). The demons here, believing they are free to torment people until the final day and expecting eternal torment in the day of judgment, recognize that their judge has just shown up, *before the appointed time.* God's ultimate intervention is yet to come, but this does not prevent us from depending on his power over the evil one in the present.

Matthew doubles Mark's demoniacs (Mt 8:28 par. Mk 5:2), as he later doubles his blind men (Mt 9:27-31; 20:29-34 par. Mk 10:46-52; compare perhaps 21:2; 26:60). In both other instances of doubling he has omitted one of Mark's accounts (the demoniac of Mk 1:23-26; the blind man of Mk 8:22-26) and hence perhaps feels justified compensating here; such a literary practice would not have been unusual in his day.

Jesus Values People More Than Animals or Property (8:30-32)
In ancient exorcism traditions, demons typically made a public scene
when they departed, melodramatically indicating their protest and the
exorcist's power (as in Jos. *Ant.* 8.48-49; Philostr. *V.A.* 4.20); but rarely
did they make this much of a scene! Pigs can normally swim for some
distance if necessary (Alexander 1980:214); given the mortality of
demons in some Jewish traditions, this account may suggest that the
demons were at least disabled or bound in hell. It would have made
sense to the earliest Jewish hearers of this story that demons wished to
enter pigs and that Jesus let the herd perish, but to the owners of the
swine (in preinsurance days) the destruction of their herd meant
financial loss, not just "deviled ham." The deliverance of the demoniacs
mattered more to Jesus than the fate of the swine (see also Hooker
1983:39).

Most People Value Property More Than God's Deliverance
(8:33-34) Gentile wonderworkers were often "magicians," whose
power others perceived as malevolent more often than not (as in Apul.
Metam. 2.5, 20, 30; 3.16-18; 9.30). Ignoring the men's deliverance and
focusing on the destruction of the property, the Gadarenes viewed Jesus
as a magician, dangerous to their interests.

People's presuppositions are so strong that even divine miracles will
not always convert them. I once debated for about seven hours with a
professor in his office, providing evidence to refute his objections to
Christianity and citing line after line of evidence for the truth of the
Christian faith, each of which he dismissed on the basis of presuppositions. Finally exasperated, I demanded, "Would you believe in Jesus if
someone were raised from the dead in front of you in his name?"

"No," he responded, "I'd say they weren't really dead."

"And you have the audacity to call *me* closed-minded for being a
Christian?" I retorted.

We cannot, however, assume in advance who will respond to our
testimony; most of us would have guessed that of all the Gadarenes, the
ones least likely to respond to Jesus would be the demoniacs. As an
atheist I argued vehemently against the gospel the first day I heard it,
and the people who witnessed to me did not learn until a year later that
I had become a Christian later that day and led ten people to Christ in

the intervening year. We are responsible to sow seed everywhere and leave the harvest with God (13:3-23).

Jesus' Authority to Forgive Sins (9:1-8) Jesus' authority to heal the body testifies to his authority to forgive (9:6-7; compare 9:12). Jesus' *authority* (vv. 6, 8) is a central focus of the context (7:29; 8:9, 27; compare 28:18). This narrative teaches us a number of lessons.

Jesus Is Moved by Our Faith, Even on Behalf of Others (9:1-2) The paralytic was not alone in his faith; his friends who brought him believed too. Thus this account teaches us about intercession: we may pray for others, not merely for ourselves. Mark's fuller narrative recounts the character of the friends' faith: they were so persistent and determined to reach Jesus, so confident that their friend would be healed if they reached him, that they dug through the roof (Mk 2:4). Faith is not simply working up a feeling or suppressing doubts, but demonstrated commitment to getting to the One on whose power we stake our trust.

We Need Forgiveness Even More Than Physical Healing (9:2) Out of his care for us, Jesus places first things first (as in Ps 119:67, 71, 75). Although Jesus' miracles teach us about his power to heal physically, these signs are meant to turn our attention to the kingdom of God (Mt 6:33; 9:12). Thus in Acts signs and wonders constitute the primary method of drawing attention to the claims of the gospel, but it is the gospel itself that is paramount (as in Acts 14:3). In this narrative, physical healing certainly earns the crowd's attention (Mt 9:8), as miracles usually did (for example, 8:27, 34; 9:26, 31, 33).

Speaking for God Usually Invites Opposition (9:3-4) Jesus' unique authority on earth to forgive sins sets him apart from other people, a claim that disturbed *the teachers of the law* (v. 3), who wrongly supposed that speaking for God was their own role. Others might pronounce sins forgiven once clear atonement was made, but no atonement was made here (compare E. Sanders 1990:62-63). Thus the theologians decided that Jesus was *blaspheming,* which in the general sense simply meant "reviling" (in this case, God). Before Jesus is done, however, he will announce that God delegated to him the authority to forgive sins in general (v. 6; compare Dan 7:13)!

Jesus' Authority to Heal Demonstrates His Authority to For-

give (9:5-7) Because healing as opposed to forgiveness is empirically verifiable, the teachers of the law would conclude that it is easier to *say "Your sins are forgiven"* (Meier 1980:91). By performing a sign that is empirically verifiable, however, Jesus argues that he is God's authorized agent and therefore has *authority . . . to forgive sins.* The reasoning runs something like a traditional Jewish *qal waḥomer* ("how much more") argument: if God would authorize Jesus to visibly heal the effects of humanity's fallenness, would he not send him to combat that fallenness itself?

Although physical healing is secondary to forgiveness, such healing is often crucial not only for compassionately meeting some of our most pressing human needs (9:36) and empowering us for greater service to the Lord (20:34) but also for drawing attention to Jesus' power to do other works. People who reason today that Jesus can heal either physically or spiritually but not both are like the radical critics who debate whether Jesus was a wisdom teacher or a prophet, a messiah or a healer. The question is forced-choice logic; why can he not be both, as the text teaches us? Without guaranteeing that God always chooses to perform miracles we might desire, I have personally witnessed how nonbelievers healed in answer to prayer sometimes end up committing their lives to the Lord Jesus.

Jesus' Signs of Authority Bring God Glory (9:8) Often God will vindicate his work despite opposition if we persevere in doing good (compare 7:28; 8:27; 9:33; 12:23). When God provides clear testimony of his power, expect hostility from those who resist God's testimony; but recognize that God's works will always bring him more glory in the end.

Sinners Need a Physician (9:9-13) Whereas the preceding narrative introduces the notion that forgiveness is a primary focus of Jesus' mission (v. 9), this narrative carries that point further and uses Jesus' healing ministry as an acted parable of his most important mission: repairing our lives broken by sin (v. 12). Surrounding narratives also demonstrate that it is the broken, such as paralytics, blind people, lepers and those in mourning, who recognize their need for God's help.

Matthew here shows us that the morally and socially reprobate sometimes humble themselves more readily than religious people. Having often witnessed the fruit of sensitive personal evangelism on the streets, I fear that sometimes we spend too much time trying to convert a few resistant sinners in the church while neglecting more sinners afraid to set foot in a church. Sometimes the latter have developed less resistance to the gospel; sometimes they are outside the church precisely because of the words or behavior of some within the church.

Jesus Calls a Collaborator with the Enemy to Be His Disciple (9:9) Jesus' call to follow was a call to be his disciple—a future teacher in training (4:19; 8:22; 10:38; 16:24; 19:21). But whereas Jesus warned a scribe who was a would-be follower about the cost (8:19-20), here he openly invites a despised tax gatherer to join his circle (compare 18:17)! The common people and nonaristocratic pietists despised tax gatherers as agents of the Romans and their aristocratic pawns (E. Sanders 1985:178), perhaps something like what the Dutch or French felt toward local collaborators with the Nazis or Africans felt toward *slatees,* African assistants to European slave traders.

The average Jewish person in ancient Palestine had several reasons to dislike tax gatherers. First, Palestine's local Jewish aristocracies undoubtedly arranged for this tax collection (E. Sanders 1990:46-47). Second, the Empire sometimes had to take precautions to keep tax gatherers from overcharging people (Lk 3:12-13; Carmon 1973:105, 226), which suggests that some tax gatherers did just that (Hoehner 1972:78; compare Philo *Leg. Gai.* 199); some also beat people to get their money (Philo *Spec. Leg.* 3.30; N. Lewis 1983:161-63). Further, nearly all scholars concur that taxes were exorbitant even without overcharges; in some parts of the Empire taxation was so oppressive that laborers fled their land, at times to the point that entire villages were depopulated (N. Lewis 1983:164-64).

Matthew's office would have made him locally prominent, possibly as a customs official. Customs officers demanded written declarations of travelers' possessions and searched baggage (Casson 1974:290-91). They may have collected some other government revenues as well (M. Stern 1974-1976:333). Some Jewish texts condemn customs officers as well as other tax gatherers (see Edersheim 1993:236), though some such officials appear to have become benefactors to local populations (Jos. *War* 2.287-88).

In the eyes of these Pharisees (v. 11), eating with sinners connoted approval of them; by contrast, a pious person normally preferred to eat with scholars (compare Jeremias 1966a:236). Some take *sinners* here to mean the *'am hā'āreṣ* common people whom the Pharisees despised for their lack of adherence to Pharisaic food laws (as in Jeremias 1972:132; thus the quotation marks in the NIV); more scholars today lean toward the view that it means sinners in a more blatant sense.

Although we make exceptions today for former sinners if they are of prominent status, many churches are embarrassed to embrace a recovering drug addict or prostitute who comes seeking help. Likewise, Christians who struggled with homosexual or lesbian behavior in the past find this one of the few sins they dare confide to no one. Some churches are even reticent to allow an unemployed person or someone who was divorced in the distant past to train for a position of leadership. Even when our churches define sin and forgiveness the Bible's way, we sometimes define status in unbiblical ways.

Sinners Are Ready to Listen and Follow (9:9-10) People's unpredictability keeps us depending on God's mandate to share the kingdom with all. Jesus, for his part, was ready to eat with people with whom many of his pious contemporaries would not associate. For Matthew to follow Jesus meant leaving behind a well-paying profession, yet even this costly repentance could not satisfy the religious elite. There are many people with whom most Christians today would not eat (for reasons of either spiritual or social incompatibility); the Pharisees went even further in having special rules governing with whom they would eat (as in *ARN* 31, §68; 32, §72B).

Religious People React (9:11) The Jewish Scriptures clearly stated that one should not fellowship with sinners (Ps 1:1; 119:63; Prov 13:20; 14:7; 28:7), but these references warn against being influenced by sinners. Jesus is eating with sinners, but even though he is the one

---

9:10 The term "recline" indicates that this was no ordinary meal (Palestinian Jews normally sat on chairs), but a banquet (when people reclined), probably in the teacher's honor (see Jeremias 1966a:20-21).

9:11 The sages desired edifying talk (Sirach 9:15; *m. 'Abot* 3:2), including at meals (Ps 154:14; *p. Ḥagiga* 2:1, §9), though most banquets emphasized music over lectures (Sirach

influencing them (9:9, 13; Lk 15:1), his ministry looks bad. Early Jewish literature indicates that, for all Judaism's emphasis on mercy and repentance, Jesus' act of actively pursuing sinners was virtually unheard of (Ladd 1974b:83); it is thus not surprising that it appeared scandalous.

This is not to play down the emphasis on repentance among Jesus' contemporaries. Jewish tradition already warned not to reproach one who had turned from sin (Sirach 8:5), but we are not always what our doctrine says we should be. I often see vibrant churches attracting young people with whom some older members (or even denominational officials) tend to be uncomfortable. Well-endowed churches reaching out to inner-city projects often encounter children with hygiene and discipline habits different from those to which their members are accustomed. At times some apparently pious members of our churches have the same spiritual depth and commitment of this passage's Pharisees.

Jesus' Mission Is for Those Who Acknowledge Their Sinfulness (9:12-13) In an honor- and shame-based culture like the ancient Mediterranean, a public complaint such as the one the Pharisees had issued constituted a challenge. Quick repartee in the face of such a challenge would not only silence the challenge but shame the challengers (as in Diog. Laert. 6.2.33). Jesus shames his opponents with some traditional and biblical wisdom. Jewish teachers often exhorted hearers to "go and find," that is, search the Scripture for examples (as in *Sipre Num.* 76.2.1), or "go and learn," that is, understand the point of a given text (*Sipre Num.* 115.5.6). But when Jesus introduces his quote from Hosea with *go and learn* in the context of a response to a challenge, he is insultingly suggesting his interlocutors' ignorance of the point of Scripture; he implies that perhaps they have never even read Hosea (compare Mt 12:5; *Ex. Rab.* 21:6). Hosea addressed a people satisfied with their ritual but displeasing to God (Hos 8:2-3).

Jesus' response would have been clear enough. Other ancient teachers

---

35:3-4). Yet in Jesus' case the influence was going one way—from Jesus to the sinners (9:9, 13; Lk 15:1); and as an early Cynic philosopher reportedly explained when charged with visiting unclean places, "the sun too visits cesspools without being defiled" (Diog. Laert. 6.2.63, *LCL* 2:64-65; contrast *Mek. Pisḥa* 1.40-41).

also used health as a metaphor for spiritual or moral wholeness and disease as a metaphor for vice or folly, seeing themselves as physicians of the soul (for example, Diog. Laert. 2.70; 6.1.4; *ARN* 23A). Writing after the spread of Christianity, Diogenes Laertius reports a much earlier philosopher who, "when he was censured for keeping company with evil men," responded, "Physicians are in attendance on their patients without getting the fever themselves" (Diog. Laert. 6.1.6, *LCL* 6-9).

Jesus came to *call* sinners—to invite them to God's final banquet (Mt 22:3, 14), a foretaste of which the present table fellowship with them may have represented. Jesus' demand for mercy is so critical that it recurs in 12:7 (see also 23:23). Many of Jesus' contemporaries who practiced sacrifice also emphasized the priority of mercy over physical sacrifice (as in Sirach 35:1-7; *Prayer of Azariah* 16-17). That Jesus' opponents agreed with his principle in theory yet invited his reprimand should force us who acknowledge his doctrine to survey our practice as well (compare Jer 2:35; 1 Jn 1:10).

After my conversion from a non-Christian background in high school, I witnessed to everyone I could, sometimes to drug users who were smoking marijuana in my presence. That kind of fellowship could have landed me in jail! But Jesus' example gave me courage to continue to engage all people with the gospel, regardless of their moral background; and some of them committed their lives to Christ. Yet I have learned that some apparently worshipful and Bible-centered churches do not welcome such persons—suggesting that ultimately Jesus who ate with sinners might not truly be welcome there either.

A Time for Everything (9:14-17) Some religious people were disturbed that Jesus would eat with sinners (Mt 9:11); in a manner of speaking, others were disturbed that he ate at all (9:14). For some, holiness meant avoiding eating with ungodly people. For others, holiness meant religious practices of self-discipline like fasting. To both, Jesus undoubtedly appeared self-indulgent (11:19). Thus Jesus responds with three illustrations about appropriateness. When sinners return to God

---

9:15 The Gospels' readers would probably catch an allusion that Jesus' first hearers missed: Jesus is the groom of God's people in the coming messianic banquet foreshadowed in their

through Jesus' ministry, celebration rather than fasting is appropriate.

Jesus Shows Little Concern for Religious Customs (9:14) Although the fasts here were not demanded in the law, they were part of current religious tradition. Most Christians today evaluate their traditions in light of the Bible so little that we generally equate the two, as some of Jesus' contemporaries did. Essentially some considered him a "liberal" (Danker 1972:72)!

Jesus Stands Up for His Disciples (9:14-15) Ancient literature regularly assumes that teachers had to answer for the behavior of their disciples (such as Socrates for Alcibiades). When we face false accusations or opposition for following Jesus, we should always remember that if he is on our side we do not need to worry about what others will say. If David Wilkerson had allowed slander to deter him from his work with New York gangs in the 1960s, we would not have the ministry of Teen Challenge today. The key to persevering in God's call is to genuinely know that we are doing God's will.

There Are Appropriate Times for Everything (9:15-17) Most of us might have responded, "Look, you want to talk about fasting? *I* fasted forty days in the wilderness." But Jesus avoids seeking human honor for what he did before God in secret (6:16-18), and makes his point instead by three illustrations.

It was inappropriate for groomsmen to fast until after a wedding banquet had ended. Weddings lasted seven days, and participants—the NIV's *guests of the bridegroom* means either the groomsmen (compare Jn 3:29) or the guests—were expected to participate joyfully. Sages even interrupted their schools to hail passing bridal processions (*ARN* 4A).

New cloth had not yet shrunk, and when it began to shrink after being patched onto a garment that had finished its shrinking, the patch would tear loose from the garment, *making the tear worse* (Mt 9:16). In the same way, *old wineskins* had been stretched to the limit as wine fermented and expanded in them. Because old wineskins had already been stretched to the limit, if they were filled with new wine it would ultimately burst them when it expanded. Traditional rituals must never

---

table fellowship (22:2; 25:10-13). Against that backdrop, the bridegroom's departure implies the crucifixion.

become a straitjacket that hinder us from celebrating sinners' embrace of the good news of God's kingdom.

□ Jesus' Authority over Disabilities and Disciples (9:18-38)

As in the previous two sections (8:1-22; 8:23—9:17), Matthew begins with three accounts of Jesus' authority in nature (9:18-34) and then articulates Jesus' authority over disciples (9:35-38).

Embracing Our Brokenness (9:18-26) When Jesus allows an impure woman to touch him and touches the hand of a corpse, he contracts ritual impurity under the law (Lev 15:19-33; Num 19:11-12). Of course we might argue that Jesus contracted no uncleanness in actuality; as in the case of his contact with sinners, the influence went from him to them rather than the reverse (Mt 9:11-13). Yet in the eyes of those present, he has assumed the status of uncleanness (see the fuller account in Mk 5:33, where Jesus even invites public attestation of the touch). He is willing to touch us in our brokenness that we might be made whole.

In a world where women were nearly always second-class citizens and where male authors who cited women as examples of heroism treated them as exceptions (as in Plut. *Bravery of Women*), the Gospels' greater balance is intriguing. Yet this balance fits the rest of Jesus' ministry and teaching: it was the socially powerless who most readily embraced him. Socially accepted Christians who are disturbed by something missing in their zeal should take note; we should humble ourselves and listen to Christians from socially marginalized groups. The point is not to insult those who are not marginalized, but that the broken and marginalized have much to teach us about humble and often desperate dependence on the grace of God.

Jesus Is Willing to Heal and Even Restore to Life (9:18-19) Matthew wrote his Gospel to tell Christians more about the Lord they worshiped. We can show devotion to the Lord about whom we read by getting to know what he is like through these accounts and acknowledging his character as we praise him.

An Example of Scandalous Faith (9:20-21) Because of this

9:18-26 John P. Meier (1994:777-88) argues from various criteria for the authenticity of this

woman's continual flow of blood, she was not permitted to move about in crowds; anyone she touched or whose cloak she touched became unclean. Abbreviating as he often does, Matthew omits Mark's crowds (Mk 5:27) but retains the woman's intention: she is so desperate that she will touch the teacher, knowing full well that this will make him unclean under the law (Lev 15:25-27; *m. Toharot* 5:8).

Her condition is desperate both for medical reasons and because of its social consequences; her ostracism would extend even to her private life. Her ailment probably had kept her from marriage if it started at puberty, and almost surely would have led to divorce if it began after she was married (which would have been within a few years after puberty), since intercourse was prohibited under such circumstances (Lev 18:19) and childlessness normally led to divorce (Keener 1991a:75). Singleness is difficult for many people in Western society, but to be a unmarriageable woman in first-century Jewish Palestine must have often been terrifying. The stigma of childlessness (compare Lk 1:24-25; *1 Enoch* 98:5), the pain of feeling "left over" and the dilemma of being unable to earn an income yet having neither husband nor children for long-term support would have made this woman's condition seem almost unbearable.

Yet her desperation also begets confidence that Jesus is an absolutely certain source of her healing. Desperation has driven many of us to a faith that refuses to be deterred. This woman was undoubtedly more desperate than most of us have been, and she pressed her way to Jesus with the determination of faith, regardless of the consequences.

Jesus Embraces Her Need (9:22) Jesus acknowledged her act as an act of faith. By failing to offer a rebuke, he demonstrated both that the healing came by God's power and not automatic magic (Hooker 1983:61) and that he was unashamed to be identified with her uncleanness. In the times of our deepest pain, the assurance of God's presence can provide comfort commensurate with the pain. This is true because the One we claim as Lord embraced our ultimate humiliation and shame on the cross, refusing even a simple narcotic to deaden the pain (27:34).

Jesus Has Authority over Death Itself (9:23-26) Death in child-

---

narrative in pre-Mark tradition.

hood was a quite frequent occurrence. Because bodies decomposed rapidly, mourners had to gather quickly (for example, *b. Sanhedrin* 47a). Later texts probably reflect the earlier view of many religious people in regarding at least two or three mourners (two flutists and one professional mourning woman) as mandatory for the funeral of the poorest person (*m. Ketubot* 4:4), but a prominent local person like this *ruler* (v. 18) would probably be able to afford more. (His wealth and status set him in stark contrast to the ailing woman earlier in the story, but his grief has reduced him to the same position of dependence on Jesus.)

"Sleep" was a common euphemism for death in antiquity (like our "passed away"), but Jesus' contrast between sleep and death here suggests that he wished his hearers to understand that the child was not truly dead. If Jesus intended his assertion that the girl was merely *asleep* (v. 24) to keep word about her resuscitation from spreading, however, the tactic did not work (v. 26). Long-term professional mourners would recognize the difference (Harris 1986:309), so they seem not to have believed him.

Corpse-uncleanness was the most serious uncleanness anyone could contract, rendering a person unclean for seven days (Num 19:11). Because others could have thought that touching the girl would render him unclean, Jesus showed his exceptional kindness and willingness to get involved by taking the girl's hand when he raised her up.

Astonishing Cures for Disabilities (9:27-34) Matthew here reports some more incidents reflecting Jesus' authority to heal.

Jesus Responds to Faith (9:27-29) See further comment on 20:29-34. The blind men's initial act of faith is approaching Jesus with a plea for mercy (5:7; 20:31; Mk 10:47), recognizing that they are dependent on his kindness rather than on any merit of their own (contrast Greek prayer—comment on Mt 6:7). Their initial faith also includes a recognition of Jesus' identity. Here two blind beggars confess Jesus' messianic identity (*Son of David*) before Peter does (16:16; compare Jn 4:25-26). Yet despite their initial acts of faith, Jesus forces them to clarify that they

---

9:27-34 The tradition behind the healing of the blind men here can make a good claim for authenticity; see Meier 1994:686-90. One particularly cogent argument for pre-Mark

not only seek his help and recognize his identity but also acknowledge his ability to heal this otherwise irreversible disability (Mt 9:28). Jesus refuses to heal without faith; he is not a magician, but one who seeks to glorify his Father (compare 13:58).

Jesus Can Cure Anything (9:30) His ability to cure includes both natural ailments (vv. 27-30) and demonically induced ailments (vv. 32-33), even though we may not always be able to discern the difference apart from divine guidance. Matthew relates these narratives in large measure to encourage us concerning the character and power of the One we serve.

Jesus Avoids Publicity, but Word Spreads Anyway (9:30-33) In regard to the messianic secret, see comment on 8:1-4. Despite Jesus' attempt to preserve some measure of the secret (9:30), perhaps to delay unnecessary hostility (v. 34), word spread and his popularity increased (vv. 31, 33).

Ridicule Is the Only Tactic Left to Jesus' Opponents (9:34) Matthew writes not only to encourage his community that Jesus can meet their needs but also to remind them that the opposition they face is not new; Jesus himself had to face it. Jesus' most religious contemporaries were so sure they were right that they were by now sure that he was wrong, preferring to explain his works as emanating from a source other than God (12:24; Mk 3:22; Jn 7:20; 8:48, 52; 10:20).

When enemies of the Christian message cannot win a debate according to traditional rules of evidence, some of them change the rules, and those who follow them blindly usually assume that they are correct. When the academy became largely anti-Christian, many Christians reacted against academics; meanwhile those who learned of Christianity only from secular academic sources were often misinformed about its character. When possible, a better response than withdrawal would be for Christians to respond reasonably to opposing arguments and maintain that posture despite the opposition, recognizing that many other hearers will listen to the truth (Mt 9:33; Acts 17:32-34).

The Pharisees were hardly antisupernaturalists; they believed mir-

---

tradition is the fact that Mark must explain "Bar Timaeus" (Mk 10:46; Meier 1994:688).

acles could happen. The consensus seems to have been, however, that though some might seek to adduce miracles in support of their claims, scholarly tradition took precedence over miracles (as in *t. Yebamot* 14:6). We ourselves recognize that charlatans and false prophets can work signs and wonders (Mt 24:24). But it is too easy, even for Christians, to use charlatans as an excuse to ignore the real workings of God. One can understand the sentiments of religious people in Jesus' day; after all, they may have reasoned, if God were still doing miracles like those he had done through Elijah and Elisha, surely he would have been doing it through them. They, after all, were sure that they were the ones with correct doctrine. When we become so sure of our theological system that we cannot listen to anyone else no matter how cogent their evidence, we may risk repeating the kind of mistake many of Jesus' contemporaries made.

More Laborers for the Harvest (9:35-38) Matthew adds a summary statement similar to 4:23-25, making clear that the incidents he has reported are merely some prominent examples of Jesus' many works and teachings. At this strategic point, however, we learn that Jesus' mission is not his alone. This section, which introduces Jesus' mission discourse in chapter 10, parallels Jesus with the disciples who must carry on his works (see also, for example, Davies and Allison 1991:411-12; Allison 1993b:138-39). As Jesus perpetuated John's message concerning the kingdom (3:2; 4:17; compare chaps. 5—7), his followers will do the same (10:7). As Jesus demonstrated the kingdom by compassionately healing (9:35; compare chaps. 8—9), his disciples must do the same (10:8). In short, at this point in the Gospel Matthew clarifies the suggestion of 3:11, 16 that much of Jesus' mission is likewise the church's mission. Matthew rearranges material from various sections of his sources in chapter 10 to emphasize not a past, historical mission with little current significance but a historical model for his community, hence for us who recognize all Scripture as relevant (2 Tim 3:16-17; compare S. Brown 1978).

Jesus Devotes Himself to Reaching People Everywhere (9:35) Jesus' ministry required much mobility on his part (see comment on 4:23-25).

Jesus' Motivation Is Compassion (9:36) Jesus knew that people needed what he brought them, both the message of the kingdom and physical healing; he came for our good, not his own (Jn 3:16-7). It is to our own hurt when we do not serve the Lord (Jer 2:13; Hos 7:1, 13; 13:9), and it hurts him because it hurts us. We can approach him with our needs precisely because we know how much he cares for us.

When lacking God-appointed leaders, God's people in the Hebrew Bible often appear as *sheep without a shepherd* (Num 27:17; 1 Kings 22:17; 2 Chron 18:16), inviting the compassionate Lord to shepherd his people himself (Ezek 34:11-16), including feeding them (Ezek 34:2-3; Mt 14:19-20), healing them (Ezek 34:4; Mt 9:35; compare *harassed* in 9:36, literally "torn") and bringing the lost sheep back (Ezek 34:4-6; Mt 18:12-14). This implies that the religious leaders of Israel who purported to be their shepherds had failed to obey God's commission (Ezek 34:2-10; Mt 23). The disciples will carry on Jesus' mission to these sheep (10:6).

We Need More Workers to Complete the Task (9:37) Jewish teachers understood that each of them could handle only so many students, even if the students were still minors (Safrai 1974-1976a:957). The term Jesus uses for *workers* here recurs in 10:10, indicating that the workers Jesus wished to send forth into the harvest were his own disciples. He trains us in our life with him so we can reach the world for him, making other disciples who in turn can carry on the work (28:19). The urgency of harvest was a potent image that sparked similar analogies among other Jewish teachers (compare *m. 'Abot* 2:15, probably concerning study and teaching of Torah).

Those of us involved with evangelism in cities have often seen the harvest falling to the ground and rotting for lack of laborers. For instance, on one evening in two hours of street ministry in the Bronx, New York, sixty-three people provided names and addresses for follow-up after praying to accept Christ as Lord and Savior; on other occasions we sometimes saw forty-four or forty-five people make a similar commitment in two hours in Brooklyn. In other parts of the city, where we were breaking new ground among other cultural groups, we might go for weeks without seeing a conversion. We nevertheless witnessed the work of the Spirit prying open the hearts of elderly people who had never before had a conversation with a Christian about the gospel. In the years following such ministry in traditionally closed groups, the gospel has begun to spread significantly as well. Yet even if we led a hundred people to Christ a day, at the end of a year the new Christians would have numbered fewer than forty thousand—not one-half of one percent of the city itself, and only about one-fifth of one percent of the whole metropolitan area.

The only hope for taking Jesus' message to all people is in Christians' multiplying their labors by training disciples to continue and expand the work (see Coleman 1963). If just one of us could win to Christ a few people a year and train them to do the same, all other factors being equal (which they are not), the results of that seed over two or three decades would be billions of people won to Christ. We each have different gifts and callings, but to the extent that we share our Lord's values and commitment to his cause, we will devote our time, energy, wealth and other resources to the task of reaching this world with the message of the kingdom and practical demonstrations of its power.

Jesus Summons His Laborers to Pray for More Laborers (9:38) Not all Christians will cross major cultural boundaries or become full-time missionaries, but all of us must be mobilized to pray for the world vision he has summoned us to share with him. An excellent resource in this respect is Patrick Johnstone's *Operation World,* which lists every nation of the world, aims to depict accurately the state of the church there, and provides important points for prayer; it ranks among those classic resources of which all missions-minded Christians should avail themselves. After praying through it, Christians may find themselves burdened for specific peoples and parts of the world and perhaps may seek ways to minister to representatives of those peoples in our own land. And who knows—in the end God may call some of us who pray to go, just as in chapter 10 Jesus sends those who shared his burden in prayer in 9:38.

PROCLAIMING THE KINGDOM (10:1-42)

Matthew explains the ethics of the kingdom (Mt 5—7), relationships in the kingdom (13), and the presence (13) and future (23—25) of the kingdom; but he does so to disciples whom he expects to further propagate the message of the kingdom (10). Just as Jesus carries on John's message (3:2; 4:17), so will his disciples carry on his (10:7; 28:19). His followers must carry on his mission of healing (9:35) because the laborers are so few (9:37). Matthew records the words of Jesus in this chapter, like those in the Sermon on the Mount, not for merely historical interest but to encourage fellow disciples in the period between the first and second comings of Jesus.

□ Jesus Commissions His Agents (10:1-4)

This passage carries on the narrative introduction to Jesus' mission discourse that began in 9:35. It describes the disciples he commissioned.

Authorizing Others to Heal (10:1) The number of disciples signifies a mission to Israel. In Jewish texts from Jesus' day, *twelve* often symbolized the twelve tribes of Israel. Although Jesus had many disciples, he apparently selected a core group of twelve (as in Mk 3:16; 1 Cor 15:5) to make a statement similar to that of the Qumran community with its twelve officers (F. Bruce 1969:75; E. Sanders 1985:104): Jesus' disciples were the leaders of the true remnant of God's people (Mt 19:28). Thus many scholars point out that the church built on this foundation of the twelve leaders of Israel's remnant represents the true heir of God's ancient promises.

The text explicitly tells us that Jesus was interested not only in proclaiming the kingdom but also in demonstrating it. In the Bible, God worked miracles most often in times of revival, times when he had raised up servants committed to his cause and full of faith. Often these servants trained others. Elijah trained Elisha and also apparently led a revival of wilderness prophets (see 2 Kings 2:3-18); Samuel also was training a prophetic movement that had not existed when God first began calling him (1 Sam 3:1; 19:20-24). We should be praying for a revival of laborers for the harvest today (Mt 9:38).

Both Jesus' proclamation and practical acts of compassion go beyond what many Christians call ministry today. Our communities are ravaged by demonic forces, violence, injustice and all kinds of human pain, while the church often remains irrelevant except to the few who venture through our doors. To follow Jesus' model of ministry, more Christians must stop simply going to church and learn rather to become the church among our communities in evangelism and ministry to social needs. (If we do not know where to begin on the latter, staff with local social services organizations may be more than happy to provide advice.)

The First Missionaries (10:2-4) For effectiveness in reaching Israel, Jesus naturally limited his disciples to free male Jews; perhaps due to the pool of available disciples, he also seems to have selected mainly Galileans. We know the occupations of roughly half of his disciples; of these, all were middle-income professions in which less than 10 percent of Jewish Palestine's population engaged (fishermen and tax gatherers), perhaps to give emphasis to socially prominent individuals who were nevertheless unassociated with any religious or social elite. Notably, Jesus did not invite any who were already religious professionals—hence already schooled in particular ideas— into his inner circle.

Despite these common features of the disciples, however, the list indicates some diversity. To include a *tax collector* (who was backed by the elite, v. 3) and possibly a revolutionary (v. 4) in the same band of disciples was noteworthy. Any of us who struggle with whether we are adequate to carry out God's purposes in the world should recall that the first ambassadors Jesus called were wholly inadequate. God uses especially those who will recognize their own inadequacy, for those who suppose their own ability adequate for God's call usually end up depending on it instead of on him.

□ **The Mission of Jesus' Agents (10:5-15)**

Jesus' instructions here show that the disciples would carry on most aspects of his mission (9:35-38). Even if one started from skeptical grounds, there is good evidence to suggest a historical basis for the account of Jesus' sending his disciples. Teachers could train disciples in part by giving them practice, and that Jesus did so best explains the disciples' rapid imitation of his miraculous ministry in the years immediately following the resurrection (compare 2 Cor 12:12). Yet Matthew

---

10:4 That Simon was a "revolutionary" is not absolutely clear. Luke's "Zealot" translates Matthew's and Mark's *Kananaios,* an Aramaic word for "zealous one" spelled in Greek letters (most scholars, e.g., Cullmann 1956b:15; F. Bruce 1972b:93). But whereas *Zealot* could mean a particular kind of "revolutionary" to writers after the first Jewish revolt (66-70), it is unclear that the term was usually limited to this sense in Jesus' day (Horsley and Hanson 1985). Even as one "zealous for the law," however, his apparently peaceable coexistence

provides these instructions not merely as a matter of historical interest—had his interest been merely historical he would not have rearranged the material in this section so thoroughly to be relevant to his readers—but as a living message to his own audience.

Thus he includes some of Jesus' teachings not strictly relevant to the first mission but which his audience would recognize as particularly relevant in their own day, including prosecution in synagogue and pagan courts (10:17-18; see F. Bruce 1972a:68; Morosco 1979; pace Schweitzer 1968:361). Likewise Matthew 11:1, unlike Mark, does not actually report the disciples' mission, because for Matthew the mission must continue in his own generation. Summoning his audience to greater commitment to the Gentile mission, he provides instructions for those who would go forth to evangelize, and in more general ways for the churches that send them.

Jesus Sends His Disciples (10:5) When *Jesus sent out* his disciples, he literally "apostled" them. Thus he provides a relevant model for his appointed agents in subsequent generations (whether they are "apostles" in the narrower sense or not). The language used here for "sending" probably connotes commissioning agents with delegated authority. Ancient Israelite circles also used formal agents or messengers (as in Prov 10:26; 13:17; 26:6); agency eventually became a legal custom so pervasive that both Roman and Jewish law recognized the use of agents, or intermediary marriage brokers, in betrothals (Cohen 1966:295-96).

Agents did not always have high legal status; some were even slaves. Yet they carried delegated authority, acting on the authority of the one who sent them. Thus later teachers commonly remarked that a person's agent is "equivalent to the person himself" (*t. Ta'anit* 3:2; *m. Berakot* 5:5). How one treats Jesus' messengers or heralds therefore represents how one treats Jesus himself (Mt 10:40-42).

Because the agent had to be trustworthy to carry out his mission,

---

with a former tax gatherer remains notable. Both nicknames and double names were fairly common.
10:5 Some later Jewish teachers viewed as agents Moses (*Sipra Behuq.* pq. 13.277.1.13-14), Aaron (*Sipra Sav Mek. DeMiluim* 98.9.6) and the Old Testament prophets (*Mek. Pisḥa* 1.87).

teachers sometimes debated the character the pious should require of such agents (*m. Demai* 4:5; *t. Demai* 2:20). This also implies, of course, that an agent's authority was entirely limited to the scope of his commission and the faithfulness with which he carried it out. The fact that Jesus authorizes us to do acts of compassion in his name (Mt 9:36) does not authorize us to use his power to get whatever we want (4:3).

Jesus' agents were not like just any legal agents: in biblical history, God's agents were the prophets. The connections in this text between Jesus' commissioned messengers and prophets should not be over-looked (10:41; compare Boring 1982:89).

To Israel Alone (10:5-6) This limitation fits the historic priority of Israel in salvation history (compare Rom 1:16; 2:9-10; 15:8-9), was practical (these disciples were not yet equipped to cross cultural boundaries) and would have undoubtedly not been objectionable to the first disciples themselves (compare Acts 10:28). Jesus did see a future hope for the Gentiles in the Scriptures (see comment on 8:11-12), but he limited his own mission primarily to Israel. In this text, however, Jesus' orders may address geography more than ethnicity (NIV mistranslates "way of Gentiles" as *among the Gentiles*); Jesus merely prohibits taking any of the roads leading to Hellenistic cities in Palestine (Manson 1979:179). Since Samaria and Gentile territories surrounded Galilee, Jesus' orders de facto limited his disciples' mission geographically, restricting their activity to Galilee (see Gundry 1982:185).

In contrast to other commandments in this chapter, however, Matthew indicates that Jesus later revokes this limitation (24:14; 28:19-20), specifically clarifying that this one command was a temporary measure during his earthly ministry. Indeed, by highlighting that the gospel's first recipients are Jewish, hence that even Jewish people may reject the kingdom and be treated as Gentiles (10:14-15), this limitation implies a supraethnic view of the kingdom that ultimately necessitates the Gentile mission.

10:6 Jesus' concern for the *lost sheep of Israel* (compare 9:36; 15:24) echoes the biblical prophets' complaint against Israel's irresponsible shepherds who allowed the sheep to go astray (Jer 50:6; Ezek 34:5); Jesus may have also recalled the price God would pay through him to restore the "lost sheep" (Is 53:6). Jewish people often thought that ten of the twelve

Good News About God's Impending Kingdom (10:7) That this good news about the kingdom remains the church's message (Acts 8:12; 20:24-25; 28:31) is clear not only from the fact that Matthew nowhere revokes it but also from the roughly parallel formulation in his Gospel's conclusion: as you go (not the imperative go as in the NIV rendering of 28:19) is a participle in both instances (10:7 and 28:19). We proclaim Jesus' lordship: he has all authority in the universe (28:18; Dan 7:13-14) and appears alongside the Father and the Spirit (28:19). To make disciples for this King is to proclaim the good news that God's future reign is already active in this age (compare 28:20).

Signs Bring Attention to the Message (10:8) "The disciples' mission (vv. 7-8) replicates and extends the mission of Jesus in preaching the coming of God's kingdom and in healing the sick (see 4:23)" (Harrington 1982:45). Matthew emphasizes the continuity between Jesus' mission and that of the disciples precisely because the model of ministry God had exemplified in Jesus remains important for Jesus' followers (see more fully Wimber with Spring 1986:113-15; Keener 1996:85-89).

Insofar as possible, we should learn to demonstrate Jesus' rule the way Jesus did. Although hardhearted people may never be satisfied with signs (15:37—16:1; compare Jn 11:47-48; 12:10-11; Acts 4:16-17), signs can draw other people's attention to the gospel (Mt 11:3-6, 21, 23; see also Jn 2:11; Acts 4:29-30; 9:35, 42). If such ministry is more difficult in our rationalistic culture, it may be for that reason all the more important. Yet some parts of today's church that are open to miracles unfortunately have missed another part of Jesus' teaching on faith and mission: God's messengers must live simply (10:8-12).

Jesus' Agents Live Simply (10:8-10) Cynic philosophers and many peasants had only one cloak. More relevant here, some Palestinian Jews known as Essenes showed their devotion to God by a simple lifestyle, especially those who lived in the wilderness (1QS 1.11-13; 6.22-23; Jos. *Ant.* 18.20; *War* 2.122). Josephus also indicates that Essenes did not take

---

tribes were lost and would be restored only in the end time (Jeremias 1971:235; E. Sanders 1985:96-97).

10:8 In one traditional Jewish proverb God commissioned Torah teachers to offer Torah freely as he did (Dalman 1929:226); some early Jewish teachers also prohibited accepting pay for teaching (Jeremias 1969:112; Gundry 1982:187).

provisions when they traveled; they expected hospitality from fellow Essenes in every city (*War* 2.124-25).

Yet perhaps most relevant is the model of Israel's ancient prophets in times of national apostasy (for example, 1 Kings 18:13). One may recall Elisha's unwillingness to accept Naaman's gifts, preferring to allow the Aramean God-fearer to remain wholly indebted to Israel's God; his servant Gehazi, however, determined to profit from Naaman and suffered for it (2 Kings 5:20-27). Elisha reminded Gehazi that the current time of spiritual crisis rendered the acquisition of material possessions a vain pursuit (2 Kings 5:26). In contrast to Elisha, many Western Christians waste their income on worldly pursuits rather than committing all their resources to the kingdom.

On long trips, one typically brought both a change of clothes and money in a bag tied to one's belt or fastened around one's neck (Stambaugh and Balch 1986:38); Jesus here forbids the normal basic apparatus for travel. By prohibiting a *bag* (Mt 10:10; Mk 6:8) Jesus forbids begging, the survival method of the otherwise almost equally simple Cynics (Meeks 1986:107). Mark allows at least staff (for self-protection) and sandals, but Matthew's demand for simplicity is still more radical, prohibiting even these. This is not a matter of asceticism but of priorities, as in 6:19-34. These prohibitions would distinguish the disciples from other kinds of wandering preachers (like the Cynics in the Greek world) "whose questionable reputation they did not want to share" (Liefeld 1967:260; see also p. 247).

Paul's examples of apostleship in 1 Corinthians 4:9-13 and 2 Cor 4:8-12; 6:3-10; 11:24-33 (presented like philosophers' lists of sufferings) show the demands of a true apostolic call. Another early church document warns that if a prophet wants to stay more than three days or asks for money, he is a false prophet (*Did.* 11:5; compare 2 Cor 11:7-15); Matthew may have even had such false teachers in mind as he dictated this warning (Gundry 1982:186).

Although Christ does not send all Christians the same way he sent these disciples, their obedience to their calling challenges us to consider

---

10:15 The prophets had employed *Sodom* as the epitome of evil that merited judgment (Is 13:19; Jer 50:40; Zeph 2:9) and regularly applied the image to Israel (Deut 32:32; Is 1:10; 3:9; Jer 23:14; Lam 4:6; Ezek 16:46-49). Sodom's rejection of angelic messengers (Gen 19)

what we can sacrifice for the work of God's kingdom. Missionaries today will not all follow these specifications exactly (just as Mark apparently toned down Q's instructions for his own community); hospitality is not as dependable in most cultures as it was in first-century Jewish Palestine. Nevertheless, the message of this text summons us to radically value our mission above all possessions and to live as simply as necessary to devote our resources to evangelism.

Those who strive to "witness" to their neighbors by demonstrating that Christ can "bless" them with abundant possessions may unwittingly witness for a false gospel, reinforcing the same materialistic goals that drive many young men in ghettos to sell drugs and many politicians to sell their souls. Non-Christians often have the spiritual sense to recognize what much of the church ignores: tacking Jesus' name onto worldly values does not sanctify those values, it just profanes Jesus' name.

God Supplies for the Mission (10:10-11) The disciples can travel light because they trust God to supply their needs where they minister. Ancient Mediterranean peoples, especially Jewish people, emphasized hospitality (as in Cicero *De Officiis* 2.18.64; Ps-Phocyl. 24; *Test. Job* 10:1-4). Because strangers could abuse this system, however, Jewish people outside Palestine depended heavily on letters of recommendation showing that the traveler was of good reputation. Jesus' messengers had better backing than a letter of recommendation, however; the authority of Jesus himself stood behind them (10:40-42; compare 2 Cor 3:1-6).

Responsibility and the Message (10:12-15) The hearers would be judged by whether they embraced Christ's messengers. The missionaries were to use one home as their base of operations for evangelizing the community (10:11-12; compare Mk 6:10; Lk 10:7). They would find the home first by inquiring regarding who might hear their message (Mt 10:11), then by finding out if the household welcomed them to stay there (vv. 12-13). Greetings constituted an essential aspect of social etiquette in Mediterranean antiquity, and social convention dictated particular rules for how to greet persons of varying rank (23:7). But Jewish people also viewed their greetings as "wish-prayers": *Shalom*

---

merited less damnation than Jesus' contemporaries' rejection of him (compare Mt 12:6, 41-42; 23:35-36).

(*šālôm*), "peace," meant "May it be well with you." Just as a curse undeserved will not take effect (Prov 26:2), Jesus declares that the disciples' blessings will be efficacious only if they prove appropriate.

Those who received the agents of Christ ultimately received Christ himself (Mt 10:40-41), even if the only hospitality they had available to offer was a cup of water (v. 42). But those who rejected Christ's agents were to be treated like spiritual pagans (v. 14). Just as Jewish people returning to the Holy Land might shake the dust of Gentile lands from their feet, so Jesus' disciples were to treat those who rejected their message as unholy (Acts 13:51). God would treat these nations not merely like Gentiles in general, but worse than Sodom and Gomorrah (Mt 10:15), for they were rejecting a greater opportunity for repentance than Sodom had (11:23-24).

☐ Persecution Is Promised (10:16-23)

Matthew's inclusion of material concerning persecution (compare Mk 13:9-13) in his discourse on the kingdom mission indicates his view that persecution and proclamation are inseparable (see likewise Acts or Paul's letters, such as Paul's defense of his apostleship in 2 Cor 11:23-33). True ministry involves suffering, especially if it is a frontline ministry to nonbelievers; I have been beaten and threatened more than once for ministry on the streets. Yet as Jesus reminds us in the next section, the worst our opponents can do to us is kill us, and we will die anyway with or without their persecution (Mt 10:24-33). Because persecution is a guarantee for a true disciple (2 Tim 3:12), we may question the strength of our witness if we are not experiencing any (compare, for example, Mt 5:11-12; Acts 5:41; 14:22; Gal 5:11; 1 Thess 3:3; Rev 1:9—though these are most applicable where the gospel seriously violates long-standing cultural traditions).

Opposition and Empowerment (10:16-20) Jesus sends his disciples (v. 16), persecution becomes an opportunity for testimony (v. 18), and the Spirit of prophecy will provide the words (v. 20). Once the church

---

10:16 While Jewish texts contain similar statements in which sheep represent Israel or the pious among them (*1 Enoch* 90.6-17; Vermes 1993:89), Jesus drives home the point still

faced persecution but possessed Jesus' power; now the church possesses more of the world's power but less of Jesus (compare Thurman 1981:11-12).

Jesus' Followers Are Powerless in Their Own Strength (10:16) Sheep, like Israel of old (v. 6; compare 9:36), were defenseless against such predators as wolves (Sirach 13:17). Christians should therefore avoid *unnecessarily* provoking their opponents *(shrewd)* while remaining "guileless" (NIV *innocent*).

Physical Suffering and Shame for Jesus' Sake (10:17) The hostility of synagogue officials (compare Jn 16:2) would extend as far as scourging (Mt 10:17; 23:34), recalling the more deadly scourging that the Lord himself would undergo (27:26). Local councils probably consisted of town elders, with special privileges for local priests. Synagogue scourgings probably resembled in some respects the custom we know from later sources: a strap of calf leather with interwoven thongs, brought against the condemned person's back twenty-six times and the breast thirteen times (*m. Makkot* 3:10-12).

God Will Empower the Disciples to Speak Before Rulers (10:18-20) That this passage speaks of Roman governors in the plural (Judea had only one governor) indicates that Matthew again points beyond the immediate mission of the Twelve to the continuing mission of the church among the nations (28:19). God allows these hearings precisely for a testimony (compare Mk 13:10-11), and God will empower the disciples by the Holy Spirit of prophecy (compare Rev 19:10; see Keener 1997). Thus despite the ancient aristocracy's valuing of rhetorical skills, disciples need not be anxious about what they will say (see also Lk 12:11-12; 21:13-15; Jn 16:1-11).

Divided Families (10:21-22) Jesus promises opposition so severe that it will divide even families. The hatred of *all* (v. 22; Mk 13:12; compare "all nations," Mt 24:9) on account of Jesus' name (5:11-12; Jn 15:19-21) will extend even to those in closest relation to us. The gospel is offensive to those who reject its demands or whose culture or tradition it

---

more graphically: his sheep are actually sent among the predators (Vermes 1993:89).

challenges. Although Judaism considered betrayal to Gentiles a heinous act (*m. Terumot* 8:12), even family members would now betray one another to death (Mt 10:21; compare 10:35; 24:9; Mk 13:9, 12; Lk 21:12, 16). In a culture dominated by honor and shame, in which the opinion of family members was paramount, such a threat demanded an incomparably high allegiance to Christ (Mt 10:37-39).

Opposition Within Israel (10:23) Even in Jewish Palestine, persecution would be so intense that disciples would have no secure refuge until Jesus' return. Persecution would cause disciples to flee (compare 2:13; Acts 14:5-6; 17:14) from one city to another (Mt 10:23; 23:34); this persecution in Israel would not subside fully until the Son of Man's return. Their missionary task and its attendant persecution would not be completed until Jesus' return (Kümmel 1957:61-62); in the end, however, Israel would repent (Mt 23:39), just as the prophets had spoken (for example, Deut 4:30; Jer 31:33; Ezek 37:23; Hos 2:14-23; 11:5-11; 14:1-7; Mal 4:6).

□ **Encouragement for the Persecuted (10:24-33)**
Too often we try to encourage people by hoping that sufferings will not come. Jesus instead warned us to get ready: evangelism is so important that we must be prepared to give our lives for it.

Like Master, like Disciple (10:24-25) Since a disciple was expected to be like a servant, since a disciple could not be greater than the Master and since servants were considered part of the household, whatever accusers could call the head of the household, they would call the servants even more.

Preach Boldly (10:26-27) In view of the impending end-time vindication (Mt 11:19), Jesus' followers should preach boldly, fearing no shame from their peers in this world. Because the flat housetops above the streets (24:17) provided easier hearing than the streets themselves, "shouting from the housetops" (10:27) underlines the boldness with which disciples must make God's message known.

Fear God Alone (10:28) Because God is judge in the end, we should not fear even persecutors who threaten death (vv. 26, 28). Mortals can destroy only one's body, while God can resurrect the body for damnation and destroy the whole person (with eternal torture; compare 3:12; 25:46). The choice is not between courage and fear but has to do with whom we will fear more (Minear 1950:169). Jesus may here recall the Jewish martyr tradition, which exhorted its followers not to fear those who think they can kill, because eternal suffering awaits the soul that disobeys God's command (4 Macc 13:14-15).

God's Care (10:29-31) Jesus assures his disciples that they can trust God's sovereignty in their protection or their death. Sparrows were the cheapest commodity sold in the markets (as food for the poor); an *assarion* was a small coin (one-sixteenth of a denarius, thus equivalent to less than an hour's wage; compare 5:26; Wheaton 1982:792). Yet as worthless as sparrows were to people, God watched over them. Jewish teachers agreed that God was sovereign over each bird's fate (*Pes. Rab Kab.* 11:16; *Gen. Rab.* 79:6; *Eccl. Rab.* 10:8, §1). "How much more" (following a standard line of Jewish reasoning) may we therefore be assured that nothing happens to us when God is "not looking" (Ps 121:4; compare 1 Kings 18:27-29). This teaching fits the biblical perspective of a God sovereign over history, who knows every hair on our heads (compare Acts 27:34; 1 Sam 14:45; 2 Sam 14:11; 1 Kings 1:52).

If we faithfully confess Jesus in our witness to others, including before earthly tribunals (Mt 10:17-20), he will also faithfully confess us before God's tribunal, justifying us before him (compare 12:36-37; Jn 12:42; 1 Tim 6:12-13; Rev 3:5). He will also deny those who deny or are ashamed to testify boldly of him (Mt 10:32-33; Mk 8:38; 2 Tim 2:12); we may all be grateful for his mercy on the repentant (Mt 26:34). Jewish people often spoke of "confessing," that is, proclaiming, God; Jesus thus probably calls for a confession of faith in himself here equivalent to confession of faith in God.

□ Jesus Matters More Than Anything (10:34-39)

The demands of the kingdom are so offensive to a world already convinced of its rightness that they provoke that world's hostility.

Opposition from Unconverted Family Members (10:34-37) Although Jesus values families (5:27-32; 15:4-6; 19:4-9), the division his mission brings is particularly evident in families (compare 10:21; 1 Cor 7:16; of course more people prefer to quote Acts 16:31). Jesus' example demonstrates how this division is accomplished: although we are "harmless" (Mt 10:16; 12:19-20), God's agents proclaim the kingdom uncompromisingly and thus face hostility from others (13:57). Jesus' mission separates us from the values of our society, and society responds with persecution. Jesus selects these specific examples of in-laws (*mother-in-law* and *daughter-in-law*) because young couples generally lived with the man's family

Jesus matters more than the approval or even the civility of our family (10:37). Many viewed honoring one's parents as the highest social obligation (*Ep. Arist.* 228; Jos. *Apion* 2.206; Ps-Phocyl. 8); for many, God alone was worthy of greater honor (Deut 13:6; 33:9; 2 Macc 7:22-23).

Love Jesus More Than Life (10:38-39) We must love Jesus not only more than our families but more than our own lives. For all our talk about low self-esteem these days (and most of us do view ourselves as less than what God has called us to be), the vast majority of people still cling desperately to life (compare Eph 5:29; Epict. *Disc.* 2.22.15-16). But the moment we become Christ's followers, our own lives and wills become forfeit; we die with Christ to sin (that is, to the right to make selfish choices; Rom 6:3-4) and choose a path that could lead any day to our execution for Christ's name (Mt 16:24). Although we may speak glibly today of "our cross" as the need to put up with Aunt Molly or a leaky roof, "taking up the cross" in Jesus' day meant being forced to bear the instrument of one's execution past a jeering mob to the site of one's imminent death as a condemned criminal (see Hengel 1977).

The promise of eternal life should be sufficient motivation for any who genuinely believe Jesus' claims—it doesn't take a math major to recognize that the greatest mortal longevity pales in comparison with eternity—but we sometimes prove less committed than we suppose (26:41). That even the first disciples were not initially prepared for such a demand (26:56) does not mitigate the level of commitment our Lord seeks from us: if we want to be followers of Jesus, we must be ready to *die*. If I value my life in this world more than I value Jesus and the life of the next world, I cannot be his disciple.

10:35-36 Micah 7:6 spoke of Israel's sin before its restoration; some Jewish interpreters thus applied the familial division of this text to the period of messianic woes, the great tribulation that would precede the Messiah's coming (*m. Soṭa* 9:15; *Pes. Rab Kah.* 5:9; see

□ **Embracing Christ's Agents (10:40-42)**

The person who relinquishes the right to his or her own life (10:38-39) becomes a representative of Jesus (10:40-42; compare 18:5; Mk 9:37; Lk 10:16; Jn 13:20), and one must receive a herald or ambassador in the same way one would receive *the one who sent* him (for the principle applied to an apostle, compare 2 Cor 5:20—6:2, 11-13; 7:2-4). Some in Jesus' day seem to have advocated receiving the sages as God's representatives, but for Jesus it was those who became like children—the epitome of dependence and powerlessness in antiquity—who were his representatives (Mt 10:42; 11:25; 18:5-6).

As people treat God's prophet, so they treat the God who sent the prophet (1 Sam 8:7). Matthew repeatedly emphasizes that disciples as Jesus' agents are his righteous ones and prophets, even greater than the prophets of old (Mt 5:11-12; 11:9; 13:17). Disciples were also *little ones* (10:42), the easily oppressed and powerless who could not or would not defend themselves, hence depended solely on God (18:3-6, 10; compare Mk 9:37; 10:14-15).

Receiving Jesus' representatives with *a cup of cold water* (Mt 10:42; Mk 9:41) probably refers to accepting into one's home missionaries who have abandoned their own homes and security to bring Christ's message (Mt 10:11; see also 25:35-40). A cup of cold water might have been all that a peasant could offer, but hospitality given in faith to a prophet who requested it would be rewarded (compare 1 Kings 17:12-16; 2 Kings 4:8-17).

The following narrative may illustrate the point twice: some would not receive a prophet who came in a prophet's name (Mt 11:7-19; compare 10:41); John the Baptist himself had to continue to *receive* Jesus, to embrace his identity in the midst of challenges to his faith (11:3-6).

QUESTIONS AND OPPOSITION (11:1—12:50)

□ **Greater Than a Prophet (11:1-19)**

John was greater than earlier prophets (11:9), for he proclaimed a fuller

---

also Edgar 1958:49) and that Jesus seems to suggest began in his ministry. Some other Jewish writers associated familial division with the final tribulation without explicitly referring to Micah's prophecy (*Jub.* 23:16, 19; compare *1 Enoch* 56:7; 2 Tim 3:2).

message (11:10; 13:17). Yet John struggled with human weaknesses, including misunderstanding and doubt (11:1-6). Aware of our own frailties, we can draw encouragement from the struggles of our biblical predecessors; God uses imperfect vessels even while he is summoning us to greater maturity in him.

The Questions of a Man of God (11:1-6) Many scholars believe that the material in verses 1-15 has a good claim to historical reliability (see Davies and Allison 1991:244; Witherington 1990:42-43, 165; E. Sanders 1993:94). After Matthew rehearses for his own missionary church Jesus' instructions to his first disciples, he moves almost directly to Jesus' own ministry in the cities where disciples had prepared the way (v. 1).

John must contact Jesus through messengers because John is in Herod's prison, soon to face execution for his bold proclamation (14:3-12). Disciples of the kingdom who prepare Jesus' way in power (11:1) need to remember the first one to prepare the way for Jesus (11:10); those who receive Jesus' power (10:7-8) must also bear his cross (10:17-39).

God Does Not Always Act As We Expect (11:1-3) John has already recognized Jesus' identity (3:14); now, in prison, he is undoubtedly discouraged and doubting, like many other men and women of God facing trials that seem greater than their power to endure. Pursued by Jezebel and finding that even the fire at Mount Carmel had not been sufficient to dislodge idolatry from the land, Elijah asked for God to take his life (1 Kings 19:4; compare Mt 17:12-13). Pursued by Saul and frustrated by continual obstacles to God's promises, David nearly committed an act that would have stained the rest of his career, had God not intervened through wise Abigail (1 Sam 25:21-35). Most of his life the only prophet of his generation speaking the truth, torn by the hatred and impending destruction of people he loved, Jeremiah cursed the day of his birth (Jer 20:14-18; compare 15:10). Dismayed by long delays in fulfillment of God's promises to Israel, the inspired psalmist protested his people's humiliation (Ps 89:38-51). All men and women of God are

---

11:4-6 Because these verses are likely authentic, E. P. Sanders thinks the historical Jesus probably did see his miracles in terms of Isaiah 35, hence either that he was fulfilling the

of like passions as we—that reminds us to always trust in God's power rather than our own (Jas 5:16-18).

Jesus' ministry had so far fulfilled none of John's eschatological promises; John had preached that the Coming One would baptize in the Spirit and fire, casting the wicked into a furnace of fire (Mt 3:10-12). It is no wonder that John doubted, and that John's questions arose *when* he heard of Jesus' deeds (11:2-3), not in spite of them. Thus when John asks if he and his disciples should look for *someone else,* this Greek expression is in an emphatic position and the specific term emphasizes "another of a different kind" (Gundry 1982:205). In contrast to the expectations of some of his contemporaries, John's expectations about the Messiah's future role were right; Jesus would baptize in fire, judging the world with justice and freeing the captives. But John did not understand that Jesus had another mission before the coming judgment. Jesus urged him to believe nonetheless.

Many Answers to Our Questions Are Already in the Bible (11:4-5) Jesus might not yet have been baptizing in fire or even in the Spirit, but his signs showed that he was clearly the Spirit-endowed One who would baptize in the Spirit later (3:11, 16). As Jesus performed miracles, he alluded to a passage in the Old Testament, Isaiah 35:5-6, which mentioned some of the same signs he was performing. In so doing he reminded John's disciples that the works he was performing might be less dramatic than a fire baptism, but Isaiah had already offered them as signs of the messianic era (Goppelt 1964:77; Jeremias 1972:116; Borg 1987:165). Besides "seeing" Jesus perform the miracles of Isaiah 35, John's messengers could *hear* the good news Jesus preached to the poor (Mt 11:4-5), fulfilling Isaiah 61:1 (compare Lk 4:18). Jesus knew his mission, and John's doubts did not make him insecure; but he knew that John would recognize the words of Scripture.

Jesus Encourages a Broken Man of God (11:6) This narrative teaches us how hard faith may seem when we are tested for our work for the kingdom (vv. 2-3), but it also demonstrates how Jesus lovingly strengthens his own to complete their task in faith (v. 6). While Jesus is

---

prophets' hopes or that their eschatological promises would soon be fulfilled (1993:168; see also Witherington 1990:44).

in Isaiah (Is 35), he reminds John that God himself will be a stumbling stone to Israel and Judah (Is 8:14-15), but not to those who trust him (Is 8:13).

One could argue that this narrative criticizes John's unbelief. Does not Jesus' response to John's question in verses 4-6 constitute a rebuke? And does not Jesus diminish John's status vis-à-vis that of the disciples in the second half of verse 11?

But an argument that views John negatively misses the whole thrust of the passage. Jesus could confront John's question no more graciously than he does in verses 4-6, quite in contrast with how he addresses his opponents and even wayward disciples (16:23; 23:13-33). Unlike those who had seen much and believed little (11:21-24), John has seen little (vv. 4-5); Jesus pronounces a blessing on him if he will persevere (v. 6). He calls John his promised forerunner (v. 10), Elijah (v. 14); he further chides a generation for not receiving that prophet (vv. 18-19; compare 10:41) and makes John the greatest figure of history so far (11:11)—even if John does not get to hear all the compliments (v. 7). When Jesus announces that disciples of the kingdom are greater than John, he is exalting the disciples, not minimizing John; he uses John for the comparison precisely because he is so significant in God's plan (v. 11).

Matthew recorded John's struggle with doubt, not to condemn John, but to encourage subsequent disciples whose faith would be tested by hardships. *Blessed is the man who does not fall away on account of me* could be translated "How happy will be the one who does not stumble on my account." In view of its serious use in the Gospel tradition (for example, 5:29-30; Mk 9:42-47; compare especially Mt 21:42-44), the language of "stumbling" here suggests that one's response to Jesus determines one's place at the final judgment (Witherington 1990:43-44).

Receiving Prophets (11:7-15) Those who received Jesus' prophets received him (10:41); most of Israel had accepted neither John the prophet nor Jesus (11:16-19) and hence invited greater judgment than wicked cities that had heard less of God's message (11:20-24). After

---

11:8 Jesus contrasts John's wilderness lifestyle favorably with the luxury of a royal court. Although Herod Antipas was only a tetrarch, he might have been the first "king" to come to most of Jesus' Galilean hearers' minds (Theissen 1991:36). Although John's public

encouraging John's faith, Jesus praises John's mission (vv. 7-15). Perhaps he does so only after the messengers' departure (v. 7; Lk 7:24) because it is not for us to know the magnitude of our service until the final day (10:26; 25:21), but in any case Jesus uses the event that has just transpired as an opportunity to provide the crowds with an object lesson about the kingdom (11:11-12).

John's Sacrificial Life Proves He Is God's Servant (11:7-8) In parallel questions, Jesus begins by affirming what John was not. First, he was not a moral weakling, easily blown about by public opinion or human authority (contrast his persecutor in 14:5; compare 21:46; 22:46). People who proved too weak for the test that awaited them were compared to papyrus reeds, easily moved by the wind (1 Kings 14:15; 2 Kings 18:21; 3 Macc 2:22; compare Is 42:3; Mt 12:20). (On the banks of the Jordan, the site of John's baptism, reeds grew as high as five meters.) John was no easily bent reed.

Second, John was no pampered prince or court prophet who might be tempted to prophesy for hire. Some prophets had found a home in royal courts, but only in those few generations when kings were godly enough to welcome their counsel (or when rare kings themselves met the ideal of being prophetically empowered themselves: compare 1 Sam 10:1, 5-6; 2 Sam 23:2-3). In most generations false prophets outnumbered true prophets; even when they claimed to prophesy for Yahweh, they were really the king's prophets (1 Kings 22:22-23). In times when true prophets were severely persecuted, some of them lived in the wilderness, as in the days of Elijah (1 Kings 17:3; 18:13; compare 2 Kings 4:38-44; 6:1-3). John was a prophet in that mold, with nothing to gain from his prophesying except the approval of his God.

The Servant's Message Is What Makes Him Great (11:9-11) Unlike Elijah and unlike the disciples, John had no signs (compare Jn 10:41), but what made him the greatest prophet until that point, even a new Elijah (see comment on Mt 3:4), was that he had the honor of introducing Jesus himself (11:9-10, 13-14). The greatness of John thus implies something about the greatness of Jesus. Because the text Jesus

---

denunciation of Antipas's sin led to his imprisonment (14:3-5), this does not lead Jesus to speak much more guardedly. (Gerd Theissen [1991:28-41] even suggests that *reed* in v. 7 is a backhanded allusion to Antipas.)

cites to prove his case refers to preparing God's way (Mal 3:1), and Jewish tradition usually viewed Elijah as preparing God's rather than the Messiah's way (compare Edgar 1958:48; Manson 1979:69), Jesus dramatically implies his own divine status here (Gundry 1975:214), although his disciples probably would not have dared assume he meant that.

Jewish people usually viewed the era of the prophets as ending with Malachi (see Keener 1991b:77-91); Jesus continues it until John, who becomes the pivotal first voice of the new order when those greater than the prophets (Mt 5:12; 10:41; 13:17; 23:34) will speak. But Jesus' concern here is hardly neat historical divisions to aid students memorizing time lines; instead he may allude to the Jewish recognition that the Law and the Prophets pointed to the coming messianic era (*b. Berakot* 34b; *Sanhedrin* 99a; compare Acts 3:24), which had now confronted them in his own ministry (12:28).

John's role was great because of the greatness of the One he introduced. If disciples of the kingdom have a greater role than John, it is not because we are more devout than he was; it is because we proclaim a fuller message of the kingdom than John could, for we can look back and understand what John did not (see above on 11:2-3): the kingdom is not only future but was present in Jesus (v. 12). Because such greatness is not dependent on us but on the roles God has assigned us, we must do his will humbly, seeking his honor alone. *The least in the kingdom is greater than* John in the sense that anyone in the kingdom has a fuller message than those who spoke beforehand. In another sense of the phrase, *the least in the kingdom* may also be the greatest in the kingdom, because God will evaluate us according to our faithfulness in

---

11:9 If the Baptist sect later provided competition, Jesus' positive evaluation of the Baptist rather than Christian imagination would seem most likely to stand behind the Gospel tradition praising John (compare Witherington 1990:34).

11:11 John Dominic Crossan's suggestion that Jesus denigrates John here (the one *who is least in the kingdom is greater than he;* this is a central argument for Crossan [1991:237-38], who thereby seeks to oppose Jesus to John's apocalyptic message) rests on inadequate understanding of ancient Jewish speech patterns. The editor of Kings allowed superlative praise of two kings to stand (2 Kings 18:5; 23:25); Jesus' contemporaries and successors developed hyperbolic and superlative praise still further. Rabbis called Johanan ben Zakkai "the least" of Hillel's eighty disciples not to demean Johanan but to praise Hillel as a teacher (*ARN* 28, §57B; see Kraeling 1951:139). Further, Jesus' division of time into eras hardly means that John would be excluded from the future kingdom; those before the kingdom nevertheless would participate in it (8:11).

deferring all honor to him rather than to ourselves (18:1-4).

The Kingdom Belongs to Those Who Contend for It (11:12-15)
Compare Luke 16:16. Our roles may be determined by grace, but grace does not erase human responsibility. Many people thought that God's kingdom would come by violent revolution against the Gentile nations, a view that Jesus clearly rejected (Mt 5:5, 9, 41); some think Jesus is rejecting such a program here, censuring revolutionaries or social bandits (for example, Cullmann 1956b:20-21). Others take the more likely approach that Jesus censures those who oppose Jesus, John and the kingdom (for example, Catchpole 1978).

But especially in Luke's form, the text does not read like censure, and it is not clear that Matthew intends the saying in this sense either. This saying may be a wisdom teacher's riddle (Stein 1978:18). Jesus regularly borrowed images from his society and applied them in shocking ways, and thus may speak favorably here of spiritual warriors who were storming their way into God's kingdom now (10:34-35; compare Vermes 1993:140). One second-century Jewish tradition praises those who passionately pursue the law; God counts it as if they had ascended to heaven and taken the law forcibly, which the tradition regards as greater than having taken it peaceably (*Sipre Deut.* 49.2.1).

These were the people actively following Jesus, not simply waiting for the kingdom to come their way. (Scholars frequently object that such language of violence is always used negatively, but Jesus' parables show that he did not hesitate to employ shocking images for the advance of God's reign, such as brutal tyrants, an unexpected thief, unjust judges and perhaps

---

11:12 Jesus' opening words about *the kingdom* and "force" may well be in the middle voice ("the kingdom has been forcing its way forward"; see Hunter 1944:55; Ladd 1974b:71); "violent persons seizing the kingdom," however, must refer, positively or negatively, to human activity in response to God's. For a survey of various views, see Hagner 1993:306-7.
11:13 The debate regarding whether John belonged to the old or new order may owe more to the ambiguities of Greek grammar than to either Matthew's or Luke's peculiar construction of salvation history. Both probably envisioned John as somewhat transitional and viewed the newness of God's kingdom in terms of salvation-historical promise and fulfillment rather than a radical discontinuity with God's past historical acts. One's reading of the rest of the Gospel, rather than grammatical matters, will decide one's reading of this passage: some see here the continuing validity of the law (Barth 1963:64; Vermes 1993:20), others its fulfillment and completion (Meier 1980:123).

a naively benevolent landowner: Mt 18:25, 34; 24:42-43; Lk 18:2; Mk 12:6.) If John is Elijah (Mt 11:14-15; see comment on vv. 9-11), then he introduced the kingdom (Mal 4:5), a time of greater blessing and greater responsibility.

Heads I Win, Tails You Lose (11:16-19) With a sharp parable Jesus pronounces judgment on his generation, which has rejected something greater than the Law and Prophets rejected by many of their ancestors (compare 12:39, 41, 42, 45; 23:29-36).

Jesus Teaches with Graphic Illustrations (11:16-17) Probably he compares his opponents to spoiled children, but this is debated; the parable of complaining children (vv. 16-17) can fit this context (vv. 18-19) in one of two ways. Some interpreters suggest that the children represent Jesus and John, Jesus addressing the generation from the vantage point of joy and John of mourning; yet the generation rejects both witnesses (for example, Wimmer 1982:108; France 1985:196-97). On this reading, the children's complaint is true: Jesus and John approached the generation from two angles, but the other children would not play either game. Jesus scandalously paints the kingdom in terms of children's play. But this assumes an exact analogy that among other things would require two groups of children, one piping and the other mourning, a picture not explicit in this text (Dodd 1961:15-16; Schweizer 1975:264).

Another interpretation is probably more likely. Children in the marketplace complaining that others would not play their games would strike most ancient hearers as spoiled. These spoiled children thus resemble Jesus' opponents, who are dissatisfied no matter what (Dodd 1961:16; Jeremias 1972:160-61). They piped to John and he would not dance; they wailed to Jesus, but he refused to mourn (vv. 17-18). This interpretation makes the analogy between the parable and its application less exact, but makes more sense of the image.

In either case, the striking image of the parable is clear: the generation is committed to refusing the truth, even if fickle in their reasons for doing so (compare Is 29:11-12). The piping refers to weddings, and the dirge

11:16-19 For a defense of the basic authenticity of this section, see Koenig 1985:20-21;

refers especially to women's role in funeral processions. Mourners expected all bystanders to join in funeral processions; rabbis might exempt their students from such duties, but only under special circumstances (*ARN* 4A; 8, §22B). On either reading, the generation rejects both John and Jesus.

The World's Dogmatic Disbelief Is Inconsistent (11:18-19) John came leading disciples to fast over Israel's sin (Mt 9:14; 11:18), but Jesus came celebrating the kingdom like a wedding feast (9:15-17; 11:19). The charge that John the prophet *has a demon* may suggest a familiar spirit, such as those that belonged to magicians (Kraeling 1951:11-12), a capital offense. Likewise, the charge that Jesus was *a glutton and a drunkard* alludes to the "rebellious son" of Deuteronomy 21:20—also a capital offense (see Jeremias 1972:160).

God has different kinds of servants for different missions, but we need all the kinds of servants God sends (Mt 11:18-19). Neither Jesus nor John accumulated earthly resources for earthly pleasure; but Jesus accepted invitations to upscale banquets, while John was a wilderness prophet. Jesus came partly as God's ambassador to initiate relations with sinners (9:10-13), whereas John primarily took the role of biblical prophets in times of persecution (3:7); Jesus was a missionary within the culture, John a critic from outside it. Both models are biblical but suit different situations. When we can influence a culture from within without compromise, we should do so; when the culture becomes so hostile to our Master that we must stand as witnesses outside it, let us do so without regret. Thus Paul had friends who were Asiarchs (Acts 19:31); but a generation later, during widespread persecution from the imperial cult, believers had to "come out from among them" (Rev 18:4). Christians today need more sensitivity to both kinds of prophets; often each kind of prophet also needs to recognize the value of the other's call.

Jesus indicts his generation for the ultimate offense: they have consummated the sins of previous generations by rejecting God's ultimate agent (Mt 23:31-32, 35). Yet Jesus' and John's opponents were like many opponents of God's message today: while claiming intellectual integrity, they merely use whatever argument works against the gospel,

Meier 1994:150.

giving no thought to its consistency with earlier arguments.

True Wisdom Is Vindicated in the Eyes of the Wise (11:19) If some people choose to reject God's message, which he has confirmed by strong evidences, this hardly brings the message into question; it merely brings into question either the sense or the moral honesty of those who reject it. Wisdom's "deeds" (NIV *actions*) here alludes loosely back to Christ's "deeds" (NIV "what Christ was doing") in verse 2 (Meier 1980:124), paving the way for the identification of Christ and Wisdom in verses 28-30 (see also 23:24).

□ Judgment and Rest (11:20-30)

Whereas Jesus pronounces judgment on the arrogant and self-satisfied, including those who thought they had some greater claim on Jesus than others (11:20-24), he embraces the meek, the broken and the little ones, for they are most like him.

Judgment on Unrepentant Cities (11:20-24) Jesus cries out laments against the Jewish cities most exposed to his miracles; none are known to have been particularly hostile to Jesus, but their reception was not close to commensurate with their opportunity. Following the ancient Near Eastern practice of judgment oracles against other nations, prophets like Isaiah (13—23), Jeremiah (46—51), Ezekiel (25—32) and Amos (1:3-2:3) denounced the sins of various nations in succession. Like the biblical prophets, however, Jesus also prophesies woes against those who claim to be God's people (as in Is 22; Jer 2—11; Ezek 24; Amos 2:4—3:8; Mic 1:9-15). Like the king of Babylon in Isaiah 14:14-15, Capernaum thought highly of itself, but Jesus teaches that people's response to himself and his message will determine their standing at the coming judgment (Witherington 1990:167).

This narrative warns that God judges peoples according to the opportunities they have had to respond to his truth. This is not to say that anyone is without some light and therefore escapes punishment, but to say that those who know best—in our day perhaps those who grow up in loving Christian homes—yet reject the truth will be punished most severely (Lk 12:47-48; Rom 2:12-16; 12:19-20; Rev 9:20-21). Those who claim to be God's people are often the most hardhearted hearers of all (see comment on Mt 2:1-12). Tyre, Sidon and Sodom would have repented, but God's people took the signs for granted (compare 2:4-11).

God often judges corporately for corporate sin. Sometimes large groups of people lead others to starve or slaughter opponents in war; those who profit from or approve of the sins of their allies will suffer judgment along with the actual perpetrators of the acts. Sometimes entire cities or nations withhold God's truth from their children, perpetuating a hardness against God for generation after generation. In such cases, judgment may be God's primary means of gaining the people's attention (as in Ex 7:5, 17; 9:14; 10:2; Is 26:9-10; 28:9-13; 29:9-14).

Rest for the Little Ones (11:25-30) Just as Israel was wrongly secure in its status before God vis-à-vis the Gentiles (vv. 20-24), so the *wise* and powerful failed to recognize that God favored the *children*, the meek (vv. 25-30). Jesus summons not the mighty or wise to follow him, but the humble laden with heavy burdens (v. 28; compare 23:4), the *weary*, like Israel in exile, hoping in God alone (Is 40:29-31).

God Favors the Weak, Not the Arrogant (11:25-26) Before the Lord of heaven and earth, human wisdom and power are nothing, so no one can protest if it was the Father's purpose (compare 3:17) to hide these things from the wise (compare 10:26; 13:11; 1 Cor 2:6-10; Job 12:24-25) and reveal them to little children (literally "infants," but applied figuratively in Greek to the helpless in general), the "little ones" (10:42; 18:10; on the revealing, see especially 16:17).

The wise of Jesus' day had careful rules for interpreting the Bible (including many we would now consider wrong); they prided themselves on their knowledge of traditional interpretations and sayings of the wise who had gone before them; they emphasized practical piety. But human tradition is hardly a dependable interpreter of God's Word (15:6-9), and faith built on mere human reason rather than the pure revelation of an unapproachably infinite God is doomed to fail, as the following narrative suggests (12:1-14). Intellectual and spiritual pride defy the fear of God, for we make our own minds and lives, rather than God, the judge, the final arbiter of right and wrong (compare 7:1-5). We should take heed; Jesus' religious contemporaries stressed humility far more than do most of our own (Bonsirven 1964:157-58).

Jesus Alone Reveals the Father (11:27) In contrast to *the wise and learned* (v. 25), Jesus alone is in a position to declare exactly what God is like (v. 27). The Father has given Jesus the sole prerogative of revealing him, so anyone who approaches God a different way will not find him. Although other images (such as of a new Moses) may also be at work, Jesus describes himself here especially in the language of divine Wisdom (Witherington 1990:227; Davies and Allison 1991:296-97). Many Christian scholars suspect that Jesus' identity is a stumbling block even today for many of the colleagues among *the wise and learned* who trust in scholarly tradition more than they fear the Lord.

Jesus Offers Rest for the Broken (11:28-30) Jesus speaks here of a figurative bondage of unprofitable labor under an inadequate understanding of God's law (23:4; Acts 15:10; Gal 5:1; compare Sirach 40:1; *Did.* 6; *1 Clement* 16). Other teachers in Jesus' day and afterward spoke of accepting the "yoke of God's kingdom," or God's rule, by submitting to the yoke of the law rather than merely human rule. Like a good sage, Jesus invites disciples to learn from him. Yet Jesus did not interpret the law, including the law of rest (Mt 12:1-14), the same way his contemporaries did; his *yoke* was lighter. In contrast to his opponents (23:4), Jesus interprets the laws according to their original purpose, to which he is privy (5:17-48; 11:27; 12:8)—for example, interpreting sabbath laws in terms of devotion to God rather than universal rules (12:7) and divorce law in terms of devotion to one's faithful wife rather than a loophole to reject her (19:4-8).

By speaking of God's law as his own, Jesus implicitly claims authority from the Father greater than that of Moses himself (11:27); other Jewish texts would have spoken only of "God's" yoke here (Smith 1951:153), or of the yoke of Torah (Davies and Allison 1991:289). Jesus models his words directly after the invitation of Ben Sira in Sirach 51:23-27, but here it is Wisdom herself who speaks (compare Sirach 24:19-21). Obeying God will bring his people *rest for [their] souls* (Jer 6:16 MT).

They will find Jesus' yoke *light* because he is a Master who will care for them (Mt 11:29). Jesus' yoke is not lighter because he demands less (5:20), but because he bears more of the load with us (23:4). In contrast

---

11:29 The end-time survivors will be the "meek and lowly" who submit to God's decrees (Zeph 3:12 LXX, with the same expression; compare Mt 5:5; Zech 9:9). Moses provides the model of a meek leader who remains firm because he acts under God's authority (Num

to unconcerned religious teachers who prided themselves on their own position, like some religious leaders today (23:4-7, 29), Jesus was going to lay down his life for the sheep (20:25-28).

When as a young Christian I first began to know what Jesus was like, I decided that no one could know what he was like and not fall madly in love with him; my new motive for obedience was not to disappoint the One who loved me as no one else had. When we learn of Jesus (see also Eph 4:20-21), we find the very Lord of the universe to be *humble*, preferring to dwell with the humble, the "little ones." If Jesus is meek, the people in whose lives he rules cannot be proud or self-centered either, for the kingdom belongs to the meek (5:3, 5).

□ Increasing Conflicts (12:1-50)

Matthew's plot, like that of the other Gospels, focuses on conflict. In the context of promises of persecution for disciples engaging in mission (Mt 10), Matthew reveals the hostility that had already begun (9:3, 11, 14, 34) but was now growing.

Conflicting Approaches to the Bible (12:1-14) Matthew writes to disciples who believe their principles of biblical interpretation differ radically from those of the Pharisees (5:20; 9:13), and he has a crucial hermeneutical point to make in this narrative (12:7). He uses two of Mark's sabbath controversy stories to illustrate the conflict between Jesus' rest and the Pharisees' rest (11:28). This conflict over the nature of the sabbath further illustrates two entirely different approaches to the law (5:20); because Jesus is himself the embodiment of divine Wisdom, his yoke brings rest (11:28). These Pharisees illustrate the principle that Jesus was "hidden . . . from the wise and learned" (11:25); may we who fancy ourselves wise choose to learn from the humble.

Some culturally conservative churches today interpret the Bible the way the Pharisees in this passage do, building an ever tighter fence around the strictest interpretation of the law to keep from breaking it. Thus, for example, I have known firsthand of some that misconstrue

---

12:3; compare generosity to enemies in Jos. *Apion* 2.211-13); Paul's depiction of his own meekness and gentleness in terms of those of Christ seems to allude back to this saying of Jesus (2 Cor 10:1).

Scripture to condemn all divorced people, women's wearing slacks to church, music relevant to youth, and anything else that violates their tradition. Conservatives can dishonor God's Word through abuse and neglect just as liberals can dishonor it through neglect and rejection. Jesus instead pursued the point of biblical texts in the situation in which they were written (19:8). The principles of God's Word actually demand far more from us than extrapolated rules: they demand the absolute integrity of our hearts before God, summoning us to devote all our actions and thoughts to his glory (5:17-48). Perhaps some Christians take refuge primarily in legal debates because we lack the courage to pursue a genuine relationship with the Father through faith in Jesus Christ. This narrative illustrates various points about biblical interpretation.

Jesus' Opponents Interpret the Law Narrowly (12:1-2) These Pharisees provide a good example if one wants to extrapolate the letter of the law; what they miss is the law's intention. Moses explicitly forbade work on the sabbath (for example, Ex 31:13-14; 35:2; Ezek 20:20), and gleaning from another's field (normally permissible—Deut 23:25; Ruth 2:2) could certainly be regarded as work, as a form of "reaping" (prohibited in *m. Šabbat* 7:2). Essenes (probably the strictest Jewish sabbath keepers) forbade so much as scooping up drinking water in a vessel (*CD* 11.1-2).

Yet just as Pharisees could disagree among themselves on some details of sabbath law (*t. Šabbat* 16:21-22), a Jewish teacher who rejected Pharisaic tradition could have interpreted the law quite differently from the Pharisees, as Jesus did. Whereas the law forbade preparing food on the sabbath (Ex 16:22-30; 35:3; Jos. *War* 2.147; *CD* 10.9), it certainly did not forbid eating it, and Jewish tradition prohibited fasting on the sabbath (*CD* 11.4-5; *Jub.* 50:12-13). Here Jesus is not a lawbreaker. Rather, that his opponents wish to kill him by the end of the narrative indicates their own unfaithfulness to the law (see comment on 12:14)!

Jesus' Ethics Are More Biblically Sensitive (12:3-8) Because Jesus differed with their tradition, these Pharisees apparently assumed that he differed with Scripture (the way some people today identify Scripture

---

12:4 Because the high priest thought that David had companions with him (1 Sam 21:2-5), his actions indicate the kind of exceptions that both David and the high priest thought

with their tradition, calling even fellow Bible believers "liberals"). As these Pharisees well knew, a challenge to the behavior of the disciples was a challenge to the teacher who was responsible to train them in proper behavior (compare Goodman 1983:79; Daube 1972:4-6). Yet in his honor-dominated culture, Jesus was quite able to respond to their challenges and defeat them at their own game. *Haven't you read . . . ?* (compare 19:4; 21:16, 42; 22:31) is a strong insult against those who claim to be Scripture experts.

Jesus' first example is the story of a breach of the law for David in an emergency—the man of God and his companions were hungry (12:3-4; see 1 Sam 21:1-6). Although Jesus' opponents may have insisted on beginning with an explicit legal text, he appeals instead to inspired narrative—a Bible story—to show how God expected legal statements to be qualified in practice. Jesus thus challenges his opponents' entire method of legal interpretation. When we fail to take into account the nature of many of Jesus' teachings (radical, succinct statements usually unqualified) by comparing them with the narratives (such as Jesus' relative patience with his disciples in not repudiating them), we repeat the mistake of Jesus' opponents (except that Jesus' opponents were more justified in their mistake, since we often treat as law texts that are not even legal statements).

Jesus' second example is the law's explicit allowance for sabbath activity of priests in the temple (Mt 12:5-8; see Num 28:9-10). After making his argument by example, Jesus proceeds with a traditional Jewish "how much more" argument. Others constructed similar arguments; for instance, an early-second-century rabbi contended that saving a human life takes precedence over the sabbath, for even the temple service overrides the sabbath (*t. Šabbat* 15:16). Others reasoned similarly from the biblical fact that the temple service overrode sabbath regulations (compare *m. 'Erubin* 10:11-15). The way ancient lawyers argued for exceptions was by showing that at least one exception was already implicit in the law (Quint. 7.6.5). Yet Jesus ranks not saving a life but his own authority above the temple: if the temple service warrants suspension of the sabbath, how much more

---

appropriate whether or not David was lying (he probably was).

the presence of one greater than the temple (12:6, 41-42). For Jesus as *Son of Man* is *Lord of the Sabbath*. Jesus' self-claim was veiled enough to prevent legal charges of blasphemy but obvious enough to enrage his opponents (see v. 14).

Jesus' third argument to validate his interpretation method is an appeal to the prophets' proclamation: the law's principles take precedence over its rituals (v. 7; compare Hos 6:6). Everyone acknowledged that an emergency need, such as a human life endangered (*CD* 11.16-17), warranted an exception to any ritual; but Jesus makes such exceptions the rule. Not merely human life but human need in general takes precedence over regulations. Kindness in response to others' genuine need—such as disciples' hunger—precedes rules whose purpose is to please the God who values such kindness more highly (compare 9:13). (As a modern example, many Christians today would look with disfavor on another Christian who, having only her tithe money and finding that her neighbors had no food, would use it to feed them.) With this third argument Jesus has appealed to all three sections of the Old Testament, treating them with equal authority: the Law, the Prophets and the Writings. (Later rabbis also liked to produce proofs from all three divisions—for example, *b. 'Aboda Zara* 19b.)

A Healing Vindicates Jesus on the Sabbath (12:9-13) Accounts of the healing of withered or paralyzed hands always suggested great power both in Jewish (1 Kings 13:6; *Test. Simeon* 2:12-13) and pagan (F. Grant 1953:56) texts. Jesus heals partly to attest God's endorsement of his ministry (Mt 9:4-7); would God heal through him on the sabbath if God disapproved of his sabbath ministry?

But before healing the man, Jesus offers another "how much more" argument by analogy. In contrast to the stricter Essenes (*CD* 11.13-14; compare F. Bruce 1969:73), Pharisees and most Jewish people accepted the necessity of rescuing an animal on the Sabbath (compare Theissen 1978:82). Yet *how much more* important is a person than a sheep (see

12:10 Some teachers considered applying medicine to be work justifiable on the sabbath only if a person's life was in danger (*m. Yoma* 8:6). But the teachers themselves found ways to circumvent some of their regulations (*m. Šabbat* 14:4), and many teachers probably permitted medicine if it had been prepared before the sabbath (*t. Šabbat* 12:12) or the act was medically urgent (*m. 'Eduyyot* 2:5; *Šabbat* 22:6), which this act was not (see E. Sanders comment on 6:26)! Jesus concludes with a summary principle: *Therefore it is lawful to do good on the Sabbath* (v. 12).

Violating Religious Custom in Favor of God's Will (12:14) That God's law was not genuinely written in these Pharisees' hearts is clear from their hostile response to Jesus' violation of their tradition (vv. 10, 14). Blatant breaches of sabbath law were punishable by public execution (Ex 31:14; 35:2; Num 15:35), but Rome prohibited its subjects from executing criminals directly. Even the ultra-strict Essenes in practice punished even intentional sabbath infringements only with detention (see E. Sanders 1990:18-19).

Jewish teachers disagreed among themselves to what extent physicians might work on the sabbath if life was not in danger. But Jesus acted as a man of prayer, not a pharmacist, and this time he does not even lay hands on the man, which some might have considered work. Instead he simply orders the man to stretch forth his hand, an act that was not considered work; God alone performs "work" in this scene (v. 13). Even the strict majority Pharisaic school in this period, the Shammaites, would have violated their own standards of ethics to have punished Jesus harshly. Although they prohibited prayer for the sick on the sabbath, they never sought to kill the minority school at the time, Hillelite Pharisees, who permitted such prayer on the sabbath (*t. Šabbat* 16:22; see E. Sanders 1993:268). If these Pharisees are upset—contradicting their own sabbath beliefs—this says more about them than it does about Jesus.

Further, even if these Pharisees are sure that Jesus is wrong, his appeal to Scripture should convince them that his "transgression" is "unintentional." No sect in early Judaism had rules that would have mandated Jesus' death for his sabbath practices. Most would have agreed that plotting to kill someone who disagrees with you is premeditated murder, which the law forbids under penalty of death (Gen 9:5-6; Num 35:29-34; Deut 21:1-9). Thus these Pharisees are so enraged with Jesus that they resort to a heinous and obvious breach of the very law they purport to

---

1990:13 and 1993:208).

12:12 Someone less scrupulous than Jesus could have used this principle to justify almost anything on the sabbath, but it is quite doubtful that Jesus himself would have used it this way; compare the similarly worded *Jubilees* 50:10-11, which clearly supports sabbath observance.

uphold (12:14). In the same vein, one can recollect numerous examples of religious people today who, defending dogmas true or false, display attitudes toward their opponents that hardly commend their faith in the Bible's law of love.

Perhaps the biggest problem with Jesus was that he was growing popular (9:33-34; 12:23-24)—a situation that might allow his teaching to attract some of the Pharisees' own populist base of support. Perhaps they were like some pious ministers today who grow jealous of others' ministries.

These Pharisees undoubtedly felt they had good reason to reject Jesus' claims. If someone were working miracles without God's approval—and how could he have God's approval if he disagreed with God's Word?—then they could only conclude that he was doing supernatural feats as a magician by the devil's power (12:24). Many Christians today defend doctrines or ideas that they insist are scriptural even though they have never seriously examined them in the Scriptures for themselves; they merely pass on what they have learned from others. Unlike those Christians, the Pharisees were at least biblically literate.

The Spirit-Anointed Humble Servant (12:15-21) Rather than contending with the Pharisees further, Jesus *withdrew* (v. 15) and warned those who were beginning to recognize his power not to tell others about it (v. 16). Jesus would not risk extinguishing a wick on the verge of going out, and so far would he go in not breaking a reed (v. 20) that he would offer his cheek to those smiting him with one (27:30; compare Mic 5:1-2). Thus Jesus demonstrated that he preferred not to fight others when it was not necessary (Mt 12:19-20; compare 10:23; Gen 26:14-22). His opponents thought him a youthful upstart, but Jesus knew his identity and his destiny (Mt 12:21). When we recognize our identity and destiny as his followers, we may also be less concerned with what the misinformed think of us.

The quotation from Isaiah 42:1-4 in this passage especially looks forward to the conflict in the following narrative: whereas Jesus' opponents misinterpret his identity, his empowerment by the Spirit demonstrates that he is the chosen one of Isaiah's prophecy (Mt 12:18, 28). Matthew quotes more of the passage than the "Spirit-endowed" or "chosen servant" part, however, to emphasize the meek character of Jesus' first coming (21:5) and especially the final line, which reinforces Matthew's theme of the Gentile mission (2:1-12; 24:14; 28:19): Gentiles will hope in Jesus.

In this passage Matthew reads Jesus as Isaiah's "servant of Yahweh." In context Isaiah 42:1-4 refers to "Israel" (44:1, 21; 49:3), but it is not hard to see how Matthew interprets the text; in contrast to some of his modern critics, Matthew read the whole context (compare Mt 8:17; 20:28). God's servant Israel failed in its mission (Is 42:18-19), so God chose one person within Israel to restore the rest of his people (49:5-7); this one would bear the punishment (compare 40:2) rightly due his people (52:13—53:12). The mission of Isaiah 42 is thus applicable to Jesus.

Translating freely from the Hebrew, Matthew conforms the language of Isaiah 42 to God's praise of his Son in Matthew 3:17 ("my Son, whom I love; with him I am well pleased"). As Matthew pointed out repeatedly earlier in his Gospel (1:1; 2:15, 18; 3:15; 4:1-2), Jesus' mission is not a wholly new event but is rooted in the history of his people. This passage may provide one window into Matthew's method of interpretation, which allowed him to draw the integral connection between Jesus and the history of his people. From this text Matthew reminds his readers that Jesus was not a political or warrior Messiah for the present time; he humbled himself as a suffering servant until the time when he would lead *justice to victory* (12:20).

Which of Us Is for the Devil? (12:22-45) Convinced that Jesus is not God's agent and annoyed by the popular response to him (v. 23; compare 7:28; 8:27; 9:8), the Pharisees resort to the only other possible explanation for his supernatural power over demons (12:22; compare 9:32-34): it comes from the devil himself (12:24). In a lengthy response, Jesus not only refutes their charge but turns it back against them (vv. 25-45). Matthew's portrayal of Jesus here is also significant for our own day in a number of ways.

God's Enemies Challenge the Way God Attests His Servants (12:22-24) Whereas ancient Jewish teachers normally characterized as a prophet or pious man one who could know others' thoughts (as in *t.*

Pisḥa 2:15), Jesus' opponents attribute his knowledge here to the same source to which they attributed his exorcisms.

People often thought magicians performed their acts through the help of spirit agents (compare *PGM* 1.88-89, 164-66, 181-85, 252-53; 2.52-54), hence the charge here is that Jesus was a sorcerer (compare Aune 1987:56). This is no small charge: magic was a capital offense (Meier 1980:134). Unable to deny Jesus' miracles, later Jewish sources continued to charge him with sorcery; these sources also complained that Christians, who were still working miracles well into the second century, were working them by Satan's power (Dalman 1973:37-38; Herford 1966:211-15; Bagatti 1971:95-96).

Those Who Work Against the Devil's Purposes Are Doing God's Work (12:25-30) Jesus presents a world sharply divided into God's kingdom and the devil's kingdom, and indicates through various arguments that one cannot be working for both kingdoms at the same time.

Jesus first asks why the devil would work at cross-purposes with himself (vv. 25-26). Perhaps the devil might permit a few exorcisms to bring fame to a sorcerer and gain ground in the long run; Jesus' widespread expulsion of demons, however, constitutes no minor strategic retreat but a wholesale assault on Satan's kingdom on earth. The necessity of concord or harmony for survival represents common wisdom in ancient society (unfortunately sometimes ignored by Christians today).

Jesus next questions why his opponents single out his ministry of exorcism while approving exorcisms performed by their own disciples (v. 27). Jewish exorcists were common and employed a variety of magical techniques (see comment on 8:17; compare Meier 1980:134-35), quite in contrast to Jesus, whose mere command the demons obeyed in fear (see also Taylor 1935:129).

Third, if Jesus was driving out demons by God's Spirit, this action

---

12:28 Matthew 12:28 par. Luke 11:20, Q material, demonstrates that where Mark depends on an earlier source like Q, Matthew, Luke or both feel free to add appropriate material from the original source. This multiple attestation also favors the authenticity of the passage. If *the kingdom* has not already *come* in some sense in this verse (which is possible; see, e.g., Dodd 1961:28 n. 1; Witherington 1990:202; Meier 1994:413-23), it is at least quite

constituted proof that the time of the kingdom was upon them (12:28). Most Pharisees apparently believed that the prophetic Spirit had been quenched when the last biblical prophets died and that the Spirit would be restored only in the time of the kingdom (Keener 1991b:77-84). Although many Pharisees apparently rejected miracles as proof of truth (Bonsirven 1964:16), Jesus summons them to consider an alternative explanation for his miracles, namely, that the promised time of the Spirit has come. Indeed, the Greek construction here could be rendered "*since* I drive out demons by the Spirit, the kingdom has come on the scene." Matthew rightly interprets "finger of God" (Lk 11:20 and probably Q) as God's *Spirit,* showing that Jesus is the promised harbinger of the Spirit (12:18), the first agent of God's kingdom. This makes good sense: as the climax of history approaches, the forces of God's kingdom and the devil's are arrayed in battle against one another.

Fourth, Jesus had defeated *the strong man,* "binding" him (tying him up) so that he could plunder the possessions in *the strong man's house* (v. 29). That is to say, Jesus invaded Satan's domain and defeated him so he could recapture the human hearts that Satan had enslaved through demon possession or other means. Far from being authorized by the demons' ruler, Jesus had authority over the devil—one spirit that no mere magical incantation could thwart (compare *Test. Sol.* 6:8)! Since Jesus claims a specific act of binding prior to his ministry of exorcism, he probably refers back to his defeat of Satan at the temptation (using language from Is 49:24-25). Jesus is saying that his integrity before God in defeating temptation has given him power over Satan.

In some modern circles, attempts at exorcism dabble in imaginary demons or recite formulas taken out of context from Scripture. Although God honors faith regardless of the formula used, exorcists do not need to say "I bind you" to demons before expelling them; they just need to make sure they are walking in integrity before God (Acts 19:11-20). In establishing the first stage of his kingdom, Jesus already defeated the

imminent (compare E. Sanders 1985:134-36 and 1993:177).
12:29 Although ancient magical texts regularly speak of "binding" or tying up spirits magically so one can rule them, Jesus' parable does not refer to magical binding (on magical exorcism see Tobit 8:1-2; Smith 1978:127; Twelftree 1986:385; in other connections, see Aramaic incantation text 3.2, 7; 5.1-2; 5.3-4; *PGM* 3.99-1004.384-85).

devil, and he has delegated his authority over evil spirits to those who are truly his followers, those who submit to his reign. The final "binding" of Satan awaits his future defeat (compare 13:30; Rev 20:2; Twelftree 1986:391-92); thus it is possible that his binding before the end of the age may have caught him by surprise (see 8:29).

Finally, this list of arguments concludes with Jesus' warning that whoever was not on his side was on the other side (12:30). This saying also reflects common wisdom in both Greek (compare Suet. *Julius* 75) and Jewish (compare Flusser 1988:510-11) life. Jesus allows no would-be disciples to straddle the fence: one either follows him or opposes him, just as one does with the devil.

A Heart Can Become Too Hard (12:31-32) Jewish teachers acknowledged that deliberate sin against God's law ("sin with a high hand" or "defiantly"—see Num 15:30-31; Deut 29:18-20; *CD* 8.8), such as deliberate blasphemy against God, was normally unforgivable (*Jub.* 15:34; 1QS 7.15-17, 22-23). Even such a sin as Peter's denial of Jesus (Mt 26:69-75) clearly does not count in the unforgivable category (28:10, 16-20); the context of blaspheming *against the Spirit* here refers specifically to the sin of the Pharisees, who are on the verge of becoming incapable of repentance. The sign of their hardness of heart is their determination to reject any proof for Jesus' divine mission, to the extent that they even attribute God's attestation of Jesus to the devil.

The equivalent today would be someone who remained so committed to rejecting Christ that she determined to find alternative explanations for any obvious proof (such as miracles) attesting him. Even in what seems to be that case, however, Paul exhorts one of his students and coworkers to remember that we humans cannot judge who has forever crossed that line (1 Tim 1:12-20). Not uncommonly young Christians read about the "unforgivable sin" and fear they have committed it. We therefore must reiterate the point in this context: the sin is unforgivable only because it reflects a heart too hard to repent. Those who desire to repent, troubled by the fear that they may have committed this sin, plainly have not committed it!

Our Words About God's Purposes Reveal Our Character (12:33-37) That one's speech reveals one's heart may represent conventional Jewish wisdom (compare Dalman 1929:227); Jesus here indicates that even the most *careless* words spoken without thought will testify concerning one's character in the judgment day. God does not listen only to what we say during Sunday-morning church services.

In this context Jesus is saying that one expects people like these Pharisees to blaspheme the Holy Spirit because their hearts are so corrupt. Because the Pharisees appeared righteous to most other observers (compare Lk 16:15), Jesus' harsh condemnation of their behavior sounds an even greater warning to those today who reject the truth of Christ yet sit in churches.

Those Who Repent with Less Evidence (12:38-42) Because God has already provided the world with sufficient evidence, he has the right to expect faith from those who have heard the truth. It is important to be ready to respond to people's objections to the faith, but sometimes we must also point out where the challengers ignore evidence already available to them. Jesus had already been providing signs, and his opponents were disputing their validity (vv. 22-24). The demand for a sign may recall Pharaoh's challenge to Moses for a sign (Ex 7:9; Allison 1993b:236).

The whole of Matthew 12:39-45 constitutes Jesus' response to his opponents' charges (*wicked . . . generation* in vv. 39, 45 frames the section). Jesus explains that his generation needs no greater sign that he is from God than his own message.

He first insists that the only sign the sign seekers would be given was the sign that God supplied to the Ninevites: Jonah's restoration after three days on the edge of death (vv. 39-40). One should keep in mind, however, that the Ninevites did not witness Jonah's resuscitation for themselves; indeed, there is no evidence he even recounted it to them (Jon 3:1-4; compare 3 Macc 6:8; Justin *Dial.* 107). The Ninevites experienced the effects of a divine sign they never recognized, and this may be Matthew's point (not clear in Lk 11:29, 32): the Ninevites repented without recognizing a sign, whereas Jesus' opponents were too hardhearted to repent despite the many signs he had been giving them (compare Mt 11:20-24; Jon 1:16; 4:2). All the Ninevites needed was Jonah's preaching of the truth, yet Jesus was greater than Jonah (Mt 12:41; compare v. 6).

Jesus' second example is that *Solomon's wisdom* was enough to prove his divine appointment, and that a distant queen heard and came to him (as some Gentile seekers had done with Jesus—2:1-12; 1 Kings 10:1-13). Yet *one greater than Solomon* was there. The images of the Ninevites and the queen of Sheba condemning Jesus' generation in Israel at the judgment would have horrified Jesus' hearers, many of whom expected Israel's final vindication against the nations on judgment day (compare Amos 5:18).

At least part of the point of the story of the queen of Sheba in context is Solomon's witness to the nations, and God's concern for Gentiles stands at the heart of the book of Jonah as well. By appealing to two repentant Gentiles in the Hebrew Bible, Matthew reemphasizes the Gentile mission: those who know little about Israel's God (like the Ninevites or the queen of Sheba, or the Magi earlier in his Gospel) are often least arrogant, hence most responsive to the gospel.

Jesus' Opponents End Up Worse Than They Started (12:43-45) Matthew specifically places this paragraph within the discussion of *this wicked generation* (vv. 39, 45) and uses it (unlike Luke) to conclude Jesus' response to his opponents. Whatever else the parable might say about exorcism, Jesus' point is what it says to that generation: although Jesus was exorcising the generation, its evil leaders were setting it up to be demonized all the more by rejecting Jesus' reign (compare Jeremias 1972:106; Argyle 1963:99).

If one translates the passage literally, a key sentence may be conditional: the demons will return *if* the house is left empty (Jeremias 1971:154). Were Jesus' opponents accusing him of being in league with Satan through his exorcisms (v. 24)? Jesus here returns the charge: it is they, not he, who are redemonizing their generation, for they leave the house empty in which God, the only true alternative to the devil, should reign (compare 23:38-39).

Jesus' True Family (12:46-50) If you have ever felt like the whole world was against you, you can at least empathize with some of the pain of Jesus' calling: not only the religious leaders (vv. 24, 38) but his

---

12:42 Jesus' contemporaries viewed *the Queen of the South* as a black African (Jos. *Ant.* 2.249; 8.159, 165, 175; *Lives of Prophets* 1.8; J. Scott 1994:536 n. 203), as did Origen and Jerome (Felder 1989:12-13; Snowden 1970:202-3); for further discussion see Felder 1989:22-

own family doubted him. Family ties were paramount (compare clan ties even in Rome—for example, Dupont 1992:106-8), and being perceived as antifamily brought even more reproach then than it does today (see Derrett 1973:39). Yet Jesus followed the practice he had demanded of others (8:21-22; 10:37): the kingdom of God comes first. Obedience to God's will (7:21; 21:31; 26:42) is what makes one Jesus' true brother, sister or mother (25:40; 28:10). When we acknowledge God as our Father, his family becomes our family, and our allegiance to him as Father must come before all earthly allegiances.

From this we learn both the importance of obedience and the futility of depending on other means of access to Jesus. Those who suppose they have some natural claim on the kingdom have no claim on it at all. But those who obey God's will for themselves have an intimate relationship with Jesus and can depend on him the way members of his immediate family can. Perhaps Jesus stresses the priority of spiritual family here because he hopes to be able to count on his disciples too.

PARABLES OF THE SECRET KINGDOM (13:1-52)

Matthew's central discourse section (13:1-52) contains seven or eight parables depicting the present character of the kingdom until the end; his final discourse section contains a roughly equal number of end-time kingdom parables (24:32—25:46). As in Mark, Jesus' parables of the kingdom's present state explain why his kingdom comes first in a hidden way and why Israel's leaders reject him (compare F. Bruce 1972a:69; Ladd 1963). These parables dramatically reinforce that Jesus' first coming was coercive neither militarily nor intellectually (11:25-27); he came as the meek burden bearer (11:28-30), and only the meek could recognize and follow him (11:25, 28).

That the parables address his people's acceptance or rejection of the kingdom message follows from the context: Jesus speaks parables *that same day* that he has confronted Pharisaic opposition (12:24-45) and offered a culturally offensive statement about his family (12:46-50). The parables section closes immediately with an account of Jesus' rejection

---

36; Hansberry 1981:33-58. Both Ethiopian and Arabic (Manson 1979:91) traditions about her claim her for themselves; if Sheba was in South Arabia, it included a mixture of African and Asian elements (Rashidi 1988:22-23).

by his hometown (13:53-58), so that rejection by his own frames his kingdom parables (compare 10:21, 34-37). This likewise implies that true disciples—those who follow the kingdom message—must be prepared to pay the ultimate price for doing so (13:20-22, 44-46).

Because modern readers often misunderstand parables, it is important to provide some brief comments about their character. Most of Jesus' parables were stories designed to illustrate a particular point or points, something like sermon illustrations today (except sometimes without the accompanying sermon that would clarify the illustration!). We should not read too much into parables; often some details of the parables merely are necessary to make a good story. Nevertheless, parables provide one creative way to explain Jesus' central point or points.

□ Setting (13:1-2)

In view of the heavy crowds, Jesus entered into a boat and pushed out slightly from the shore, a technique that had enabled him to speak to large crowds at other times (Lk 5:3). Many natural acoustic settings existed in Galilee, including a cove near Capernaum, that would enable thousands to hear the voice of someone properly positioned (Crisler 1976:134-37).

□ The Sower and the Soils (13:3-23)

Jesus tells the "parable of the sower" (v. 18) in verses 3-9; in verses 18-23 he provides the interpretation, in which only one who "hears the word and understands it" perseveres to eternal life (v. 23). In the intervening section (vv. 10-17) Jesus emphasizes that only his inner circle will understand, because the parables make sense only in the context of Jesus' ministry. Thus prospective disciples have a measure of choice: only those who press into his inner circle, those who persevere to mature discipleship, will prove to be good soil.

13:3 When one compares Jesus' parables with the illustrations of other preachers from the Roman period, most illustrations (including those of later Christians) provide only a relatively distant comparison. Full-fledged story parables are a largely Jewish phenomenon (Young 1989:1).

In the Greek version of the Old Testament, the Greek term *parabolē* ("parable") roughly translates the Hebrew māšal, which includes stories, proverbs, taunt songs and riddles. Parables appear in some apocalyptic literature (*1 Enoch* 1:2-3; 37-71) but were especially

Various Soils Respond to the Seed (13:3-9) Jesus draws from commonplace agricultural conventions to illustrate his kingdom principles, as one might expect from a teacher sensitive to rural Galilean hearers. Whereas the later rabbinic parables often focus on such settings as royal courts (compare 22:2; see comment on Mt 18:23), Jesus most often told stories about agriculture and the daily life of his common hearers (as in 20:1).

Other ancient writers employed the seed image; perhaps most significantly, 4 Ezra declares that just as not all the seeds a farmer sows survive or put down roots, so not all people will persevere to eternal life (4 Ezra 8:41). But whereas the harvest would be completed in the end time (Mt 13:39; 3:12; 21:34; compare 9:37-38), Jesus portrays the present as a time of sowing to prepare for that harvest.

The sower must sow widely to ensure a good harvest. It made more sense, in a field like the one in Jesus' parable, to plow up the ground before sowing; this was a frequent practice in ancient Israel (Is 28:24-25; Jer 4:3; compare Hos 10:11-12; K. White 1964). Later literature, however, repeatedly speaks of plowing after sowing (although some plowed both before and after sowing); farmers who knew their fields apparently felt comfortable sowing first, then plowing the seed into the ground (*Jub.* 11:11; Jeremias 1972:11 and 1966b; see especially P. Payne 1978:128-29, contending that both practices occurred). Because we cannot know the conditions of given hearers' hearts before we preach, Jesus uses the second analogy of sowing before plowing; we must sow as widely as possible and let God bring forth the appropriate fruit (compare the agricultural counsel in Eccl 11:6).

Not all ground will yield good fruit. The path probably represents one of the footpaths running through or around the field (A. Bruce 1979:195). Some of the grain accidentally fell on or beside it, exposing the seed there to hungry birds (compare *Jub.* 11:11). The sower's field in this

common property of the sages (Sirach 1:24; 3:29; 20:20). In rabbinic literature, the *māšal* specifically includes the kind of story parables told by Jesus and later rabbis (D. Stern 1991:9-10; cf. B. Scott 1989:7-11). Because Jesus did not directly influence most later rabbis (pace Jeremias 1972:12), we may assume that both Jesus and these rabbis drew on and adapted standard Palestinian Jewish teaching techniques of their day (Abrahams 1917:106; Johnston 1977:43).

parable also includes some land where the soil is shallow over rock. Palestine includes much land like this; though seed springs up quickly on such soil, which holds its warmth, the seed readily dies because it cannot put down roots (Argyle 1963:101).

The fruitful soil yields enough to make up for the useless soil. Italy and Sicily averaged fivefold or sixfold return on grain sown; irrigated fields in Egypt averaged around a sevenfold yield for wheat (N. Lewis 1983:121-22). The average Palestinian harvest may have yielded seven and a half to ten times the seed sown. Thus harvests yielding thirty to a hundred times the seed invested are extraordinarily abundant (Gen 26:12; *Jub.* 24:15; *Sib. Or.* 3.264-65), and one rarely exceeded one hundredfold (P. Payne 1980:183-84). The fruit from the good soil more than makes up for any seed wasted on the bad soil.

Secrets for Disciples Only (13:10-17) Jesus reveals special truth to his disciples through parables. Jewish teachers used parables as sermon illustrations to explain a point they were teaching (for examples, see Johnston 1977:507). To offer an illustration without stating the point, however, was like presenting a riddle instead (compare *Test. Ab.* 12-13A). By articulating his principles only in parables, Jesus offers riddles whose answer can be fathomed only by those who understand them in the context of his own ministry (for example, events like the Pharisees' rejection—12:24-45) or who patiently press into his inner circle to wait for the interpretation (13:12; compare Irenaeus *Adversus haereses* 2.27.3).

Jesus spoke in parables because the kingdom involved end-time

13:11 This concept of mystery derives from Daniel (2:28; 4:9) and possibly *1 Enoch* (Nock 1964:30; Gibbard 1956:109; Caragounis 1977:126); compare also the Qumran Scrolls dependent on them (see R. Brown 1958-1959 and 1968; E. Ellis 1977:208; Ramirez 1976). The mysteries of Daniel (2:18, 19, 22-23, 27-30, 47) include the mystery of God's coming kingdom (2:44-45).

13:13 Some other teachers similarly instructed disciples only privately in their secrets. Compare especially Qumran's Teacher of Righteousness; the Qumran community believed that God had revealed to its leaders mysteries hidden from other readers of Scripture (e.g., 1QpHab 7.4-5, 13-14; 1QH 2.13-14; 1QS 8.1-2, 12; compare 4 Ezra 14:45-47). Further, whereas parables usually illustrated, even rabbis sometimes used them for secret speech (D. Stern 1991:202).

13:16-17 "Happy are those who see [God's long-awaited blessings on Israel, his Messiah,

"mysteries" (NIV *secrets*, v. 11) now being revealed to those with ears to hear. The disciples were more special than the prophets of old only because they lived in a time when they could receive a greater revelation than the prophets, as Jesus' blessing on them makes clear. The disciples' eyes and ears were blessed (v. 16) because of the greater one among them (v. 17). The rest of the hearers, unable to fathom his message, fulfilled the prophecy of Isaiah about penal blindness: because of Israel's sin, they would be unable to truly *see, hear* and *understand* God's message (vv. 13-15; 15:14; Is 6:9-10; compare Is 29:9-10; Evans 1981). Yet those who did turn to the truth would be "healed" (Mt 13:15); Jesus' physical healings were concrete signs of the spiritual healing of which Isaiah spoke (Mt 8:17; compare Is 6:10; 53:5; Hos 11:3; 14:4).

The disciples alone had pressed close enough to Jesus to understand the rest of what he was giving them. To those who had some revelation, more revelation would be given (Mt 13:11-12). In other words, the disciples alone proved to be good soil (v. 23).

Only Disciples Who Understand Persevere (13:18-23) The only conversions that count in the kingdom are those confirmed by a life of discipleship. Jesus sowed the Word widely, but not all his hearers persevered in discipleship. What was true of the crowds that followed Jesus is also true of the crowds who claim to be his disciples today. Many who have raised their hands in evangelistic crusades or even attended church regularly will be surprised on the day of judgment that Jesus never knew them (7:21-22). Whether the message went in one ear and out the other (13:19), whether someone began the Christian life

etc.]" was a fairly common Jewish beatitude (*Ps. Sol.* 17:44; 18:6-7; Sirach 48:11). But it was also customary to praise one person by blessing another related to that person: for example, "happy is the one who bore so-and-so" is a means of praising so-and-so (Lk 11:27; *Jub.* 25:19; *m. 'Abot* 2:8; *t. Ḥagiga* 2:1; *ARN* 13, §32B; Petr. *Sat.* 94).

13:18 Jewish parables customarily included interpretation (Johnston 1977:561-62, 565-66, 638; D. Stern 1991:24); thus, against some earlier scholars, current scholars increasingly recognize that the interpretations here may be authentic. Jewish parables often included multiple points of comparison (Johnston 1977:601-2; D. Stern 1991:11), allowing for these to be authentic in Jesus' teaching (Johnston 1977:608, 638-39; Witherington 1990:72; Blomberg 1990; pace Jülicher, Jeremias). As here (13:10, 36), disciples regularly asked their rabbis questions (*t. Sanhedrin* 7:10) and sometimes sought a private interpretation after a purposely vague or hostile public statement (*Num. Rab.* 9:48).

eagerly and then abandoned it because it entailed too much hardship or persecution (vv. 20-21), whether one accepted the gospel but then backslid into complacency, seduced by other interests (v. 22), such people prove useless to the kingdom. Yet others will more than make up for the seed invested in them, becoming true disciples of the kingdom and spreading the true message of the kingdom to others (v. 23).

In One Ear and out the Other (13:19) Jewish teachers exhorted students to listen intently and memorize their teachings (for example, *Mek. Pisha* 1.135-36; *Sipre Deut.* 306.19.1-3). Yet many who listened to Jesus would forget the message of his kingdom. Such neglect, Jesus says, is the devil's work. Sometimes in counseling I encounter people who have heard the gospel every week in church yet insist that they do not know how to be saved. Simply hearing the gospel does not guarantee understanding or embracing it.

Shallow Commitment (13:20-21) Matthew warns us that even disciples who spent years with Jesus proved susceptible to such hardship, although their roots were secure enough to return (26:56, 75). I soberly recall that many friends who became followers of Jesus at the same time I did, including some of my witnessing partners, later abandoned the faith. God is less interested in how quickly we run at the beginning of the race than in whether we truly finish it (compare Jn 8:30-47). Some will fall no matter how plainly we preach the truth, but we definitely set people up for failure when we fail to instruct new believers that suffering comes with following Christ (Acts 14:22; 1 Thess 3:3-4).

The World's Distractions (13:22) Some embrace the gospel, but gradually other interests—wealth, security, family and the like—choke it out of first place. Christ's apostles proclaimed that Jesus must hold first place in our lives (see 1 Cor 10:31; Col 3:17). The Bible often warns against the dangers of wealth (as in Mt 6:24; Deut 6:10-12), and Matthew provides some examples of would-be disciples lured away by desire for wealth (Mt 19:21-23; 26:14-16). Even in parts of the world that include many professing Christians, many churches are full of barely committed people who never win a soul to Christ, rarely speak a word on his behalf and accept Christianity as a nice addition to their lives—which are devoted to the same basic goals as their neighbors'. Jesus' kingdom demands suggest that such people may not believe the reality of the gospel enough to stake their lives on it, hence may not prove true disciples of Jesus Christ (compare 3:8-10; Marshall 1974:62-63). One reason we may have so many shallow Christians in some churches today is that many of us have preached a shallow gospel rather than the demands of God's kingdom, and they are (to paraphrase a lament of D. L. Moody) our converts rather than our Lord's.

Daring to Believe the Gospel (13:23) Sometimes daring to believe in opposition to the values around us means believing the gospel even in contrast to the practice of Christianity we see around us! These people dare to make a difference in the world for the name of their Lord Jesus. Jesus already understood what many of us who work for him have yet to learn: in the long run, drawing crowds is less significant for the kingdom than training those who will multiply the work by training others in turn. Perhaps many of us prefer numbers in the short term over spiritual depth because we lack the faith to believe that such depth is essential (compare v. 12); but fifty disciples with spiritual depth will produce greater numbers in the end than a million raised hands without commitment ever could.

We should take careful note, however, of Matthew's description of the fruitful person: the fruitful person is the one who *understands* the message (v. 23). Only those who press close to Jesus, persevering until they understand the real point of his teaching, will prove to be long-term disciples (vv. 10-17; compare Jn 8:31-32; Marshall 1974:62-63).

□ The Future Revelation of Kingdom People (13:24-43)

Just as Matthew presents the purpose for Jesus' opaque teachings (vv. 10-17) in the midst of a parable explaining that not all will receive the gospel and persevere for him (vv. 3-9, 18-23), he now presents the parables of the mustard seed and the yeast (vv. 31-33) in the midst of the parable of the weeds (vv. 24-30, 36-43), with more words about the nature of parables (vv. 34-35). The parable of the weeds (vv. 24-30, 36-40) emphasizes that children of the kingdom must coexist with children of the evil one in this world until their vindication at the end. The parable may also reinforce images of conversion, perseverance and apostasy in the parable of the sower (vv. 3-9, 18-23): especially in places where disciples can blend into the world (v. 22), it is hard to know for sure who will persevere until the final judgment. The glorious kingdom of the future is present in this age only in an obscure and hidden way, except to those with eyes of faith (vv. 31-33).

The Enemy's Weeds (13:24-30) As in verses 3-9, Jesus tells an agricultural story that is relatively realistic. Although the color is local, the central character of the story is not a peasant like many of Jesus' hearers; he is a wealthy landowner (v. 27), whereas the farmer in the parable of the sower could easily have been a tenant farmer, a peasant like many of Jesus' hearers. The main character's authority makes him a clearer analogy for God, as in other Jewish parables (such as *Sipra Behuq.* pq. 3.263.1.8).

"Tares" (KJV) or *weeds* (NIV) here are darnel *(Lolium temulentum)*, a poisonous weed organically related to wheat and difficult to distinguish from wheat in the early stages of its growth (Jeremias 1972:224). (Calling them "tares" may tempt a preacher given to puns to title a sermon on this passage a "tare-ible parable.") Given the occasional feuding of rival farmers (Derrett 1973:43), it is not surprising that Roman law would specifically forbid sowing such poisonous plants in another's field (Hepper et al. 1982:948) or that one who found an abundance of such weeds would suspect an enemy's hand (v. 28).

Despite the workers' willingness to try (v. 28)—workers regularly uprooted weeds before their roots were entangled with those of the wheat (Jeremias 1972:225; Kümmel 1957:134-35)—it would be difficult for them to root out the many tares at this stage (Manson 1979:193; Meier 1980:147). The weeds had grown enough that their roots were already intertwined with those of the wheat but not far enough that it would be easy to distinguish them from the wheat; uprooting thus might endanger the wheat (v. 29).

After the wheat and darnel were grown, they were easily distinguished, and reapers could gather the darnel, which did have one use: given the scarcity of fuel, it would be burned (v. 30; Jeremias 1972:225; A. Bruce 1979:200). Wheat was normally gathered and bound in sheaves, then transported, probably on donkeys, to the village (or in this case the large estate's own) threshing floor (N. Lewis 1983:123), then stored.

13:24 Jesus also introduces the parable with a standard means of comparison; *the kingdom . . . is like* reflects standard Jewish idiom for "it is this way with the kingdom," rather than

The Hidden Kingdom of the Present (13:31-35) Jesus insists that the glorious anticipated kingdom of God is also present in a hidden way in his ministry and that of his followers. These parables most clearly declare that God's kingdom has arrived in some sense in Jesus' ministry, in a hidden and anticipatory way. Far from baptizing the wicked in fire and overthrowing the nations at his first coming, Jesus came as a meek servant (12:18-20), wandering around Galilee with a group of obscure disciples and healing some sick people.

In a world characterized by political turmoil and filled with wandering teachers and magicians, Jesus' initial arrival as a politically inconspicuous servant had rendered his mission as opaque as his parables, except to people of faith. We Christians sound foolish to those outside Jesus' circle when we speak of a final judgment and living for a future kingdom; what does that have to do with the troubles of daily life in the present? But those who have pressed into Jesus' circle today, like those who did so two thousand years ago, know who Jesus really is. Despite the magnitude of the task before us, we dare not despise the "smallness" of our own works, for God's entire program long ago came hidden in a small package.

The Kingdom Is like a Mustard Seed (13:31-32) Despite some dispute today over which plant Jesus intended, the mustard seed had become proverbial for small size (17:20; *m. Niddah* 5:2; *Toharot* 8:8). Although not literally the smallest of seeds, and yielding a shrub rather than a *tree* in the technical botanical sense in English, the mustard plant hyperbolically conveyed Jesus' point (the inconspicuous becomes mighty) better than any other. (It commonly reaches eight to ten feet around the Lake of Galilee.)

The Power of a Little Bit of Leaven (13:33) Jewish writers used *yeast* in a variety of symbolic ways, but Jesus stresses here the factor all had in common: its ultimately pervasive character. One leavens unleavened meal until the finished product is thoroughly leavened. The amount of flour involved here represents roughly fifty pounds, providing enough bread for over one hundred people. A housewife would not normally fix so much meal and could not knead more than this; the unnatural

---

implying that the kingdom is equivalent to the landowner (*t. Sukka* 2:6; *Sipre Num.* 84.1.1; *Sipre Deut.* 3.1.1).

magnitude of the illustration probably suggests that the kingdom far exceeds daily examples to which it may be compared (so Jeremias 1972:147). That she "hid" (NIV *mixed* obscures this point) the yeast in the dough also exceeds the comparison and reinforces the image of the hiddenness of the kingdom in this age.

Jesus Tells Parables to Reveal God's Long-Hidden Mysteries (13:34-35) Although the parables were riddles to outsiders, they conveyed God's hidden revelation to his followers (compare 13:10-17; 1 Cor 2:7-10; Col 2:2-3). As in the central section of the parable of the sower (Mt 13:10-17), Jesus justifies this principle from Scripture.

The Coming Separation (13:36-43) Jesus explains that God tolerates the wicked in the present for the sake of his elect, but will publicly distinguish between the two in the day when the secrets of the kingdom are revealed. That will be the end of present ambiguities! The landowner avoids uprooting the young darnel, which still looks like wheat, because he values the wheat; in the same way, God endures the wicked in the present to provide all those who will receive him time to become his followers (Rom 9:22-24; 2 Pet 3:9, 15).

Jesus observed these principles when he embraced sinners at table fellowship and denounced the Pharisees; but the principle offers abundant applications for Jesus' followers as well. Jesus' primary point is the coexistence of kingdom people with the world's people in this age. Though the context also suggests some application to the church (Mt 13:19-23, 47-50), the point here is not that we should abandon efforts to keep the church pure (18:15-20), although that agenda could be easily carried too far (18:7-14, 21-35). The point is that the kingdom remains obscure in the present world and only the final day will bring God's true children into their vindicated glory and banish the wicked from among them (Ladd 1974b:97).

□ **Those Who Know the Kingdom's Value (13:44-52)**
The kingdom might be hidden to the world (vv. 24-43, 47-50) like a

---

13:38-39 Jesus' portrayal of the final judgment is graphic and contains numerous images familiar from contemporary Judaism and early Christianity. For example, a later writer depicts the end time as a harvest when the seed of the evil ones and of the good ones is

hidden treasure or a special pearl that only a merchant searching for it would find (vv. 44-46; compare 6:20), but a few people would recognize its value and live accordingly. Such people would relinquish everything they had to obtain it (13:44-46; compare 6:19-24; 19:21).

Having made this point, Jesus returns to his earlier theme (13:36-43) about only the final time distinguishing the *righteous* from the *wicked* (vv. 47-50), reminding his hearers that a single sacrifice for the kingdom may be insufficient: "It's not over till it's over." Jesus then returns to his theme of the kingdom's value: teachers of the kingdom are like well-to-do householders with new treasure, the kingdom (vv. 51-52). Just as each of the previous parable sections (vv. 3-23; vv. 24-43) contained a central section essential to its interpretation (vv. 10-17; vv. 31-35), so verses 47-50 provide a warning that many will profess to be true disciples but that only the end will reveal whose commitment has been adequate (vv. 44-46, 50-52). This warning may reiterate a recurrent theme of the chapter: the uncertainty of the identity of those who will persevere to salvation (vv. 19-23, 37-43).

The Kingdom Costs True Disciples Everything (13:44-46) True, the kingdom is available to us only by grace through faith; but genuine faith means genuinely embracing and yielding to God's reign, not simply acknowledging it and then passing it by as if it did not exist. The kingdom is a treasure, and those who really believe it will sacrifice everything else in their lives for its agendas (compare Ladd 1974b:99; Fenton 1977:227; Gundry 1982:276). Professed Christians who desire worldly wealth and status but are far less consumed with the furtherance of God's kingdom must reconsider the true state of their souls. When we preach that people who simply pray a prayer will automatically be saved from hell regardless of whether they truly commit their lives to Christ in trust that he is saving them from sin (from selfishness, from going their way instead of his), we preach a message other than the one our Lord has taught us.

Treasure Hidden in a Field (13:44) People in Palestine often hid

---

ripe for harvest (*2 Baruch* 70:2).

13:43 The shining of *the righteous* in the future was a motif in Jewish end-time texts (Wisdom 3:7-8; Qumran's commentary on Is 54:11-12; Ps-Philo 26:13; 4 Ezra 7:97).

treasures, and a treasure might remain concealed if the hider died before he could retrieve it. Probably the central character of this parable is a peasant working a wealthy landowner's field who when plowing turns up a strongbox or jar containing coins. Once he buys the field, the field's contents legally belongs to him (compare *m. Baba Batra* 4:8-9), freeing him to later "rediscover" the treasure. Whereas most discovered-treasure stories emphasized the finder's extravagant lifestyle afterward or some compromise between the field's seller and buyer (*Gen. Rab.* 33:1; Jeremias 1972:200), Jesus lays the entire emphasis on the price the man is ready to pay to invest in this treasure far greater than any he already owns. Although this treasure, like the kingdom, is hidden to most of the world, not only does the man recognize that its value outweighs all he has, but (unlike most of us today) he acts accordingly.

A Prosperous Merchant Seeks Pearls (13:44-45) In contrast to the tenant worker, the central figure of this story is a *merchant,* a man with capital, hence of greater means. Ancient reports tell of *pearls* worth tens of millions of dollars in modern currency (Jeremias 1972:199). This merchant, uniquely sensitive to the value of the pearl, wisely invests all he has to purchase it. Other Jewish accounts of finding expensive pearls typically emphasized the finder's piety; thus a Jewish tailor pays an outrageous price for a fish because he needs it to keep the sabbath, yet finds in it a pearl that supplies his needs the rest of his life (*Pes. Rab.* 23:6). Jesus, however, emphasizes only the value of the pearl and the joy of finding it (Jeremias 1972:199).

The Coming Separation (13:47-50) Jesus closed the last parable section (vv. 24-43) with the coming separation, a theme that recurs here. Only the final judgment will reveal who was truly committed to the kingdom and how wise the committed were to invest their lives in it. Fruits often reveal true and false disciples in the present (7:15-23), but some who seem to be genuine today may not persevere to the end, and some who will become believers may not have yet heard the gospel (13:23).

Of at least twenty-four species of fish counted in the Lake of Galilee, many were unclean or inedible, and the net would not discriminate in its catch. Until the final day, Jesus will continue eating with sinners to seek and save the lost (vv. 28-29, 48-50). The kingdom had not consumed the wicked with fire (3:10-12) or come "with signs to be observed" (compare Lk 17:20); it had invaded the world in a hidden way and would remain hidden until the end. But while the parable probably applies primarily to the world, those who apply the parable to the church are not wholly amiss: the same line between righteous and wicked will ultimately divide Jesus' professing disciples (13:20-23).

Revealing the Kingdom's Treasures (13:51-52) True teachers of the kingdom display the kingdom's treasure for all to see. Matthew concludes this central discourse of his Gospel with a final, eighth parable. If Jesus' disciples have truly understood his teaching (v. 51), they are prepared to teach others the value of the kingdom (v. 52). Jesus expects his disciples to build both on the biblical teachings that had come before him and on his gospel of the kingdom; the heavy New Testament dependence on both shows that they did so. Because these disciples understand (v. 51), they prove that they are the good soil, those who pressed in close enough to Jesus to know him (v. 23; compare 13:11-12, 16).

THE REJECTED PROPHET (13:53—17:27)

The theme of this section is not hard to discern: even more than in previous sections, it alternates between opposition and miracles, thus showing the spiritual blindness of those who oppose Jesus. Because Jesus is a rejected prophet (13:53-58), John's martyrdom (14:1-12) foreshadows his own. His miracles reveal his identity to disciples (14:33) and even to Gentiles (15:22), but the elite among his own people trifle over irrelevant matters (15:2) and prove unable to recognize his signs (16:1-4). Yet even the disciples fail to understand fully (14:31; 15:15-16, 33; 16:8-12; 17:20), although Jesus' revelation begins to make his identity clearer to them (16:13—17:13).

In contrast to the continuity of material in this section, its only clear structure is on the level of individual paragraphs, but here it will be divided into three rough segments that may help reveal both the development of the opposition to Jesus and his self-revelation to his followers. In 13:53—14:36 Jesus confronts opposition but performs dramatic miracles. In 15:1-39 he confronts more direct opposition from people of influence but again performs dramatic miracles, even for a Canaanite. In 16:1—17:27 Jesus faces opposition from a united political front (16:1) but grapples especially with revealing himself to his disciples.

□ The Threatened Prophet (13:53—14:36)

Like Moses, Elijah and Jeremiah, Jesus was rejected among his own people (13:53-58); the prophet John's execution thus prefigures his own (14:1-12). But like Moses and Elisha of old, Jesus feeds the multitude (14:13-21) and ultimately reveals himself in an act that characterizes no mere prophet, but God alone (14:22-33); the multitudes continue to seek him for healing (14:34-36).

A Prophet Visits Home (13:53-58) Himself greater than a prophet (5:12; 11:11-14), Jesus would face rejection greater than the prophets had (23:29-36). Like Jeremiah (Jer 1:1; 11:21-23), Jesus faced the rejection of those closest to him through the ties that usually mattered most in his society—geography and blood (Mt 13:53-58; compare 10:21, 35; 12:46-50).

These accounts of breaking traditional ties frame the kingdom parables (12:46—13:58), forcefully illustrating the message of those parables: the kingdom comes in an obscure way like a mustard seed, and only those with the eyes of faith will recognize it. How could anyone believe that God had stepped into history in the person of a boy who had grown up in their own community? Today we may often have the opposite problem: the familiarity of church tradition too easily obscures the reality that the God we confess as having stepped into history came in the flesh as a little boy in a particular time and place. We may also risk missing the character of Jesus of Nazareth.

Knowing much about Jesus without obeying him leads to taking him for granted. One might cite here the saying that familiarity breeds contempt. The people among whom Jesus had grown up were unprepared to embrace his *wisdom and . . . miraculous powers.* Those who know most about Jesus without obeying him risk taking him for granted

13:55 That Joseph found employment in carpentry is historically likely: starting immediately after its destruction in A.D. 6, Antipas began rebuilding the devastated Galilean capital of Sepphoris (compare Jos. *War* 2.68), only four miles from Nazareth (see F. Grant 1959:99;

(v. 54; see also Jn 6:42; 7:15). In a town of probably five hundred or fewer inhabitants (Stanton 1993:112), everyone would have thought they knew Jesus already (compare Lk 13:26-28); indeed, Nazareth was a small town from which even Nazarenes would not expect a great prophet (2:23; compare Jn 1:46). They never expected the kingdom to come in a hidden way or to come as close to them as it did (13:31-33); hence those closest to the kingdom did not recognize it, and it passed them by (compare 2:1-12).

Prophets—both Jesus and his true followers—will be rejected. This principle so permeated the early Christian understanding of Jesus' rejection by the leaders of his people that it figures prominently in the Gospels (13:57; Mk 6:4; compare Lk 4:24; Jn 4:44). "If the world hates you, keep in mind that it hated me first" (Jn 15:18). Jesus' contemporaries already knew and emphasized that prophets were rejected (as in Mt 23:37; Acts 7:52, 58; *CD* 7.17-18; *1 Enoch* 95:7), but never thought to apply concretely in this case what they professed abstractly.

God allows our unbelief to limit his activity. Mark says that Jesus "could not" do a miracle in Nazareth because of the people's unbelief (Mk 6:5), probably meaning that Jesus refused to act as a mere magician but demanded faith (Goppelt 1981:148). Matthew clarifies the wording: Jesus *did not* (would not) act because of their unbelief (13:58). Those who are hostile to God's purposes cannot complain because they do not receive the attestations of his power that appear regularly among those who believe him. We should keep in mind, however, that the issue here is the hostility of antibelief, not a young Christian's struggles with doubt (compare Moule 1965:47); sometimes God does sovereignly act on behalf of his own to develop faith, not just to reward it (compare 17:2-7; 28:5-10, 17; Ex 3:2; Judg 6:12-14).

A Prophet Martyred (14:1-12) The parallels between the missions of John and Jesus have been building toward the climax of this paragraph. John has introduced Jesus, proclaiming the same message that Jesus

Thurman 1981:18). That Jesus himself would have labored as a carpenter (Mk 6:3) is also likely; Jewish fathers sought to equip their sons with a trade (Moore 1971:2:127; Meeks 1986:62), and most trades were learned by apprenticeship (N. Lewis 1983:135).

would (3:2; 4:17). After Jesus promises persecution and speaks of prophets (10:17-42), he praises John in prison as his ally (11:2-19); narratives about those who reject Jesus follow that account (11:20-25; 12:1-14). But nowhere does John's fate prefigure that of Jesus so clearly as here: if Jesus himself proves to be "a prophet without honor" among his people (13:53-58), what is to keep him from the fate of John the Baptist (14:1-12; 17:12)? And if for Jesus, how much more for us who follow him (5:12)?

Herod Antipas's Guilty Conscience (14:1-2) Antipas believes that John has returned *from the dead* in the temporary sense exhibited in some biblical resuscitations (1 Kings 17:21-22; 2 Kings 4:34-36), not the final resurrection, which Jewish people generally understood as a corporate event (Dan 12:2). Although Antipas had executed John, he knew very well that John was a righteous man and feared his influence. The more evil a society becomes, the more likely its members are to kill the righteous whose words or lives reproach its character, even if they recognize that the righteous speak truth.

The Powerful Can Mistake Moral Reproof for Political Pronouncements (14:3-4) Those ensnared in adultery often become blind to common sense, including the warnings of those close to them. Antipas, son of Herod the Great (2:1) and a Samaritan mother, hence Archelaus's full brother (2:22), had functioned as *tetrarch* over Galilee and Perea since about 4 B.C. He had entered into a politically prudent marriage with a Nabatean princess, perhaps seeking to secure further loyalty from Nabatean subjects within his territory of Perea (Kraeling 1951:89).

But when Antipas divorced his first wife to take his brother's wife, he violated not only Jesus' teaching on the moral indissolubility of marriage (5:31-32) but also the Mosaic law concerning incest (Lev 18:16; 20:21). John thus publicly reproached a public example of immorality. But what John viewed in moral terms Antipas undoubtedly saw in political terms as well (compare Jos. *Ant.* 18.118; Kraeling 1951:85,

---

14:2 Although some Jews apparently explained Jewish doctrines to Greeks in terms of reincarnation (Jos. *Ant.* 18.14; compare Plato *Meno* 81B-C), the view was not predominant, and Herod is not thinking in such terms here (John could hardly have been reincarnated and then grown to adulthood again in a few months or even years).

90-91, 143-45). Antipas's plans to divorce his first wife had provoked trouble with her father, the powerful Nabatean king Aretas (on whom see 2 Cor 11:32-33). This trouble ultimately led to war and public humiliation for Antipas (Jos. *Ant.* 18.113-14, 124-25). That many Nabateans in Perea presumably remained loyal to Aretas further extended the political implications of Herod's affair. A prophet harping on the tetrarch's misbehavior was therefore politically dangerous.

Christians today who take a stand against abortion, exploitation of the poor or racism may be taking a moral stand, but in our polarized society many will read such a stand as politically partisan even when we do not intend it in such terms. The major difference at this point is that John's society did not recognize freedom of speech; publicly denouncing a ruler's character was essentially suicidal. Israel had a long-standing tradition exempting prophets from severe punishment for their speech—a rule that only the most vicious rulers broke. Unfortunately for John, Antipas proved to be such a ruler.

God Can Use Various Means to Restrain Evil (14:5) In another case the government might be more sensitive to justice than the masses are (compare 27:24-25), but in this case John's popularity with the people protects him from the power of a populist politician. After John's execution, when King Aretas soundly defeated Antipas in war to avenge the latter's rejection of Aretas's daughter, many people believed that Antipas's loss was divine judgment for the execution of John, which by this point had occurred some years before (Jos. *Ant.* 18.116-19; compare Meier 1992:233).

Antipas Ensnares Himself in Deeper Sin Through Lust and Oaths (14:6-7) Birthday celebrations were a Greek and Roman rather than Jewish custom, which Antipas readily accommodated (compare also *m. 'Aboda Zara* 1:3); his full brother Archelaus had also been known for drunken parties (see Jos. *War* 2.29). According to Josephus's briefer account of John's execution, this scene must have taken place at Herod's fortress Machaerus in Perea, near where John had often preached

---

14:3 The Gospels call him Philip, Josephus by the more general title Herod; but Herod the Great sometimes gave various sons the same name (if they had different mothers) and elsewhere showed a liking for the name Philip. Herod Philip was likely son of Herod the Great and Mariamne II (Hoehner 1972:133-36; pace Anderson 1976:168).

(compare Kraeling 1951:9-10, 92-93). This fortress included a dungeon where John was kept.

Nearly all Jews would have found Herod's lust disgusting: because the girl was the daughter of a woman with whom Antipas was sleeping, desire for her constituted incest (compare Amos 2:7). According to some accounts the girl, Salome, may have been between six and eight years old; more likely she was a virgin of marriageable age (twelve to fourteen), but possibly she was already betrothed or married to Philip the tetrarch (see Hoehner 1972:155-56; Theissen 1991:90-91).

Jewish scholars had devised ways to release people from oaths that would lead to more evil, so no one would have faulted Herod for breaking his promise: life took precedence over oaths. But Antipas is concerned about more than his oath itself. Once Herod has given his oath in front of dinner guests, his "honor" is at stake (compare Esther 1:10-19; Jos. *Ant.* 18.299); here short-range political considerations take precedence over the long-term ones, and Antipas remains captive to what others may think. In this account Matthew graphically illustrates his earlier principles about the dangers of lust, divorce and oaths (5:27-37).

Speaking for Righteousness Can Elicit Enmity in High Places (14:8) Antipas had wronged his brother Philip by taking the man's wife; this was an act of adultery in God's sight (5:31-32) and also qualified as incest under the Mosaic law (Lev 20:21). But Herodias wanted vengeance on John for daring to publicly denounce her sin; John must have known that if Antipas's new wife wanted his death, she would ultimately have more influence with Antipas than he would.

John's Friends and Enemies React to His Martyrdom (14:9-12) Jewish law forbade execution without trial, but the Romans had granted Antipas capital jurisdiction. Freely disregarding Jewish scruples, he granted execution in the least painful Roman style—beheading with a sword (see O'Rourke 1971:174). The delivery of John's head *on a platter* (v. 11) was a grisly conclusion to the feast presupposed by a birthday party (v. 6) and dinner guests (v. 9).

John's disciples, however, risked their own lives to show up and bury John's body in one final act of love (v. 12). With nowhere else to go, these disciples then find Jesus, the One to whom John had borne witness

(3:11-15) and to whom John had sent messengers when in prison (11:2-6). In John's final direct portrayal in the Gospel, then, his martyrdom has sent his remaining disciples to Jesus, the Coming One. May all of us lay such a groundwork that after we are gone those who recall our service may look beyond us to the Lord we proclaimed.

Feeding the Five Thousand (14:13-21) Although Jesus attempted to withdraw to a solitary place (v. 13), he was now too popular to escape notice. This narrative teaches us about the host sponsoring the messianic banquet it foreshadows (5:6; 22:2). In the context of other attempted signs workers in the wilderness in Jesus' day, Jesus' sign in the wilderness involves a clear messianic statement (Witherington 1990:91, 100). But the narrative especially instructs us concerning God's caring provision for his people in this age (6:11; 7:9-10; 15:25-28, 29-39). It also stands in deliberate contrast to the drunken feast of the evil ruler Herod Antipas in 14:6-11 (Lane 1974:227); had we titled the former "Herod's party," we might have titled this passage "God's party."

Some problems require God's direct intervention. The disciples were right to be concerned about the people's hunger but intended to solve the problem in a purely natural way (vv. 15, 17). Our expectations of what God can do often are too small; providing food in the wilderness was technically impossible, but God had used Moses, Elijah and Elisha for feeding miracles. (The present miracle especially resembles one performed by Elisha—2 Kings 4:42-44.)

Feeding multitudes by natural means is, of course, appropriate (as in 2 Kings 6:22); rabbis also delegated to disciples the task of managing an academy's food (for example, *Pes. Rab.* 25:2). But few towns were nearby, and towns were generally small, at most accommodating only a few visitors in towns of a few thousand people. Further, most of the day's bread would be consumed by evening (Mt 14:15). It would have been nearly impossible for roughly ten thousand people (five thousand men plus women and children—v. 21) to fend for themselves in the countryside.

In this light, the disciples' practical objection (v. 17) merely recalls that of Elisha's disciple (2 Kings 4:43): the master's command (Mt 14:16; 2 Kings 4:42; compare 1 Kings 17:16) was impossible. But both Elisha's disciple and Jesus' disciples should have been with their master long enough to expect that what the master said he had power from God to perform. The God of the exodus, who divided waters (Ex 14:21) and provided manna from heaven (Ex 16:14-18), was at work in history again (2 Kings 2:8-14; 4:38-44; Mt 14:13-33).

God often begins with what we have. Jesus often takes what we bring to him and multiplies it (vv. 16-19). When Moses insisted that he needed a sign to take with him, God asked him what was already in his hand and then transformed it (Ex 4:1-3), using what had been merely a shepherd's rod even to part the sea (Ex 14:16). When a widow needed financial help, Elisha asked what she had in her house; she responded that she had only a small amount of oil, so he commanded her to borrow jars into which to pour the oil and then multiplied it until all the jars were full (2 Kings 4:1-7). Although God created the universe from nothing, he normally takes the ordinary things of our lives and transforms them for his honor (see, for example, Judg 6:14; 15:15-19). The narrative does not even report that Jesus prayed for the food to multiply; confident that he represents the Father's will, he merely *gave thanks* (the meaning of the Greek expression that some translations render "blessed"; "blessing" food merely means giving thanks for it), which was the standard Jewish custom before and normally after meals (as in *m. Berakot* 6:5-6; Safrai 1974-1976c:802).

God does miracles only when we need them. This miracle is greater than the manna of the exodus; none of the manna would be left over (Hooker 1983:50). But manna was never left over because it was to be provided every day, whereas this miracle is a rare one. So much was left over that each of the twelve disciples gathered food in his wicker basket (v. 20). The leftovers stress the lavish abundance of God's miraculous power in Christ (compare Theissen 1983:67); many people felt that a good host should provide enough food that some would always be left over (as in Plut. *Table-Talk* 7.4 and *Mor.* 702D-704B).

Yet the gathering of the leftovers (compare 2 Kings 4:7, 44; 7:1-2, 16-20; 1 Kings 17:16; Jn 6:12) teaches us something further. Most moralists condemned wastefulness and emphasized thrift (for example, Juv. *Sat.* 1.58-60; Ps-Phocyl. 138). Jesus trusted that God's provision would always be available when it was needed (compare 16:9-11), but like most moralists he refused to squander what was available. The extra bread, which was more than the amount started with, could be used for other meals.

Everett Cook, a retired Pentecostal minister running a street mission, confronted an associate who had a growth on his nose but refused to see a doctor. "God will heal me," the man insisted.

"If you needed a miracle, God would give you one," Everett retorted, "but right now he's given you a doctor and medical insurance. You need to use what he's given you."

The next time they met the man's growth was much bigger, but the man still insisted, "I am healed." The third time they met the growth had spread further, and finally the man was thinking that perhaps he needed to see a doctor.

God performed a miracle when he created the world and set its laws in motion, and we are often wise to start with natural means when those are available. God performs miracles to meet our genuine needs, but he will not perform them merely to entertain us.

God is not intimidated by the magnitude of our problem. The disciples saw the size of the need and the littleness of the human resources available; Jesus saw the size of the need and the greatness of God's resources available. Often God calls us to do tasks for him that are technically impossible—barring a miracle.

The day before I was going to call my prospective Ph.D. program to say I was not coming because I had no money, God unexpectedly met my need. And in the summer after I finished my Ph.D., I found myself still unable to locate a teaching position for the fall. After much prayer, one night I finally determined the bare minimum I needed to live on and to store my research that year, and I cried out in despair. *Barring a miracle,* I thought, *I will be on the street this year.* Less than twenty-four hours later Rodney Clapp called from InterVarsity Press and offered me a contract to write the *IVP Bible Background Commentary: New Testament* I had proposed—plus an unexpected advance that was, to the dollar, what I'd decided I needed for the year. Undaunted by the magnitude of my need, God was teaching me that he alone has the power to meet my needs.

Lord of the Sea (14:22-33) By providing for the crowds, Jesus showed himself greater than a human magician who could just heal some individuals or turn some stones into bread. At the least, Jesus was a prophet like Moses or Elisha (vv. 13-21; Ex 16:14-18; 2 Kings 4:42-44). But by treading on the sea, Jesus now takes a role that the Hebrew Bible had reserved for God alone (Job 9:8; see also Ps 77:19; Hab 3:15; Davies and Allison 1991:504). Nevertheless, as in an earlier storm scene, Matthew is interested here in teaching us not only Christology but also about the requisite faith for disciples (Mt 8:26). Of all the disciples, Peter alone begins to walk, but Jesus regards even his faith as less than what a disciple should have.

The Setting for the Miracle (14:22-24) From the setting we already see Jesus as a man of prayer (v. 23). Rather than sticking around to reap the political benefits of his miracle, Jesus retires to prayer, which, unlike political advancement, is central to his mission (compare Jn 6:15). We also learn that the fact that disciples face difficult situations does not mean that Jesus is not the One who sent us (Mt 14:22, 24).

Jesus' Coming Should Bring an End to Fear (14:25-27) If the disciples were still struggling against the winds at the fourth watch of the night—the Romans divided the night into four instead of the Jewish three watches—the disciples must have been exhausted. Probably accustomed to awakening around 6:00 a.m., they instead found themselves still trying to cross the lake between 3:00 and 6:00 a.m. We may chide the disciples for accepting the popular notion of ghosts, but the biggest offense here is that they still underestimate Jesus' power. It has not occurred to them that he could know their plight, walk on water to come to them or catch up to them in a storm! To their credit, however, the fear issue seems to be solved once they recognize that their teacher is with them. They knew him well enough to know that if he was there, he would bring them through their storm.

Jesus Wants Us to Imitate His Works (14:28-31) Although the proposal that Peter walk on water is first Peter's idea (v. 28), Jesus' response indicates that he approves of it (v. 29). Peter is gently reproved not for presumptuously stepping from the boat but for presumptuously

14:25 The same passage in Job had spoken of God "passing by" (Job 9:11), as in Matthew's source (Mk 6:48). Commentators also often recognize Jesus' deity in his *It is I* in Matthew 14:27, which literally declares, "I am" (Argyle 1963:115; Lane 1974:236-37). Further, as W. D. Davies and Dale Allison (1991:503) point out, Jewish tradition acknowledges only God as deliverer at sea.

doubting in the very presence of Jesus (v. 31; compare 6:30; 8:26; 16:8; 17:20; see Manson 1979:206; France 1985:239). Disciples were expected to imitate their masters, and Jesus is training disciples who will not simply regurgitate his oral teachings but will have the faith to demonstrate his authority in practice as well.

Once Jesus has given the command, walking on water is simply a matter of trusting the One who has performed so many miracles in the past. Peter's failure comes as he observes the wind (14:30), looking to his situation rather than to God's power that is sustaining him. Still, Peter knows by this point whom to cry out to; his feeble attempt to walk on water is no more feeble than our first attempts to walk on land. Our faith may be more infantile than Peter's if we have never even tried to step out in obedience to Jesus' commands or direction for our lives; many of us have less practice walking in faith than two-year-olds have walking physically.

It is important to note that while Jesus is disappointed with Peter's inadequate faith, Peter has acted in greater faith than the other disciples—he is *learning*. Faith cannot be worked up by formulas or emotion, but it grows through various tests as we continue to trust our Lord and he continues to teach us. *Faith grows out of a relationship with the Person of Jesus, and in no other way.*

Jesus Has Authority to Settle Any Crisis (14:32) As soon as they enter the boat, the wind grows still. Stilling storms was a sign of God's authority in the biblical record (see Davies and Allison 1991:509-10). The disciples may recall an earlier occasion on which Jesus simply commanded and the storm died down (8:26); this time, however, the storm acts out of respect for him—apparently without so much as requiring a word on his part.

Jesus' Power Leads the Disciples to Acknowledge His Identity (14:33) Their knowledge will still need to be tested outside the excitement of miracles (16:15), but the disciples nevertheless offer the correct response. When we recognize Jesus' works, thereby learning

---

14:26 The *lilin,* or night spirits, were thought extremely dangerous, especially to night travelers (Alexander 1980:30-31); many pagans also believed that spirits of those drowned at sea never could descend to the realm of the dead, but wandered endlessly above the waters (Ach. Tat. 5.16.1-2).

more of his character, the appropriate response is to worship him. This will deepen our relationship of faith with the Lord we love.

Jesus Heals All Who Come (14:34-36) Jesus had welcomed the crowds (v. 13), temporal though their needs may have been (v. 14). As word continued to spread, ailing people from throughout Galilee came to Gennesaret seeking the only One who could meet their need. Those who had heard of how a woman had been healed by touching the tassel of his *ṭallît*, his shawl (9:20), sought similar healings for themselves (14:36). Such activity may not have been at the heart of Jesus' mission, but it reflected the heart that motivated his mission: compassion (v. 14).

□ **Pharisees and Canaanites (15:1-39)**
The educated religious elite of Jesus' day opposed him (vv. 1-20), his own disciples trusted but could not understand him (vv. 15-16), but a Canaanite woman recognized his identity as Son of David (vv. 21-28). Matthew again reminds the reader of what the religious elite would not guess: Jesus does another sign like Moses and Elisha (vv. 29-39).

Moral Versus Ritual Cleanness (15:1-20) The reader recognizes Jesus as God's Son who acts not only as the prophets of old (14:13-21) but as the Lord of creation himself (14:22-32). The disciples acclaim him as God's Son (14:33), and the masses approach him for healing (14:34-36). In this context the pedantic response of the Pharisees and scribes, a sort of religious and academic elite, stands in all the starker contrast to reality. (They were no denser than some ministers and religious academicians today who likewise seem able to obscure the forest of God's saving message with far less relevant trees.)

Jesus points out that though the Pharisees use their traditions as a standard for righteousness, some of their traditions can be extended to contradict the written law. Christians today who strongly advocate particular views as biblical, yet cannot demonstrate them from Scripture understood in context, follow tradition rather than Scripture just as did many of Jesus' contemporaries. (I have unfortuantely witnessed this problem in some circles where most members insist they are biblical, led by the Spirit and devoid of tradition.) A religious community may have helpful cumulative wisdom (especially if it has remained faithful to God's earlier revelations), but ultimately the revelation comes only from God himself, and especially from his word to his apostles and prophets preserved for us in Scripture. When we really hear God in Scripture, its message can awaken us and transform us (for example, 2 Kings 22:11-13).

Judging Purely on the Basis of Tradition (15:1-2) The religious elite insist that their way is right, even though it is based only on tradition. Once again they object to a practice of Jesus' disciples, implying a deficiency in the training Jesus has supplied to them (see comment on 12:3-8). People commonly recognized that the Pharisees passed on ancestral laws not written in the law of Moses (Jos. *Ant.* 13.297). Hand washing was one such extrabiblical tradition, perhaps originally adopted from foreign Jews (*Sib. Or.* 3.591-94; E. Sanders 1990:39-40, 228, 260-71), concerning which the Pharisees were especially meticulous (compare *m. Yadayim* 1:1-2:4).

Jesus Challenges Their Tradition as Unbiblical (15:3-11) This observation need not denigrate all tradition; some "traditions" are more biblical than others, and some traditions, like many customs in many cultures, are morally neutral. Among those who accept the Bible as God's Word and as canon (a measuring stick), the test of a statement's authority should be its conformity to biblical principles. Yet many of us, for all our insistence on the authority of Scripture, pay surprisingly little attention to it—little time researching context, background or other factors essential for understanding the Bible. We may work hard to assimilate various trends of popular culture yet spend little time assimilating our lives to the Bible's teachings. I have watched some contemporary churches denigrate the traditions of older churches, yet recite verses out of context or follow extrabiblical routines that reflect traditions no less (albeit newer ones).

Jesus begins by showing how easily a tradition can conflict with the moral purpose of Scripture (15:3-6). One could dedicate an object for sacred use; one could also prohibit others from using one's property (say, eating one's figs) by declaring the property dedicated to the temple or perhaps "as if they were" so dedicated, hence "forbidden to you" (*m. Nedarim* 3:2; Baumgarten 1984-1985; E. Sanders 1990:54-55). Even far from the Holy

Land some Jewish teachers could use such vows to keep property from other family members (see E. Sanders 1990:57). By expanding certain common traditional practices, an unscrupulous person could get around biblical principles about unselfishly meeting others' needs.

Jesus deliberately picks an issue that will provoke thought and argues from a principle with which his opponents will have to agree. A Pharisaic teacher could have offered the same sort of argument Jesus offers here, for Pharisees could argue by laying one text against the interpretation of another. Judaism also heavily stressed honoring and obeying one's parents (for example, Sirach 3:7-8; Jos. *Apion* 2.206) and the obligation to support one's parents in their old age (compare Sirach 3:12-15).

Jewish teachers who debated legal details never contended that such details were at the heart of the law nor approved of exploiting loopholes (see, for example, Urbach 1979:1:576). Nevertheless, exploitation is bound to result in some instances if we spend more time, in religious institutions or in society, debating laws as laws than in teaching ethical principles behind the laws. Jesus is not challenging Pharisaic views about parental support, but the danger of evaluating morality on the basis of extrabiblical traditions.

Jesus then compares this behavior to Scripture's warning about following human rules rather than an intimate relationship with God (15:7-9, citing Is 29:13). Scribes and Pharisees would have taken offense at the appellation *hypocrites* (6:2; 22:18; 23:13; 24:51). Like Jesus, Pharisees were willing to suspend the letter of the law to uphold its spirit (as in *m. Šebi'it* 10:3-4; compare Moore 1971:2:31). But the Pharisees frequently determined morality by extrapolating from tradition. By demanding that we extrapolate morality instead from biblical principles, Jesus takes ethics out of the domain of the academy and courtroom and places it in the daily lives of his followers. To follow Jesus' guidelines here, church members need to know more Scripture, not more churchly rules not founded in Scripture.

Jesus finally publicly opposes his challengers by declaring a more basic principle (15:10-11). Some Pharisees may have agreed with the principle, but they normally stated it only in private (*Pes. Rab Kab.* 4:7),

---

15:14 Leading the blind may have been a well-known image (Plut. *Bride* 6, *Mor.* 139A);

perhaps fearing that some would cease to observe the literal requirements of the law (compare Philo *Migr. Abr.* 89-93). Although Jesus explains his point in private, he first makes it publicly.

Speaking Truth Can Alienate Influential Opponents (15:12-14) Jesus is interested in speaking God's truth, not in winning influential allies. Although many people respected blunt, radical teachers, polite Mediterranean society generally emphasized public respect toward persons of appropriate rank. When one is planning to get crucified anyway, however, one does not need to accommodate the opinions of those who lead God's people astray.

Scholars may debate how much political power the Pharisees held in this period (the Sadducees certainly held more official power), but they were highly influential with the people (Jos. *Ant.* 18.17; E. Sanders 1992:402-4). Jesus' disciples are thus concerned that he has publicly shamed his influential interlocutors instead of reaching out to them (v. 12). Jesus responds by alluding back to the prophetic image of building or tearing down, planting or uprooting people according to God's message (v. 13; compare 3:10; Jer 42:10; 45:4); God has concealed his revelation from "the wise and learned" (11:25-27; 13:11-17; 16:16-17; compare 14:33).

Jesus then graphically compares his self-assured opponents to people who offer to lead the blind but cannot see themselves (15:14; compare 7:3-5; 13:13; 23:16; Rom 2:19). Even were the interpretation of such an image difficult, the disciples should have understood him perfectly well: earlier prophets had also complained that the leaders of God's people were blind (for example, Is 3:12, 14; 6:10; 9:16).

Jesus Demands a Pure Heart and Ethics, Not Mere Ritual (15:15-20) Jesus illustrates his point with a vice list, a standard literary form in both Jewish (for example, Wisdom 14:25-26; 1QS 4.9-11) and broader Greco-Roman (for example, Arist. *E.E.* 2.3.4, 1220b-21; *V.V.* 1249-51b) circles.

Not food that enters the mouth (Ezek 4:14-15; Acts 10:11-16; Rom 14:1-4; 1 Tim 4:3) but what comes forth (Mt 12:34-37; Eph 4:29; Jas 1:19) renders a person *unclean*. Alluding to the Isaiah passage he has quoted (Is 29:13; compare 59:13), Jesus emphasizes the heart (compare Mt

---

Brad Young (1989:241-42) cites Plato *Republic* 8.554B.

5:21—6:18), as did some of his contemporaries (*m. 'Abot* 2:9). The Pharisees of Jesus' day would have agreed with his emphasis on inwardness, although not that the outward did not defile.

In a church I know well, a deacon I respect in most other matters rebuked a person for wearing work clothes to church (even though she had just gotten off work); another leader in the same church had gone unrebuked for sleeping with a woman to whom he was not married. Many of us modern Christians have a lot of nerve to compare ourselves favorably with the Pharisees!

A Canaanite Woman's Faith (15:21-28) Placed immediately after a discussion of purity in both Matthew and Mark, Jesus' encounter with this Gentile woman brings out the implications the Evangelists find in his view of purity: Gentiles will no longer be separated from Israel (compare Acts 10:15, 28; 11:9-18). Like an earlier Gentile in Matthew's Gospel (8:10), this woman becomes an illustration of faith. Also like the centurion, this outsider's faith compares favorably with that of some religious insiders among Jesus' contemporaries (15:1-20).

Matthew reinforces this point by specifying exactly what Mark's Hellenistic Syro-Phoenician woman (Mk 7:26) means. She is a descendant of the ancient Canaanites, the bitter biblical enemies of Israel whose paganism had often led Israel into idolatry (compare *Jub.* 22:20-22). "Yes," Matthew seems to reply; "God's compassion extends to *all* Gentiles." If *Tyre and Sidon* (15:21) lead some readers to recall Jezebel, others must recall instead the widow who supported Elijah (1 Kings 17:8-24; Lk 4:26). The narrative thus constitutes another of Matthew's invitations to the Gentile mission (like 2:1-11; 8:5-13), reinforcing the message of 11:21-24 (where Tyre and Sidon were more open to repentance than Galilean towns were).

The Woman Will Not Take No for an Answer (15:21-25) In our culture we might consider this woman rude, but ancient Mediterranean judges were sometimes so corrupt that among the poor only a persistent, desperate, otherwise powerless woman could obtain justice from them

---

15:21-28 Even on skeptical presuppositions, one should presume this account authentic. That the only available samples of Jesus' adult interaction with Gentiles in the Gospel tradition included some measure of rejection (see also 8:7, as a question) indicates that the

(Lk 18:2-5; Bailey 1980:134-35). Both men and women in the Old Testament (Gen 18:22-32; 32:26-30; Ex 33:12—34:9; 1 Kings 18:36-37; 2 Kings 2:2, 4, 6, 9; 4:14-28) and in the Gospel tradition (Mk 5:28-29; Jn 2:3-5) show courage by refusing to take no for an answer to a desperate need. When we recognize that we have nowhere else to turn, clinging to the only One who can answer us is an act of faith.

Jesus' Mission Is Specifically for Israel (15:26) Jesus had left Jewish territory because the masses crowded him and he needed a short vacation to rest with and teach his disciples (v. 21; compare 16:13); but this stage of his mission was for Israel alone (compare 28:19). Thus when his disciples ask him to send the woman away (15:23), he notes the limitation of his mission (v. 24; compare 10:6; Rom 15:8). Yet he did not send her away as his disciples requested, which may have encouraged her to persevere (compare 19:13; 20:31). To her own insistent entreaty (15:25) Jesus responds with almost equal firmness (v. 26). Some Jewish teachers would have reached out to the woman, hoping to make her a proselyte (see, for example, Jos. *Ant.* 20.34-36; *Apion* 2.210; *m. 'Abot* 1:12; Goppelt 1964:54); Jesus simply snubs her.

The language in Mark is somewhat milder: that the children must be fed "first" (Mk 7:27) allows for the possibility of a later healing and a window for the coming Gentile mission (Hurtado 1983:103), but even in Mark the woman's need is too urgent for that. Jesus probably refers to children's pet dogs; well-to-do Greeks, unlike Jews, could raise dogs as pets and not view them merely as troublesome pests (compare Lk 16:21; Ex 22:31). The image is thus simply one of children's needs (compare 7:9) taking temporal precedence over those of pets (Lane 1974:262; Anderson 1976:191). Such an admission, however, hardly transforms the image into a compliment (compare 7:6).

Jesus is not cursing the woman, but he is putting her off (compare 8:7). It is possible that he is testing her, as teachers sometimes tested their disciples (Jn 6:6; *Lev. Rab.* 22:6), but he is certainly reluctant to grant her request and is providing an obstacle for her faith (compare Jn 2:4). Perhaps he is requiring her to understand his true mission and

---

Gospel writers did not fabricate stories to bolster appeal for the Gentile mission. It is unlikely that Christians would lightly attribute to Jesus a view they no longer held (Theissen 1991:63-64).

identity, lest she treat him as one of the many wandering magicians to whom Gentiles sometimes appealed for exorcisms. Yet he is surely also summoning her to recognize Israel's priority in the divine plan, a recognition that for her will include an admission of her dependent status. (One may compare Elisha's requirement that Naaman dip in the Jordan despite Naaman's preference for the Aramean rivers Abana and Pharpar in 2 Kings 5:10-12, ultimately leading to Naaman's acknowledgment of Israel's God and land in 2 Kings 5:17-18.) For one of her social status (an elite "Greek" citizen of Syro-Phoenician race, in Mark's account) this was a dramatic reversal indeed (see Theissen 1991:66-80); but by calling her a Canaanite, Matthew's account mutes the class issue, properly focusing instead on the racial issue, which is more relevant to his own audience.

The Woman Shows Her Faith (15:27-28) The woman recognizes that Jesus is no mere magician who performs feats for fame or money. By hailing Jesus as *Son of David* (v. 22; compare *Ps. Sol.* 17:21), she has already acknowledged him as the rightful king over a nation that had conquered her ancestors (Josh 12:7-24; 2 Sam 8:1-15)—more than many of his own people had done (Mt 15:2; 21:15-16; 23:39). Like John's woman at the well (Jn 4:25-29; 6:69), this Canaanite woman publicly acknowledged Jesus' identity before the disciples who wished her to leave had done so (Mt 16:16). Now she refuses to dispute that Jesus' mission is to Israel first and that her status is secondary to that of Israelites (Jeremias 1958:30; Rhoads and Michie 1982:131); nevertheless, she believes Jesus will have more than enough power left over from what Israel does not need or want. Jesus responds to such striking faith. Jesus has enough bread for Israel, but the following narrative reinforces that plenty of scraps remain over for others (15:37). Matthew reminds his community that all, both Jew and Gentile, can approach God only through faith in his Messiah (8:10; compare Acts 15:8-11).

Feeding the Four Thousand (15:29-39) This narrative, like the feeding of the five thousand (14:15-21), teaches us about Jesus' power and care for us. He heals the multitudes (15:29-31), acts out of compassion for

---

15:32 Many suggest that the two feedings are two versions of a single event (Burkill 1972:48-70); others contend that two distinct events occurred (Knackstedt 1964). Many of the parallels between the two accounts are those necessary to depict the multiplying of

their need (v. 32; compare 9:36; 14:14; 20:34) and provides for them (15:33-39).

Jesus Meets People's Needs (15:29-31) After some time alone with his disciples (v. 21), Jesus returns to meeting the people's needs. Jesus here meets people's physical needs (v. 30). Those ultraconservative Christians who have considered ministry to people's physical needs "liberal" need to read the Bible more carefully themselves (compare vv. 3, 7-9; Is 1:10-17; 58:3-9; Jer 22:16; Amos 5:21-24). Some theologians have critiqued some forms of Christianity for focusing on "meeting our needs" instead of on glorifying God. The critique is partly right and partly wrong. Jesus met the broken where they were, meeting their needs. Nevertheless, only those who pressed on to become his servant-disciples would really come to know who he was. Even his initial acts of compassion led to God's glory; though the crowds had exercised some faith in bringing the ailing to Jesus, they still were *amazed* by the miracles and *praised the God of Israel* (Mt 15:30-31).

Recognizing Our Need, Showing Compassion (15:32) The text does not suggest that people were complaining about the food situation. Although one should not argue from silence (especially on the historical level), it is possible that the passage implies that Jesus, like his Father, recognizes our need before we ask (6:8, 32). Indeed, sometimes he protects us from dangers of which we are not even aware.

Disciples Should Grow in Faith (15:33-34) Jesus acts even though his disciples "don't get it." In contrast to the multitudes who flock to Jesus for miracles, the disciples seem blind to his true character (compare Weeden 1971:28); despite Jesus' earlier feeding miracle, they assume again that they must procure bread by purely natural means (v. 33). They are still learning, and Jesus does not yet reprove their unbelief—although he will if it continues (16:8-11). He demands more of maturer Christians who have seen his works than he does from young Christians who have seen fewer (compare Ex 17:5-6; 32:10; Num 14:22-23). Some contemporary writers say that God acts

---

food (Carson 1984:357-58). Perhaps the tradition reports both to imitate the double feeding miracles of Elijah and Elisha (see Blomberg 1992:245).

only in response to faith; in the Bible, however, he sometimes acts in advance of faith to teach us how to trust him.

Jesus Organizes His Ministry for Efficiency (15:35-36) What was not humanly possible, Jesus performed as a miracle; the distribution of the food was humanly possible, however, and Jesus organized it efficiently. The fact that the Lord empowers us is all the more reason for us to be good stewards of what he gives and to observe principles like delegated responsibility (Ex 18:14-26). Tremendous revivals followed the ministries of George Whitefield and John Wesley. But because Wesley organized his converts (Noll 1992:92), his results have made a greater direct impact on subsequent generations.

Jesus Again Supplies More Than Enough (15:37-39) See comment on 14:20-21. Matthew provides both a literal lesson taken from the story and a figurative lesson based on the context. Figuratively, the leftovers symbolize that plenty of the "children's bread" remains for other seekers (15:26-28). But on the literal level Matthew teaches about God's limitless power and design in providing his children's needs. One might think that more food would remain after this feeding miracle than the previous one; after all, this time Jesus started with more food and fewer people (although the baskets used this time may have been larger). But such was not the case, reminding us that God's design rather than natural considerations determines the magnitude of any miracle.

Everett and Esther Cook pioneered many churches during and after the Great Depression, trusting God to supply their needs. In one town, having drawn a small number of women to their opening meetings, they prayed that God would send them some men as well. Everett decided to "put some legs to my prayers," as he put it, and went out to the streets to invite some men; he found only one, but promised him, "I can definitely guarantee you a seat."

The man did not come that night, but Everett concluded this was fortunate, because he would have broken his promise: no seats were available! Some men had driven into town from a nearby army camp, spotted the tent and entered the meeting. Many were converted and began bringing their

---

15:39 This verse probably belongs more naturally with the following paragraph (16:1-4), but I include it in the preceding passage to accommodate the chapter break (added later)

friends, and from that day forward the Cooks' meetings never lacked for men. God does not always answer prayers so quickly, but we can be confident that no request offered for his honor is too hard for him.

□ The Son Revealed—to Some (16:1—17:13)

Jesus' opponents prove too blind to recognize the signs he has already offered them (16:1-4), and even his own disciples are slow to understand (16:5-12). Peter finally recognizes Jesus' secret identity, though he misunderstands its character (16:13-28). Jesus reveals his glory more dramatically, and his inner circle (including Peter) gains insight (17:1-13). Yet the other disciples still are of little faith (17:14-23), and Peter himself requires further instruction in basic matters (17:25; 18:21).

Jesus' Opponents Seek a Sign (16:1-4) This passage offers some significant lessons, both for Matthew's first audience and for us today.

Asking for a sign after the Lord has already revealed himself is testing him (16:1; compare Ex 17:7; Ps 78:18-20). Pharisees and Sadducees were generally at odds, joining forces only under external duress (compare, for example, Jos. *Life* 21-22); Matthew reports that Jesus' mission was one such case of duress (3:7).

This passage refers not to those who genuinely fear God yet ask for signs as an assurance of God's promise (Gen 15:6, 8; Judg 6:17, 36-39; 2 Kings 20:8), but to those who seek grounds to disbelieve. Religious leaders had challenged Jesus after other miracles (Mt 15:1-20); the Gospel's first reference to testing (4:1; compare 6:13; 19:3; 22:35) may suggest that the devil is the theological source of their opposition. Now they ignore the signs of a prophet (15:21-39) and demand instead *a sign from heaven* (16:1). A *sign from heaven* probably means a sign in the heavens, like those that many people believed presaged the fall of Jerusalem (Jos. *War* 6.288-91) and the end of the age (compare 24:29-31; 27:45, 51-53). Presumably these leaders ask Jesus to predict a sign in the sky—which essentially reduces them to the level of astrologers or

---

as easily as possible. *Magadan* may have been the large fishing village Tarichaea, and may refer to Mary Magdalene's hometown.

diviners, something forbidden in the Hebrew Bible (Deut 18:10). The religious leaders here contrast starkly with some pagan astrologers who came to worship King Jesus (2:1-12)!

Jesus is giving them a clearer sign than a sign in heaven would be (16:3-4). Jesus' questioners could predict many celestial phenomena with no supernatural inspiration at all; a red sky in the morning, for example, meant that Mediterranean winds from the west would be bringing rain. But Jesus was not interested in predicting events in the sky or using such events to predict the future; they were overlooking an explicit sign that was nearer at hand. The sinfulness of that generation could itself constitute one sign, for many Jewish people understood that a sinful generation would immediately precede the coming of God's kingdom (*CD* 20.14-15; *2 Baruch* 26:12; *m. Soṭa* 9:15). The description of that generation resembles Moses' complaint against Israel (Deut 32:5), a generation that had repeatedly tested God in the wilderness and rejected his prophet Moses (Ps 78:18-20).

Jesus' own ministry and resurrection constituted the decisive sign to that generation (16:4). The resurrection was an end-time event (Dan 12:2); Jesus' resurrection was a clear indication that the kingdom time was at hand (Mt 12:39-40).

Religious Cancer and Doubting Disciples (16:5-12) If Jesus' opponents were active in their unbelief (vv. 1-4), his disciples were passive in their unbelief. Unlike the Pharisees, Jesus' disciples had stayed with him and witnessed the miracles of the loaves; nevertheless, they still fail to understand his power.

Jesus warns against testing God as his opponents had just done. When Jesus warns against Pharisaic leaven (vv. 5-6), hence Pharisaic teaching (vv. 11-12), he is not implying that he disagrees with all Pharisaic teaching (23:2); the context specifies which teaching he means. *The Pharisees and Sadducees* have posed challenges intended to discredit Jesus (16:1-4); Jesus' words against the yeast of the Pharisees and Sadducees in this context must constitute a warning against such cynicism, which rapidly poisons the attitudes of others. *Yeast* was an appropriate metaphor for something that spreads; today we might employ the negative image of cancer. The disciples' passive unbelief (v. 8) suggests that the threat of Pharisaic leaven is closer to them that they would have guessed.

The disciples misunderstand Jesus' point because they are "of little faith." Perhaps they were headed for "the sparsely populated east side" of the lake, where bread would be in short supply (Hoehner 1972:204). At any rate, the disciples had inadvertently neglected their responsibility to bring bread (v. 5; see comment on 14:15), and they were so concerned about what their teacher would think about their lapse that they assumed he was addressing their own failure (16:7). Yet given what had just transpired (vv. 1-4), how could they assume that *the yeast of the Pharisees and Sadducees* referred to forgetting to take bread? Did they think Jesus was instructing them to bake bread from scratch once they had crossed the lake, but to make sure not to borrow yeast from the spiritually unclean religious elite? The disciples here appear inordinately dense. Thus they misunderstand because they are self-absorbed (v. 7).

But Jesus is crystal clear why they cannot understand him. Spiritual understanding cannot come apart from faith (v. 8). Had they simply forgotten to take bread—a technical rather than a moral failure—Jesus could have provided bread (vv. 9-10). That Jesus could miraculously supply bread had already eluded them twice (14:15-17; 15:33; compare 6:11, 25-34); by this point his disciples should have more faith, so he corrects them. Their real problem is that they are learning faith so slowly (compare 15:10, 16). He has serious reason for concern: these are his disciples, by definition apprentices expected to take over his earthly ministry after his departure! Yet other instances of his "little-faith" rebuke demonstrate that it represents a reproof like that of a concerned parent, not that of a harsh drill sergeant (compare 6:30; 8:26; 14:31; 17:20).

God's Plan Established on Christ (16:13-20) The religious elite repudiated Jesus (vv. 1-4); the disciples lacked sufficient faith in him to understand his most basic warnings (vv. 5-12). But now, informed by Jesus' works (14:33) and perhaps by a new understanding of Jesus' role vis-à-vis that of their people's religious establishment (16:1-12), the disciples are on the verge of a new level of revelation. Even at this point, however, they do not fully understand their Master's mission (vv. 21-28).

The Revelation of the Gospel Occurs in Pagan Territory (16:13) Jesus has taken his disciples northward from predominantly Jewish territory, presumably to escape the crowds and spend time privately with his disciples. They have journeyed some twenty-five miles (and seventeen hundred feet uphill) from the Lake of Galilee to the source of the Jordan near the ancient city of Dan, the northern boundary of ancient Israel. The recently renamed Caesarea Philippi was as pagan a territory as one could find. It was famous for its grotto where people worshiped the Greek god Pan; its earlier name Paneas persisted even in its modern Arabic name, Baneas (compare Jos. *War* 1.404), and public pagan rites reportedly continued there until a later Christian miraculously demonstrated that Jesus was more powerful (Euseb. *H.E.* 7.17). Following Mark, Matthew emphasizes that God moves where he wills, fitting the theme of Jesus' universal mission in his Gospel (for example, 1:3, 5-6; 2:1-12; 3:9; 4:15).

People Must Recognize Jesus as the Christ (16:14-16) Outsiders' recognition of Jesus as a prophet is inadequate (16:14); those who follow Jesus closely know him as the Christ, God's Son (vv. 15-16). Herod Antipas thought Jesus was John (14:2); many Jewish people anticipated the return of Elijah and other prophets like Baruch. Viewing Jesus in such terms thus fit him into categories of thought that already existed, rather than letting the Lord redefine their categories by his identity (see comment on 4:1-11). *Christ* designates Jesus as the rightful king of Israel (see introduction).

A Foundational Revelation (16:17-18) Peter did not receive his revelation from *man,* literally "flesh and blood" (compare Gal 1:16), a common expression for "mortals" or "humans" (as in 1 Cor 15:50; Eph 6:12; Heb 2:14; *1 Enoch* 15:4; *Mek. Pisha* 1.120). Peter's understanding of Jesus' identity came by divine revelation (Mt 16:17; 11:25), undoubtedly including God's revelation through Jesus' miraculous acts (14:33; compare 15:22). This revelation of Jesus' identity was foundational for God's purposes in history.

16:13-20 Many Protestant interpreters have doubted the authenticity of this section (especially the blessing of Peter, specific to Matthew), but more recent interpreters have shown less skepticism. Davies and Allison (1991:609-15) argue for authenticity on the following grounds: (1) evidence in Paul (especially Gal 1:11-21), (2) Semitic expressions, (3) indications of a Palestinian origin (comparisons with the Dead Sea Scrolls), (4) consistency with Jesus' other teachings, (5) dissimilarity from other sources (*gates of Hades, keys of the kingdom,* and binding and loosing are not distinctively Christian; the promise to Peter is not pre-Christian Jewish), (6) geographical setting and (7) the weakness of the

Jesus then plays on Simon's nickname, *Peter*, which would be roughly the English "Rocky": Peter is rocky, and on this rock Jesus will build his church (16:18). Scholars have debated precisely what Jesus means by *rock*. Protestants, following Augustine and Luther, have sometimes contended that the rock in this passage is only Jesus himself (references in Cullmann 1953:162 n. 13). But by Jesus' day the Greek terms *petros (Peter)* and *petra (rock)* were interchangeable, and the original Aramaic form of Peter's nickname that Jesus probably used *(kēphas)* means simply "rock" (Cullmann 1953:18-19; Ladd 1974b:110; Carson 1984:368; France 1985:254; Blomberg 1992:252).

Further, Jesus does not say, "You are Peter, but on this rock I will build my church"; he says, *And on this rock I will build my church*. Jesus' teaching is the ultimate foundation for our lives (7:24-27; compare 1 Cor 3:11), but here Peter functions as the foundation rock like the apostles and prophets in Ephesians 2:20-21. Jesus does not simply assign this role to Peter arbitrarily, however; Peter is the "rock" because in this context he is the one who confesses Jesus as the Christ (Mt 16:15-16; Cullmann 1953:162; Ladd 1974b:110; C. Brown 1978:386). Others who share his proclamation also share his authority in building the church (18:18 with 16:19).

The Community Built on This Foundation Will Prevail (16:18)

Ancient teachers from Greek philosophers to Qumran's founding teacher established communities of followers to perpetuate their teachings (as in Culpepper 1975:123; compare Albright and Mann 1971:195; Flusser 1988:35). The Qumran community described themselves as the *qāhāl*, the Hebrew word for God's congregation in the exodus narrative, which the Greek versions sometimes translate as *ekklēsia* or "church." Jesus thus depicts his followers, his *church*, as the true, faithful remnant of God's people in continuity with the Old Testament covenant community

---

objections to the contrary.

16:18 *Gates of Hades* appears in the Hebrew Bible (Job 38:17; Ps 9:13; 107:18; Is 38:10), in subsequent Jewish literature (Wisdom 16:13; 3 Macc 5:51; *Ps. Sol.* 16:2; 1QH 6.24; *Sib. Or.* 2.228) and in Greek literature as well (Diog. Laert. 10.126; Char. *Chaer.* 4.1.3; *Orphic Hymn* 18.15). The gates of the realm of the dead appear widely in ancient Near Eastern literature, but the image here may especially evoke Isaiah 28:15-19, where the cornerstone in Zion withstands the assault of water from those in covenant with Sheol (Davies and Allison 1991:630).

(Ridderbos 1975:328; F. Bruce 1963:84). What marked it as new, however, was Jesus' specific designation "*my* community" (Ladd 1974b:110; France 1985:255).

Biblical tradition had often spoken of "building up" the community of God (as in Ps 51:18; 69:35; Jer 24:6; 31:4, 28). *The gates of Hades* is a familiar Semitic expression for the threshold of the realm of death. The words used here suggest that death itself assaults Christ's church, but death cannot crush us (Ladd 1974b:116). The church will endure until Christ's return, and no opposition, even widespread martyrdom of Christians or the oppression of the final antichrist (compare Jeremias 1968:927), can prevent the ultimate triumph of God's purposes in history.

Jesus Authorizes His Agents to Admit People to the Kingdom (16:19) The authority belongs not only to Peter (v. 19) but to all who share his proclamation of Jesus' identity (18:18). The realm of *heaven* here contrasts strikingly with the powers of *Hades,* or "Sheol," the realm of the dead thought to lie beneath the earth (16:18; compare Heb 2:14; Rev 1:18). *Keys* opened locked doors or gates, but the carrying of keys especially symbolized the authority of the person who bore them. One who carried keys to a royal palace was the majordomo, as in Isaiah 22:22 and Revelation 3:7. Supervisors held the keys to the temple courts among Jesus' contemporaries (as in *ARN* 7, §21B), and in Jewish lore prominent angels carried certain keys (for example, 3 Baruch 1:2; compare *b. Ta'anit* 2a).

Whether Peter thus acts as "prime minister" for the kingdom (see Brown, Donfried and Reumann 1973:96-97) or perhaps as a "chief rabbi" making halakhic rulings based on Jesus' teachings (Meier in Brown and Meier 1983:67), he clearly acts with enough delegated authority (compare Acts 10:44; Gal 2:7). Whereas Israel's religious elite was shutting people out of the kingdom (23:13; compare Lk 11:52), those who confessed Jesus' identity along with Peter were authorized to usher

---

16:19 Some later Jewish teachers also applied the image of *keys* to their teaching authority (Davies and Allison 1991:635). Some see in "binding" and "loosing" the ability to evaluate actions as sinful or not, as in 18:18 (Derrett 1983), releasing death's bonds in the context (Basser 1985), dissolving vows (Falk 1974) or Jesus' authorization for exorcisms, which Matthew reapplied more generally (Hiers 1985). Noting the magical usage of "binding,"

people into God's kingdom.

Scholars have proposed many interpretations of "binding and loosing," but in Jewish texts these terms (*'āsar* and *hittîr* or *š^erā'*) could refer to authority to interpret the law, hence to evaluate individuals' fidelity to the law as in 18:18 (see comment there). In this context, however, the nuance may be somewhat different from 18:18: Peter and those who share his role (others share it in 18:18) evaluate not those who are in the community, but those who would enter it (10:14-15, 40; this is a role assigned to overseers in the Qumran community—compare 1QS 5.20-21; 6:13-14). In both functions—evaluating entrants and evaluating those already within the church—God's people must evaluate on the authority of the heavenly court. The verb tenses allow (and according to some scholars even suggest) that they merely ratify the heavenly decree (see comment on 18:18; compare Mantey 1973 and 1981; Keener 1987).

Peter must thus accept into the church only those who share his confession of Jesus' true identity (16:16). Of course the church should emulate Jesus' practice of welcoming the unconverted (9:10), but this is not the same as acting as if all comers were true disciples of Christ regardless of their commitment. Today some churches both admit into membership the unconverted and fail to take the message of Jesus' identity to the unconverted outside their walls. The danger of building a church on those not committed to Christ's agendas is that in time the church will reflect more of the world's values than Christ's; this was one way some originally abolitionist churches compromised with the slave trade (Usry and Keener 1996:102-5).

Jesus Admonishes the Disciples Not to Reveal His Identity (16:20) The context suggests why Jesus admonished his disciples to keep his identity secret. Until after the resurrection (17:9) the disciples were unprepared to understand the cross; and apart from the cross they could not understand the real nature of Jesus' messianic mission (16:21-28).

---

some might suggest disciplinary language for demons; people might also tell demons to get "behind" them (Incant. text 5.7; compare Mt 16:23) or put them under the "ban" (text 14.1-2). But the immediate context of the church's triumph against death does not support this interpretation.

The Cost of the Kingdom (16:21-27) It is not enough to confess that Jesus is Messiah (16:16) if we do not understand that his messiahship involves suffering and death (vv. 21-23). And if Jesus' mission involves the cross, those who would follow him must embrace the same price (vv. 24-27).

The Cross Is Central to Jesus' Mission (16:21) The gospel message is incomplete without the cross. Recognizing Jesus as the Messiah was a good first step (vv. 13-20), but not very helpful when the disciples' concept of Jesus' messiahship differed so greatly from his own. Jesus' messiahship meant that he would suffer and die (v. 21); those who wish to follow him must be ready to pay the same price (v. 24). The cross was the most scandalous form of criminal execution in Jesus' day (see Hengel 1977:8-9). Even the term sounded terrible to ancient readers (Hengel 1977:10), and we may not blame the disciples if they hoped he was speaking metaphorically.

The Devil Offers the Kingdom Without the Cross (16:22-23) If verses 18-19 grant Peter special authority, this passage qualifies it: his authority functions only when he speaks from God, not when he speaks human or demonic wisdom (compare Meier 1979:118). When Peter rebukes Jesus, he oversteps his appropriate bounds as a disciple. Correcting a teacher was rare (*ARN* 1A), and some sages believed teaching the law even in the presence of one's teacher merited death from God (as in *Sipra Shem. Mek. deMil.* 99.5.6). Disciples "followed" their teachers (Mt 8:22; 9:9-10; 10:38; 19:21), literally remaining behind them out of respect when they walked. Thus though Jesus *turned* to confront Peter literally behind him, he now ordered him to *get behind*

16:21 Some scholars doubt that Jesus could have predicted his own death (Wrede 1971:82-92), but even if one discounted the possibility that God could grant insight to one of his agents concerning his mission (which is merely a philosophical a priori; see R. Brown 1994:1468), their doubts are untenable for several reasons (see more fully R. Brown 1994:1468-91). First, the saying reflects an early Aramaic construction and three characteristics of Jesus' distinctive style (Jeremias 1971:282; Hill 1979:61). Further, Jesus taught the common Jewish view that sufferings precede the kingdom and accepted the Jewish view, confirmed in John's death, that prophets are martyred; the Gospel tradition reports numerous conflicts Jesus had experienced up to this point, which could have shown where Jesus' confrontations were headed; and some of Jesus' other sayings, such as that disciples must share his cup (20:22-23) and his words at the Last Supper (26:26-29), point in the same direction (Jeremias 1971:277-86; Dodd 1961:57; Stauffer 1960:171-73). Finally, Jesus could not but have foreknown his death: he ultimately provoked it, showing his control

him figuratively (16:23), returning to a position of discipleship.

But Peter was not only out of order; he was the devil's agent. At the wilderness temptation Satan offered Jesus the kingdom without the cross (4:8-9); Peter now offers the same temptation and encounters the same title (Cullmann 1956b:27). The devil has influenced this world so deeply that the world's values are quite often the devil's values (Jas 3:15; 4:7); by valuing the things human beings value (like lack of suffering), Peter shows himself in league with the devil. The religious leaders later echoed Satan's temptation as well (Mt 27:42-43). That Peter is a *stumbling block* (16:23; not in Mk) again plays on his name: *rock* (see comment on 16:18) could have negative as well as positive functions (Meier 1979:117 and 1980:185).

That some of Jesus' religious contemporaries were Satan's mouthpieces need not surprise us: think how many of us prefer comfortable beliefs to the cross today. (We can wear crosses as jewelry mainly because the Christian symbol has lost much of its original significance; as some preachers point out, few of us would enjoy sporting a miniature electric chair or gallows around our neck.) Some Western Christians expect unlimited prosperity or teach that Christians will escape all tribulation, while many of our brothers and sisters elsewhere (such as in Iran or the Sudan) die for their faith. Is it not possible that some Christians today still speak for the devil?

Jesus Expects Disciples to Follow Him to Death (16:24) Summoning others to his revolutionary cause, Garibaldi cried, "He that loves Italy, let him follow me! I promise him hardship . . . suffering . . . death. But he that loves Italy, let him follow me!" (Strong 1907:766). Only a

---

over its timing, by his assault on an institution by which the aristocracy symbolized its power (21:12-17). If Jesus expected a prophet's death in Jerusalem, political conditions being what they were he had to expect the chief priests and Romans to play a role.

It also makes sense that if Jesus expected to face rejection and death for an offensive message like many earlier prophets, he might also expect God's vindication in swiftly establishing the kingdom (R. Brown 1994:514), hence raising the dead. That Jesus may have expected his own resurrection ahead of that of others would be distinctive—we know of no direct precedents for the view—but is reasonable if, as argued above (on 16:18-19), Jesus expected a community to carry on after him in the intermediate eschatological era.

16:24 Crosses did become a natural metaphor for sufferings (Apul. *Metam.* 10.9) or the pain of grief (Apul. *Metam.* 9.31) or anxiety (Apul. *Metam.* 9.23). But consistent with his teaching elsewhere, Jesus probably means the point more graphically: his disciples must be prepared to die literally for his honor.

cause worth dying for is truly worth living for, and a generation of Western youth, deprived of causes worth their lives and of elders personally committed enough to point the way, have become restless and disillusioned.

"Taking up one's cross" in antiquity hardly meant simply putting up with an annoying roommate or having to live with ingrown toenails. It meant marching on the way to one's execution, shamefully carrying the heavy horizontal beam (the *patibulum*) of one's own death-instrument through a jeering mob (Jeremias 1972:218-19 and 1971:242). Jesus anticipated literal martyrdom for himself and many of his followers by the Romans' standard means of executing lower-class criminals and slaves; his kingdom was ultimately incompatible with Rome's claims (Manson 1979:131; F. Bruce 1972a:19). If disciples "come after" and imitate their teachers, Christians' lives are forfeit from the moment they begin following Christ; to *come after* Jesus, Peter himself had to return to walking behind him (v. 23).

Although genuine Christians may fall short on their commitment at times (26:69-75), those who wish to follow Christ should understand from the start that they are surrendering their lives to Christ. Those who do not acknowledge Jesus as Lord—as having the right to demand of them anything, including their lives—have yet to be truly converted. Today Christians continue to debate the character of the gospel: to be saved, does one need to accept Christ as Lord or only as Savior? Throughout the New Testament, however, the question is more or less a moot one. Jesus came to save us from our sin, and accepting him must include recognizing his right to rule our lives. This does not imply that Christians are perfect; it does indicate that they recognize who their Lord is.

Jesus Is Worth Any Price We Must Pay to Follow Him (16:25-27)

Losing one's life in this age would be a small price to preserve it in the eternal age to come (compare *2 Baruch* 51:15-16; *m. 'Abot* 4:17). We

---

16:28 Some apply the promise especially to Pentecost (see Dunn 1970:40), others to Jesus' resurrection (F. Bruce 1972a:25-26); others suggest that it refers to the end of the age and was left unfulfilled (Mattill 1979:59-67). Probably the transfiguration proleptically introduces the whole eschatological sphere, which Jesus' resurrection inaugurates and his return consummates; on the blending of successive future events in prophetic time, compare 24:3

must decide whether we "want" to come after Jesus (Mt 16:24; NIV *would*) or "want" (the same Greek term; NIV *wants*) to save our lives (v. 25); we cannot have it both ways. The cross means death, and nothing less (10:38-39; Jn 12:25).

Yet the only way to ultimately preserve one's life is to relinquish it in faith that the Son of Man will someday come with his angels to execute judgment (Mt 16:27; compare 25:31; 2 Thess 1:7-8; Dan 7:9-14) according to each person's works (for example, Ps 62:12; Prov 24:12; Rom 2:6; 2 Cor 11:15; Rev 22:12). Those who expected a period of great suffering before the time of the kingdom, as most Jewish people did, would hear in such words a radical call to perseverance (Mt 24:9-13).

In the end God will reward us for what we have done, and eternal life matters more than our temporary lives in this age. I once shared Christ with an associate who cared deeply about his friends, prompting him to consider that eternal life is a gift of far greater significance than any other he could offer them, but he could not give what he did not have himself. God's Spirit prompted him to forsake status and worldly plans, and he became a committed Christian who has touched countless lives since that day. John dared to believe that God's eternal riches outweigh any cost in the present, so he became a true disciple of Jesus Christ. Yet how few disciples we have; except for going to church and paying tithes, many Christians today do with their time and money much the same as what morally upright non-Christians do.

The Son of Man's Glory (16:28—17:13) Had the disciples any doubt that Jesus would someday come to reign in glory (16:27), he promises them a proleptic vision of his glory in the present (16:28). In a narrative that resembles Moses' revelation on Mount Sinai, the disciples become witnesses like Moses of Jesus' divine glory (17:1-8). The *six days* (17:1) probably allude to Exodus 24:15-18 (see, for example, Mauser 1963:111). The *bright cloud* (Mt 17:5; Ex 24:15) and other features of the narrative

and the following discourse.

17:1 Qumran had not only a special group of twelve but also a special group of three (1QS 8.1-8; Hill 1972:267). But in this case it may be most relevant that Moses had three specific companions in Exodus 24:1, 9, although they were joined by the seventy elders (France 1985:262).

likewise recall the revelation on Mount Sinai. The appearance in Matthew 17:3 of the literal Moses and Elijah (both of whom had experiences with God on Mount Horeb) invite the reader to consider the other allusions to Moses (17:2-5) and Elijah (17:10-13) later in the narrative.

Jesus the Glorious Lord (16:28—17:3) When Jesus again takes some disciples aside for private instruction (15:21; 16:13; see comment on 13:10-17), his transfiguration among them provides a foretaste of his glory when he will return to judge the earth (16:28). Various suggestions for the background for Jesus' proleptic "glorification" could be offered here, but a variety of allusions combine to point to Moses in the Old Testament. After Moses beheld God's glory, his own face shone with that glory (Ex 34:29-35; compare Ps-Philo 12:1; 19:16). Despite the clear testimony of Deuteronomy 34 (see also *1 Enoch* 89:38), some of Jesus' contemporaries doubted that Moses had died (*Sipre Deut.* 357.10.5; *ARN* 12A), living on like Elijah and some other figures (compare 4 Ezra 6:27; pace Jos. *Ant.* 9.28). The Bible itself claimed that both Elijah (Mal 4:4-5) and a prophet like Moses (Deut 18:15-19) would return. Most important, this literal Moses and Elijah also capture the reader's attention for the figurative new Elijah (Mt 17:12) and new Moses—Jesus—of whom this text speaks.

But while the text may present Jesus as a new Moses (especially 17:5), it also presents him as something more. It portrays the disciples as witnesses of his glory on the mountain, just as Moses and Elijah heard God on Mount Sinai (see Moiser 1985). The presence of Moses and Elijah indicates that Jesus is incomparably greater than the prophets with whom some were comparing him (16:14; compare Thrall 1970:316).

We Are Called to Heed Jesus As We Would God's Law (17:4-5) The *bright cloud* that *enveloped* or "overshadowed" them is described in language reminiscent of the Jewish doctrine of the Shekinah, God's presence, especially recalling God's presence in the tabernacle in the

---

17:2 Jewish texts sometimes described angels and archangels as brighter than the sun (Mt 28:3; Dan 10:6; Rev 10:1; *2 Enoch* 19:1; *3 Enoch* 18:25). The righteous after death would shine in the same way (4 Ezra 7:97), as could Noah (*1 Enoch* 106:2, 10; 1QpGen. Apoc. col. 2), Abel (*Test. Ab.* 12A) and God himself (Dan 7:9-10; *1 Enoch* 14:18-20).
17:6 Falling on one's face or being terrified was a customary response to superhuman

wilderness (Ex 40:34-38; Daube 1973:30; W. Davies 1966b:22-23; Argyle 1963:132). God then repeats in a *baṭ qôl* some of the commendation oracle he uttered at Jesus' baptism, revealing Jesus' identity as both Messiah and suffering servant (Ps 2:7; Is 42:1; see comment on Mt 3:17); to this he adds an allusion that indicates that Jesus is the promised "prophet like Moses" as well, for of that prophet God said, *Listen to him* (17:5; Deut 18:15).

Jesus Does Not Flaunt His Power (17:6-8) The disciples fall on their faces, afraid. As he often did, Jesus crosses barriers and communicates his kindness by touching (v. 7; compare 8:3, 15; 9:20, 25, 29). He then speaks words of assurance customary for divine and angelic revelations: *Get up. . . . Don't be afraid* (compare 28:5, 10).

God's Way Is the Way of Martyrdom (17:9-13) Although scholars disagree concerning how widespread and early was the explicit view of Elijah as the Messiah's forerunner, his end-time function in general is clear from Malachi 4:5-6 (compare Sirach 48:10; see note on 3:4 above), which also presents him as a "restorer."

□ Miracles and Disciples (17:14-27)

Even after three of Jesus' disciples had seen his glory, the other disciples lacked adequate faith (vv. 14-22), and one of those who had seen him still required further instruction (vv. 23-27).

Lacking a Mustard Seed of Faith (17:14-23) As Moses found that those he had left in charge were unable to control the people (Ex 24:14; 32:1-8), Jesus found that those he had left behind could not cast out a particularly troublesome demon. Jesus casts out the demon immediately, demonstrating how it should be done (17:18; compare 8:26), but the disciples' inability twice invites Jesus' reproof of their weak faith (17:17, 20).

Jesus Honors One Person's Faith on Behalf of Another (17:14-

---

revelations both in Israel's ancient history (Gen 15:12; Dan 8:17-18; 10:9-9; Ezek 1:28) and in contemporary Jewish accounts (Rev 1:17; Tobit 12:16; *Jub.* 18:10; *1 Enoch* 14:13-14; 4 Macc 4:11; 4 Ezra 4:12).

17:7 On the commands to arise or not to fear after an overwhelming revelation, see, for example, Ezekiel 2:1-2; Daniel 8:18; Tobit 12:17; *1 Enoch* 60:4; 4 Ezra 5:15; *2 Baruch* 13:1-2.

15) A man brings his son to the One with power to deliver him. Some of the symptoms depicted here resemble those of epilepsy (for example, Alexander 1980:83), which may imply that demons gaining control over the human central nervous system can sometimes cause epileptic-type phenomena. This observation does not, however, mean that epilepsy is always caused by demons; both the differentiation of the two in 4:24 and the numbers of committed Christians who suffer from epilepsy invite us to distinguish the two. Some contemporary accounts of spirit possession tell of spirits seeking to make people burn themselves (Kaplan and Johnson 1964:211).

Jesus accepts the father's faith on behalf of his son. Those who support infant baptism have found in this text a principle they believe supports it (Richardson 1958:359-60); those who emphasize the importance of personal faith at baptism are not persuaded by the analogy. But in either case the principle applies for many other kinds of prayer (compare, for example, 10:8; 18:15-20; 1 Jn 5:16) and encourages us in our faith for others' needs (compare 8:13; 9:2; 15:28).

Jesus Summons Us to Grow in Active Faith (17:16-18) Jesus expected his disciples to have sufficient faith to repeat his miracles by this point (vv. 16-17, 20). *Unbelieving . . . generation* (v. 17) applied generally to Jesus' contemporaries (11:16; 12:39-45; 13:39, 45; 16:4; 23:36; 24:34), but in this case specifically to his disciples, who proved unable to stand in for him in his absence (17:16). Disciples were by definition apprentices in training to assume the role of their teachers. Jesus had already sent his disciples out, and they had healed the sick and driven out demons (10:8). Had they not seen enough to believe (compare 8:26)?

Matthew expected his audience to learn from these recorded signs of Jesus, just as the first disciples did when they witnessed them. We who read these accounts in the Bible should be growing in our faith

---

17:20 Jewish teachers often depicted mastering difficult subjects as "moving mountains"— for example, by one bird scraping off one piece at a time (see *b. Berakot* 63b); presumably they, like Jesus, echo a more popular and generally applicable idiom for what was beyond human power (compare Ps 46:3; Is 54:10; Hab 3:10). Isaiah promised that Israel would be powerful enough to crush mountains (Is 41:15); Zechariah promised that mighty mountains would become like plains before God's Spirit-empowered leaders for his people (Zech 4:6-7), and especially before the Lord himself (Zech 14:3-5).

relationship with Jesus, as the disciples did who first walked with him. How often do needs around us go unmet because we neglect radical trust in God, especially on behalf of others' needs?

The Disciples Lacked the Most Basic Level of Faith (17:19-20) Jesus explicitly attributes their inability to the smallness of their faith (compare 6:30; 8:26; 14:21; 16:8), pointing out that even a mustard seed's worth of faith would be sufficient to cast out not merely demons but mountains (17:20; 21:21; 1 Cor 13:2). The disciples already recognized how small a mustard seed was (Mt 13:32). Ancient peoples thought of mountains as rooted far beneath the earth (Gundry 1982:353), so "moving mountains" was a typical Jewish teacher's image for doing what was virtually impossible. With this illustration Jesus indicates that even were we casting out mountains rather than demons, we would only be scratching the surface of a life of faith. What could we do with faith greater than that of a tiny mustard seed! Like children who have only begun to walk, most of us have only begun our adventure of faith.

Faithful Obedience to God Invites Martyrdom As Well As God's Power (17:22-23) We may become too infatuated with God's power and protection (v. 20); God sometimes calls us into danger. God twice honored Elijah's call for fire from heaven (2 Kings 1:10-12), but then instructed him to accompany the third captain (who by this point, at least, feared God enough to provide the prophet safe passage). Jesus' disciples had preferred the glories of the messianic kingdom to suffering (Mt 16:16, 21-22; 17:4); like them, we must avoid missing the point of his triumphant empowerment (compare 1 Cor 13:2; Lk 10:17-20). Faith means willingness to go where God leads, not power to avert all unpleasant circumstances. We mature as the Lord leads us through hard tests for his name's sake, forcing us to actively trust his provision and power.

Jesus gives us access to tremendous power for accomplishing his will.

17:21 Many of the earliest manuscripts over a wide geographical distribution omit this verse, which may derive from Mark 9:29. Possibly Matthew's comment about the littleness of their faith is an application of Mark's comment "only by prayer" or "because you don't pray enough," linked with remarks about unbelief in Mark 9:19, 23. A lifestyle of faithful prayer (and fasting, though it is missing even from some of Mark's manuscripts) can produce a stronger life of faith.

Jesus' own example shows us, however, that those who have an intimate faith relationship with God act in compassion for others' needs rather than exploiting power frivolously (Mt 4:3-10).

Upholding Society's Requirements (17:24-27) Adult Jewish males throughout the Empire paid an annual two-drachma tax, based on Exodus 30:13-16, for the upkeep of the Jerusalem temple (compare E. Sanders 1992:156). Even in Matthew's day, (probably) after the temple was destroyed, this tax remained important: after 70, the Romans required all Jewish people (including Jewish Christians maintaining allegiance to their Jewish heritage) to pay that tax to the Roman government (see *CPJ* 1:80-81; 2:119-36, §§160-229; Hemer 1973; Carlebach 1975). For the sake of maintaining public identification with their Jewish heritage, Jewish Christians should join non-Christian Jews in paying the tax. The principle is that we must sometimes engage in otherwise unprofitable pursuits for the sake of upholding our witness as citizens of the communities where God has placed us.

Jesus Cares About Our Social Obligations (17:24-26) Like a good prophet, Jesus knows in advance Peter's question (17:25). He also does not regard the poll tax as binding on himself or Peter (vv. 25-26), but recognizes that the tax collectors may (v. 24). He thus does not rebuke Peter for committing him (v. 25); he wishes to avoid unnecessary cause for misunderstandings (v. 27) that might turn people away from his gospel unnecessarily (compare 5:29-30; 13:41; 16:23; 18:6). Jesus has offended (literally "caused to stumble") members of the religious establishment before (15:12-14), but this is an unnecessary "stumbling block" because it addresses one's own rights rather than the truth of God's kingdom (18:6).

Surrendering "Rights" for the Sake of the Gospel (17:27) Jesus'

17:24 There are various possible reasons the tax gatherers were unsure whether Jesus would pay. They did not impose the tax on those living off charity (Derrett 1970:253); Jesus and his disciples were essentially dependent on monetary sponsors during their period of frequent itinerant ministry (27:55; Lk 8:1-3; compare 2 Kings 4:42). Sadducees disapproved of the tax (France 1985:267), and some ancient pietists, notably wilderness Essenes who regarded the temple as impure, apparently paid the tax only once in a lifetime (4QOrdinances; Derrett 1970:252; Davies and Allison 1991:743). Probably they also know Jesus' reputation of conflict with other religious teachers.

point here is similar to Paul's point in 1 Corinthians 9 and 10:29-33: one should sacrifice one's own privileges for the sake of the gospel. Head or poll taxes normally listed specific exceptions who would not have to pay (for example, N. Lewis 1983:169). Conquerors subjected conquered peoples, not their own subjects, to taxation. Priests were exempt from the two-drachma tax cited here (Reicke 1974:168; E. Sanders 1990:50); so in later times were rabbis (France 1985:268). Most significant here, dependents of a king were naturally exempt from his taxes (Derrett 1970:255).

Jesus Supplies These Needs As Well As Other Needs (17:27) The *four-drachma coin* probably is a Tyrian stater, precisely enough to pay two persons' temple dues (Avi-Yonah 1974-1976:60-61). Following an old Greek story, some Jewish stories of uncertain date speak of God blessing pious people by leading them to find precious objects in fish (Bultmann 1968:238; Jeremias 1971:87). If Peter knew of such stories, the moral of Jesus' causing him to find money in a fish would not be lost on him. This is irony of a sort: the King's children can pay the tax because the King gives them the money to do so (Patte 1987:247). Jesus can take care of his people who walk close to him.

RELATIONSHIPS IN THE KINGDOM (18:1-35)

Here Jesus begins the fourth discourse in Matthew, addressing relationships in the church, the community of the kingdom (18:1-35). Relations with the state (17:24-27), with one's spouse (19:1-9) and with children (19:13-16) surround this section. Yet Jesus' teaching on relationships here especially addresses relationships among disciples. As God's community, they are to watch out for one another, expressing patience toward the spiritually young as well as seeking to restore the straying, gently disciplining the erring and forgiving the repentant.

17:27 *Offend* is literally "cause to stumble." Placing a literal stumbling block before an unsuspecting person was illegal (Lev 19:14), but Jesus was hardly the first to reapply the image figuratively; Greek texts use it for obstacles or opposition (compare Plut. *Cato the Younger* 30.2; Marc. Aur. 7.22). Jewish texts developed the Old Testament (Ezek 14:3, 7; 18:30) sense of the term as falling into or leading someone into sin to their destruction (1QS 2.12; 3.24; 1QpHab 11.7-8) or like the righteous stumbling stone of Isaiah (Sirach 34:15; 39:24).

□ Serving the Little Ones (18:1-14)

The unifying theme in this section is the importance of honoring children and others who lack worldly status in the kingdom (vv. 1-5). Those who cause a *little child* (literally, "little one") to fall from the faith will themselves be damned—a fate to be avoided at all costs (vv. 6-9). Not only must we not be the cause of a lowly person leaving Jesus' fellowship, but we must take the responsibility to seek those who are straying (vv. 10-14), as God had long desired his shepherds to do (Ezek 34:1-16). Many church offices today depend on honor shown to those with higher rank; but rank in the kingdom depends especially on how we treat those least honored among us.

The Greatest Is the Child (18:1-5) Compare Mark 9:33-37 and Luke 9:46-48. The disciples are concerned with an issue naturally prominent in status-conscious Mediterranean antiquity: who will be greatest in the kingdom (v. 1; compare 5:19; 20:26; 23:11). Jesus declares that the kingdom belongs to children (compare 19:14). This paragraph urges at least two lessons.

Kingdom Status May Be Inverse to Worldly Status (18:1-4) Ancient moralists regularly trotted forth models of heroes and states- men for their students to imitate; Jesus instead points to a child. More so then than today, children were powerless, without status and utterly dependent on their parents (Harrington 1982:74). Yet we must imitate such people of no status, people who recognize their dependence (compare France 1985:270). To "turn" (NIV *change*) reflects the Jewish concept of repentance (as in Jer 34:15); com- pare John 3:3, 5.

Embracing the Weak, We Embrace Christ (18:5) True disciples are "little ones who believe in" Jesus (18:6; compare 10:42), out to make Christ great alone. In Jesus' day parents loved children, but children held little status. Jesus calls us to notice and welcome the "nobodies," to esteem those without status or social respect.

18:6 Rabbis sometimes described a great burden as a millstone around the neck (though Jesus clearly means the language more strongly here—Vermes 1993:84). Most significantly, "better never to have been born" was also a typically Jewish expression (26:24; *1 Enoch* 38:2; 4 Ezra 7:69; *2 Baruch* 10:6; *ARN* 29A).

Causing a Little One to Stumble (18:6-9) Compare Mark 9:42-50 and Luke 17:1-2. Causing one to *sin,* or literally to "stumble," meant causing the person to fall from the way of Christ and be damned (as in Jn 6:61; 1 Cor 8:9). Matthew often uses the Greek term in the same manner as here (Mt 17:27; 26:31; compare 5:29-30; 11:6; 13:41; 16:23; Mk 9:42-47).

God Will Avenge the Little Ones, Whom He Favors (18:6-7) The cruelest legal punishment in Jesus' day was crucifixion, but this image of drowning represents a Roman punishment more horrifying to Jewish hearers than crucifixion and one only rarely tolerated among them (Jeremias 1972:180; for an exception see Jos. *Ant.* 14.450). When people in a community had much grain to grind, they took it to the community mill, pouring it between an upper and lower millstone. Jesus refers here not to the lighter millstone turned by a woman's hand but to the heavier community kind turned by an ass—heavy enough to take one quickly to the bottom of the sea (Deissmann 1978:81; compare *1 Enoch* 48:9). Jesus says this punishment would be an act of mercy compared to what is in store for those who turn *little ones* from Christ's way—be they arrogant university professors, torturers enforcing Islamic law or gossipers within the church.

Avoiding Hell Is Worth Any Price (18:8-9) To paraphrase Malcolm X out of context (which is unfortunately how he is usually quoted), we must avoid hell "by any means necessary." Here the image shifts from others as the cause of stumbling to personal responsibility. Because Judaism abhorred self-mutilation (Dalman 1929:227), this is an especially stark image of the cost one must be willing to pay to avoid spiritual death. *Enter life* was standard shorthand for "enter the life of the coming age" (compare 19:17). The language of losing limbs was reminiscent of the price martyrs paid for their devotion to God (2 Macc 7:11; 4 Macc 10:20). According to a common Jewish belief (as in *2 Baruch* 50:2-4; compare 2 Macc 7:11; 14:46), a person with missing members would be resurrected in that form before being restored.

18:8-9 *Life* literally indicates the life of the coming world, after the resurrection (Dan 12:2). Compare the common Jewish expressions "life of the world to come" (*m. 'Abot* 2:7; *Sipre Deut.* 305.3.2-3), "eternal life" (= "life of the world"; e.g., *Ps. Sol.* 3:12; 13:11; *CIJ* 1:422, §569) and "life" (Tobit 12:9-10).

Go After the Straying Sheep (18:10-14) Compare Luke 15:3-7. The similar parable in the context of Luke 15:1-32 emphasizes Christ's pursuit of the lost sheep (see also Mt 9:36; 10:6); in this context, however, the parable summons those who share God's concerns to pursue the lost sheep (Jeremias 1972:39-40). By his ingenious arrangement of the material, Matthew demonstrates that overbearing leaders unwilling to forgive the repentant fall into the same category as those who caused the stumbling to begin with. Matthew opposes leaders in the religious community who are more concerned with their own reputation and position than with the needs of the people (20:25-28; 23:5-12; 24:45-51).

God cares for each believer, even the weakest. This paragraph begins and ends with God's care for his sheep (18:10, 13-14). Although scholars have proposed various interpretations for verse 10 (for example, that *angels* simply means the spirits of the little ones after death, Acts 12:15; Mt 22:30; *2 Baruch* 51:5, 12; Carson 1984:401), the majority view—and the most satisfactory interpretation of this passage in light of ancient Jewish ways of speaking—is that it refers to guardian angels (see Davies and Allison 1991:770-72). The guardian angels of these children were of the highest rank, indicating their special place before God (compare Jeremias 1971:182; Meier 1980:203-4). In view of the full Palestinian Jewish background, verse 14 even more clearly reiterates that "it is not God's will for even the very least to be lost" (see Jeremias 1971:10, 39 and 1972:39-40; compare 2 Pet 3:9).

This text summons those who share God's agendas to go after those who stray. It is not enough not to cause stumbling; we must also actively seek to prevent anyone from stumbling. Higher-status urban people generally looked down on shepherds (*b. Sanhedrin* 25b; Jeremias 1972:132-33; MacMullen 1974:1-2, 15), but biblical heroes like Moses, David and Amos had been shepherds (Ex 3:1; 1 Sam 16:11; 17:15, 28, 34-37; Amos 1:1; 7:14-15), and the Bible especially portrayed God in these terms (for example, Ps 23:1; 78:52; Is 40:11). *A hundred* represents an average-size flock (Jeremias 1972:133). Contemporary evidence

---

18:10 On guardian angels in Judaism, see, for example, Hebrews 1:14; Ps-Philo 11:12; 59:4; *Sipre Num.* 40.1.5; Philo *Giants* 9.
18:12 God appears as shepherd repeatedly in the Psalms (Ps 23:1-4; 28:9; 74:1-2) and elsewhere in the Bible (Is 40:11; Jer 13:17; 31:10; Ezek 34:11-17; Mic 7:14) and Jewish texts

indicates that shepherds and cowherds did leave their flocks or herds to search for lost animals (1 Sam 9:3; Diog. Laert. 1.109; Hock 1988:139); often shepherds would leave sheep with other shepherds (compare Lk 2:8; Bailey 1976:149). Like God, a true shepherd for God will search for the straying sheep (Ezek 34:4, 11).

When I returned from college, I went to visit a friend who had always been faithful in church attendance and witnessing. He had left the church a year before, yet no one from the church had so much as called to see how he was doing. Whether it was because he was single or because his income was minimal I do not know, but he became one of many examples I saw of wounded Christians neglected by our churches. We cannot ultimately make people's decisions for them, but we can certainly help them. Former members who no longer attend church and the people who pray for salvation at our altars and then leave remain our responsibility as Christ's church. God does not send them just to improve our statistics and self-esteem.

☐ Discipline and Forgiveness (18:15-35)

The paragraph on discipline fits closely with the preceding paragraph on seeking the straying sheep and the paragraph before that warning against causing little ones to stumble. It also fits with the following story about conditional forgiveness. By holding discipline and grace in their proper tension (with a greater but not imbalanced emphasis on grace), Matthew summons the church to practice tough love.

Addressing Stumbling Blocks Seriously (18:15-20) Compare Luke 17:3. We must pursue the straying sheep (Mt 18:10-14), but certain very exceptional circumstances demand expulsion of wolves in sheep's clothing who may not wish to leave (vv. 15-20; compare 7:15-23). In this context of forgiveness to the greatest possible extent (18:21-27), however, our ultimate goal must be restoration whenever possible, even when we must expel someone from the church (compare vv. 19-20; 1

(Sirach 18:13; *1 Enoch* 89.18; Ps-Philo 28.5; 30.5). Thus God led and protected his people, for whom he cared. Israel nearly always appears as God's flock, in the Psalms (Ps 74:1; 77:20), Prophets (Is 49:9; 63:11; Zech 9:16; 10:3) and other Jewish texts (*1 Enoch* 89-90; 4 Ezra 5:23-24; Ps-Philo 23:12; *Mek. Pisḥa* 1.162).

Cor 5:5; 2 Cor 2:5-11; 1 Tim 1:20). The greatest sin of this context is being a continuing stumbling block to others (18:6-7, 15), which must include unwillingness to accept them back (vv. 28-33; compare vv. 1-14)—a sin that results in damnation (vv. 34-35). The principle would apply to many kinds of sin, but in this context such a sin, whether committed by those expelled or by those expelling others, is most probably an unrepented and continuing sin against the community or its members.

Admonish the Brother or Sister Privately First (18:15) Although Jewish teachers preferred that the offender seek forgiveness first, Jewish law also emphasized proper giving and receiving of reproof (as in *Sipre Deut.* 1.3.2), which continued until the offender repented or decisively repulsed the reprover (Moore 1971:2:153). Rabbis emphasized that reproof was to be private whenever possible (as in *b. Sanhedrin* 101a); a sage could thus rule that publicly shaming one's fellow warrants exclusion from the coming age (*m. 'Abot* 3:11). The Dead Sea Scrolls also emphasize this sequence: private reproof, then before witnesses, and finally before the gathered assembly (compare Schiffman 1983:97-98). Public admonition was reserved for the severest of circumstances (compare Gal 2:14).

Witnesses Must Gather Evidence (18:16) Although we hope for reconciliation, we must gather evidence in the proper order in case we later need proof of what transpired. As community centers, synagogues doubled as local courts, a function they maintained when evaluating internal disputes in Diaspora Jewish communities (see comment on 10:17); Christians transferred the same function to churches (1 Cor 5:4-5; 6:1-5). Later Jewish teachers regularly echoed the judicial requirement of Deuteronomy 17:6-7 and 19:15; under such rules to speak evil of another without supporting witnesses warranted a public beating (Belkin 1940:267). The requirement of two witnesses remained standard judicial procedure among Christians (2 Cor 13:1-2; 1 Tim 5:19-20).

The Church Must Discipline False Christians (18:17) Jesus' repeated condemnations of "hypocrisy" apply to professed disciples, not

---

18:18 In later Jewish literature "binding" and "loosing" signify legislative authority through interpreting the law; they mean "prohibiting" and "permitting," respectively, regularly in rabbinic texts (*m. Giṭṭin* 9:1; *t. Sanhedrin* 7:2). This legislative authority could be extended just to the religious establishment of his day (24:51). If all else fails, the Christian community must publicly dissociate itself from a habitually sinning professed Christian: neither outsiders nor the sinner should continue under the delusion that this person is truly saved. Thus one should treat such a person as a tax gatherer (9:9; 21:32) or a Gentile (5:47; 6:7; 20:25)—unclean and to be avoided. Although lesser forms of discipline existed (as in 1QS 6.25 vs. 5.16-17; 2 Thess 3:6), this discipline was full excommunication, implying spiritual death (1 Cor 5:5; 1 Tim 1:20; Tit 3:10-11). Professing Christians never repudiated by the church have perpetrated many evils throughout history, bringing shame to the body of Christ.

In Such Cases the Church Acts on God's Authority (18:18) God authorizes the Christian judicial assembly that follows these procedures to act on the authority of *heaven*. The unrepentant person has already left God's way and cannot be restored without repentance. The verb tenses allow (though do not demand) the meaning the context suggests: the earthly action follows the heavenly decree (compare Mantey 1973). By removing an unrepentant sinner from the Christian community, believers merely ratify the heavenly court's decree (see Keener 1991a:141-43; in Jewish courts, compare *t. Roš Haššana* 1:18), removing branches already dead on the vine (compare Jn 15:2, 6).

Bind and *loose* refer to the judicial authority of gathered Christians to decide cases on the basis of God's law. Most scholars thus recognize that this passage applies to church discipline (Cullmann 1953:204-5; R. Fuller 1971:141). The more popular use of "binding" today in many circles (exercising authority over the devil) resembles instead an ancient practice in the magical papyri—also called "binding" (see note on 12:29)—of manipulating demons to carry out a magician's will. (The Bible does support Christians' authority to cast out real demons—compare comment on 17:17—but the only "devils" in *this* passage are fully human ones, and they are being cast out of the church!)

Witnesses Are to Pray, Not Act Vindictively (18:19) Given the

---

judicially, and the terms also naturally apply figuratively to judicial action, given the literal use for detaining and releasing prisoners (Jos. *War* 1.111). The neuter *hosa* ("whatever") can include persons (Carson 1984:372).

context, the *two or three* gathered for prayer in verses 19-20 must be the *two or three witnesses* of 18:16. Whereas in Deuteronomy 17:6-7 the two or three witnesses were to be the first to cast stones, here they are to be the first to pray. While this could refer to the negative prayer of execration (which may have been more of a curse—compare 1 Cor 5:5), in this context of forgiveness the prayer may represent a prayer for ultimate restoration (though compare 1 Jn 5:16). Jewish excommunication even in its long-term form was normally reversible if repentance took place (*p. Mo'ed Qaṭan* 3:1, §11; though compare the extreme cases in 1QS 7.1-2, 16-17, 24-25).

Jesus Himself Is the Presence of God (18:20) An ancient Jewish saying promised God's presence for even two or three gathered to study his law (*m. 'Abot* 3:2, 6; *Mek. Bahodesh* 11.48ff.; compare *m. Berakot* 7:3). Here Jesus himself fills the role of the Shekinah, God's presence, in the traditional Jewish saying (compare Smith 1951:152-53; Meier 1980:206; Barth 1963:135; Ziesler 1984). Jewish teachers often called God "the Place," that is, "the Omnipresent One" (see Keener 1991a:150 n. 27); Jesus is "God with us" (Mt 1:23; 28:20).

Forgiveness (18:21-35) On verses 21-22, compare Luke 17:4. This parable's point is that our fellow disciples (vv. 28-29) are Christ's representatives no less than we are (vv. 5-6), and God will avenge their harsh treatment at the hands of those who claim his mercy for themselves.

Our Forgiveness Should Be Unlimited (18:21-22) Judaism also stressed forgiveness, though some teachers saw the need to limit forgiveness to three instances of premeditated sin, pointing out that repentance was otherwise not genuine (ARN 40A). But Jesus here reverses the principle of 490-fold (compare Gen 4:24 LXX) or seventy-sevenfold (Gen 4:24, where LXX uses the exact phrase; Carson 1984:405) vengeance, demanding unlimited forgiveness toward the truly repentant.

18:24 One very late rabbinic parable pictures God forgiving human debts owed to him (*Ex. Rab.* 31:1; Marmorstein 1968:63-64). An earlier parable compares sins that squander the merits of one's righteous ancestors to borrowing more and more from a king (*Sipre Deut.* 349.1.1).
18:26 "I will repay" was a standard IOU form in ancient business documents (Deissmann

God's Grace Is the Model for Forgiveness (18:23-27) Jesus portrays the magnitude of God's grace in terms that would have stretched his hearers' imagination: each of us owes God more than we could ever repay. Galileans were quite aware of some features of royal courts outside Palestine, and Jesus presents such a setting to emphasize the severity of the punishment (Derrett 1970:35). Later Jewish parables frequently include a king as a symbol for God's majesty (for example, *t. Berakot* 6:18; Johnston 1977:583). No one can offend our moral sensibilities as much as everyone offends the moral sensibilities of a perfect God!

Servants could refer to the king's high officials, like provincial satraps (Jeremias 1972:210, 212; Via 1967:138). Then again, *servants* could also be tax farmers working for the king; in earlier days some Gentile tax farmers would bid on collecting taxes for the king and could generally turn a profit—provided everyone paid their taxes (Derrett 1970:37; B. Scott 1989:270). Because tax farmers were responsible to collect the taxes for the king, they could become quite ruthless in their efficiency. Business documents from Jesus' day sometimes depict peasants with such overwhelming tax indebtedness that they fled their own land (N. Lewis 1983:164-65; Avi-Yonah 1978:216; M. Grant 1992:90).

At the appropriate time of year the king wanted to *settle accounts* with his servants. Although the talent's worth varied in different periods, ten thousand talents represented between sixty and one hundred million denarii, or between thirty and one hundred million days' wages for an average peasant—a lot of work. The combined annual tribute of Galilee and Perea just after the death of the repressive Herod the Great came to only two hundred talents (Jos. *Ant.* 17.318; Jeremias 1972:30); the tribute of Judea, Samaria and Idumea came to six hundred talents (Jos. *Ant.* 17.320). This fact starkly reveals the laughably hyperbolic character of the illustration: the poor man owes the king more money than existed in circulation in the whole country at the time! The man was a fool to

---

1978:331). Compare with this parable the public gratitude (and economic recovery) when imperial benefactors released the debts of peasants or other economically ravaged people (M. Grant 1992:88-89; Bowersock 1965:85). Such a royal release of a city's debt serves as an early third-century parable of God's forgiveness of Israel on Rosh Hashanah (*Pes. Rab.* 51:8); compare a possibly earlier comparison in Derrett 1970:46.

get so far in debt, and the king had been a fool to let him get away with it. Jesus could compare God with a father (Lk 15:12) or landowner (Mt 21:33-37) so merciful that hearers would consider him shamelessly indulgent. So here he compares God with a king who let a subordinate get too far into debt to ever pay him back. The grace of God is so deep and unimaginable that it repeatedly bursts the bounds of Jesus' metaphor.

Selling the man into slavery would recover virtually none of the loss, though it might abate some of the king's anger: the most expensive slave recorded would sell for only a talent, the average being one-twentieth to one-fifth of that (Jeremias 1972:211). Jewish custom prohibited the sale of women and children, but Jesus' hearers recognized that a pagan king wouldn't care about such just technicalities (compare *m. Soṭa* 3:8; *t. Soṭa* 2:9; Jeremias 1972:180, 211; Derrett 1970:38; Via 1967:138-39). In all, the king was bound to lose at least 9,999 talents (as much as 99,990,000 days' wages, or roughly 275,000 years' wages for an average worker) despite the sale. Perhaps this was one reason the king canceled the debt at the pitiable sight of the fool offering to pay it all back.

Unforgiveness Toward a Fellow Servant Betrays Arrogance (18:28-30) When poor crops or other circumstances forced a ruler to forgive taxes, he did so with the understanding that his people would respect his benevolence. If he released his subordinate ministers' debts, they in turn must release the debts of those indebted to them. This principle was widely known, and the first servant should have understood it (Derrett 1970:42); but as we have seen, this servant is a fool.

Although creditors could come up with money quickly by demanding immediate payment on loans (Stambaugh and Balch 1986:72), the sum the other man owes the first servant is impossibly small compared to what that higher official owes the king. Perhaps the sum is so small that the first man previously overlooked it. Yet this first servant, perhaps still determined to repay his debt to the king, has now decided to become ruthlessly efficient in exacting what is owed him—a sum less than one-fifth of the minimum he himself would have fetched on the slave market. In other words, the forgiven servant has failed to embrace the principle of grace.

Once the unforgiven man is jailed, he is unable to settle his own debts with the king (it is still the time of accounting—Derrett 1970:41); he also is away from his active duties, costing the king more money. Further, he must depend especially on his relatives and political allies—and perhaps the king himself, as his patron—to pay his way out.

The Consequences of Unforgiveness (18:31-35) Although the other servants offer no money to release the imprisoned man, they are *distressed* or "grieved" (the same Greek term as in 17:23; 19:22; 26:22) and do not hesitate to report the forgiven servant's act, which has now cost the king (and thus ultimately them) still more money (Manson 1979:214). Ancient documents indicate that this practice of imprisoning debtors was legal—and that officials could severely punish those who abused it (Deissmann 1978:269-70).

The first servant's debt is reinstated, and he is handed over to the torturers. Jewish law forbade torture—though exceptionally cruel persons were known to practice it (as in Jos. *War* 2.448)—but pagan rulers customarily employed torture against tardy officials to extort money from their friends (Jeremias 1972:212). Yet who would be so politically naive as to come to the rescue of one who had obviously fallen from the king's favor? The magnitude of the debt was simply unpayable by any means, and the man would never escape the torturers.

Forgiveness must issue *from the heart* (18:35)—it must be sincere (compare Is 59:13). God has forgiven us; if we fail to show grace to others who have repented—guilty parties in a divorce, former gang members, adulterers, homosexuals, gossipers, crafty politicians—then this text simply promises us hellfire (compare Mt 5:7; 6:12, 14-15). One need not agree with all of Marcus Garvey's views to appreciate his indictment of professed Christians who reject Christ's teachings on love and forgiveness: "If hell is what we are taught it is, then there will be more Christians there than days in all creation" (Garvey 1923:27).

THE FINAL JOURNEY (19:1—22:46)

Jesus continues to face conflicts with the establishment and misunderstanding among his disciples, but especially once he arrives in Jerusalem, the conflicts with the municipal aristocracy—the local religious and political establishment backed by the Roman Empire—grow more intense. Without an army to support him, Jesus challenges the leadership in Jerusalem, an act that would, apart from God's intervention, inevitably invite his execution.

□ Inverting the World's Values (19:1—20:16)

Jesus' male contemporaries valued the great and powerful; Jesus summoned status-seeking men to love their wives and children. The world valued wealth; Jesus summoned his followers to sacrifice all for the kingdom, caring for the poor (19:21; compare 6:19-24). Only those who prepared for such sacrifices could enter the coming kingdom.

Grounds for Divorce in God's Law (19:1-12) The hardhearted person who cannot forgive or live in proper relation to others in Christ's body (18:1-35) will also despise weaker people in society—in Jesus' day, these included wives (19:1-12; compare Mal 2:14-16) and children (Mt 19:13-15). By contrast, Jesus, who is not hardhearted, remains unimpressed by worldly status (vv. 16-22). When we hold grudges against a genuinely repentant spouse and remain hardhearted toward her or him—whether or not we officially cast the person away—we hinder our own communication with God (1 Pet 3:7-12) and ultimately can invite our own damnation (Mt 18:34-35).

It is thus no coincidence that in Matthew Jesus' teaching on marital commitment directly follows his teaching on forgiveness (18:21-35), just as in Mark it follows a discussion of sinning against a "little one" (Mk 9:42-50; compare Mt 18:7-9). The more intimate the relationship, the deeper the wounds of interpersonal friction sear; marriage without forgiveness and reconciliation would be difficult. Some of Jesus' contemporaries for this reason either emotionally neglected or divorced their wives; many of our contemporaries refuse to form close bonds of commitment to begin with. This passage provides a number of essential principles.

Jesus Summons Us to Work Toward God's Ideals (19:1-6) God wants us to work for the purposes he intended for the world before it was marred by sin. Matthew introduces the setting of Jesus' debate in a

---

19:3 Some doubt the relevance of the Shammaite and Hillelite debate here. William Heth and Gordon Wenham rightly suggest (1984:129) that Jesus must have been stricter than Shammaites since his disciples said, *If this is the situation . . . it is better not to marry* (v.

manner similar to Mark 10:1, but again notes Jesus' healings (19:1-2). The religious elite, perhaps provoked again by Jesus' indisputable signs (compare 9:34; 12:14, 24; 14:36—15:1; 15:38; 16:1), try to lure him into a debate on the sorts of issues in which they had sharpened their own debating skills.

The two main schools of Pharisaic teachers debated the meaning of Deuteronomy 24:1, in which a man finds "any matter of indecency" (my translation) in his wife and hence divorces her. The School of Shammai interpreted Deuteronomy 24 as indicating that a man could divorce his wife for the cause of unfaithfulness ("indecency"); the School of Hillel understood the passage to mean that a man could divorce his wife for any cause, even burning his toast ("any matter"—*m. Giṭṭin* 9:10; *Sipre Deut.* 269.1.1). In practice both schools agreed that the law at least often granted the man a right to divorce, regrettable as divorce was (as in *b. Sanhedrin* 22a).

Jesus, however, circumvents their whole argument based on Deuteronomy 24. The ultimate issue should not be the right to divorce, but God's original desire for husbands and wives to be one flesh (compare Belkin 1940:231); "one flesh" is the language of family ties and alliances (as in 2 Sam 5:1). The Genesis principle from which Jesus draws this application goes beyond opposing divorce; it opposes marital disharmony altogether. Indeed, the purpose of the Deuteronomy 24 law itself was probably "to check haste in divorce" (Gundry 1982:380), hence to provide some legal protection for the wife (Luck 1987:109; compare Coiner 1968:368-69). Jesus' call to follow and proclaim him comes first (Mt 10:34-39; 19:27-30), but one's relationship with a spouse must take priority over any other relationship but one's relationship with Christ.

Although his opponents claim Scripture for their purposes, Jesus challenges their actual knowledge of Scripture by showing that they are proof texting rather than reading it in light of God's whole plan: *Haven't you read . . . ?* (v. 4; compare 12:3; 21:16, 42; 22:31). Some Pharisees might have considered Jesus "liberal" (as we would put it) in his interpretations, but his objection was not to Scripture but to human traditions of interpretation (15:2-9; compare 5:17-20; 8:4; 22:24, 32); here

---

10). I suspect, however, that he is stricter merely in calling remarriage adultery (v. 9); Shammaites could not invalidate Hillelite marriages.

he even attributes a saying of the biblical narrator directly to God (19:4-5; J. Wenham 1977:28).

Some People Interpret the Bible in a Way That Treats Others Unjustly (19:7-8) God sometimes allowed what was less than ideal because people's hard hearts made the ideal unattainable (for example, Ex 13:17; 1 Sam 12:12-13). To be able to exercise some restraint over human injustice, Moses' civil laws regulated some institutions rather than seeking to abolish them altogether: divorce, polygyny, the avengers of blood, and slavery (Keener 1992b:192-96). Jewish lawyers themselves recognized that God had allowed some behavior as a concession to human weakness (Daube 1959).

Nevertheless, Jesus' opponents here assume that whatever the law addresses it permits (Mt 19:7). Jesus responds that Moses permitted this merely as a concession to Israel's hard hearts, implying that his questioners who exploit this concession also have hard hearts. Thus in Matthew (in contrast to Mark) the Pharisees even exploit Moses' concession as a command (Gundry 1982:380). American slaveholders were similarly sure that the practice of slavery in biblical times proved the Bible's approval of slavery (Sawyer 1858), the same way Muslim slaveholders applied the Qur'an (Gordon 1989:xi; B. Lewis 1990:78). Some husbands today twist biblical teachings to justify abusing their wives (see, for example, Alsdurf and Alsdurf 1989). And some churches use Jesus' words in this very passage—words that may have been meant to protect an innocent Jewish wife from being wrongfully divorced by her husband (Kysar and Kysar 1978:43; France 1985:280; M. Davies 1993:54)—to batter innocent parties in divorces. Human nature has

---

19:9 Many interpreters take the adultery view: for example, Hauck/Schulz 1968:592; Keener 1991a:31-33; Hill 1972:125, 281; Schweizer 1975:124; Christiaens 1983; Carson 1984:414, 417; France 1985:123; Stein 1992:195; M. Davies 1993:132; tentatively, Davies and Allison 1988:529-31.

I have surveyed other views more fully in Keener 1991a:28-31; for a more extensive and favorable survey, see Heth and Wenham 1984. Many alternatives deny that a valid marriage exists (Leeming and Dawson 1956:82); some argue, for example, that the woman here is a nonmarried sexual partner (Byron 1963) or that the reference is to unions after the first in a polygynous marriage (Ramaroson 1971) or, most commonly, an incestuous union (Meier 1980:52-53; Caron 1982:312; Schedl 1982; Wambacq 1982; Witherington 1985), though nothing in the context supports such a narrow reading of the term here (if anything, *porneia* should mean more than adulterous infidelity; see Belkin 1940:230-31). Considine

changed very little in two millennia.

An Exception for the Innocent Party (19:9) God's ideal was always that we should avoid divorce; the preservation of a marriage depends on both wills, however, and one partner can sometimes end a marriage unilaterally against the other's will (see comment on 1:19). Roman law permitted either party to divorce the other; Jewish law permitted the husband to divorce the wife, regardless of the wife's wishes (Keener 1991a:51).

Matthew mentions an exception to the general rule about divorce: *except for marital unfaithfulness,* or literally (and more ambiguously) except for *porneia,* sexual immorality. The NIV probably rightly interprets the sense for this context, which provides a specific exception for those already married. When Matthew speaks of this exception, his readers very probably would have understood this as a legal charge (as in Quint. 7.4.11; Suet. *Julius* 6, 74), hence as referring to unfaithfulness; thus, for example, the wife's adultery exempted the husband from returning her funds to her (Safrai 1974-1976b:790). Jewish and Roman law both required divorce for these grounds (Safrai 1974-1976b:762; see comment on 1:19). Matthew's audience would thus probably interpret these words in line with the typical meaning of "infidelity," namely, sexual unfaithfulness to the marriage, as grounds for divorce. Mark and Luke probably could assume such an exception without explicitly stating it (Carson 1984:418). As France puts it (1985:124):

> To repudiate a wife after she had committed adultery was therefore simply the recognition that the marriage had already been terminated

---

1956 proposes ecclesiastical annulments here based on rejecting Christ; Fleming 1963 that Jesus' public view allowed an exception for adultery, but his more private comments later forbade even that; Sabatowich 1987 that one does not cause the unfaithful woman to become adulterous because she already is (this seems too self-evident and tautological to require Matthew to include an exception clause); Lehmann 1960:265 that the exception is only for Jews.

Heth and Wenham 1984 helpfully summarize various positions, but while they repeatedly point out that none of the other views concurs with the infidelity interpretation (which they characterize as the "Erasmian" and "evangelical" view), we should note that the other views also conflict with one another. *All* positions are minority positions, but the infidelity position probably claims more adherents than any other.

by the creation of a new union. . . . The Matthaean exceptive clause is . . . making explicit what any Jewish reader would have taken for granted when Jesus made the apparently unqualified pronouncements of Mark 10:9-12.

I believe that most other views of *porneia* in this text fail to treat Matthew's specific cultural setting adequately (taking into account the "charge") beyond their own proposal. Most of these views also give *porneia* ("immorality," "infidelity") a more restricted meaning than it normally bears unless explicitly qualified, which it is not here (as noted by many commentators, such as Hagner 1993:124). They also miss how such a term (used in its unqualified, general sense) would function in a usual legal context (see above). Most views other than the infidelity view imply that Matthew permits divorce only when the original marriage is not valid, but divorce was unnecessary in the case of invalid marriages; further, such marriages were not common enough to warrant Matthew's mention.

"Except for infidelity" may modify Jesus' statement about divorce rather than remarriage (Heth and Wenham 1984:117; G. Wenham 1984 and 1986; compare against this position Murray 1953:39-43), but if it does, it does so precisely because in Jesus' graphic statement it is the validity of the divorce that is in question. No one permitted remarriage if a divorce was invalid, but a valid divorce by definition included the right to remarry, as is attested by ancient divorce contracts (see, for example, *m. Giṭṭin* 9:3; *CPJ* 2:10-12, §144; Carmon 1973:90-91, 200-201) and the very meaning of the term (besides sources in Keener 1991a, see, for example, Jos. *Ant.* 4.253; Blomberg 1992:111). Jesus' point is at any rate not to break up second and third marriages (even for guilty parties)—as if the hyperbolic element in his graphic statement might be missed—but to underline in no uncertain terms the sanctity of marriage and our solemn responsibility to preserve it when this is at all possible. Thus most conservative Christian writers acknowledge some cases where divorce and remarriage are permitted (for example, Dobson 1986:68; Adams 1980:86-87).

19:10-12 Some scholars have argued that Jesus here recommends celibacy specifically for all men divorced for the sake of the kingdom, but this reads Jesus' response as if he simply appealed back to verse 9 and the disciples had not raised an objection in verse 10. Yet in

***Remaining Single Is Sometimes the Price of Following Jesus
(19:10-12)*** The disciples are concerned about the danger of marrying
without an escape clause, and Jesus responds to their question (Carson
1984:418-19; France 1985:282). Parents arranged marriages, and in
Galilee at least prospective spouses could not spend time alone until
after the wedding (Safrai 1974-1976b:756-57; Finkelstein 1962:1:45).
Then, more so than today, marriage partners could not know in advance
how their spouse would turn out. To marry without the possibility of
divorce in a painful marriage seemed worse than not marrying at all!
Responding to this objection, Jesus replied that some would indeed be
better off not marrying; perhaps because of the intensity of their calling,
it would be difficult for them to find a compatible spouse who would
share their commitment (this is not only an ancient situation).

Jesus' remark about celibacy is graphic and would certainly seize the
attention of Jewish listeners; Jewish people did not allow eunuchs into
the covenant (Deut 23:1; though compare Is 56:4-5; Tannehill 1975:136-
37). Although some sectarians in the wilderness may have preferred
celibacy, mainstream Jewish society regarded marriage and childbearing
as solemn responsibilities (Keener 1991a:72-78). A metaphor of such
shame and sacrifice testifies to the value of the kingdom of God for
which anyone would pay such a price (Tannehill 1975:138-40). By
embracing both shame and temporary self-control, Joseph to a lesser
extent models the nature of this demand (1:25; compare 1 Cor 7).

The Kingdom Belongs to Children (19:13-15) Jesus here reiterates
his teaching in 18:1-6, which his disciples have apparently forgotten
(compare again 21:15). Like their culture, they think "children should
be seen and not heard." Children were low-status dependents; they had
to trust adults and receive what they provided (compare Best 1976:133-
34). Disciples did not want their teacher interrupted (2 Kings 4:27; Diog.
Laert. 7.7.182), and Jesus' disciples did not want these children, low in
status, to deter Jesus from more important matters (Mt 19:13).

Later, lest Jesus be delayed in his mission to Jerusalem, crowds tried

---

contrast to their argument, even verse 26 may refer back to the question of verse 25; further,
Jesus normally answers disciples' questions directly (13:10-11, 36-37, 24:3-4), though
sometimes impatiently (15:15-16).

to silence blind beggars (20:31). It seems that in both 19:13 and 20:31, as in the parallel passages in Mark, disciples and crowds alike fail to understand what Jesus' kingdom is really about—caring for the weakest, rather than engaging in political or military triumphalism.

The Cost of Discipleship (19:16-22) If the kingdom belongs to children (19:13-15)—those who receive the kingdom as humble dependents (18:1-6)—then someone accustomed to being powerful and supporting dependents might find it difficult to enter the kingdom (compare 5:20; 7:14; 18:8; 25:46). This is the illustration with which 19:16-24 confronts us: wealth and status make perfect surrender to God's will more difficult, because we think we have more to lose.

Many examples of faith in the Bible are acts of desperation; few are the acts of self-satisfied individuals. Ultimately one who would receive the kingdom must not only obey like a trusting child but also relinquish worldly possessions and cares, acknowledging the absolute authority of our King.

Those Who Want Eternal Life Must Obey God's Commands (19:16-20) The *good thing* the man must do is show his fidelity toward God's covenant by obeying his laws. These laws were part of first-century Jewish culture, and the young man is convinced that he has kept them, as many of us have avoided breaking the laws of our society (compare Odeberg 1964:60). But if he is really ready to submit to the yoke of God's kingdom, he must also become a follower of Jesus and submit to Jesus' demands. That he is unwilling to spare all his goods to help the poor will soon bring into question whether he really loves his neighbor as himself (vv. 19-22).

Jesus Summons Disciples to Absolute Commitment (19:21-22) The commandments listed in verses 18-19 are humanward, summarized in the decree *Love your neighbor as yourself* (Lev 19:18); by adding these words from 22:39, Matthew underlines this point. Yet if God alone is *good* (19:17), the man is lacking in some way (he himself admits it in v.

19:17 Jewish teachers recognized that just as they praised God as good (Philo *Change of Names* 7; *m. Berakot* 9:2), so also his commandments are good (*p. Roš Haššana* 3:8, §5; Abrahams 1924:186).
19:21 Diogenes also successfully exhorted Crates to discard all his money into the sea

20, allowing Jesus to echo in 19:21 the call in 5:48 to "perfect obedience"). Now the man's allegiance to the Godward love commandment (22:37-38) is tested: does he serve God or money (6:24)? Loss of our wealth or fear of how our needs will be met can test us in this way (6:19-34); the needs of the poor can test us in the same way, as here. Love for God demands a true love for neighbors that not only avoids harming them but actively serves them. The young man wants a *teacher* (19:16); he does not want a Lord who demands sacrifice (20:20-28).

By "going" (19:21; also 8:4; 20:4; compare 10:6; 28:19) and abandoning all else (compare especially 13:44), the man could have "followed" Jesus, that is, become his disciple (compare 4:19; 8:22; 9:9; 16:24). The kingdom demands more than merely keeping many commandments; if we recognize Christ as our King, we must surrender to him everything we have and are (compare L. Johnson 1981:17). Whether he then allows us to use some of what he has given us is his choice. Disciples do not always lose all possessions upon conversion—but they lose all ownership of them, for they themselves belong to a new ruler.

Jesus generally called his own chief disciples (Mt 4:19, 21). Yet on some occasions prospective disciples did approach him (8:19); as here, Jesus sometimes thrust them aside—probably, like some other ancient teachers, to test the would-be student's real willingness to become a learner (as in Diog. Laert. 6.2.21, 36; 7.1.22; compare *Sipre Num.* 115.5.7). When Jesus turned away prospective disciples with heavy demands, he probably intended the same as some other teachers did: disciples must count the cost, repudiate their prior assets and recognize the incomparable value of his teaching.

Persistent seekers throughout the Gospels display the appropriate response: the Canaanite woman (Mt 15:25-28), the blind men (20:31-34), the Gentile centurion (8:7-13) and Jesus' own mother (Jn 2:3-9). Jesus' sorrow over the unwilling disciple (Mk 10:23-25) indicates that he hoped not to turn inquirers away but rather to make them genuine disciples, which they could become only if they counted the cost and chose the

---

(Diog. Laert. 6.5.87). Diogenes was happy to attract disciples—provided they were willing to pay the appropriate price for following him, which could include forsaking family (Diog. Laert. 6.2.75-76; compare Mt 4:22; 8:21-22; 10:35-37; see Young 1989:214).

narrow way of following him.

When we tell prospective disciples today, "Just ask Jesus to forgive your sins and you can go to heaven," we are not telling the whole truth of the gospel. Jesus is available for the asking, but accepting Jesus means accepting the reign of God and God's right to determine what we do with our lives. When we invite our Lord to free us from sin, we are inviting him to rule our life; and while we may yet fall short in submission to his will, we must actively acknowledge his right to determine our lives, acting on the knowledge that he has begun to transform us by his Spirit. If we accept Jesus' terms of unconditional surrender to him, however, he promises an unlimited supply of what truly matters (Mt 19:23-30).

The wealthy would-be disciple was not the only person whose attachment to possessions proved a challenge to his commitment to Christ. As Dietrich Bonhoeffer, martyred by the Nazis, pointed out, the difference between us and the rich man in the story is that Jesus stood before him and did not allow him to reinterpret the Master's words in a more convenient manner. Bonhoeffer claims that the man's honesty in rejecting Jesus' command was better than disobedience that pretends to be obedience today (1963:88). He compares a boy told by his father to go to bed; the boy has studied theology, however, so he is now intelligent enough to reason, "Father tells me to go to bed, but he really means that I am tired, and he does not want me to be tired. I can overcome my tiredness just as well if I go out and play." But a child offering such arguments to his father would likely meet with language or an experience he would have to interpret more literally, as would a citizen with her government—or a disciple who reasons away God's demands (Bonhoeffer 1963:90).

Sacrifice and Reward (19:23-30) Jesus had promised a man treasure in heaven if he followed him (v. 21; compare 6:20); the man preferred to keep his treasure on earth (19:22). The well-to-do young man of 19:16-22 was like many "First World" Christians today. We want God to

---

19:24 Some commentators speculated that *eye of a needle* referred to a low gate in Jerusalem peasant homes into which a camel could enter if it cast off its load; there is no evidence,

affirm that we are religious enough without costing us anything more than we have already been offering him. We trust only tentatively the value of heaven's kingdom and hence are prepared to sacrifice only little for it; but one who is not sufficiently convinced of the gospel's truth to sacrifice everything (compare 13:44-46) will not prove worthy of it. This is not to say that we are justified by our merit—we must receive the kingdom like a child (19:13-15). But genuine, saving faith is practically shown not by merely reciting a prayer but by living consistently with what we profess.

Jesus promises to more than make up for our sacrifices; do we believe him enough to sacrifice whatever our calling demands? As Craig Blomberg (1992:301) comments: "This entire episode should challenge First-World Christians, virtually all of whom are among the wealthiest people in the history of the world, to radical changes in their personal and institutional spending."

The Powerful Can Scarcely Enter the Kingdom at All (19:23-24) Jesus apparently employs a common figure of speech when he speaks of a camel passing through a needle's eye (see Abrahams 1924:208; Dalman 1929:230). As much as we want Jesus to have said something else, he said that the rich and powerful could barely enter the kingdom at all. This statement shocked the sensibilities of the disciples even more than verse 10 had; they share the values of Jesus' enemies (Rhoads and Michie 1982:91-92; Mt 16:23). Presumably because many of their contemporaries viewed wealth as a mark of God's blessing (for example, *Ep. Arist.* 204-5; *m. Qiddušin* 4:14), the disciples may have assumed that Jesus' standard for people who were not rich was even stricter. If not the rich, *who then can be saved?* (19:25). Yet because God alone is good (v. 17), salvation by merely human means is impossible for anyone.

Jesus Promises the Kingdom to Whoever Follows Him (19:25-30) The disciples emphasize that they have forsaken all to follow Jesus, and he does not dispute their claim (vv. 27-28; 4:22). Nevertheless, even once we have committed our lives to him, we must watch and pray to be ready for still other tests. Faced with loss of possessions, the rich

---

however, for such a gate (see Bailey 1980:166), and "needle's eye" meant then essentially what it means today; compare *m. Šabbat* 6:3.

young man walked away (19:22); faced with possible death, Jesus' disciples would later abandon him and flee (26:56).

Because families may oppose Christ's call to discipleship, a true disciple must be prepared to abandon not only possessions but also family (19:29; compare 8:21-22; 10:21, 34-37) for Christ's name (compare 5:11; 10:22; 24:9). Jesus himself (12:46-50; 13:55-57) and probably many in Matthew's Jewish Christian audience had suffered rejection by their families, a pain felt much more severely in that culture than in ours.

The modern Christian emphasis on family values is important, but we must beware lest family become idolatry: for instance, parental opposition or concern for our children is not an adequate excuse to reject God's call to the mission field. In response to such sacrifices God multiplies our resources (19:29) precisely because in the kingdom we find a new and larger family than the one we have left behind, and as a family true believers share their resources with one another (Acts 2:44-45; 4:32-35; Kee 1977:109-10; Tannehill 1975:147-52). This assumes that the church will live like the community of God's kingdom, that his will may be done on earth as it is in heaven. While such words may have encouraged early faith missionaries (Trocmé 1975:203; Rhoads and Michie 1982:92), they just as readily address a persecuted church (Heb 10:34).

Specifically to these twelve who forsook their livelihoods to follow Jesus' call, Jesus promises that they will sit on thrones judging the twelve tribes of Israel (Mt 19:28). That Jesus would reward his loyal followers would not have surprised them; they seem to have expected as much (16:16, 21-22; 20:20-22). Thus *when the Son of Man sits on his glorious throne* (19:28; compare 25:31; for "glory," 24:30) those who have

---

19:28-29 *Inherit* (v. 29) frequently appears in end-time contexts in Matthew (5:5; 21:38; 25:34), biblical and apocryphal texts (Ezek 47:13; 1 Macc 2:57; Wisdom 3:14; 5:5; Rom 8:17; 1 Cor 6:9; 1 Pet 1:4) and other Jewish literature (*Ps. Sol.* 12:6; 4 Ezra 7:96; *1 Enoch* 40:9; *m. 'Abot* 3:11), perhaps evoking a new exodus (Ex 32:13; 1 Macc 2:56; 11QTemple 51:15-16; see Hester 1968:22-36). The language Matthew uses for *renewal* could suggest the Stoic idea of a cosmic conflagration, ending one of the universe's periodic cycles (see description in F. Bruce 1972b:44); but in a Jewish context this must refer to the time of the new creation (Manson 1979:216). From Isaiah (65:17) on, this was a familiar Jewish hope (see Black 1961:135-36; Gaster 1976:23).

19:30 The rhyming meter suggests authenticity (see Jeremias 1971:27; compare Dalman 1929:228). For one defense of probable authenticity of the following parable (20:1-16) see

followed him in his humble estate will rule (a common sense of "judge"; compare, for example, Judg 4:4; 10:3; 12:7-14; 15:20; 1 Macc 9:73) Israel's twelve tribes. Indeed, Jesus probably chose exactly twelve disciples with such a connection in mind; see comment on 10:1.

In Matthew's context the lesson extends beyond the Twelve (5:19; 20:23): those who sacrifice now and become least in this age will inherit the place of honor in the coming age (19:30—20:16; 19:30 and 20:16 function as an inclusio, bracketing the enclosed parable). The disciples' reward in the kingdom will be commensurate with their sacrifice.

Reversal of Fortunes (19:30—20:16) The parable in 20:1-16 explicitly illustrates the point that *the first will be last* and *the last . . . first* (19:30; 20:16); Matthew uses this principle to frame the parable and hence summarize its primary point. The principle appears at the same point in Mark, though Matthew alone includes this parable of laborers in the vineyard.

Jesus may have defended outcasts in this parable. Whether one thinks of Gentiles or of other excluded classes, recognizing the exaltation of the socially, ethnically or morally excluded fits Jesus' emphasis elsewhere (as in 22:1-14; 23:12; Lk 14:11; compare 1 Cor 1:26-31). In Matthew's context the emphasis is probably on disciples who humble themselves and sacrifice much but are amply rewarded, in contrast to those who only pretend to follow without sacrifice (19:21-30; 23:2-12). Jesus speaks of rank in the day of judgment (5:19).

Jesus' hearers could relate to the story he told. Rich landowners (Jas 5:1-5), vineyards (Song 8:11; *m. Kil'ayim* 4:1—8:1) and hirelings (Jn 10:12) were important features of Galilean life in this period. Other

---

Fortna 1990, where also the realism of 20:1-7 is contrasted with the unthinkable, hence dramatic, conflict of 20:8-15.

20:1 Two later rabbinic parables may reflect a common story line; the first is *Sipra Behuq.* pq. 2.262.1.9, in which a king pays other workers a modest wage but to an especially hard worker, symbolizing Israel, he provides much pay. Matthew's version may deliberately contradict this older parable (Smith 1951:50-51), flouting conventional values (Johnston 1977:633-35; see also Young 1989:262-66). Jeremias also cites a fourth-century parable he thinks is dependent on Jesus here (1972:138-39); it speaks of laborers receiving equal wages for different tasks, but it was because some (representing a diligent rabbi who died young) had worked harder (1972:37; compare Young 1989:261-62; Vermes 1993:105-6).

Palestinian texts support the plausibility of various details of the text (such as the way idle workers are hired). Other Jewish teachers also could portray God as the master of one's labor, who would pay the reward of one's work (*m. 'Abot* 2:14). Many Galileans seem to have owned small homes and worked their own fields or crafts (Goodman 1983:34), but many others were peasants working the estates of a handful of well-to-do absentee landlords (see Horsley and Hanson 1985:59). Sometimes workers hired themselves out to work for others for a period of time up to six years (Klausner 1979:180), but temporary help was cheaper for employers. Harvest required an influx of extra workers—most to harvest, and some to guard crops in the fields and gathered sheaves against thieves and animals. A few lesser-paid donkey drivers, sometimes boys, were often required as well (N. Lewis 1983:122-23). Landowners typically drew from the ranks of the landless—sometimes homeless—poor for such brief and urgent tasks (Goodman 1983:38-39).

A day officially began at sunset, but Jewish people reckoned hours from sunrise at about 6:00 a.m. (Jeremias 1972:136 n. 21); the third hour was thus between 8:00 and 9:00 a.m. and the eleventh hour (v. 6) between 4:00 and 5:00. Twelve-hour workdays were customary only during harvest time. In Jesus' story the landowner finds extra workers sitting idle in the marketplace because they have not been hired.

God rewards his servants according to grace. As in verse 8, employers paid wages in the evening (Lev 19:13; Deut 24:14-15; Jeremias 1972:136; Goodman 1983:39). The landowner pays equal wages to all the workers, a full day's work for each. Those who have worked all day lose nothing; justice is served, but mercy is added. Jewish hearers would consider it pious to give wages even to those not expecting it (*Test. Job* 12:3-4; *p. Baba Meṣi'a* 6:1, §2; compare Jos. *Ant.* 20.219-20).

Those who treat God's grace as his obligation are evil. Nevertheless, those who have labored all day complain (Mt 20:11; compare Lk 15:2); Jesus' hearers may have been shocked that workers would openly react

---

20:7 Jeremias thinks "because no one has hired us" is a cover for laziness (1972:37; compare Acts 17:5; Plut. *Precepts of Statecraft* 2, *Mor.* 798C). But while they intend their response to avoid shame, they may have simply spent the morning harvesting their own smaller field. Throughout the Empire, many small holders found part-time employment only during harvest or by serving on larger estates (Finley 1973:107). Unemployed day laborers were

so negatively to a benevolent landowner from whom they might need future favors. But the landowner puts them in their place, politely shaming them by reminding them that they are objecting not to injustice but to generosity. In verse 15 he is *generous* (literally "good"; compare 19:17); they are *envious* (literally, have an "evil eye"—are stingy; see comment on 6:23). In verse 13 he singles out one, perhaps the primary murmurer (Jeremias 1972:137), but whereas the workers have neglected to greet him with the requisite title (20:12; compare Lk 15:29), he offers a polite title, *Friend* (Mt 20:13)—which Matthew always uses to shame one who has arrogantly presumed on another's grace (22:13; 26:50).

In later rabbinic parables a landowner provides one who labored two hours with pay equal to that of others who labored all day because he accomplished more in his two hours than they had all day; or he pays a hard worker, symbolizing Israel, much extra. By contrast, the image in Jesus' parable is of unmerited grace; the owner realizes that an hour's fraction of a day's wage would not sustain a family (Jeremias 1972:37; France 1985:289). But a parable of grace also challenges those who operate only on a principle of merit, despising the showing of mercy because they feel it unfairly raises others to their own standing (Jeremias 1972:38, comparing Lk 15:25-32).

☐ The Price of Jesus' Mission (20:17—21:16)

After encountering another prediction of Jesus' imminent death (20:17-19), the reader of Matthew learns the relationship between his death and his mission (20:28). Shortly after this, Jesus shames the authorities with such deliberate provocation that they must eventually arrest him or lose face (21:12-13).

Suffering for the Kingdom (20:17-19) As in Mark, Matthew's repeated passion predictions (16:21; 17:22-23) keep the reader focused on where the story of Jesus is heading. Disciples may sacrifice much and be

---

common (Horsley and Hanson 1985:58-59; Applebaum 1974-1976:657), but most of those were probably already hired in the morning.

20:15 The parable does not lack an "absolute standard of justice" (pace B. Scott 1989:296-97) so much as it points to grace that exceeds justice. But Scott is right that this parable subverts the standard mytheme in the earlier Jewish story line.

rewarded (19:21—20:16), but the ultimate sacrifice is martyrdom, the price paid by Jesus and many who would follow him all the way (20:17-19).

The placement of this prediction exposes the disciples' selfish conception of the kingdom in verses 20-22, 24: for them the kingdom is about reigning, but Jesus recognizes that reigning first requires suffering (vv. 22-28). Significantly, this passion prediction adds the notion of mocking by Gentiles, a horrifying image in a culture emphasizing shame (as in Epict. *Disc.* 1.4.10) and diametrically opposed to the picture of a militant Messiah triumphing over the nations.

The disciples had managed to ignore Jesus' warnings that did not make sense on their cultural and theological presuppositions; undoubtedly they felt that other sayings confirmed their predispositions (19:28). In this respect they were not unlike most Christians today.

The Reign of a Suffering Servant (20:20-28) This passage shows us that the disciples had misunderstood both the preceding passion predictions and Jesus' teaching concerning the kingdom's nature. Hearing Jesus' promise of a special place for the Twelve (19:28), James and John wanted to establish a special place among the Twelve. While each of us is special to the Lord, we must not fail to recognize, as the sons of Zebedee did, that all other disciples are special to him as well. To accomplish their petition they enlisted their mother; Jewish tradition accorded aged women a special place of respect that younger women did not hold (compare Judg 5:7; 2 Sam 14:2; 20:16-22; Tit 2:4). Further, women could get away with asking requests men dare not ask, both in Jewish (Lk 18:2-5; 2 Sam 14:1-21; 20:16-22; 1 Kings 1:11-16; 2:17; Bailey 1980:134) and broader Greco-Roman culture (Dixon 1988:179).

To the disciples, recognizing that Jesus was Messiah and would soon reign was an expression of faith (16:17); unfortunately, they failed to grasp the seriousness of the sacrifice that constituted the prerequisite

20:23 Because early Christian tradition has John living into the late first century, in contrast to James, the prophecy here seems not to arise after the event; hence it is likely authentic (Jeremias 1971:243-44; Hill 1972:288; E. Sanders 1985:147; pace Theissen [1991:197], who misses Gal 2:9).
20:28 Burton Mack (1988:368-76) charges that the Gospel of Mark's "myth of innocent

for his kingdom (16:21-27). Outsiders recognized Jesus' Davidic rule in truth (15:22; 20:30-31), but here James and John function more like the crowds that recognize Jesus' Davidic role when it is popular (21:9). Those crowds never became disciples who submitted to Jesus' rule; they preferred a revolutionary (27:17-25).

The Lord Evaluates the Motivation for Our Prayers (20:20-21) The context of this passage explicitly contrasts this prayer for costless glory with a desperate prayer of true need in verses 29-34. Both groups recognized Jesus as the coming King, but the first group sought Jesus for personal advancement, the latter out of genuine need.

Only Those Who Suffer with Jesus Will Reign with Him (20:22-23) This principle became a standard teaching of early Christians (Rom 8:17; 2 Thess 1:5; 2 Tim 2:12). The *cup* disciples must share is his death (26:27-28, 39), borrowed from one image of God's wrath in the Prophets (Ps 11:6; Is 51:17; Jer 25:15-17; 51:7; Hab 2:16; Zech 12:2). Jesus later tells them as much at the Last Supper (Mt 26:27-28). As R. A. Cole notes, "This price they will in any case pay, for this is not the price of Christian greatness but the price of following Christ at all" (Cole 1961:170).

The Greatest Role Belongs to the Self-Sacrificial Servant (20:24-28) James and John were not the only ones with a problem; the other disciples were angry with them because they too wanted a high position. Competition for status among peers was important in their culture (v. 24; see Derrett 1973:54; Malina 1993:133). But the world's models for status differ from those in God's kingdom; because honor ultimately belongs to God alone, we should humble ourselves and serve, allowing God to exalt us. Rank in the day of judgment (5:19) will confound many of our expectations (18:4; 23:11): it will expose the pride of many who are respected in today's church, while conversely, God's revelation of the lives of many humble and unknown servants of Christ will bring him much honor.

Jesus argues his point by means of both negative and positive

power" stands behind most of the existential troubles in the United States today (as well as behind Christian anti-Semitism). But Mark teaches disciples to abandon power rather than to seek it (Mk 10:42-45), contrary to Mack's counterreading; what Mack may dislike is how the oppressed resonate with the way the theme of justice is expressed in apocalyptic vindication.

example. Negatively, one should not be like the pagans (20:25; compare 5:47; 6:7; 18:17). Not only those in Jesus' day but all the tyrants and empires of history confirm his point: absolute power always corrupts precisely because the desire for power over others, to whatever extent we may achieve it, shows that we ourselves are slaves to self-centeredness.

Positively, Jesus himself was a suffering servant who laid down his life for us (compare Jn 13:13-15, 31-35). This is a typical Jewish "how much more" argument: if our Master was a servant, how much more should we humble ourselves! Matthew sees in this an allusion to the suffering servant of Isaiah (Mt 12:18), particularly in offering his "soul" or "life" as "a ransom" or redemption price on behalf of "many" ("the many"; Is 53:10-12; compare Mt 26:28; Rom 5:15; see Cullmann 1959:64-65; pace Hooker 1959:74-79).

The language here is that of substitutionary atonement (see especially Morris 1965:34; Gundry 1982:404; compare Ladd 1974b:187-88). As in Philippians 2:1-11, however, the Evangelists treat us to this summary of Jesus' mission not to rehearse the doctrine of salvation but to provide an active model for Christian living. To what extent would Jesus serve? Fulfilling the servant's mission, he would lay down his life on behalf of his people; of disciples he expects no less.

Persistent Prayer (20:29-34) Despite the notorious dangers of roads like the one from Jericho to Jerusalem (v. 29; compare Lk 10:30), many beggars would have sought alms from Passover pilgrims there in this season (Lane 1974:387). Although Matthew, abbreviating Mark's account, omits the label "faith" here (Mk 10:52), he illustrates the same principle (Mt 9:29). While this text does not promote selfish prayers like the one illustrated in 20:20-21, it does provide principles for one with a desperate need (vv. 32-33). Like many other passages, this one provides a model for how to approach our risen Lord today.

These Suppliants Recognize Jesus' Identity (20:29-30) They could entreat Jesus in faith because they recognized his authority. They recognized that he was *Son of David*—rightful ruler in God's coming kingdom (1:1; 15:22; 21:9). They also acknowledged their need of *mercy* (5:7; compare 6:2-4—"alms" originally literally meant "acts of mercy"), humbly depending on his favor rather than their own merit or formulas.

They Refuse to Let Others' Priorities Deter Them (20:31) The crowd already "following" Jesus (vv. 29, 31; compare 8:1; 19:2) did not want a figure of Jesus' caliber to be interrupted by a beggar. Many probably wanted him to get on with the business of setting up the kingdom they hoped he would establish (21:9). It is easy for us to want to get on with "ministry," with what we suppose are the agendas of the kingdom, and forget that God's agendas demand that we serve people in need (20:28; compare 19:13). We must exercise sufficient faith in our Lord's authority and concern so that no one else's impatient dismissal of our need will hinder our dependence on God (compare 8:7; 15:24-26).

Compassion Is Jesus' Ultimate Motivation (20:32-34) Although the men's need for sight was obvious, Jesus allowed them to voice their need (vv. 32-33); then he acted from his compassion (v. 34). God knows the pain in his people's lives. Whether he gives us the strength to endure pain or (quite often) heals us in response to persistent prayer, it is not because we have mastered formulas of prayer. It is because he cares for us intimately (6:8; compare 9:36; 14:14; 15:32).

Recipients of Jesus' Gifts Should Follow Him (20:34) Responding to Jesus' compassionate healing, the formerly blind men now choose to follow him, becoming models of discipleship. We who have seen both Jesus' power and his compassion best show our love by following him as disciples (Matthew's primary sense of "follow"—8:19, 22; 19:21). We should remember, however, that following Jesus means following to the cross (20:17-28).

Jerusalem's King Enters Its Gates (21:1-11) Despite the prevalence of skepticism in our culture, there is little reason to question the substance of this account. Later storytellers would probably not have thought to have invented accurate allusions to Jerusalem Passover customs, such as an acclamation from Psalm 118 (which was recited during festivals); this suggests genuine historic tradition in the triumphal entry. If Jesus rode an ass into Jerusalem, he himself probably intended an allusion to Zechariah (E. Sanders 1993:254). And why not, if Jesus both read the Hebrew Bible and knew himself to be descended from David?

More important, this narrative both portrays Jesus as a king and defines the significance of his kingship. Because his kingship was so different from worldly models of authority (20:25), Jesus subverts the worldly understanding of kingship to suggest a reign of a different order.

All Our Possessions Belong to Our King (21:1-3) Matthew devotes less space than Mark to Jesus' "impressing" or commandeering an animal, but in both Gospels Jesus exercises a prerogative of royalty. Although household servants could think of *the Lord* as the donkey's absent earthly owner, the borrowing more likely testifies to Jesus' status. Whether or not the owner is a disciple, he has heard of Jesus, and Jesus foreknows his response; this testifies first of all to the man's respect for Jesus. More important, the passage testifies to Jesus' foreknowledge (that he would have prearranged the situation with the man without the knowledge of his disciples—who would have been his agents—is unlikely; compare 26:18). Thus Matthew is making a statement not so much about possessions here as about Christ: as the rightful King he has the right to anything in creation, certainly among his people (compare Gundry 1982:408; Blomberg 1992:311-12).

Jesus Chose to Define the Kind of King He Is (21:4-6) Mark seems unaware of Zechariah 9:9 (see Gundry 1975:197-98), but Matthew and John, the Gospels bearing the most Palestinian flavor and most apt to recognize the source of the allusion, explicitly cite this text. Although later teachers and probably Jesus' contemporaries regarded this prophecy as messianic (*b. Sanhedrin* 98a; 99a; *Gen. Rab.* 75:6; Edgar 1958:48-49), it was not such a popular text that his first followers need have grasped the full significance of his actions immediately. Jesus was announcing that he was indeed a king, but not a warrior-king (Moule 1965:87; E. Sanders 1993:242). Jesus was the meek one (11:29; 12:18-21; compare 5:5).

Many of Jesus' People Did Offer Homage (21:7-11) Even many who did not understand the nature of Jesus' kingship paid him royal

21:3 Rulers (as Jesus is here) and officials could impress animals; Jewish teachers (as the man presumably regards Jesus) apparently could also borrow animals from those who respected these teachers (Derrett 1971).
21:12 Later reports suggest that the authorities allowed moneychangers in the temple for only one week, beginning to change money on Adar 25, several days before the temple tax was due (*m. Šeqalim* 1.3). Some later reports suggest that moneychanging, originally

homage. Matthew specifically upgrades the Christology of Mark's crowd; his coming leads not only to cries that the Davidic kingdom must be imminent but to hailing Jesus himself as *Son of David*, the promised King. Yet even in Matthew, Jerusalem itself does not know Jesus (v. 10; compare 8:27); the crowds of Passover pilgrims (presumably from Galilee) must announce him (21:11).

Although the crowds had to honor Jesus by casting something before him (2 Kings 9:12-13) and branches were appropriate to the festal setting (Ps 118:27; compare Rev 7:9; 2 Macc 10:7), another Gospel's specific mention of palm branches (Jn 12:13) is significant, for they normally were more in use at the Feast of Tabernacles—or for triumphal entries. Whereas Jesus by riding the donkey implies his renunciation of revolutionary aspirations, the crowd's use of palm branches, an allusion to the Maccabean triumphs, implies that they still see him in more revolutionary messianic terms (1 Macc 13:51; 2 Macc 10:7; Rev 7:9; Cullmann 1956b:38; Stauffer 1960:110).

Jesus now accepts such public homage, which is appropriate (Mt 21:16). Nevertheless, the crowds understand the meaning of his messianic identity no more than the disciples had (16:20-22; 27:20); *Son of David* reflects a true but inadequate Christology (22:41-45). Even today many people call themselves Christians but have not pressed far enough in Jesus' teachings to understand the real character of his lordship or his demands on their lives. The praises of the masses are good, but it is the disciples who truly submit to Christ's will—those who read his kingship in light of the cross—who will carry out his purposes in the world.

Judgment on the Temple Establishment (21:12-16) The Gospel has been building toward a confrontation between Jesus and the leaders in Jerusalem. Now Jesus indirectly confronts the most powerful Jerusalem leaders, who to this point have felt less threatened by him than the more populist Pharisees. Such a move can only foreshadow Jesus' death.

restricted to the Mount of Olives, had been moved to the temple shortly before Jesus' arrival, undoubtedly drawing considerable opposition (Eppstein 1964). The practice would have helped the buyers, reducing the risk of an animal's becoming blemished in transit between the Mount of Olives and the temple, an expensive risk for most people; the problem was paying money in the temple (Chilton 1994:165).

Jesus courageously confronts injustice. First-century Jewish theologians debated various issues, but it was most likely those actions of Jesus which could be interpreted politically that led to his execution (Young 1989:296). Protest actions are common today in the West; in many cases they excite little attention because they provoke little danger. When ancient philosophers like the Cynics criticized the authorities, however, they invited both persecution and general suspicion of itinerant teachers (Liefeld 1967:162). By challenging nationalism and rulers' policy, the biblical prophets had invited retribution even more consistently (despite a frequently observed tradition of "prophetic immunity" in Judah and Israel). Many Christians today are able to avoid persecution in part because some of us live in more tolerant societies and in part because we do little to challenge the sinful practices of our societies.

The *money changers* probably did not see themselves as taking advantage of the pilgrims. Even in Galilee the varieties of local currency required money changers to convert coinage for use in the temple (and local economy); changing coins was necessary, not an option (see Goodman 1983:57; E. Sanders 1992: 63-65). Further, the temple money changers seem to have made little if any profit (*m. Šeqalim* 1.6-7), though Jerusalem undoubtedly profited from the resultant trade. We have no evidence that the priestly aristocracy made a direct profit (pace Reicke 1974:168).

Because Jesus opposed the buyers as well as the sellers, he probably was not criticizing economic exploitation or high prices (pace Gundry 1982:413). Jesus probably viewed the temple as morally and spiritually impure, as the Qumran sect also believed (compare 1QpHab 9.4-5; *CD* 5.6-7). Yet Jesus was not simply seeking to renew the temple's holiness (compare *m. Berakot* 9:5; Mal 3:1-4). He could have symbolized a mere purifying of the temple by pouring out water; overturning tables signified something more ominous (E. Sanders 1985:70).

Jesus defends Gentiles' worship. That the selling occurred in the outer court, beyond which Gentiles could not travel, may have been significant (compare Jos. *Ant.* 12.145; 15.417). Later reports claim that the front

---

21:14 This exclusion presumably related to purity laws prohibiting the entrance of those with physical abnormalities (1QS 2.8-9; 1QM 7.4-6; 12.7-9). Even under Levitical regulations,

court of the temple was normally to be kept clear as a sacred area (compare *m. Berakot* 9.5), but the many temporary shops for selling animals inside would have violated this custom even if they took up but a small part of the temple area.

Matthew claims that Jesus quoted two texts, Isaiah 56:7 and Jeremiah 7:11. In Isaiah 56 God promises to accept foreigners and eunuchs (previously banned—Deut 23:1) as members of his people, declaring that his temple will welcome all peoples; indeed, its purpose had been universalistic from the start (1 Kings 8:41-43). But by Jesus' day (in contrast to the Old Testament temple) a partition with warning signs segregated Gentiles from the Israelite section of the outer court (Jos. *War* 5.194; 6.124-26; *Ant.* 15.417), probably for purity reasons (women were similarly considered less pure than men; compare also 11QTemple 3-48). Concern for the sanctity of this outer court, hence for the worship of the Gentiles, may have been part of Jesus' objection to the current temple order (pace E. Sanders 1985:67-68). But that Matthew deletes the words "for all nations" from Mark's quotation may suggest that he wishes to lay the emphasis elsewhere—perhaps especially on the next quotation (Jer 7:11).

Jesus warns that religious symbols cannot protect us from God's wrath. Jeremiah 7 promised judgment on God's people who treated his temple as a safe haven for robbers. Jeremiah warns his contemporaries that the presence of the temple will not stay God's wrath against them; Matthew, probably writing after A.D. 70, wishes to stress judgment against a temple establishment that rejected Jesus (Mt 23:31-36; 24:15; 27:25). Not so much the brigands in the wilderness as the temple authorities are the real bandits. Even today it is arrogance to think that merely having coins that claim "In God we trust," or a state church, or any other mere symbol of religious attachment can prove sufficient to stay God's wrath if we do not live according to his will.

True prophets must face the consequences of their message. Of all Jesus' acts, his attack on the temple came closest to appearing as a revolutionary challenge to the political order, but this action was a prophetic

---

members of priestly families could not enter the sanctuary as priests if they were blind or lame (Lev 21:17-18); that such rules were carried further by the time of Jesus is likely.

declaration rather than the challenge of a Zealot leader seeking a following. The act itself was undoubtedly more symbolic than efficacious; the sellers undoubtedly set up their tables again soon after the disruption. Jesus probably symbolized prophetically what Jeremiah's smashing of the pot in the temple did (Jer 19): impending judgment (for example, Harvey 1982:131-32; Aune 1983:136; Catchpole 1984:334; E. Sanders 1985:70). Yet Jesus' action was politically dangerous: merely prophesying the temple's destruction invited scourging and the threat of death (Jer 26:11; Jos. *War* 6.300-309), especially if one had a significant gathering of followers (E. Sanders 1985:302-3).

Jesus embraced the blind and lame. It is easy for readers today to miss the significance of the disabled approaching Jesus in the temple (21:14). Jewish teachers did not require blind or lame people to make the journey to the temple (*m. Ḥagiga* 1:1), and at least some traditions excluded them from the temple (2 Sam 5:8 LXX). Here again Jesus apparently challenges the way the temple hierarchy has conducted temple affairs (for example, Hill 1972:294). Even today it is easy for us to marginalize those who cannot participate in our own activities; many of us fail to make necessary sacrifices to give special attention to those whom others leave out, whether it be a blind person or someone whose mobility is limited by muscular dystrophy. When we fail to care for those disabled in this way, we are unlike Jesus (on serving the disabled, see Newman and Tada 1987).

God can speak through children. Jesus' deeds were not the only cause for the chief priests' and legal experts' discomfort; Jesus was accepting public praise as the *Son of David,* and even if the priestly aristocracy was gentler than their opponents' portraits of them suggest, Roman rule left them no choice but to correct him or betray him to the governor (vv. 15-16). To them he appeared to be simply another charismatic leader whose ego had gotten out of hand; Josephus provides many examples of such leaders in first-century Palestine.

Jesus, who again defends the receptiveness of children (v. 16; compare 18:1-5; 19:13-15), responds from Scripture (since he now

---

21:21 Jesus may also allude to Zechariah 4:6-9, where Zerubbabel's obstacles in building the temple are compared to a mountain; the Spirit of God would bring the obstacles down. In this case Jesus is saying that no challenge to the work God has called his servants to do

addresses those educated in Scripture): from the lips of children God has *ordained praise*. And if children praise him, how much more (borrowing a standard line of argument from Jesus' day) ought the religious leaders to join in!

☐ Jesus Debates Jerusalem's Leaders (21:17—22:46)

Because of the flow of context, it is not clear whether the first passage of this unit (21:17-22) belongs in this section or the preceding one, if Matthew himself would have made such a distinction. The rest of the passages in this section, however, reveal a common theme: Jesus offers his closing public debates with Jerusalem's elite, debates that increase his populist support and further threaten their base of power. Because he is headed for the cross, he can afford to cut through their self-delusions unapologetically. Because he cares about the people as a whole (20:28), he is especially angry with those who claim to lead God's people but in fact have usurped prerogatives that belong to God alone (21:33-45). Christian leaders must beware lest we fall prey to the same temptation (24:48-51).

Faith to Accomplish the Impossible (21:17-22) Here Jesus provides an acted parable for his disciples, symbolizing another prophetic act of judgment. Matthew's audience, probably native to Syro-Palestine, are likely aware of what Mark states explicitly: it was not yet the season for figs (Mk 11:13). At Passover season in late March or early April, fig trees are often in leaf on the eastern side of the Mount of Olives. At this time of year the trees contain only green figs (Arabs call them *taqsh*); they ripen around June but often fall off before that time, leaving only leaves on the tree. Because of their unpalatable taste, these early figs rarely were eaten; but someone too hungry to care about taste would eat them anyway, as some do today. A leafy tree lacking early figs, however, would bear no figs at all that year (F. Bruce 1980:73-74; Witherington 1990:173).

Although Matthew retains Mark's emphasis from the context—judgment on the temple (compare fruitless trees in 3:10; 12:44-45; compare

---

may stand. Jesus himself, like his Davidic ruling ancestor Zerubbabel (Mt 1:12), was preparing a new temple (21:42; compare Zech 4:7); beyond the price paid by Zerubbabel, however, the price of this act of faith will be Jesus' own life (Mt 21:37-39, 42; 26:61).

also 24:32; Jer 24)—his arrangement of the material lays primary stress on Jesus' lesson of faith. "Moving mountains" was a Jewish metaphor for accomplishing what was difficult or virtually impossible (as in *ARN* 6A; 12, §29B). Like the prophets of old, Jesus' disciples could do whatever God called them to do (compare 7:7-11; 10:8; 17:20). Faith, of course, implies obedience to God's wishes, not simply acting on our own. Given the surrounding context of conflict, Jesus' model of faith includes facing death bravely in obedience to God's call—and trusting his power over death itself.

The Source of Jesus' Authority (21:23-27) The reader who has witnessed in the text of Matthew miracles such as the cursing of the fig tree understands that Jesus' authority is from God (vv. 21-22); the reader who has seen the fate of John the Baptist, an earlier representative of God, also recognizes what Jesus will face (compare 21:32, 38-39). The political leaders here are not, however, privy to the information Matthew's audience shares. Like many contemporary politicians—and the rest of us—Jesus' adversaries were more interested in making their opponent, in this case Jesus, look bad than in uncovering further truth about his claims. Undoubtedly they view Jesus as a "populist" (see Rhoads and Michie 1982:82), the sort of demagogue aristocrats normally despised (as in Isoc. *Nic.* 48 and *Or.* 2).

Pretend Obedience Versus Delayed Obedience (21:28-32) The three parables in 21:28—22:14 together respond to the Jewish leaders, critiquing them harshly (compare van Tilborg 1972:47-52). Ancient Mediterranean culture demanded that sons honor and obey their parents, especially when they still lived on the father's estate (see Keener 1991:98, 197). The parable's point is obvious enough in Matthew's context: the repentant (3:2) son does the father's will (7:21; 12:50); the unrepentant

---

21:28-32 Story lines similar to this passage appear in later Jewish parables. Rudolf Bultmann (1968:201) and Bernard Scott (1989:83-84), following Strack-Billerbeck, cite the late *Exodus Rabbah* 27/88a; compare Johnston 1977:635, citing a purportedly earlier tradition in *Deuteronomy Rabbah* 7:4. More to the point, Jewish parables sometimes proceeded by contrasting positive and negative characters (*Sipre Deut.* 349.1.1), including brothers dealing with money from their father (*Sipre Deut.* 48.1.4; compare Lk 15:11-13) as here; the basic moral of this story is also not foreign to Palestinian Judaism (*Gen. Rab.* 85:3).

son is unfruitful (3:8), claiming to do but not doing (23:3). Thus the latter stands for Israel's religious leaders, in contrast to the humble who heed John and Jesus.The issue is not that *the tax collectors and the prostitutes* were good (compare 9:9; 18:17; cf. 19:17); it is that the religious and political elite were worse, being treasonous (22:5-10). Jesus provides a question after a parable (as in Is 5:3-4; Mt 21:40).

The interpretation of this parable follows naturally after 21:23-27: Jesus and John represent the same source of moral authority, and those who rejected John's *way of righteousness* showed the hypocrisy of their own claims to be God's servants. The repentance of more openly sinful people did not provoke them to jealousy for their own spiritual status (compare Rom 11:14).

The Murderous Tenants (21:33-44) As one expects from Jesus' rural parables, this one is true to life. The viticulture is accurate enough (although most of these details stem from Isaiah allusions): fences (often a *wall* of loosely fitted stones) protected vineyards from animals (Ps 80:12-14; N. Lewis 1983:125), and watchmen used the tower (2 Chron 26:10; Is 1:8), often "a hut of leaf-covered wood or possibly of stone which served both as a look-out . . . and as a shelter for the vinedressers at harvest time" (Anderson 1976:272).

The religious leaders were wicked. Because the *vineyard* probably refers to Israel (Is 5:2; compare 3:14; Ezek 17:6; Hos 9:10; Jeremias 1972:70, 76-77), the *farmers* stand for the nation's religious leaders (Mt 21:45). Thus while Jesus borrows the imagery of Isaiah, he adapts it so that the primary evildoers represent not Israel but its leaders. Neither Jesus nor Matthew contends for God's rejection of Israel as a people, but for his rejection of the religious leaders (23:13-36; compare Kee 1977:113; pace Ladd 1974b:114). Israel was unprepared for its Master because Israel's leaders failed in their stewardship to acknowledge the

---

21:34 Tenant farming was familiar enough that later rabbis also told parables of vineyards tended by tenants (e.g., *Pes. Rab Kah.* Supplement 1:11); they also could tell of an owner uprooting a vineyard that provided no fruit to portray God's judgment on a people who refused to repent (*Gen. Rab.* 38:9). Robert M. Johnston (1977:594) points out that in rabbinic parables the landlord always represents God, although the sharecropping tenants are ad hoc.

true Lord; when the cat is gone, the mice will play, but a day of reckoning is coming (compare Prov 7:19, 22-27). This threat from Jesus' day also provides a warning for Christian leaders in Matthew's day and our own (24:45-51). The church and many of its leaders have repeated Israel's disobedience enough in history and to a great extent continue to do so today. Many ministers regard the church as "our" field of ministry rather than keeping in mind who our Lord is.

Although small holders may have predominated in Palestine, Galilee had many tenant farmers. Tenant farmers worked the land for its owners, often absentee landlords, and paid them as much as half the resulting produce. While peasants did not enjoy their economic situation, they would not have identified with the foolish tenants in this story; everyone regarded as treacherous the killing of unarmed messengers. The rejected messengers symbolize the biblical prophets (23:29-38; compare 5:12); Jewish tradition not only acknowledged but amplified their sufferings.

God is incomprehensibly kind to his enemies. The *landowner* here is too nice; whether aristocrats, artisans or peasants, no one would recognize in this figure the benevolence of any patron they knew. But even had hearers not recognized the image of God and his prophets here, no one would expect the benevolent landowner to remain benevolent indefinitely; indeed, the worse landlords sometimes even had their own hit squads to take out troublesome tenant farmers. Everyone also knew that the state would always side with the landlord (even if he was a bad one); in a case of obvious wrong like this one, the murderers of his servants would be excuted or enslaved.

The landowner has no reason to continue his benevolence. At the very least, he must know that the tenants hate him; in antiquity the way people treated a messenger was the way they would treat the sender (compare 10:40-42; *t. Ta'anit* 3:2). By continuing to appeal to their sense of honor, the landowner has made himself appear a fool; to maintain any vestige of honor, he must retaliate against their repeating shaming of him (B. Scott 1989:250).

Quite in contrast to expectations, however, the landowner acts with

---

21:44 Assuming, as is likely, that this verse is authentic, its point resembles that of the later *Esther Rabbah* 7:10, often cited in this connection: Israel is like a rock and the nations like

such benevolence that ancient hearers could have regarded his action merely as utter folly: he believes that the murderous tenants will at least respect his *son* as his own representative. Jesus tells us about the death of the landowner's son, the tenants' ultimate act of treachery. Casting him outside the vineyard (compare Heb 13:13), they kill him.

Even God's patience eventually comes to an end. As benevolent as the landowner is, no one will be surprised that he finally retaliates. No law would have actually granted the vineyard to tenants who had murdered the owner's son. As if asking for a legal ruling, Jesus questions the religious leaders what this patient landowner will finally do to the murderers. The answer is obvious. The evil tenant farmers, no match for the landlord's power, were utter fools to doubt that they would die.

It may be no coincidence (compare 21:13; 24:2) that Jesus' contemporaries understood Isaiah's parable of the vineyard (Is 5:1-7) on which this parable draws as referring to the temple's destruction. Jesus concludes by again challenging their knowledge of the Scriptures (which should have made the object of his parable obvious to begin with), as in 12:3, 19:4, 21:16 and 22:31.

Here Jesus cites Psalm 118:22 from the Hallel (Ps 113—18, recited during Passover season), only a few verses away from the praise recently uttered by the children (Ps 118:25-26 in Mt 21:15; compare 21:9). All his hearers would recognize the source of the quotation, and probably its context. (By contrast, many of us today sing "This is the day the Lord has made" [Ps 118:24] out of the context of the day and event the psalmist was celebrating.) In context, the cornerstone or *capstone* to which Jesus refers is probably part of the architecture of the temple. Hearers might have recognized that he was comparing the covenant community to a temple; some others in his day made that comparison (for example, 1QS 8.5, 8-9; 9.6; *CD* 2.10, 13; Gärtner 1965:16-46). Most clearly they would recognize that he was challenging the *builders,* here the temple authorities.

Jesus adds a clarifying comment that expands the reproof to all Israel with no vestige of subtlety (v. 43). Thus, he says, these leaders will no longer administer God's reign among his people as God's stewards

---

vessels; whether the rock falls on the pot or the pot on the rock, it is the pot that will suffer.

(compare 23:13; 16:19). Henceforth the holy nation of the new exodus (Ex 19:5-6) will bring forth their *fruit*—the landowner's rightful portion of the vintage—for God (3:10; Hos 14:4-8; Lk 13:6-9; Jn 15:1-8).

Using the Jewish interpretation method called *g^ezerâh šāwâh,* which links verses on the basis of key terms they share, this passage develops the cornerstone idea (compare 1 Pet 2:6-8). *Crushed* probably reflects Daniel 2:44; *falls on this stone,* the stumbling stone of Isaiah 8:15 and 28:16. Neither alternative is intended to be pleasant; the Greek term for *but* here is the weaker one, in this case probably meaning virtually "and."

Finally understanding that he is addressing them, the religious leaders look for a way to seize him (compare Mt 26:5, 50). Because the Jewish crowds believe that Jesus was a prophet, however (21:11), the leaders must bide their time; they are cowardly politicians (21:45-46).

The Cowardly Politicians (21:45-46) This character of Jesus' opponents fits their later actions. Concerned about the populace's response, they both choose a more advantageous time to seize Jesus (26:4-5, 55; compare Lk 22:53) and allow Pilate and the Romans to carry out a death sentence. Without a degree of favor from the people whom they had to keep quiet as well as from the Romans, the household of Caiaphas could not have stayed in power so long.

Scorning the King's Son (22:1-14) Those who dishonor the Son shame and dishonor the Father who sent him. It was common for kings or important personages to throw wedding banquets for sons, to which they might invite the entire village (compare, for example, Char. *Chaer.* 3.2.10). But the *banquet* here makes special allusion to the promised banquet of the messianic era. In the narrative logic of the Gospel, Jesus is finally ready to unveil his identity in the final week (see Kingsbury, 1986:81-84).

Other Jewish prophets had also applied the principle of special accountability to those closest to the Word (for example, Amos 3:2; 9:7). Whether the parable emphasizes judgment on all Israel (compare

---

22:2 Matthew's parable more closely resembles the format of a standard rabbinic parable in which God as a king throws a wedding banquet for his son, Israel, and his daughter,

Sandmel 1978a:60; Mt 27:25), on Israel as a whole but not individual Jews (Hare 1979:39) or on the Judean leadership in particular (21:43-45) is debated, but the burning of the city in Matthew probably refers to the destruction of Jerusalem (Jeremias 1972:33; Hare 1979:39). In the context, Jesus' harsh words condemn Israel's leaders. Yet as often in his Gospel, Matthew apparently uses the community's opponents to warn members of his own community not to be like them. Not only Jesus' enemies but even some of his supposed friends (22:11-14) would betray him.

Refusing the King's Invitation Is a Grievous Insult (22:1-6)
Papyri testify to the practice of double invitations, both among upper classes and in regular village life (B. Scott 1989:169; Rohrbaugh 1991:139-41). The king long ago honored the guests with an invitation, and they appropriately responded with a promise to come; the second invitation in the parable is merely to inform them that the dinner is now ready (v. 4). Because the exact time of completion of preparations was difficult to determine in advance, a second invitation at the appropriate hour was standard procedure, and the lower a person's status, the more punctual the person was expected to be. Attendance at weddings was a social obligation in Palestinian Judaism (Bonsirven 1964:151); attendance at a patron's banquet was incumbent on social dependents throughout the Empire (compare Sirach 13:9-10). In such a society, not inviting the right person, or inviting the wrong person, could have disastrous, even fatal, consequences (*b. Giṭṭin* 55b-56a). Thus, for example, one who invited the townsfolk but not the king to a town banquet merited much severer punishment than one who invited neither (*t. Baba Qamma* 7:2). Ignoring a king's proclamation or invitation warranted severe punishment (as in *Ruth Rab. Proem* 7).

By refusing to come, the guests deliberately insult the dignity of the king who has counted on their attendance and graciously prepared food for them. For all the invited guests to refuse to come would greatly shame the host; the unanimous refusal (and in Lk 14:18-20, absurd excuses given) barely disguises what must be a concerted plan to

---

Torah. Kings in Jewish parables almost always represent God (Johnston 1977:583; Mt 18:23).

deliberately insult the host (B. Scott 1989:171).

This Act of Treason Warrants Serious Judgment (22:7) For the king to graciously extend the honor of an invitation to a banquet and be rebuffed as if his benefaction were meaningless was a traumatic breach of the social order, an act of rebellion. The king can salvage some honor only by getting others to attend the banquet and by punishing these who have insulted his kindness; even in less dramatic circumstances, Jewish stories could envisage a king avenging his honor by executing those who have scorned his invitation to eat (*Gen. Rab.* 9:10).

Slaughtering messengers (v. 6) constituted an explicitly revolutionary act (compare Jos. *War* 2.450-56; *Ant.* 9.264-66). The parable's audience would naturally applaud the king's rage as just—except those who were aware that the lesson was aimed at them (21:45). The violence is realistic: after such an insult to a king's honor, nothing less than such vengeance as verse 7 depicts would satisfy his honor. Of course the parable is at the same time unrealistic to suppose that the king would engage in a military expedition while his banquet food was getting cold (Young 1989:171)! The expedition is noted here so the parable can climax with its primary point at the end—a point that also bursts the bounds of realism to show the horrible fate of the disobedient.

The Kingdom Belongs to the Humble, Not the Proud (22:8-10) The arrogant often ignore God; God seeks the lowly of this world who will humbly acknowledge his reign. Vengeance restores some of the king's honor, but to recoup it more fully the king must invite other guests who will accept his invitation, even if they are of much lower status than the first invitees (compare *p. Ḥagiga* 2:2, §5; Vermes 1993:113). The matter is urgent: otherwise the freshly prepared food will spoil. Commentators generally believe that those gathered from outside the destroyed city represent the Gentiles (Meier 1980:248; Theissen 1991:272). This view would fit Matthew's emphasis on the Jewish-Christian mission to the Gentiles.

The welcoming of *both good and bad* (v. 10) echoes Jesus' own

---

22:11-14 The parable of the wedding garment may borrow a familiar Jewish story line (compare *b. Šabbat* 153a; *Eccl. Rab.* 9:8, §1) to make its point.
22:16 The Pharisees and more revolutionary Jews had many ideas in common (Jos. *Ant.* 18.23); Herodians were partisans of the Herodian dynasty, who held their power by Rome's

mission to sinners (9:11-13), but it may also remind us that grace not only forgives but also transforms. All are welcome, but no one dare remain the way he or she entered, in view of the final separation of "the wicked from the righteous" (13:49). Such echoes of earlier passages in the Gospel prepare the reader for the parable that follows (22:11-14): salvation is not simply a matter of those who begin the race, for we must finish it (compare 13:20-23).

Those Inside the Church May Also Dishonor God (22:11-14) Once the newly chosen guests have begun to dine, the host enters after the banquet has begun, as was customary (Jeremias 1972:187). Some hold that hosts may have provided wedding garments to guests at the door (A. Bruce 1979:272; Gundry 1982:439). But *wedding clothes* may simply refer to clean garments as opposed to soiled ones (Jeremias 1972:187-88); to come to a wedding in a soiled garment insulted the host, and this host was in no further mood to be insulted. Patrons invited their social dependents to banquets, expecting due honor in return; this man, like the first guests the king invited, has responded to grace with an insult.

Just as most of the Jewish leaders were unprepared at Jesus' first coming (compare 23:13-33), some professing disciples of Jesus will be unprepared at his second (24:45-51). (Judas proves merely a case in point—compare *friend* in 22:12; 26:50; see also 20:13.) Professing Christians who insult God's grace by presuming on it, failing to honor his Son, will be banished to outer darkness (compare 8:12; 25:30) and weeping with gnashing of teeth (13:42; 24:51; 25:30; compare Meier 1980:248-49). Many are "called" or *invited* with the message of repentance (22:14; 21:32), but only those who respond worthily will share the inheritance of the chosen covenant people (also Jeremias 1971:131); compare 7:13-23.

Caesar or God (22:15-22) Devotion to God demands a higher allegiance to him than to anything else, but it is not an excuse to avoid our other responsibilities that do not conflict with it.

God's Mission Sometimes Produces Powerful Enemies (22:15-

favor and hoped for the full restoration of Herodian authority (see Simon 1967:86; Smallwood 1976:164). An attempt to *trap* Jesus fits what we know of legal procedure in that period, which depended on *delatores,* accusers (in Roman custom, see O'Neal 1978; Hemer 1986:67).

17) Courageously speaking God's message as Jesus did can yield adversaries among those who suppose themselves his spokespersons. The Herodians (v. 16) were unlikely allies with the Pharisees. Pharisees generally cooperated with the aristocracy only when grave national interests were at stake, providing an essential coalition between populist and institutional leadership (as in Jos. *Life* 21-22). Here the extreme situation presented by Jesus brings the two groups together (Smallwood 1976:164; Bowker 1973:41; compare Mk 3:6). The coalition hopes to catch Jesus coming or going: either he will support taxes to Rome, undercutting his popular messianic support, or he will challenge taxes, thereby aligning with the views that had sparked a disastrous revolt two decades earlier. In the latter case, the Herodians could charge him with being a revolutionary—hence showing that he should be executed, and executed quickly.

Locally minted copper coins omitted the emperor's portrait due to Jerusalem's sensitivities, but because only the imperial mint could legally produce silver and gold coins, Palestine had many foreign coins in circulation. The silver denarius of Tiberius, including a portrait of his head, minted especially at Lyon, circulated there in this period and is probably in view here (Reicke 1974:137). The coin related directly to pagan Roman religion and the imperial cult in the East: one side bore Caesar's image and the words "Tiberius Caesar, son of the Divine Augustus," while the other side referred to the high priest of Roman religion (Ferguson 1987:70-71). Like it or not, Jews had to use this coin; it was the one required for the poll tax in all provinces (Lane 1974:424).

Jesus Reveals His Opponents' Hypocrisy and Greed (22:19-22)
To render to Caesar what was Caesar's was to return his own coin to him (compare 17:25; Rom 13:6-7; 1 Pet 2:13-14; Jer 26:8-9; 27:6-22; 29:4-9; Ezek 8—9); to render to God what was God's was to render worship to him alone (compare 4:10). Neither the image nor the superscription on coins in common usage could prevent Jewish people's single-minded devotion to God. The appropriate response to living in

---

22:23-33 Even on minimal historical grounds, the tradition behind this passage is likely authentic. Later Christians had little reason to create a dialogue in which Sadducees figured as opponents; although Sadducees persecuted the early Jewish Christians, we have no evidence of theological dialogue between them (Witherington 1990:15 n. 58).
22:32 Jesus also cites a line of argument intelligible in his culture, as contemporary sources

a society whose beliefs differ from one's own is to critically evaluate and withstand its claims, not to censor such claims from being heard or to boycott all participation in the society.

Further, some suggest that Jesus was challenging the idea that his opponents needed to hold on to the coins at all; why not return them to Caesar? Jerusalemites preferred death to allowing Caesar's image to enter Jerusalem on standards (Jos. *Ant.* 18.59), yet they carried it in on coins. Those who hated Caesar's image to such an extent would make an exception for coinage only if they valued money too much (W. White 1971:233; Witherington 1990:102). By contrast, surrendering to God *what is God's* implies the surrender of all one is and possesses (Patte 1987:309-10). In Jesus' teaching elsewhere, possessions have a zero value, and those who seek them are not the simple who trust in God (6:19-34). Rather than compromising his popular support, Jesus ends up embarrassing his challengers; they, not he, are the ones carrying the offensive coin, so scruples against it cannot be their own (Danker 1972:202-3). Thus they rightly earn his derisive title for them: *hypocrites* (22:18; 6:2; 15:7; 23:13-29; 24:51).

Proving the Resurrection (22:23-33) This story line would make some sense in a variety of cultures. Levirate marriage (Deut 25:5-6; compare Gen 38:8-26) and widow inheritance (see Belkin 1970; as in Ruth 3:12-13) perpetuate the name of the deceased and serve to provide for widows in many traditional societies where women cannot earn sufficient wages for sustenance (for example, Mbiti 1970:188-89). Yet many ancient hearers would assume a woman who had outlived seven husbands was dangerous (Mart. *Epig.* 9.15; *t. Šabbat* 15:8). The Sadducees borrow the story line of a woman with seven husbands from the popular Jewish folktale in Tobit 3:8; they want to illustrate the impossible dilemmas they believe the doctrine of *resurrection* creates.

The Sadducees were known for their opposition to the doctrine of

---

attest: Philo also found in Exodus 3:6 that the patriarchs continued to live (*On Abraham* 50-55 in Downing 1982): 4 Maccabees declares that the patriarchs did not die, but live to God (4 Macc 7:18-19; 16:25); some later rabbis also inferred from the promise to the patriarchs (Ex 33:1) that "the righteous are called living even in their death" (*Eccl. Rab.* 9:5, §1).

the resurrection (Acts 23:6-8; perhaps Jos. *Ant.* 18.16; *War* 2.164-65). When Jesus declares that they deny *the power of God* (compare 2 Thess 3:5), he may evoke the traditional Jewish view that God expresses his power most visibly in *the resurrection of the dead,* a view attested in the second of the regularly prayed Eighteen Benedictions (abbreviated as "Power"; compare *m. Roš Haššana* 4:5; see also Rom 1:4).

Most Jewish people agreed that angels did not eat, drink or propagate (*1 Enoch* 15:6-7; *Test. Ab.* 4, 6A; *ARN* 1, 37A). Some Jewish traditions also compared the righteous after death with angels (*1 Enoch* 39:5; 104:2-4; *2 Baruch* 51:10-11). Since angels did not die (unless God destroyed them), they had no need to procreate. Jesus' statement about lack of marriage and procreation in heaven (Mt 22:30) follows largely from the logic of the resurrection, to which he now turns (vv. 31-32).

Early Jewish teachers regularly argued apart from the Bible with Gentiles or scoffers, but from Scripture for those who knew Scripture (Moore 1971:2:381). When debating the views of Sadducees who doubted the resurrection and demanded proof from the law of Moses, later rabbis found ample proof for this doctrine in the Bible's first five books (*Sipre Deut.* 329.2.1; *b. Sanhedrin* 90b). One later rabbi went so far as to say that all texts implied the resurrection if one simply had the ingenuity to find it (Moore 1971:2:383; *Sipre Deut.* 306.28.3); however, this often meant reading it into the text! As an expert Scripture interpreter, Jesus here exposes his opponents' lack of Scripture knowledge with his standard formula, *have you not read . . . ?* (v. 31; see 12:3; 19:4; 21:42, 46).

Jesus may be arguing for God's continuing purposes with an individual after death, which for many Palestinian Jews would imply ultimate resurrection. He implies that God would not claim to be the God of someone who no longer existed (compare Doeve 1954:106; Longenecker 1975:68-69); he also evokes God's covenant faithfulness to his people, which Palestinian Jewish prayers regularly associated with the "God of the fathers," Abraham, Isaac and Jacob (Jeremias 1971:187). If God was still God of Abraham, Isaac and Jacob, and if his power was unlimited, then he would ultimately fulfill his promise to them—not only corporately through their descendants, but personally to them. The crowds are again astounded by Jesus' quick wit (compare 7:28; 22:22), just as they are by his signs (8:27; 9:8; 12:23).

Love God and Neighbor (22:34-40) "Testing" scholars with riddles—and God's vindication of the divine wisdom given to his servant—is at least as old as King Solomon (1 Kings 10:1; elsewhere, for example, *Ep. Arist.* 187-291). In this context, however, the intent is more malicious (compare 16:1; 19:3), related to that of the supreme tempter (4:1).

Some Pharisees ask a question they had probably practiced before, since their own teachers debated among themselves which *command-ment* was the *greatest*. Although all commandments were equally weighty in one sense (see comment on 5:19), rabbis had to distinguish between "light" and "heavy" commandments in practice (see comment on 23:23).

Jesus' view does not contrast dramatically with views held by his contemporaries. In the late first century Rabbi Akiba regarded love of neighbor in Leviticus 19:18 as the greatest commandment in the law (*Gen. Rab.* 24:7; Vermes 1993:42); while this is not where Jesus ranks it, it is close. Other Jewish teachers also conjoined love of God with love of neighbor (*Test. Iss.* 5:2; 7:6; *Test. Dan* 5:3; Philo *Decal.* 108-10). Following the Jewish interpretive principle *gᵉzerâh šāwâh*, it was natural to link two commandments on the basis of the common opening Hebrew word *uᵉ'ahaḇtā* ("you shall love"; Diezinger 1978; Flusser 1988:479).

Yet Jesus' combination of the two as the greatest commandments, which exercised an authoritative influence on subsequent Christian formulations (including Paul's frequent triad of virtues with love as the greatest—1 Cor 13:13), is distinctive (see Vermes 1993:43). Amid the multiplicity of proposals concerning the greatest commandment in antiquity, only Jesus wielded the moral authority among his followers to focus their ethics so profoundly on a single theme (compare Meier 1980:257). Thence comes the early Christian "law of love" (as in Rom 13:8-10; Gal 5:14; Jas 2:8; Jn 13:34-35; compare Manson 1963:80).

The first passage Jesus cites in fact portrays the love of God as a summary of the law (Deut 6:1-7); one who loved God would fulfill the whole Torah (Deut 5:29). This passage about loving God was the central and best-known text of Judaism, the *Shema (šᵉma')*. Likewise, the command to love one's neighbor as oneself (Lev 19:18; compare Lev 19:34; Mt 5:43; Rom 13:9) expresses a general principle, though its original context applied it to a more specific situation. As in 7:12, Matthew reminds us that these commandments epitomize all the commandments in the Bible.

If left to ourselves, we tend to grasp for power rather than seeking to serve, and this can apply even to the ways we interpret the Bible. In contrast to some modern readings, Jesus here assumes rather than commands self-love (so also Piper 1977; Gundry 1982:449). Thus he elsewhere emphasizes that true love for neighbor is demonstrated beyond one's own circle of favored people (5:43-47; Lk 10:29-37); some texts in Scripture even warn us against self-centered love (2 Tim 3:2; Paul here warns against selfishness, however, rather than advocating masochism or self-punishment, which is also self-centered). But while Scripture summons us to love that is other-directed, it also assumes that all of us—including Christians—need other people's love. Perhaps as we Christians learn to love and affirm one another better (for example, Prov 12:18; 16:24; Eph 4:29), especially the most wounded and vulnerable among us, we will not require as much talk about self-love. Until we learn to behave that biblically, however, it is difficult to blame broken people who desperately try to affirm themselves when no one else will.

David's Son, David's Lord (22:41-46) How can Jesus be David's *Lord* yet at the same time David's *son,* younger in age yet superior in rank (Moule 1965:99)? Jewish teachers often asked didactic questions that functioned as "haggadic antinomy," in which both sides of a question were correct but their relationship needed to be resolved (Jeremias 1971:259). The Messiah, the "anointed" king, was by definition *son of David* in various circles of Jewish expectation, but the title *Lord* describes him far more adequately.

If David spoke to a Lord besides Yahweh, a Lord who would be enthroned at God's right hand as his vice regent, then the eternal King was someone greater than David, more than merely a descendant of David—perhaps to be understood on the Near Eastern analogy of divine kings. Yet *Lord* was sufficiently ambiguous (in contrast to, say, Is 9:6) to make the point without yet giving the temple authorities words with which to condemn Jesus from his own mouth. Early Christians often followed Jesus' use of Psalm 110 (as in Acts 2:34-35; Eph 1:20; Heb 1:13; Justin *1 Apol.* 45).

Mark announced that "they dared ask him no further questions" earlier in the narrative (Mk 12:34, my translation), but Matthew reserves this "punch" for the end of Jesus' public controversies. He had silenced and shamed his adversaries. The capacity of a wise speaker's wisdom to overwhelm hearers was a common motif in narratives meant to glorify their protagonists (for example, 1 Esdras 4:41-42; compare *Ep. Arist.* 186, 200). Matthew's audience could see in Jesus their hero who could answer all the objections raised by their opponents. Jesus must remain both our Lord and our hero today as well.

THE FUTURE AND THE KINGDOM (23:1—25:46)

Matthew's final discourse (chaps. 23—25) approximately balances the first discourse (chaps. 5—7) in length and concludes with the same summary statement as the other discourses: "When Jesus had finished saying all these things" (26:1). But whereas Jesus' first sermon in Matthew opens with blessings for the meek (5:3-12), his last opens with woes against the religious elite. Jesus here condemns much of the religious leadership of his and Matthew's day. Judgment against both the religious teachers (scribes and Pharisees) and the temple blend together with the final judgment in this final sermon of the Gospel. Matthew's audience, probably facing increasing pressure from the religious elite of their own day (very possibly successors of the Pharisaic scribes), would have heard in these warnings cause for hope.

At the same time, scribes and Pharisees are hardly the address's main audience; these words function instead to warn Christians. The explicit audience, as in the first discourse section (5:1-2; 7:28), consists of both disciples and crowds (23:1). Sometimes Christian preachers have caricatured Pharisaic piety to avoid the demands that Jesus' condemnations otherwise would make on Christians today (see Odeberg 1964). Just as judgment separated true from false religion at Jesus' first coming, it would do the same at his second, laying bare the hearts of church leaders (24:45—25:30).

□ Judgment on the Religious Elite (23:1-39)

Jesus opens his prophecy of end-time judgment with a severe critique of the religious establishment of his day—the same establishment that had been challenging him in the previous chapter. Although Matthew's first audience would hear in this critique a promise of judgment on the Judean leaders of their own day, who continued to oppose their message, Matthew also wanted them—and us—to look deeper. Jesus' own professed servants can belong among the "hypocrites" (24:51). Like Paul in Romans 1—2 and Amos in Amos 1—3, Matthew forces leaders in his own community to see themselves through the prism of a disobedient religious establishment that opposed its Lord and thereby summons them to take warning.

Religion for Show (23:1-12) *Teachers of the law* are literally "scribes," which throughout the Empire included those who wrote legal documents for others, but in Judea and Galilee included educated teachers who instructed children in the law and in some cases taught adults as well. Pharisees were a particularly scrupulous brotherhood of teachers and laypersons committed to interpreting the law according to the traditions received from earlier Pharisees. Both groups (which overlapped at points) probably derived from families with some means, and Pharisees clustered especially (though not exclusively) in Jerusalem, where some of them belonged to the urban elite.

Luke correctly distinguishes scribes and Pharisees (Lk 11:39-54), but like modern preachers, Matthew is telling the story in a manner that addresses the enemies of his own community, of whom Pharisaic scribes seem to be the dominant element (compare Hare 1967:81). Matthew is sensitive to the Jewish orthodoxy of his own audience, which probably included some Christian scribes (Mt 13:52; 23:34) and Pharisees (Acts 15:5; compare 23:6), but by Matthew's day the non-Christian Pharisaic leadership had probably marginalized all Christians, Pharisaic or not.

Religious Leaders Must Live What They Teach (23:1-4) Jesus agrees that many of the scribes and Pharisees' ethical teachings are good;

23:2 Scholars regularly observe that later Palestinian synagogues often had a special chair for teaching, which came to be known as a "chair of Moses" (Manson 1979:228; Filson 1960:243; Avi-Yonah 1974-1976:53; Ferguson 1987:400). Not all agree that the "seat of Moses"

the problem is not their teaching but their lives (vv. 2-3; Rom 2:21), a dichotomy known to exist among many religious professionals and other religious people today. The religious leaders here have seated themselves *in Moses' seat,* probably meaning that they have adopted the role of the law's interpreters (compare Carson 1984:472). Although Pharisaic ethics emphasized being as lenient or strict with others as one was with oneself (*ARN* 23, §46B), in practice Jesus accuses them of being too strict with others and too lenient with their own failings (compare 5:18-20; 15:1-20), which fits the way Christians often evaluate sins today.

Religious Leaders Must Not Seek Marks of Honor (23:5) Many Greek philosophical teachers wore identifying apparel that elicited respectful greetings (as in Justin *Dial.* 1), and Jewish scribes may have preferred identifying raiment as well (see *b. Baba Batra* 98a). Whereas phylacteries were supposed to glorify God (Bonsirven 1964:61), the wearers here use them to draw attention to themselves. Jewish sources associated phylacteries, *t̄pillîn,* with *ṣiṣṣîm,* tassels or fringes attached to the outer cloak's four corners (Num 15:38-40; Deut 22:12). Following the law, Jesus himself presumably wore *ṣiṣṣîm* (9:20; 14:36) and used *t̄pillîn.* The issue here is not about wearing fringes or not, but whether we seek honor for ourselves or for God alone.

Religious Leaders Must Not Seek Honored Treatment (23:6) As in much of the Mediterranean world, Palestinian Jewish society included a heavy emphasis on honor and even hierarchy. Seating was normally by rank (as in *t. Sanhedrin* 7:8; 8:1; Lk 14:7-11; 1QS 2.19-23), and greetings (Mt 23:7; compare 26:49) were virtually mandated by social custom.

Religious Leaders Must Not Seek Honorary Titles (23:7-11) Social etiquette dictated the manner of greetings: one must greet one's social superior first (Manson 1979:99; Goodman 1983:78). Sages were objects of special honor (as in *t. Mo'ed Qaṭan* 2:17). Fitting this context of public honor and salutations (vv. 6-7), in Jesus' day *Rabbi* was probably an honorary greeting, "my master" (vv. 7-8; only gradually did

---

was already a literal seat in first-century synagogues, however (also Meier 1980:262), and Jesus in any case applies the expression figuratively here.

it come to be added as a title to a given teacher's name). But whereas Jesus' disciples will carry on his mission of teaching, they will make disciples for him rather than for themselves (28:19).

Some people used *abba* ("papa") as a respectful title for older men and other prominent individuals (Jeremias 1971:68), and may have especially viewed Bible teachers in these terms (see, for example, *Sipre Deut.* 34.3.1-3). But with God as their Father, Jesus' disciples are all siblings (compare 12:48-50; 18:15; 28:10). Matthew's original readers, who knew all about the titles and power Pharisaic teachers were claiming for themselves, would hear Jesus' teaching as a warning not to be like their competitors by seeking honorary titles or a position above others.

John Meier, a Roman Catholic scholar, notes Jesus' prohibition of the title *father* and questions the use of ecclesiastical titles, which arose even in Matthew's church in Syria a few decades after his Gospel (1980:265). But while we Protestants may determine "pecking order" by different means, most of our churches offer the same temptations for personal advancement. In most church services, ministers (including guest ministers performing no function in the service) grace the platform; many churches use various forms of social conformity to increase offerings. In some circles ordained ministers are taken aback if they are not greeted with the title "Reverend," which literally means "one worthy of reverence, one who should be revered." Is it possible that the very criticisms Jesus laid against the religious establishments of his day now stand institutionalized in most of his church?

God Alone Exalts in the End (23:12) Sometimes we grow jealous of others' ministries or spiritual gifts. But Jesus teaches here that exalting remains God's business alone. He echoes the biblical (as in Is 2:11-12; 5:15-16; Ezek 21:26) and later Jewish (as in Sirach 11:5-6; *1 Enoch* 104:2; 1QM 14.10-11) emphasis on end-time reversal of present status.

Woes Against Human Religion (23:13-32) Jesus' woes are the angry

---

23:13 We should note that later rabbis themselves were quick to condemn the hypocrisy of some kinds of Pharisees whose motives were less than holy (*m. Soṭa* 3:4; *ARN* 37A; 45, §124B; Moore 1971:2:193; Sandmel 1978b:160-61); they also regarded hypocrisy in general as morally reprehensible (Moore 1971:2:190). Matthew's critiques, like these, are Jewish laments of wounded love, incited by compassion for those whom religious leaders have led astray (see 23:37). Second-century rabbis, probably passing on many ideas from the Pharisees of Jesus' day, harshly condemned hypocrisy (for example, *t. Yoma* 5:12). Christians today often think of "Pharisees" as hypocrites and hence do not feel threatened when hearing them denounced. But the Pharisees' contemporaries thought of them as very devoted practitioners of the Bible, and of the scribes as experts in biblical laws. In today's terms, Jesus was thundering against many popular preachers and people who seemed to be living holy lives—because they were practicing human religion rather than serving God with purified hearts.

I suspect that much of what passes for Christianity today is little more than human religion with the name of Jesus tacked onto it, because like most of the religion of Jesus' contemporaries, it has failed to transform its followers into Christ's servants passionately devoted to his mission in the world. When rightly understood, Jesus' woes may strike too close to home for comfort. When religion becomes a veneer of holiness to conceal unholy character, it makes its bearers less receptive to God's transforming grace.

Religious Leaders Sometimes Do More Harm Than Good (23:13-15) Jesus first accuses these religious leaders of "shutting" off *the kingdom,* using the image of a majordomo, a prominent official who carried keys (16:19; Is 22:22; Rev 3:7). This may allude to scribes' purported authority to "bind" and "loose" by their knowledge of the law (Mt 16:19), here used to hinder would-be followers of Christ (Meier 1980:268-69). Thus they are *blind guides* of the blind (23:16, 19, 24; compare 15:14).

They are eager to make converts, but their converts simply mimic and accentuate their flaws. (One thinks by contrast of the stone-drunk man who told D. L. Moody, "I'm one of your converts," to which Moody reportedly replied, "I can certainly see you're not one of the *Lord's.*") Although Judaism had no central sending agency, hence no "missionaries" in the formal sense, plenty of evidence testifies that many Jewish

---

critiques within Judaism, not intended for exploitation by Gentile anti-Judaism.
23:14 Textual evidence favors viewing this verse as an interpolation (Mk 12:40; Lk 20:47), leaving a total of seven woes.

people were winning Gentiles to Judaism (for example, Jos. *Ant.* 20.17, 34-36; *Apion* 2.210; Tac. *History* 5.5). Jewish people actively courted many conversions in the Gentile world until Christian emperors began enforcing earlier Roman laws to shut down Jewish proselytism (see Jeremias 1958:11-12). Presumably by exposing converts to the truth of God's standards while allowing hypocrisy through their own bad example (23:3, 13), these Pharisees were leading their converts to be doubly damned.

Inconsistency in Standards of Holiness Dishonors God (23:16-22) See comments on 5:33-37. An oath involved invoking a deity as witness to the veracity of one's claim. On the popular level, people had begun using many surrogate phrases for God's name, hoping to avoid judgment if they broke the oath. Pharisees endeavored to distinguish which oath phrases were actually binding, but Jesus rejected such casuistry (E. Sanders 1990:55, 91; compare *CD* 16.6-13). On *blind guides* (23:16, 24; compare 23:17, 19; Lk 6:39), see 15:14 and the principles in 6:22-23, 7:3-5 and 13:14-17.

As in 23:19, Jewish people viewed the altar as consecrating whatever was offered on it (Bonsirven 1964:124). Pharisees may have prohibited swearing *by the gold of the temple* because they believed that it, unlike the temple or the *altar,* was subject to lien (Gundry 1982:463); in any case, Jesus rejects their reasoning. Jesus rails in part against traditions that have created inconsistent standards of holiness. (We might compare churches today that rightly condemn smoking or overeating as polluting the body yet remain silent on watching television programs that pollute the mind. Some traditional churches regard particular styles of clothing or music as "worldly" yet harbor jealousy, materialism and other attitudes the Bible explicitly condemns as worldly. Some churches fight for the authority of Scripture yet care so little for it in practice that they ignore the context of verses or explain away passages that seem too difficult, like God's demand that Christians care for the poor or witness to their neighbor.) But Jesus' attack is ultimately directed against the profanation

---

23:23 *Dill* (this was probably not anise as in the KJV) and *cummin* were aromatic plants; rabbis settled on dill (probably *m. Ma'aerot* 4:5) and cummin (*m. Demai* 2:1) being tithed but later denied mint (see Goulder 1974:22); first-century Shammaites doubted that black cummin need be tithed, in contrast to Hillelites (*m. 'Uqsin* 3:6; E. Sanders 1990:48). By the

of God's name. Because any surrogate oath nevertheless represents God's name and implicitly calls him to witness, any breach of truthfulness demands judgment no less severe.

Religion Should Not Miss the Forest for the Trees (23:23-28)
While emphasizing what we believe to be holiness in the details, we can miss more critical issues of holiness; some older churches, for example, condemned wearing earrings yet did so in a spirit of self-righteousness or anger—hardly reflecting the "gentle and quiet spirit" (1 Pet 3:4 NASB) they wished to promote. Having remarked on the religious leaders' inconsistency in ritual matters (vv. 16-22), Jesus now turns to their inconsistency in other respects, beginning with tithing. Ancient Israel had been an agrarian society, and Israelites brought one-tenth of their produce into storehouses to provide for all the (landless) Levites and priests, and once every third year for a major festival, paying the way of the poor who otherwise could not participate (Lev 27:30; Num 18:21-32; Deut 14:22-29; Neh 13:10-12). (Modern ministers who use Mal 3:8-10 to warn nontithers they are "robbing God" ought to beware: to be consistent we must use these tithes for what the Bible commands—the support of ministers and those in need. Yet Jesus' more radical standard is that everything we are and have belongs to God and the work of his kingdom—Lk 12:33; 14:33.)

Pharisees were particularly known for their scrupulousness in tithing (as in *ARN* 41A; Borg 1987:89). Building their fence around the law, these religious people were careful about tithing even substances whose status as foodstuffs was disputed, so that it was not clear whether the Old Testament agrarian tithe applied to them (compare Jeremias 1969:254). Jesus accepts that the leaders should have kept these biblical laws but insists that they have missed the forest for the trees (compare 7:3-5); their neglect of the law's basic requirements (Deut 10:12-13; Mic 6:8) is inexcusable.

Like Jesus, most Jewish teachers recognized some commandments

---

second century, rabbis exempted "rue" (Lk 11:42) from requirement for tithe, suggesting that Matthew may preserve the more original wording here (*m. Šebiʿit* 9:1; McNamara 1983:204; Gundry 1982:463, who usually favors Luke).

as *more important,* literally "weightier," than others (compare Johnston 1982:207). Although he, like his contemporaries, regarded no commandment as light (see comment on 5:19; compare Jas 2:10-11; *m. 'Abot* 4:2), Jesus himself taught much about "weightier" matters, even in this context (Mt 23:5, 17, 19). Today as well, many of us separate from or condemn other Christians on the basis of our interpretations of isolated passages while neglecting broader principles (like charity or the equal standing of all believers in Christ).

Jesus illustrates the inconsistency in verse 24 with a witty illustration about Pharisees who were more scrupulous than Pharisaic legal rulings required. If a fly fell into one's drink, Pharisees taught that it must be strained out before it died, lest it contaminate the drink (compare Lev 11:34); but they decided that any organism smaller than a lentil (such as a gnat) was exempt (E. Sanders 1990:32). Since most of us today would not want a gnat dying in our drink either, we may have sympathy with a Pharisee who for a different reason—passion for purity—went beyond the letter of the law to remove it (see E. Sanders 1990:38). Nevertheless, these Pharisees were so inconsistent, Jesus said, that they concerned themselves with purity issues as trifling as a gnat but did not mind swallowing a camel whole. In ancient writings gnats are cited as the prototypically smallest of creatures (Ach. Tat. 2.21.4-5; 2.22); camels, which were explicitly unclean under biblical law (Lev 11:4), were the largest animal in Palestine (see comment on 19:24).

Although Jesus speaks metaphorically about the *inside* of a *cup* (that is, the human heart) in Matthew 23:25-26, he may allude to a matter of some debate among his contemporaries. The Shammaite school of Pharisees were less concerned whether one cleansed the inner or outer part first. In contrast, the Hillelite Pharisees thought that the *outside* of a cup was typically unclean anyway and thus, like Jesus, insisted on cleansing the inner part first (Neusner 1976:492-94; *m. Berakot* 8:2). On the surface Jesus' statement challenges Shammaite practice (though for the effect of the metaphor); but he actually addresses the purity of our hearts, a point he reinforces in his next illustration.

23:29 Veneration of holy persons' tombs is an ancient practice in the Middle East (Argyle 1963:176; Hill 1972:313), but Jewish care for prophets' tombs may have particularly

Although dead creatures in a beverage produced impurity (23:24), corpse uncleanness (v. 27) was more severe, extending seven days (Num 19:11-14; Jos. *Ant.* 18.38; *m. Kelim* 1:4). If so much as one's shadow touched a corpse or a tomb, one contracted impurity (E. Sanders 1990:34, 232). Although Jesus may have originally alluded to the springtime practice of using *whitewash* to warn passersby and Passover pilgrims to avoid unclean *tombs* lest they become impure and hence barred from the feast (*m. Mo'ed Qaṭan* 1:2; *Ma'aser Šeni* 5:1; *Šeqalim* 1:1), as in Luke 11:44, Matthew focuses on an incidental effect of the marking. For him whitewash is a beautifying agent to cover a tomb's corruption (borrowing the image from Ezek 13:10-12). The leaders' outward appearance (compare Mt 23:5, 28) merely provided a veneer for the impurity, hence lawlessness (literally; NIV *wickedness*), of their hearts. To those who prided themselves on obedience to Torah, the charge of lawlessness would be deeply offensive and shaming.

Those Who Hate Prophets Have a Long Line of Predecessors (23:29-32) It is possible to be very religious yet hate God's message and messengers! In verses 29-36 Jesus challenges the hypocrisy of those who honor *the prophets* by caring for their *tombs,* yet like their ancestors will kill the Prophet who has come to them. Their behavior proves that, spiritually speaking, they are not descendants of the prophets, but rather descendants of those who killed them. (A parallel today would be to claim, "If I had lived in 1830, I would have opposed slavery," while treating others in racist or otherwise demeaning ways today; or to say, "If I had lived in Nazi Germany, I would have helped Jewish people escape Hitler," while fearing to speak against abortion or racism lest someone think us too reactionary.)

Employing irony in a manner typical of the prophets (who sometimes told the people to go on sinning but to expect God's judgment for it—Is 6:9; 29:9; Jer 23:28; 44:25-26; Ezek 3:27; Amos 4:4-5), Jesus tells the leaders to fill to the brim the role of prophet murderers they have inherited, so that the judgment accumulating for generations will finally be poured out (Mt 23:36).

---

flourished around Jesus' time (Jeremias 1971:146 n. 2; Schweizer 1975:442-43).

Impending Judgment on the Religious Establishment (23:33-39)

Many of us today do not like to preach on judgment, but the prophets of Scripture, including Jesus, heavily emphasized warnings about judgment. If we are to be faithful to our calling as Christ's followers and if we care about others, we dare not shortchange Scripture's message of judgment on individuals and nations. We must recognize that every nation, including our own, will face divine punishment (if Israel, how much more Gentiles!). Yet we must remember that God's heart of judgment sometimes sounds most like a lament (v. 37).

Persecutors of God's Servants Will Face Judgment (23:33-36)
Just as the religious people had murdered God's spokespeople in the past (vv. 29-31), they would do to Jesus (v. 32) and his followers (v. 34). But whatever judgments past generations might have suffered, the true guilt had been saved up for the climactic murder of this generation—the execution of Jesus (27:25). Like Matthew 24, this section views the destruction of the temple, due to occur in the leaders' generation (23:35-38), in the context of the final period of judgment (vv. 33, 39).

John the Baptist had demanded to know who warned these offspring of *vipers* (see comment on 3:7; compare 12:34) to flee approaching hellfire yet failed to call them to bear fruits of repentance (3:7-8). Jesus offers the same message (23:33). The *prophets, wise men* (*ḥokmîm,* "sages") and *teachers* ("scribes") Jesus would send represent the various missions of his own followers (5:12; 13:52; compare "apostles" in Lk 11:49), whether they came as prophetic or teaching figures (see 11:18-19). Jesus here fills a role that God filled in the biblical tradition (as in 2 Chron 36:15-16). These prophets, like the earlier prophets Jesus mentioned (Mt 23:29-31; compare 21:35-36) and himself (23:32, 36; compare 21:39), would face persecution (see again 10:17, 23).

Filling up the cup to the brim refers to meriting all the *blood* (bloodguilt) saved up among past generations, never punished as was deserved (compare Deut 32:43; Ps 79:10; Is 40:2; Rev 6:10). The blood of *Abel,* a prototypical martyr (as in Ps-Philo 16:2), had cried for

---

23:34 That Luke (11:49) and probably Q attribute this saying to divine wisdom may suggest that Matthew here understands Jesus as deity or divine wisdom (Hamerton-Kelly 1973:31, following Suggs).

23:37 Jewish teachers also came to speak of one who converted a Gentile as bringing him

vengeance against his fraternal slayer (Gen 4:10; Heb 11:4; 12:24; *Jub.* 4:3; *1 Enoch* 22:6-7). Jesus' second example is probably the Zechariah of 2 Chronicles 24:20-22, martyred in the temple. According to Jewish tradition, Zechariah's blood, like Abel's, cried against the murderers for vengeance, yielding the massacre of many priests (*b. Giṭṭin* 57b; *p. Ta'anit* 4:5, §14; *Pes. Rab Kah.* 15:7). The bloodguilt for Jesus' death would fall on that generation (Mt 27:25). And as Zechariah's blood had once desecrated the priestly sanctuary and so invited judgment (*Lives of Prophets* 23:1; *Sipra Behuq.* pq. 6.267.2.1), so would the blood of the priests in A.D. 66 as the "abomination that causes desolation" (24:15).

Jesus Longs for Repentance Rather Than Judgment (23:37-39) In contrast to the woes earlier in the chapter (vv. 13-29), verse 37 represents a true lament. That Jesus wishes to gather his people under his wings recalls the image of God sheltering his people under his wings (as in Ex 19:4; Deut 32:11; Ps 17:8; 36:7; 63:7; 91:4; *1 Enoch* 39:7). But as often in the case of God in the Old Testament, Jesus' love for Jerusalem here gives way to the brokenhearted pain of their rejection. God also weeps over his judgment of Israel (for example, Jer 8:21-22; 9:1, 10). Israel had killed (Jer 26:20-23; here especially 2 Chron 25:16) and persecuted (Is 30:10; Amos 2:12) the prophets God had sent; Jewish tradition amplified prophetic martyrology further (Manson 1979:126-27), as did Christian tradition (the interpolation in *Sib. Or.* 2.248). After A.D. 70, Jewish prayers also confessed that Israel's sins had brought on the calamity of exile.

This passage reminds us that God does not forget his promises to his people. For Luke, Jesus' grief and his promise that they will see him later (Lk 13:34-35) precedes, hence is fulfilled in, the triumphal entry (19:41); Matthew places it among the woes of coming judgment, but in so doing transforms this into a promise of future hope (compare Mt 10:23; Glasson 1963:96-98; Aune 1983:176). Israel's restoration was a major theme of the biblical prophets and reappeared at least occasionally in early Christianity (Rom 11:26), though the emphasis of early Christian apologetic came to focus on the Gentile mission.

---

or her under the wings of the Shekinah (compare Ruth 2:12; *2 Baruch* 41:4; *Sipre Num.* 80.1.1). The protective instincts of a mother bird were proverbial (4 Macc 14:14-17); if Luke's context is original, it also recalls Jesus' physical vulnerability to his enemies on Israel's behalf (Lk 13:32).

In this context, the impending judgment Jesus promises for the climactic shedding of his blood is the "desolation" of their *house*—the temple's destruction. To this theme the discussion quickly turns (24:1-3, 15).

□ Judgment on the Temple and the World (24:1-31)

Jesus pronounces woes against religious leaders of his day (23:13-32) and then hints about judgment against the temple, the ultimate symbol of the religious establishment's power (23:38; compare 21:13). As in many Old Testament prophets, nearer judgments foreshadow the final judgment; Matthew recognizes in the temple's destruction in A.D. 70 a vindication of Jesus' prophecy and an assurance that his other prophecies will also come to pass.

The Temple's Destruction (24:1-3) In much of Matthew 24, Jesus is warning followers who, like Peter, want an optimistic promise of the future (16:21-23) that realism is more important. His followers must prepare themselves to die for his honor before the coming of the end (compare 16:24-28). The introduction to this part of the discourse makes some crucial points.

Jesus Is Not Impressed with Splendid Monuments (24:1-2) The temple was renowned for its beauty (*ARN* 28A; 48, §132B), even throughout the Roman world (2 Macc 2:22; *Ep. Arist.* 84-91; *CIJ* 1:378, §515); Israel had traditionally viewed the temple as invincible (Jer 7:4; *Ep. Arist.* 100-101; Philo *Spec. Leg.* 1.76). Jesus, however, is not impressed.

Swift Judgment to Come Against the Temple Establishment (24:2) The temple, as the ultimate symbol of the Judean religious establishment, which the people took to be the symbol of God's glory (compare Jer 7:4), would be utterly destroyed.

It is difficult to deny that Jesus accurately predicted the temple's destruction. Even on minimal historical grounds, we have good reason to agree with Matthew that Jesus did so (see, for example, Hill 1979:62-63; Aune 1983:174-75; E. Sanders 1993:257). First, although the

---

24:2 Some of Jesus' sectarian contemporaries predicted judgment on the temple as well (e.g., *Test. Levi* 15:1; *Test. Moses* 6:8-9); before 70, Qumran sectarians (1QpHab 9.6-7) and Joshua ben Hananiah (Jos. *War* 6.301) also expected judgment on Jerusalem and its priesthood.

later church may have forgotten the significance of some of Jesus' words and deeds against the temple, they preserved them. Thus we learn of a symbolic act of judgment there (Mt 21:12), testimony of witnesses the Christians believed to be false (26:61; compare Mk 15:29; Jn 2:19; Acts 6:14), and a tradition about its destruction that must come from before it was destroyed (Q tradition in Mt 23:38 par. Lk 13:35). Jewish Christians who continued to worship in the temple (Acts 2:46; 21:26-27) nevertheless remained faithful to a saying of Jesus which they would surely not have created (compare Hare 1967:6). Finally, someone making up Jesus' prediction after the event would have fitted it more literally to its fulfillment, whereas Jesus' saying retains its prophetic hyperbole (such as *not one stone . . . on another*).

The End of Both the Temple and the Age (24:3) This chapter will address two issues: (1) the time of the temple's destruction and (2) the *sign* indicating his coming and the close of this *age*. Although biblical prophecy often linked events according to the kind of event rather than their sequence (for example, a near plague of locusts coalesces with eschatological armies in Joel), clarity was essential for Matthew (probably writing after 70) in a way that it was not for Mark (Mk 13:2, probably before 70; compare F. Bruce 1972a:71; S. Brown 1979). Modern prophecy teachers who require a restored temple and another abomination of desolation to precede Christ's return may be missing the point of Matthew's careful division of questions in 24:3. The final prerequisite for Jesus' coming is the evangelization of all nations (v. 14); the most specific prerequisite is the temple's desecration (v. 15), but the only *sign* of his immediate coming mentioned in the passage appears in the heavens when or just before Jesus appears (v. 30; compare J. Wenham 1977:72; pace Walvoord 1971b).

Not Yet the End (24:4-14) Many modern readers have felt uncomfortable with the picture of Jesus as an end-time prophet. Nevertheless, even if one starts with historical skepticism, Jesus clearly taught on the end

---

24:3 Grammatically the coming and close of the age are linked by the single sign and represent a single question; the single definite article governing them may identify them as well (see Gundry 1982:476; pace P. Ellis 1974:87-88).

time. Much of Jesus' final discourse in Matthew comes from Mark and Q, but even where Matthew adds elements (such as the trumpet in 24:31), we often have other evidence that Jesus spoke these words. Our earliest extant Christian document, 1 Thessalonians, alludes to some of the same words of Jesus ("according to the Lord's own word," 1 Thess 4:15): clouds, gathering of the elect, angel(s), lawlessness, apostasy, defilement of God's temple, the parousia, coming as a thief, sudden destruction on the wicked, and so on (4:13—5:11; compare 2 Thess 2:1-12; Waterman 1975; D. Wenham 1984). Some of Jesus' other words, for instance about unknown times and seasons (Acts 1:7), also appear there. But this common ground not only helps us defend the reliability of the Gospels; it also reminds us that Paul, unlike some Bible teachers today, saw no difference between Jesus' coming for the saints and his coming at the end of the age to judge the world.

Modern prophecy teachers have traditionally looked to current events for signs of the end, to stir end-time enthusiasm among Christians. While the goal may be worthy, the methodology runs counter to Jesus' own teaching. After listing many of the signs (usually hardships) that characterized the end among contemporary Jewish thinkers and visionaries, Jesus declares that *the end is still to come* (v. 6; compare Rev 6:1-8). Jewish people called such events the "birth-pangs of the Messiah" (Morris 1972:23), but Jesus declares that these are merely *the beginning of birth pains* (Mt 24:8). Besides missing Jesus' point, modern prophecy teachers are also almost always wrong; for one survey of missed prophecies—often reinterpreting the same biblical texts differently from decade to decade, as headlines change—see Wilson 1977.

While catastrophic events do not allow us to predict how soon the Lord is coming—such events have happened throughout history (Ladd 1956:72 n. 1; pace Frost 1924:18-19)—they do remind us that such

24:8 When Jewish people spoke of the messianic birth pangs (compare 1QH 3.3-18; *1 Enoch* 62:4; *b. Sanhedrin* 98b), they thought of Israel's travail before the end of the age (for samples of hardships at the end of the age, see, e.g., *Jub.* 23:11-25; *Sib. Or.* 3.213-15; 4 Ezra 8:63-9:8; 13:30; *m. Soṭa* 9:15). The early Christians seem to have applied the image to the entire period between the first and second comings (Rom 8:22), just as the Qumran sect viewed its "final generation" as extending until the imminently expected end.
24:9 Matthew and Mark clearly write for the church. Although I mean no disrespect for differing positions, I thus interpret this passage quite differently from those North American

problems characterize this age, summoning us to long for our Lord's coming all the more fervently. Jesus warns us what kind of sufferings we must face. His teaching presupposes important knowledge about the end time, but its repeated exhortations show that its emphasis is on how to live in light of that reality (see Lane 1974:446; Hill 1979:63). Thus it makes good sermon material if we catch Jesus' point!

Christians Must Be Ready for False Messiahs (24:4-5) The danger of being misled is mentioned frequently (vv. 4, 11, 24), and Matthew elsewhere has cause to report Jesus' warnings against signs-working prophets (7:15, 22; on signs prophets, see the introduction), a warning that is clearly part of the Jesus tradition (2 Thess 2:9). Today we might think of Jim Jones, David Koresh and New Age Christ figures (see Groothuis 1990). The death toll under Jones and Koresh, incidentally, serves as a helpful rebuttal to those who claim that all religions are the same and it matters not what one believes. But false messianic figures abounded in the first century as well (for example, Jos. *War* 2.259-63; 6.285-88; *Ant.* 20.97-98).

Be Ready for Both Human and Natural Disasters (24:6-8) Jesus borrows traditional biblical language here (compare 2 Chron 15:6; Is 19:2; Jer 51:46; for rumors of wars, compare Dan 11:44). Most of the events of Matthew 24:5-14 occurred between A.D. 30 and 70 (Blomberg 1992:356, following W. G. Thompson 1974). Some even believe *the gospel of the kingdom* was proclaimed among the nations in a representative sense (Rom 10:18; Col 1:6; Blomberg 1992:356-57). The general character of the language prohibits us from limiting it to any such events, however (Beasley-Murray 1957:35, 39). Such events occurred throughout the period of 30-70 and have been occurring ever since.

Be Ready for Persecution; Some Professing Christians Will Fall Away (24:9-13) So heart wrenching is this reality that the New

scholars who deny that the church is addressed (Walvoord 1971a and 1976:73-74; Ware 1981; contrast Beechick 1980:231-51, who, though supporting pretribulationism, agrees that the text addresses the church). Historically, addressing the disciples, Jesus was also addressing the nucleus of the church, no less than in, say, John 14—17 (see Katterjohn 1976:17). As D. A. Carson (1984:490) notes, "Most will agree that no passage in the Bible unambiguously teaches a two-stage return" (i.e., pretribulationalism). In practice, of course, readiness to suffer and persevere in hope of Jesus' future coming makes more difference than one's official position on this doctrine.

Testament writers had to warn Christians about it repeatedly (2 Thess 2:3; 1 Tim 4:1-3; 2 Tim 3:1-9; 2 Pet 3:3; 1 Jn 2:18-19; Rev 13:12-17). Early Christian exhortation regularly portrayed perseverance and apostasy as the alternatives in times of serious testing (S. Brown 1969:146). Like Mark, Matthew connects the suffering of believers with that of Christ, even prefacing his passion narrative with the promise of believers' suffering (compare Feuillet 1980b; Graham 1986).

Wickedness, or more literally and specifically "lawlessness," could characterize especially the outwardly religious (Mt 23:28; compare Jude 4) but probably applies to the society as a whole, including wicked rulers (2 Thess 2:3, 7-8). Nevertheless, as a consequence even the hearts of *most* (literally, "the many," perhaps denoting disciples—compare Mt 20:28) will become loveless (compare 22:37-39), hence capable of betrayal. Although the promise that one who *stands firm to the end will be saved* (24:13; compare v. 22) could refer to survival (as in 4 Ezra 6:25), the context of apostasy suggests that enduring to salvation here may refer to the same demand that phrase implies in most New Testament passages: that only those who continue in the faith will receive salvation at the final day (compare 7:13-14; Marshall 1974:73).

True Christians Will Spread the Gospel Among All Nations (24:14) Whereas Jesus says that other phenomena do not mark the end (v. 6), here he explicitly declares that the spread of the gospel does mark *the end.* The world controls many other factors, but this is the one factor the church itself determines: we must complete the commission of discipling all nations before this age will come to a close (28:19-20; compare Acts 1:6-11; Rom 11:25-26; 2 Pet 3:9-15). This prerequisite for the end does not imply that all peoples will be converted, but that the kingdom will not come in its fullness until all peoples have had the opportunity to embrace or reject the King who will be their judge (Mt 25:31-32). Jesus' early followers recognized that he would rule a remnant with representatives from all peoples (Rev 5:9; 7:9), just as the world system would (Rev 13:7).

Perhaps just as Israel, because of disobedience, ruled the land promised to Abraham only twice in its history (Gen 15:18; 1 Kings 4:21; 2 Chron 34:5-7), so the Lord's return has been delayed and the world's suffering prolonged by the church's disobedience to the Great Commission (see 2 Pet 3:9-15; Ford 1979:76). While some generations have come much closer than others, the Lord will not return until he has found a generation of servants devoted enough to fulfill the worldwide missions task he has commanded.

Whereas Matthew 28:18-20 is a commission, 24:14 is also a promise that some generation will succeed in finishing the task others have begun. African, Asian and Latin American Christians are in the forefront of world evangelism today; Christ's followers among many peoples must labor together for the harvest. But this mission cannot be done in human strength. The first generation of the church experienced the most rapid exponential growth while lacking all the resources Western Christians think necessary to accomplish the task today, such as money, literature, mass transportation and communication. But they had what much of the Western church today lacks: a faithful dependence on the Holy Spirit (compare 10:20; Mk 13:11; Acts 1:8). With a world population five times what it was a mere century and a half ago, the stakes have never been as high as they are now. Let us pray for laborers for the Lord's harvest (Mt 9:38), that we may become that promised generation.

We should note the context in which this worldwide evangelism occurs: suffering (24:9-13; more explicitly in Mk 13:9-11, earlier applied by Matthew to his fuller discourse on evangelism). Many early Christians recognized suffering as a prerequisite for the end (Col 1:24; Rev 6:10-11; compare 4 Ezra 4:3-37), because Christians' suffering is inseparable from our witness. It is when we are least comfortable with the world that we most dramatically proclaim the kingdom of our Lord. Further, just as most mission fields in history were opened through the blood of martyrs, many peoples will not be reached today without Christians who are prepared to lay down their lives for the gospel Jesus has called us to proclaim.

The Tribulation in History (24:15-28) Various New Testament passages seem to have reapplied Daniel's image of tribulation in different ways; but all agree in warning Christians to be vigilant when they face such testing. In contrast to the false prophets who till the end exhorted Jerusalemites to stand firm and expect sudden deliverance (Jos. *War* 6.285-86), Jesus warns his followers to accept the perils of this age and escape them when possible. Eusebius reports that the church in

Jerusalem responded to true prophets and fled the city before its destruction came (Euseb. *H.E.* 3.5.3); probably Jesus' words had guided the Christian prophets to a realistic appraisal of the danger, in contrast to some other Jerusalemites. His words likewise may instruct believers facing peril today. They also remind us that judgments, persecution and other sufferings characterize life in this age, summoning us to yearn for our Lord's coming rather than to become complacent with this world.

No Religious Symbol Provides Refuge from Divinely Decreed Judgment (24:15) The sanctuary, once desecrated, was doomed, as Jesus had earlier warned (23:38). Earlier desecrations had led others to recognize this pattern in history as well. Over two centuries earlier, a Syrian ruler had defiled the altar, causing an "abomination" that ruined the sanctuary with "desolation" (1 Macc 4:38). Daniel contains three references to an *abomination that causes desolation,* a sacrilege or defilement that will inevitably lead to destruction. One or two of the passages refer to events surrounding Antiochus Epiphanes, who claimed to be a deity and oppressed Israel (Dan 8:13; 11:31, 36-39); another text associates the same kind of "abomination" with the cutting off of an anointed ruler, close to the time of Jesus (Dan 9:26; compare J. Payne 1962:146; Beckwith 1981). Jewish speculation concerning the end time regularly reapplied Daniel's descriptions in various ways (see F. Bruce 1956:177; Russell 1964:198-201); Revelation may even reapply Daniel's tribulation period to the period between Jesus' first and second comings (Rev 12:1-6, 10).

Jewish people recognized that shedding innocent blood in the sanctuary would profane it (1 Macc 1:37; Jos. *Ant.* 9.152; so also Mt 23:35), and some saw this defilement as a desolation (1 Macc 1:39; 2:12). Josephus indicated that the shedding of priestly blood in the sanctuary (Jos. *War* 4.147-201; 4.343; 5.17-18) was the desecration, or abomination, that invited the ultimate desolation of A.D. 70 (Jos. *War* 5.17-19). Very close to three and a half years after this abomination, the temple was destroyed and violated even more terribly: the Romans erected on its site their standards, which bore the emperor's image, then offered sacrifice to them (Jos. *War* 6.316). But Jesus' warning must apply to the earlier (66) rather than the final (70) desecration, because shortly after the Romans surrounded Jerusalem, escape (Mt 24:16-18) became increasingly difficult (as in Jos. *War* 5.420-23, 449).

In Matthew, the tribulation *(distress)* seems to begin with the sanctuary's desecration in 66 and concludes with Jesus' return (24:29). If this observation is correct, it requires a "tribulation" longer than three and a half years or some other way to bridge the gap between 66 and the end. Scholars offer several explanations for this gap: in Matthew 24 Jesus (1) skips from this tribulation to the next eschatologically significant event, his return (G. Fuller 1966; compare Lk 21:24); (2) regards the whole interim between the temple's demise and his return as an extended tribulation period ("immediately"—Mt 24:29; see Carson 1984:507); (3) prophetically blends the tribulation of 66-70 with the final one, which it prefigures (see Bock 1994:332-33; compare Frost 1924:15-19); (4) begins the tribulation in 66 but postpones the rest of it until the end time; (5) intends his "return" in verses 29-31 symbolically for the fall of Jerusalem (see Tasker 1961:224-26; J. Wenham 1977:71; Barclay 1959; France 1985:333).

Not all these views are mutually exclusive. I currently favor option 1 or 2 with elements of 3. Although many scholars (including a number of conservative scholars) prefer option 5, the many emphatic statements about a personal, visible coming in the context probably rule out a symbolic coming the way they would a "spiritual" one. The third option may in fact deserve more attention than my current inclination has given it: certainly the prophetic perspective naturally viewed nearer historical events as precursors of the final events; see Ladd 1974b:196-201 (with Old Testament examples) and 1978a:36-37; compare Beasley-Murray 1960; Everson 1974:337; Bock 1994:332-33. Early Jewish texts also telescope the generations of history with the final generation (*Jub.* 23:11-32). As in Mark, the tribulation of 66-70 remains somehow connected with the future parousia, if only as a final prerequisite.

In any case, the view that the whole of Matthew 24 addresses only a future tribulation (often assumed automatically in circles unaware of the history of 66-70) is not tenable; Matthew understands that "all these things" (probably referring to the question about the temple's demise—24:2; Mk 13:4) will happen within a generation (Mt 24:34), language that throughout Jesus' teachings in Matthew refers to the generation then living (as in 12:39, 45; 16:4; 23:36; compare 27:25).

Believers Must Flee Impending Judgment with Haste (24:16-20)

Once the Romans surrounded Jerusalem, its inhabitants could still leave the city safely until the spring of A.D. 68 (Jos. *War* 4.377-80, 410; Lane 1974:468). Later deserters to the Romans, suspected of having swallowed jewels to escape with them, were often cut open by Syrian auxiliaries (Jos. *War* 5.550-52). Jesus' command to *flee to the mountains* (v. 16) makes good sense; Palestine's central mountain range provided a natural refuge (as in 1 Sam 23:14; Ezek 7:15-16; Jos. *War* 2.504).

The admonitions to leave the rooftop without entering the *house* (v. 17) and to leave *the field* without returning for one's *cloak* (v. 18) indicate that life matters more than even its basic necessities, which might later be replaced (compare 1 Macc 2:28). Because outside staircases led up to the flat rooftops, one could descend without entering the house to retrieve possessions (Lane 1974:470). One normally slept in one's outer garment and wore it during the cold of morning labor in the fields, but left it at the edge of the field as the day grew warmer (Anderson 1976:296). As essential as this outer cloak was, Jesus declares that running at the news of impending destruction was more urgent still.

The "woe" over the pregnant and nursing (*how dreadful*, v. 19) signifies the difficulty of flight and survival (Lk 23:29), implying the sorrow of losing infants in the trauma (compare *2 Baruch* 10:13-15). Verse 20 also reveals foresight concerning the sabbath and winter. On the former (mentioned only by Matthew) one could not secure animals for transport. Winter's cold limited travel; even armies stopped traveling campaigns during this season (as in Jos. *War* 4.442; *Ant.* 18.262). Further, winter rains could flood the roads and bury them deep in mud (*m. Ta'anit* 1:3; Jeremias 1969:58); indeed, in spring 68, because the Jordan was flowing high, Gadarene fugitives were delayed in crossing and were slaughtered by the Romans (Jos. *War* 4.433; Lane 1974:470-71).

Although Jesus' words specifically address the fall of Jerusalem, they provide us with some important principles. Christians who remember the nature of the time ought not to be attached to worldly possessions; we should value our lives enough to flee immediately. Indeed, God may

---

24:28 *Vultures* gathering around the slain is a biblical image of judgment, especially in the final battle (Lk 17:37; Ezek 39:17-20; Rev 19:11-21). Certainly in context this is not carnage

judge materialistic Western and other societies at times to turn us from our pursuit of what does not matter so we may learn to pursue what really does. Nor ought we to believe false prophets of peace proclaiming that judgment will never strike our own locality (for example, Jer 6:14); rather than sparing a locality, God sometimes warns his servants to leave (Gen 19:15-30).

God Cares About His Servants in Distress (24:21-28) Daniel spoke of an end-time tribulation greater than any that had preceded it (Dan 12:1); by indicating that no tribulation before or after this one would rival it, Matthew may suggest that it is a tribulation within history, not necessarily the final one (compare Jos. *War* 1.12). In any case, he warns against believing anyone who claims to be Christ, for when our Lord really returns even the sky will declare it (24:23-28).

When faith is tested, patience may wane; like Abraham and Sarah, we may be tempted to look for less difficult solutions than trusting God to fulfill his promise literally (Gen 16:1-2). But if our allegiance is to the Lord of the universe, we dare not settle for counterfeits. Signs and wonders (Mt 24:24) alone are inadequate to demonstrate a prophet's authenticity (7:21; Deut 13:1-5; 2 Thess 2:9). At what time will Jesus return? The same day *the vultures* gather around the corpses of the wicked slain in judgment (Mt 24:28).

Jesus' Return (24:29-31) Compare Mark 13:24-27; Luke 21:25-28. *Immediately* ties the tribulation of those days to the unidentified final tribulation, a tribulation that, on our reading, can be clearly identified as the final one only by the fact that the parousia (Jesus' return) concludes it. Like the day of the Lord in the Old Testament (Amos 5:18-20), Jesus' return is not good news for everyone.

The Effects of Jesus' Revelation Will Be Cosmic (24:29) End-time events explicitly reported in the Bible include no secretive coming as in some popular current eschatology (pace Strombeck 1982:151-53); as Leon Morris notes of the only return of Christ of which Scripture speaks, "It is difficult to see how he could more plainly describe something that

---

merely during the tribulation (pace Strombeck 1982:71).

is open and public" (1959:145).

The Nations Will Respond with Terror (24:30) The nations have good reason to fear. When applied to a king or other prominent dignitary, the term for Jesus' coming *(parousia)* was a quasi-technical expression that implied considerable demands for preparation on the part of the local populace (Ladd 1967:92). That the Son of Man has authority to dispatch *his* angels to gather *his* elect (v. 31; Mk 13:27) portrays Jesus as divine (Meier 1980:288). As in Mark 13:26, the language of *the Son of Man* coming with *the clouds* alludes to Daniel 7:13, but Matthew includes an additional allusion to Zechariah 12:10, in which the nations *mourn.*

The Church Will Ultimately Be Delivered (24:31) Paul likewise observes that deliverance from tribulation in this age arrives when Jesus comes as King and judges the wicked (2 Thess 1:6-7). *From one end of the heavens to the other* means the whole earth (Mk 13:27; compare Is 11:12; *1 Enoch* 57:2).

The figure of the *trumpet* is appropriate, and is one feature noted by Matthew but missing in Mark, yet earlier cited also by Paul (1 Thess 4:17). Paul refers to the "last trumpet" at the resurrection of the righteous (1 Cor 15:52), when the final enemy, death, is subdued (1 Cor 15:24-26). Most often trumpets assembled God's people for war or alerted them to an attack (as in Num 10:9; Judg 3:27; Is 18:3; Jer 4:19; Ezek 33:3-6; Joel 2:1; Zeph 1:16); such a trumpet blast often came with a shout (Jos. *War* 3.265; 1 Thess 4:16) and could symbolize the final battle (compare 1QM 8.9-12).

24:30 We can especially expect the term *parousia* (which bears various possible meanings) to convey the image of a royal appearance when writers conjoin the term with another quasi-technical expression, *apantēsis,* "meeting," as in 1 Thessalonians 4:17 (see Milligan 1908:62; F. Bruce 1963:68-69, 1977:527 n. 26, and 1982:102; Best 1977:199; Marshall 1983:131). Like other New Testament terms for Jesus' coming, this one is applied "indiscriminately for what [pretribulationists] regard as the two phases of Jesus' return," more likely than not suggesting that the New Testament picture, like the historic Christian picture till J. N. Darby's formulation of pretribulationism in 1830, was of only one return of Jesus, at the very end of the age (Gundry 1973:158; see also Ladd 1956:61-70; pace Strombeck 1982:147-48, who appears to simply presuppose what he hopes to prove).

Clouds are a recurrent motif in early Christian parousia language (Acts 1:9, 11; 1 Thess 4:17; Rev 1:7; 11:12; 14:14; see Rissi 1966:103 n. 168); if, as is likely, Paul alludes to Daniel by way of Jesus here, Paul places Jesus' coming for the saints at the end of the tribulation of this age (Mt 24:29-30; 1 Thess 4:17).

24:31 *Elect* here most likely means Christians, as in this eschatological tradition (2 Thess

☐ Parables of the Future Kingdom (24:32—25:46)

In Matthew 13 Jesus used seven or eight parables to illustrate how God's kingdom could be present in a hidden way until the day of judgment. Now he closes his final sermon in this Gospel with a roughly equal number of parables about the consummation of his kingdom at the end of the age.

Neither the Day Nor the Hour (24:32-44) Many popular prophecy teachers have created an end-time scenario very different from, and far more complex than, the one taught by Jesus. At the same time, they have rightly reminded many in the body of Christ that we should be ready for Christ's unexpected return.

Since the Temple's Desolation, the End Has Been Imminent (24:32-35) This passage probably suggests that the temple's desolation constitutes the final visible prerequisite for the kingdom before the cosmic signs of Jesus' return. Because fig trees, unlike most trees in Palestine, lost their leaves seasonally, their fruit indicated the season (Jeremias 1971:106; Song 2:13). The temple establishment was like fig trees with the veneer of maturity yet without fruit (Mt 21:19; compare Mk 11:12-25). Though some wish to take *generation (genea)* as "race," Matthew 23:35-36 leaves no doubt that Jesus uses the term normally and, as elsewhere in Matthew, refers to the climactic generation. Jerusalem fell about forty years after Jesus' warning. Once God had judged the fruitless authorities who dominate the temple, Jesus could return at any time.

2:13) and usually in the New Testament (Mt 22:14; Rom 8:33; 1 Pet 1:1; 2:9); so also, for example, Katterjohn 1976:20; Sandmel 1978a:38. John Walvoord (1971a) is forced to argue that the church is removed before the tribulation of verses 15-28, although no such event is mentioned there (nor explicitly mentioned elsewhere in the New Testament or other Christian literature before 1830).

In biblical and Jewish tradition, the remnant of Israel was "chosen" and would be "gathered" at the end time (Is 11:12; 43:5; 49:5; 56:8; *Ps. Sol.* 8:28; 11:2-5; 17:26; 4 Ezra 13:39-40; *4 Baruch* 3:11; *Test. Asher* 7:7); but early Christian texts regularly apply the image of Israel's remnant to the church, consisting of all those in covenant relationship with God in Christ, who thereby share in Israel's messianic hope. Further, Jesus has been addressing his followers throughout the rest of the discourse (J. Payne 1962:55). Paul applies this "gathering" to followers of Jesus; see 2 Thessalonians 2:1, where the Granville Sharpe rule links the "gathering" and parousia (Waterman 1975:112; Best 1977:274), and the context places the parousia at the end (2 Thess 2:8); see also 1 Thessalonians 4:15-17.

Jesus' Coming Will Catch Most People Unawares (24:36-44) The *day* in this passage may well refer to the day of the Lord (as in 1 Thess 5:2; see Cullmann 1950:43). Such a warning prevents suffering believers from building up undue expectations that would set them up for exploitation (Mt 24:23-27); this sort of warning was especially critical in view of the tendency of many of Jesus' contemporaries to predict signs of the end (see comment on 24:6-8).

Like the flood, the Son of Man's coming (Dan 7:13-14) would arrive as sudden and unexpected judgment, without explicit warning. Jesus' followers might recognize the completion of requisite signs (compare 1 Thess 5:4-6), but for outsiders, life would be business as usual (banquets and weddings, or *grinding with a hand mill*). This passage echoes the damnable folly of outsiders repeated throughout the Gospel tradition in general and Matthew in particular (as in 13:19; 15:10): they do not understand (24:27, 39). If Jesus means "taken in judgment" (Jer 6:11; 8:13; compare *Ps. Sol.* 13:11), the "taking" parallels the different expression in Matthew 24:39, where the flood *took* the wicked *away* (see Lk 17:34-37; contrast Sirach 44:16-17).

Keep watch does not mean "look for" or "anticipate immediately," but borrows the image of a night watchman at his post (Mt 24:42; 25:13; Ladd 1974b:208): the believer must remain prepared for the Lord's coming, remaining alert and awake (26:38, 40-41, 43-46). That the time of Jesus' coming is unknown does not preclude that some signs mentioned earlier in the passage will precede it (compare Gundry 1982:491-92; Katterjohn and Fackler 1976:118-19), any more than such ideas were incompatible in various ancient Jewish end-time

---

24:36 Although Allen Beechick (1980:231-51) admits that the imminence passages are in the context of Jesus' return after the tribulation, he argues that since we know on other grounds that the Lord will also return before the tribulation, the same principle of imminence applies to Jesus' coming before the tribulation. This argument for a pretribulational coming falters, however. First, Beechick admits that the text's statements about imminence do not by themselves teach a pretribulation coming. Second, the imminence statements are in a posttribulation context, hence one cannot calculate the time of Jesus' coming after the tribulation. Third, if exhortations to watchfulness and readiness do not imply that return after the tribulation to which they explicitly refer will occur at "any moment," they cannot imply it for a coming to which the text never explicitly refers. Fourth, to have Jesus return for his saints before the tribulation of Matthew 24 would place his return before A.D. 66. Finally, it is not surprising that history reports no one who followed the same divisions of

views (see, for example, Bonsirven 1964:53). The early Christians often reused Jesus' image of a householder unprepared for a nocturnal *thief* (compare Joel 2:9) for Jesus' return at the end (1 Thess 5:2, 4; 2 Pet 3:10; Rev 3:3; 16:15).

Christ's Servants Judged (24:45-51) After Jesus exhorts the disciples to "keep watch," to stay awake, he illustrates what he means. We stay alert not by artificially and perpetually stirring expectation that he will come at a given time, but by living in such a manner that we would have no cause for shame if he did come at any time, since he may in fact do so. Paul may echo the warning against living an unexpectant, self-serving life here (compare 1 Thess 5:3-9).

Of the one to whom much is given, much is required. Ministers have special responsibilities to serve others (Lk 12:41-42; compare Hos 4:6-9; 1 Pet 5:1-4). This parable shows that Jesus' assault on hypocritical leaders in Israel (Mt 23) is also applicable to those in the church at the Second Coming who prove equally unprepared (compare 25:14-30; Jas 3:1; see Meier 1980:293-94; Gundry 1982:497). Here the ruling servant exploits the resources meant for others through his gluttony and drunkenness (Mt 24:49; compare the demand for sobriety in Lk 21:34; 1 Thess 5:6-7). "You have ruled [my sheep] harshly and brutally" (Ezek 34:4).

Some servants of Christ will be as unprepared at his Second Coming as was much of the religious establishment at his first. Sharing hell with the *hypocrites* (Mt 24:51) explicitly recalls the false servants of 23:13-29. Like the tenants of 21:35-37 or the shepherds failing to feed the sheep

---

the context Beechick finds, since, ingenious though they are, they do not fit the natural flow of context.

24:39 Jesus parallels the flood not with the tribulation (as in some pretribulational views) but with the more final end-time destruction at the tribulation's end (see also 2 Pet 2:5-6).

24:43 Because "day of the Lord" appears in the related saying of 1 Thessalonians 5:2 (see later 2 Pet 3:10) but not here (compare also Rev 3:3; 16:15), Robert Gundry (1987) suggests that Paul introduced the phrase there; for the sense of "day of the Lord" in Paul, see Ladd 1974b:364, 555 (it cannot include the tribulation, pace Walvoord 1967:81, 117 and 1972:160-63 and Strombeck 1982:46-54, which contradict 2 Thess 2:1-4; see F. Bruce 1982:163).

in Ezekiel 34:15 (compare Mt 24:45), these leaders forgot their true role as servants (23:12) and acted as if they could do as they pleased with those God had entrusted to their care.

Ministers who exploit the flock for their own interests will be damned. See also 2 Peter 2:3. Jesus is severe on leaders who are responsible for crushing or misleading others, not because he does not love these leaders but because he also loves the people they are exploiting. Jesus calls us ministers to serve our fellow servants, and we do ourselves a disservice by toning down Jesus' willfully strong language about the lostness of those who do not. If we are (for example) more concerned about getting a good "altar call" for our own self-esteem than about building up the flock with sound teaching or sharing Christ beyond the church's walls, we are using church members for our own interests. Ministers who use churches merely as stepping stones for personal ambition or who are more interested in preserving their wages than fulfilling their calling (see Mic 3:11-12; 1 Tim 6:5) could discover on the day of judgment that they will not spend eternity with the Lord they proclaimed.

Awaiting the Bridegroom (25:1-13) Since the time of Jesus' coming is unknown, we must watch and be ready (24:36). Although some rabbinic parables also address the theme of readiness (see *Sipre Deut.* 43.15.2), Jesus' parables about the end time especially focus on readiness for the Son of Man (for example, 24:42—25:13). To live ready for Jesus' return involves living in light of the day of judgment, when our deeds and motives will be revealed.

Wise disciples remain vigilant for Jesus' return. In this parable the bridesmaids, rather than the bride herself, constitute the primary characters. Wedding processions from the bride's to the groom's home, accompanied by singing and dancing, normally happened at night and hence required light. The *lamps* in ancient weddings were not the small, hand-held lamps used under normal circumstances, but torches (as in Plut. *Roman Questions* 2, *Mor.* 263F; Ach. Tat. 2.11.1), perhaps sticks wrapped with oiled rags, as in traditional

---

25:10 The door would hardly be locked throughout the feast, which lasted seven days (Judg 14:12, 17; Tobit 11:19; *Sipra Behuq.* pq. 5.266.1.7). New guests sometimes arrived during those days, requiring the repeating of the blessings (Safrai 1974-1976b:760).

Palestinian Arab weddings (Jeremias 1972:174-75). Women torchbearers probably led the bride to the bridegroom's home, joined by the groom and his male friends (Jeremias 1972:173). Presumably the bridesmaids are thus waiting outside the bride's home for his coming, to escort her to his home (Argyle 1963:189).

In this particular parable (in contrast to 24:42-44) the issue is not that the virgins went to sleep—both the wise and foolish did so; this detail is merely part of the narrative's setting. The issue is that some were not watchful enough to have sufficient *oil* (Beare 1981:482; Schweizer 1975:467). Some suggest that the torches could burn only fifteen minutes before being rewrapped with more oiled cloth (for example, France 1985:351; Witherington 1984:43). In traditional Palestinian weddings, messengers may repeatedly announce the bridegroom's coming, yet it can be delayed for hours (Jeremias 1972:173). Delays occur while the bride's relatives haggle over the value of presents given them, emphasizing the bride's great value and thus the wisdom of the groom's selection (Jeremias 1972:173-74; compare Eickelman 1989:174).

Disciples should not lose heart if Jesus does not return as quickly as we expect him to. All the virgins would have been ready for the groom had he arrived when they expected, but grooms' delays were common enough that they should have anticipated it. This provides clear warning that the parousia may be delayed. The term used for the meeting or rendezvous with the bridegroom (*meet*, v. 6) often suggested a party going out to meet someone and forming his escort to a place where he would be honored (as in 1 Thess 4:17; see Milligan 1908:62; F. Bruce 1963:68-69).

Those unprepared for Christ's banquet insult him and warrant judgment. The wise virgins' unwillingness to share their oil reflects their concern for their friend's wedding; since they had only enough for their own torches, sharing would cause all the torches to be extinguished, ruining the whole procession (Meier 1980:295; Gundry 1982:500). Bridal processions were so important that later rabbis even suspended their lectures so they could hail a passing bride (*ARN* 4A; 8, §22B); for the

---

25:12 The expression "I do not know you" was sometimes used when one wished to treat another as a stranger and keep them from approaching (Blomberg 1992:371 n. 76).

groom and (some held) for the attendants, weddings even took precedence over some ritual obligations (as in *t. Berakot* 2:10), so a breach of etiquette was serious.

Thus the foolish virgins were not excluded simply because the door was locked (25:10-11), nor because the host actually did not recognize them (v. 12), but because they had insulted the bride and groom as well as all their relatives! They would never be allowed to forget such an offense. To participate in their friend's wedding was a great honor; as *virgins*, these young women were in a sense practicing for their own impending weddings around the age of twelve to sixteen. To have spoiled the wedding for their friend by failing to do their part was a great insult to everyone else at the wedding. That they would be shut out of the feast in punishment suits their case, but the language used to depict this nightmare points beyond itself to severer, eternal judgment, probably echoing the sayings in 7:21-23. Wedding feasts epitomized joy (as in Jn 3:29); the transgressors have been shut out.

The Industrious and the Lazy Managers (25:14-30) As in 24:45-51, readiness for Jesus' return here demands faithfulness in doing the work he has called us to do. This warning applies to all disciples, but perhaps most seriously to church leaders: "A Christian leader who does not lead is damned" (Meier 1980:300).

We have the opportunity to multiply what Christ has entrusted to us. Matthew seems to make a special point in noting that the master gave to *each according to his ability*—he already knew which slaves would be most industrious, but expected all to show *some* industry. In the Roman Empire slaves could earn wages and bonuses and acquire property (as in Apul. *Metam.* 10.13; Cohen 1966:179-278), hence they would have more incentive to look out for the master's property than slaves in many cultures do. Householders going on long journeys might entrust their estate to slaves to oversee (compare 24:45-51), since household slaves often held managerial roles (for example, Treggiari 1975:49). Thus the servants understood very well what was required of them.

Most people lacked capital, but those who had it could multiply their

---

25:26 The word often translated *lazy* normally means "fearful," suggesting that fear was

investment fivefold or even tenfold (Lk 19:16-18); doubling one's investment (Mt 25:20, 22) might be regarded as a reasonable minimum return in the ancient economy (Derrett 1970:24). Burying money (v. 18) kept the capital safe, but the money would have been no less safe with bankers (*m. Baba Meṣi'a* 3:11; Gundry 1982:509).

Jesus promises eternal reward for those who prove worthy of his trust. The servants' rewards were commensurate with their faithfulness in pursuing the master's interest. Elsewhere we encounter the principle that one untrustworthy in what is his own will not be trustworthy in what concerns others (Lk 16:10-12; *m. Demai* 2:2); here we find the principle that only those proved in small leadership positions will be prepared for bigger ones (compare, for example, *Ep. Arist.* 264; *t. Ḥagiga* 2:9). In the context of the preceding parable (Mt 25:10), sharing the *master's happiness* probably connotes banqueting with the master.

Professed disciples who insult Christ's grace by neglecting his commission in this world are damned. But as in the preceding parable (25:12), the exclusion of the unfaithful, who insult their patron's trust in them, is explicit: it involves hell's *darkness* (8:12; 22:13) and wailing (22:13). When the lazy servant declares, "Here is your own money back!" he refuses to acknowledge responsibility, a responsibility he could have easily enough fulfilled. Having already failed the master's trust, he now proceeds to insult the master. He offers an excuse no master would have accepted: knowing the master's reputation for sternness, he was paralyzed with fear (25:24-25). He is like too many Christians so overwhelmed by the magnitude of God's task that we put off contributing anything to it. The master rightly responds, "On the assumption that I am indeed hard and merciless, you should have been all the more diligent!" (vv. 26-27).

Whereas the other servants are rewarded by the master's benevolence, this servant, fearing the master's harshness but unaware of his benevolence (compare Patte 1987:346), experiences the very wrath he feared. This, says Jesus, is what will happen to those who claim to be his followers but do not invest their lives in the work of the kingdom.

the source of the slave's passivity (Nielsen 1990).

The Division of the Sheep and the Goats (25:31-46) This final parable in Jesus' final sermon in Matthew brings home the reality of judgment. As the missionaries from Matthew's churches spread the good news of the kingdom both among fellow Jews and among Gentiles, they faced hostility as well as welcome. This parable brings together some themes from the rest of the Gospel: Christ, like the kingdom, had been present in a hidden way (compare chap. 13), and one's response to his agents represented one's response to him (chap. 10).

Jesus is the judge on the day of judgment. The parable assumes Jesus' deity. Whereas others sometimes fill the role of final judge in Jewish tradition (as in *Test. Ab.* 13A; 11B), the central biblical and Jewish role of final judge that Jesus here assumes normally belongs to God himself (see, for example, *1 Enoch* 9:4; 60:2). As noted earlier, the king in rabbinic parables is nearly always God. Likewise, coming with *all the angels* (Mt 25:31; compare 13:41; 16:27; 24:31; 2 Thess 1:7) alludes to various versions of Zechariah 14:5 (see Gundry 1982:511), where God is in view. Further, Jesus' claim that whatever others have done to his servants they have done to him fits a rabbinic perspective about God (Smith 1951:154). Finally, although shepherds could represent Moses, David and others in biblical and Jewish tradition, the chief *shepherd* remained God himself (as in Ps 23:1-4; 74:1-2; Is 40:11; Ezek 34:11-17; Zech 10:3; Sirach 18:13; *1 Enoch* 89:18; Ps-Philo 28.5; 30.5). Jesus is both judge and the focus of the final judgment, spelling disaster to those who ignored him on this side of that day.

The nations will be judged according to how they respond to the gospel and its messengers. The *nations* or "Gentiles" in Jewish literature would be judged according to how they treated Israel (4 Ezra 7:37; Klausner 1979:200). As in other parables, here they are *gathered* (compare 13:40; Is 2:4; Rev 16:16) and separated (Mt 13:30, 49), in this instance the way a shepherd would separate *sheep* from *goats* (compare Ezek 34:17), to keep the goats warm at night while keeping the sheep in open air as they preferred (Jeremias 1972:206). Sheep cost more than goats (Jere-

---

25:40 That the "siblings" are here disciples is the majority view in church history and among contemporary New Testament scholars, though scholars divide over whether they are Christian missionaries or the Christian poor (Michaels 1965; Grassi 1965:46; Cope 1969;

mias 1972:206) and because of their greater utility and value were nearly always more numerous on a farm (N. Lewis 1983:131-32).

The older dispensational scheme viewed this passage as the judgment of the nations based on their treatment of Israel. This suggestion could fit Jewish perceptions of the judgment, as noted above (compare Manson 1979:249-50). But this suggestion does not fit well Jesus' own designation of his *brothers* in the Gospels elsewhere (Mt 12:50; 28:10; see below). Because the passage explicitly declares that this judgment determines people's *eternal* destinies (25:46), it cannot refer to a judgment concerning who will enter the millennium, as in some older dispensational schemes (Ladd 1977:38; compare Ladd 1978b:98-102).

Nor is the popular view that this text refers to treatment of the poor or those in need (as in Gross 1964; Hare 1967:124; Catchpole 1979; Feuillet 1980a) exegetically compelling, although on other grounds it would be entirely consonant with the Jesus tradition (such as Mk 10:21; Lk 16:19-25) and biblical ethics as a whole (for example, Ex 22:22-27; Prov 19:17; 21:13). Jewish lists of loving works include showing hospitality and visiting the sick, though not visiting prisoners; such acts were found praiseworthy in the day of judgment (*2 Enoch* 63:1-2; Jeremias 1972:207-8; compare Bonsirven 1964:151-52).

In the context of Jesus' teachings, especially in the context of Matthew (as opposed to Luke), this parable addresses not serving all the poor but receiving the gospel's messengers. Elsewhere in Matthew, disciples are Jesus' *brothers* (12:50; 28:10; compare also *the least*—5:19; 11:11; 18:3-6, 10-14). Likewise, one treats Jesus as one treats his representatives (10:40-42), who should be received with hospitality, food and drink (10:8-13, 42). Imprisonment could refer to detention until trial before magistrates (10:18-19), and sickness to physical conditions brought on by the hardship of the mission (compare Phil 2:27-30; perhaps Gal 4:13-14; 2 Tim 4:20). Being poorly clothed appears in Pauline lists of sufferings (Rom 8:35), including specifically apostolic sufferings (1 Cor 4:11). The King thus judges the nations based on how they have responded to the gospel of the kingdom already preached to them

Ladd 1974a:191-99; Harrington 1982:101; Gundry 1982:511-14; France 1985:355; Blomberg 1992:377-78).

before the time of his kingdom (Mt 24:14; 28:19-20). The passage thus also implies that true messengers of the gospel will successfully evangelize the world only if they can also embrace poverty and suffering for Christ's name (compare Matthey 1980).

The stakes involved in our witness are eternal. The horrifying conclusion (25:46) is the damnation of people who did not actively embrace messengers of the gospel but nevertheless were oblivious to how they had offended God. The goats thus depart (7:23) into eternal fire (the worst possible conception of hell; see comment on 3:8, 10, 12), but tragically, God had not originally created them for the fire or the fire for them (compare 4 Ezra 8:59-60). Rather, it had been *prepared* (compare Mt 25:34) by God for the devil and his angels (compare 2 Pet 2:4; 1QM 13.11-12).

We too must "receive" one another with grace. In the context of the surrounding parables, welcoming Christ's messengers probably involves more than only initially embracing the message of the kingdom: it means treating one's fellow servants properly (24:45-49). Unless we "receive" one another in God's household, we in some way reject Christ whose representatives our fellow disciples are (18:5-6, 28-29). Paul likewise reminds the Corinthians that to be reconciled to him is to be reconciled to God himself (2 Cor 5:11—7:1).

ARREST, MARTYRDOM, RESURRECTION (26:1—28:20)

Because the accounts of Jesus' death and resurrection are central to Christian faith, they have been subjected to special challenge. Nevertheless, strong evidence supports the essential Gospel reports about Jesus' death and resurrection. Other narratives may have figured as much in early Christian ethical preaching, but early Christians probably would have told and retold the passion story, which lay at the heart of their gospel. No record remains of any form of early Christianity that lacked the basic structure of the story of Jesus' death and resurrection. Paul's sequence is similar to Mark's (1 Cor 11:23; 15:3-5; compare Jewish and Roman responsibility in 1 Cor 1:23; 1 Thess 2:14-15), and if, as is probable, John represents an independent tradition, his passion narrative again confirms the outline Mark follows, suggesting a passion narrative that existed before Mark (R. Brown 1994:53-55, 77-80).

Other evidence suggests the substantial reliability of these accounts.

First of all, the basic story seems to have been established among Jerusalem Christians within a decade after the resurrection. The basic components of the story and their outline are surely earlier than Mark; Paul and John independently attest the same material. Mark himself appears to presuppose that his audience is familiar with some details of the story (especially Barabbas and other insurrectionists, despite Pilate's many confrontations with such revolutionaries; Theissen 1991:171, 182-83).

Further, the "criterion of embarrassment" makes it nearly impossible to believe that the early Christians could have invented the account. Christians would not invent one disciple's betrayal or other disciples' abandonment (both shameful in their milieu); the earliest Christians, who were Jewish, probably would not invent condemnation by the majority of their own people's leaders; Christians would never have invented shameful death by crucifixion; and they would never have invented the treason charge "King of the Jews," which would have made all Christians look seditious and invited Roman retribution.

Finally, the accounts of Jesus' arrest, trials and execution fit what we know of the period in question. Craig Evans (1995:108) accurately compares Josephus's account of Jesus ben Ananias, who similarly entered the temple area during a festival (Jos. *War* 6.300-301). Like Jesus, he predicted doom on Jerusalem and its sanctuary, even referring (again like Jesus) to the context of Jeremiah's prophecy of judgment against the temple (Jer 7:34 in *War* 6.301; compare Jer 7:11 in Mk 11:17). The Jewish authorities arrested and beat Jesus ben Ananias (*War* 6.302) and handed him over to the Roman governor (*War* 6.303), who interrogated him (*War* 6.305). He refused to answer the governor (*War* 6.305), was scourged (6.304) and—in this case unlike Jesus (though compare Mk 15:9)—was released (6.305).

The primary difference, that Jesus of Nazareth was executed whereas Jesus son of Ananias was not, also makes good sense: unlike Jesus ben Ananias, Jesus of Nazareth was not viewed as insane and already had a band of followers, plus a growing reputation that could support messianic claims (compare E. Sanders 1993:267). Jesus ben Ananias could simply be punished; Jesus of Nazareth had to be executed. The basic points of the passion story—including those most apt to be questioned—make excellent historical sense.

□ The Betrayal (26:1-56)

Matthew concludes his grand eschatological vision of the exalted Son of Man with the harsh reality of present suffering, leading directly into his account of Jesus' betrayal, arrest and execution. As Mark connects Jesus' suffering (Mk 14—15) with that of the disciples (Mk 13) in a climax that fits the rest of his narrative, so for Matthew the passion narrative reminds disciples in this age of our present testing until our final, end-time deliverance (for example, 24:42-43; 25:13; 26:41). Because the story of our Lord's death provides the historical record of our once-for-all redemption, it reveals to us in intimate detail the concrete expression of God's love for us, as well as the awfulness of sin. At the same time, because Jesus' sacrifice becomes the model for that of his disciples (16:24), it invites us to count the cost of discipleship in a world hostile to the purposes and agendas of a God of justice, holiness and compassion.

In one of the opening scenes of this section, a woman plays the role that women continue to play in the accounts of Jesus' death, burial and resurrection: a foil that reveals the inadequate commitment of the male disciples. But most significant, her sacrifice provides a stark contrast to Judas's determination to profit somehow from Jesus, and his ultimate betrayal of Jesus to his enemies. That Jesus suffered at the hands of a close associate and disciple should encourage us when we experience rejection from those we seek to help. That most of the male disciples failed to stand firm challenges us to watch and pray that we may be ready for testing.

How Much Is Jesus Worth? (26:1-16) The extravagant anointing at Bethany (vv. 6-13) is framed by a plot to arrest Jesus (vv. 3-5, 14-16). The disciples, who can appear less wise than the women they seek to silence in the Gospels (as in 15:23; compare Lk 24:11), protest this extravagance. One disciple, Judas, who realizes that Jesus is a martyr

---

26:2 Theissen (1991:166-99) argues that the original passion narrative was in use by A.D. 40 in Jerusalem and Judea. Thus, for example, Mark preserves names (e.g., sons who identify the second Mary and Simon) that serve no visible purpose in his own narrative but may well have been important to the transmitters of the tradition behind his early Jerusalem source (Mk 15:40, 43; Theissen 1991:176-77). Names of small Palestinian towns would mean nothing to audiences outside Palestine; while one normally identifies local persons through their father's name, most persons in the passion narrative are identified by their place of

messiah, decides that following Jesus will not be profitable and determines to gain at least some profit.

Jesus Faces God's Calling Obediently (26:1-2) By adding another passion announcement here (contrast Mk 14:1-2), Matthew reminds us that whatever the power of those who plotted against Jesus, Jesus moved according to his Father's plan and not theirs. No matter how strong the forces arrayed against God's servants, God will ultimately fulfill his purposes. In contrast with Judas in this passage (Mt 26:14-16), Jesus obeys God's calling at great cost to himself and provides a model for those who would follow him.

Not All Who Claim to Lead God's People Follow the Rules (26:3-5) The high-priestly office constituted the most powerful religious, and one of the most powerful political, positions in Jewish Palestine; Caiaphas (high priest A.D. 18-36) retained it by giving the Romans what they wanted (E. Sanders 1993:265). That meant, of course, that threats to the political stability of Jerusalem would need to be dealt with swiftly and efficiently. And someone who caused a commotion in the temple in the dangerously crowded period just before Passover was clearly a threat to the public order. Although the plan to arrest Jesus away from the crowds was politically prudent, it was a stratagem of those who could not win by persuasion or demonstrations of God's power (21:46). When someone can win only by subterfuge and force, that person is not serving God—although, as here, God may well use such a one to execute his own purposes.

Jesus Is Worth Our Best (26:6-13) We disciples who are grieved by the failure of every single one of our male spiritual predecessors to stand with our Lord in his time of testing (vv. 40-56) can at least find some solace in the love shown by the women disciples (v. 7; 27:61; 28:1; compare Mk 15:40-41). Although the threat to their safety may have been less grave, they nevertheless put us men to shame in the passion

origin instead. This practice makes the most sense in the church's first generation in Jerusalem, when (and where) it consisted of people from elsewhere (Theissen 1991:179-80). Finally, some central characters in the account remain anonymous, probably to protect living persons who could face criminal charges in Jerusalem (Theissen 1991:186-88). Some argue that Mark completely rewrote the passion story, but Soardes 1994 makes a strong case both that Mark uses a source and that we probably cannot separate that tradition from his editing.

narrative. By contrast, it is male disciples here (Mt 26:8) who oppose the woman who anoints Jesus, more clearly than in Mark (Mk 14:4). Particularly in contrast to Judas, who (like many professed worshipers of God today) seeks only what he can get from Jesus (Mt 26:14-16), this woman seeks what she can offer to Jesus. The extravagance of our love is but an infinitesimal symbol compared to the price of his love for us (vv. 26-29), but Jesus both accepts it and gives us all the more (vv. 10, 13).

People often used expensive alabaster bottles, which were semitransparent and resembled marble, to store costly ointments (Argyle 1963:195). They would seal the ointment to prevent evaporation, requiring the long neck of the jar to be broken and the ointment to be expended at once (Meier 1980:312). Nard was a costly ointment imported from India, and its expense might suggest an heirloom passed from one generation to the next (Lane 1974:492). We may contrast Jesus' response to that of the disciples. He honors this obscure woman (despite significant exceptions women generally were obscure) more highly than any of the male disciples: her act would henceforth be preserved as part of the passion tradition relating to Jesus' burial (compare Judith 14:7).

Some modern readers take Jesus' reproof in 26:9-11 as playing down the priority of the poor, and then they inexplicably apply the example of this woman's extravagance to their church building programs or other projects. (That the disciples would have thought of the needs of the poor shortly before Passover fit their culture's custom—m. Pesaḥim 9:11; 10:1.) The needs of human beings always remain closer to Jesus' heart than most other monetary agendas (as in 5:42), and his very words about the poor remaining with them allude to Deuteronomy 15:11, where the context demands caring for the poor (Deut 15:1-10). This woman supplied something for Jesus shortly before his death that none of the rest of us can repeat (hence Mt 26:13), but she provides a model of sacrificial love. We show that sacrificial love to Jesus now by using all our resources for the work of his kingdom (13:44-46), including serving the poor (6:2, 19-24; compare Lk 12:33-34).

Judas Follows Jesus for What He Can Get out of Him (26:14-16) Ancient narrators sometimes contrasted positive and negative moral examples; as Judas contrasts with Peter in 26:69—27:10, he contrasts here with the extravagant love of the woman in 26:6-13. Jesus has continued to discuss his death (vv. 2, 12), and perhaps at least Judas has now caught on. But when Judas finds that Jesus' kingdom will not profit him materially (and may even cost him his life), he chooses to get what he still can from his lengthy investment in Jesus: he sells him for the price of a slave (v. 15; Ex 21:32). Like another disciple of old (2 Kings 5:26-27), Judas abandoned his spiritual birthright for better material conditions, and in saving his own life lost it for eternity (Mt 16:24-27; 27:1-10). Judas represents all those who follow Jesus only for what they can get from him, not for how they can serve him: eventually they may decide that the cost of serving him is higher than it is worth.

The Meaning of Jesus' Death (26:17-30) As Jesus' death approaches, he instructs his disciples more fully in the meaning of his mission. The disciples could not guess that their Teacher's death was part of God's sovereign plan, and they would scatter in fear once it came; but by reinterpreting a familiar ritual (the Passover, an annual celebration of how God delivered Israel from slavery in Egypt), Jesus gave them a new way of looking at God's purposes, which would make sense once he had risen.

Jesus' Mission Signifies a New Passover (26:17-20) In the context of the Passover, Jesus shows that his own mission provides a new act of redemption (vv. 17-20, 26). The *first day of the Feast of Unleavened Bread* (v. 17) had come to be applied in popular parlance to the Passover as well (see Gundry 1982:524). Passover pilgrims tried to find refuge with Jerusalemites during the actual Passover celebration, to eat the Passover within the city walls as tradition demanded (*m. Pesaḥim* 7:9); thus Jesus and the disciples located a place to spend the evening. The Passover meal began after sunset, around 6:00 p.m. (compare 26:20; Jn 13:30; 1 Cor 11:23; *t. Pisha* 5:2). Jewish people sat for ordinary meals, but by this period they normally reclined in Greek fashion at banquets like Passover (see Jeremias 1966a:48-49); Luke is explicit that this is a Passover meal (Lk 22:15). By identifying his own mission with the Passover, Jesus indicates that he has come to enact the new redemption and new exodus promised by the biblical prophets.

Some Who Claim to Follow Christ May Betray Him (26:21-25) Scripture indicated that the Son of Man's destiny included betrayal, but this did not relieve from responsibility the particular betrayer, who acted from personal choice (v. 24). Matthew clarifies Mark to show that Jesus here foreknows the specific betrayer (v. 25).

Yet Judas would not be the only one to betray Jesus; the context reminds us that all of us are capable of denying the Lord (vv. 33, 35; 26:69—27:10). The joyous occasion of Passover becomes a sorrowful one (26:22; compare 17:23; 18:31; 19:22) by the announcement of betrayal. By dipping with Jesus in the bowl containing the sauce of bitter herbs (26:23), the betrayer had shown himself a treacherous person indeed; rising against one with whom one had eaten violated the sanctity of tradition (compare Ps 41:9).

Jesus' Body and Blood Provide a New Covenant (26:26-30) Salvation is free to us, but it was never cheap; nothing in all human history has ever been so costly. Jesus probably alludes to Isaiah 52—53 (for example, Cullmann 1956b:64-65; pace Hooker 1959:80-82); still more probably, many of his words (such as *body, blood* and *poured out*) suggest sacrificial terminology, especially since crucifixion itself required no blood. (Romans sometimes fixed criminals to crosses with rope; Jeremias 1966a:220-22.) *For the forgiveness of sins* appears in *Targum Neofiti* with reference to sacrifices (McNamara 1972:129).

The Last Supper was a symbolic act, like the triumphal entry and "cleansing" of the temple (E. Sanders 1993:263). Interpreting the elements of the Passover feast (the bread, the bitter herbs and so on) was a standard part of Passover tradition (Jeremias 1966a:56), but instead of using standard explanations Jesus interprets two elements (those representative of food and drink in blessings at Jewish meals) in a strikingly new way.

That the bread *is* Jesus' body means that it "represents" it (compare the Aramaic in Martin 1982:153). We should interpret his words here no more literally than the disciples would have taken the normal words of

---

26:23 Some have also compared the Qumran custom in which members partook of a meal in sequence by rank (1QS 6.4-5), suggesting that we read "dip with me" temporally: by stretching out his hand simultaneously with Jesus, Judas deliberately indicated his rebellion (Fensham 1965; Albright and Mann 1971:321). While this view is plausible (compare how one respects others by allowing them to grab first—Sirach 31:14-18), it does leave us to question why no one seems to have understood the act already (Mt 26:22).

26:24 Jesus' "woe" (compare 18:7) that the betrayer would have been left better unborn resembles biblical (Job 3:3-26; Jer 20:14-18), Greek and Jewish (*ARN* 29A; *1 Enoch* 38:2; 4 Ezra 7:69; *2 Baruch* 10:6) lamentations.

the Passover liturgy: "This is the bread of affliction which our ancestors ate when they came from the land of Egypt." (Even had that bread not been eaten already, one might fear it a trifle stale after some thirteen centuries!) That Jesus was also in his body at the time he uttered the words further militates against interpreting the bread as literally equivalent to his body (Moffatt 1938:168).

The head of the household, who had been reclining, would now sit up to bless (give thanks for) the bread before the meal. After the meal, Jesus interprets the third or fourth of the Passover meal's four cups: this represents *the blood of the covenant* (compare Ex 24:8). After partaking of this cup, Jesus utters what resembles a traditional vow of abstention (compare Num 6:4; 30:2; 11QTemple 53-54), in this case vowing not to drink wine until the coming of his reign (Jeremias 1966a:182-85). After a few hours of discussion, here perhaps abbreviated, a household would sing the remaining hymns of the Hallel (Ps 113—18), undoubtedly the *hymn* to which Matthew 26:30 refers (Daube 1963:45; Ellington 1979).

Jesus' Turmoil and the Disciples' Weakness (26:31-46) Even in events that seem as disastrous as Jesus' arrest and execution seemed to the first disciples, God may be preparing his sovereign purposes (compare 2:16-17). Nevertheless, he gives us a part to play—and in this case all of our spiritual forebears failed. The disciples would deny him, despite their protestations (26:31-34); indeed, in their failure to remain prayerful in advance, they had failed the test before it arrived (vv. 40-45).

I weep when I remember how often these disciples stand for us. We forget too easily that Jesus became one of us, became flesh. He made himself vulnerable, depending in his most difficult hour on the support of his friends—and we let him down. Reigning as Lord of the universe,

26:26 Because Paul as well as Synoptic tradition attests Jesus' Passover language, it remains among the most secure elements of the Jesus tradition (E. Sanders 1993:263; compare Bornkamm 1969:135). Paul's claim that he "received" and "delivered" to the Corinthian church the Lord's Supper tradition (1 Cor 11:23) probably reflects Jewish language for the passing on of traditions (Jos. *Ant.* 13.297, 408; *m. 'Abot* 1:1).

26:29 F. F. Bruce even suggests that early Christians recited the passion narrative in this context as a new Passover Haggadah, recalling Paul's phrase "proclaim the Lord's death until he comes" (1971:113 and 1972a:16).

he does not depend on our support in the same way now; but is it possible that Matthew still intends us to hear the plaintive cry of the Lord of harvest in this narrative? The burden of his heart remains the mission of the world's redemption, yet he continues to cry out to a sleeping church governed by other agendas.

Jesus knows better than we do what we are made of. This theme appears in verses 31-32, 34, 41. Jesus thus tells us what it will take for us to succeed in his mission (v. 41)—for testing must come (vv. 45-46). When Jesus warns that they would *fall away* because of him (v. 31; compare Is 8:14), he probably refers to apostasy (compare Mt 5:29-30; 13:41; 16:23; 17:27; 18:6-9). Despite Peter's objection that he would not stumble (compare *Test. Job* 4:2; 5:1), Jesus responds that he will indeed do so, and three times at that (26:34; compare Jn 13:36-38). Jesus promises that the denial will happen before daybreak—which means that this Peter who is vigorously protesting that he will never deny Jesus is already on the verge of renouncing him.

Yet in promising to meet them in Galilee (which normally has positive associations in Matthew—4:12, 23; 10:5) after he has risen (28:7), Jesus promises a restoration beyond their apostasy (26:32; see Petersen 1978:76). Jesus' demands are high (10:33), but he does not automatically repudiate those who fail; this is important for us to remember as we encounter frustration while seeking to bring both ourselves and our fellow disciples to maturity.

Only devotion to prayer can carry us through the hardest times. Our best intentions (26:33, 35) cannot protect us in the time of severest testing unless we have learned how to seek God in prayer (v. 41). The three disciples worthy of special censure here (vv. 37, 40) are the three who had witnessed Jesus' glory on the mountain (17:1), including the disciple most adamant about his faithfulness (26:35). *Spirit* (v. 41) refers to the purpose of the human spirit versus the weakness of mortal humanity (in contrast to Paul's usual contrast between God's Spirit and human flesh). Jesus had already warned his disciples to pray lest they succumb to the test, a warning applicable to all disciples (6:13); his admonitions

---

26:34 The cock's crowing, which usually lasted no more than five minutes, may mark the third Roman watch, which was punctuated with such rooster crows (reportedly c. 12:30, 1:30 and 2:30 a.m.; Kosmala 1963). Yet most people slept through that crowing and

to *watch* likewise apply to all disciples in all eras (24:42-43; 25:13; compare F. Bruce 1972a:71 n. 14; Jeremias 1972:44, 55; pace Barrett 1967:47). The lesson of Gethsemane is thus for all generations.

The disciples' failure reminds us that they were people of flesh and blood just like us, not superspiritual people whom God would use because they had earned his favor. Even the big meal should not have put them to sleep so quickly; it was customary to discuss God's redemptive acts for a few hours after the meal before singing the Hallel (*t. Ketubot* 5:5). Some Jewish tradition suggested that those who fell asleep to the point they could not even answer thereby dissolved their Passover group—which the disciples inexplicably did by the time Jesus had finished praying (Daube 1956:342). Jesus did not regularly hold "all-night prayer" as a mark of being spiritual, but he did expect the disciples to take seriously his need in this emergency situation. If staying awake on this one night was a test, the disciples failed it. Peter undoubtedly comes in for special rebuke (v. 40) because he had most vehemently pledged his faithfulness till death (v. 33).

God's call may lead through unbearable pain. If this was the case with Jesus (vv. 37-39, 42, 44), his servants should expect no less (10:24-25). By describing his *sorrow* as *to the point of death* (26:38), Jesus underlines the intensity of his grief: of itself the grief could kill him (Meier 1980:323).

When we are in such pain, we need the strength of others' presence. Jesus' disciples provide a stark contrast in this narrative, a foil that reveals our Lord's own sacrifice all the more powerfully. Some popular authors and speakers emphasize "being positive" in all circumstances without exception, but despite the importance of a cheerful disposition (Prov 15:13, 15; 17:27; 18:14) and the normalcy of Christian joy (Gal 5:22; Phil 4:4; 1 Thess 5:16), in the psalms God's servants also repeatedly pour out broken hearts to him (for example, Ps 39:10-13; 40:13-17; 89:46-51). Jesus does not complain, but he does ask for support in prayer, and finds strength for his mission in God alone. The world and the church around us are full of suffering; they will hear God's heart for them best

---

especially identified the rooster crow with dawn (Horace *Satires* 1.1.9-10; Apul. *Metam.* 2.26; 3 Macc 5:23; *b. Berakot* 60b). Raymond Brown (1994:607) rightly concludes that cocks crowed at various times throughout the morning before dawn.

if we share their suffering in prayer (Mt 26:38-41) rather than if we dismiss genuine pain with platitudes about "being positive."

Cup refers to Jesus' sufferings and death on the cross (20:22; 26:27-28; compare 27:48). The image probably alludes as well to the frequent biblical picture of God's "cup of wrath" against the nations (Ps 60:3; 75:8; Is 29:9-10; 51:17, 21-23; Jer 25:15-29; Lam 4:21; Zech 12:2). Thus Jesus may shrink not merely from death but from dying as a sacrifice under his Father's wrath (Gundry 1982:533; Is 53:10).

No matter what the pain, we must obey the mission God has given us. Jesus had lived his life in filial obedience to his Father's will; now he chose the Father's plan over his own desire (Mt 26:39, 42, 44). Being fully human, Jesus experienced the full human dread of death; because the Son is distinct from the Father, his own desire might differ from the Father's, though he was ready to submit to the Father. Jesus' obedience is thus an example for us (12:50; compare 7:21). Loving God does not always mean that we *want* to face what God calls us to face; it does mean that we choose to face it anyway. Thus when the test arrives, Jesus summons all his disciples to *rise* to face it—ready or not (26:45).

From this point forward, passive verbs depicting Jesus' suffering and actions done to Jesus dominate most of the narrative (Perrin 1976:91); having labored until his hour, he now relinquishes his destiny to the Father. Yet even in his surrender, he remains in majestic control; only his own words (v. 64) will allow his accusers to condemn him (see Rhoads and Michie 1982:88).

The Betrayal (26:47-56) In this passage everyone who was close to Jesus—from Judas to the disciples who planned to follow him to the death—either betrays or abandons him to his opponents. As Jesus faces injustice alone as a victim, he shows us the depth of his love: when not another human being stood with him, our Lord nevertheless continued in the Father's plan to save us.

Jesus' enemies (here probably the Levite temple police) came armed as if he were a *lēstē* (26:55), the term Josephus most frequently applies

---

26:48 Besides Mark 14:43-52 (Lk 22:47-53), the betrayal to the high priests probably appears independently in John 18:2-12 and 1 Corinthians 11:23 (see Fee 1987:549,

to revolutionaries (Moule 1965:119). They did not understand that the real threat Jesus posed was quite different—and that his execution would signal the beginning of his messianic triumph.

One May Betray Jesus with Outwardly "Pious" Acts (26:47-49) By having a disciple trusted by his colleagues approach the group, the priests might hope to catch the disciples off guard and reduce resistance; and the high priests undoubtedly considered Judas expendable if the ploy failed (compare 27:3-10). People often greeted those they respected—for example, disciples to rabbis—with a kiss as a sign of intimacy and respect (for example, 1 Esdras 4:47; *t. Hagiga* 2:1). That Judas should betray Jesus with an outward gesture of devotion makes his act all the more heinous, and an ancient audience might grasp something of the depth of such betrayal's pain (Lk 22:48; compare 2 Sam 20:9-10; Prov 27:6).

When we feign love for Jesus but our lives serve purposes more in line with his enemies' mission, we follow in the footsteps of the son of Simon Iscariot. Jesus responds by confronting Judas with his crime—after addressing him as *friend,* an appropriate title for a disciple (A. Bruce 1979:316) but earlier applied in Matthew to those behaving in a shameful manner (20:13; 22:12).

We Must Not Fight the Kingdom's Battles Our Way (26:50-54) World hunger, racism, abortion, freedom to evangelize openly and a variety of other matters are literally life-and-death issues, but the very urgency of these issues sometimes tempts us to fight the battle with human passion or incendiary rhetoric. Protecting Jesus seemed the greatest of life-and-death issues, yet Jesus did not want his disciples to protect him. He came to conquer by way of the cross, not by way of the sword. We disciples are sometimes ready to fight for our cause, but rarely willing simply to be martyred for it without resistance; and once Jesus' disciples realized that martyrdom without resistance was the price of following Jesus, they fled (v. 56). For disciples to abandon their teacher in this way was a betrayal that would have deeply shamed the teacher (Malina 1993:18).

---

although "handing over to the Romans" was also dramatic enough that it could figure in the tradition, e.g., Mk 10:33-34).

We who cannot love our enemies today (5:44) would have failed this test as readily as our spiritual forebears did. Jesus was doing the Father's will, and the Father still would have granted him twelve legions of angels (one for himself and each disciple) had he asked (26:53); but the Father had called him to face death for us. Angels will assist at the end (compare 13:41-42; 16:27; 24:30-31), but in the present time, for Jesus to depend on them for deliverance would be giving in to Satan's test (compare 4:5-7).

A disciple (named only in John) cut off the ear of the high priest's servant (presumably aiming for the man's neck, he missed, probably because the man moved). Jesus' response to the disciple—and to Matthew's community, which has probably survived the crisis of a Judean-Roman war—provides three reasons for rejecting violence (26:52-54; compare 5:39-42): violence destroys those who employ it (26:52); Jesus trusts the Father's ability to protect him (v. 53); and Jesus recognizes that his Father's will for him includes suffering (v. 54; Meier 1980:328).

Jesus Confronts Injustice but Submits to Scripture's Plan (26:55-56) The authorities act unjustly as well as in political cowardice, and Jesus does not mind telling them so (v. 55). But Scripture dictates his own mission, so he submits to the Father's will (as in 4:1-11). Jesus' model of confronting injustice contrasts starkly with that of his disciples, who still don't quite get it.

□ The Trials (26:57—27:26)

The disciples proved inept, but the opposition was quite competent. After Judas handed Jesus over to the leaders of Jerusalem's aristocracy, they quickly came to their expected conclusion and sent him off to the Roman governor for execution; before evening he was dead. If we did not know the end of the story, would we have had any confidence at this point that God was executing his own purposes? But like the first disciples, we should have: by this point in the Gospel, both they and

---

26:56 Oscar Cullmann (1956b:40-41) may be right about the disciples' motivation: at last the disciples realized that Jesus was not a revolutionary messiah and would not fight.
26:57-68 Some scholars are skeptical about the account of Jesus' trial (Winter 1961 and 1964), but others have shown that the arguments against authenticity are fallacious (Sherwin-White 1978:34-47 and 1965). Some doubt whether any witness could have told the account to the early Christians. But a variety of possible sources exist: Joseph of

we have seen who Jesus is. Is any opposition severe enough to make us doubt that in the end God really has everything under control though we do not? The disciples doubted, but they should have known better.

Religious Leaders Versus Jesus (26:57-68) Some scholars wonder why the Gospels' accounts of Jesus' trial (possibly a brief hearing) seem to contradict later Jewish laws. But in the first place, it is unlikely that these first-century aristocrats were as concerned with legal procedure as later rabbis were. It is also unlikely that they would have agreed with all the careful stipulations of later rabbinic legal theories. Perhaps most important, the Gospel writers probably intended to convey breach of procedure, not to pretend that the mock trial and abuse they depict were standard Jewish custom (see Hooker 1983:86; Rhoads and Michie 1982:120-21). Based on what we know of first-century Jerusalem leaders' practice, the Gospels' portrait of Jesus' trial actually fits quite well (see E. Sanders 1992:487). The Romans usually executed only those brought to them as condemned by the local aristocracies.

The people respected the law teachers, elders and priests as their spiritual leaders (representatives of these groups constituted the Sanhedrin), but here most of these spiritual leaders prove too hostile to Jesus to concern themselves with legal ethics. Although exceptions historically existed (Mk 15:43), the overwhelming picture of religious leaders in the Gospels provides a warning to us today. Many follow those in eminent positions, and if we in authority positions in the church dare forget whose servants we are, we can easily become enemies of our own Lord, vying for the power and honor that rightfully belong to him alone (Mt 21:38).

The High Priest and Council Ignore Judicial Procedure (26:57-61) Given reports about the aristocratic priests from their Pharisaic and Essene enemies, the improprieties of the priests here should hardly surprise us. Power and dogmatic certainty that one's cause is right prove

---

Arimathea (Mk 15:43), connections within the high priest's household (Jn 18:15-16), others who later became disciples or sympathizers (Jn 19:39; compare perhaps Acts 6:7), Jesus himself. Certainly other information was leaked from the Jerusalem council (Jos. *Life* 204); if someone leaked information to Josephus, why not to some well-to-do members of the early church (e.g., to John Mark's mother)?

a deadly combination for those who do not play by the rules, for whom the end justifies the means. Their possible breaches of legality (at least by legal theory as reported by later rabbis more concerned with it) were several. Judges were to conduct and conclude capital trials during daylight (*m. Sanhedrin* 4:1). Further, trials were not to occur on the eve of a sabbath or festival day (compare *m. Yom Tob* 5:2). Pharisaic rules (which the Sadducees would have ignored) probably also required a day to pass before a verdict of condemnation could be issued (*m. Sanhedrin* 4:1). Likewise, the Sanhedrin should not meet in the high priest's palace (though they would soon move, probably to their normal meeting place on or near the Temple Mount).

Most obviously, Jewish law opposed false witnesses. The biblical penalty for false witnesses in a capital case was execution (Deut 19:16-21). Cross-examination of witnesses was standard in Jewish law (as in Susanna 48-62; *m. 'Abot* 1:9), and apparently the examiners did their job well enough here to produce contradictions they did not expect. In the end, the witnesses could provide only a garbled account of Jesus' proclamation of judgment against the temple (compare Jn 2:19; Acts 6:14), which could have seemed to the Sanhedrin political reason enough to convict him (see comment on 21:12-17; R. Brown 1994:458). But the high priest ultimately must choose another tack; even a court as slanted as this one will not admit evidence from witnesses whose testimony is inconsistent (see Trites 1977:186; Stauffer 1960:123-24). Thus for the Jewish court (as opposed to Pilate) the chief priest seeks a new charge in Matthew 26:62-68: blasphemy (Blinzler 1959:170).

Truth Engenders Opposition (26:62-68) The high priest stands (following biblical legal custom—see Trites 1977:187) and gives Jesus the opportunity to defend himself, as Jewish law demanded (v. 62), but Jesus chooses to remain silent (v. 63; compare Is 53:7). Perhaps exasperated, the high priest seeks to place Jesus under the curse of an oath, crying, *I charge you under oath,* or "I adjure you" (the beginning of an oath formula often used to secure testimony—*m. Šebu 'ot* 4:5-13). Here the high priest explicitly asks Jesus whether he claims messianic authority (v. 63).

Jesus' answer is probably a reluctant yes (Catchpole 1971:226; Marshall 1990:86). He *is* the Messiah—but this was the priest's choice of wording rather than his (see F. Bruce 1972b:176 n. 45). Now that there remains no need to continue the messianic secret, Jesus reveals publicly that he is God's Son (again, 27:54; compare Kingsbury 1983:122; Perrin 1976:95; Hooker 1983:58-59). But Jesus must define that sonship, not allow the leaders' cultural preconceptions to define it for him (compare comment on 4:1-11). Thus by responding in scriptural allusions (26:64), Jesus defines his mission in terms his interrogators cannot misapprehend: he is both *Son of Man* (compare Dan 7:13-14; Mt 24:30) and Lord (Ps 110:1; Mt 22:44; see Dodd 1961:91). Jesus was greater than merely a messiah, a son of David (22:44).

By declaring that "from this point forward" (not simply *in the future* as in the NIV) he would reign (26:64), Jesus may seem to the Sanhedrin to claim that he is going to rule politically despite their power over him. But undoubtedly he means that his reign opens not with power but with the cross. In the words of the Fourth Gospel, the time has come for the Son of Man to be lifted up and glorified (Jn 12:23, 32-33; compare Is 52:13 LXX). Yet the ultimate fulfillment will be when even his enemies will see him at his coming in triumph as heavenly ruler (Mt 26:64; compare 24:30; Rev 1:7). That is, though they claim to judge Jesus now, he will ultimately prove their judge (see Kingsbury 1983: 124)—a claim certain to enrage unbelieving leaders who demand honor.

Such words would be offensive, but even if false they were not technically blasphemous (*m. Sanhedrin* 7:5). Nevertheless, most uses of *blasphemy* were nontechnical (R. Brown 1994:522-23), and the high priest might admit whatever he needed as blasphemy. Because the priestly aristocracy perceives Jesus as a political threat to the temple establishment and the peace of the nation, and because the charge of threatening the temple remains unproved by strict standards of investigation, they need another basis for conviction quickly. Again the leaders twist the rules to get the job done. By whatever means they construe his words as blasphemy, the high priest stands to rend his cloak as custom required when one heard blasphemy (*m. Sanhedrin* 7:5), following a traditional custom in mourning (as in 1 Macc 4:39-40; 5:14; 11:71).

The spirit of Jewish law opposed condemning a criminal on his own admission, but the Sanhedrin treats Jesus' words here not as admission of a crime but as a crime itself—blasphemy—to which they themselves are witnesses, obviating the need for other witnesses (Blinzler 1959:137; Stauffer 1960:125). Although the spirit of Jewish law probably prohibited witnesses from participating in sentencing the accused (Blinzler 1959:135), the court acts as witness. Finally, whatever else may have been illegal, the physical mistreatment of a prisoner certainly was; this would have shamed Jesus as well, for such treatment was inappropriate to the status he had claimed.

Jesus' Opponents Ironically Confirm His Identity (26:68) By ridiculing Jesus' prophet status—challenging him to a child's game of guessing—his opponents may imply that they have condemned him as a false prophet according to the rules of Deuteronomy 18:20 (Hill 1979:52). His very condemnation and likely imminent execution disproved for them his prophecies about the temple and his own imminent enthronement (26:61, 64; Gundry 1982:547; R. Brown 1994:575, 580). The informed reader, by contrast, knows that Jesus predicted accurately both his mistreatment and the temple's destruction; the reader thus sees Jesus as the truest prophet of all (Deut 18:15-18; compare Mt 2:16; 4:2; 5:1; 17:1-5), meaning that it was his accusers who merit judgment (Deut 18:19). Yet when they treat Jesus as a false prophet (compare Mt 5:12) and offer unrequited blows to the cheek (5:39; 26:53), they demonstrate Jesus' integrity to the audience familiar with his teachings; earlier prophets had also been struck on the cheek for their prophecies (1 Kings 22:24; Is 50:6; compare Mt 5:12). Likewise, Jesus' opponents mock him "as a false prophet at the very moment when his prophecy about Peter is being fulfilled" (26:69-75; Donahue 1976:78-79, on Mk 14:65-66).

This sort of irony runs throughout the narrative. The religious leaders condemn Jesus for blasphemy for claiming simply what God had claimed about him all along (Mt 3:17; 17:5; see Kingsbury 1983:151). From Jesus' condemnation as "God's Son" (26:63-68) to the centurion's recognition that Jesus really is God's Son (27:54), the dominant christological title will be "King of the Jews" (so Kingsbury 1983:151). This title constitutes a double irony: those who apply it intend it ironically, but the Gospel tradition inverts the irony so that they have described him accurately. God's irony is vital: even in the deepest of trials, God provides hints of his coming triumph to those with the eyes of faith. If

Jesus accurately prophesied his hardships, one can likewise depend on the victory he promised.

The First Response to Betrayal (26:69-75) By including the denial account, Matthew warns disciples against apostasy in the face of persecution. By placing two responses to betrayal side by side, Matthew also points out how disciples should respond to failures of their discipleship. Peter wept with remorse (v. 75); Judas killed himself (27:5). Only the former was able to return to Jesus.

Even Disciples Must Watch Lest They Fall (26:69-74) In this account Peter cares more about his own life than about his Lord's honor, and this is unacceptable for a disciple (10:32-33). Peter sought to be a disciple: while Jesus' enemies "assembled" or "gathered" (26:57; compare 13:40), Peter "followed" (compare 4:19; 8:22), though from "a distance, . . . to see the outcome," or the "end" (*telos;* 26:58). That he would renounce his faith before one of minimal social status (a "slave girl"; Matthew underlines this point with two servant girls—26:69, 71) increases the heinousness of the denial. Peter's wording does the same; "I do not know what you say" and similar formulas represent an emphatic form standard in Jewish law "for formal, legal denial" (as in *m. Šebu'ot* 8:3, 6; Smith 1951:35). Denials with cursing imply not profanity but invoking a curse upon himself if he were lying (Beare 1981:524)—directly violating Jesus' teaching in 5:33-37. Most significantly, Peter was denying the Lord he had promised never to deny (10:33; 26:35).

Peter had hoped to follow a Messiah whose kingdom did not involve the cross (16:22); thus he proved unprepared when the time came to take up his cross and follow the Lord (16:24; compare Dewey 1976:111). That Peter illustrates Jesus' teaching about discipleship in 16:24-27 indicates his function as a paradigm for us: only by counting the cost of following Jesus, only by watching and praying, will we be ready when the hour comes for us to share the sufferings of our Lord for his name's sake.

The Appropriate Response to Failure Is Repentance (26:75) By placing the failures of Peter and Judas side by side, Matthew presents Peter's response to his failure as the appropriate model for disciples. The exposure of our weakness is cause for repentance (v. 75; compare

26:31-32), not sorrow unto death (27:5; compare 2 Cor 7:10). Peter's example warns us to be ready for testing; but it also summons us to start afresh if we have failed, and to show mercy to those who have already stumbled but wish to return to the way of Christ (compare 18:10-35).

The Other Response to Betrayal (27:1-10) Like Peter, Judas is guilty of apostasy, but unlike that of Peter, Judas's was premeditated. Whereas Peter's remorse leads to repentance, Judas's leads to terminal despair.

This narrative further reveals the heartlessness of the religious leaders, who value laws of ritual purity more highly than their responsibility to human life. They are not unlike some Christians today, more concerned for petty church rules than for the life-and-death needs in the communities around them, except that the religious leaders of Jesus' day probably could have justified more of their rules from Scripture.

Finally, this narrative shows us that even to the smallest details, the events of the passion fulfilled God's purposes previously revealed in his Word.

Consenting to Wrong Judgments, We Participate in Guilt (27:1-2) The Christian view of sin is not that only the individual or only the society is responsible: all guilty parties are responsible. By framing Judas's end with the account of Jesus' being brought before Pilate (27:1-2, 11), Matthew contrasts Judas not only with Peter but also with the courageous Lord he had betrayed. The theme of shedding innocent blood connects Judas, Pilate, the high-priestly authorities and the people (vv. 4-6, 24-25): like Pilate (v. 24), the priestly officials wish nothing further to do with the situation (v. 4) and likewise imply that the *blood* was innocent (v. 6).

Meanwhile, leading characters in the narrative who foreshadow oppressors of Matthew's community try to pass off responsibility (compare Jer 38:5); both aristocratic priests and Pilate declare, "See to that yourself," or *"That's your responsibility"* (Mt 27:4, 24, the "you" being

---

27:9-10 Matthew may interpret Zechariah 11:13 as if "potter" could be read "treasury" (slightly revocalizing the Hebrew to provide a new interpretation, as later Jewish interpreters often did; Longenecker 1975:150). By appealing to "Jeremiah" rather than to Zechariah, however, Matthew also intends his biblically literate audience to recall an analogous passage in Jeremiah (32:6-14) and to interpret them together (see Lindars 1961:120; R. Brown

emphatic). But contrary to their own interpretation, the whole generation that betrayed Jesus shared in Judas's guilt (27:25). Matthew knows nothing of the modern dichotomy between personal and societal responsibility for injustice. Religious and social leaders who make decisions, as well as the people to whose demands they give way, share in the guilt; thus, for example, television networks that incite moral depravity are guilty, but so are those who choose to watch their programming.

The Hypocrisy of the Chief Priests (27:3-8) These leaders were willing to pay out blood money for Jesus' capture, willing to allow Judas's suicide, but too pious to accept their own blood money into the temple treasury. Jewish law prescribed for false witnesses the penalty they had wished to inflict on others (Deut 19:16-21; 11QTemple 61.7-1); since the chief priests refuse to serve the cause of justice, Judas has to see to his own execution (Meier 1980:338-39). Although Roman society regarded suicide as an honorable and noble way to die, all readers would recognize Judas's act as one of despair, a dishonorable suicide (compare 2 Sam 17:23; Philo *Mut.* 61-62; see also Acts 1:18-19). Hanging oneself in a sanctuary (F. Grant 1953:12) would defile it, and while Judas left the temple to perform the deed, the leaders' blatant unconcern for justice or for his life contrasts starkly with their attention to purity in details. By sentencing Judas to take care of his own guilt, they have unconsciously sentenced themselves before God (Mt 12:34-37).

Scripture Is Fulfilled (27:9-10) All the events of the passion story fulfill God's plan recorded in Scripture. Matthew therefore expects us to take Scripture very seriously (though he applies it in a way particularly suited to persuade his own late first-century audience).

Politics Versus Justice (27:11-26) Even skeptics should admit that Jesus undoubtedly appeared before Pilate; only the governor could order him crucified, and this required a prior hearing. Likewise, his own

1994:651). (Given Matthew's ability to retranslate the entire Hebrew text based on revocalization, it is unlikely that he would simply get his attribution wrong.) In so doing, Matthew reapplies Zechariah's prophecy with a message of Israel's coming restoration in Jeremiah. Matthew may well allude to Jeremiah 18—19 as well; in this case he also evokes a prophecy of the impending destruction of Jerusalem (Jer 19:10-13; Mt 27:25).

countrymen would normally perform the function of *delatorēs,* or accusers, to charge him with sedition (Harvey 1982:16; see Sherwin-White 1978:47). Whatever the leaders' possible religious or personal motivations, the charge they bring against Jesus before Pilate here is political: by claiming to be a king, Jesus implied a worldly kingdom that would challenge Rome (for example, F. Bruce 1972b:199). This is easily the charge of *lese majesty* (Blinzler 1959:213; see also Bammel 1984:357), for which the normal punishment in the provinces was crucifixion (Blinzler 1959:238). What we know of ancient proceedings fits the Gospels' record of what happened.

This part of Matthew's account has less to do with Jesus than with Pilate, however: it is not Jesus but the character of Pilate that is on trial. Though Pilate knows the unjust motivation of the charges (v. 18) and receives a divine warning (v. 19), political expediency takes precedence over justice. We are guilty of the same crime whenever we side with views because they are popular in our society or political party even though we know that someone is suffering unjustly (whether the poor, the unborn, racial minorities, abused wives or children, crime victims, prisoners of war, refugees or others).

But the narrative does not implicate Pilate alone: the insistent people, blindly following their blind leaders (v. 20; compare 15:14; 23:16), embrace the moral responsibility Pilate seeks to evade. In the narrative world of Matthew, their acceptance of guilt for Jesus' blood on themselves and the generation of their children (27:24-25) directly invites the catastrophic events of 66-70 (23:29-39).

Jesus Bravely Chose to Suffer for Us (27:11-14) Only the Roman governor could approve a capital sentence (see, for example, Sherwin-White 1978:32-43). Pilate's initial interrogation of Jesus clarifies the charge the Sanhedrin has brought to Pilate: Jesus claims to be a king, which Rome, like the priestly aristocracy, would understand in revolutionary terms (v. 11). The hearing is swift not only because Pilate is more concerned with the stability of his political position than with justice but also because Jesus refuses to defend himself. By Roman law, a defendant

---

27:25 Many later professing Christians abused this passage in an anti-Jewish manner (forgetting the ethnic Jewishness of Matthew's own Jewish Christian community). But while this abuse of Matthew is an important warning, it is an issue quite different from what

who refused to make a defense had to be assumed guilty (Lane 1974:551); yet Roman officials typically offered "a defendant three opportunities to respond before convicting by default" (France 1985:389), and Pilate offers Jesus at least two here (v. 13). It is no wonder, then, that Pilate is amazed by Jesus' silence (v. 14). Such astonishment on the part of judges appears also in Jewish accounts of defiant martyrs who—in contrast to their judges—valued God's kingdom more than their lives (Stanton 1974:36).

We Cannot Pass Off Responsibility (27:15-23) But warned by his wife's dream, Pilate can avoid the conflict between justice and political expediency only by letting the crowds take responsibility for freeing Jesus. He apparently thought himself indulgent on special occasions; his otherwise brutal disposition, however, is evident in all the other brief Jewish reports of his activity that remain extant. Pilate presumably thought that it was safer to release Jesus, the "so-called Christ" (vv. 17, 22), than alternatives like Barabbas, who, like those ultimately executed with Jesus, was a "robber" (vv. 38, 44; Mk 15:7), the aristocracy's derisive title (shared by Josephus) for insurrectionists. Pilate probably saw Jesus in the terms suggested in John 18:36-38: as one of the relatively harmless wandering philosopher-kings known to him from Greco-Roman tradition. Roman officials were generally not inclined to execute (hence, perhaps, make martyrs of) those they saw as harmless fools (compare Jos. *War* 6.305).

Both Pilate and the Crowds Were Guilty (27:24-26) Perhaps because the high priests have reported Jesus' popular appeal along with the charge, Pilate gambles that the people will prefer Jesus to Barabbas; if so, his hope is disappointed. Ancient literature is replete with examples of masses' being easily swayed by leaders (including these priests: for example, Jos. *War* 2.237-38, 316-17, 321-25) and being fickle in the populist favor they bestowed on various figures (as in Tac. *History* 1.32, 45; 3.85; Ps-Phocyl. 95-96). On a literary and theological level, Pilate may be offering this generation of Israel the "two ways," one of life and the other of death (7:13-14; compare Deut 30:15-19). Given the dangers

---

Matthew intended; for Matthew, the curse invoked in this verse was fulfilled in the year 70, *children* in this instance referring to the generation immediately following that of the multitude (Albright and Mann 1971:345; Saldarini 1994:33).

of riots, Pilate's acquiescence to the masses at the Passover (Mt 27:24) was likely (R. Brown 1994:722).

Finally, Matthew underlines in obvious ways that the crowds shared the guilt for Jesus' execution—though he also refuses to let Pilate absolve himself as easily as Pilate desires. Pilate, having handed Jesus over to the crowds' wishes, is no less guilty than weak-willed Zedekiah, who hands over Jeremiah in Jeremiah 38:5. By accepting the bloodguilt on themselves and their children, however (compare 2 Sam 3:28-29; 21:6, 14), Matthew's crowds directly fulfill Jesus' warning in Matthew 23:29-36, thereby inviting the destruction of their temple at the end of the generation, in their children's days.

Pilate decrees the sentence, as his position required him to do (27:26): *Ibis in crucem* ("you will mount the cross"; Blinzler 1959:238). The preliminary scourging here was quite serious; it accompanied the death sentence and sometimes caused death by itself (see F. Bruce 1977a:445; R. Brown 1970:2:874 and 1994:851). Probably stripped and tied to a pillar or post, Jesus was beaten with flagella—leather whips made of thongs knitted together with pieces of iron or bone, or a spike; such a scourging left skin hanging from the back in bloody strips (Blinzler 1959:222). That Pilate *handed him over* or "delivered" him up to the soldiers (perhaps foreign auxiliaries) links him to Judas and the chief priests, who had also "handed Jesus over" (26:48, Greek; 27:2-3; see Patte 1987:376). Far from escaping responsibility, Pilate forms the next link in the chain of guilt in which members of all involved parties participated.

□ The Crucifixion and Burial (27:27-66)

The rest of the passion narrative merely carries through the expected plan set in motion by the events in the earlier part of the Gospel: Jesus' refugee status in childhood, the way his teachings infuriated the religious establishment, and his deliberate provocation of the rulers of the temple. Jesus' death defines the nature of his messiahship for a world accustomed to identifying rulers with human power.

The World Ridicules God's Son (27:27-44) One cannot doubt historically that Jesus was crucified by the Romans; Christians would hardly have invented the execution, and certainly not Roman execution, and never Roman execution on the charge of high treason (the claim to be *king of the Jews*)! Worshiping one crucified for treason would have painted all Christians as seditious and hence directly invited repression from the Roman authorities.

Pilate often went to great lengths to quell even public complaints; his violent suppression of a crowd once led to many deaths (Jos. *War* 2.176-77; *Ant.* 18.60-62). Although slaves (as in Suet. *Domitian* 10) and dangerous criminals (Suet. *Julius* 4) were regularly crucified, crucifixions of free persons in Palestine usually involved the charge of rebellion against Rome (Harvey 1982:12; for example, Jos. *War* 2.75, 241, 253, 306; 3.321; 5.449; *Ant.* 20.102).

Genuinely following Jesus to the cross means we follow a road that may quite well cost us our lives physically (16:24); it also means sacrificing our own honor for Christ's along the way. Ridicule was often the social backdrop of public executions, especially naked crucifixion, which constituted the ultimate form of shame. Those of us who value our dignity too much to live with unjust criticisms and the world's hatred must seek a different messiah to follow.

Soldiers often taunted captives, and here they mock Jesus' kingship (27:27-31), not for a moment considering the possibility that he really is a king. That Jesus submits to such abuse teaches us that power does not function in the kingdom the way it does in the world. In the next paragraph Jesus bears public humiliation in front of and from the crowds he had come to save (vv. 32-40). The soldiers draft a bystander to suffer with Jesus (v. 32); this man performs the role disciples should have been performing (16:24). As Jesus participated with us in our suffering under injustice in the world, he summons us to endure the unjust treatment visited on us for his name's sake. Also, here Jesus refuses a beverage that could have dulled his agony; he came to embrace our pain and would accept nothing less than the full impact of his bloody death (27:34). When we are so convinced of God's will that we forsake the world's power and wealth to perform his mission, we show ourselves disciples of the One who redeemed us at the cost of his own life.

The crowds invite Jesus to prove his divine sonship by escaping the death of the cross (vv. 39-40); thereby they act as Satan's final mouthpieces to turn Jesus from his divine mission (4:3-10; 16:21-23). In the final section of this unit, the religious authorities (at the top of the Jewish social order) and the dying robbers (at the bottom) join the crowds in functioning as Satan's mouthpieces. Neither outward piety nor being oppressed necessarily guarantees a heart obedient to God.

Jesus Is Ridiculed by Those Who Should Honor Him (27:27-31) The Gospels reveal Jesus' status as a servant-king in part by revealing how unlike a king the world thought him to be: if Jewish opponents ridiculed his claim to be a prophet (26:68), Roman opponents mocked his pretentious claim to royalty (27:29). Auxiliaries stationed in Palestine might be happy to ridicule the notion of a Jewish king—thereby also ridiculing the people among whom they were stationed (Malina and Rohrbaugh 1992:163). Those in the East who worshiped Caesar or Hellenistic rulers would kneel and cry, *"Ave* [Hail], Caesar!"* (Blinzler 1959:227; R. Brown 1970:2:875). The soldiers here offer the same to Christ, but the narrative inverts their irony: he is the rightful ruler whom they sarcastically claim him to be.

The *scarlet robe* (v. 28) is undoubtedly a faded red soldier's cloak, the *staff* or scepter probably a bamboo cane used for military floggings, and the *crown of thorns* probably woven from the branches of an available shrub like acanthus (Blinzler 1959:227). The long thorns may have turned outward to imitate contemporary crowns rather than inward to draw blood (Blinzler 1959:244-45). After the mockery the soldiers turn to abusing Jesus physically (though the blows are also insulting; see 5:39; Dupont 1992:126-27).

A Bystander Is Drafted for a Disciple's Task (27:32) After the passage emphasizes the suffering Jesus chose to endure for his followers (vv. 11, 14, 34), we might expect at least some of his followers to share his cross—as he had called them all to do (16:24). But the soldiers had

27:32 Boykin Sanders (1995:62-63) makes a reasonable case for Simon's ancestry being native Cyrenian rather than immigrant Jewish Cyrenian. Yet at Jerusalem's festivals, full of pilgrims from other parts of the world (e.g., Acts 2:5-11), one might simply identify oneself by one's place of origin, especially if (see France 1985:395; R. Brown 1994:913) Simon or his sons remained part of the Christian community in Jerusalem, which probably passed on the passion narrative (see Theissen 1991:166-99). Cyrene was as much as a quarter Jewish (Jos. *Ant.* 14.115-18; see also R. Brown 1994:915), and its Jewish community is well known (Acts 2:10; see especially Applebaum 1979); Simon is a common (though not

to draft a bystander instead—putting to shame all the claims we disciples make about how committed we are (26:33-35). The unfaithfulness of the disciples underlines Jesus' faithfulness all the more.

Normally a condemned prisoner carried his own *patibulum,* or transverse beam of the cross, to the site of the execution, where soldiers would fix it to an upright stake *(palus, stipes, staticulum)* that they regularly reused for executions (R. Brown 1994:913). It was unlikely that the soldiers would simply show mercy. Jesus was probably too weak to carry the cross (perhaps exhausted in part from Gethsemane—26:38); his executioners preferred to have him alive on the cross than dead on the way. In such circumstances, the soldiers would naturally draft a bystander rather than carry the beam themselves (see comment on 5:41). Whether Simon was from an ethnically African family converted to Judaism or one of the many Jewish families settled in Cyrene is unclear.

Jesus Endured a Slow, Agonizing Death for Us (27:33-38) The *wine . . . mixed with gall* (v. 34) may have been meant to dull Jesus' pain. Once he tasted the wine, he may have refused it in part because of his vow in 26:29; but Jesus probably refused it also because he had come to share our pain and had to experience it in full. He endured this pain alone, for a world that hated him and for disciples who had forsaken him and denied him.

It is difficult to communicate adequately the torture Jesus, like others who were crucified, endured. Although some features remained common, executioners could perform crucifixions in a variety of ways, limited only by the extent of their sadistic creativity (Hengel 1977:25). Executioners usually tied victims to the cross, but in some cases hastened their death by also nailing their wrists (see Artem. 2.56; *m. Šabbat* 6.10). Yet in a symbolic sense a song by musician Michael Card puts it well:

---

exclusively) Jewish name, but certainly appropriate in a family of proselytes as well.
27:34 Myrrhed *wine* (Mk 15:23) may have been used to deaden pain (*b. Sanhedrin* 43a; Blinzler 1959:252-53), though some have doubted this connection (R. Brown 1994:941). In either case, by changing Mark's "myrrh" to *gall,* Matthew reduced the emphasis on its narcotic effect, emphasizing instead its bitterness. But the wine itself could exercise this painkilling function (Prov 31:6-7), so Jesus' refusal to drink it probably meant that he came to embrace humanity's suffering in full measure.

had the soldiers not nailed Jesus to the cross, his love for us would have held him there.

Romans crucified their victims naked (Artem. 2.61; R. Brown 1994:870), and public nakedness could cause shame (as in Juv. *Sat.* 1.71; Plut. *Roman Questions* 40, *Mor.* 274A), especially for Palestinian Jews (for example, *Jub.* 3:21-22, 30-31; 7:8-10, 20; 1QS 7.12). Anyone so executed could not brush flies away from wounds, nor control bodily functions while hanging naked for hours and sometimes days (Klausner 1979:350).

The specific mention of divided clothing (27:35) may well recall Psalm 22:18 but can hardly be a mere accommodation to it without historical substance. Roman law allowed execution squads to seize the few possessions a condemned might have on his person (Justinian *Digest* 48.20.6; Sherwin-White 1978:46). The *charge* posted above Jesus' head reveals the irony of the situation: Jesus is executed for being king of Israel (v. 37). Romans crucified many self-proclaimed kings and their followers under the *Lex Iulia de maiestate* (Jos. *Ant.* 17.285, 295; R. Brown 1994:968), and both Jesus' royal triumphal entry and his temple "cleansing" marked him as a troublemaker. On other known occasions a member of the execution squad would carry in front of or beside the condemned a small tablet *(tabula)* declaring the charge *(titulus)*, the cause of execution *(causa poenae)*, which he might later post on the cross (Cullmann 1956b:42-43; R. Brown 1994:963).

Jesus Is Offered One Final Satanic Temptation (27:39-44) When we realize that the *robbers* are probably revolutionaries who sought to facilitate the establishment of God's earthly kingdom (as in Jos. *War* 4.138), the irony and pathos of their ridicule become all the clearer. Both lay and aristocratic mockers pass by, perhaps along a road, *shaking their heads* (Ps 22:7; Lam 2:15), repeating the slanderous charge of Matthew 26:61, seeking a sign (compare 16:1) and serving as mouthpieces for Satan's desire for a kingdom without the cross (compare 4:3, 7). Perhaps they are trying to get Jesus to admit the justice of the court's sentence (compare *m. Sanhedrin* 6:2-3; Ps-Philo 25:6-7; 27:15).

27:37 The location of the charge identifies the shape of the cross as in Christian tradition, rather than the T- or X-shaped crosses also used (see R. Brown 1994:948). The upright stakes were ten feet at the highest, more often closer to six or seven feet so that the man hung barely above the ground, with a seat *(sedile)* in the middle (Blinzler 1959:249; Reicke

Amid the derisive comments one might expect at an execution of a misled pietist, the mockers from the Sanhedrin (Mt 27:41-43) unwittingly cite Psalm 22:8 (Matthew presumably conforms the wording of their mockery to that text)—showing themselves enemies of God's anointed servant, hence of God himself. Their language probably also echoes Wisdom 2:18 in the Septuagint: "For if the righteous man is a son of God, God will help him, and deliver him from the hand of those who resist him." In the Wisdom of Solomon, those words are uttered by the wicked who want to condemn a righteous person to death unjustly because he claims to be a child of God and to have a good future (Wisdom 2:16-20). Meanwhile, they echo the devil's earlier temptation of Jesus (Mt 4:3, 6). In other words, by their own words Jesus' enemies are condemned (12:37; compare Lk 19:22). The King of Judeans refuses to respond (5:39; compare Is 53:7).

Again irony saturates the narrative: they are right that he cannot *save himself* if he would save others (Mt 27:42). That they offer to believe if he will *come down,* just as Satan offered him the kingdom if he would bow down, tests Jesus: he can have people's allegiance if he will just forsake the Father's way of getting it (26:39, 42). God's mission for us will not always be pleasant, but the more pleasant alternatives actually forfeit our right to fulfill that mission. (For example, ministers who win great numbers only by sidestepping the demands of the kingdom have won statistics but not transformed hearts, and have failed a very costly test that Jesus here resists.)

Signs at Jesus' Death (27:45-54) As Jesus dies broken, his Father vindicates him with signs in nature—signs that only Jesus' pagan executioners are shown to understand.

Jesus Dies Wounded but Trusting His Father (27:45-46) That Jesus utters the complaint of the righteous sufferer (Ps 22:1) suggests that he participated in our ultimate alienation from God in experiencing

1974:186); animals sometimes assaulted the feet of the crucified. Romans could employ high crosses to increase visibility for significant public executions (Suet. *Galba* 9.1), and given the reed here (27:48; Mk 15:36), Jesus may have been slightly higher than usual (Blinzler 1959:249); Raymond Brown (1994:948-49) guesses seven feet.

the pain of death. Yet he would also know that the psalm goes on to declare the psalmist's triumph (Ps 22:22-24), and the phrase *my God* indicates continuing trust.

To the End, His Opponents Do Not Understand His Identity (27:47-49) Jesus' own people did not recognize what was happening; they knew that rabbis in distress sometimes looked to Elijah for help (as in *b. 'Aboda Zara* 17b; *p. Ketubot* 12:3, §6), and they assumed that Jesus was doing likewise. Clearly they expected no supernatural intervention—expectations seemingly confirmed because Elijah would not come.

The narrative again bristles with irony: far from being able to help Jesus, Elijah was his forerunner in martyrdom (17:10-13; Kingsbury 1983:130). The *wine vinegar* (27:48) was probably an attempt to revive him (Reicke 1974:187), perhaps to prolong the torment in mocking pretense that Elijah had come to relieve him. But Jesus had come to drink the cup of suffering (26:39), the cup of God's wrath (Jer 25:15-29). Our Lord is both our model, obedient and uncomplaining as he serves the Father no matter what the cost, and our Savior, who offers himself for the sins of the world.

The Father Vindicates His Murdered Son (27:50-53) Elijah did not come to deliver Jesus, but signs that Jews regularly expected to accompany the death of the righteous did follow Jesus' death (vv. 51-53). To both pagan and Jewish audiences these signs would indicate divine approval of Jesus and disapproval of his executioners (see Kee 1983:189; Best 1965:98; R. Brown 1994:1113-14). The raising of dead persons at Jesus' death (vv. 52-53) reminds us that by refusing to save himself, Jesus did save others (v. 42). Yet by mentioning only *many* of the saints, Matthew clearly intends this sign merely to prefigure the final resurrection, proleptically signified in Jesus' death and resurrection (Cullmann 1956a:168). Popular folk religion venerated the *tombs* of saints (Meyers and Strange 1981:162), and the very people who sought Jesus' death built those tombs (23:29-32); but Jesus, the holiest saint of all, had power to raise them.

27:45 The *darkness* may recall the three-day plague immediately preceding the sacrifice of the first paschal lamb (Ex 10:21-23), as well as end-time judgment imagery (4 Ezra 7:38-42; Ps-Philo 3:10). By expiring at 3:00 p.m., Jesus died about the official time of the evening lamb offering in the temple (*m. Pesaḥim* 5:1).

The rending of the veil (probably the inner veil—compare Heb 6:19-20; 9:3; 10:19-20) around the time of the evening sacrifice (Mt 27:45-46) could symbolize the departure of God's presence that preceded his judgment against the temple (Ezek 9:3; 10:4-18; compare Mt 23:35-38; 24:1-2).

Gentile Oppressors Become Models of Faith in Christ (27:54) Whereas Jesus' own people had not believed, the supervising centurion and those with him recognized Jesus' identity the way Peter had some time before (16:16). In contrast to Peter, however (16:21-22), these Gentiles recognize Jesus' sonship in the cross rather than by ignoring the cross, all the more remarkable because this defied Gentile models of leadership (20:25).

The Gospel has come full circle: again the religious leaders of Israel have missed the significance of Jesus, whereas the pagans one would expect to be most hostile to Christ have understood and embraced his true identity (2:1-12). Matthew's message to his Jewish Christian audience is clear: regardless of the response of the Jewish religious leaders, you must evangelize the Gentiles. His message to us today is no less clear: although church people often live in disobedience to the gospel and take Christ for granted, we must take him beyond the walls of our churches to a waiting world.

Guardians of Jesus' Body (27:55-66) The identity of the actors in this narrative is significant. Because John's disciples took great risk and buried their teacher (14:12), we may expect at least as much courage from Jesus' disciples here (Rhoads and Michie 1982:133). But Jesus' disciples disappoint us, leaving the task to characters Matthew's audience would not anticipate unless they had heard the story before (they probably had heard it, but might still be struck by the contrast).

The Women's Courage (27:55-56) Whereas the male disciples feared for their lives and were nowhere to be found, the women followed all the way to the tomb. In that culture women were

---

27:50 The Docetic idea of a wraith substituted for Jesus on the cross, followed in the Qur'an, derives not from the New Testament itself but from popular stories such as those in Greek mythology, for instance in Euripides *Helen.*

relegated to a marginal role in discipleship at best, not permitted to be disciples (see Keener 1992:83-84; Witherington 1984). Thus women, unlike men, would not be suspected as potential coconspirators with Jesus; their courage is nonetheless telling. These women had followed Jesus as disciples in whatever ways they could, even ways that would have appeared scandalous in that culture (v. 55; compare Stanton 1989:202; Stambaugh and Balch 1986:104; Liefeld 1967:240).

Joseph of Arimathea: A Rare Wealthy Ally (27:57-61) Rich people rarely showed up among Jesus' disciples, especially when pressure became serious (19:24; 26:18). Yet Joseph here is *a disciple of Jesus*, a model to be imitated, one of the few rich men who squeezed through a needle's eye by God's grace (19:23-24). The Romans normally preferred for the bodies of condemned criminals to rot on crosses (Petr. *Sat.* 112), but Jewish custom prohibited this final indignity (Deut 21:23; compare *m. Sanhedrin* 6:5-6), and the Romans sometimes surrendered a corpse to friends or relatives who sought permission to bury it (Philo *Flaccus* 83-84). But unless Joseph already held special favor before Pilate (compare Jos. *Life* 420-21), which is unlikely, only a courageous ally would identify himself before the governor as "friend" or patron of one condemned for conspiracy against Rome.

Matthew explicitly notes the use of Joseph's own family tomb, fulfilling Isaiah 53:12. To bury Jesus in his own tomb (Mt 27:60) fits the situation of haste and location, but also suggests a special love normally reserved for family members or those equally esteemed (compare 1 Kings 13:30-31). Archaeological evidence for the tombs in this area may suggest that the tomb belonged to a person of material substance (Craig 1995:148).

Most Judean burial sites were private family tombs scattered around

27:60 The traditional Protestant "Garden Tomb" is a later, Byzantine site and cannot represent the site of Jesus' burial; by contrast, the Catholic Holy Sepulcher and tombs in its vicinity date to the right period (on the latter, see R. Brown 1994:1279-83). The tradition of the latter vicinity is as early as the second century (when Hadrian erected a pagan temple there; he defiled many Jewish holy sites in this manner) and probably earlier. Good evidence exists, in fact, that this site dates to within the first two decades after the resurrection. This is because (1) Christian tradition is unanimous that Jesus was buried outside the city walls and no one would make up a site inside (compare Heb 13:12; Jn 19:41), (2) Jewish custom made it common knowledge that burials would be outside the city walls (4 Baruch 7:13;

Jerusalem and elsewhere (Safrai 1974-1976b:779-80). Often these were caves with an opening covered by a large stone rolled in a groove; such stones could not be removed from within (Reicke 1974:187; Yamauchi 1972:112). Because Joseph was well-to-do, he probably owned a more ornate tomb, whose disk-shaped stone would be too large (a yard in diameter) for a single man to move even from outside (Lane 1974:581).

Trying to Keep Jesus Buried (27:62-66) In contrast to the women and Joseph, the other participants in the tomb narrative—the religious leaders—have quite different motives: they want Jesus to stay buried lest his promises to reign stir hope. They want the whole Jesus movement to stay buried in the tomb. This paragraph inaugurates a contrast between the alleged deceitfulness of Jesus (v. 63) and of his disciples (v. 64) on the one hand and, not long after, the actual deceitfulness of his enemies on the other (28:13-15; compare Gundry 1982:582). The authorities' behavior is not unlike that of some religious people today, whether conservative or liberal, who insist on being viewed as right even when they are wrong.

But the primary focus of this paragraph and its conclusion in 28:11-15 is the incontrovertible evidence for Jesus' resurrection. Sealing the stone (27:66) would make it impossible for anyone to enter the tomb and then merely replace the stone (see Filson 1960:299). Although Jesus has already left the tomb, the stone is not removed until 28:2. Because Matthew would hardly create a charge that did not exist, we may be sure that the primary polemic against the Christian claim concerning Jesus' resurrection was theft of the body (compare Craig 1984; Meier 1980:356).

□ **The Risen Christ (28:1-20)**

The Gospel concludes with the resurrection and the commissioning of

---

Wilkinson 1978:146), (3) the traditional vicinity of the Holy Sepulcher is inside Jerusalem's walls, and (4) Agrippa I expanded the walls of Jerusalem sometime in the A.D. 40s (R. Brown 1994:1282).

27:64 Corpses were used for magic (N. Lewis 1983:96), and people suspected that witches sometimes stole bodies for magic (see especially the tale of Telephron in Apul. *Metam.* bk. 2), though it seems not to have been common; corpses of those who died violent deaths were considered particularly potent for magic (*PGM* 1.248-49; 2.49-50; 4.342-43). If Jesus' enemies considered him a magician (12:24), some Jewish leaders may have anticipated the theft of the body as here.

the disciples. The gospel is good news because it does end with the cross; following Jesus demands from us all that we are and have, but it gives us a new and eternal life in return. The narrative of the resurrection paves the way for the commissioning: the witness of the women contrasts starkly with the fearful falsehood of the guards and provides a positive model for the witness of the church.

The Report of the Women (28:1-10) The resurrection narratives in the four Gospels differ in detail, but in all four the women become the first witnesses, and Mary Magdalene is explicitly named as one witness among them (also *Gospel of Peter* 12:50—13:57). One could harmonize the accounts, but as they stand they present strong evidence for the basic story: E. P. Sanders (1993:280) may be right to argue that "a calculated deception should have produced greater unanimity." Two matters remain clear: (1) the differences in accounts demonstrate that the Gospel writers were aware of a variety of independent traditions, and (2) these divergent traditions overlap significantly and hence independently corroborate the basic outlines of the story.

God Often Sends His Message Through the Least (28:1) Jesus' Jewish contemporaries held little esteem for the testimony of women (Jos. *Ant.* 4.219; *m. Yebamot* 15:1, 8-10; 16:7; *Ketubot* 1:6-9; compare Lk 24:11); this reflects the broader Mediterranean culture's limited trust of women's testimony, a mistrust enshrined in Roman law (Gardner 1986:165; Kee 1980:89). By contrast, the guards' report that the disciples had stolen the body (Mt 28:11-15) would command much greater respect then, as well as in an antisupernaturalistic culture like much of modern academia. Later Christians thus had to depend on the testimony of men for the public forum (1 Cor 15:5-8). No one had apologetic reason to invent the testimony of these women, but the Gospel writers may have a profound theological purpose in preserving it.

Matthew lays these two reports, the true and the false, side by side,

---

28:6 For a fuller defense of the empty tomb traditions, see Craig 1981, 1985 and 1995:146-52; on the bodily character of the resurrection, see Craig 1980:47-74. For responses to Mack,

forcing his audience to declare their choice. The testimony of the women thus becomes a model for the disciples who will follow them (28:16-20). Jesus commissions them as his *š^elûḥîm* (sg., *šālîaḥ*)— agents or apostled ones (see comment on 10:5)—to brings news of his resurrection to his own disciples. Their faithfulness, like Joseph's (27:55-61), is laid over against the authorities' deceitful accusation of deceit (27:62-66); Matthew thereby calls his audience to suffer rejection and dishonor at the hands of the hostile authorities of their own day.

God's Power Is Revealed (28:2-3) The angelic revelation exhibits points of contact with biblical theophanies, and the description of glory recalls Jesus' own in 17:2 (compare further Dan 7:9; 10:5-6; 4 Ezra 10:25-27; *3 Enoch* 22:9). Jewish angels traditionally appeared in linen (Ps-Philo 9:10; Rev 15:6) or white garments (*1 Enoch* 71:1; 87:2; 90:31-33; 2 Macc 3:26; 11:8) or clothed in glory (3 Macc 6:18; *1 Enoch* 71:1). That the angel *sat on* the stone is also a dramatic statement of supernatural triumph, since the stone, probably disk-shaped, would not naturally accommodate one sitting on it. Although the guards feared for their lives, God had no intention of slaying them.

God Is Selective in His Revelation (28:4-10) Although the *guards* witnessed God's power, the angel spoke only to the *women*. Often when people fell before a revelation as if they were dead, the revealer declared, "Do not be afraid" (compare v. 10; 17:7; Mk 16:6; Dan 10:11-12; for other parallels, see notes on Mt 17:6-7). But here the angel says *Do not be afraid* to the women, not to the guards who had fainted before him (28:4-5). Jesus appears directly to the women as well, but not to people who did not believe (vv. 8-10; compare Acts 10:41).

The men's initial dependence on the testimony of the women reflects the gospel's power to transcend gender restrictions (W. M. Thompson 1985:233). When the women met Jesus, they *worshiped* (Mt 28:9)—finally responding as the wise Gentiles had (2:2, 11), yet—again with an ironic touch—before the male disciples (28:17).

Crossan and others, see Boyd 1995; Witherington 1995; L. Johnson 1996.

Nevertheless, Jesus does not cast off the male disciples here; he identifies the disciples to whom he is sending them as his *brothers* (v. 10; 12:50; 25:40; Jn 20:17).

Because Paul explicitly reports only resurrection "appearances," some suppose that the empty tomb tradition was a myth. But while Paul's language can apply to visionary experiences, nearly all scholars concur that he is reporting earlier Palestinian tradition in 1 Corinthians 15:3-7 (see, for example, Dibelius 1971:18-20), and Palestinian Jews did not speak of nonbodily resurrections. Nor would anyone have persecuted the early Christians for simply affirming that they had seen someone who had been dead; apart from the specifically bodily character of the resurrection—the sort that would leave an empty tomb—people would merely assume they claimed to see a ghost, a noncontroversial phenomenon (compare comment on 14:26; note on 1:20). Further, very little evidence suggests the plausibility of successive and mass, corporate visions (Schweizer 1971:48-49). Those inventing an empty-tomb tradition would hardly have included women as the first witnesses (see above), and "Jesus' resurrection could hardly have been proclaimed in Jerusalem if people knew of a tomb still containing Jesus' body" (Schweizer 1971:48).

Many who claimed they had seen Jesus alive from the dead (as in 1 Cor 15:1-8; virtually all the narrative accounts also suggest significant conversation with him, rather than fleeting appearances) were so sure that they devoted their lives to proclaiming what they had seen, and some died for it; clearly their testimony was not fabricated (E. Sanders 1993:280). Supposed pagan parallels to the resurrection stories are weak (see Aune 1981:48). To most ancient Mediterranean peoples the concept of corporeal resurrection was barely intelligible; to Jewish people it was a strictly end-time event. Yet once one grants the possibility of a bodily resurrection of Jesus within past history, the appearances follow natu-

---

28:15 Roman guards from whom a prisoner escaped could be executed (Codex Justinian 9.4.4; Lake and Cadbury 1979:139; compare Acts 16:27-28; 28:42), and while the priests would not execute guards (Acts 5:22-24), some Jewish authorities followed the practice (Acts 12:19). One could sometimes strike deals, however, and some careless sentries escaped execution (Tac. *Hist.* 5.22; see also R. Brown 1994:1311, though he does not argue

rally with or without parallels.

The Report of the Guards (28:11-15) Just as Josephus's response to the anti-Jewish polemic of *Apion* has inadvertently preserved the basic outline of anti-Jewish polemic in his day, Matthew's response to arguments against the early Christian claims about the resurrection preserves what must have been the basic charge of his day: the disciples stole the body (compare later sources in Stauffer 1960:144-45; Tert. *Apol.* 21). But it is exceedingly doubtful that disciples would deliberately steal the body yet later prove prepared to die for the claim that they had seen Jesus alive from the dead!

Jesus' enemies could not account for the body's disappearance. Indirectly this suggests that opponents of Christianity conceded that Jesus' body was missing and that no simpler explanation (such as the body's being deposited in the wrong tomb) was available (also Craig 1984; Meier 1980:356). Although Paul does not appeal to the empty-tomb tradition in 1 Corinthians 15, his account necessarily implies it. Many people in antiquity claimed to see "ghosts," but for Palestinian Jews "resurrection" meant bodily resurrection and nothing else. Against some commentators, it is quite difficult to imagine that the disciples would have begun proclaiming the resurrection, and the authorities opposing them, without anyone's having checked the tomb (Craig 1995:151). Yet the church depended on the testimony of witnesses of the risen Christ, not simply on an empty tomb (Ladd 1974b:325). The empty tomb tells us about the nature of the resurrection (and the body and history), but the witnesses attest to its facticity.

In contrast to the disciples' claims, the report of the guards is not credible. Stones were rolled away so graves could be robbed (Char. *Chaer.* 3.3.1), but not with guards posted (at least, not unless the robbers had subdued the guards, normally fatally). Moreover,

---

for the historicity of the guards). Because sleeping on duty was a punishable offense, one would doubt that the guards would normally publicly admit it (Beare 1981:543); but because the missing body could spell their execution either way, they have reason to please the authorities, who promise conditional amnesty (Gundry 1982:585).

whereas tomb robbers normally carried off wealth, carrying off the body was so rare that it would shock those who heard of it (Char. *Chaer.* 3.3).

If the disciples did not protect Jesus while he was alive, surely they would not have risked their lives to rob his tomb after his death (grave robbing was a capital offense—for example, *SEG* 8.13). Nor could they have rolled away the massive stone without waking the guards. Penalties for falling asleep on guard duty could be severe, and guards who claimed to have slept through the stealing of the body, yet suffered no harm, would sound very suspicious. (Thus, for example, a soldier assigned to guard corpses hanging on crosses to prevent burial found a body stolen and preferred suicide to court-martial and execution—Petr. *Sat.* 112.) Under normal circumstances, people might suppose that such guards and those who failed to punish them had collaborated in the disappearance of the body, but in this situation those who failed to punish the guards had too much to lose.

It might be argued that someone took the body but guards were not actually present. But then why would the establishment circulate a rumor that guards were present, which would weaken rather than strengthen their case? The testimony of guards who slept through the theft would be less credible than the guesses of investigators after a theft. The story makes the most sense if guards had been present but somehow failed to protect the body, and the officials had to strike a deal to cover their embarrassment.

The narrative's irony announces both God's power and human weakness. Guards who saw an angel were ready, like Judas (26:15), to betray the truth for money (28:12); like Peter (26:69-75), they were ready to deny the unbelievable to protect their lives (28:14). Yet the guards only pretended to have slept through the Messiah's deliverance (28:15), whereas when Jesus needed his disciples the most, they slept through his time of testing (26:40-45). Disciples and enemies alike proved weak, but Jesus' resurrection was an act of God's power.

28:19 Albright and Mann (1971:362) point out that the trinitarian formula is established by the period of our first extant Christian documents (1 Cor 12:4-6; 2 Cor 13:14; see most thoroughly Fee 1994:839-42) and widespread in the church (1 Pet 1:2; 1 Jn 3:23-24; *Did.* 7; *Ode Sol.* 23:22; Athenagoras *Plea* 24). Mark already pairs "Father" and "Son," as do Q (Mt 16:27) and Johannine tradition; the saying could even derive from a lost ending of Mark.

The Report of the Church (28:16-20) The *mountain* (v. 16) recalls the other sites of revelation in the Gospel (5:1; 17:1). All our earliest evidence indicates the Christian missionary impetus; this suggests that it originated with Jesus, as various Gospel accounts independently attest. The women offered a true report (28:1-10) and the guards a false one (vv. 11-15); Matthew's closing paragraph announces that we, like the women at the tomb, must offer a true report and resist temptations like money and protection to which the guards succumbed.

The narrative teaches us about faith and unbelief. Some of those who see Jesus worship him (compare v. 9), which suggests that they recognize him for who he is—"God with them" (1:23; 28:18-20). Others, however, despite seeing him, doubt (v. 17; compare Lk 24:40). Matthew here agrees with Mark (Mk 16:8) that disciples often are foolishly unbelieving (Mt 6:30; 14:31; 17:20), even after the resurrection. If even seeing is not necessarily believing, we ought not to wait to see before we will believe, as if God had not provided enough evidence already.

The narrative teaches us about Jesus' identity. Jesus holds *all authority* as does the son of man in Daniel 7 (28:18; compare 7:29; Jn 17:2; Dan 7:13-14). One may contrast here Satan's offer in Matthew 4:8-9; by pursuing obedience Jesus received more than Satan offered. Jewish teachers felt that confessing the one Lord by means of the *Shema (š^ema')* expressed submission to God's royal authority (*m. Berakot* 2:5); in this passage we learn that such submission requires confession of Jesus (compare 10:32). Disciples of rabbis normally made *disciples* of their own when they became rabbis, but Jesus is more than a normal rabbi (28:19) and summons us to make disciples for him alone and not for ourselves (23:8-10).

Disciples baptize not only in the name of the *Father* and the *Holy Spirit,* whom biblical and Jewish tradition regarded as divine, but also in the name of the *Son.* Placing Jesus on the same level with the Father

---

The formula distinguishes Christian from other Jewish proselyte baptism (see comments on 3:5-9). In Acts, baptism "in Jesus' name" means baptism distinguished by the faith confession of the person receiving baptism rather than the one giving it (Acts 2:21; 22:16), as suggested by the passive voice of the verbs; the matter is less clear in Matthew 28:19.

and Spirit (28:19) makes even more explicit what is implicit in Acts's "baptism in Jesus' name" (Acts 2:38; 8:16; 10:48; 19:5; compare 22:16)—that Jesus is divine (Mt 1:23). One other aspect of this pericope emphasizes Matthew's high Christology. Jesus' continuing presence with his followers even after his departure (28:20) suggests his omnipresence—an attribute limited to deity alone (see comment on 1:23; 18:20).

Finally, the narrative teaches us about our mission. Because Jesus' future reign (28:18) has begun in the lives of his followers in the present age (v. 20), his people should exemplify his reign on earth as it is in heaven, as people of the kingdom, people of the future era (compare 6:10). Most significant in this passage, because Jesus has all authority, because he is King in the kingdom of God, disciples must carry on the mission of *teaching* the kingdom (10:7). Jesus' instructions include an imperative (a command) surrounded by three participial clauses: one should make disciples for Jesus by going, baptizing and teaching. Making disciples involves more than getting people to an altar; it involves training them as thoroughly as Jewish teachers instructed their own students. Most of modern Christendom falls far short on this count.

Making disciples involves "going" (28:19), as it had before (10:7). Because "going" (NIV *go*) is a participle, we could read, "as you go"—essentially, "on your way," implying that one need not cross cultural boundaries to fulfill this commission (compare Culver 1968). But this misses the parallel between the final commission and the model mission in chapter 10: even while remaining within Galilee, the disciples had to proclaim the kingdom to those who had not yet heard the message (10:7; compare Mk 1:38). Nevertheless, the commission probably emphasizes teaching and baptizing while presupposing that disciples have already done the necessary work of crossing cultural boundaries. "Going" might mean "having gone" (the Greek aorist); the aorist participle "going" may represent part of the command, the aorist imperative "make disciples," while the two present participles explain how to make disciples (Rogers 1973; compare R. White 1960:127 n. 3). But this does not require us to excessively subordinate "going," since Matthew often uses this participle in a sense coordinate with the main verb (compare 2:8; 11:4; 17:27; 28:7; Blomberg 1992:431). Given Matthew's similar expression in 10:7, we must still regard crossing cultural boundaries as an integral part of the commission.

Unlike other ancient teachers, Jesus' disciples would not raise disciples for themselves but only for Jesus (23:8). Greek tradition could praise those who made many disciples (as in Diog. Laert. 8.1.16). Greek philosophers thought in terms of "conversion" to philosophy (see Nock 1933), and various pagan religious cults were propagated by travelers in antiquity (Stambaugh and Balch 1986:42; compare Acts 8:4). Judaism also spoke of sages as having disciples (see comment on 4:19; 19:21-22) and sometimes even persuading large numbers of people to become students of Torah (as in *ARN* 26, §54); they also separately recognized the conversion of Gentiles (see comment on 23:15; see De Ridder 1971). But ancient hearers would, and modern hearers should, recognize a drastic innovation in a command to disciple *nations*.

All nations may signify all groups of "peoples," rather than the modern concept of "nation-states" (McGavran and Arn 1977:38); in many nations a variety of different peoples coexist. Thus Christ commands us to sensitively reach each culture, not merely some people from each nation. Also far from abandoning the mission to Matthew's own people, his commission represents "peoples" and not simply "Gentiles" (Saldarini 1994:59-60, 78-81; compare Meier 1977), although in the context of his whole Gospel he lays the emphasis on Gentile peoples, whom his community most needs to be encouraged in evangelizing.

As long as unreached peoples exist, we disobey the Great Commission by refusing to cross those boundaries. Given the explicitness of Jesus' command, perhaps many use the lack of "call" to missions as an excuse; yet it may be that the Lord of the harvest has been calling us through the need of the world but we are not willing to hear. If Christ has already called his disciples to *go*, is it not possible that it is those of us who stay who need an explicit message from God?

Matthew needed to encourage Jewish Christians in their commitment to reach Gentiles, but he could not have imagined the present situation: a huge Gentile church with Jewish Christians as a small and marginalized minority. If Matthew were writing his Gospel to the church today, he would certainly plead with Gentile Christians to remember, pray for and minister to his own people, who gave them the gospel (compare

10:6; Rom 15:25-27).

But wherever God leads particular disciples to carry out this commission, the text is clear how one makes disciples. First of all, one baptizes them under the lordship of Christ. Baptism was an act of initiation and conversion (see comment on 3:6), so this text suggests that we initiate people into the faith, introducing them to Jesus' lordship. But once they are initiated, we must also build them into stronger discipleship by *teaching* them Jesus' message. The summaries of Jesus' teachings earlier in Matthew's Gospel work well as a discipling manual for young believers. Here, as in Jewish instruction of converts to Judaism, the process of teaching continues subsequent to initiation.

The Gospel closes with a promise: as Jesus' disciples carry out the Great Commission, he will be with them to the end of the age (28:20). The text probably specifies *the end of the age* because at that time the Son of Man would return in his kingdom—after the nations had heard the good news of the kingdom (24:14) and hence been prepared for the judgment (25:32-36). If many Christians today have lost a sense of Jesus' presence and purpose among us, it may be because we have lost sight of the mission our Lord has given us. If we would be his disciples, then we must prepare the way for our Lord's second coming and his kingdom, as John the Baptist did for his first coming (3:1-3). If we truly long for our Lord's return, our mission is laid out before us until he comes.

BIBLIOGRAPHY

Abelson, Joshua
1969   *The Immanence of God in Rabbinical Literature*. 2nd ed. New York: Hermon.

Abrahams, I.
1917   *Studies in Pharisaism and the Gospels*. 1st series. Cambridge: Cambridge University Press.

1924   *Studies in Pharisaism and the Gospels*. 2nd series. Cambridge: Cambridge University Press.

Adams, Jay E.
1980   *Marriage, Divorce and Remarriage in the Bible*. Grand Rapids, Mich.: Baker Book House.

Albright, William Foxwell, and C. S. Mann
1971   *Matthew*. Anchor Bible 26. Garden City, N.Y.: Doubleday.

Alexander, William Menzies
1980   *Demonic Possession in the New Testament: Its Historical, Medical and Theological Aspects*. Grand Rapids, Mich.: Baker Book House (original ed. Edinburgh: T & T Clark, 1902).

Allen, Lloyd
1992   "The Sermon on the Mount in the History of the Church." *Review and Expositor* 89:245-62.

Allison, Dale C., Jr.
1993a   "Divorce, Celibacy and Joseph (Matthew 1.18-25 and 19. 1-12)." *Journal for the Study of the New Testament* 49:3-10.

1993b   *The New Moses: A Matthean Typology*. Minneapolis: Fortress.

Alsdurf, James, and Phyllis Alsdurf
1989   *Battered into Submission*. Downers Grove, Ill.: InterVarsity Press.

Anderson, Hugh
1976   *The Gospel of Mark. New Century Bible*. London: Oliphants/Marshall, Morgan & Scott.

Applebaum, Shim'on
1974-1976   "Economic Life in Palestine." In *The Jewish People in the First*

Century: Historical Geography, Political History, Social, Cultural and Religious Life and Institutions, pp. 631-700. Edited by S. Safrai and M. Stern with D. Flusser and W. C. van Unnik. 2 vols. Section 1 of Compendia Rerum Iudaicarum ad Novum Testamentum. Vol. 1: Assen, Netherlands: Van Gorcum. Vol. 2: Philadelphia: Fortress.

1979   Jews and Greeks in Ancient Cyrene. Studies in Judaism in Late Antiquity 28. Leiden: E. J. Brill.

Argyle, A. W.
1963   *The Gospel According to Matthew*. Cambridge: Cambridge University Press.

Aune, David Edward
1981   "The Problem of the Genre of the Gospels: A Critique of C. H. Talbert's *What Is a Gospel?*" In *Studies of History and Tradition in the Four Gospels II*, pp. 9-60. Vol. 2 of *Gospel Perspectives*. Edited by R. T. France and David Wenham. 6 vols. Sheffield, U.K.: JSOT Press.

1983   *Prophecy in Early Christianity and the Ancient Mediterranean World*. Grand Rapids, Mich.: Eerdmans.

1987   *The New Testament in Its Literary Environment*. Library of Early Christianity 8. Philadelphia: Westminster Press.

1988   "Greco-Roman Biography." In *Greco-Roman Literature and the New Testament: Selected Forms and Genres*, pp. 107-26. Edited by David E. Aune. Society of Biblical Literature Sources for Biblical Study 21. Atlanta: Scholars Press.

Avi-Yonah, Michael
1974-1976   "Archaeological Sources." In *The Jewish People in the First Century: Historical Geography, Political History, Social, Cultural and Religious Life and Institutions*, pp. 46-62. Edited by S. Safrai and M. Stern with D. Flusser and W. C. van Unnik. 2 vols. Section 1 of Compendia Rerum Iudaicarum ad Novum Testamentum. Vol. 1: Assen, Netherlands: Van Gorcum. Vol. 2: Philadelphia: Fortress.

1978   *Hellenism and the East: Contacts and Interrelations from Alexander to the Roman Conquest*. Jerusalem: Institute of Languages, Literature and the Arts, Hebrew University/University Microfilms International.

Bagatti, Bellarmino
1971   *The Church from the Circumcision*. Jerusalem: Franciscan.

Bailey, Kenneth Ewing
1976   *Poet and Peasant: A Literary Cultural Approach to the Parables in Luke*. Grand Rapids, Mich.: Eerdmans.

1980   *Through Peasant Eyes: More Lucan Parables, Their Culture and Style.* Grand Rapids, Mich.: Eerdmans.

Bammel, Ernst
1984   "The *Titulus.*" In *Jesus and the Politics of His Day,* pp. 353-64. Edited by Ernst Bammel and C. F. D. Moule. Cambridge: Cambridge University Press.

Bandstra, Andrew J.
1981   "The Original Form of the Lord's Prayer." *Calvin Theological Journal* 16:15-37.

Barclay, William
1959   "Great Themes of the NT—VI. Matthew xxiv." *Expository Times* 70:326-30. 376-79.

Barna, George
1991   *What Americans Believe: An Annual Survey of Values and Religious Views in the United States.* Ventura, Calif.: Regal.

Barrett, C. K.
1966   *The Holy Spirit and the Gospel Tradition.* London: S.P.C.K.

1967   *Jesus and the Gospel Tradition.* London: S.P.C.K.

Barth, Gerhard
1963   "Matthew's Understanding of the Law." In Günther Bornkamm, Gerhard Barth and Heinz Joachim Held, *Tradition and Interpretation in Matthew,* pp. 58-164. Philadelphia: Westminster Press.

Basser, Herbert W.
1985   "Derrett's 'Binding' Reopened." *Journal of Biblical Literature* 104:297-300.

Bauer, David R.
1988   *The Structure of Matthew's Gospel: A Study in Literary Design. Journal for the Study of the New Testament* Supplement 31. Sheffield, U.K.: Sheffield Academic Press/Almond.

Baumgarten, Albert I.
1984-1985   "*Korban* and the Pharisaic *Paradosis.*" *Journal of the Ancient Near East Society* 16-17:5-17.

Beare, Francis Wright
1981   *The Gospel According to Matthew.* San Francisco: Harper & Row.

Beasley-Murray, G. R.
1957   *A Commentary on Mark 13.* London: Macmillan.

1960   "The Eschatological Discourse of Jesus." *Review and Expositor* 57:153-66.

Beckwith, Roger T.
1981   "Daniel 9 and the Date of Messiah's Coming in Essene, Hellenistic, Pharisaic, Zealot and Early Christian Computation." *Revue de Qumran* 10:521-42.

Beechick, Allen
1980   *The Pre-tribulation Rapture.* Denver: Accent.

Belkin, Samuel
1940   *Philo and the Oral Law: The Philonic Interpretation of Biblical Law in Relation to the Palestinian Halakah.* Harvard Semitic Series 11. Cambridge, Mass.: Harvard University Press.

1970   "Levirate and Agnate Marriage in Rabbinic and Cognate Literature." *Jewish Quarterly Review* 60:275-329.

Bennett, Lerone, Jr.
1966   *Before the Mayflower: A History of the Negro in America, 1619-1964.* Rev. ed. Baltimore, Md.: Penguin.

Benoit, Pierre
1973-1974   *Jesus and the Gospels.* Translated by Benet Weatherhead. 2 vols. Vol. 1: New York: Herder & Herder; London: Darton, Longman & Todd. Vol. 2: New York: Seabury/Crossroad; London: Darton, Longman & Todd.

Berger, David, and
Michael Wyschogrod
1978   *Jews and "Jewish Christianity."* New York: KTAV.

Best, Ernest
1965   *The Temptation and the Passion: The Markan Soteriology.* Society for New Testament Studies Monograph 2. Cambridge: Cambridge University Press.

1976   "Mark 10:13-16: The Child as Model Recipient." In *Biblical Studies: Essays in Honor of William Barclay,* pp. 119-34. Edited by J. R. McKay and J. F. Miller. Philadelphia: Westminster Press.

1977   *A Commentary on the First and Second Epistles to the Thessalonians.* Black's New Testament Commentaries. London: Adam & Charles Black.

1983   *Mark: The Gospel as Story.* Studies of the New Testament and Its World. Edinburgh: T & T Clark.

Betz, Otto
1968   *What Do We Know About Jesus?* Philadelphia: Westminster Press; London: SCM Press.

Black, Matthew
1961   *The Scrolls and Christian Origins.* London: Thomas Nelson & Sons.

1967   *An Aramaic Approach to the Gospels and Acts.* Oxford: Clarendon.

Blackburn, Barry L.
1986   " 'Miracle Working ΘΕΙΟΙ ΑΝΔΡΕΣ' in Hellenism (and Hellenistic Judaism)." In *The Miracles of Jesus,* pp. 185-218. Vol. 6 of *Gospel Perspectives.* Edited by David Wenham and Craig Blomberg. 6 vols. Sheffield, U.K.: JSOT Press.

Blinzler, Josef
1959   *The Trial of Jesus: The Jewish and Roman Proceedings Against
               Jesus Christ Described and Assessed from the Oldest Accounts.*
               Translated by Isabel McHugh and Florence McHugh. Westmin-
               ster, Md.: Newman.
Blomberg, Craig L.
1987   *The Historical Reliability of the Gospels.* Downers Grove, Ill.:
               InterVarsity Press.

1990   *Interpreting the Parables.* Downers Grove, Ill.: InterVarsity
               Press.

1992   *Matthew.* New American Commentary 22. Nashville: Broadman.

1995   "Where Do We Start Studying Jesus?" In *Jesus Under Fire,* pp.
               17-50. Edited by Michael J. Wilkins and J. P. Moreland. Grand
               Rapids, Mich.: Zondervan.
Bock, Darrell L.
1994   *Luke.* IVP New Testament Commentary Series. Downers
               Grove, Ill.: InterVarsity Press.

1995   "The Words of Jesus in the Gospels: Live, Jive or Memorex?"
               In *Jesus Under Fire,* pp. 73-99. Edited by Michael J. Wilkins
               and J. P. Moreland. Grand Rapids, Mich.: Zondervan.
Bockmuehl, Klaus
1988   *The Unreal God of Modern Theology: Bultmann, Barth and
               the Theology of Atheism—A Call to Recovering the Truth of
               God's Reality.* Translated by Geoffrey W. Bromiley. Colorado
               Springs, Colo.: Helmers & Howard.
Bonhoeffer, Dietrich
1963   *The Cost of Discipleship.* Rev. ed. New York: Macmillan; Lon-
               don: SCM Press.
Bonsirven, Joseph
1964   *Palestinian Judaism in the Time of Jesus Christ.* New York:
               Holt, Rinehart & Winston.
Borg, Marcus J.
1987   *Jesus: A New Vision (Spirit, Culture and the Life of Disci-
               pleship).* San Francisco: Harper & Row.
Boring, M. Eugene
1982   *Sayings of the Risen Jesus: Christian Prophecy in the Synoptic
               Tradition.* Society for New Testament Studies Monograph 46.
               Cambridge: Cambridge University Press.
Bornkamm, Günther
1969   *Early Christian Experience.* New York: Harper & Row; Lon-
               don: SCM Press.   *ist*

Bourke, Myles M.
1960   "The Literary Genius of Matthew 1-2." *Catholic Biblical Quar-
               terly* 22:160-75.

Bowersock, G. W.
1965   *Augustus and the Greek World*. Oxford: Clarendon.

Bowker, John
1973   *Jesus and the Pharisees*. Cambridge: Cambridge University Press.

Boyd, Gregory A.
1995   *Cynic Sage or Son of God?* Wheaton, Ill.: Victor.

Brown, Colin
1978   " 'Rock' in Matt. 16:18." In *The New International Dictionary of New Testament Theology*, 3:385-88. Edited by Colin Brown. 3 vols. Grand Rapids, Mich.: Zondervan.

Brown, Raymond E.
1958-1959   "The Semitic Background of the New Testament *Mysterion* (II)." *Biblica* 39:426-48; 40:70-87.

1968   *The Semitic Background of the Term "Mystery" in the New Testament*. Philadelphia: Fortress.

1970   *The Gospel According to John*. Anchor Bible 29A. Garden City, N.Y.: Doubleday.

1977   *The Birth of the Messiah*. Garden City, N.Y.: Doubleday.

1994   *The Death of the Messiah: From Gethsemane to Grave. A Commentary on the Passion Narratives in the Four Gospels*. 2 vols. New York: Doubleday.

Brown, Raymond E.,
Karl P. Donfried and
John Reumann, eds.
1973   *Peter in the New Testament*. New York: Paramus; Toronto: Paulist.

Brown, Raymond E.,
and John P. Meier
1983   *Antioch and Rome: New Testament Cradles of Catholic Christianity*. New York: Paulist.

Brown, Schuyler
1969   *Apostasy and Perseverance in the Theology of Luke*. Rome: Pontifical Biblical Institute.

1978   "The Mission to Israel in Matthew's Central Section (Mt 9:35-11:1)." *Zeitschrift für die Neutestamentliche Wissenschaft* 69:73-90.

1979   "The Matthean Apocalypse." *Journal for the Study of the New Testament* 4:2-27.

Bruce, Alexander
Balmain
1979   "The Gospel According to Matthew." In *The Expositor's Greek Testament*, 1:61-340. Edited by W. Robertson Nicoll. Reprint ed. 5 vols. Grand Rapids, Mich.: Eerdmans.

Bruce, F. F.
1956   "Qumrân and Early Christianity." *New Testament Studies* 2:176-90.

1963   *The Books and the Parchments*. Old Tappan, N.J.: Fleming H. Revell.

1966   "Holy Spirit in the Qumran Texts." *The Annual of Leeds University Oriental Society* 6:49-55.

1969   "Jesus and the Gospels in the Light of the Scrolls." In *The Scrolls and Christianity: Historical and Theological Significance*, pp. 70-82. Edited by Matthew Black. London: S.P.C.K.

1971   *1 and 2 Corinthians*. New Century Bible 38. Greenwood, S.C.: Attic; London: Marshall, Morgan & Scott.

1972a   *The Message of the New Testament*. Grand Rapids, Mich.: Eerdmans.

1972b   *New Testament History*. Garden City, N.Y.: Doubleday.

1977   *Commentary on the Book of the Acts: The English Text with Introduction, Exposition and Notes*. New International Commentary on the New Testament. Grand Rapids, Mich.: Eerdmans.

1978   *The Time Is Fulfilled*. Grand Rapids, Mich.: Eerdmans.

1980   *The New Testament Documents: Are They Reliable?* 5th ed. Grand Rapids, Mich.: Eerdmans.

1982   *1 and 2 Thessalonians*. Word Biblical Commentary 45. Waco, Tex.: Word.

Bruns, J. Edgar
1961   "The Magi Episode in Matthew 2." *Catholic Biblical Quarterly* 23:51-54.

Bryant, David
1984   *In the Gap: What It Means to Be a World Christian*. Ventura, Calif.: Regal.

Bultmann, Rudolf
1968   *The History of the Synoptic Tradition*. 2nd ed. Translated by John Marsh. Oxford: Basil Blackwell.

Burkert, Walter
1985   *Greek Religion*. Translated by John Raffan. Cambridge, Mass.:

Harvard University Press.

Burkill, T. A.
1972   *New Light on the Earliest Gospel: Seven Markan Studies*. Ithaca, N.Y.: Cornell University Press.

Burkitt, F. Crawford
1910   *The Earliest Sources for the Life of Jesus*. Boston: Houghton Mifflin.

Burridge, Richard A.
1992   *What Are the Gospels? A Comparison with Graeco-Roman Biography*. Society for New Testament Studies Monograph 70. Cambridge: Cambridge University Press.

Byron, B.
1963   "The Meaning of 'Except It Be for Fornication.' " *Australasian Catholic Record* 40:90-95.

Caragounis, Chrys C.
1977   *The Ephesian Mysterion: Meaning and Content*. Coniectanea Biblica New Testament 8. Lund, Sweden: Gleerup.

Carcopino, Jérôme
1940   *Daily Life in Ancient Rome: The People and the City at the Height of the Empire*. Edited by Henry T. Rowell. Translated by E. O. Lorimer. New Haven, Conn.: Yale University Press.

Carlebach, A.
1975   "Rabbinic References to Fiscus Judaicus." *Jewish Quarterly Review* 66:57-61.

Carmon, Efrat, ed.
1973   *Inscriptions Reveal: Documents from the Time of the Bible, the Mishna and the Talmud*. Translated by R. Grafman. Jerusalem: Israel Museum.

Caron, Gerard
1982   "Did Jesus Allow Divorce? (Mt. 5:31-32)." *African Ecclesiastical Review* 24:309-16.

Carson, D. A.
1984   "Matthew." In *The Expositor's Bible Commentary*, 8:3-599. Edited by Frank Gaebelein. 12 vols. Grand Rapids, Mich.: Zondervan.

Carson, D. A.,
Douglas J. Moo
and Leon Morris
1992   *An Introduction to the New Testament*. Grand Rapids, Mich.: Zondervan.

Cary, M., and T. J.
  Haarhoff
1946   *Life and Thought in the Greek and Roman World*. 4th ed. London: Methuen.

Casson, Lionel
1974   *Travel in the Ancient World*. London: George Allen & Unwin

Catchpole, David R.
1971   "The Answer of Jesus to Caiaphas (Matt. XXVI.64)." *New Testament Studies* 17:213-26.

1978   "On Doing Violence to the Kingdom." *Journal of Theology for
                Southern Africa* 25:50-61.

1979   "The Poor on Earth and the Son of Man in Heaven: A Re-
                appraisal of Matthew xxv.31-46." *Bulletin of the John Rylands
                University Library of Manchester* 61:355-97.

1984   "The 'Triumphal' Entry." In *Jesus and the Politics of His Day*,
                pp. 319-34. Edited by Ernst Bammel and C. F. D. Moule.
                Cambridge: Cambridge University Press.

1993   *The Quest for Q*. Edinburgh: T & T Clark.

Chilton, Bruce
1994   *Judaic Approaches to the Gospels*. University of South Florida
                International Studies in Formative Christianity and Judaism 2.
                Atlanta: Scholars Press.

Christiaens, M.
1983   "Pastoraal van de Echtscheiding volgens Matteüs: Vragen rond
                de 'Ontuchtclausule.' " *Tijdschrift voor Theologie* 23:3-23; *New
                Testament Abstracts* 27:255.

Clavier, Henri
1957   "Matthieu 5:39 et la non-résistance." *Revue d'Histoire et de Phi-
                losophie Religieuses* 37:44-57.

Cohen, Boaz
1966   *Jewish and Roman Law: A Comparative Study*. 2 vols. New
                York: Jewish Theological Seminary of America.

Coiner, H. G.
1968   "Those 'Divorce and Remarriage' Passages (Matt. 5:32; 19:9;
                1 Cor. 7:10-16)." *Concordia Theological Monthly* 39:367-84.

Cole, R. A.
1961   *The Gospel According to St. Mark*. Tyndale New Testament
                Commentary. Grand Rapids, Mich.: Eerdmans.

Coleman, Robert E.
1963   *The Master Plan of Evangelism*. Huntingdon Valley, Penn.:
                Christian Outreach.

Considine, T.
1956   "Except It Be for Fornication." *Australasian Catholic Record*
                33:214-23; *New Testament Abstracts* 1:177.

Cope, O. Lamar
1969   "Matthew xxv 31-46: 'The Sheep and the Goats' Reinter-
                preted." *Novum Testamentum* 11:32-44.

1976   *Matthew: A Scribe Trained for the Kingdom of Heaven*.
                Catholic Biblical Quarterly Monograph 5. Washington, D.C.:
                Catholic Biblical Association of America.

Craig, William Lane
1980   "The Bodily Resurrection of Jesus." In *Studies of History and
                Tradition in the Four Gospels I*, pp. 47-74. Vol. 1 of *Gospel*

Perspectives. Edited by R. T. France and David Wenham. 6 vols. Sheffield, U.K.: JSOT Press.

1981 "The Empty Tomb of Jesus." In *Studies of History and Tradition in the Four Gospels II,* pp. 173-200. Vol. 2 of *Gospel Perspectives.* Edited by R. T. France and David Wenham. 6 vols. Sheffield, U.K.: JSOT Press.

1984 "The Guard at the Tomb." *New Testament Studies* 30:273-81.

1985 "The Historicity of the Empty Tomb of Jesus." *New Testament Studies* 31:39-67.

1986 "The Problem of Miracles: A Historical and Philosophical Perspective." In *The Miracles of Jesus,* pp. 9-48. Vol. 6 of *Gospel Perspectives.* Edited by David Wenham and Craig Blomberg. 6 vols. Sheffield, U.K.: JSOT Press.

1995 "Did Jesus Rise from the Dead?" In *Jesus Under Fire,* pp. 141-76. Edited by Michael J. Wilkins and J. P. Moreland. Grand Rapids, Mich.: Zondervan.

Craigie, Peter C.
1978 *The Problem of War in the Old Testament.* Grand Rapids, Mich.: Eerdmans.

Cranfield, C. E. B.
1955 "The Baptism of our Lord: A Study of St. Mark 1.9-11." *Scottish Journal of Theology* 8:53-63.

Cranford, Lorin L.
1992 "Bibliography for the Sermon on the Mount." *Southwestern Journal of Theology* 35:34-38.

Crisler, B. Cobbey
1976 "The Acoustics and Crowd Capacity of Natural Theaters in Palestine." *Biblical Archaeologist* 39:128-41.

Crossan, John Dominic
1986 "From Moses to Jesus: Parallel Themes." *Bible Review* 2:18-27.

1991 *The Historical Jesus: The Life of a Mediterranean Jewish Peasant.* San Francisco: HarperSanFrancisco.

Cullmann, Oscar
1950 *Christ and Time.* Translated by Floyd V. Filson. Philadelphia: Westminster Press.

1953 *Peter: Disciple, Apostle, Martyr.* Philadelphia: Westminster Press.

1956a *The Early Church.* Edited by A. J. B. Higgins. London: SCM Press.

1956b *The State in the New Testament.* New York: Charles Scribner's Sons.

1959	*The Christology of the New Testament.* Philadelphia: Westminster Press; London: SCM Press.

Culpepper, R. Alan
1975   *The Johannine School: An Evaluation of the Johannine-School Hypothesis Based on an Investigation of the Nature of Ancient Schools.* Society of Biblical Literature Dissertation Series 26. Missoula, Mont.: Scholars Press.

Culver, R. D.
1968   "What Is the Church's Commission? Some Exegetical Issues in Matthew 28:16-20." *Bibliotheca Sacra* 125:239-53.

Cunningham, Scott,
and Darrell L. Bock
1987   "Is Matthew Midrash?" *Bibliotheca Sacra* 144:157-80.

Dalman, Gustaf
1929   *Jesus-Jeshua: Studies in the Gospels.* New York: Macmillan.

1973   *Jesus Christ in the Talmud, Midrash, Zohar and the Liturgy of the Synagogue.* New York: Arno (original ed. Cambridge: Deighton, Bell, 1893).

Danker, Frederick W.
1972   *Jesus and the New Age.* St. Louis: Clayton.

Daube, David
1956   "The Gospels and the Rabbis." *The Listener* 56:342-46.

1959   "Concessions to Sinfulness in Jewish Law." *Journal of Jewish Studies* 10:1-13.

1963   *The Exodus Pattern in the Bible.* All Souls Studies 2. London: Faber & Faber.

1972   "Responsibilities of Master and Disciples in the Gospels." *New Testament Studies* 19:1-15.

1973   *The New Testament and Rabbinic Judaism.* New York: Arno (original ed. London: University of London, 1956).

Davids, Peter H.
1980   "The Gospels and Jewish Tradition: Twenty Years After Gerhardsson." In *Studies of History and Tradition in the Four Gospels I,* pp. 75-99. Vol. 1 of *Gospel Perspectives.* Edited by R. T. France and David Wenham. 6 vols. Sheffield, U.K.: JSOT Press.

Davies, Margaret
1993   *Matthew.* Readings: A New Biblical Commentary. Sheffield, U.K.: JSOT Press/Sheffield Academic Press.

Davies, Stevan L.
1983   "John the Baptist and Essene Kashruth." *New Testament Studies* 29:569-71.

Davies, W. D.
1966   *Invitation to the New Testament: A Guide to Its Main
            Witnesses.* Garden City, N.Y.: Doubleday.
1966b   *The Sermon on the Mount.* Cambridge: Cambridge University
            Press.

1967   "Reflexions on Tradition: The Aboth Revisited." In *Christian
            History and Interpretation: Studies Presented to John Knox,*
            pp. 129-37. Edited by W. R. Farmer, C. F. D. Moule and R. R.
            Niebuhr. Cambridge: Cambridge University Press.

Davies, W. D., and
Dale C. Allison
1988   *Introduction and Commentary on Matthew I-VII.* Vol. 1 of *A
            Critical and Exegetical Commentary on the Gospel According
            to Saint Matthew.* International Critical Commentaries. 3 vols.
            Edinburgh: T & T Clark.

1991   *Introduction and Commentary on Matthew VIII-XVIII.* Vol. 2
            of *A Critical and Exegetical Commentary on the Gospel Ac-
            cording to Saint Matthew.* International Critical Commentaries.
            3 vols. Edinburgh: T & T Clark.

Deere, Jack
1993   *Surprised by the Power of the Spirit.* Grand Rapids, Mich.:
            Zondervan.

Deissmann, G. Adolf
1978   *Light from the Ancient East.* Grand Rapids, Mich.: Baker Book
            House (reprint of 4th ed., 1922).

Delaney, Carol
1987   "Seeds of Honor, Fields of Shame." In *Honor and Shame and
            the Unity of the Mediterranean,* pp. 35-48. Edited by David D.
            Gilmore. American Anthropological Association 22. Washing-
            ton, D.C.: American Anthropological Association.

De Ridder, Richard R.
1971   *Discipling the Nations.* Grand Rapids, Mich.: Baker Book
            House.

Derrett, J. Duncan M.
1970   *Law in the New Testament.* London: Darton, Longman & Todd.

1971   "Law in the New Testament: The Palm Sunday Colt." *Novum
            Testamentum* 13:241-58.

1973   *Jesus's Audience: The Social and Psychological Environment
            in Which He Worked.* New York: Seabury.

1983   "Binding and Loosing (Matt 16:19; 18:18; John 20:23)." *Jour-
            nal of Biblical Literature* 102:112-17.

Dewey, Kim E.
1976   "Peter's Curse and Cursed Peter (Mark 14:53-54, 66-72)." In
            The Passion in Mark: Studies in Mark 14—16, pp. 96-114. Ed-

ited by Werner H. Kelber. Philadelphia: Fortress.

Dibelius, Martin
1971   *From Tradition to Gospel.* Translated from the 2nd (1933) German ed. by Bertram Lee Woolf. Cambridge: James Clarke.

Diezinger, W.
1978   "Zum Liebesgebot Mk xii,28-34 und Parr." *Novum Testamentum* 20:81-83.

Dixon, Suzanne
1988   *The Roman Mother.* Norman: Oklahoma University Press.

Dobson, Edward G.
1986   *What the Bible Really Says About Marriage, Divorce and Remarriage.* Old Tappan, N.J.: Fleming H. Revell.

Dodd, Charles Harold
1961   *The Parables of the Kingdom.* Rev. ed. New York: Charles Scribner's Sons (original ed. 1936).

1980   *The Apostolic Preaching and Its Developments.* Grand Rapids, Mich.: Baker Book House (original ed. London: Hodder & Stoughton, 1936).

Doeve, J. W.
1954   *Jewish Hermeneutics in the Synoptic Gospels and Acts.* Assen, Netherlands: Van Gorcum.

Donahue, John R.
1976   "Temple, Trial and Royal Christology (Mark 14:53-65)." In *The Passion in Mark: Studies in Mark 14—16,* pp. 61-79. Edited by Werner H. Kelber. Philadelphia: Fortress.

Down, M. J.
1978   "The Matthaean Birth Narratives: Matthew 1:18—2:23." *Expository Times* 90:51-52.

1984   "The Sayings of Jesus About Marriage and Divorce." *Expository Times* 95:332-34.

Downing, F. Gerald
1982   "The Resurrection of the Dead: Jesus and Philo." *Journal for the Study of the New Testament* 15:42-50.

1988   "Compositional Conventions and the Synoptic Problem." *Journal of Biblical Literature* 107:69-85.

Draper, Jonathan
1984   "The Jesus Tradition in the Didache." In *The Jesus Tradition Outside the Gospels,* pp. 269-87. Vol. 5 of *Gospel Perspectives.* Edited by David Wenham. 6 vols. Sheffield, U.K.: JSOT Press.

Drury, John
1976   *Tradition and Design in Luke's Gospel: A Study in Early Christian Historiography.* London: Darton, Longman & Todd.

Dunn, James D. G.
1970   "Spirit and Kingdom." *The Expository Times* 82:36-40.

Du Plessis, I. J.
1967   "The Ethics of Marriage According to Matt. 5:27-32." *Neo-testamentica* 1:16-27.

Dupont, Florence
1992   *Daily Life in Ancient Rome.* Translated by Christopher Woodall. Oxford: Basil Blackwell.

Easton, Burton Scott
1940   "Divorce in the New Testament." *Anglican Theological Review* 22:78-87.

Edersheim, Alfred
1993   *The Life and Times of Jesus the Messiah.* Reprint ed. Peabody, Mass.: Hendrickson.

Edgar, S. L.
1958   "The New Testament and Rabbinic Messianic Interpretation." *New Testament Studies* 5:47-54.

Efird, James M.
1985   *Marriage and Divorce: What the Bible Says.* Nashville: Abingdon.

Eickelman, Dale F.
1989   *The Middle East: An Anthropological Approach.* 2nd ed. Englewood Cliffs, N.J.: Prentice-Hall.

Ellington, J.
1979   "The Translation of *humnéo*, 'Sing a Hymn,' in Mark 14.26 and Matthew 26.30." *Bible Translator* 30:445-46.

Ellis, E. Earle
1977   "How the New Testament Uses the Old." In *New Testament Interpretation: Essays on Principles and Methods,* pp. 199-219. Edited by I. Howard Marshall. Grand Rapids, Mich.: Eerdmans.

Ellis, Peter F.
1974   *Matthew: His Mind and His Message.* Collegeville, Minn.: Liturgical Press.

Eppstein, Victor
1964   "The Historicity of the Gospel Account of the Cleansing of the Temple." *Zeitschrift für die Neutestamentliche Wissenschaft* 55:42-58.

Evans, Craig A.
1981   "A Note on the Function of Isaiah, VI." *Revista Biblica* 88:234-35.

1995   "What Did Jesus Do?" In *Jesus Under Fire,* pp. 101-15. Edited by Michael J. Wilkins and J. P. Moreland. Grand Rapids, Mich.: Zondervan.

Everson, A. Joseph
1974   "The Days of Yahweh." *Journal of Biblical Literature* 93:329-37.

Falk, Z. W.
1974   "Binding and Loosing." *Journal of Jewish Studies* 25:92-100.

Fee, Gordon D.
1987   *The First Epistle to the Corinthians.* New International Com-

mentary on the New Testament. Grand Rapids, Mich.: Eerd-mans.

1994   *God's Empowering Presence: The Holy Spirit in the Letters of Paul.* Peabody, Mass.: Hendrickson.

Felder, Cain Hope

1989   *Troubling Biblical Waters: Race, Class and Family.* Bishop Henry McNeal Turner Studies in North American Black Religion 3. Maryknoll, N.Y.: Orbis.

Fensham, F. Charles

1965   "Judas' Hand in the Bowl and Qumran." *Revue de Qumran* 5:259-61.

Fenton, J. C.

1977   *Saint Matthew.* Philadelphia: Westminster Press.

Ferguson, Everett

1987   *Backgrounds of Early Christianity.* Grand Rapids, Mich.: Eerdmans.

Feuillet, André

1980a   "Le caractère universel du jugement et la charité sans fron-tières en Mt 25, 31-46." *Nouvelle Revue Théologique* 102:179-96.

1980b   "La signification fondamentale de Marc XIII: Recherches sur l'eschatologie des Synoptiques." *Revue Thomiste* 80:181-215.

Filson, Floyd V.

1960   *A Commentary on the Gospel According to St. Matthew.* New York: Harper & Row.

Finegan, Jack

1969   *The Archeology of the New Testament.* Princeton, N.J.: Prince-ton University Press.

Finkelstein, Louis

1962   *The Pharisees: The Sociological Background of Their Faith.* 3rd ed. 2 vols. Philadelphia: Jewish Publication Society of America.

Finley, M. I.

1973   *The Ancient Economy.* Sather Classical Lectures 43. Berkeley: University of California Press.

Finney, Charles G.

1869   *Lectures on Revivals of Religion.* New York: Fleming H. Revell.

1965   *Prevailing Prayer: Sermons on Prayer.* Grand Rapids, Mich.: Kregel.

Fitzmyer, Joseph A.

1974   *Essays on the Semitic Background of the New Testament.* 2nd ed. Studies in Biblical Theology 5. Missoula, Mont.: Scholars Press.

Fleming, T. V.

1963   "Christ and Divorce." *Theological Studies* 24:106-20.

Flowers, Harold J.
1953   "En pneumati hagió kai puri." *Expository Times* 64:155-56.

Flusser, David
1988   *Judaism and the Origins of Christianity.* Jerusalem: Mag-
              nes/Hebrew University Press.

Ford, Desmond
1979   *The Abomination of Desolation in Biblical Eschatology.* Wash-
              ington, D.C.: University Press of America.

Fortna, Robert T.
1990   " 'You Have Made Them Equal to Us!' (Mt 20:1-16)." *Journal
              of Theology for Southern Africa* 72:66-72.

France, R. T.
1976   "The Authenticity of the Sayings of Jesus." In *History, Criti-
              cism and Faith,* pp. 101-43. Edited by Colin Brown. Downers
              Grove, Ill.: InterVarsity Press.

1977   "Exegesis in Practice: Two Examples." In *New Testament Inter-
              pretation: Essays on Principles and Methods,* pp. 252-81.
              Edited by I. Howard Marshall. Grand Rapids, Mich.: Eerdmans.

1979   "Herod and the Children of Bethlehem." *Novum Testamentum*
              21:98-120.

1981   "Scripture, Tradition and History in the Infancy Narratives of
              Matthew." In *Studies of History and Tradition in the Four Gos-
pels II,   pels II,* pp. 239-66. Vol. 2 of *Gospel Perspectives.* Edited by R. T.
France   France and David Wenham. 6 vols. Sheffield, U.K.: JSOT Press.

1985   *Matthew.* Tyndale New Testament Commentaries. Grand Rap-
              ids, Mich.: Eerdmans.

1986   *The Evidence for Jesus.* Downers Grove, Ill.: InterVarsity Press.

Freyne, Sean
1988   *Galilee, Jesus and the Gospels: Literary Approaches and
              Historical Investigations.* Philadelphia: Fortress.

Frost, Henry W.
1924   *Matthew Twenty-four and the Revelation.* New York: Oxford
              University Press.

Fuller, G. C.
1966   "The Olivet Discourse: An Apocalyptic Timetable." *Westmin-
              ster Theological Journal* 28:157-63.

Fuller, Reginald H.
1971   *The Formation of the Resurrection Narratives.* New York:
              Macmillan.

Gallup, George H., Jr.,
and Timothy Jones
1992   "Uncovering America's Hidden Saints." *Christianity Today,*

August 17, pp. 26-29.

Gardner, Jane F.

1986   *Women in Roman Law and Society.* Bloomington: Indiana University Press.

Gärtner, Bertril

1965   *The Temple and the Community in Qumran and the New Testament: A Comparative Study in the Temple Symbolism of the Qumran Texts and the New Testament.* Cambridge: Cambridge University Press.

Garvey, Marcus

1923   *The Philosophy and Opinions of Marcus Garvey.* Vol. 1. New York: Universal. (Reprint edited by Amy Jacques-Garvey; New York: Atheneum, 1993.)

Gaster, Theodor H.

1976   *The Dead Sea Scriptures.* Garden City, N.Y.: Doubleday.

Gempf, Conrad

1993   "Public Speaking and Published Accounts." In *The Book of Acts in Its Ancient Literary Setting,* pp. 259-303. Edited by Bruce W. Winter and Andrew D. Clarke. Vol. 1 of *The Book of Acts in Its First-Century Setting.* Edited by Bruce W. Winter. 6 vols. Grand Rapids, Mich.: Eerdmans; Carlisle, U.K.: Paternoster.

Gerhardsson, Birger

1961   *Memory and Manuscript: Oral Tradition and Written Transmission in Rabbinic Judaism and Early Christianity.* Acta Seminarii Neotestamentici Upsaliensis 22. Uppsala, Sweden: Gleerup.

Gibbard, S. M.

1956   "The Christian Mystery." In *Studies in Ephesians,* pp. 97-120. Edited by F. L. Cross. London: A. R. Mowbray.

Glasson, T. Francis

1963   *The Second Advent: The Origin of the New Testament Doctrine.* 3rd rev. ed. London: Epworth.

Goldingay, John

1977   "Expounding the New Testament." In *New Testament Interpretation: Essays on Principles and Methods,* pp. 351-65. Edited by I. Howard Marshall. Grand Rapids, Mich.: Eerdmans.

Goodman, Martin

1983   *State and Society in Roman Galilee, A.D. 132-212.* Oxford Centre for Postgraduate Hebrew Studies. Totowa, N.J.: Rowman & Allanheld.

Goppelt, Leonhard

1964   *Jesus, Paul and Judaism.* Translated by Edward Schroeder. New York: Thomas Nelson & Sons.

1981   *Theology of the New Testament.* Vol. 1. Translated by John E. Alsup. Edited by Jürgen Roloff. 2 vols. Grand Rapids, Mich.: Eerdmans.

1982   *Theology of the New Testament*. Vol. 2. Translated by John E.
               Alsup. Edited by Jürgen Roloff. 2 vols. Grand Rapids, Mich.:
               Eerdmans.

Gordon, Murray
1989   *Slavery in the Arab World*. New York: New Amsterdam Books
               (originally published as *L'esclavage dans le monde arabe*
               [Paris: Editions Robert Laffont, 1987]).

Goulder, M. D.
1974   *Midrash and Lection in Matthew*. Speaker's Lectures in Bibli-
               cal Studies, 1969-71. London: S.P.C.K.

Graham, H. R.
1986   "A Passion Prediction for Mark's Community: Mark 13:9-13."
               Biblical Theology Bulletin 16:18-22.

Grant, Frederick C.
1953   *Hellenistic Religions: The Age of Syncretism*. Library of Liberal
               Arts. Indianapolis: Bobbs-Merrill/Liberal Arts.

1959   *Ancient Judaism and the New Testament*. New York: Macmil-
               lan.

Grant, Michael
1992   *A Social History of Greece and Rome*. New York: Charles Scrib-
               ner's Sons; Oxford: Maxwell Macmillan International.

Grant, Robert M.
1986   *Gods and the One God*. Library of Early Christianity 1. Phila-
               delphia: Westminster Press.

Grassi, Joseph A.
1965   *A World to Win: The Missionary Methods of Paul the Apostle*.
               Maryknoll, N.Y.: Orbis.

Grelot, Pierre
1979   "La quatrième demande du 'Pater' et son arrière-plan sémi-
               tique." *New Testament Studies* 25:299-314.

Grenz, Stanley J.
1992   *The Millennial Maze: Sorting Out Evangelical Options*. Down-
               ers Grove, Ill.: InterVarsity Press.

Groothuis, Douglas
1990   *Revealing the New Age Jesus: Challenges to Orthodox Views of
               Christ*. Downers Grove, Ill.: InterVarsity Press.

Gross, G.
1964   "Die 'geringsten Brüder' Jesu in Mt 25,40 in Auseinan-
               dersetzung mit der neueren Ezegese." *Bibel und Leben*
               5:172-80.

Grudem, Wayne A.
1982   *The Gift of Prophecy in 1 Corinthians*. Lanham, Md.: Univer-
               sity Press of America.

Guelich, Robert A.
1982   *The Sermon on the Mount: A Foundation for Understanding*.
               Waco, Tex.: Word.

Gundry, Robert H.
1973   *The Church and the Tribulation*. Grand Rapids, Mich.: Zondervan.

1975   *The Use of the Old Testament in St. Matthew's Gospel: With Spe-
                cial Reference to the Messianic Hope.* Supplements to *Novum
                Testamentum* 18. Leiden, Netherlands: E. J. Brill.

1982   *Matthew: A Commentary on His Literary and Theological Art.*
                Grand Rapids, Mich.: Eerdmans.

1987   "The Hellenization of Dominical Tradition and Christianiza-
                tion of Jewish Tradition in the Eschatology of 1-2 Thessaloni-
                ans." *New Testament Studies* 33:161-78.

Guy, Harold A.
1959   "The Golden Rule." *Expository Times* 70:184.

Hagner, Donald A.
1993   *Matthew 1—13.* Word Biblical Commentary 33A. Dallas: Word.

Hamerton-Kelly, R. G.
1973   *Pre-existence, Wisdom and the Son: A Study of the Idea of Pre-
                existence in the New Testament.* Cambridge: Cambridge Uni-
                versity Press.

Hansberry,
William Leo
1981   *Pillars in Ethiopian History.* William Leo Hansberry African
                History Notebook 1. Edited by Joseph E. Harris. Washington,
                D.C.: Howard University Press.

Hare, Douglas R. A.
1967   *The Theme of Jewish Persecution of Christians in the Gospel Ac-
                cording to St. Matthew.* Cambridge: Cambridge University Press.

1979   "The Rejection of the Jews in the Synoptic Gospels and Acts."
                In *Anti-Semitism and the Foundations of Christianity,* pp. 27-
                47. Edited by Alan T. Davies. New York: Paulist.

Harrell, Pat Edwin
1967   *Divorce and Remarriage in the Early Church: A History of Di-
                vorce and Remarriage in the Ante-Nicene Church.* Austin,
                Tex.: R. B. Sweet.

Harrington, Daniel J.
1982   *The Gospel According to Matthew.* Collegeville, Minn.: Liturgi-
                cal Press.

Harris, Murray J.
1986   " 'The Dead Are Restored to Life': Miracles of Revivification in
                the Gospels." In *The Miracles of Jesus,* pp. 295-326. Vol. 6 of
                Gospel Perspectives. Edited by David Wenham and Craig
                Blomberg. 6 vols. Sheffield, U.K.: JSOT Press.

Harvey, A. E.
1982   *Jesus and the Constraints of History.* Philadelphia: Westminster
                Press.

Hata, Gohei
1975   "Is the Greek Version of Josephus' *Jewish War* a Translation

or a Rewriting of the First Version?" *Jewish Quarterly Review* 66:89-108.

Hauck, Friedrich,
and Siegfried Schulz
1968   "πόρνη κτλ." In *Theological Dictionary of the New Testament*, 6:579-95. Edited by Gerhard Kittel and Gerhard Friedrich. 10 vols. Grand Rapids, Mich.: Eerdmans.

Hemer, Colin J.
1973   "The Edfu *Ostraka* and the Jewish Tax." *Palestine Exploration Quarterly* 105:6-12.

1986   *The Letters to the Seven Churches of Asia in Their Local Setting.* Journal for the Study of the New Testament Supplement 11. Sheffield, U.K.: Department of Biblical Studies, University of Sheffield.

Hengel, Martin
1974   *Property and Riches in the Early Church: Aspects of Social History of Early Christianity.* Philadelphia: Fortress.

1977   *Crucifixion in the Ancient World and the Folly of the Message of the Cross.* Philadelphia: Fortress.

1985   *Studies in the Gospel of Mark.* Translated by John Bowden. Philadelphia: Fortress.

Hepper, F. N., et al.
1982   "Plants." In *New Bible Dictionary*, pp. 945-48. 2nd ed. Edited by J. D. Douglas and Norman Hillyer. Leicester, U.K.: Inter-Varsity Press.

Herford, R. Travers
1966   *Christianity in Talmud and Midrash.* Library of Philosophical and Religious Thought. Clifton, N.J.: Reference Book Publishers (reprint of 1903 ed.).

Hester, James D.
1968   *Paul's Concept of Inheritance: A Contribution to the Understanding of Heilsgeschichte.* Scottish Journal of Theology Occasional Papers 14. Edinburgh: Oliver & Boyd.

Heth, William A., and
Gordon J. Wenham
1984   *Jesus and Divorce: The Problem with the Evangelical Consensus.* Nashville: Thomas Nelson.

Hiers, Richard H.
1985   " 'Binding' and 'Loosing': The Matthean Authorizations." *Journal of Biblical Literature* 104:233-50.

Hill, David
1972   *The Gospel of Matthew.* New Century Bible. Grand Rapids, Mich.: Eerdmans; London: Marshall, Morgan & Scott.

1979   *New Testament Prophecy.* New Foundations Theological Library. Atlanta: John Knox.

1980   "Son and Servant: An Essay on Matthean Christology." *Journal for the Study of the New Testament* 6:2-16.

Hock, Ronald F.

1988   "The Greek Novel." In *Greco-Roman Literature and the New Testament: Selected Forms and Genres*, pp. 127-46. Edited by David E. Aune. Society of Biblical Literature Sources for Biblical Study 21. Atlanta: Scholars Press.

Hoehner, Harold W.

1972   *Herod Antipas*. Society for New Testament Studies Monograph 17. Cambridge: Cambridge University Press.

Hooker, Morna D.

1959   *Jesus and the Servant*. London: S.P.C.K.

1983   *The Message of Mark*. London: Epworth.

Horsley, Richard A.

1985   " 'Like One of the Prophets of Old': Two Types of Popular Prophets at the Time of Jesus." *Catholic Biblical Quarterly* 47:435-63.

1986   "Ethics and Exegesis: 'Love Your Enemies' and the Doctrine of Non-violence." *Journal of the American Academy of Religion* 54:3-31.

Horsley, Richard A., and John S. Hanson

1985   *Bandits, Prophets and Messiahs: Popular Movements in the Time of Jesus*. Minneapolis: Seabury/Winston.

Hunter, Archibald M.

1944   *The Message of the New Testament*. Philadelphia: Westminster Press.

Hurtado, Larry W.

1983   *Mark*. Good News Commentary. San Francisco: Harper & Row.

Jennings, Theodore W., Jr.

1990   *Good News to the Poor: John Wesley's Evangelical Economics*. Nashville: Abingdon.

Jeremias, Joachim

1958   *Jesus' Promise to the Nations*. Translated by S. H. Hooke. Franz Delitzsch Lectures for 1953. Studies in Biblical Theology 24. London: SCM Press.

1963   *The Sermon on the Mount*. Translated by Norman Perrin. Philadelphia: Fortress.

1964   *The Prayers of Jesus*. Philadelphia: Fortress.

1966a   *The Eucharistic Words of Jesus*. Philadelphia: Fortress.

1966b	"Palästinakundliches zum Gleichnis vom Säemann (Mark. IV.3-8 Par.)." *New Testament Studies* 13:48-53.
1968	"πύλη, πυλών." In *Theological Dictionary of the New Testament,* 6:921-28. Edited by Gerhard Kittel and Gerhard Friedrich. 10 vols. Grand Rapids, Mich.: Eerdmans.
1969	*Jerusalem in the Time of Jesus.* Philadelphia: Fortress; London: SCM Press.
1971	*New Testament Theology.* New York: Charles Scribner's Sons.
1972	*The Parables of Jesus.* 2nd rev. ed. New York: Charles Scribner's Sons.

Jochim, Christian

1986	*Chinese Religions: A Cultural Perspective.* Prentice-Hall Series in World Religions. Englewood Cliffs, N.J.: Prentice-Hall.

Johnson, Luke
Timothy

1981	*Sharing Possessions: Mandate and Symbol of Faith.* Philadelphia: Fortress.
1996	*The Real Jesus: The Misguided Quest for the Historical Jesus and the Truth of the Traditional Gospels.* San Francisco: HarperSanFrancisco.

Johnson, M. D.

1988	*The Purpose of the Biblical Genealogies: With Special Reference to the Setting of the Genealogies of Jesus.* 2nd ed. Society of New Testament Studies Monograph 8. Cambridge: Cambridge University Press.

Johnston, Robert
Morris

1977	"Parabolic Interpretations Attributed to Tannaim." Ph.D. dissertation, Hartford Seminary Foundation. (Ann Arbor, Mich.: University Microfilms International, 1978.)
1982	" 'The Least of the Commandments': Deuteronomy 22:6-7 in Rabbinic Judaism and Early Christianity." *Andrews University Seminary Studies* 20:205-15.

Johnstone, Patrick

1993	*Operation World: The Day-by-Day Guide to Praying for the World.* 5th ed. Grand Rapids, Mich.: Zondervan.

Jones, A. M. H.

1970	*The Empire.* Vol. 2 of *A History of Rome Through the Fifth Century.* New York: Walker.

Jones, James L.

1971	"The Roman Army." In *The Catacombs and the Colosseum: The Roman Empire as the Setting of Primitive Christianity,* pp. 187-217. Edited by Stephen Benko and John J. O'Rourke. Valley Forge, Penn.: Judson.

Kaplan, Bert, and
Dale Johnson
1964   "The Social Meaning of Navaho Psychopathology and Psycho-
               therapy." In *Magic, Faith and Healing: Studies in Primitive
               Psychotherapy Today*, pp. 203-29. Edited by Ari Kiev. New
               York: Free Press.

Katterjohn, Arthur D.,
with Mark Fackler
1976   *The Tribulation People*. Carol Stream, Ill.: Creation House.

Kee, Howard Clark
1977   *Community of the New Age: Studies in Mark's Gospel*. Philadel-
               phia: Westminster Press.

1980   *Christian Origins in Sociological Perspective: Methods and Re-
               sources*. Philadelphia: Westminster Press.

1983   *Miracle in the Early Christian World: A Study in Sociohistori-
               cal Method*. New Haven, Conn.: Yale University Press.

Keener, Craig S.
1987   "Matthew 5:22 and the Heavenly Court." *Expository Times*
               99:46.

1991a   *. . . And Marries Another: Divorce and Remarriage in the Teach-
               ing of the New Testament*. Peabody, Mass.: Hendrickson.

1991b   "The Function of Johannine Pneumatology in the Context of
               Late First-Century Judaism." Ph.D. dissertation, Duke Univer-
               sity Graduate School. (Ann Arbor, Mich.: University Microfilms
               International.)

1991c   "Nonviolence in the Face of Oppression: A Perspective on the
               Letter of James." *ESA [Evangelicals for Social Action] Advocate*
               12 (April): 14-15.

1992   *Paul, Women and Wives: Marriage and Women's Ministry in
               the Letters of Paul*. Peabody, Mass.: Hendrickson.

1993   *The IVP Bible Background Commentary: New Testament*.
               Downers Grove, Ill.: InterVarsity Press.

1995   "A Critique of Burton Mack's *Lost Gospel.*" *Paper presented at
               a meeting of the Evangelical Theological Society, Philadelphia,
               November 18. (Available from Theological Research Exchange
               Network, P.O. Box 30183, Portland, OR 97294-3183.)*

1996   *Three Crucial Questions About the Holy Spirit*. Grand Rapids,
               Mich.: Baker Book House.

1997   *The Spirit in the Gospels and Acts*. Peabody, Mass.: Hendrickson.

Kennedy, George A.
1980   *Classical Rhetoric and Its Christian and Secular Tradition
               from Ancient to Modern Times*. Chapel Hill: University of
               North Carolina Press.

1984   *New Testament Interpretation Through Rhetorical Criticism*.
               Chapel Hill: University of North Carolina Press.
Kingsbury, Jack Dean
1975   *Matthew: Structure, Christology, Kingdom*. Philadelphia: Fortress.

1983   *The Christology of Mark's Gospel*. Philadelphia: Fortress.

1986   *Matthew as Story*. Philadelphia: Fortress.

Klausner, Joseph
1979   *Jesus: His Life, Times and Teaching*. Translated by Herbert
               Danby. New York: Menorah (original ed. n.p.: Macmillan, 1925).
Knackstedt, J.
1964   "Die beiden Brotvermekrungen im Evangelium." *New Testa-
               ment Studies* 10:309-35.
Koenig, John
1985   *New Testament Hospitality: Partnership with Strangers as
               Promise and Mission*. Overtures to Biblical Theology 17.
               Philadelphia: Fortress.
Koester, Helmut
1990   *Ancient Christian Gospels: Their History and Development*.
               Philadelphia: Trinity Press International; London: SCM Press.

1994   "Written Gospels or Oral Tradition?" *Journal of Biblical Litera-
               ture* 113:293-97.
Kosmala, Hans
1963   "The Time of the Cock-Crow." *Annual of the Swedish Theo-
               logical Institute* 2:118-20.
Kraeling, Carl H.
1951   *John the Baptist*. New York: Charles Scribner's Sons.

Kümmel, Werner
   George
1957   *Promise and Fulfilment: The Eschatological Message of Jesus*.
               Translated by Dorothea M. Barton. Studies in Biblical Theol-
               ogy 23. Naperville, Ill.: Alec R. Allenson.
Kysar, Myrna, and
   Robert Kysar
1978   *The Asundered: Biblical Teachings on Divorce and Remar-
               riage*. Atlanta: John Knox Press.
Ladd, George Eldon
1956   *The Blessed Hope*. Grand Rapids, Mich.: Eerdmans.

1963	"The Life-Setting of the Parables of the Kingdom." *Journal of Bible and Religion* 31:193-99.
1967	*The New Testament and Criticism*. Grand Rapids, Mich.: Eerdmans.
1974a	"The Parable of the Sheep and the Goats in Recent Interpretation." In *New Dimensions in New Testament Study*, pp. 191-99. Edited by Richard N. Longenecker and Merrill C. Tenney. Grand Rapids, Mich.: Zondervan.
1974b	*A Theology of the New Testament*. Grand Rapids, Mich.: Eerdmans.
1977	"The Historic Premillennial View." In *The Meaning of the Millennium: Four Views*, pp. 17-40. Edited by Robert G. Clouse. Downers Grove, Ill.: InterVarsity Press.
1978a	*The Gospel of the Kingdom*. Grand Rapids, Mich.: Eerdmans (original ed. Exeter, U.K.: Paternoster, 1959).
1978b	*The Last Things*. Grand Rapids, Mich.: Eerdmans.

Lake, Kirsopp, and
Henry J. Cadbury

1979	*English Translation and Commentary*. Vol. 4 of *The Beginnings of Christianity*. Edited by F. J. Foakes Jackson and Kirsopp Lake. Reprint ed. 5 vols. Grand Rapids, Mich.: Baker Book House.

Lampe, G. W. H.

1951	*The Seal of the Spirit*. New York: Longmans, Green.

Lane, William L.

1974	*The Gospel According to Mark*. New International Commentary on the New Testament. Grand Rapids, Mich.: Eerdmans.

Lapide, Pinchas E.

1984	*Hebrew in the Church: The Foundations of Jewish-Christian Dialogue*. Translated by Erroll F. Rhodes. Grand Rapids, Mich.: Eerdmans.

Leeming, Bernard,
and R. A. Dawson

1956	"Except It Be for Fornication?" *Scripture* 8:75-82.

Lefkowitz, Mary R.,
and Maureen B. Fant

1982	*Women's Life in Greece and Rome*. Baltimore, Md.: Johns Hopkins University Press; London: Gerald Duckworth.

Lehmann, Manfred R.

1960	"Gen 2.24 as the Basis for Divorce in Halakhah and New Testament." *Zeitschrift für die Neutestamentliche Wissenschaft* 72:263-67.

Lewis, Bernard
1990   *Race and Slavery in the Middle East: An Historical Enquiry.*
              New York: Oxford University Press.
Lewis, Naphtali
1983   *Life in Egypt Under Roman Rule.* Oxford: Clarendon.

Liefeld, Walter L.
1967   "The Wandering Preacher as a Social Figure in the Roman
              Empire." Ph.D. dissertation, Columbia University. (Ann Arbor:
              University Microfilms International, 1976.)
Lindars, Barnabas
1961   *New Testament Apologetic.* London: SCM Press.

Longenecker, Richard N.
1975   *Biblical Exegesis in the Apostolic Period.* Grand Rapids, Mich.:
              Eerdmans.

1981   *The Christology of Early Jewish Christianity.* Grand Rapids,
              Mich.: Baker Book House (original ed. London: SCM Press,
              1970).
Luck, William F.
1987   *Divorce and Remarriage: Recovering the Biblical View.* San
              Francisco: Harper & Row.
Luz, Ulrich
1989   *Matthew 1—7: A Commentary.* Translated by Wilhelm C.
              Linss. Minneapolis: Fortress.
Lyons, George
1985   *Pauline Autobiography: Toward a New Understanding.* Society
              of Biblical Literature Dissertation 73. Atlanta: Scholars Press.
Mack, Burton L.
1988   *A Myth of Innocence: Mark and Christian Origins.* Philadel-
              phia: Fortress.

1993   *The Lost Gospel: The Book of Q and Christian Origins.* San
              Francisco: HarperSanFrancisco.
MacMullen, Ramsay
1966   *Enemies of the Roman Order: Treason, Unrest and Alienation
              in the Empire.* Cambridge, Mass.: Harvard University Press.

1974   *Roman Social Relations: 50 B.C. to A.D. 284.* New Haven,
              Conn.: Yale University Press.
Maddox, Robert
1982   *The Purpose of Luke-Acts.* Edinburgh: T & T Clark.

Malina, Bruce J.
1981   *The New Testament World: Insights from Cultural Anthropol-
              ogy.* Atlanta: John Knox Press.

1993   *Windows on the World of Jesus: Time Travel to Ancient Judea.*

Louisville, Ky.: Westminster/John Knox.

Malina, Bruce J., and
Richard L. Rohrbaugh
1992   *Social Science Commentary on the Synoptic Gospels.* Minneapolis: Augsburg Fortress.

Manson, T. W.
1963   *On Paul and John: Some Selected Theological Themes.* Studies in Biblical Theology 38. Edited by Matthew Black. London: SCM Press.

1979   *The Sayings of Jesus.* Grand Rapids, Mich.: Eerdmans (original ed. London: SCM Press, 1957).

Mantey, Julius R.
1973   "Evidence That the Perfect Tense in John 20:23, and Matthew 16:19 Is Mistranslated." *Journal of the Evangelical Theological Society* 16:129-38.

1981   "Distorted Translations in John 20:23, Matthew 16:18-19 and 18:18." *Review and Expositor* 78:409-16.

Marmorstein, A.
1968   *The Old Rabbinic Doctrine of God: The Names and Attributes of God.* New York: KTAV (original ed. 1927).

Marshall, I. Howard
1969   "Son of God or Servant of Yahweh? A Reconsideration of Mark i.11." *New Testament Studies* 15:326-36.

1974   *Kept by the Power of God: A Study in Perseverance and Falling Away.* Minneapolis: Bethany Fellowship (original ed. London: Epworth, 1969).

1978   *Commentary on Luke.* New International Greek Testament Commentary. Grand Rapids, Mich.: Eerdmans.

1983   *1 and 2 Thessalonians.* New Century Bible. Grand Rapids, Mich.: Eerdmans.

1990   *The Origins of New Testament Christology.* 2nd ed. Downers Grove, Ill.: InterVarsity Press.

Martin, Ralph P.
1982   *The Worship of God.* Grand Rapids, Mich.: Eerdmans.

Mason, Steven
1992   *Josephus and the New Testament.* Peabody, Mass.: Hendrickson.

Matthey, J.
1980   "The Great Commission According to Matthew." *International Review of Mission* 69:161-73.

Mattill, Andrew J., Jr.
1979   *Luke and the Last Things: A Perspective for the Understanding*

of Lukan Thought. Dillsboro, N.C.: Western North Carolina Press.

Mauser, Ulrich
1963   *Christ in the Wilderness*. Studies in Biblical Theology 39. London: SCM Press.

Mbiti, John S.
1970   *African Religions and Philosophies*. Garden City, N.Y.: Doubleday.

McCane, Byron R.
1990   " 'Let the Dead Bury Their Own Dead': Secondary Burial and Matt 8:21-22." *Harvard Theological Review* 83:31-43.

McGavran, D. A., and W. C. Arn
1977   *Ten Steps for Church Growth*. San Francisco: Harper & Row.

McNamara, Martin
1972   *Targum and Testament*. Grand Rapids, Mich.: Eerdmans.

1983   *Palestinian Judaism and the New Testament*. Good News Studies 4. Wilmington, Del.: Michael Glazier.

Meeks, Wayne A.
1967   *The Prophet-King: Moses Traditions and the Johannine Christology*. Supplements to *Novum Testamentum* 14. Leiden, Netherlands: E. J. Brill.

1986   *The Moral World of the First Christians*. Library of Early Christianity 6. Philadelphia: Westminster Press.

Meier, John P.
1977   "Nations or Gentiles in Matthew 28:19?" *Catholic Biblical Quarterly* 39:94-102.

1979   *The Vision of Matthew: Christ, Church and Morality in the First Gospel*. Theological Inquiries. New York: Paulist.

1980   *Matthew*. New Testament Message 3. Wilmington, Del.: Michael Glazier.

1991   *The Roots of the Problem and the Person*. Vol. 1 of *A Marginal Jew: Rethinking the Historical Jesus*. Anchor Bible Reference Library. New York: Doubleday.

1992   "John the Baptist in Josephus: Philology and Exegesis." *Journal of Biblical Literature* 111:225-37.

1994   *Mentor, Message and Miracles*. Vol. 2 of *A Marginal Jew: Rethinking the Historical Jesus*. Anchor Bible Reference Library. New York: Doubleday.

Metzger, Bruce M.
1968   *The Text of the New Testament*. New York: Oxford University Press.

Meyers, Eric M., and
James F. Strange
    1981   *Archaeology, the Rabbis and Early Christianity.* Nashville: Abingdon.

Michaels, J. Ramsey
    1965   "Apostolic Hardships and Righteous Gentiles." *Journal of Biblical Literature* 84:27-38.

    1976   "Christian Prophecy and Matthew 23:8-12: A Test Exegesis." In *SBL Seminar Papers 1976,* pp. 305-10. Missoula, Mont.: Scholars Press.

Milligan, George
    1908   *St Paul's Epistles to the Thessalonians: The Greek Text with Introduction and Notes.* London: Macmillan.

Minear, Paul S.
    1950   *The Kingdom and the Power: An Exposition of the New Testament Gospel.* Philadelphia: Westminster Press.

    1954   *Christian Hope and the Second Coming.* Philadelphia: Westminster Press.

Moffatt, James D.
    1938   *The First Epistle of Paul to the Corinthians.* Moffatt New Testament Commentary. London: Hodder & Stoughton.

Moiser, Jeremy
    1985   "Moses and Elijah." *Expository Times* 96:216-17.

Momigliano, Arnaldo
    1977   *Essays in Ancient and Modern Historiography.* Middletown, Conn.: Wesleyan University Press; Oxford: Basil Blackwell.

Montefiore, C. G.
    1968   *The Synoptic Gospels.* 2 vols. Library of Biblical Studies. New York: KTAV (original ed. 1927).

Montefiore, C. G.,
and Herbert Loewe
    1974   *A Rabbinic Anthology.* New York: Schocken (original ed. London: Macmillan, 1938).

Moore, George Foot
    1971   *Judaism in the First Centuries of the Christian Era.* 2 vols. New York: Schocken (original ed. Cambridge, Mass.: Harvard University Press, 1927).

Morosco, Robert E.
    1979   "Redaction Criticism and the Evangelical: Matthew 10, a Test Case." *Journal of the Evangelical Theological Society* 22:323-31.

Morris, Leon
    1959   *The First and Second Epistles to the Thessalonians.* New International Commentary on the New Testament. Grand Rapids, Mich.: Eerdmans.

    1965   *The Apostolic Preaching of the Cross.* 3rd ed. Grand Rapids,

Mich.: Eerdmans.

1972   *Apocalyptic.* Grand Rapids, Mich.: Eerdmans.

Moulder, James
1978   "Who Are My Enemies? An Exploration of the Semantic Back-
            ground of Christ's Command." *Journal of Theology for South-
            ern Africa* 25:41-49.
Moule, C. F. D.
1965   *The Gospel According to Mark.* Cambridge: Cambridge
            University Press.
Murray, John
1953   *Divorce.* Philadelphia: Committee on Christian Education,
            Orthodox Presbyterian Church.
National Conference
of Catholic Bishops
1986   *Economic Justice for All: Pastoral Letter on Catholic Social
            Teaching and the U.S. Economy.* Washington, D.C.: National
            Conference of Catholic Bishops.
Neil, William
1976   "Five Hard Sayings of Jesus." In *Biblical Studies: Essays in Honor
            of William Barclay,* pp. 157-71. Philadelphia: Westminster Press.
Neusner, Jacob
1976   "First Cleanse the Inside." *New Testament Studies* 22:486-95.

Newman, Gene, and
Joni Eareckson Tada
1987   *All God's Children: Ministry to the Disabled.* Grand Rapids,
            Mich.: Zondervan.
Nielsen, Helge Kjaer
1990   "Er den 'dovne' tjener doven? Om oversaettelsen af ὀκνηρός
            i Matth 25, 26." *Dansk Teologisk Tidsskrift* 53:106-15; *New
            Testament Abstracts* 35:27.
Nineham, D. E.
1977   *Saint Mark.* Pelican New Testament Commentaries. Philadel-
            phia: Westminster Press; London: SCM Press.
Nock, Arthur Darby
1933   *Conversion: The Old and the New in Religion from Alexander
            the Great to Augustine of Hippo.* Oxford: Clarendon.

1964   *Early Gentile Christianity and Its Hellenistic Background.*
            New York: Harper & Row.
Noll, Mark A.
1992   *A History of Christianity in the United States and Canada.*
            Grand Rapids, Mich.: Eerdmans.
Odeberg, Hugo
1964   *Pharisaism and Christianity.* Translated by J. M. Moe. St.
            Louis: Concordia (original Swedish ed. 1943).

Oesterley, William
Oscar Emil
1925   *The Jewish Background of the Christian Liturgy*. Oxford:
                Clarendon.
O'Neal, W. J.
1978   "Delation in the Early Empire." *Classical Bulletin* 55:24-28.

O'Rourke, John J.
1971   "Roman Law and the Early Church." In *The Catacombs and
                the Colosseum: The Roman Empire as the Setting of Primitive
                Christianity*, pp. 165-86. Edited by Stephen Benko and John J.
                O'Rourke. Valley Forge, Penn.: Judson.
Overman, John
Andrew
1990   "Deciphering the Origins of Christianity." Review of *A Myth of
                Innocence: Mark and Christian Origins*, by Burton L. Mack.
                Interpretation 44:193-95.
Palmer, Darryl W.
1993   "Acts and the Ancient Historical Monograph." In *The Book of
                Acts in Its Literary Setting*, pp. 1-29. Edited by Bruce W.
                Winter and Andrew D. Clarke. Vol. 1 of *The Book of Acts in Its
                First-Century Setting*. Edited by Bruce W. Winter. 6 vols.
                Grand Rapids, Mich.: Eerdmans; Carlisle, U.K.: Paternoster.
Patte, Daniel
1987   *The Gospel According to Matthew: A Structural Commentary
                on Matthew's Faith*. Philadelphia: Fortress.
Payne, J. Barton
1962   *The Imminent Appearing of Christ*. Grand Rapids, Mich.:
                Eerdmans.
Payne, Philip Barton
1978   "The Order of Sowing and Ploughing in the Parable of the
                Sower." *New Testament Studies* 25:123-29.

1980   "The Authenticity of the Parable of the Sower and Its Interpre-
                tation." In *Studies of History and Tradition in the Four Gospels
                I*, pp. 163-207. Vol. 1 of *Gospel Perspectives*. Edited by R. T.
                France and David Wenham. 6 vols. Sheffield, U.K.: JSOT Press.

1983   "Midrash and History in the Gospels, with Special Reference
                to R. H. Gundry's *Matthew*." *In Studies in Midrash and Historiog-
                raphy*, pp. 177-215. Vol. 3 of *Gospel Perspectives*. Edited by R. T.
                France and David Wenham. 6 vols. Sheffield, U.K.: JSOT Press.
Perrin, Norman
1963   *The Kingdom of God in the Teaching of Jesus*. Philadelphia:
                Westminster Press.

1976   "The High Priest's Question and Jesus' Answer (Mark 14:61-
                62)." In *The Passion in Mark: Studies in Mark 14—16*, pp.
                80-95. Edited by Werner H. Kelber. Philadelphia: Fortress.

Petersen, Norman R.
1978   *Literary Criticism for New Testament Critics.* Philadelphia:
              Fortress.
Piper, John
1977   "Is Self-Love Biblical?" *Christianity Today* 21:1150-53.

Pritchard, James, ed.
1955   *Ancient Near Eastern Texts Relating to the Old Testament.* 2nd
              ed. Princeton, N.J.: Princeton University Press.
Pusey, Karen
1984   "Jewish Proselyte Baptism." *Expository Times* 95:141-45.

Ramaroson, Leonard
1971   "Une nouvelle interprétation de la 'clausule' de Mt 19,9."
              Science et Esprit 23:247-51.
Ramirez, J. M. Casciaro
1976   "El 'misterio' divino en los escritos posteriores de Qumran."
              Scripta Theologica 8:445-75.
Ramsay, William M.
1898   *Was Christ Born at Bethlehem? A Study on the Credibility of St.
              Luke.* London: Hodder & Stoughton (reprint ed. Grand
              Rapids, Mich.: Baker Book House, 1979).
Rapske, Brian M.
1994   "Acts, Travel and Shipwreck." In *The Book of Acts in Its
              Graeco-Roman Setting,* pp. 1-47. Edited by David W. J. Gill
              and Conrad Gempf. Vol. 2 of *The Book of Acts in Its First-
              Century Setting.* Edited by Bruce W. Winter. 6 vols. Grand
              Rapids, Mich.: Eerdmans; Carlisle, U.K.: Paternoster.
Rashidi, Runoko
1988   "Africans in Early Asian Civilizations: A Historical Overview."
              In *African Presence in Early Asia,* pp. 15-52. Edited by Ivan
              Van Sertima and Runoko Rashidi. New Brunswick, N.J.:
              Transaction (Rutgers)/Journal of African Civilizations.
Reicke, Bo
1974   *The New Testament Era: The World of the Bible from 500 B.C. to
              A.D. 100.* Translated by David E. Green. Philadelphia: Fortress.
Rhoads, David, and
  Donald Michie
1982   *Mark as Story: An Introduction to the Narrative of a Gospel.*
              Philadelpia: Fortress.
Richardson, Alan
1958   *An Introduction to the Theology of the New Testament.* New
              York: Harper & Brothers.
Richlin, Amy
1981   "Approaches to the Sources on Adultery at Rome." *Women's
              Studies* 8:225-50.
Ridderbos, Herman N.
1975   *Paul: An Outline of His Theology.* Translated by John Richard
              De Witt. Grand Rapids, Mich.: Eerdmans.

Rissi, Mathias
1966   *Time and History: A Study on the Revelation.* Translated by
               Gordon C. Winsor. Richmond, Va.: John Knox Press.
Robbins, Vernon K.
1992   *Jesus the Teacher: A Socio-rhetorical Interpretation of Mark.*
               Minneapolis: Augsburg Fortress.
Robinson, John A. T.
1977   *Can We Trust the New Testament?* Grand Rapids, Mich.:
               Eerdmans.
Rogers, Cleon
1973   "The Great Commission." *Bibliotheca Sacra* 130:258-67.

Rohrbaugh, Richard L.
1991   "The Pre-industrial City in Luke-Acts: Urban Social Rela-
               tions." In *The Social World of Luke-Acts: Models for Interpreta-
               tion,* pp. 125-49. Edited by Jerome H. Neyrey. Peabody,
               Mass.: Hendrickson.
Russell, D. S.
1964   *The Method and Message of Jewish Apocalyptic.* Philadelphia:
               Westminster Press.
Sabatowich, J. J.
1987   "Christian Divorce and Remarriage." *Bible Today* 25:253-55.

Safrai, S.
1974-1976a   "Education and the Study of the Torah." In *The Jewish People
               in the First Century: Historical Geography, Political History,
               Social, Cultural and Religious Life and Institutions,* pp. 945-
               70. Edited by S. Safrai and M. Stern with D. Flusser and W. C.
               van Unnik. 2 vols. Section 1 of Compendia Rerum Iudaicarum
               ad Novum Testamentum. Vol. 1: Assen, Netherlands: Van
               Gorcum. Vol. 2: Philadelphia: Fortress.

1974-1976b   "Home and Family." In *The Jewish People in the First Century:
               Historical Geography, Political History, Social, Cultural and
               Religious Life and Institutions,* pp. 728-92. Edited by S. Safrai
               and M. Stern with D. Flusser and W. C. van Unnik. 2 vols.
               Section 1 of Compendia Rerum Iudaicarum ad Novum Testa-
               mentum. Vol. 1: Assen, Netherlands: Van Gorcum. Vol. 2:
               Philadelphia: Fortress.

1974-1976c   "Religion in Everyday Life." In *The Jewish People in the First
               Century: Historical Geography, Political History, Social,
               Cultural and Religious Life and Institutions,* pp. 793-833.
               Edited by S. Safrai and M. Stern with D. Flusser and W. C. van
               Unnik. 2 vols. Section 1 of Compendia Rerum Iudaicarum ad
               Novum Testamentum. Vol. 1: Assen, Netherlands: Van Gor-
               cum. Vol. 2: Philadelphia: Fortress.
Saldarini, Anthony J.
1994   *Matthew's Christian-Jewish Community.* Chicago Studies in

the History of Judaism. Chicago: University of Chicago Press.

Sanders, Boykin
1995   "In Search of a Face for Simon the Cyrene." In *The Recovery of Black Presence: An Interdisciplinary Exploration—Essays in Honor of Dr. Charles B. Copher*, pp. 51-63. Nashville: Abingdon.

Sanders, E. P.
1969   *The Tendencies of the Synoptic Tradition*. Society for New Testament Studies Monograph 9. Cambridge: Cambridge University Press.

1977   *Paul and Palestinian Judaism*. Philadelphia: Fortress.

1985   *Jesus and Judaism*. Philadelphia: Fortress.

1990   *Jewish Law from Jesus to the Mishnah: Five Studies*. London: SCM Press; Philadelphia: Trinity Press International.

1992   *Judaism: Practice and Belief, 63 BCE 66 CE*. London: SCM Press; Philadelphia: Trinity Press International.

1993   *The Historical Figure of Jesus*. New York: Allen Lane/Penguin.

Sandmel, Samuel
1978a   *Anti-Semitism in the New Testament?* Philadelphia: Fortress.

1978b   *Judaism and Christian Beginnings*. New York: Oxford University Press.

Satterthwaite, Philip E.
1993   "Acts Against the Background of Classical Rhetoric." In *The Book of Acts in Its Ancient Literary Setting*, pp. 337-79. Edited by Bruce W. Winter and Andrew D. Clarke. Vol. 1 of *The Book of Acts in Its First-Century Setting*. Edited by Bruce W. Winter. 6 vols. Grand Rapids, Mich.: Eerdmans; Carlisle, U.K.: Paternoster.

Saucy, Robert L.
1993   *The Case for Progressive Dispensationalism: The Interface Between Dispensational and Non-dispensational Theology*. Grand Rapids, Mich.: Zondervan.

Sawyer, George S.
1858   *Southern Institutes: Or, An Inquiry into the Origin and Early Prevalence of Slavery and the Slave-Trade*. Philadelphia: J. B. Lippincott.

Schechter, Solomon
1900   "Some Rabbinic Parallels to the New Testament." *Jewish Quarterly Review* 12:415-33.

Schedl, Claus
1982   "Zur Ehebruchklausel der Bergpredigt im Lichte der neu gefundenen Tempelrolle." *Theologische-Praktische Quartalschrift* 130:362-65.

Schiffman, Lawrence H.
1983   *Sectarian Law in the Dead Sea Scrolls: Courts, Testimony and
               the Penal Code.* Brown Judaic Studies 33. Chico, Calif.: Schol-
               ars Press.
Schuler, Philip L.
1982   *A Genre for the Gospels: The Biographical Character of
               Matthew.* Philadelphia: Fortress.
Schweizer, Eduard
1970   *The Good News According to Mark.* Atlanta: John Knox Press.

1971   *Jesus.* Translated by David E. Green. New Testament Library.
               London: SCM Press.

1975   *The Good News According to Matthew.* Translated by David E.
               Green. Atlanta: John Knox Press.
Schweitzer, Albert
1968   *The Quest of the Historical Jesus.* Translated by W.
               Montgomery from 1906 ed. New York: Macmillan.
Scobie, Charles H. H.
1969   "John the Baptist." In *The Scrolls and Christianity: Historical
               and Theological Significance,* pp. 58-69. Edited by Matthew
               Black. London: S.P.C.K.
Scott, Bernard
   Brandon
1989   *Hear Then the Parable: A Commentary on the Parables of
               Jesus.* Minneapolis: Augsburg Fortress.
Scott, James M.
1994   "Luke's Geographical Horizon." In *The Book of Acts in Its
               Graeco-Roman Setting,* pp. 483-544. Edited by David W. J.
               Gill and Conrad Gempf. Vol. 2 of *The Book of Acts in its
               First-Century Setting.* Edited by Bruce W. Winter. 6 vols.
               Grand Rapids, Mich.: Eerdmans; Carlisle, U.K.: Paternoster.
Senior, Donald
1983   *What Are They Saying About Matthew?* New York: Paulist.

Sherk, Robert K.,
   ed. and trans.
1988   *The Roman Empire: Augustus to Hadrian.* Translated Docu-
               ments of Greece and Rome 6. New York: Cambridge Univer-
               sity Press.
Sherwin-White, A. N.
1965   "The Trial of Christ." In D. E. Nineham et al., *Historicity and
               Chronology in the New Testament,* pp. 97-116. London: S.P.C.K.

1978   *Roman Society and Roman Law in the New Testament.* Grand
               Rapids, Mich.: Baker Book House (original ed. Oxford:
               Oxford University Press, 1963).
Sider, Ronald J.
1979   *Christ and Violence.* Scottsdale, Penn.: Herald.

| 1990 | *Rich Christians in an Age of Hunger.* 3rd ed. Dallas: Word. |

1993   *One-Sided Christianity? Uniting the Church to Heal a Lost and Broken World.* Grand Rapids, Mich.: Zondervan; San Francisco: HarperSanFrancisco.

Simon, Marcel
1967   *Jewish Sects at the Time of Jesus.* Philadelphia: Fortress.

Smallwood, E. Mary
1976   *The Jews Under Roman Rule: From Pompey to Diocletian.* Studies in Judaism in Late Antiquity 20. Leiden, Netherlands: E. J. Brill.

Smith, Morton
1951   *Tannaitic Parallels to the Gospels.* Philadelphia: Society of Biblical Literature.

1978   *Jesus the Magician.* San Francisco: Harper & Row.

Snowden, Frank M., Jr.
1970   *Blacks in Antiquity: Ethiopians in the Greco-Roman Experience.* Cambridge, Mass.: Harvard University Press.

Soardes, Marion L.
1994   "Appendix IX: The Question of a Premarcan Passion Narrative." In *The Death of the Messiah: From Gethsemane to Grave—A Commentary on the Passion Narratives in the Four Gospels,* pp. 1492-1524. 2 vols. New York: Doubleday.

Soares Prabhu, George M.
1976   *The Formula Quotations in the Infancy Narrative of Matthew: An Enquiry into the Tradition History of Mt 1—2.* Rome: Biblical Institute Press.

Spencer, F. Scott
1993   "Acts and Modern Literary Approaches." In *The Book of Acts in its Ancient Literary Setting,* pp. 381-414. Edited by Bruce W. Winter and Andrew D. Clarke. Vol. 1 of *The Book of Acts in Its First-Century Setting.* Edited by Bruce W. Winter. 6 vols. Grand Rapids, Mich.: Eerdmans; Carlisle, U.K.: Paternoster.

Stambaugh, John E., and David L. Balch
1986   *The New Testament in Its Social Environment.* Library of Early Christianity 2. Philadelphia: Westminster Press.

Stanton, Graham N.
1974   *Jesus of Nazareth in New Testament Preaching.* Cambridge: Cambridge University Press.

1989   *The Gospels and Jesus.* Oxford Biblical Studies. Oxford: Oxford University Press.

1992   "Matthew: ΒΙΒΛΟΣ, ΕΥΑΓΓΕΛΙΟΝ, or ΒΙΟΣ?" In *The Four Gospels 1992: Festschrift for Franz Neirynck,* pp. 1187-1201. Edited by F. Van Segbroeck et al. Leuven, Belgium: Leuven University Press.

1993   *A Gospel for a New People: Studies in Matthew.* Louisville, Ky.: Westminster/John Knox; Edinburgh: T & T Clark, 1992.

Stauffer, Ethelbert

1960   *Jesus and His Story.* Translated by Richard Winston and Clara Winston. New York: Alfred A. Knopf.

Stegner, W. R.

1985   "The Baptism of Jesus: A Story Modeled on the Binding of Isaac." *Bible Review* 1:36-46.

Stein, Robert H.

1978   *The Method and Message of Jesus' Teachings.* Philadelphia: Westminster Press.

1979   " 'Is It Lawful for a Man to Divorce His Wife?' " *Journal of the Evangelical Theological Society* 22:115-21.

1980   "The 'Criteria' for Authenticity." In *Studies of History and Tradition in the Four Gospels I,* pp. 225-63. Vol. 1 of *Gospel Perspectives.* Edited by R. T. France and David Wenham. 6 vols. Sheffield, U.K.: JSOT Press.

1992   "Divorce." In *Dictionary of Jesus and the Gospels,* pp. 192-99. Edited by Joel B. Green, Scot McKnight and I. Howard Marshall. Downers Grove, Ill.: InterVarsity Press.

Stephen (pseudonym)

1993   "Don't Blame Divorce's Victims." *Christianity Today,* September 13, p. 14.

Stern, David

1991   *Parables in Midrash: Narrative and Exegesis in Rabbinic Literature.* Cambridge, Mich.: Harvard University Press.

Stern, Menahem

1974-1976   "The Province of Judaea." In *The Jewish People in the First Century: Historical Geography, Political History, Social, Cultural and Religious Life and Institutions,* pp. 308-76. Edited by S. Safrai and M. Stern with D. Flusser and W. C. van Unnik. 2 vols. Section 1 of Compendia Rerum Iudaicarum ad Novum Testamentum. Vol. 1: Assen, Netherlands: Van Gorcum. Vol. 2: Philadelphia: Fortress.

Stowers, Stanley K.

1988   "The Diatribe." In *Greco-Roman Literature and the New Testament: Selected Forms and Genres,* pp. 71-83. Edited by David E. Aune. Society of Biblical Literature Sources for Biblical Study 21. Atlanta: Scholars Press.

Streeter, B. H.

1925   *The Four Gospels.* New York: Macmillan.

Strombeck, J. F.
 1982   *First the Rapture*. Eugene, Ore.: Harvest House.

Strong, Augustus
 Hopkins
 1907   *Systematic Theology: A Compendium Designed for the Use of
                Theological Students*. Old Tappan, N.J.: Fleming H. Revell
                (reprint 1979).

Suder, R. N.
 1982   "Epiphany Texts and the Akedah." *Lutheran Theological
                Seminary Bulletin* 62:3-7; *New Testament Abstracts* 27:144.

Sutcliffe, Edmund
 Felix
 1960   "Hatred at Qumran." *Revue de Qumran* 2:345-56.

Talbert, Charles H.
 1977   *What Is a Gospel? The Genre of the Canonical Gospels*. Phila-
                delphia: Fortress.

Tannehill, Robert C.
 1975   *The Sword of His Mouth*. Society of Biblical Literature Semeia
                Supplements 1. Missoula, Mont.: Scholars Press.

Tasker, R. V. G.
 1961   *The Gospel According to St. Matthew*. Tyndale Commentaries.
                Grand Rapids, Mich.: Eerdmans.

Taylor, Vincent
 1935   *The Formation of the Gospel Tradition*. 2nd ed. London:
                Macmillan.

 1952   *The Gospel According to St. Mark*. London: Macmillan.

Teeple, Howard M.
 1957   *The Mosaic Eschatological Prophet. Journal of Biblical Literature*
                Monograph Series 10. Philadelphia: Society of Biblical Literature.

Theissen, Gerd
 1978   *Sociology of Early Palestinian Christianity*. Philadelphia: Fortress.

 1983   *The Miracle Stories of the Early Christian Tradition*.
                Translated by Francis McDonagh. Edited by John Riches.
                Philadelphia: Fortress.

 1991   *The Gospels in Context: Social and Political History in the
                Synoptic Tradition*. Translated by Linda M. Maloney. Minnea-
                polis: Fortress.

Thielman, Frank
 1994   *Paul and the Law: A Contextual Approach*. Downers Grove,
                Ill.: InterVarsity Press.

Thompson, Barbara
 1987   "A Fellowship of Suffering." *Christianity Today,* February 20,
                pp. 24-29.

Thompson, William G.
1974   "An Historical Perspective on the Gospel of Matthew." *Journal of Biblical Literature* 93:243-62.

Thompson, William M.
1985   *The Jesus Debate: A Survey and Synthesis*. New York: Paulist.

Thrall, Margaret
1970   "Elijah and Moses in Mark's Account of the Transfiguration." *New Testament Studies* 16:305-17.

Thurman, Howard
1981   *Jesus and the Disinherited*. Richmond, Ind.: Friends United Press (original ed. Abingdon, 1949).

Trapnell, D. H.
1982   "Health, Disease and Healing." In *New Bible Dictionary*, pp. 457-65. 2nd ed. Edited by J. D. Douglas and N. Hillyer. Downers Grove, Ill.: InterVarsity Press.

Travis, Stephen H.
1977   "Form Criticism." In *New Testament Interpretation: Essays on Principles and Methods*, pp. 153-64. Edited by I. Howard Marshall. Grand Rapids, Mich.: Eerdmans.

Treggiari, Susan
1975   "Jobs in the Household of Livia." *Papers of the British School at Rome* 43:48-77.

Trites, Allison A.
1977   *The New Testament Concept of Witness*. Society of New Testament Studies Monograph 31. Cambridge: Cambridge University Press.

Trocmé, Etienne
1975   *The Formation of the Gospel According to Mark*. Translated by Pamela Gaughan. Philadelphia: Westminster Press.

Twelftree, Graham H.
1986   "ΕΙ ΔΕ . . . ΕΓΩ ΕΚΒΑΛΛΩ ΤΑ ΔΑΙΜΟΝΙΑ . . ." In *The Miracles of Jesus*, pp. 361-400. Vol. 6 of *Gospel Perspectives*. Edited by David Wenham and Craig Blomberg. 6 vols. Sheffield, U.K.: JSOT Press.

Urbach, Ephraim E.
1979   *The Sages: Their Concepts and Beliefs*. Translated by Israel Abrahams. 2nd ed. 2 vols. Jerusalem: Magnes/Hebrew University Press.

Usry, Glenn J., and Craig S. Keener
1996   *Black Man's Religion: Can Christianity Be Afrocentric?* Downers Grove, Ill.: InterVarsity Press.

VanderBroek, Lyle D.
1983   *The Markan Sitz im Leben: A Critical Investigation into the Possibility of a Palestinian Setting for the Gospel*. Ph.D. dissertation, Drew University. (Ann Arbor, Mich.: University Microfilms International.)

Van Tilborg, Sjef
1972   *The Jewish Leaders in Matthew*. Leiden, Netherlands: E. J. Brill.

Vermes, Geza
1984   *Jesus and the World of Judaism*. Philadelphia: Fortress (original ed. London: SCM Press, 1983).

1993   *The Religion of Jesus the Jew*. Minneapolis: Augsburg Fortress.

Via, Dan Otto, Jr.
1967   *The Parables: Their Literary and Existential Dimension*. Philadelphia: Fortress.

Walvoord, John F.
1967   *The Thessalonian Epistles*. Grand Rapids, Mich.: Zondervan.

1971a   "Christ's Olivet Discourse on the End of the Age." *Bibliotheca Sacra* 128:109-16.

1971b   "Christ's Olivet Discourse on the End of the Age: Signs of the End of the Age." *Bibliotheca Sacra* 128:316-26.

1972   *The Rapture Question*. Grand Rapids, Mich.: Zondervan.

1976   *The Blessed Hope and the Tribulation*. Grand Rapids, Mich.: Zondervan.

Wambacq, B. N.
1982   "Matthieu 5,31-32: Possibilité de divorce ou obligation de rompre une union illégitime." *Nouvelle Revue Théologique* 104:34-49.

Ware, B. A.
1981   "Is the Church in View in Matthew 24—25?" *Bibliotheca Sacra* 138:158-72.

Waterman, G. Henry
1975   "The Sources of Paul's Teaching on the Second Coming of Christ in 1 and 2 Thessalonians." *Journal of the Evangelical Theological Society* 18:105-13.

Weeden, Theodore J., Sr.
1971   *Mark: Traditions in Conflict*. Philadelphia: Fortress.

Wenham, David
1979   "Jesus and the Law: An Exegesis on Matthew 5:17-20." *Themelios* 4:92-96.

1984   *The Rediscovery of Jesus' Eschatological Discourse*. Vol. 4 of *Gospel Perspectives*. Edited by R. T. France and David Wenham. 6 vols. Sheffield, U.K.: JSOT Press.

Wenham, Gordon J.
1984   "Matthew and Divorce: An Old Crux Revisited." *Journal for the Study of the New Testament* 22:95-107.

1986   "The Syntax of Matthew 19.9." *Journal for the Study of the
                     New Testament* 28:17-23.
Wenham, John W.
1977   *Christ and the Bible*. Downers Grove, Ill.: InterVarsity Press.

Wheaton, D. H.
1982   "Money." In *New Bible Dictionary*, pp. 790-93. 2nd ed. Edited
                     by J. D. Douglas and Norman Hillyer. Leicester, U.K.:
                     Inter-Varsity Press.
White, K. D.
1964   "The Parable of the Sower." *Journal of Theological Studies*
                     15:300-307.
White, R. E. O.
1960   *The Biblical Doctrine of Initiation*. Grand Rapids, Mich.:
                     Eerdmans.
White, William, Jr.
1971   "Finances." In *The Catacombs and the Colosseum: The Ro-
                     man Empire as the Setting of Primitive Christianity*, pp. 218-36.
                     Edited by Stephen Benko and John J. O'Rourke. Valley
                     Forge, Penn.: Judson.
Wilkinson, John
1978   *Jerusalem As Jesus Knew It*. London: Thames & Hudson.

Williams, Chandran,
and Sal Williams
1992   "Sri Lanka: Coming Apart at the Seams." *ESA [Evangelicals for
                     Social Action] Advocate*, June, pp. 10-11.
Wilson, Dwight
1977   *Armageddon Now!* Grand Rapids, Mich.: Baker Book House.

Wimber, John, with
Kevin Springer
1986   *Power Evangelism*. San Francisco: Harper & Row.

Wimmer, Joseph F.
1982   *Fasting in the New Testament: A Study in Biblical Theology*.
                     New York: Paulist.
Winter, Paul
1961   *On the Trial of Jesus*. Studia Judaica Forschungen zur
                     Wissenschaft des Judentums 1. Berlin: Walter de Gruyter.

1964   "The Trial of Jesus and the Competence of the Sanhedrin."
                     New Testament Studies 10:494-99.
Witherington,   ed
Ben, III
1984   *Women in the Ministry of Jesus: A Study of Jesus' Attitudes to
                     Women and Their Roles As Reflected in His Earthly Life*. Soci-
                     ety for New Testament Studies Monograph 51. Cambridge:

Cambridge University Press.

| 1985 | "Matthew 5.32 and 19.9: Exception or Exceptional Situation?" *New Testament Studies* 31:571-76. |

| 1990 | *The Christology of Jesus*. Minneapolis: Augsburg Fortress. |

| 1992 | *Jesus, Paul and the End of the World: A Comparative Study in New Testament Eschatology*. Downers Grove, Ill.: InterVarsity Press. |

| 1995 | *The Jesus Quest: The Third Search for the Jew of Nazareth*. Downers Grove, Ill.: InterVarsity Press. |

Wrede, William

| 1971 | *The Messianic Secret*. Translated by J. C. G. Greig. Cambridge, U.K.: James Clarke. |

Wright, Addison G.

| 1966 | "The Literary Genre Midrash." *Catholic Biblical Quarterly* 28:417-57. |

Yamauchi, Edwin M.

| 1966 | "The 'Daily Bread' Motif in Antiquity." *Westminster Theological Journal* 28:145-56. |

| 1972 | *The Stones and the Scriptures: An Introduction to Biblical Archaeology*. Grand Rapids, Mich.: Baker Book House. |

Young, Brad H.

| 1989 | *Jesus and His Jewish Parables: Rediscovering the Roots of Jesus' Teaching*. New York: Paulist. |

Ziesler, J. A.

| 1984 | "Matthew and the Presence of Jesus (2)." *Epworth Review* 11:90-97. |